Ancient African Christianity

An Introduction to a Unique Context and Tradition

Christianity spread across North Africa early, and it remained there as a powerful force much longer than anticipated. While this African form of Christianity largely shared the Latin language and Roman culture of the wider empire, it also represented a unique tradition that was shaped by its context. *Ancient African Christianity* attempts to tell the story of Christianity in Africa from its inception to its eventual disappearance. Well-known writers such as Tertullian, Cyprian, and Augustine are studied in light of their African identity, and this tradition is explored in all its various expressions.

This book is ideal for all students of African Christianity and also a key introduction for anyone wanting to know more about the history, religion, and philosophy of these early influential Christians whose impact has extended far beyond the African landscape.

David E. Wilhite is currently Professor of Theology at Baylor University's George W. Truett Theological Seminary, USA.

Ancient African Christianity
An Introduction to a Unique Context and Tradition

David E. Wilhite

Routledge
Taylor & Francis Group

LONDON AND NEW YORK

First published 2017
by Routledge
2 Park Square, Milton Park, Abingdon, Oxon OX14 4RN

Simultaneously published in the USA and Canada
by Routledge
711 Third Avenue, New York, NY 10017

Routledge is an imprint of the Taylor & Francis Group, an informa business

British Library Cataloguing-in-Publication Data
A catalogue record for this book is available from the British Library

Library of Congress Cataloging-in-Publication Data
Names: Wilhite, David E., author.
Title: Ancient African Christianity: an introduction to a unique
    context and tradition / David E. Wilhite.
Description: New York : Routledge, 2017. | Includes bibliographical
    references and index.
Identifiers: LCCN 2016056770 | ISBN 9780415643757 (hardback) |
    ISBN 9780415643771 (pbk.) | ISBN 9780203075678 (ebook)
Subjects: LCSH: Church history—Primitive and early church,
    ca. 30–600. | Africa, North—Church history. | Africa, North—
    History—To 647. | Africa, North—History—647–1517.
Classification: LCC BR190. W55 2017 | DDC 276.101—dc23
LC record available at https://lccn.loc.gov/2016056770

ISBN: 978-0-415-64375-7 (hbk)
ISBN: 978-0-415-64377-1 (pbk)
ISBN: 978-0-203-07567-8 (eBook)

Typeset in Sabon
by Apex CoVantage, LLC

Contents

Preface   ix

1   Introduction   1
Preliminary concerns   1
   Question 1: what is meant by "ancient African
     Christianity"?   2
   Question 2: why study ancient African Christianity?   3
   Question 3: what makes African Christians unique?   5
   Question 4: what is the purpose of this book?   10
Introducing ancient African Christians: an overview   10
   Pre-Christian Africa   11
   The beginnings of Christian Africa   15
   Christian Africa in the fourth century   19
   The last days of ancient African Christianity   22
History and ancient African Christians   29

2   Backgrounds to early African Christianity   45
Romanization: from culture to ethnicity to identity   45
African (identity) politics   49
African languages   52
African art   56
African religions   59
African appearance   63

3   The earliest evidence of African Christianity   79
Tertullian on the earliest African Christians   80
African Christian origins   82
The Scillitan martyrs   85
Perpetua, Felicity, and their fellow martyrs   87

African Christianity in the late second and early third
    century   89
Legacies and later trajectories   96

4 **Tertullian**   108
Tertullian's life   108
    Tertullian the legalist   109
    Tertullian the fideist   110
    Tertullian the priest   111
    Tertullian the Montanist   112
    Tertullian the misogynist   114
    Tertullian the Roman   115
    Tertullian the African   116
Works and teachings   116
Tertullian the African   122
Legacy and later trajectories   126

5 **Cyprian and the later third century**   136
Minucius Felix   136
Cyprian   141
    Persecution   142
    Controversies   144
    His works and teachings   146
    Cyprian the African   147
That Idols Are Not Gods (Quod idola dii non sint)   154
Commodian   155
Late third-century martyrdoms   158

6 **The early fourth century in Africa**   170
Christian records from the early fourth century   171
Arnobius of Sicca   176
    Arnobian theology   177
    What was African about Arnobius?   178
Lactantius   181
    Works and teachings   182
    What was African about Lactantius?   183

7 **The Donatist controversy**   195
Identifying Donatists   195
The beginning of the schism   196
Appeals to Constantine   199

Escalation of violence and persecution   201
Donatist diversity and decline   203
The end of Donatism?   210
Reassessing Donatist characteristics   214
What was African about the Donatists?   217
  Donatists and the Punic language   218
  Donatists and African identity   220
  Donatists and conflict with Romans   221
Conclusions and caveats   225

8 **Augustine the African**   240
Augustine's life and legacy   240
Augustine's works and teachings   244
What was African about Augustine?   250
  Augustine's African background   250
  Accusations about Augustine's identity   251
  Self-identifying as an African   253

9 **The Vandal era of African Christianity**   264
The Vandal invasion of Africa   264
Vandals, Catholics, and Donatists   266
Vandal expansion of power   272
The end of the Vandal kingdom   276

10 **The late Byzantine era in Africa**   287
Justinian's reconquest of Africa   287
The African Three Chapters controversy   295
Gregory the Great   301
Maximus the Confessor   308
Conclusions about Byzantine Africa   311

11 **The Arab conquests in Africa**   321
Understanding the sources and background   321
History of the conquest   325
Survival of evidence and evidence of survival   330
Characteristics of late African Christianity   335
Reasons for African Christianity's disappearance   338
  Political power theory   340
  Christian exodus theory   341
  Decapitation theory   342
  House divided theory   343

Cultural gap theory   344
Theological syncretism theory   345
Political pragmatism theory   347
Tentative conclusions on African Christianity's end   348

12 **Conclusion: What was African about ancient
    African Christianity?**   357
Summary of findings   357
Elements found in the "African School"   360
Further considerations   360
Potential implications   362

Bibliography   366
  Abbreviations   366
  Ancient sources cited   366
  Secondary sources   375
Subject Index   405
Ancient Source Index   418
Scripture Index   425

Preface

In this work I attempt to retell the story of Christianity in North Africa from its inception to its disappearance. In doing so, my primary aim is to treat this history as one, unique tradition. My intended audience is all students of African Christianity, be they experts or not. Therefore, while I have attempted to make a contribution to this field of study, I made an effort to do so in a way that makes this history accessible to non-specialists. I have consulted the critical editions for all sources used here, but provided translations for all them, using those already published where possible (see the section on primary texts in the bibliography) and providing my own where needed (indicated as such in the notes). Furthermore, I have attempted to give credit to the secondary literature and point the reader to further studies, even though the documentation of scholarly debates has been kept to a minimum and relegated to footnotes wherever possible. Of course, finding the proper balance in this area has not been easy, and so I must beg forgiveness where others would judge that more or less citation of secondary literature is needed. Whatever success I have had in this area is to be credited to the many colleagues and friends who read drafts and/or chapters of this work. In particular I wish to thank the following for offering feedback that helped improve this project: Ian Balfour, Charles Bobertz, Frédéric Chapot, Jonathan Conant, Anthony Dupont, Eric Fournier, Sean Hannan, Erika Hermanowicz, Jesse Hoover, Matthew McCarty, Beth DePalma Digeser, Edwina Murphy, Éric Rebillard, James Rives, Kiran Sebastian, Michael Simmons, Jonathan Young, and the anonymous reviewers enlisted by Routledge Press. I should also express my indebtedness to the participants in the "Contextualizing North African Christianity" unit of the Society of Biblical Literature, whose interaction with my work – both formally and informally – has done much to shape my thinking. I also thank them in particular because much of what follows is indebted to their research. Of course, none of these are to be blamed for any problems or mistakes remaining in this work.

I also wish to thank Baylor University, and in particular Baylor's Truett Theological Seminary. My deans and colleagues have supported me in various ways, including sabbaticals and travel funding that allowed me to carry out various parts of research and writing that have finally come to fruition in this book. I also wish to thank my graduate assistant, Jeremy "The Machine" Crews, who logged numerous hours in helping with various parts of this project. I could not have stayed on pace without his help. My students – some of whom even accompanied me to North Africa – also deserve credit for participating in the various courses in which I explored these ancient sources. Their feedback and insights, not to mention their enthusiasm for the subject matter, both challenged and inspired me in this process.

A special word of thanks goes to my friend and former doctoral supervisor, Mario Aguilar. He encouraged me to write this book before I even completed my thesis, and now more than ten years later the faith he had in me and in this project has something to show for it. My doctoral thesis attempted to read Tertullian and the earliest African Christians in light of the Carthaginian and Romano-African context. The chapters that follow represent my attempt to carry out the same line of research, and whatever skill I have been able to utilize in this work is a direct result of the careful guidance and insights offered by my former supervisor. More than that, he instilled in me both a confidence to explore new methodologies and a rigorous demand for precision when it comes to categories and conceptions that shape the results of research. Mario, I am ever grateful and indebted.

Finally, my wife and family deserve much more than the meager thanks I can offer in the preface of a book. Their patience over the years as I have spent countless hours on this project and their eagerness to celebrate all the minor victories along the way mean more to me than words can express. I am eternally grateful for you. *Deo gratias. Deo laudes.*

1 Introduction

Wearing his toga and holding a ripe fig, Cato asked the Roman senate, "How many days ago would you guess I plucked this fruit?" With parliamentary-like rumbles, the senators murmured guesses of a "day or two," based on the fruit's pristine condition.

"Correct!" thundered Cato, and yet "This fig came from Carthage." Carthage, the hated and much feared arch-enemy of Rome, was not far away and distant, but a mere two days journey across the sea. If Rome knew the moment her enemies were leaving their port, she would not have time to prepare a defense before they arrived!

Cato forced the Romans to realize just how imminent a threat resided in Carthage, and in response Rome launched the third Punic war. He ended this speech, like every one he gave on the senate floor, no matter the subject, with the cry, *Carthago delenda est!* "Carthage must be destroyed!"

Preliminary concerns

Christianity arrived in Africa early, and within a few centuries the whole region was heavily Christianized. What has Cato to do with Christianity? Often enough the answer can simply be, "Nothing." On a closer reading, however, this assumption misses something in our understanding of the influential Christian thinkers from this region. Perhaps Cato and the Punic wars were important to African Christian writers who belonged to the Punic heritage, and perhaps an omission of their heritage results in an oversight in our interpretation of their writings.

In fact, famous African Christians like Tertullian and Augustine knew of Cato's famous speech, referencing the Roman senator by name. Allusions to the Punic wars and to Africa's heritage can be found in many of the North African church fathers, and in addition to an implicit non-Roman identity, or other-than-Roman identity,[1] which can be detected in most of the works from this region, these writers often explicitly described themselves as "African."

The present book is devoted to studying the entirety of ancient African Christianity. In other words, the story of Christianity in the geographic region of Africa during the first millennium needs to be told as one continuous story. In carrying out this task, the story needs to question what ancient African Christians shared with the wider church (something that has often been done) and what was unique to their experiences (something that has rarely been done). For these tasks to be completed a few initial questions need to be answered.

Question 1: what is meant by "ancient African Christianity"?

At the risk of being pedantic, it will help to define each word in this phrase in order to avoid any initial confusion. By "ancient" I am referring roughly to the first millennium of Christianity, or late antiquity into the middle ages – pre-modern, if you like. The first undisputed evidence for Christianity in Africa dates to the mid-second century, which itself is evidence that Christianity had probably been established in some way previous to this – perhaps with ties to the first century. Moreover, the literary sources continue through the mid-seventh century, when the spread of Islam begins to replace Christianity in the region.

By "Africa" I primarily refer to the Roman province known as *Africa Proconsularis,* but I secondarily include the entire region of North Africa west of *Aegyptius* (Egypt). It is here argued that the early African Christians were not only African in a categorical sense because of the modern map (which is a modern expansion of a Roman invention), but also because the ancient Christians themselves embraced a self-identity as African. This self-understanding is especially acute in the Roman province of Africa, while the Christian residents of the ancient provinces connected with Egypt were far less likely to identify themselves as African. In other words, my usage represents the way people spoke of Africa in late antiquity. "Africa" (which the Latin writers generally preferred) or "Libya" (which the Greek writers generally used) could refer to the whole region,[2] but usually with the connotation that excludes Egypt. More precisely, Rome divided the province of Africa Proconsularis from Numidia (to the west) and Cyrenaica (to the east). Even when, under the emperor Diocletian (284–305), Africa was subdivided into seven provinces,[3] the whole region could still be referred to as "Africa." It is also helpful to remember that the dominant language of Egypt and Cyrenaica to the east was Greek, while Latin dominated in the western provinces. When Christianity became prominent throughout these western African provinces, Christians adopted this category of "Africa" so that they could speak of specific provinces, such as Africa Proconsularis, and yet they could also refer to the general region.[4] Therefore, keeping this designation aligned with the view of the ancient African Christians enables us to understand them better.[5]

Lastly, by "Christianity" I include everyone who understood themselves in these terms, which includes some groups formerly known as "heretics." The reason for this is that the boundaries of "Orthodox Christianity" became solidified only during the period of the ecumenical councils (325–787). By this time Christianity in North Africa had already divided into what will later be understood as "orthodoxy" and "heresy"; the internal split in the North African church predates the councils. Moreover, oftentimes the historian is hard pressed to identify who belonged to which group, since all such groups normally referred to themselves simply as "Christian." In sum, ancient African Christians includes the whole of African Christian history, from the earliest records to the mysterious disappearance of a Christian presence around the end of the first millennium.

But beyond such elementary definitions of terms, the following work is devoted to studying ancient African Christianity *as* African Christianity. One recent group of scholars have concluded that much like the "Antiochene school" and the "Alexandrian school," African Christians had their own theological tradition and their own unique expression of their faith.[6] This school, therefore, deserves to be studied further and on its own terms.

Question 2: why study ancient African Christianity?

If this question were asked more broadly (i.e. Why study *any* ancient Christians?), then it would demand a longer answer than I can provide here. Suffice it to say that the discipline of Christian history is an important one.

When this question is asked more narrowly (i.e. Why limit the study of Christian history to one particular region?), then the question is about how to subdivide history. It is common practice for historians to divide history into periods (e.g. ancient, medieval, modern), and it is common practice to focus on specific persons from history (i.e. biographies) or groups and movements (e.g. monastics, scholastics, the Charismatic movement, etc.). In any one approach the historian could fall into a range of problems, such as overgeneralizations and misrepresentations, or – to the other extreme – losing the proverbial forest for the trees. In studying the history of a religion in a certain region, one hopes to avoid both pitfalls and to focus on patterns, recurring themes, and common context (generalizations) which can be identified in particular groups and persons (specifics). In short, Christianity in ancient Africa needs to be told as one story.

The topic of ancient African Christianity has too often been, if not neglected, than eclipsed by larger narratives. While most histories of Christianity include major African figures such as Cyprian and Augustine, few treat these subjects as Africans. Too often the fact that Africa was a western Roman province has meant that scholars can categorize African Christian history into the history of western Christianity, without paying closer attention to the uniqueness of Christianity in this region. While there are many commonalities between ancient African Christians and ancient Italian Christians, for example, there are also many differences. These differences are important. Just as one could not adequately understand the apostle Paul without identifying his commonalities with Greeks, so one should also identify his differences from Greeks. Paul, "the apostle to the Gentiles" (Rom. 11:13), could become "all things to all people" (1 Cor. 9:21–22), and yet he always remained "a Hebrew of Hebrews" (Phil. 3:5). With ancient Africans, however, such a clear statement of otherness is more difficult to define – after all, no one claimed to be "an African of Africans."

Or did they? Occasionally, ancient writers from North Africa will claim just such a unique North African identity, and some specific examples are worth examining at the start of this discussion. Although Africa was conquered by Rome during the Punic wars (264–146 BCE), the actual rule of Africa by Rome was more complex. After the third Punic war (149–146 CE), Rome's control of Africa began in the area around Carthage and only gradually spread from there over the next century. Furthermore, Rome's presence in North Africa in no way negated the indigenous populations or their local languages, religions, and customs. Inhabitants of Africa often embraced their new Roman identity alongside their indigenous heritage. We will explore this more fully in Chapter 2, but a few examples will help introduce our discussion here.

Fronto (c.100–166 CE) was from the North African city of Cirta, but he moved to Rome and joined the highest ranks of imperial society. Nevertheless, Fronto could still claim, "I am a Libyan of the Libyan nomads" – an uncanny parallel to Paul's self-description as a "Hebrew of Hebrews."[7] Fronto's point, of course, is rhetorical and serves a different purpose than Paul's statement, but he nevertheless nicely illustrates how easily Africans could claim a non-Roman identity.

Another example is Apuleius of Madauros (c.124–180 CE), who stated, "I proclaimed myself to be 'half Numidian' and 'half Gaetulian.'"[8] The Numidians and Gaetulians were people groups in northwestern Africa. Apuleius's claim to be of mixed heritage is making a very particular rhetorical point about how he has embraced the highest of ideals of the empire, such as education and political involvement, despite what some think is a barbaric background.[9] Again, Apuleius's case demonstrates how someone can be categorized as non-Roman in one sense and still fully belong to Roman society. The important point for this study is that the wider Roman context should not negate our appreciation of the local context.

This point will be evident in Christian writers as well: Augustine, who studied in Madauros, will need to invoke Apuleius's memory in order to speak to his non-Roman context, saying, "Apuleius of whom I choose rather to speak, because, as our own countryman, he is better known to us Africans."[10] Apparently, the memory and local heritage mattered to people who could classify themselves as "us Africans."

Fronto and Apuleius both represent very specific groups within North Africa, namely the civic identity of Cirta and the ethnic identities of the Numidians and Gaetulians. So we must also not allow our category of "African" to eclipse the many local people groups who were from this region, because most of the individuals from these groups would not necessarily think of themselves as "African." In all likelihood, the Africans primarily thought of themselves as Carthaginians, or Numidians, or some other expression of local identity.[11] Even so, the phenomenon of a more general African identity does emerge in response to the presence of Romans. Princeton historian Brent Shaw explains this for all inhabitants of Roman Africa:

> The split was between the official identity of an empire and the local identities of regional communities. In this situation, they repressed the smaller identities nested within the larger potential one, and they claimed, more simply to be Africans. The evidence of Africans resident in Rome and Latium, for example, shows this systematic repression of local or civic identities in favor of the larger claim to be an African.[12]

We must proceed, therefore, by looking for the "African" aspects of early Christian writers from this region, while allowing that any given individual needs to be understood in more specific terms. What Fronto meant by a "Libyan" and what Augustine meant by an "African" may mean very different things. Nevertheless, since these various individuals and groups could claim to be "more simply Africans," as Shaw notes, we should take this aspect of their history into consideration.

In sum, there are (at least) two sides to studying ancient African Christians. Since most of our Christian writers from this region wrote in Latin, they have been classified as part of Latin Christianity – which is certainly correct. Nevertheless, these Christians also belong to their own unique context, and their African locale should be considered as well. To recall the apostle Paul again, both his Jewish context and his Greco-Roman milieu should be considered in any attempt to study this one apostle. The same is true of writers from "Roman Africa," which leads us to our next point.

Question 3: what makes African Christians unique?

This question is one of the most important for the current discussion, and so to answer this question fully is to write this entire book. At the end of this introductory chapter, a more concrete answer can be given, but for now a short clarification is in order. On the one hand we must avoid any claims that something inherent in Africans makes them unique (what is known in scholarly discussions as "essentialism"). On the other hand, we can identify a shared heritage and history of ancient Africa (what is often summarized with the word "culture"). While answering this question is one of the primary tasks of this present work, the notion that all Africans were alike or could be stereotyped must be avoided. Instead of looking for something "essentially African," we hope to trace the common history of Africans and to detect various expressions of African identity.

A brief apology is in order regarding this question. In an earlier study, I applied this question and a specialized methodology to Tertullian, the first significant African Christian writer.[13] Although much work has been done to analyze Tertullian's own teachings and his contribution to the later Latin tradition, little to no attention has been given to the fact that Tertullian writes from Africa with a distinct African identity.[14] To be sure, Tertullian – and for that matter every individual – can inhabit multiple identities: Christian, male, educated, Roman citizen, etc. (to give just a few examples). However, the fact that Tertullian likely coined the term *Romanitas* ("Roman-ness"), and he did so in contrast to his own *Punicitas* ("Punic-ness"), indicates that his own self-identity as a Carthaginian should be taken into account when studying him.[15] To be sure, Tertullian's African identity should not eclipse all his other forms of identities in our study of him – especially not his Christian identity! Some reviewers have critiqued my work for exactly that mistake.[16] In particular, I have allegedly erred on two points, which are worth considering here.

First, my work is compared to W.H.C. Frend's *The Donatist Church*, which focuses on "an indigenous movement of rebellion against the Roman empire."[17] I would point out that my work nowhere describes Tertullian nor his North African context in terms of "rebellion." Instead, I outline the numerous forms of "resistance" available to subjects under imperial pressure, including the phenomenon taught in the rhetorical schools throughout the empire at this time known as the Second Sophistic movement. Furthermore, while I agree that Frend's work is methodologically flawed, his underlying point that there is an indigenous aspect to some members of the Donatist party (discussed further in Chapter 7) has been shown to still have validity,[18] and there is an element of self-identity involved in such an indigenous response to Romanization.[19] I merely cited Frend in my earlier work in order to draw attention to this non-Roman aspect of the identities of Tertullian's North Africa; I nowhere attempt to follow Frend in identifying Tertullian as "Berber" or his compatriots as "nationalistic."

Second, my work is said to presuppose "a fixed and unequivocal concept of identity," instead of assuming identity to be something that is fluid and responsive to particular situations.[20] Individuals should be understood as inhabiting multiple identities, such as Roman and African.[21] This critique, however, is unfounded: my definition of identity is repeatedly stated to be fluid, manifold, and occasioned by the situation at hand. I prefer, in fact, to speak of Tertullian's numerous "identities," and my chapters are devoted to certain social identities that illustrate his non-Roman self-descriptions, such as kinship identity, class identity, ethnic identity, and religious identity. My work nowhere describes Tertullian as inhabiting a singular African identity. Instead, I intentionally challenge the notion of the fixed categories of "Roman" and "indigenous" by showing how those individuals we call "elites" could and did inhabit numerous and even apparently conflicting identities, such as Roman and African.[22]

My focus, in that earlier study, was simply to explore the non-Roman aspects of Tertullian's self-description that sometimes take center stage in his writings. In order to clarify this focus, I cited part of Robert Sider's conclusion from his monumental study of Tertullian's rhetoric, and that passage is worth repeating here:

> We have, in fact, proceeded on the assumption that the perceptions of the early Christians can be understood and appreciated only when we have unraveled the intricately woven fabric of their experience. That this "experience" was a highly composite one has long been known, but still too little has been done to distinguish its strands. Our work in this study has attempted to set in conspicuous clarity a major, and, I have argued, a crucial strand, of the early Christian mentality.[23]

In order to acknowledge the limitations of my focus in that earlier study, I then concluded by admitting to the intentional narrowness of my own study: I did not attempt "to treat Tertullian in his entirety or even to exhaust the whole array of his identities constructed in his writings, but instead, this project has chosen to select Tertullian's 'Africanity' as a starting point and, borrowing Sider's phrase, to 'set in conspicuous clarity' an aspect of his writings. From this vantage point, scholars can revisit traditional discussions of Tertullian's life"[24]

Despite dissatisfaction among some reviewers, I stand by this approach since Tertullian's Africanity is a much-overlooked aspect of his surviving works.[25] In what follows I will again take up this one "strand" in order to address the uniquely African aspects of Christians from this context, only I now extend this approach to the whole story of ancient African Christianity. While the following chapters offer a broader introduction to the lives, writings, and experiences of ancient African Christians, this study is by no means exhaustive. Nevertheless, running throughout the various chapters is the unifying theme of the Africanity of these Christians, and it must be reiterated that this approach is needed since this theme has been too often overlooked.

Why has the African identity of these Christians been so neglected, if not taboo, in recent scholarship? I suspect that one answer to this question lies in the French history of colonization of Africa in modern times. It has been well documented that many of the earliest modern histories of ancient African Christianity were written by French scholars who unwittingly employed their own colonialist lenses to read the ancient African sources.[26] Many modern Europeans saw their own work of colonization as the heir to Rome's history of "civilizing" places like Africa. For example, Maurice Caudel compared the "Berbers" to his own race ("Les Aryens") and found them to be "an inferior race."[27] Similarly, Gabriel Médina spoke of how the Africans were always conquered by "the superior races."[28] Similarly, Philip Schaff, who was born in Switzerland, educated in Germany, and who taught in the United States, believed certain heresies attracted African Christians because "the Punic national character leaned naturally towards gloomy and rigorous acerbity."[29] To return to the example of Tertullian in particular, the French scholar René Braun described him as a "man of combat" part of an "aggressive and archaic Christianity," and Braun traced these flaws to "the Punico-Berber religiosity."[30]

This mentality undoubtedly also affected the theological assessment of other African Christians. François Decret, for example, commented on "The African church's independent spirit, one of its key characteristics."[31] For Decret, however, this is not a compliment: it "should not be understood as a very spiritual reaction. In fact, it was this 'African autonomy' that also characterized violent resistance movements."[32] This kind of theological assessment suffers from a stereotyping of all African Christians, be they independent-minded bishops like Cyprian or violent rebels against Rome.[33]

With these sorts of stated assumptions, it is no surprise that there has been a needed backlash to this colonialist approach. First, the whole field of historical study into African Christian history has largely turned away from the African-ness of these early Christian writers. Timothy Barnes, for example, responded to the statement by Braun (quoted above) to comment on Tertullian's African heritage

> Tertullian's name proves nothing, and cannot be invoked in aid of any thesis. For all that it can reveal, he could be the son of a soldier or not, of immigrant Italian stock or of native (Punic or other) extraction. But what does that matter? Attention should concentrate, not on his supposed racial characteristics, but on his definable place in Carthaginian society.[34]

Barnes cannot be faulted for wishing to correct the blatant racism of previous scholars. The correction, however, seems to have come with its own cost: the next wave of scholars attempted to purge their field of nationalist and "racial" (and too often racist) notions, but they did so in such a way as to make ethnic and social identity questions almost taboo and therefore neglected.[35]

The other kind of response to the colonialist bias in modern history has come from postcolonial approaches. For more than a century, many belonging to the modern African diaspora have looked to "African Christians" as their spiritual ancestors, and in doing so have invoked a Black and/or pan-African identity shared by ancients and modern African Christians alike.[36] Two more recent historians wrote from the context of North Africa itself: 'Abd Allāh 'Arawī (or "Abdullah Laroui" as his name appeared in print) in his work, *L'histoire du Maghreb*,[37] argued that the Africans under Roman rule perpetually revolted against the empire, and Marcel Benabou's study, *La résistance africaine à la romanisation*,[38] concurred but broadened the concept of "resistance" beyond strict military and political resistance to forms such as cultural resistance. These studies received harsh reviews by contemporary historians.[39] While these two authors can be critiqued for an agenda-driven study of history, the dismissal of their concerns established a climate that erased the discussion of ethnicity and colonialism from the field altogether, a veritable "white-washing of history" wherein the agendas remain but remain hidden.[40]

In the aftermath of colonialist and postcolonialist approaches, as well as critiques of both, there has been a shift away from any absolute distinction between "Roman" and "African." David Mattingly has rightly identified a problem in allowing such distinctions:

> The explicit dichotomies are questionable as generalizations, but were widely adopted as explanations of a supposed historical reality. . . . Once again, this has the effect of segregating "us" (the colonizers or latterly European scholars) from "them" (the unruly African people) and ignores all possible gradations (social, spatial, and temporal) between, for instance, nomad and sedentarist.[41]

In this current book, we must constantly heed Mattingly's warning[42] and recognize how many "Africans" were also "Roman" or at least participated in various levels of *Romanitas*. Thereby, we face a tension in our attempt to categorize this history: on the one hand, we must not allow any absolute dichotomy between "Romans" and "Africans"; on the other hand, we cannot dismiss the differences that remained (at least at times) between Romans and Africans.

By focusing on who or what is "African," we also bring to light another problem: how to define who or what is "Roman." One could identify as a Roman by living in the city of Rome itself, by being a citizen of the Roman Empire, or even by belonging to a Roman province, such as Africa. Therefore, we constantly have to remind ourselves about how an African under Roman rule may just as easily identify him- or herself as a Roman, perhaps even primarily as a Roman. The purpose of this discussion is to focus on what made a Roman African an African, since this question is often neglected at the expense of focusing on (or simply assuming) how the Roman African was Roman.

Part of the difficulty in speaking of Romanization is the tendency to see Rome's presence in Africa as one that eclipses all pre-Roman and non-Roman elements. Although Africa's archaeological record suggests that the region was thoroughly "Romanized," Roman historians have come to recognize how much of the pre-Roman African elements of society remained throughout the Roman period.[43]

It appears that there has been a subtle and positive correction in recent studies wherein the concept of an African identity as something social or even ethnic can be retrieved and utilized when studying the ancient Christians from North Africa.[44] To cite David Mattingly again, "More work is urgently needed on tribal settlements and on the exploration of African and Punic influences in Roman-period Africa."[45] For example, an international group of Augustine scholars met in Algeria in 2001 for a conference with the theme "Saint Augustine: Africanity and Universality."[46] African Christians, like Augustine, can belong to the "universal" church while also having an "African" identity. I am here proposing that the study of ancient African Christianity should attempt to understand the unique African context and identities throughout its history.

Question 4: what is the purpose of this book?

The student of ancient African Christianity can utilize many helpful resources. Reference works, recent translations, technical monographs, and many other sources are all at the disposal of someone with access to a good library. And yet, somewhat surprisingly, no single work has adequately synthesized all of these materials into a single volume.[47]

This book is an introduction to the primary and secondary sources of ancient African Christianity. It is written in a style that is accessible to non-specialists and with the aim to be comprehensive in its treatment of ancient African Christians. This book also aims to study ancient African Christians with the key question in mind: what makes these Christians "African"? This agenda will not be formatted as a technical monograph because it will not (a) assume prior knowledge on the part of the reader nor (b) sideline material that seems irrelevant to our key question. Instead, each section will incorporate the data about the subjects whether or not it helps answer the question. In other words, our key question is one we will *also* ask before leaving any subject, but it will not be the *only* question.

In short, this work is written for all students of ancient African Christianity, be they specialists in this field or newcomers to the conversation. Therefore I have written with the assumption of no prior knowledge, and yet there is an argument made here that will hopefully affect future scholarship. Debate with other scholars must be kept to a minimum in this book, but the facts themselves inevitably invoke different interpretations, and these will be explicitly identified as such, even though most of the secondary literature will be relegated to the footnotes. The reader who wishes to engage these debates more precisely can find the necessary literature in these notes.

This book is an introduction to ancient African Christianity, one that spans the whole of its history yet focuses on the specifics of the people involved. But ancient African Christianity blossomed in the societal soil of ancient Africa, and so we must begin by understanding some of the African history and heritage that predates Christianity.

Introducing ancient African Christians: an overview

To return to our initial question, what does Cato, the Punic wars, and the rest of pre-Christian history in Africa have to do with our study? Tertullian, addressing a different matter around the year 197 CE, noted "how near was that province of the enemy [i.e. Africa] whose subjugation [Cato] was constantly urging."[48] How near indeed is the history of ancient Africa to Roman history, and the encounter between the two has significantly shaped Christian history in Africa. Before turning directly to specific chapters on ancient African Christian history, it will benefit the reader to glimpse the overarching story, beginning in pre-Christian times, following through to the introduction and spread of Christianity in the region, and finally culminating with the inner turmoil and eventual disappearance of the Christian religion in North Africa. What follows is a "bird's eye view," or what is now called "history from above." That is, we are going to give the political and military account of this region, even though in the chapters that follow we will be more interested in the day-to-day life of ancient African Christians. The following account, however, will repeatedly show how this political history affects the Christians on the ground. This overarching account is helpful because it enables the reader to place the specific studies in each of the following chapters within the larger story of African history.

Pre-Christian Africa

While our project cannot do justice to the entire history of ancient Africa, we do need to summarize the major episodes leading up to the Christianization of the region.[49] In reviewing this history, a helpful theme that ties various events together is conflict, especially the conflict between the Roman Empire and the African societies. Of course there is much that could be said apart from the conflict between these two, such as the spread of Greek influence or the establishment of Jewish communities. However, as will be discussed further in Chapter 2, most of the surviving evidence, especially the literary and Christian evidence, focuses on Rome and its conquests.

Greek influence is rare compared with other provinces of the empire, and the evidence is primarily found along coastal cities, especially to the eastern sectors of North Africa. The Greeks established trade colonies in Cyrenaica as early as the sixth century BCE. Alexander the Great conquered Egypt in 332 BCE, although his influence did not pass from Egypt to the west into the rest of North Africa. The Greek influence, therefore, is primarily through trade in Punic ports. To be sure, Carthage before its defeat by Rome was very cosmopolitan, but the Carthaginian accommodation of Hellenism was minimal compared to other regions of the Mediterranean. The Greek influence all across North Africa was filtered through Egyptian and Punic accommodation rather than being imported by a direct process of Hellenization.

Another social group found in North Africa at this time is the population of diaspora Jews. The earliest archaeological remains of Judaism dates to the second century CE, but it is possible that such remains testify to a pre-established community that could have arrived after the Jewish War (66–70 CE). While the evidence for Judaism in North Africa cannot be treated in full here, African Judaism provides a helpful comparison because the remaining records suggest that these Jews took on unique African practices and traits in contrast to those in Judaea.[50]

Instead of arbitrarily choosing a precise date from which to begin this telling of pre-Christian history in Africa, let us start by acknowledging the *Afri*. Romans referred to this group and to the region from which they came as *Africa*, the land of the Afri, when in fact what became the Roman province of Africa Proconsularis in particular and the whole region of Africa in general consisted of many different people groups. The Greek writers referred to these peoples as *Libyoi*, usually Anglicized as "Libyans," and so most ancient languages and artifacts from this region are commonly deemed "Libyan." Although less common in recent discussions, scholars also refer to these people groups as "Berbers," based on the later Arabic term (which itself is derived from the Latin word for barbarian). Beyond these labels, the various "tribes" mentioned in ancient sources of North Africa are numerous.[51] Very little is known about these groups, who ranged from nomadic to sedentary. More specific information can be found when this Libyan "culture" (or better, "cultures") encountered a wave of Punic influence, centered in ancient Carthage.[52]

The legend of Carthage's founding tells of a beautiful princess who fled Phoenician Tyre, a city on the eastern coast of the Mediterranean (modern Lebanon). According to most ancient sources, Queen Elissa – or "Dido" – founded the city in 814 BCE, which (coincidentally?) is the same year as Rome's founding according to one source.[53] Dido's life remains shrouded in legend, but the most famous account is from the poet-laureate of imperial Rome, Virgil.

Virgil tells of how the soon-to-be founder of Rome, Aeneas, himself fleeing the destroyed city of Troy, stopped in the port of Carthage for respite from his travels. Dido first provided hospitality to Aeneas and his comrades, but then fell in love with her guest. Aeneas eventually left Dido because he was duty-bound to establish Rome. Jilted, Dido cast herself upon her own funeral pyre and extinguished her life in a tragic display of fury. At least, that is the story, according to Virgil. As we will soon see, others in Africa remembered things differently.

More verifiable events emerge with the rise of the Punic empire. Whereas the culture of the eastern Mediterranean is referred to as "Phoenician," the influence of Carthage is deemed "Punic," a Latinization of "Phoenician."[54] Carthage quickly grew in its economic influence and in its political power.[55] Like Tyre, Carthage's strength especially resided in its navy. Because of this use of the sea, Punic influence is primarily laced along the southern coastline of the Mediterranean. Carthaginian trade and religion also spread further inland in Africa and further abroad: Punic settlements had already been established in Iberia (modern Spain and Portugal) and Corsica, and Carthage established colonies in Sardinia and Sicily. The encroachment of this Punic empire into Roman territory pushed what had been an ongoing economic competition into what eventually became total war between these two Mediterranean powers.[56]

The Punic wars, for the present purposes, can be summarized in terms of the conflict between Rome and Carthage over who would control, and benefit from, trade, beginning in Sicily and ultimately throughout the western Mediterranean. The first Punic war (261–241 BCE) consisted of an extended deadlock between the superior Roman army and the superior Carthaginian navy. Ironically, however, Carthage's troops succeeded often enough in the land war in Sicily, whereas Rome strengthened its navy to the point of eventual success over the Punics at sea. When the war ended, the peace agreement exacted a heavy toll on Carthaginians as a means of preventing any resurgence of Rome's enemy. A resurgence, however, did occur in what became the second Punic war (218–201 BCE).

The second war between Carthage and Rome produced some of the most iconic figures of military history. Carthage's general, Hannibal, claimed initial success in Iberia and Gaul as he marched toward Rome. Rome, however, stalled the Carthaginian progress at several key junctures. In an unprecedented move, Hannibal marched his troops, including war elephants, across the Alps through the middle of winter, thereby surprising the Romans and earning himself an immortal reputation for his military prowess.

Rome was slowly able to turn the tide against Hannibal. Despite several devastating defeats, Rome staved off Hannibal's army with its superior infantry skills and with its ability to win over Carthage's allies. Hannibal's army, in turn, weakened by multiple battles and its treacherous Alpine crossing, and ultimately unable to win over Rome's Italian allies, could never muster an attack on Rome itself. Eventually, the Roman general Scipio received authority to lead an invasion into Africa, which forced Carthage to recall Hannibal from Italy.

In Africa, Scipio and Hannibal met in the battle of Zama, a titanic clash of elephants, cavalry, and infantry. Other African groups, such as the Numidians, defected and pledged their support to Rome, and so Scipio's army soundly defeated Hannibal's. For his ultimate defeat of Carthage and its influence on the surrounding region, the Roman general was awarded the title *Africanus*, or "Defeater of the Africans."

Even though Hannibal escaped from the war and served King Antiochus III in Syria, he remained forever the iconic image of anti-Roman sentiment. The historian Polybius recounts how Hannibal had at age 9 sworn an oath "never to be the friend of the Romans."[57] If Hannibal becomes paradigmatic for all Punic Africans, then this animosity will haunt Rome for some time to come.

The second Punic war ended with an even heavier toll on Carthage: Rome sought to ensure that Carthage could never again raise an army. On top of heavy fees paid each year to Rome, Carthage had to appeal for Roman permission before waging any battles against any enemy. Numidia, immediately west of Carthaginian territory, had divided during the second Punic war, partly supporting Rome. Later, when Numidians raided Punic cities near Carthage, Rome prohibited Carthage from responding. Eventually,

Carthage ignored the Roman senate and fought against a Numidian attack, an action that initiated the third Punic war (149–146 BCE). Even though Carthage lost this battle, Rome declared war on Carthage, issued impossible terms for its citizens, and eventually besieged the city and burned it to the ground. The Punic empire was the only one conquered entirely by Rome, and even though the Roman sources largely depicted the Punic presence as having crumbled to dust along with Carthage's walls, the sources from later centuries reveal an ongoing presence of the Punic-speaking population.

With Carthage destroyed, over time the rest of Africa became the grain supply for Rome. To return to Cato the Elder's famous speech wherein he displayed a still-ripe African fig and with which he inspired the Romans to go to war again with Carthage, one may ask whether the senate, more than being struck with fear of Africa as a military threat (an impossibility given the heavy taxes since the last Punic war), realized the possibility that Africa could provide inexpensive and accessible food for the growing population of Rome.

The city of Carthage died, but it would rise again like a phoenix from its ashes.[58] The battle of Carthage (146 BCE) resulted in the entire city being leveled, its population being sold into slavery, and all of North Africa eventually being claimed as Roman territory. The scene of burning Carthage included the moment when the Carthaginian general, Hasdrubal, who had already fled the city and surrendered to Scipio Africanus the Younger, looked up at the burning walls only to see his wife there holding his two sons: she spat at his cowardice and, rather than accepting imprisonment by Romans, cast herself and her children into the burning rubble. When the fires died, the Roman senate declared that the city could never be rebuilt, and – according to a much later telling – claimed that the fields of Carthage were salted to prevent them from ever being used again. However, in 49 BCE Julius Caesar rebuilt Carthage, re-establishing it as the capital of Africa. The new city of Carthage was modeled after Rome, and over time Roman trade and Roman legions spread throughout North Africa – overlapping the Libyan and Punic layers of society.[59]

Rome's influence in Africa was once seen by scholars to be ubiquitous, almost totalizing in its effects on the surrounding region. No province was as Romanized as Africa. The basis for this was primarily in the linguistic spread of the Latin language and the architectural evidence of Roman presence that peppered the landscape. Some of Rome's most impressive architectural artifacts can still be seen in modern Algeria, Tunisia, and Libya. Even so, this understanding of Roman Africa as entirely Romanized has been significantly revised.

Scholars now understand Africa to have retained its pre-Roman heritage throughout the Roman period (roughly until around 650 CE). Africa was not as much Romanized as it was *legionized*. In other words, despite Roman colonization, which was meant to facilitate trade for Rome's economic improvement, African languages (like Libyan and Punic), African religions, and African practices survived and even thrived.[60] More details about pre-Roman heritage will be discussed in the Chapter 2. But for now, suffice it to say that Africa was never a target of Romanization. Instead, many Africans welcomed and sought after *Romanitas*, or Roman-ness – a phenomenon especially prominent during the early Christian era.[61]

The beginnings of Christian Africa

The first evidence for Christians in North Africa emerges at a time when Africans began claiming prominence in the Roman Empire. In 180 a group of martyrs from outside of Carthage were beheaded for claiming Jesus as *Dominus*, or Lord. Within two decades, Tertullian, the first prolific Latin writer, begins writing tracts in defense of Christianity, especially Christianity in Carthage. The martyrdom of Perpetua and Felicity and their compatriots occurs in 203, and Cyprian ascends to the bishop's chair in 248, from which he will write numerous treatises addressing the persecutions and internal problems of the church in Africa. We will devote more attention to each of these in the following chapters, but for now it is helpful to note the dynamic of African/Roman relations at large during this period.

In the following sections, we will repeatedly draw attention to points of comparison between the events of the time and the writings of African Christians. For the sake of brevity, these comparisons will simply be noted without any attempt to prove connections between the events at large and the thoughts of Christians – arguments such as these, however, will be addressed in the main chapters. Also, we do not intend at this time to make any claims about these events and writings as being unique to Africa. Much of the subject matter, such as martyrdom, can be found in many Roman provinces. We simply wish to supplement our summary of the history of Africa during the Roman period with examples of how Christians from this time reflect their context. In order to do so, let us begin by looking at how Africans adapted to the Roman presence.

Africans, be they Roman colonizers or those of indigenous descent, had assumed prominent roles in the empire by the turn of the second century. For example, Marcus Cornelius Fronto, whom we mentioned on p. 4, came from Cirta, the capital city of Numidia, and yet he became a senator and lived in Rome. Whereas Numidia had partly sided with Rome during the Punic wars, Cirta itself later became a target of Roman expansion and was eventually conquered by Julius Caesar. Cirta's prominence continued to increase as Roman use of African granaries grew. Regardless of past relations between Cirta and Rome, someone like Fronto could ascend to the prominence of the senatorial class and serve in Rome, in which he continued to act as a patron to his hometown.[62]

Fronto is not unique, either: "For most of the second century [the Africans] were to dominate the intellectual life of the Empire, and by the 180s nearly a third of the Roman senate was of African origin."[63] Fronto provides an illuminating example of an African who embraced *Romanitas*, especially given his claim to be "a Libyan of the Libyan nomads."[64] Perhaps a similar dynamic occurs in the life of Victor the African, who became the bishop of Rome around 189.[65] One scholar has argued that Victor's prominence is due to the large number of Africans who had migrated to Rome, bearing considerable influence on the city's population.[66]

Not only would Africans climb the social ladder of Rome by way of political status, education, and public service of other sorts, but they would also allow many indigenous Africans to come to prominence in Roman society. As Rome expanded both south and east, a movement arose known as the "Second Sophistic." This phenomenon by and large consisted of the retrieval of classical Greek rhetoric, which is to say polished oratory skills and the ability to draw upon the Homeric myths.[67] The Second Sophistic movement is an important occurrence for our study because it often functioned as a means of asserting social legitimacy. Even though Romans had conquered the Greeks, Greeks could claim superiority in terms of their artistic skills, something highly valued across the Mediterranean world. Not only would Greeks tout their art and artisanship, but Romans themselves would adopt and spread Greek architecture, literature, and even religion throughout their empire. Unsurprisingly, Africans also valued and adopted the practices of the Second Sophistic movement. One prominent example is Apuleius of Madauros.

Madauros became a center for learning in North Africa under Roman rule, and none mastered the skills of oration better than Apuleius. This city, roughly fifty miles inland in what is modern Algeria, represents the southern portion of Numidia, which is probably why in his famous *Apology*, Apuleius will claim to be "half Numidian . . . half Gaetulian."[68] The Gaetulians were peoples further south who were often characterized as nomadic and had less contact with Roman trade.[69] Despite this seemingly provincial and marginal place of birth, Apuleius will be appointed as the provincial priest who presided over the cult of the emperor. Apuleius's path will be followed by many Africans who used education as a means of social mobility. Even Christians such as Tertullian, who is often located within the Second Sophistic[70] for his education and rhetorical talent, and Augustine, who also studied in Madauros, will obtain the ability to transcend their "Punicitas" with their oratory skills.[71] In one letter, Augustine even claims Apuleius as a compatriot: "Apuleius of whom I choose rather to speak, because, as our own countryman, he is better known to us Africans."[72]

While Fronto accommodated himself to the political system of Rome, and Apuleius similarly capitalized on education and speaking talent, one other avenue remained for Africans to acquire higher social cache and status in terms of *Romanitas*: military service.

In 193 the emperor was murdered, and Septimius Severus, or "Severus of Africa," was declared the rightful successor by his own troops.[73] After a few years of war with other claimants, he became the sole ruler of Rome and the first emperor from Africa. Severus always remained loyal to his hometown of Leptis Magna (in modern Libya). His African background, however, was never a source of pride, seeing as how he tried to hide his "Punic" looks and speech.[74] Although Severus ruled by transferring power from the senate to the military, his ascendency to the summit of Roman power and status is part of a wider phenomenon of African upward mobility – a phenomenon one historian has labeled "the advance of Africans."[75]

Of course, one cannot find an exact Christian parallel to Septimius Severus in that Christians at this time generally refused military service. One can, however, see numerous instances where African Christians employ military motifs as a way to communicate their faith to others and to subvert the values of the Roman Empire. It seems that the heritage of warfare and the ongoing presence of Roman legions left an indelible imprint upon the thinking of many African Christians.[76] One early example is in the heroine-martyr Perpetua.

The martyrdom account of Perpetua and her cohort remains one of the most memorable texts from early Christianity. In terms of military imagery, the major scene takes place in the "military camp" as a sort of gladiatorial game to honor Severus's son, Geta. In her diary, Perpetua tells of a vision where she transformed into a gladiator and defeated an "ugly Egyptian." This vision informed her that her battle would be waged, not with flesh and blood, but in a spiritual arena: "I realized that it was not with wild animals that I would fight, but with the Devil, but I knew that I would win the victory."[77] Perpetua's understanding of Christian warfare represents the accepted teachings of her church. And yet, there is evidence that Septimius Severus's pro-military policies at this time were attracting many of Perpetua's "brothers."

Soon after (c.208), and possibly partly in response to Severus's successful recruitment of troops in Africa, Tertullian wrote a treatise against military service entitled *On the Military Crown*.[78] This treatise is evidence that Christians in fact were serving in the military at this time, although the case at hand seems to be of a soldier who converted, and then refused to participate in unscriptural behavior.

At another point, Tertullian himself seems to have suggested that Christians could serve in Rome's army. In his *Apology*, written soon after Severus's rise to power (c.197), he argues, "We sail with you, and fight with you."[79] The "we" of course is "we Christians" and the "you" is "you Romans/persecutors." This admission of military cooperation, however, seems to be rhetorical: Christians are not necessarily enemies of the empire; they are desirable citizens who contribute to society. In his later work, Tertullian insisted that Christians cannot serve in the army of this world. Instead, they must shift from the "military camp [same word used in the *Passion of Perpetua*] of darkness" to the "military camp of light."[80] Whether this later statement is a change of Tertullian's beliefs or a more carefully stated position he held all along is debatable. What is certain is the fact that the military imagery becomes a recurring motif in North African Christian writing.

After the military legacy of Severus and his successors, the martyrdoms in North Africa continue to employ military imagery. The later martyrdom accounts, however, further reflect the changing political landscape of the third and fourth centuries: namely, the internal turmoil of civil wars. Let us briefly recount the internal conflicts of the Roman Empire by focusing on the role played by Africans. We have already mentioned how Severus's son, Caracalla, took control of the empire after his father's death by murdering his brother Geta in 211. In turn, Caracalla was murdered by his own supporter and fellow African, Macrinus.[81] Macrinus ruled for only a short time, for he, and then the rest of the Severan dynasty, met an untimely death. The next emperor, Maximinus Thrax, dealt with a conflict arising out of Africa known as the "Gordian revolt."

Since Maximinus, like Severus, ruled by exalting the military, the price for the elevated salaries of soldiers had to be paid by undesirable means, such as increased taxes. One Roman official in Africa pressed too hard, which led to an uprising of landowners and farmers. "The Africans" declared the local proconsul, Gordian I, as the new emperor; Gordian recruited his son, Gordian II, to reign with him; and the Roman senate, which never truly approved of Maximinus, officially declared the Gordians *Augusti*.[82]

While the new co-emperors enjoyed widespread support in North Africa, the III Augustan Legion in Numidia remained under the control of Maximinus's supporter, Governor Capellianus. His well-trained soldiers marched through Africa to Carthage with easy success. Gordian II died in battle, and then his father committed suicide.

Meanwhile in Rome, the senate continued its resistance to Maximinus and appointed Gordian's grandson, Gordian III, as the new emperor.[83] Maximinus's attempt to reclaim the city of Rome failed, and his own troops assassinated him in 238. Gordian III gained the support of many in Rome, and yet in Carthage loyalties were at times still divided. The African proconsul, Sabinianus, declared himself emperor in 240, but the governor of Mauretania, a supporter of Gordian III, swiftly defeated the rebellion.[84] The civil wars took their toll on the African landscape: Roman legions retreated from the southern borders, and the already damaged agricultural economy continued to face increasing taxes. This deadly mixture led to a series of local uprisings, and such uprisings would continue sporadically across Africa for generations to come.[85] The military imagery can even be seen in the Christian writings from this time, such as Cyprian's letters.

From 248 to 258 Cyprian served as bishop during two of the more severe persecutions known to the African church. Early in his career, he wrote a letter addressing the martyrdoms taking place under the emperor Decius (251), and referred to martyrs as "spiritual soldiers."[86] Cyprian's use of military imagery pervaded much of his work, as seen even at the end of his life when he receives word that his own death was imminent. He boldly asserts, "soldiers of God and of Christ are not slain but crowned."[87] Cyprian's church seems to have embraced this imagery, for upon his death they honor him with a *triumphus*, a term that normally indicates the parade celebrating a general's military conquest.[88] Many African martyrdom accounts follow Cyprian's example both in terms of imitating his Christian witness and in terms of the military imagery used to color the accounts.[89] The military struggles in Africa continue to impact Christian thinking into the fourth century; only the rhetoric sharpens by focusing on division and betrayal.

Christian Africa in the fourth century

The fourth century in Africa, and elsewhere, witnessed dramatic shifts in the political landscape. In Rome, Constantine converted to Christianity and conquered his rivals.[90] In Carthage, schism broke out over who should be the rightful bishop – which later became known as the Donatist schism (see Chapter 7). Throughout Africa, the simultaneous increase of "very oppressive . . . taxes" and decrease of military protection resulted in another civil war.[91]

Across the vast geographical diversity of fourth-century Africa, many had grown impatient with imperial policies. In Tripolitania to the east of Carthage (a region in what is now modern Libya), the once-influential port cities came under attack by the "madness of savages [*barbarica rabies*]" from the south.[92] The Roman official in Carthage, however, failed to provide any defense for these citizens. In Numidia and across the Mauretanian regions to the west, the lack of any Roman legions left a disorganized and weakened infrastructure that was unable to maintain imperial control. The blame for these matters, although stemming from older problems, fell largely on the count of Africa, Romanus.[93] Romanus had withheld military support in Tripolitania because the citizens there refused to bribe him. In the west his governance was no better.

When (in c.372) the Mauretanian ruler, Nubel, died, his sons fought over his estate. Count Romanus had supported Jubel's son, Zammac, but the other son, Firmus, killed Zammac over an inheritance dispute. Romanus then lobbied the emperor against Firmus, and in response Firmus revolted. Nubel and his sons belonged to the Jubaleni, which was one of the many people groups on the frontier of Rome's southern provinces. Because Rome could no longer sustain an army in these regions, the empire employed these vassal-like kingdoms as border patrol. This practice, however, left open the likelihood of a powerful ruler such as Firmus betraying any allegiance to Rome.

For three years Firmus led successful campaigns against the Roman presence in Africa, until allies handed him over to General Theodosius.[94] Upon his defeat, we are told, Firmus committed suicide rather than undergo humiliation and torture. As for Theodosius, although he had shown himself to be an able military leader and though he was revered by the chroniclers, he suffered arrest and execution in Carthage in 376 for reasons lost to history.[95]

For a few years a relative peace settled over Africa, but it would not be long lived. The emperor tolerated Donatist Christians, probably with a clear understanding that times required such compromises. A similar appointment came in 386, when Emperor Theodosius (the son of the general), appointed Firmus's brother, Gildo, as the new count of Africa.

Betraying ties of kinship, Gildo had supported the elder Theodosius in his campaign against Firmus, and he then continued in service to the emperor as an army official. For reasons not entirely clear, Gildo then rebelled in 398. Theodosius had died in 395, leaving the empire divided between east and west. Theodosius's two sons, Arcadius and Honorius, ruled each half respectively. Gildo halted Africa's grain shipment to Rome, and Honorius in turn had Gildo declared an enemy of the state.

The battle with Gildo would be led by Gildo's younger brother, Mascazel. Just as Gildo had betrayed his brother Firmus and brought about his defeat, so Gildo in turn lost the fight with Rome because of Mascazel, who reportedly fought him like a "crazy barbarian."[96] Gildo, again reminiscent of his older brother, committed suicide after his capture. The recurring motif of betrayal from Africa's civil wars also arises thematically in the Christian literature from this time as well.

In the fourth-century African Christian martyrdoms, the military motif continues as a dominant theme. One of the most influential accounts is that of the Abitinian martyrs.[97] The narrator explains, "I begin an account of celestial battles and struggles undertaken anew by the bravest of soldiers of Christ [*milites Christi*],"[98] language that echoes the words of Cyprian and which fills virtually every page of the Abitinians' story. What emerges as a new theme in this era is the concern with *traditores*, or traitors.

To understand the concern with treachery in these so-called Donatist martyrdoms, one scholar explains, "one might quote the analogy of the feuds which sprang up in western European countries after the Second World War between 'collaborators' and 'men of Resistance.'"[99] While such comparisons may be an overstatement of the connection between the political turmoil and the Christian communities, the analogy is helpful in describing the climate in which the North African Christians lived.

In *The Acts of the Abitinian Martyrs*, the narrator uses the strongest language when it comes to the *traditores*. Just before the sentencing, the author clarifies how the purpose is to remember "the glory of the martyrs and the condemnation of the traitors."[100] The importance of this battle line must be repeated, so that "one may know the rewards of the martyrs and the punishments of the traitors."[101] Exactly who, or what, the betrayal refers to needs further discussion.

When the Donatist schism occurs in the early fourth century, the primary concern is with those who have betrayed Christ during the persecution. This betrayal could occur by way of verbal denial ("Caesar is Lord"), by way of sacrificing to the Roman gods, or simply by "handing over" (*traditio*) the sacred scriptures. *The Acts of the Abitinian Martyrs* begins with a focus on this last form of betrayal: "Some fell from faith at the critical moment by handing over to unbelievers the scriptures of the Lord and the divine testaments so they could be burned in unholy fires."[102] The concern with betrayal, however, likely includes more than the scriptures alone. The martyrs themselves were "handed over" by "local officials" to the proconsul. Moreover, the proconsul tortures the Christians in order to ascertain who was "the leader of their congregation,"[103] and, embarrassingly, it seems that Dativus did single out his presbyter.[104] This slip, however, seems to be a pardonable moment of weakness, given the fact that Dativus and Saturninus, the outed presbyter, died together as martyrs. In another case, however, the betrayal seems to run deeper.

The final pages of the martyrdom allow the narrator to demonstrate the ongoing relevance of these events: "When Mensurius, so-called bishop of Carthage, polluted by the recent handing over of scripture, repented for the malice of his misdeeds and then began to reveal greater crimes."[105] These "greater crimes [*flagitiis maioribus*]" turn out to be the scene where Mensurius betrayed the martyrs themselves. The bishop ordered the deacon (and soon to be head of the "Catholic" party) Caecilian to assault any Christians who offered food to the martyrs-to-be in prison. Caecilian stationed himself at the door to the prison, apparently in full view of – and perhaps in total cooperation with – the Roman officials. "Caecilian was more ruthless than the tyrant, more bloody than the executioner."[106] Sentiments such as these reflect an African context torn by divided loyalties.

The word *traditor* itself bears an interesting history in ancient African Christian writings. In its oldest known Christian usage, Tertullian and Arnobius employ the term simply to mean "teacher" or one who "hands over" truth (thus our term "tradition").[107] It is not until the Donatist controversy that Christians begin to use the word to mean "traitor."[108] Seemingly unaware of the earlier benign meaning of this term, Augustine quotes a contemporary of Cyprian, a certain Marcus of Mactaris, who stated, "What is marvelous is that some of us, *traitors* to the truth, uphold heretics and oppose Christians; therefore we decree that heretics should be baptized."[109] Augustine delights in Marcus's admission that Cyprian's party communed and identified with *traditores*, for Augustine's so-called Catholic party does the same.[110]

Augustine, however, has overlooked two important items: First, Marcus is not proud that some in his region of Africa[111] have in fact betrayed the truth. He is urging them to reconsider. Second, and more to the point of our discussion, Marcus used the Latin word *praevaricator*, not *traditor*, to refer to those who abandon the truth. Augustine correctly quotes him as using *praevaricator* but then proceeds to replace the word with *traditor* in his commentary on Marcus's quote.

In Marcus's day, *traditor* still meant one who "hands over," "passes along," or "teaches" something, and so he must use a stronger word to call someone a "traitor." By Augustine's time, however, the literal idea "to hand over" has become politically charged with the idea of treachery. In the fourth century, Augustine (and in modern times his translators) failed to notice how *praevaricator* and *traditor* are not synonymous for an earlier writer like Marcus.

The shift in meaning for *traditor* coincided with the civil wars recounted here, in which betrayal played such a dominant motif in Africa's history. In recounting the lot of Gordian, one ancient historian concludes, "the same thing that is related [*traditus*] of [Julius] Caesar happened to Gordian."[112] The use of the archetypal betrayal of Julius Caesar by Brutus and his conspirators suggests that many who followed the events of these civil wars understood them in terms of political "traitors." Whether or not the Christians of the third and fourth centuries knew of this particular historical account is beside the point: both reflect the common mentality of this African context.

The backdrop of political treachery accentuates the concern with the *traditores* in African Christian writings. Although many of the Christian texts cited predate Firmus's and Gildo's rebellions (but not that of the Gordians), they reflect the same widespread anxiety of fourth-century Africa, namely, a society plagued with divided loyalties that often produced bloody battles between neighbors and kin. We will return to the specific writers of this time in our sixth chapter. But before we conclude our overview of ancient African Christian history, we need to cover the period of the Vandal invasion until the supposed end of ancient African Christianity.

The last days of ancient African Christianity

In 429 the political focus in Africa shifted from internal disputes to foreign invaders. The Donatist controversy that had riddled Africa for over a century had come to a climax in 411. Augustine, who would die in 430, had successfully lobbied the emperor to have legislation passed and enforced against the so-called Donatist party, and the latest enforcer of this situation was Count Boniface.

Boniface, appointed by the western emperor Honorius (mentioned in the previous section), held together Africa's fragile frontier reasonably well. Although many "barbarians"[113] raided the Roman provinces from time to time, the records suggest Boniface ruled successfully in Africa. When Honorius died in 423, the throne of the western empire fell into the hands of Johannes, or John the Usurper. Boniface, however, remained loyal to Honorius's lineage and supported Valentinian III, who received the appointment to be the western *Augustus* from his uncle Theodosius II, the eastern emperor. Reminiscent of Gildo from the previous generation, Boniface withheld the grain supply to Italy. This move weakened Johannes's position, until he was finally defeated and Valentinian claimed the throne.

Boniface's control over Africa came to an end at the hands of the so-called barbarian hordes plaguing the Roman Empire at this time. Augustine knew firsthand the limits of Roman control in his province. In answer to a friend's letter, Augustine justified the need to accept the oath of a "barbarian": "For not only at the frontier, but in all the provinces peace is won by the oaths of barbarians."[114] This letter, written in Augustine's early career, was then book-ended by his correspondence with Count Boniface, wherein he pleaded for intervention with the "African barbarians."[115] At the end of Augustine's life he also addressed the ensuing Vandal invasion,[116] the same invasion that besieged the city of Hippo as Augustine lay dying, and the same invasion that many blamed on Boniface's political miscalculation.

Boniface, despite his display of loyalty to Valentinian, soon became suspect in the eyes of Valentinian's mother, Placidia. According to one source, Boniface then attempted to strengthen his position against a possible attack from Italy by inviting the Vandals from their recently established position in Spain into Africa. When suspicions died down, Boniface asked the Vandals to return to Spain. The Vandals declined and declared war on Boniface and his troops.[117] After a brief conflict in which Boniface and his reinforcements from Placidia lost decisively, the Vandal king, Geiseric, signed a treaty with Emperor Valentinian. The treaty conceded all of the western African provinces to the Vandals, the newest ally of the Roman Empire. Geiseric, however, heeded the borders of this treaty for only a short time and by 439 he had conquered all of North Africa, forcing a new treaty, and marking the last time Italy would control Africa.[118]

One of the bishops of Carthage who served during Geiseric's rule was Quodvultdeus. Because Geiseric held to an Arian view of Christ (which will be discussed further in Chapters 7 and 9), he sent Quodvultdeus into exile as the bishop of the so-called Catholic party. Sometime during this controversy, Quodvultdeus commented on how fickle earthly authorities can be: "Kings have persecuted Christ in his Christians . . . let no one conspire with a usurper [*invasori*]."[119] This last word of warning about an "invader" is couched within Quodvultdeus's inspiring exhortation about fidelity to Christ – and yet no audience from this time period would miss the political overtones of the bishop's message, especially during a time of constant change in foreign control over Africa.[120]

In a wider perspective, Geiseric's new treaty with Theodosius II conceded the Mauretanian provinces back to Constantinople's jurisdiction.[121] This political redistricting made little difference, however, to everyday life: much of western Africa had long been untamable by the empire, and so the eastern emperor's alleged authority over these regions could never be fully enforced. Therefore, when Geiseric chose to interrupt the supply of grain from the western African provinces to Italy (a now-familiar tactic for African-based rulers), the eastern emperor could do little to stop him. One contemporary bemoaned the loss of "the imperial storehouses . . . they have captured Africa itself, which is to say, the heart of the Empire."[122]

The severed tie between these western African provinces and Rome not only applied to political jurisdiction, but it also affected the churches of the region, as found in the letters of Pope Leo I. In one letter he expresses his concern about the Mauretanian bishops because they allowed a certain person to be ordained. The person's election occurred by "the over-bearing conduct of intriguers or the rioting of the people had so much weight with you in a time of disorder."[123] The towns in these provinces seem to be in such an uproar because of "the violence of barbarians."[124] The whole tone of this letter suggests that Leo believed the provinces to be in complete anarchy, and Leo implicitly claims Roman jurisdiction over Africa.[125] Leo's claim raises a major debate among Christians today, namely between Roman Catholics and non-Catholics, over papal supremacy – a matter that need not distract us here. For the sake of our discussion, we simply note this episode because it again reflects the context of Africa, where the matter of foreign control and jurisdiction was constantly in question. Also, it should be noted that bishops of Rome had earlier assumed their responsibility for areas like Italy, Africa, and Illyricum. The point here is that Leo's assumptions about jurisdiction further illustrates the view that Romans had of Africa, which was not necessarily shared or appreciated by the Africans.

Returning to the Vandals' posture toward Rome, since Geiseric had conquered Africa's land, he could now turn his attention across the sea. The legendary naval power of Carthage from the times of the Punic wars had long since been replaced by fleets of Roman ships (themselves modeled after Punic designs) and merchant trade ships from around the Mediterranean. Geiseric converted these means of maritime transport into a veritable armada that controlled the western half of the Mediterranean. Geiseric's navy not only blocked the grain supply to Italy, but he also frequently sent his fleet on raids into various provinces on the northern coast, culminating in his sacking of Rome in 455. Although it occurred at the hand of a foreign ruler, the historical irony cannot be missed in this event: Carthage had finally defeated Rome. Susan Raven even conjectures that many of the indigenous Punic sailors continued to work in Carthage and contributed to its naval success.[126] Whatever Punic heritage may have fueled Geiseric's forays, the North African peoples' reception of and cooperation with the 80,000 Vandals (easily less than 5 percent of the population of North Africa), suggests that Rome's enemies were seen as allies.[127] The Carthaginians had not even resisted Geiseric when he marched on the city in 439. For much of the population, life in North Africa continued largely unchanged, only now the authority had passed from a Roman governor to a Vandal king.[128]

To return to Geiseric's reign in Carthage, the Roman Empire continued to strike back. However, with Rome no longer able to put up any resistance, the lot fell to Constantinople to reclaim Africa. In 468 the eastern empire's navy attacked Geiseric, but Geiseric emerged as the victor. Until his death in 477 the Vandal king ruled North Africa without threat from outside forces. Geiseric's successors, however, could not say the same.

In our discussion of the Vandal invasion in this section, we often relied on the account of Victor of Vita. His *History of the Vandal Persecution* is one of the few (roughly) contemporary accounts of these events. Without discounting any religious motivation for writing this work, we also should note how Victor's stated purpose is to appeal to "the fathers of the East," that is, to Constantinople, for help.[129] Victor's plea, which serves as one more example of how Christians must address the matter of jurisdiction over Africa, will soon receive an answer.

Geiseric's successors ruled over North Africa during the decline of Vandal control. The Mauretanians and other people groups from the southern borders repeatedly and successfully attacked Vandal territory. Decades after such attacks had weakened the Vandal kingdom, the new Byzantine emperor, Justinian, easily defeated the Vandals in 533. On the one hand, Vandal rule no longer appealed to the North Africans, seeing as how this Byzantine army marched on Carthage aided by local supplies. On the other hand, the Byzantine reconquest did not establish itself as firmly as Justinian hoped it would.

First, although the Vandals were defeated in 553, it took Byzantium years to subdue the Mauretanians, who refused to recognize the re-established *Romaiōn archēs*, "Roman rule."[130] Moreover, the empire once again used the African provinces for a cheap food supply, meaning that the natural resources were extracted (this time, taken east), and this also coincided with a much higher tax than the Vandals had required. Such a combination made for a volatile situation.

Justinian's official in Africa, Solomon, understood the dangerous reality of the people groups in the frontier zones. He sought truces with them while simultaneously erecting numerous fortifications throughout the African provinces. Despite his efforts, and because of additional turmoil within the Byzantine ranks, the Byzantine soldiers mutinied against Solomon in 536, pledging their allegiance to the Numidians. Solomon regained control of the area by 539, but his authority did not last. A Numidian leader brought about Solomon's defeat and death in 543, and for a few years North Africa fell back into a period of civil war, or wars, fought mostly between the various people groups.

For some time, Constantinople could do nothing to re-enforce its own authority in Africa. Finally, in 546 a new "Roman" general, John Troglita, established relative peace in the name of the empire, although it took him years to do so.[131] For almost a century after Troglita's tenure, Africa prospered. Although sporadic fighting continued to arise, the Byzantine leaders allowed the local peoples to rule themselves, so long as trade and some taxation continued east. On the heels of this reconquest of Africa, Constantinople also faced challenges to its jurisdiction from Christian writers. In what later became known as the Three Chapters controversy, African Christians led the charge against Emperor Justinian.

In the same year Solomon was defeated in Africa, the emperor Justinian attempted to reconcile two Christian parties within his empire, namely the Chalcedonians and the Alexandrians, and in order to accommodate the

Alexandrians he declared the writings of three theologians heretical.[132] This move in turn created three problems: (a) these writers were dead, and to excommunicate dead people would open a can of worms – no pun intended; (b) no emperor had so boldly interfered in the decisions of the church, and Justinian it seemed had overstepped his bounds; (c) these theologians had been validated by the Council of Chalcedon, and now the Chalcedonian party would react.

Although we will treat this controversy in full in Chapter 10, the doctrinal concerns are listed here so as to avoid any simplistic claim that the civil wars in Africa directly caused the African Christians' response to Justinian. The relationship between two events requires a much more nuanced explanation; we do, however, once again see a parallel between the African political context and the inner workings of the Christian churches. On the northern shore of the Mediterranean, the bishop of Rome, Vigilius, after some persuasion agreed with Justinian's action. Meanwhile, on the southern shore, the Africans continued to resist: by 553 they had denounced the emperor and in 554 they even excommunicated the pope. Facundus, the African bishop of Hermiane, declared the pope to be a "Roman traitor [*praevaricator*]."[133]

During this controversy, Justinian convicted Reparatus, the bishop of Carthage who refused to support Justinian's declaration, for conspiring with "Rome's" enemies – the African "barbarians."[134] Reparatus's replacement, selected and installed by Justinian, met a mob of protestors upon his arrival in Carthage, and he entered into his office only with the help of an armed guard. In Africa the Christian opponents of Justinian, like the Mauretanian resistance, continued to reject the emperor's claim to their province.

The next major disruption to Africa's history also involved the question of foreign control over Africa. In 602 the usurper Phocas murdered the Byzantine emperor, Maurice. Maurice had once spent time in Africa and as emperor he enjoyed the loyalty of Heraclius, the exarch of Africa (many provinces at this time could be collectively referred to as an "exarchate," and the exarch functioned as both a governor and a military commander).[135] Heraclius, according to most of the sources, came from Armenia, but had so proven himself in warfare that the emperor entrusted the rule of Africa to him. When Phocas seized the throne, Heraclius – after a few years of calculated delay – invoked the classical African maneuver of halting grain shipments to Constantinople. Heraclius then sent his son, Heraclius the Younger, to attack Phocas. Upon his arrival in Constantinople, the people overthrew Phocas and embraced the younger Heraclius as the new emperor. Heraclius's appointment to the throne illustrates how significant a role Africa played at this time, so much so that the new emperor considered relocating the capital of the Roman Empire from Constantinople to the safety of Carthage.[136] The move, however, never occurred, since Heraclius had to devote most of his rule to quelling the Persian armies. Next, a new opponent arose: the Arab disciples of Muhammad.[137]

When the Arab armies gained control of Palestine and then Egypt, the African exarch at the time, Gregory, decided to declare himself emperor. This title, however, refers not to the Byzantine or "Roman" empire, but to the African. With the new threat from Arabia coming across Egypt, "the Africans" encouraged Gregory to declare Africa independent of Rome.[138] Gregory, as the emperor of Africa, moved his headquarters to Sufetula (central Tunisia) and awaited the invading army.

During this time a Byzantine monk named Maximus (who would later earn the title, "the Confessor") arrived on the scene in Africa. Maximus had been born into a noble family in Constantinople, and he likely would have known about Emperor Maurice's inclination to move the capital to Carthage. Although Maurice never took this action, Maximus fled the Persian invasion of 626 and moved to Carthage. As discussed on the previous page, Justinian had systematically replaced bishops in Africa who opposed his actions against the Three Chapters, and in their place he installed bishops who appeased the Monophysite party. Maximus took it upon himself to debate these Monophysites, and his actions won him the approval of Christians in the region. It is hard to imagine that the African resistance to Justinian did not impact Maximus' own thinking, for – if accusations are to be believed – Maximus and the African bishops encouraged Gregory the exarch to declare Africa independent of "Rome."[139]

The African independent spirit has caused great debate among scholars. The evidence comes not only from Maximus the Confessor, but also from letters of Pope Gregory I (known as Gregory the Great) written during this period to African leaders (see Chapter 10). Gregory voiced concerns with a resurgence of "Donatism," but many scholars find this hard to accept at face value. Instead, it is argued, the African churches champion their independence throughout their history. As examples, historians find this shared value among early African martyrs, fourth-century "Donatists," and seventh-century supporters of Gregory the exarch. As R. A. Markus has explained,

> Whatever the answer, the persistence and volume of dissent throughout the history of African Christianity is striking enough to prompt the historian to seek an underlying thread behind the changing forms. The Church of Tertullian and Cyprian, the Church of Donatus and Parmenian, the Church of Ferrandus and Facundus, are all stamped with a common character; and some of its features are to be discerned even in the Church of Augustine and Aurelius. It is a character with a vitality which made itself felt again in the seventh century, when the opposition to monothelitism, rallied around Maximus, had its mainstay in the African Church.[140]

We must be careful not to claim too much about this "common character" of African Christianity, for many exceptions can be found and we should take each writer and subject on a case-by-case basis. Markus, however, does touch upon a recurring theme we will encounter throughout our study. This theme of independence, moreover, is understood better when we locate it within the broad scope of Africa's political history of competing claims for foreign control.

Another new foreign presence attempted to seize control of Africa: the Arab invasion from Egypt. In response the Africans once again divided their support. At the battle of Sufetula in 648, "Berbers" fought on both sides. When this battle concluded in Exarch Gregory's defeat and death, the African empire officially ended, but the African populations continued to struggle in deciding where to pledge their loyalty.[141] The Arabs, after a hefty payment from the Africans, returned to Egypt. Control of Africa, many thought, belonged once more to Constantinople, when in reality Byzantine control extended little past the port cities, while many of the inland areas operated independently. The local populations resented and at times resisted the empire's reinstated taxes, which posed a "crushing burden" to the local populations.[142]

In 683, after Arab raids had gained much ground in regions south of Byzantine control, the Egypt-based general, Uqba Ibn Nafi, led a force west in order to expand Arab rule.[143] While historians may doubt the stories of Uqba reaching the Atlantic, his westward march was undeniably impressive. His fatal mistake, however, lay in the fact that his long march left him vulnerable.

Against the last alliance between the various people groups of the African provinces and the Byzantine army, Uqba's force met its defeat. The architect of this alliance, Kusayla, ruled the Awrabas in the Aures Mountains. Upon his death in 690 another leader arose, called Kahina ("the Seer"), and she led the last major resistance to the Egypt-based Arabs.[144] Kahina, according to later sources, announced a simple strategy: inspire the peoples of Africa to desolate their own lands. If Africa could no longer produce wealth, then the foreign invaders would no longer desire Africa. Such a policy, however, proved too radical for her lowland allies, and many even welcomed Muslim conquest as preferable.[145]

Kahina's death around 703 marked the end of any real dispute over Arab rule. This rule, it should be noted, for many centuries remained decentralized, and many Africans thrived during this period. In the words of one Arab source:

> The Rum [i.e. "Romans" or Byzantines] who were occupying these lands were forced to leave, but the Afāriq [i.e. Africans] who were subject to the Rum remained, paying a tribute which they were accustomed to render to all who occupied their county.[146]

The only major objection of the inhabitants, of course, was the dominance of a new religion – something which will be discussed further in Chapter 11.[147]

As we recount this final scene in North African Christian history, we can find no parallel in the Christian writings from this period in Africa, for there the Christian voices fall silent in the late seventh century. Fleeting glimpses of an ongoing Christian presence in Africa arise in archaeological sources and in a few European references to Africa, but on the whole the supposed disappearance of Christianity in seventh-century Africa occurs as mysteriously as Christianity's first appearance in Africa during the second century. Reflecting on this entire history, one Muslim writer concluded:

> When these people [from the Northern Mediterranean] coveted the possession of the southern shore, as the Byzantines (coveted) Ifrîqiyah and as the Goths (coveted) the Maghrib, they achieved superiority over the Berbers and deprived them of their power. . . . The ancient master of Carthage used to fight the master of Rome and to send fleets loaded with armies and equipment to wage war against him.[148]

As with every point in our story, our treatment has only been introductory, and the material will receive more detailed discussion in the following chapters. But before turning to those chapters, let us attempt to resituate our aims with this introductory chapter and for this book as a whole.

History and ancient African Christians

In the previous section we have attempted to provide the backdrop to North African Christianity by tracing the political history and listing examples where this history is reflected in Christian writings from this time. Our approach, therefore, has largely been what scholars now call "history from above." In other words we have focused on rulers and wars. Hopefully, this has helped the reader gain a bird's-eye view (i.e. "from above") of ancient African Christian history.

In the following chapters we will shift our perspective and focus more on the specific writers and events that occurred in the life of the North African churches. Our approach, then, will be closer to what historians now call "history from below."[149] Although most of our sources will be texts written by the literate elite class, we aim to learn about the majority of African Christians addressed by and reflected in their works. Hopefully, this will enable the reader to appreciate the many textures and voices from ancient African Christian history.

A bit more needs to be said about the difference between history "from above" and "from below." In choosing to focus on the "below" side of things, we do not disparage the big-picture approach; instead we rely upon it, and situate our discussion within the larger framework. Also, we need to be clear what this method entails.

As we treat each time period and person in more detail, we will continually discuss the "cultural" distinctions. We must place this word, "culture," in quotation marks because it has been notoriously difficult to define. A precise definition of this term, however, does not need to be provided here, because in the following chapters we will mostly avoid the word and instead speak about more clearly defined topics that are usually lumped together under this broad category – topics such as language, religion, art, and customs. What we do need to clarify, however, is the way in which a "history from below" understands the relationship between two "cultures." Since much of the following study is an attempt to understand Christians who are both "Roman" and "African," we must pause to clarify the method that will be used in order to avoid some disastrous mistakes.

1   The first mistake we must avoid is assumptions about the word "race." In a collection entitled *New Stories from the South*, a southern child in Mississippi learns about the martyrs, Perpetua and Felicity. When she hears that these women were from Carthage, the child responds, " 'Well, if Carthage is in Africa, were [they] colored?' That had never occurred to me. I thought that if it was true it was wonderful."[150] While we will have the opportunity to address the ethnicity and even the skin color of North Africans in the following chapters, we need to clarify that a person's ethnicity has nothing to do with "race." The old idea of race – one still common in popular conversation – must be rejected. A people's body type, skin color, DNA, or any such physical characteristic have absolutely nothing to do with their behavior, temperament, or disposition. An ethnic group may be described by any number of shared characteristics or practices, such as language, religion, or land of origin – to name but a few. This point will be important in the following chapters because we will not be looking for an African "race," or even racial features. Instead, we will focus on what it meant to be "African" in each individual circumstance and time period.

2   The second mistake we must avoid is the assumption that "culture" and "ethnicity" go hand in hand. To again take a popular example, one can cook "ethnic food," such as lasagna, without belonging to a certain "ethnicity," such as Italian. In other words, "culture" can cross ethnic boundaries.[151] This will be important in the following chapters because we will often find examples where Roman "culture" has been embraced by African people groups, the most famous being the Latin language itself.[152] And yet, such an embrace of *Romanitas*, or Roman-ness, makes these people no less African.

3   The third mistake we must avoid is the assumption about labels and "identity." Given what was said in the previous statement about cultural content crossing ethnic boundaries, we can recognize someone as "African" in one sense, such as being born on African soil, but also look for ways in which they are "not African" in another sense, such as speaking the "Roman" language. In fact, in most instances we will see that "African" and "non-African" is a false dichotomy, for many

people we will study bear multiple identities: African by homeland, Roman by citizenship, Christian by religion, poet by trade, etc. In any given instance we must seek to understand the person or group on their own terms, which may include several different – even seemingly conflicting – self-descriptions.

4   One last mistake we must seek to avoid is separating our material into overly rigid categories, such as religion, politics, and economics. While we have used and will use these terms, we do so with the awareness that many acts, such as sacrificing to Caesar, entail multiple meanings, such as political significance, religious significance, and economic significance. While we do not wish to diminish the religious and spiritual motivations in the thoughts of Tertullian, Augustine, and other Christian writers, we must also avoid claiming that their thoughts are "only" religious. In the ancient world (as in ours!) there was no such thing as "only religious," or "only political," or "only economic," to name but a few examples.[153] One area that will not receive sufficient treatment in this book is what could be called "theology proper." That is to say that the nuances of what the North African Christians believed about God and God's ordering of creation will not be explored in depth. To be sure, the main contributions of each author will be introduced, and certain theological trends will be traced throughout this history. The following work, however, is not an attempt to offer a systematic treatment of the African Christians' doctrines. Partly, this is because no strict divorce can be made even between "theology proper" and Christian practice for our subjects. Also, before a more in depth treatment can be attempted for such a broad historical tradition, more work needs to be done to situate this African tradition in its historical context, which is the main focus of the following chapters.

With these four mistakes identified – and hopefully avoided – we can now also acknowledge a specific problem that scholars face in regard to ancient African Christians. The relationship between these categories – religious and social, in particular – have troubled modern scholars of North African Christianity. The problem can especially be seen when looking to sources from the fourth and early fifth century. This is the time of the Donatist controversy, which will be discussed in Chapter 7. Since more sources from this era survive than any other period in African Christian history, scholars have naturally focused on it. Our understanding of the unique expression of Christianity in Africa owes much to this time period and to this controversy. The Donatists claimed to be the traditional expression of Christianity in Africa, as opposed to the "Catholic" party of Augustine, which was tied to the traditions of Italy. Scholars who wished to test this claim often took the next logical step and inquired about the "African" nature of the Donatists themselves. While space does not allow for a full review of the literature, a summary will help illustrate the kind of mistake we must avoid in the present discussion.[154] The scholarly views can be summarized in terms of a Hegelian dialectic:[155] (a) the traditionalist thesis, (b) the revisionist antithesis, and from these two views is (c) an emerging synthesis.

1   The traditionalist thesis views Donatism in the paradigm outlined by Irenaeus, wherein heresy is a deviation from pre-established orthodoxy.[156] This is the view forwarded by the two major opponents of the Donatists, Optatus of Milevis (late fourth cent.) and Augustine of Hippo (354–430).[157] Their view was then largely accepted by the "Catholic" tradition that followed them. The main difficulty with such a paradigm is that the Donatists themselves utilized the exact same framework, only with the Caecilianists representing the deviation from the pre-established (in this case Cyprianic) orthodoxy. Both sides claimed to be Catholic.[158]

2   The revisionist thesis follows the approach of Gottfried Arnold, who in 1699 attempted an "Impartial History" of the heretics, a view later modified and brought into the mainstream of scholarship by Walter Bauer.[159] In this framework, the chronological binary of orthodoxy and heresy is essentially replaced with an emphasis on the diversity of "Christianities." Some groups formerly known as "heretics" are now understood as the earliest form of Christianity in their locale.[160] The Donatists in particular will be seen as an indigenous group who were especially prone to religious extremism, violence, and therefore eager to align themselves with militant rebellions against Rome.[161] The objection to such a view is the inherent reductionism that eclipses any sincere religious conviction on the part of the Donatists, as well as the clear evidence that Donatists often appealed to the Roman legal system and thus were not unanimously or absolutely anti-Roman in their behavior.[162]

3   A few scholars have attempted a synthesis between these two views, wherein both social and religious factors can cohere.[163] While these scholars in no way champion a view of the Donatists as essentially "indigenous," they do focus equally on the "social" aspects of the movement. Of course, the categories of traditional thesis and revisionist antithesis should not be viewed rigidly: most scholars from each category devote study to the "social" and to the "religious." The difference is primarily one of emphasis: which aspect of Donatism was its driving force? The scholars I classify here as offering a synthesis represent an approach that does not require a choice between the social and the religious. With the Donatists in particular, and with ancient African Christians in general, I suspect that this is the way forward in future studies.

Peter Brown is helpful here: even though he preferred to understand Donatism in conjunction with the wider Christianization of late antiquity rather than focus on the local,[164] his insights can simply be synthesized with aspects of Donatism that were social, not nationalist or strictly social in a reductionistic sense, but social nonetheless – an approach Brown went on to model in his later works for Christianity in late antiquity writ large.[165] Therefore, in answer to the question, were the Donatists a social movement in disguise? We firmly answer in the negative. But then again this is the wrong question. They were a socio-religious group at times exhibiting a regional social identity. In fact, as Brown long ago acknowledged, Donatism was not a "movement" at all, for it was Augustine's "Catholic" party that had to establish itself in North Africa.[166] Concurring with Brown, R. A. Markus insisted,

> Donatism was no new creation. It was the representative in the fourth century of an older African theological tradition with deep roots in its characteristic religious mentality. . . . Donatism was, quite simply, the continuation of the old African Christian tradition in the post-Constantinian world. It was the world that had changed, not African Christianity. . . . It is the catholic church of Optatus and Augustine, between Constantine and the disappearance of Roman rule in 430, that constitutes the anomaly in African Christianity.[167]

In other words, Brown and Markus, while critical of the indigenous antithesis per se, are equally unwilling to revert to the traditional thesis – that Donatists were a deviation from their region's pre-established orthodoxy. Therefore, a new synthesis must emerge in the study of ancient African Christians, wherein both the religious and the social aspects are considered together. This view of Donatism in particular can be broadened to include the whole of ancient African Christianity.

All of these points about identity and how to study an "African identity" will be further discussed in Chapter 2, when we look at the background and context to African Christianity. At this point, we can conclude this introductory discussion by restating our opening question, which is the primary question that guides the following study. Who were the ancient African Christians and what about them was "African"? We hope to answer this question in sufficient detail in the chapters that follow.

Notes

1 As will be explained throughout this book, "non-Roman" does not necessarily imply "anti-Roman" or not-Roman-at-all. How to understand "identity" will be discussed at length in chapter two.
2 E.g. in Strabo, *Geography*, 17.3.1.
3 Africa Proconsularis, Byzacena, Tripolitania, Numidia Cirtensis, Numidia Militiana, Mauretania Sitifensis, and Mauretania Caesariensis.
4 For an example of "Africa" encompassing all of the provinces, including Africa Proconsularis, see a letter from an African Christian quoted in Augustine's *Expositions on the Psalms* 36.2.36.20, "To our most holy brethren and colleagues throughout the whole of Africa, that is, those dwelling in Africa Proconsularis, Numidia, Mauretania, Byzacena and Tripoli [*sanctissimis fratribus*

atque collegis per uniuersam Africam, hoc est per prouinciam proconsularem, Numidiam, Mauritaniam, Byzacenam et Tripolim constitutis]."

5 Cf. Karen B. Stern, *Inscribing Devotion and Death: Archaeological Evidence for Jewish Populations of North Africa* (Leiden: Brill, 2007), who argues that Jewish material remains in North Africa are better understood in comparison with local African culture rather than looking for only unique Jewish characteristics, as defined by Palestinian Judaism. Also, see David Frankfurter, *Religion in Roman Egypt: Assimilation and Resistance* (Princeton, NJ: Princeton University Press, 2000), or a study of Egypt comparable to the one undertaken here for Africa.

6 J. Patout Burns and Robin Margaret Jensen, et al., *Christianity in Roman Africa: The Development of Its Practices and Beliefs* (Grand Rapids, MI: Eerdmans, 2014), xlvi–xlvii. It should be noted that the category of "schools" for Antioch and Alexandria has now been challenged by scholars (see Paul L. Gavrilyuk, *The Suffering of the Impassible God: The Dialectics of Patristic Thought* [Oxford: Oxford University Press, 2004], 137–139). Nevertheless, if "school" is understood loosely to mean something like a collective heritage of doctrines and practices, then Burns, Jensen, et al. have demonstrated the heuristic benefit of studying the North African Christians as a collective because the transgenerational continuities can be better appreciated and understood.

7 *Letter to the Mother of Caesar* 5: ἐγὼ δὲ Λίβυς τῶν Λιβύων τῶν νομάδων.

8 *Apology* 24: *professus sum . . . Seminumidam et Semigaetulum*; cf. *Florida* 9.36–40, where Apuleius represents himself as a spokesman for the whole province of Africa.

9 Even though Carthage and Punic populations in general are understood by historians as advanced civilizations, the Romans readily dismissed them as "barbarians." E.g. the Roman Scipio called the Carthaginian general Hasdrubal "a barbarian, a mass of effeminacy and cowardice [βάρβαρος ἀνὴρ καὶ τρυφῆς γέμων καὶ δέους]" (in Appian, *The Punic Wars* 4.20).

10 *Letter* 138.19: *Apuleius, enim, ut de illo potissimum loquamur, qui nobis Afris Afer est notior.*

11 One of the earliest classical sources on "Libya" is Herodotus, *Histories*, who in book four discusses many different people groups in the region in order from east to west. In the first century CE, Pliny the Elder, *Natural History* 5.4.29, counted 516 such groups who were in allegiance with Rome, and there he is reporting on only one region within Africa.

12 Brent D. Shaw, "Who Are You? Africa and Africans," in *A Companion to Ethnicity in the Ancient Mediterranean*, ed. Jeremy McInerny (Oxford: Wiley Blackwell, 2014), 530.

13 Wilhite, *Tertullian the African: An Anthropological Reading of Tertullian's Context and Identities* (Berlin: Walter De Gruyter, 2007).

14 While some scholars may point to the social analysis of Georg Schöllgen, *Ecclesia sordida? Zur Frage der socialen Schichtung frühchristlichen Gemeinden am Beispiel Karthagos zur Zeit Tertullians* (Münster: Aschendorff, 1984), Schöllgen's focus was on the economic status of Christians, and not their socio-ethnic identity.

15 See his work *On the Cloak*, discussed in chapter four.

16 Jérôme Lagouanere, "Tertullien et la littérature chrétienne d'Afrique: problématiques et enjeux," in *Tertullianus Afer: Tertullien et le littérature Chrétienne d'Afrique (IIe-Vie siècles)*, ed. Jérôme Lagouanere and Sabine Fialon (Turnhout: Brepols, 2015), 10–11, following the reservation expressed by Frédéric Chapot in his brief summary of my work (in *Chronica Tertullianae et Cyprianae* in *Revue des Études augustiniennes et patristiques* 54 [2 2007], 326–327).

17 Lagouanere, "Tertullien et la literature chrétienne d'Afrique," 11 (my trans.): "un mouvement autochtone de rébellion contre l'impérialisme romain."

18 Éric Rebillard, "William Hugh Clifford Frend (1916–2005): The Legacy of the Donatist Church," *Studia Patristica* 53 (2013), 55–71.

19 See Yves Modéran, *Les Maures et L'Afrique romaine* (Bibliothèque des écoles françaises d'Athènes et de Rome 314; Rome: Ecole française de Rome, 2003), 526–530.

20 Lagouanere, "Tertullien et la literature chrétienne d'Afrique," 11 (my trans.): "une conception fixiste et univoque de l'identité."

21 Lagouanere therefore recommends the work of Rebillard, *Christians and Their Many Identities in Late Antiquity, North Africa, 200–450 CE* (Ithaca, NY: Cornell University Press, 2012). I found, however, that Rebillard's approach and my own in fact have much in common; cf. the papers from the 2015 Oxford International Patristics Conference (forthcoming in *Studia Patristica* as Rebillard, "Early African Martyr Narratives"; and Wilhite, "Were the 'Donatists' a National or Social Movement in Disguise?"), wherein we both presented as part of a pre-planned session on the African Christian tradition.

22 See esp. Wilhite, *Tertullian the African*, 44. This phenomenon is discussed more generally in chapter two of this present work.

23 Robert D. Sider, *Ancient Rhetoric and the Art of Tertullian* (Oxford: Oxford University Press, 1971), 132, cited in Wilhite, *Tertullian the African*, 177. It is also worth noting that Jean-Claude Fredouille, *Tertullien et la Conversion de la Culture Antique* (Paris: Études Augustiniennes, 1972), 24, had to make a similar disclaimer in his study of classical culture in Tertullian.

24 Wilhite, *Tertullian the African*, 177.

25 For positive reviews of my work, see Geoffrey D. Dunn in *Bryn Mawr Classical Review* (2008.02.16); Ilaria Ramelli in *Review of Biblical Literature* 9 (2009); Dongsun Cho in *Southwestern Journal of Theology* 52 (2, 2010), 245–246; and Ivor J. Davidson in *Scottish Journal of Theology* 66 (February 2013), 120–121. Positive citations of my work need not be documented here.

26 For surveys, see David John Mattingly, "From One Colonialism to Another: Imperialism and the Maghreb," in *Roman Imperialism: Post-Colonial Perspectives*, ed. J. Webster and N. J. Cooper (Leicester Archaeology Monographs 3; Leicester: University of Leicester, 1996), 49–69; Patricia M. E. Lorcin, "Rome and France in Africa: Recovering Colonial Algeria's Latin Past," *French Historical Studies* 25 (2, 2002), 295–329; Walter E. Kaegi, *Muslim Expansion and Byzantine Collapse in North Africa* (Cambridge: Cambridge University Press, 2010), 18–29; and Matthew M. McCarty, "French Archaeology and History in the Colonial Maghreb: Inheritance, Presence, and Absence," in *Unmasking Ideology: Archaeology and Colonialism*, ed. Bonnie Effros and Guolong Lai (Los Angeles, CA: Cotsen Institute of Archaeology, forthcoming).

27 *Premières invasions Arabes dans l'Afrique du nord* (Paris: Ernest Leroux, 1900), 21: "une race . . . inférieure."

28 "Le christianisme dans le nord d l'Afrique avant l'Islam," *Revue Tunisienne* 8 (1901), 427: "les races supérieures."

29 *History of the Christian Church* (New York: C. Scribner's Sons, 1882), 2:420.

30 René Braun, "Aux origines de la chrétienté d'Afrique: un homme de combat, Tertullien," *Bulletin de l'Association Guillaume Budé*, fourth series (1965), 194: "un Christianisme agressif et archaïsant . . . religiosité punico-berbère" (my trans).

31 *Early Christianity in North Africa*, trans. Edward L. Smither (Eugene, OR: Wipf and Stock Publishers/Cascade Books, 2009 [French orig. 1996]), 59.

32 *Early Christianity in North Africa*, 60.

33 On how the earliest archaeology of North Africa was driven by colonialist assumptions, see Stern, *Inscribing Devotion*, 6–11.

34 Timothy David Barnes, *Tertullian: An Historical and Literary Study* (Oxford: Clarendon Press, 1971), 243.

35 For my more complete argument about what could be construed as a thesis/ antithesis in the last century, and the need for an emerging synthesis, see Wilhite, "Were the 'Donatists' a National or Social Movement in Disguise? Reframing the Question."

36 See my survey of these sources with regard to Augustine in particular in Wilhite, "Black Augustine," in *Oxford Guide to the Historical Reception of Augustine*, ed. Karla Pollmann and Willemien Otten (Oxford: Oxford University Press, 2013), 126–133.

37 *L'histoire du Maghreb: un essai de synthèse* (Paris: Maspero, 1970); available in English: Abdullah Laroui, *The History of the Maghrib: An Interpretive Essay*, trans. Ralph Manheim (Princeton, NJ: Princeton University Press, 1979).

38 Benabou, *La résistance africaine à la romanisation* (Paris: Maspéro, 1976).

39 See D. J. Mattingly and R. B. Hitchner, "Roman Africa: An Archeological Review," *Journal of Roman Studies* 85 (1995), 170, who find the responses to Laroui and Benabou to be unjustifiably vitriolic.

40 See the essays in Michael K. Brown, et al., *Whitewashing Race: The Myth of a Color-Blind Society* (Berkeley, CA: University of California Press, 2003).

41 "From One Colonialism to Another," 53.

42 Edward Said, *Orientalism* (London: Routledge, 1978), had earlier warned against any such us/them dichotomy.

43 See further discussion in chapter two.

44 As I have argued elsewhere, in particular for the Donatist controversy; see Wilhite, "Were the 'Donatists' a National or Social Movement in Disguise?" (cited in n.21).

45 Mattingly, "From One Colonialism to Another," 62.

46 Pierre-Yves Fux, Jean-Michel Roessli, and Otto Wermelinger (eds.), *Augustinus Afer: saint Augustin, africanité et universalité* (Fribourg: Editions Universitaires, 2003).

47 At least, such a volume has not been produced in a long time and not in English. See "Resources for Further Study" at the end of this chapter.

48 *Against the Nations* 2.16.4 (trans. ANF 3:165). Tertullian refers to his own homeland as "the enemy" sarcastically, a device for which he is known to be exceptionally gifted.

49 For a more complete introduction, see the first two volumes of *The Cambridge History of Africa*, and the detailed essays by Josephine Crawley Quinn, "North Africa," in *The Blackwell Companion to Ancient History*, ed. Andrew Erskine (Blackwell Companions to the Ancient World 49; New York: John Wiley and Sons, 2009), 260–272; and Brent D. Shaw, "Who Are You?"

50 See Stern, *Inscribing Devotion* (2008).

51 See chapter two.

52 Livy 21.22, refers to the "Libyphoenicians – a race of mixed Punic and African blood [*Libyphoenices, mixtum Punicum Afris genus*]," which has no historical value as demarcating a specific people group (such as the Numidians and the Mauretanians, which he also mentions in this section), but does indicate how the Punics and Libyans appeared to the Romans to have amalgamated into one non-Roman group.

53 The date of Rome's founding varies widely in the ancient sources. The more traditional date is 753. Even though Dido is shrouded in legend, archaeological studies can date evidence of Phoenician settlement in Carthage to the time the literary sources claim it was founded: see details on the possible dates in Edward Lipiński, *On the Skirts of Canaan in the Iron Age: Historical and Topographical Researches* (Orientalia Lovaniensia Analecta 153; Leuven: Peeters, 2006), 168.

54 See Richard Miles, *Carthage Must Be Destroyed* (London: Allen Lane, 2010); Nigel Bagnall, *The Punic Wars 264–146 BC* (New York: Routledge, 2003); and Adrian Keith Goldsworthy, *The Punic Wars* (London: Cassell, 2001).

55 For a detailed study of this "power" and the whole question of imperialism as it relates to Rome and Africa, see Josephine Mary Crawley, *Imperialism and Culture in North Africa: The Hellenistic and Early Roman Eras* (PhD dissertation for the University of California, Berkeley, 2003).

56 The distinction between eastern Phoenician and western Punic civilizations is a modern invention. At the same time, throughout Punic cities, there was much greater diversity than has previously been imagined by modern scholars. See both of these points discussed by the contributors to Josephine Crawley Quinn and Nicholas C. Vella (eds.), *The Punic Mediterranean: Identities and Identification from Phoenician Settlement to Roman Rule* (Cambridge: Cambridge University Press, 2014).

57 *Histories* 3.11.7.

58 The phoenix is thought to have derived its name from Phoenicia, a point that will be discussed in later chapters when African writers identify with the phoenix.

59 For discussion of material remains that illustrate the negotiation of Punic/Roman symbols and rituals in the rebuilding of Carthage, see Allen Brent, *Cyprian and Roman Carthage* (Cambridge: Cambridge University Press, 2010), 29–40. It should be noted that there is a methodological tension between identifying the "layers" (e.g. Libyan, Punic, and Roman) as distinct and between stratifying them too much; see discussion in Matthew M. McCarty, "Transforming Religion Under the Roman Empire," in *Companion to Roman Africa*, ed. Bruce Hitchner (Oxford: Wiley-Blackwell, forthcoming).

60 Again, there is a need to acknowledge both how Punic language and religion persisted and how Punic elements were re-imagined as ways of constructing an African identity; see Josephine Crawley Quinn and Matthew M. McCarty, "Echos puniques: langue, culte, et gouvernement en Numidie hellénistique," in *Massinissa, au Coeur de la consecration d'un premier Etat numide*, ed. D. Badi (Algiers: 2015), 167–198. Nevertheless, when African towns and cities accommodated Carthaginian/Punic practices, especially in reaction to the new Roman presence, the "Punic" identity often came to the forefront, as McCarty elsewhere concludes ("Africa Punica? Child Sacrifice and Other Invented Traditions in Early Roman Africa," in *Religion in the Roman Empire* [forthcoming]).

61 For the revised view, see esp. T.R.S. Broughton, *The Romanization of Africa Proconsularis* (Baltimore, MD: John Hopkins Press, 1929); Laroui, *The History of the Maghrib*; Benabou, *La Résistance Africaine*; Brent D. Shaw, *Rulers, Nomads, and Christians in Roman North Africa* (Aldershot, UK: Variorum, 1995); Brent D. Shaw, *Environment and Society in Roman North Africa* (Aldershot, UK: Variorum, 1995); David Cherry, *Frontier and Society in Roman North Africa* (Oxford: Clarendon Press, 1998); and Jonathan Conant, *Staying Roman: Conquest and Identity in Africa and the Mediterranean, 439–700* (Cambridge: Cambridge University Press, 2012), esp. 3–9.

62 For Fronto's loyalty to his homeland, see Edwin Champlin, *Fronto and Antonine Rome* (Cambridge, MA: Harvard University Press, 1980), 15. And for an interesting, if dated, study relevant to the current discussion, see M. Dorothy Brock, *Studies in Fronto and His Age; With an Appendix on African Latinity Illustrated by Selections From the Correspondence of Fronto* (Cambridge: Cambridge University Press, 1910).

63 Susan Raven, *Rome in Africa* (London: Routledge, 1993), 122.

64 Cited on p. 4.

65 The dates of Victor's episcopate are confused in the primary sources (Jerome, *Lives of Illustrious Men* 34; and Eusebius, *Church History* 5.22.1). Most scholars agree with the assigned date. His African birth is known from the *The Book of the Popes* (see Raymond Davis, *The Book of Pontiffs [Liber pontificalis]: The Ancient Biographies of the First Ninety Roman Bishops to AD 715* [Liverpool: Liverpool University Press, 2000], 6).

66 William Tefler, "The Origins of Christianity in Africa," *Studia patristica* 4 (1961), 515.

67 Admittedly, the differences between the Latin and Greek writers, to name but one example, deserves further discussion. However, the nuances of defining this movement need not detain us here, since they do not – I think – affect my conclusions here. For a more complete introduction, see Tim Whitmarsh, *The Second Sophistic* (New Surveys in the Classics, 35; Oxford: Oxford University Press, 2005).

68 *Apologia* 24 (cited on p. 4).

69 See Michael Brett and Elizabeth Fentress, *The Berbers* (Oxford: Blackwell, 1996), 32–49.

70 More will be said on how specific writers belong to the Second Sophistic movement in later chapters.

71 Although Tertullian is not listed as a Second Sophistic writer by classics scholars (e.g. Simon Swain, *Hellenism and Empire: Language, Classicism, and Power in the Greek World, AD 50–250* [Oxford: Oxford University Press, 1996]), many who specialize in Tertullian have found this to be an appropriate way to understand him (e.g. Eric Osborn, *Tertullian: First Theologian of the West* [Cambridge: Cambridge University Press, 2003], 29). Debate ensues when the precise meaning of "Second Sophistic" comes into play (e.g. Geoffrey Dunn, *Tertullian's Aduersus Iudaeos: A Rhetorical Analysis* [Patristic Monograph 19; Washington, DC: The Catholic University of America Press, 2008], 32ff.)

72 *Letter* 138.19 (trans. NPNF[2] 12:487). For more on Apuleius, see S. J. Harrison, *Apuleius: A Latin Sophist* (Oxford: Oxford University Press, 2004).

73 *The Augustan History: Severus* 1: *Severus Africa oriundus*. It should be noted that the *Augustan History* (*Scriptores Historiae Augustae*) is late and often proves to be problematic. Although it is ostensibly a collection of works by different authors, scholars today believe it to be the work (or at least the heavy redaction) of one author. Nevertheless, even if some of the details from this source cannot be accepted uncritically, historians use it to help understand how Septimius was remembered by Romans. For further discussion on the sources on Septimius Severus, see Rowan, *Under Divine Auspices: Divine Ideology and the Visualisation of Imperial Power in the Severan Period* (Cambridge: Cambridge University Press, 2012).

74 See *The Augustan History: Severus* 15 and 19.

75 Anthony R. Birley, *The African Emperor: Septimius Severus*, rev. ed. (London: B. T. Batsford LTD, 1988).

76 In addition to other sources of military imagery, such as passages from Paul (e.g. Phil. 2:25 and Eph. 6:10–18).

77 *Passion of Perpetua and Felicitas* 10 (trans. Herbert Musurillo, *The Acts of the Christian Martyrs* [Oxford: Clarendon Press, 1972], 119).

78 I am following the chronology of Barnes, *Tertullian: An Historical and Literary Study*, rev. ed. (Oxford: Clarendon Press, 1985). For the more common dating of 211, see Excursus I in René Braun, *Deus Christianorum* (Paris: Presses universitaires de France, 1962).

79 *Apology* 42.3.

80 *On the Military Crown* 11.

81 Macrinus was born in Caesarea, Mauretania.
82 Zosimus, *New History* 1.14.
83 Gordian III in fact was the second choice. The senate had first appointed Pupienus and Balbinus as co-emperors, but the Roman citizens rioted in objection.
84 Cf. Zosimus, *New History* 1.17 (Ridley 6); and Julius Capitolinus, *Augustine History: The Three Gordians* 23 (LCL 140:422–423).
85 For discussion, see Muhammad Jamal al-Din Mukhtar, *Ancient Civilization of Africa*, vol. 2 of *General History of Africa* (Berkley, CA: University of California Press, 1981), 264ff.
86 *Letter* 39.3.1 (trans. G. W. Clarke, *The Letters of Cyprian of Carthage*, vol. 2 [ACW 44; New York: Newman Press, 1984], 55).
87 *Letter* 80.2 (ACW 47:105).
88 *Acts of Cyprian* 5: *triumpho magno*.
89 See esp. *The Martyrdom of Marian and Jacob* 8; *The Martyrdom of Montanus and Lucius* 4; and *The Acts of Maximilian* 1.
90 The debate over Constantine's "conversion" will be treated on p. 183 in chapter six.
91 Zosimus, *New History* 4.16.
92 Ammianus Marcellinus, *History* 27.9.1
93 "Count [*comes*]" was a relatively new position of enormous power. Romanus was in effect the commander in chief of all Roman military in Africa.
94 Ammianus Marcellinus, *History* 29.5.44–56.
95 Orosius 7.33.
96 Zosimus, *New History* 5.11.
97 The events occurred in 304, but the dating of the martyrdom itself is debatable. Maureen A. Tilley, *Donatist Martyr Stories: The Church in Conflict in Roman North Africa* (Liverpool: Liverpool University Press, 1996), 26, insists on a pre-312 dating because Caecilian is known only as a deacon. But the narrator (§19) locates the audience in the "time of schism" (see further discussion of dating in chapter seven).
98 *The Acts of the Abitinian Martyrs* 1.
99 W.H.C. Frend, *The Donatist Church* (Oxford: Clarendon Press, 1952), 10.
100 *The Acts of the Abitinian Martyrs* 1. The problems of authenticity involved with this text will be discussed in detail later in this work (see chapter seven).
101 *The Acts of the Abitinian Martyrs* 1.
102 *The Acts of the Abitinian Martyrs* 2 and passim.
103 *The Acts of the Abitinian Martyrs* 6 and passim.
104 *The Acts of the Abitinian Martyrs* 9.
105 *The Acts of the Abitinian Martyrs* 20.
106 *The Acts of the Abitinian Martyrs* 20.
107 Tertullian, *On the Military Crown* 4.7; Thelwall translates the term "teacher" (ANF 3:94). Arnobius, *Against the Nations* 3.22; George E. McCkracken, *Arnobius of Sicca: The Case Against the Pagans* (Westminister, MD: Newman Press, 1949), 1:209, translates this term as "he who gives training."
108 Even when translating the Gospels into Latin for his Vulgate, Jerome has Judas as a *proditor*, not *traditor*; see discussion in Anthony Cane, *The Place of Judas Iscariot in Christology* (Hampshire, UK: Ashgate Publishing, 2005), 114ff.
109 Augustine, *On Baptism* 7.2 (emphasis added).
110 Augustine, *On Baptism* 7.3.
111 Cf. Cyprian, *Letter* 70.
112 Julius Capitolinus, *Augustine History: The Three Gordians* 33.4.
113 Augustine, *Letters* 111 (WSA 2.2:88–94).
114 *Letters* 47.2.

115 *Letter* 220.7.
116 E.g. *Letter* 228.
117 This incident is from Procopius, *The History of the Wars* 3.3, whose account has been called into question by historians. One may compare the *Chronicle* of Prosper of Aquitaine.
118 That is, until modern colonialism.
119 *The Barbaric Age* 1.10 (text CCL 40:436–437; trans. R.G. Kalkmann, *Two Sermons De tempore barbarico Attributed to St. Quodvultdeus, Bishop of Carthage: A Study of Text and Attribution with Translation and Commentary* [PhD dissertation for Catholic University of America, 1963], 156–157).
120 For further discussion of the Vandal invasion, see Andrew Merrills and Richard Miles, *The Vandals* (Malden, MA: Wiley-Blackwell, 2010); Daniel Van Slyke, *Quodvultdeus of Carthage: The Apocalyptic Theology of a Roman African in Exile* (Early Christian Studies 5; Strathfield, Australia: St Paul's Publications, 2003), chapter five (147–202); and Frank M. Clover, *The Late Roman West and the Vandals* (Aldershot: Variorum, 1993).
121 The sources are less than clear as to which provinces. Victor, *The History of the Vandal Persecution* 1.13 (trans. John Moorhead, *Victor of Vita: History of the Vandal Persecution* [Liverpool: Liverpool University Press, 1992], 7), is the most specific. See also Procopius, *The History of the Wars* 3.4 (LCL 81:36–39); and Prosper, *Chronicle* 439 (PL 51:0596B), for "Africae portione."
122 Salvian, *On the Government of God* 6.12.
123 Leo, *Letter* 12.1.
124 Leo, *Letter* 12.8.
125 For his explicit claim, see *Letter* 2.
126 *Rome in Africa*, 199.
127 W.H.C. Frend, "The Christian Period in Mediterranean Africa, *c.* AD 200 to 700," in *The Cambridge History of Africa* vol. 2, ed. J. D. Fage (Cambridge: Cambridge University Press, 1978), 480, understands the indigenous population to have welcomed the Vandals, because the latter removed the wealthy landowners who had become oppressive to the former. For the number 80,000, see Victor, *History of the Vandal Persecution* 1.2. However, this number was said to be exaggerated by Procopius, *The History of the Wars* 3.5; cf. Salvian, *On the Government of God*, 7.7.27–7.8.30. "Five per cent [sic]," is Raven's estimate (*Rome in Africa*, 198).
128 For a helpful treatment of this topic and the way in which Africans (indigenous, Vandal, and others) attempted to legitimate their status by claims to "Romanness," see Conant, *Staying Roman*.
129 *The History of the Vandal Persecution* 3.68.
130 Procopius, *The History of the Wars* 4.28, line 47 (cf. LCL 81:457, which translates this phrase as "Roman territory.") For further reading on the Byzantine reconquest of Africa, see Denys Pringle, *The Defence of Byzantine Africa from Justinian to the Arab Conquest: An Account of the Military History and Archaeology of the African Provinces in the Sixth and Seventh Centuries*, 2 vols. (British Archaeological Reports 99; Oxford: John and Erica Hodges, 2001).
131 See Corippus, *Iohannes*.
132 Namely, Theodore of Mopsuestia, Theodoret of Cyrrhus, and Ibas of Edessa.
133 Facundus, *Epistle on the Catholic Faith in Defense of the Three Chapters*.
134 However, see Procopius, *The History of the Wars* 4.26.
135 See Procopius, *The History of the Wars* 3.4, for his alleged agreement with Geiseric.
136 In what is likely rhetorical flourish, many sources laud Heraclius as a new Scipio Africanus. See sources and discussion in Walter Emil Kaegi, *Heraclius: Emperor of Byzantium* (Cambridge: Cambridge University Press, 2003), 29.

137 See Vassilios Christides, *Byzantine Libya and the March of the Arabs Towards the West of North Africa* (British Archaeological Reports 851; Oxford: J. and E. Hedges, 2000).

138 Theophanes, *Chronicle 645/6* (trans. Cyril Mango and Roger Scott, *The Chronicle of Theophanes Confessor: Byzantine and Near Eastern History AD 284–813* [Oxford: Clarendon Press, 1997], 477); cf. Walter Emil Kaegi, *Byzantium and the Early Islamic Conquests* (Cambridge: Cambridge University Press, 1992).

139 Andrew Louth, *Maximus the Confessor* (London: Routledge, 1996), 16.

140 "Reflections on Religious Dissent in North Africa in the Byzantine Period," essay VII in *From Augustine to Gregory the Great* (London: Variorum, 1983), 149.

141 In another recurring theme in Africa's history, Gregory's daughter committed suicide after this defeat so as to avoid marriage to an enemy; cf. Dido, Hannibal, Hasdrubal's wife, Gordian I, Firmus, and Gildo.

142 P. Salama, "The Roman and Post-Roman Period in North Africa, Part II: From Rome to Islam," in *General History of Africa, vol. 2: Ancient Civilizations of Africa*, ed. G. Mokhtar (Heinemann, CA: Unesco, 1981), 503.

143 See the account of Ibn 'Abd al-H'akam 194–196 (trans. J.F.P. Hopkins, *Corpus of Early Arabic Sources for West African History*, rev. ed. [Princeton, NJ: Markus Wiener Publishers, 2000], 12–13; see also pp. 63, 157, and 237).

144 For sources and discussion, see Abdelmajid Hannoum, *Colonial Histories, Post-Colonial Memories: The Legend of the Kahina, a North African Heroine* (Studies in African literature; Portsmouth, NH: Heinemann, 2001).

145 For citation of primary sources, see L. R. Holme, *The Extinction of the Christian Churches in North Africa* (New York: Burt Franklin, 1895), 223–225.

146 Quoted in Frend, "The Christian Period in Mediterranean Africa," 489.

147 The conversions occurred at a much slower rate than is often assumed. See Rodney Stark, *The Triumph of Christianity: How the Jesus Movement Became the World's Largest Religion* (San Francisco, CA: HarperCollins, 2011), 199–211.

148 Ibn Khaldûn, *The Muqaddimah* (Franz Rosenthal [trans.], *The Muqaddimah: An Introduction to History*, rev. ed. [Princeton, NJ: Princeton University Press, 1967], 2:38–39).

149 For an introduction to "history from below" in early Christian studies, see the first three volumes of the series, *A People's History of Christianity*, from Fortress Press (2005–2006).

150 Ingrid Hill, "Valor," in *New Stories From the South: The Year's Best 2004*, ed. Shannon Ravenel (Chapel Hill, NC: Algonquin Books, 2004), 63.

151 This is the terminology and theory put forth by Fredrik Barth, "Introduction," in *Ethnic Groups and Boundaries*, ed. Fredrik Barth (Boston, MA: Little, Brown and Co., 1969), 9–38. For a more complete discussion of these theories, see my work, *Tertullian the African*.

152 Crawley, "Roman Africa?" in *"Romanization"?*, ed. J. Prag and A. Merryweather *Digressus* Supplement 1 (2003), 9, rightly argues, "categorization by culture is not the best basis for interpreting this society." More generally, see Edward Herring, "Ethnicity and Culture," in *The Blackwell Companion to Ancient History*, ed. Andrew Erskine (Blackwell Companions to the Ancient World 49; New York: John Wiley and Sons, 2009), 112–122.

153 For further discussion, see Elizabeth Clark, *History, Theory, Text: Historians and the Linguistic Turn* (Cambridge, MA: Harvard University Press, 2004).

154 The following paragraphs are adapted from my essay, "Were the 'Donatists' a National or Social Movement in Disguise? Reframing the Question."

155 Unlike the popular reading of Hegel, my proposed "synthesis" is in fact an aporia between the thesis and antithesis, not a progressing past the two. Here I follow Derrida's Kierkegaardian inversion of the so-called Hegelian dialectic,

wherein the both/and (and/or the neither/nor) remains inescapable; see Jacques Derrida, "Différance," in *Margins of Philosophy*, trans. Alan Bass (Chicago: University of Chicago Press, 1986), [1–28] 13–14; for commentary, see John D. Caputo, *Radical Hermeneutics: Repetition, Deconstruction, and the Hermeneutic Project* (Bloomington, IN: Indiana University Press, 1987); and Caputo, *More Radical Hermeneutics: On Not Knowing Who We Are* (Bloomington, IN: Indiana University Press, 2000).

156 E.g. *Against Heresies* 1.23; 3.2–5.

157 Although Augustine carefully identified the Donatists as schismatics and not heretics, he worked to have the anti-heretical laws applied to the Donatists, and he used this same Irenaean paradigm where the "Catholic" church was original and the Donatists deviated from it into schism.

158 Donatists claimed this status before Constantine (see Augustine, *Letter* 88.2), and throughout the controversy (cf. the *Gesta* of the Conference of Carthage 411). Optatus's claim (Optatus of Milevis, *Against the Donatists* 3.3) that they referred to themselves as *Donatistae* is too polemical to be accepted uncritically.

159 Arnold, *The Impartial History of the Church and the Heretics*. For discussion, see Philip Schaff, *History of the Christian Church*, 1:27–54. Walter Bauer, *Orthodoxy and Heresy in Earliest Christianity*, ed. Robert A. Kraft and Gerhard Kroedel (Philadelphia, PA: Fortress Press, [orig. 1934] 1979).

160 Bauer, *Orthodoxy and Heresy*, xxii, suggests,

> Perhaps – I repeat, perhaps – certain manifestations of Christian life that the authors of the church renounce as 'heresies' originally had not been such at all, but, at least here and there, were the only form of the new religion – that is, for those regions they were simply "Christianity."

161 E.g. Wilhelm Thümmel, *Zur Beurtheilung des Donatismus: Eine kirchengeschichtliche Untersuchung* (Halle: Ehrhardt Karras, 1893), 27, found the Donatists to have "nationalen Elementen" (explicitly defined as common ancestry, language, and religion; similarly, Henri Leclercq, *L'Afrique Chretienne* (Paris: Librairie Victor Lecoffre, 1904), 1:343–346, viewed the movement, especially the Circumcellions, as Punic resistance to Rome, that is "patriotisme provincial et municipal" (1:308–311); Frend, *The Donatist Church*, especially saw evidence of indigenous Berbers identity for the Numidian Donatists; similarly, Jean-Paul Brisson, *Autonomisme et christianime dans l'Afrique romaine: Dans l'Afrique Romaine de Septime Sévère à l'invasion vandale* (Paris: Éditions E. de Boccard, 1958), found the Donatist schism attractive to local peasant workers, and thus grew into a social movement as much as a theological party.

162 E.g. Andre Mandouze, "Encore le donatisme: Problèmes de méthode posés par la thèse de Jean-Paul Brisson, *Autonomisme et christianisme dans l'Afrique romaine de Septime Sévère à l'invasion vandale*," *L'Antiquité classique* 29 (1, 1960), 61–107; Mandouze, "Les donatistes entre ville et campagne," *Histoire et archéologie de l'Afrique du Nord. Actes du IIIème Colloque international réuni dans le cadre du CXè Congrès national des sociétés savantes, Montpellier, 1er-15 avril 1985* (Paris, 1986), 193–217; Emin Tengström, *Donatisten und Katholiken: soziale, wirtschaftliche, und politische Aspekte einer nordafrikanischen Kirchenspaltung* (Götenborg: Acta Universitatis Gothoburgensis, 1964); Peter Brown, "Christianity and Local Culture in Late Roman Africa," *Journal of Roman Studies* 58 (1968), 85–95; and Alexander Evers, "A Fine Line: Catholics and Donatists in Roman North Africa," in *Frontiers in the Roman World: Proceedings of the Ninth Workshop of the International Network Impact of Empire (Durham, 16–19 April 2009)*, ed. Olivier Hekster and Ted Kaizer (Leiden: Brill, 2011), 175–198. The many works of Maureen Tilley should also be included here, since she has emphasized the sincere religious

commitments of the Donatists against Augustine's caricature of them (see bibliography).

163 Primary examples of this synthesis include Leslie Dossey, *Peasant and Empire in Christian North Africa* (Berkeley, CA: University of California Press, 2010); Shaw, *Sacred Violence: African Christians and Sectarian Hatred in the Age of Augustine* (Cambridge: Cambridge University Press, 2011); Rebillard, "William Hugh Clifford Frend (1916–2005)"; and Burns, Jensen, et al., *Christianity in Roman Africa*.

164 Brown, "Christianity and Local Culture in Late Roman Africa".

165 Most famously, his *Augustine of Hippo: A Biography* (London: 1967); *The World of Late Antiquity* (London: Faber and Faber, 1971); and *The Body and Society: Men, Women, and Sexual Renunciation in Early Christianity* (New York: Thames and Hudson, 1988).

166 Brown, "Religious Dissent in the Later Roman Empire: The Case of North Africa," *History* 48 (1963), 282–305; reprinted in *Religion and Society in the Age of Augustine* (1972), 301–331; and "Religious Coercion in the Later Roman Empire: The Case of North Africa," *Journal of Roman Studies* 58 (1968), 85–95.

167 "Christianity and Dissent in Roman North Africa: Changing Perspectives in Recent Work," in *Schism, Heresy, and Religious Protest*, ed. Derek Baker (Cambridge: Cambridge University Press, 1972), 28–29, 35. Cf. Shaw, "African Christianity: Disputes, Definitions, and 'Donatists,' " originally in *Orthodoxy and Heresy in Religious Movements: Discipline and Dissent*, ed. M. R. Greenshields and T. A. Robinson (Lampeter: The Edwin Mellen Press, 1992), 5–34; reprinted in *Rulers, Nomads and Christians in Roman North Africa* (Aldershot: Variorum, 1995).

Resources for further study

For overviews of this time period, the English reader can turn to three works (listed below). Decret's work is very introductory and does not often engage the sources critically. Raven's work is an introduction for the whole of Roman African history, but it does also include chapters on Christianity. The work of Burns, Jensen, et al., is a masterpiece that provides details about specific practices of African Christians; although it offers introductory chapters, the whole of the work focuses on the third, fourth, and early fifth centuries. Finally, the works of Thomas Oden can also be considered, although they represent more of an argument for studying African Christianity than detailed accounts.

Burns, J. Patout, Jr., Robin M. Jensen, et al. *Christianity in Roman Africa: The Development of Its Practices and Beliefs* (Grand Rapids: Eerdmans, 2014).

Decret, François. *Early Christianity in North Africa*, trans. Edward L. Smither (Eugene, OR: Wipf and Stock Publishers/Cascade Books, 2009 [orig. 1996]).

Raven, Susan. *Rome in Africa* (London: Routledge, 1993).

Oden, Thomas C. *How Africa Shaped the Christian Mind* (Downers Grove, IL: InterVarsity Press, 2008).

Oden, Thomas C. *The African Memory of Mark: Reassessing Early Church Tradition* (Downers Grove, IL: InterVarsity Press, 2011).

Oden, Thomas C. *Early Libyan Christianity: Uncovering a North African Tradition* (Downers Grove, IL: InterVarsity Press, 2011).

For more detailed history of both Africa in late antiquity generally as well African Christian history in particular, see the following works.

Gsell, Stéphane. *Histoire ancienne de l'Afrique du Nord*, 8 vols. (Paris: Hachette et Cie., 1913–1929).

Leclercq, Henri. *L'Afrique chrétienne*, 2 vols. (Paris: Lecoffre, 1914).

Lepelley, Claude. *Les cités de l'Afrique romaine au bas-empire* (Paris: Études augustiniennes, 1979).

Mandouze, André. *Prosopographie chrétienne du Bas-Empire*. I. *Prosopographie de l'Afrique chrétienne (303–533)* (Paris: Éditions du Centre National de la Recherche Scientifique, 1982).

Monceaux, Paul. *Histoire littéraire de l'Afrique chrétienne depuis les origins jusqu'a l'invasion arabe*, 7 vols. (Paris: Leroux, 1901–1923).

Charles-Picard, Gilbert. *La Civilisation de l'Afrique romaine* (Paris: Etudes Augustiniaennes, 1990).

2 Backgrounds to early African Christianity

"African Christianity was shaped by an environment marked by the remnants of *Punic* culture, including its religion, making it different from other forms of Christianity."[1] This observation, made by Maureen Tilley in her influential book, *The Bible in Christian North Africa*, provides us with a helpful starting point for the following study.

Whereas in the opening chapter we reviewed the overall history of ancient Africa, as well as the methods that will be used in this study, the current chapter turns to various kinds of "backgrounds" to our subject. This chapter title is deliberately alluding to Everett Ferguson's *Backgrounds to Early Christianity*, which has proven to be a helpful text for many who want to understand better the New Testament and early Christianity by looking into the "world behind the text."[2] Not only should a student of the New Testament learn about the major historical events that predate Christ, but the "backgrounds" to the New Testament include a whole array of socio-economic and religious data. In other words, in addition to studying the empires of Persia, Greece, and Rome, studying Second Temple Judaism in particular and the ancient near east in general is vital to a robust understanding of early Christianity. In what follows, several kinds of backgrounds will be given, which are arguably just as vital to understanding early Christianity in Africa. Of course, Professor Ferguson's book covers many areas that would equally serve as a helpful backdrop to early African Christianity, because backgrounds such as Jewish diaspora, Greek philosophy, and Roman law (to name but a few examples) illuminate virtually any region of the ancient Mediterranean world. What follows, therefore, is not a replacement of such studies but a supplement to them. In addition to these kinds of generally applicable fields of study, we should also focus on the backgrounds unique to the region of Africa. Therefore, it will prove helpful if we start this chapter about backgrounds by explaining how the large-scale history of empires intersects with the lived experiences of people living in ancient Africa.

Romanization: from culture to ethnicity to identity

Whereas at one time North Africa appeared thoroughly Romanized, more recent historians have had to nuance this view greatly. To understand

"Roman Africa" better, we need to define terms like "Romanization," *Romanitas*, and – what is often thought to be their antithesis – "resistance." The notion of *Romanitas* is in fact old; Tertullian himself may have even coined the term.[3] Nevertheless, this concept allows for an array of phenomena, ranging from military enforcement of Roman practices (very rare) to economic incentives that enticed provincials to embrace their new Roman patrons (very common). The full range of this spectrum often is summarized under the term "Romanization," which is only moderately helpful since it begs for further elaboration: who was doing the Romanizing? Why were they doing it? How were they Romanizing/being Romanized? Furthermore, what did Romanizing involve, since people could accommodate *Romanitas* in various ways? The old model of colonialism assumes the dominant culture imposed its will on the conquered peoples, and this act occurred as if it were both natural and inevitable, a concept known as "social Darwinism." This model has now been revised, and scholars must take into account how locals were agents capable of negotiating Roman values and customs in light of their own indigenous ones.[4]

To be sure, there were specific acts of Romanization enacted in Africa. After Julius Caesar defeated the last of his enemies in Africa, he launched an aggressive campaign of colonization of Africa.[5] Eventually, he and his successor, Caesar Augustus, transferred more than 50,000 veterans and settlers to the region, which meant confiscating lands from the local population. The Roman legions in Africa built walls for the cities and built roads connecting them. All of this work protected the African grain supply, and these sweeping changes to the African landscape caused much of the region to experience "Romanization." Just what did this mean?

Rome's colonizing presence did not eradicate the local population, nor did it erase the pre-Roman society's language and customs. Those colonized reacted in various ways. Much work remains to be done in order to better define who or what was Roman/-ized. Conversely, what does it mean to be non-Roman, provincial, and/or indigenous? Along with the idea of dominant and conquered "cultures," we also have to explain what we mean when we classify these different groups.

There was no African "race," as explained in the first chapter, but there were many different African ethnic groups, such as the *Afri* themselves who are largely lost to our historical record and the later Punic and "Berber" (or "Libyan") groups.[6] However, even the concepts of ethnic groups and ethnicity are in danger of describing something static and unchanging: people who were once and forever identifiable by skin color, language, religion, etc. This is not at all what anthropologists mean when they use the term "ethnicity." Instead, they speak of the "construction" of ethnicity, because some practices can be shared by varying people groups while at other times these same practices can be constructed as the boundary separating people groups.[7] Punics can dress Roman, but still speak Punic.[8] Or, Punics could speak Latin, while still worshipping Punic deities, even under Latin names.

Therefore, while there is a need to study ethnic groups in North Africa,[9] the current study focuses instead on social identity.[10]

This shift from ethnicity to identity helps nuance our discussion in various ways. To return to the example of the Donatists discussed at the close of the previous chapter, this focus on social identity circumvents the central objection of Peter Brown to the understanding of the Donatists as consisting of indigenous Africans. In opposition to scholars who see the Donatists as in some sense African "nationalists," Brown contends:

> The Donatist bishops, their clergy, and their followers had gained, by their conversion to Christianity, a culture which they shared with the rest of the Latin world, and, having gained it in Latin, they not unnaturally claimed to be right, in Latin.[11]

There is, however, a problem in Brown's objection: his linking of language (i.e. Latin) and nationality or ethnicity (i.e. non-African) fails to acknowledge that Latin speakers could retain a non-Latin identity. The tension Brown does not attempt to resolve is the fact that while *some* Donatists can embrace Latin language and societal practices, those same Donatists can also (and other Donatists can primarily) embrace a local identity. In short, Brown risks confusing the cultural content for the ethnic identity.

Even after acknowledging the disjunction that can occur between "culture" and "ethnicity," any future study of this question will benefit from a more precise definition of identity.[12] Once we understand how social identities can function, we can apply a more nuanced reading of the ancient sources from Africa that takes into account how complex identities can be.

The particulars of social identity cannot be adequately treated in the space allotted here,[13] but the following general principles will be used to analyze the identities of the ancient African Christians.

1   Identities are not fixed. Like the examples given with ethnicity, they often arise in response to another (or an-Other) identity. Africans in late antiquity probably saw themselves as Africans only when encountering Romans, or some other sort of outside group. Otherwise, they would have self-identified as Carthaginian, senatorial, Christian, or some other category, depending on the situation.

2   Identities are plural. Individuals and groups can self-identify in multiple ways: one may be African, Carthaginian, plebian, masculine, and an adherent of Christianity – to name but a few examples.

3   No single identity can be assumed as more fundamental than others. For example, individuals may strongly declare themselves to be Christians, but their Christian identity may play little to no role when they decide about economic practices or even public practices that include religious ceremony.[14] This point will be especially important for the following chapters, because it is tempting to understand the Christian

writers as speaking *only* in terms of Christian/non-Christian identities. While Christian writers certainly did construct their identity over and against the "idolaters," they also spoke in terms conditioned by their African context, even at times doing so by embracing an African identity.

4   Apparently contradicting identities can be inhabited by the same individual or group. While our modern categories relentlessly pressure us to accept binary oppositions (i.e. either/or), we must allow for the ancient evidence to transcend these categories (i.e. both/and). In other words, certain identities seem to us to be almost mutually exclusive, such as "Roman African," so we are tempted to oversimplify: Roman Africans must have been Romans or at least thoroughly Romanized, who merely resided in Africa. This oversimplification, however, neglects to account for the way the individuals and groups can inhabit both identities without having to choose. In postcolonial theory, this is called "hybridity."[15] Hybridity, much like Romanization, could describe an array of concepts, ranging from full acceptance of the colonial culture at one end of the spectrum to a resistance to the colonial presence cloaked in the colonial language, dress, and social practices. Most case studies will find that few people inhabiting a hybridity of identities are at either extreme of this spectrum, and so any analysis must proceed on a case-by-case basis. The point here is to allow for individuals who were to greater or lesser degrees Romanized to also inhabit a non-Roman identity as well – and "non-Roman" may or may not mean "anti-Roman."

It will be important to keep this complex view of identity in mind when surveying the evidence, because classifying a certain ancient person as "African," "Punic," or "non-Roman" in some way still assumes that this same individual could also be Roman, Latin, elite (etc.) in other ways. Since the Christians from ancient North Africa have been thoroughly studied as "Latin" writers, the current focus is on the more neglected aspect of their identity, their Africanity.

This idea of hybridity is also helpful for our discussion of Romanization, and for what often seems to be an antithesis to it: resistance. Against such binary opposition (i.e. either/or), the concepts of Romanization and resistance no longer need to be mutually exclusive, when seen in terms of social identities. In fact, neither "Romanization" nor "resistance" on their own function well as categories. Partly, the rejection of Romanization and resistance as static categories belongs to a larger trend in the study of history. Eric R. Wolfe criticized past approaches to studying different "nations" and "cultures" as if they were each billiard balls bouncing off each other whenever they come into contact.[16] Instead, Wolfe urged us to view history as people groups whose cultures overlap and permeate each other, even when the encounter creates two distinct identities, such as Roman and African. Wolfe's approach has influenced many classical studies,[17] and it should be remembered in what follows so that the categories of Roman and African

can be seen to overlap as much as they differ. Groups and individuals in Africa may have responded to Romanization in any number of ways, such as acceptance, resistance, or some hybrid of the two.

When we do attempt to pinpoint an "African" identity as distinct from a "Roman" one, we begin to see how ill-defined this last concept can be. Does this refer to citizens of the city of Rome, citizens of the empire, or any inhabitant under the rule of the Roman emperor? The answer, of course, is that it depends. In the current study, we do not intend to set "Roman" and "African" as fixed identities, but instead we need to recognize how the African identity can be constructed (sometimes) in opposition to the Roman other.

When we speak of either Romanization or resistance in the following chapters, we do so acknowledging how varied the individual cases may be, and the point will be to inquire as to what degree any given expression of Romanization and/or resistance can be determined. For example, given the repeated rebellions that arose in Africa against Rome (see Chapter 1), some scholars believed that Africans under Rome should be characterized in terms of military resistance. However, this view fails to account for the numerous instances where Africans supported Rome. Even if one rejects the notion of military resistance as widespread in Roman Africa (it would be better to say it was sporadic), one could speak of what is called "cultural resistance."[18] It should be obvious by now, however, that even when we find examples of so-called cultural resistance, such as retaining Punic deities or Libyan language, that alone does not prove someone was to any degree anti-Roman. Instead, we have to allow that sometimes individuals inhabit non-Roman expressions of identity, such as Punic or Libyan, while at other times those same individuals may embrace *Romanitas* and wear the toga and speak Latin. To ignore either aspect of their hybrid identities would be a mistake.

In the rest of this chapter we will turn to specific examples of social backgrounds unique to ancient Africa. Much of what is discussed would commonly be labeled "culture." However, it must be remembered that all artifacts, be they material or literary, require interpretation, and we are reviewing these various artifacts in order to better interpret the identities of ancient African Christians.[19] Finally, it should be noted that this pre-Roman background to African Christian history is being reviewed in order to understand what non-Roman elements continued in North African society throughout the Roman period, for many of the elements found to express an African identity remained prevalent even into the Vandal, Byzantine, and Arab periods.[20] We can, therefore, turn now to the pre-Christian background of Africa and learn how this context was unique.

African (identity) politics

Our interest in a uniquely African social identity need not mean that our evidence must be limited to armed uprisings and governments. One complicating factor in discussing "African" uprisings is that many who rebelled against Rome were also Romans.[21] The rebellions almost always entailed an attempt to gain control of Rome, not independence from Rome. At least, this was the stated aims of the leaders in these uprisings; the motives of the masses who supported them is less clear. Nevertheless, the politics in Africa did at times identify individuals there as Africans. Even Septimius Severus, the first African declared emperor of Rome, had to forgo the traditional celebratory march into the capital after defeating some of his opponents, "lest he seem to triumph for a victory over Romans."[22]

We have already reviewed the political history in the introductory chapter. What remains to be seen is how these political events shaped the identity of the Africans, and how this African identity surfaces in the surviving sources. As an example, let us consider the symbolism of elephants in early African sources. While Roman authors knew of elephants from India and Ethiopia, they tended to think first of North Africa.[23] When depicting Afra, the spirit or goddess of Africa, ancient artists would have her wearing an elephant headdress.[24] Most notoriously, Hannibal's use of elephants solidified them as symbolic of the Punics in particular and their threat to Rome. Perhaps it is more than coincidental that references to elephants in Christian sources are found almost exclusively in the writings of African Christians.[25] While they do not always refer to Hannibal or endorse his antipathy towards Rome, we should not ignore how this African heritage influenced the thought of the Christian writers from this region. A brief explanation is in order here.

As an analogy, let us say we read a modern author who refers to a lion. All things being equal, this lion is simply an animal, the king of the jungle. However, if we knew the author's context to be Israel, Britain, or Detroit, we would then pause to consider whether this reference is an allusion to the Lion of Judah, the royal family, or to a football team. In such cases what is ostensibly just an animal is imbued with more significance given the context, and whether it is potentially religious, political, or social in some other way depends on that context. If an American were to refer to a bald eagle, this would in all likelihood entail more significance than simply an eagle. Moreover, even if an American referred to a bald eagle on the fourth of July, that same American could be an Anglophile who closely follows British royal news and vacations in the lake district of England. In such an example, the reference to a bald eagle would still involve more than a mere animal; it would be a reference to the individual's heritage, which is in turn tied to the individual's identity.

The same is true when Christians from North Africa refer to elephants. At the very least, we should pause to consider the possible significance of the reference. Lactantius, for example, an African writer from the early fourth century, refers to a certain "Donatus" who had been persecuted under Diocletian. Lactantius praises Donatus's ability to overcome the tortures by saying, "How pleasing was that spectacle to God when He beheld you as victor, not bringing under subjection to your chariot white horses or huge elephants, but, best of all, the very triumphant ones themselves."[26] White horses famously pulled the chariot of a Roman general in a triumph. In one unique instance, the general Pompey attempted to celebrate his victories in Africa by riding into Rome on a chariot pulled by elephants, instead of white horses. His attempt, however, failed because the beasts were too large to enter the gate.[27] Pompey's attempt to coopt and dominate Hannibal's elephants certainly would be seen as an insult to North Africans who had fought against Rome.[28] Just how widespread such sentiments were in Lactantius's Africa requires further investigation (see discussion in Chapter 6). Suffice it to say that Lactantius's statement would likely have evoked political significance from an African audience at the time.

It should also be remembered that even Africans who embraced *Romanitas* (like Lactantius) would be capable of inhabiting a non-Roman identity. To take another modern example, one could consider people from India today who may be "more English than the English,"[29] and yet they may celebrate Indian independence every 15th of August. Analogously, the political history of North Africa should be considered when reading texts from North Africa. Even Christian texts primarily devoted to religious matters invoke political symbolism that can help us understand the social identities at play. Lactantius's statement is an example of how we should consider the context, even the military background, of early African Christians.

The political history and symbolism for Carthage in particular will be important for understanding many of the surviving sources from North Africa. Although the city was destroyed in the third Punic war, Julius Caesar initiated its rebuilding, and the project was continued under Caesar Augustus. Roman Carthage utilized the best of Roman engineering and design.[30] Its population, furthermore, swelled and served as the largest and most important of Africa.[31]

Of course, Carthage had already loomed large in the Roman imagination, and now that Romans could move there to capitalize on the region's productivity, Carthage in many ways became more Roman than Rome – to adapt the phrase used two paragraphs prior about being "more English than the English."[32] Even so, Carthage symbolized a proud local heritage in addition to its Roman re-founding. Apuleius, whom we discussed in the introductory chapter, once celebrated Carthage as "the venerated teacher of our province . . . the celestial muse of Africa."[33] In one way, Apuleius, who could be described as very Romanized, celebrates in this statement how Carthage is the hub of *Romanitas* to be spread throughout Africa. Even so, Apuleius, who is a master of developing a rapport with his audience, is not shaming the non-Roman aspects of Africa: instead, his statement is a "proud claim . . . [which] informs rather than contradicts the 'Punicity' of the city."[34]

The remark by Apuleius can be compared with the Christian writer Tertullian, who will be discussed further in Chapter 4. For now, suffice it to say, Tertullian can also invoke Carthage's current state within the empire:

> Men of Carthage, ever princes of Africa, ennobled by ancient memories, blest with modern felicities, I rejoice that times are so prosperous. . . . These are the "piping times of peace" and plenty. Blessings rain from the empire and from the sky.[35]

Tertullian's tone, however, quickly reveals itself as sardonic, for he next reminds the Carthaginian's of their city's destruction by Rome.[36] He then offers a more conciliatory tone, acknowledging the shame caused by his remarks: "Draw we now our material from some other source, lest Punichood either blush or else grieve in the midst of Romans."[37] Tertullian's statement belongs within his wider rhetorical aim and deserves further attention.[38] For our immediate purposes, however, his statement illustrates how Africans, even Christian Africans, can use Carthage itself as a symbol of Punic history.

Another noteworthy example that cites Carthage's political history is Augustine's discussion about the fall of Rome (410 CE). He cites Sallust (c.86–c.35 BCE), a former Roman governor of Africa, who had claimed that the apex of Roman morality was during the Punic wars.[39] Augustine uses this very Roman sentiment with a surprising twist: while the Romans after 410 were blaming the Christians for the fall of their city, Augustine blames the fall of Rome on the Romans and their destruction of Carthage![40] This action was in fact the beginning of moral decline and internal decay for the Romans.[41] Again, Augustine's statement should not be exaggerated; in many ways, he was pro-Rome. Nevertheless, his statement should not be minimized either: his reference to Carthage invokes the political history and heritage of this chief city of Africa. As part of our reading of his work, we should ask how Augustine's audience in Africa might have interpreted this passage.

The focus on Carthage illustrates how the political identities emerge in the writings of North African Christians. Carthage itself, however, is only one example, and it should not be forgotten that many North Africans (the so-called Berbers) fought against Carthage at various stages in its history.[42] The diversity of sources and identities in North Africa must always be remembered, while at the same time the political significance of Carthage should not be overlooked, even when it is deployed by Christian writers. The example of Carthage, therefore, helps to demonstrate the need to focus on political history and heritage in our sources.

African languages

Along with the Libyan, Punic, and Roman political history, scholars can trace North Africa's history in terms of these groups' respective languages. Inscriptions in the Libyan language dating from the seventh to fifth centuries BCE can be found across North Africa.[43] The surviving evidence is mostly from funeral monuments, and so scholars still struggle to decipher the language.[44] While the Libyan dialect seems to have been largely replaced by Punic and then Latin, there are some surviving inscriptions that can be dated well into the Roman period, and this ancient language group has links to the "Berber" dialects still spoken across North Africa today. Moreover, while the Libyan population should be understood as largely assimilated into the later Punic and Roman social systems, their ongoing retention of the Libyan language suggests a distinct self-identity.[45]

When the Phoenicians asserted their dominance across the coast of North Africa, they established cities and took control of existing cities. Punic customs and language then spread into inland Africa. The replacement of Libyan mentioned in the previous paragraph likely entailed a creolizing of the two languages, so that the replacement was not sudden and complete. The Punic language continued to be spoken throughout North Africa, lasting throughout the Roman era, even if Punic literature all but disappeared in late antiquity.[46] The second-century Latin writer Apuleius came from a wealthy family, one we would consider very Romanized, and yet he did not speak Latin as a child, but spoke "Punic [*punice*]."[47] Writing much later, in the mid-sixth century, Procopius still understood North Africa to be largely Punic: "And they established numerous cities and took possession of the whole of Libya as far as the Pillars of Heracles, and there they have lived even up to my time, using the Phoenician tongue."[48]

Another indication of Punic language is the preponderance of Punic names that became Latinized.[49] Terentius Afer, or Terence the African, is an early example of someone being given a thoroughly Roman name (in this case, it was Terence's former owner), but still being remembered as Afer ("the African"). To be sure, Latin names in the records do not necessarily imply that the person was Roman, to the exclusion of holding to other identities, such as African. For example, Joyce Reynolds has studied many funeral busts of North Africans who had Latin names and Greek style of dress, but who nevertheless had "what are generally accepted as typical Libyan facial traits."[50] Reynolds's attempt to find an African identity in "facial traits" is an admittedly dubious enterprise, and so more on appearance will be said on pp. 63–66. Her point remains, however, that Latin names and dress in Africa cannot be taken to indicate that these individuals were not also African in some sense.

Other names of North Africans serve as clues as to their indigenous origin. Names like Saturus and Donatus are Latinized versions of popular Punic names, and often the ancient sources report very little about a certain person but their indigenous status can be gleaned from their name alone. For example, very little is known about Septimius Severus's first wife, Paccia Marciana, but her name indicates Punic or Libyan origin, and so scholars can conclude that she was a native African.[51] Beyond specifically Punic names, many Latin names statistically speaking belong to Africa, and therefore in some cases historians can with a high probability identify an individual's *patria*, or homeland, simply by their name.[52]

Christian examples include the martyrs named in two of the earliest Christian records of North Africa, the *Acts of the Scillitan Martyrs* and *The Passion of Perpetua and Felicity*. These record several individuals whose names indicate Punic heritage.[53] One of the martyr's names, Saturninus, derives from the popularity of the cult of Saturn in North Africa, because Saturn was a Latinization of the name of the Punic god Baal (see further discussion on p. 60). One inscription even records a hybrid version of this name: "Saturbalius" (i.e. Saturn/Baal).[54]

Examples of Christians utilizing Latinized Punic names can be found throughout the later centuries as well. Augustine's mother, Monica, is likely Libyan or Punic; her name points to the Libyan deity, Mon, who was worshipped in the nearby town of Thibilis.[55] Augustine's father, Patricius, has a Roman name, and yet some scholars still believe he was "a native Numidian."[56] Augustine's only child, born from his African concubine, was named Adeodatus. This name, according to Peter Brown, was a case of translating into Latin the Punic name Iatanbaal.[57] Brown's source for this is I. Kajanto's *Onomastic Studies in the Early Christian Inscriptions of Rome and Carthage*, wherein Kajanto demonstrates the common occurrence of this name. It is also possible that Adeodatus was a translation of the less common yet more literal rendering of Hannibal (Punic = Gift of God; cf. Lat. "Adeodatus"). If this last interpretation were correct, then even more of an indigenous identity could be inferred in that to name one's child after the great antagonist of Rome and defender of Carthage would be a blatant display of African pride.[58] Either way, the ongoing use of Punic names (even in translation) may be important in helping us better understand many Africans' self-identity from this time.

Another way that many Africans' native language became apparent is that even when they spoke Latin, they often did so with an accent.[59] Because speaking Latin with a provincial accent carried with it a stigma, Fronto once had to excuse his accent by comparing himself to Anacharsis[60] who, despite being a "barbarian," was known for his wisdom: "for he was a Scythian of the nomad Scythians, while I am a Libyan of the nomad Libyans."[61] In other words, even though he could overcome the language barrier, the residue of his native tongue meant that Fronto must admit to being African or "Libyan."[62] Fronto's statements convinced some modern scholars that there was an African dialect of Latin.[63] While the notion of such a dialect has now been dismissed, we can see how Fronto and many Africans struggled to lose their accent when speaking Latin, something which marked them in the eyes – or ears – of a Roman audience as Africans.

Recognizing *patria*, or homeland, as a constructed ethnic boundary by some, Apuleius also defended himself first by stating, "I proclaimed myself to be 'half Numidian' and 'half Gaetulian.' . . . You must not judge a man's district of origin but his disposition, not *where* but *how* he has commenced to live."[64] Therefore, we can conclude that Apuleius's native language was "probably Punic. . . . His linguistic background is therefore complex and this was no doubt the reason why he had to watch his words carefully."[65] In his defense, Apuleius next proceeds to mock his opponent who "never speaks any language save Punic," and how another of his accusers was "hardly able to stammer out single syllables" of Latin.[66] In other words, despite his ostensibly "barbarian" or non-Roman origin, Apuleius proudly boasts that he has transcended his Numidian-Gaetulian background and embraced *Romani-tas*, unlike his opponents, who are fellow Africans still speaking only Punic or only Latin with a Punic accent.

Other sources also imply that new elites from North Africa struggled with a stigmatized African identity due to language. Similar to Apuleius, Septimius Severus spoke well, "but retained an African accent even to his old age."[67] Even so, one modern commentator has noted the self-awareness of Septimius Severus:

> An African from Leptis Magna, named Septimius Severus, was once congratulated by the poet Martial "that nothing in his looks or speech betrayed his Punic origin." His relative of the same name who became the first African emperor "never lost his African accent, and his Punic-speaking sister, on a visit, is said to have shamed him with her broken Latin."[68]

The claim that nothing in his speech betrays the emperor as being from Africa is a notion found in Statius, who exclaimed, "Your speech was not Punic, nor foreign your dress or your mind: Italian, Italian!"[69] This claim seems to be flattery and not factual; Septimius's multilingual abilities probably did not mask his accent altogether. Another ancient source describes the emperor as "sufficiently well educated in Latin letters, competent in conversation in Greek, and more proficient and eloquent in Punic seeing that he grew up in Leptis in the province of Africa."[70]

In short, several sources from Africa indicate that non-Latin languages continued to be spoken well into the Roman era. While we should probably assume a bilingual model, rather than think strictly in terms of a "native" Punic language (for example) with Latin as a "secondary" language, it is worth reconsidering how to go about classifying the African population from this time linguistically. We cannot simply assume that an African who writes in Latin was strictly or even primarily a Latin speaker, something that must even be said about Christian writers from this context.

The background of Punic language can be detected in Christian sources from Africa. The account of Perpetua's death (in 203), which was written in Latin, boasts of her ability to speak Greek, which is not surprising since she was of noble birth.[71] Nevertheless, other clues in the text suggest to Thomas Heffernan that Perpetua "likely would have spoken a dialect of Punic in running her household."[72] Several generations later in Christian history, Augustine and his son, Adeodatus, spoke Punic,[73] as did Augustine's mother, Monica, although she never lost her accent when speaking Latin.[74] More details about the use of Punic from Augustine's time will be discussed in later chapters. More generally, the recurring instances of Punic in the various African Christian sources may indicate that Punic continued to be the language of Christian teaching in North Africa, even though Latin became the default written language.[75]

More generally, regarding new elite usage of language, Richard Miles explains,

> In north Africa, with the emergence of a Romano-African elite in the first century AD, bilingual inscriptions in both Latin and Punic reflect this elite's need to not only maintain its local power base with a self-consciously constructed "African" cultural identity, but also to articulate its position as an important group of people within the framework of the Roman empire.[76]

Apuleius, Septimius Severus, and even Christian examples like Augustine and Monica illustrate how new elites, conscious of language as an ethnic boundary marker established by the Roman "Other," attempted to transcend their own African origins.

Closely related to language is the use of rhetoric. Across the empire, many young men were schooled in rhetoric so that they could improve their social status through a public career. This trend, which in modern times came to be known as the Second Sophistic movement, especially celebrated classical Hellenism, and it served as means for Greek heritage to flaunt its social cache, even though Greece had been conquered by the Romans. Beyond Greece and Italy, schools of rhetoric in places like North Africa enabled local elites to educate their sons and prepare them to climb the social ladder of the Roman Empire. Fronto and Apuleius are often classified as part of the Second Sophistic since their surviving works display many of the movement's characteristics. The Christian writer, Tertullian, has been read as belonging to this movement in rhetoric.[77] Later, Augustine, who was schooled in Apuleius's hometown of Madauros and who frequently cited "Apuleius the African [*Apuleius Afer*],"[78] went on to teach rhetoric in Carthage, Rome, and Milan, before he was baptized and retreated from public life back to his hometown in North Africa. According to Peter Brown, Africans like Apuleius and Augustine had a penchant for using rhetorical skills in an extreme form, a practice he called "African fire."[79] In fact, understanding the strategies of rhetoric will be essential for the following chapters that attempt to read the North African Christian writers. The shift from language to rhetoric, however, moves us into another category, that of art.

African art

Another background to ancient African Christianity is African artwork. The category of "art" is given here only to draw attention to what has often been generically called "culture." We are avoiding "culture" in this study because it is ill defined, and often includes an amalgamation of other items, like language and religion, which we are dealing with in other sections. In this section, however, we need to acknowledge some of the unique African expressions of identity that can be detected in the artisanship and in the artistic remains from this era.

Along with Libyan and Punic languages and religions, evidence can be found for Libyan and Punic artwork not only in pre-Roman times but throughout the Roman era.

A previous generation of scholars sought to investigate these artifacts with an eye to finding a tie to an indigenous African expression of Christianity.[80] This kind of evidence, however, is very slim, and so most recent scholars have looked to how Roman "culture" has been appropriated by the Christians from this region. By now, however, it should be clear that we do not expect or need the indigenous elements to be pure and isolated from the Roman. Instead, we can see how the Roman expressions of art have been assimilated.[81]

One art form in North Africa is the literary art. The Romans found that Punic authors wrote books that survived late into the Roman period.[82] Writing in the fifth century, Augustine can still refer to Punic books.[83] No Punic literature, however, has survived for historians to investigate further.

Apart from a Punic literary tradition, the heritage of Carthage in particular inspired art and artisanship. The name itself, in Punic, *Qart-hadasht*, means "New City," and Carthage's influence certainly spread throughout North Africa soon after it was established. The quotation from Apuleius, partially cited on p. 51, helps illustrate this idea. In the full paragraph Apuleius praised Carthage's political heritage as well as its artistic role in Africa and throughout the empire. He especially lauds the fact that Carthage's

> citizens are full of learning . . . [and] teach all manner of knowledge. Carthage is the venerable instructress of our province, Carthage is the heavenly muse of Africa, Carthage is the fount whence all the Roman world draws draughts of inspiration.[84]

Apuleius certainly exaggerates, which is understandable given his role as an elite speaking to both indigenous and Roman(/-ized) Carthaginians. Even so, Apuleius's claim can be verified to some extent by noting how important African red slip pottery was in the region and throughout the empire[85]: the "draughts" of inspiration were literally imbibed from African dishware, and this form of pottery was one prized by those who could afford it. In the fourth century, smaller towns and villages begin to acquire more independence and the lower classes begin to acquire more wealth, as evidenced by the archaeological remains of this African pottery, which previously was afforded only by the upper classes. This social shift influences how we think about the Donatist controversy, since the local bishops in these towns functioned in such a way as to provide these smaller but ascending municipalities with a degree of independence.[86]

Another example can be found in African food. If we allow food supplies exported to count as art, then the culinary influence of Africa extended beyond its famous agricultural production. In terms of cuisine, it was one of the primary producers of *garum*, a salted fish paste beloved by the Romans that first belonged to Punic practices.[87]

To turn to another example of African artwork and artisanship, we can see assimilation between African and Roman practices in the burial steles and inscriptions from this region.[88] The surviving pre-Roman Punic steles have a distinct style. Later, in what looks to be Romanization, the same religious and funerary monuments utilize Roman sculpture and style. However, it should be noted that the accommodation of Roman style does not negate the indigenous significance of these artifacts. In fact, the Roman style artwork on the later steles show less impact than one might expect on the content of these material remains.[89] Pre-Roman dedications invoking Punic deities, for example, will continue throughout the Roman period – only then the Punic deities appear "Romanized" in the sculptures.[90] (We will return to the Punic religion in particular on in the next section.) Even with the clear development in style, many indigenous symbols and images continue to appear on these artifacts well into the Roman period.[91]

Burial sites were important for Christianity in North Africa.[92] While little to no material artifacts remain from second and third century Christians,[93] we can detect the importance of burial and funerary practices for the early African Christians by comparing the literary records with later archaeological remains.[94] It was once commonly agreed by scholars that early Christians in North Africa maintained cemeteries and burial sites that were strictly for Christians.[95] However, recent scholars have challenged this view, arguing that the earliest Christians would have buried their dead in burial grounds for non-Christians.[96] More work is needed in revisiting the potential influence and overlap between African burial monuments and African Christian practices.[97]

Some of the earliest records of African Christianity indicate that Christians found burial sites to be important.[98] This becomes especially apparent in later centuries with the burial shrines of the martyrs. The martyr stories not only played an important role in the liturgy of the African churches,[99] but the Christians also performed certain rituals on site in the cemeteries, eventually building shrines and basilicas over these sacred spaces.[100]

Of course, banqueting with the dead was a common practice throughout the Mediterranean, and Christians across the Roman Empire often practiced what looks to modern historians like a syncretism of ancestor worship and Christianity. Often graves were marked with a *mensa*, or table for feasting. In Africa, however, the *refrigerium* or banquet at a burial site of a deceased Christian was especially lively.[101] An inscription dating from around 309 reads "The Mensa of Januarius, the Martyr. Drink up and live long!"[102] When Augustine's own mother, after following him to Italy, practiced this kind of banquet in Milan, "as she normally did in Africa [*sicut in Africa solebat*]," she was rebuked by the famous bishop Ambrose.[103] Notable bishops in Africa, like Augustine, will attempt to temper the celebrations in the cemeteries.[104] Meanwhile, the Donatist party will continue this practice with no apparent reservations.[105]

It should be reiterated that the earliest Christians in North Africa have left no material remains, and so a direct comparison with African burial artifacts is difficult.[106] Moreover, the demographics are skewed in the funerary remains throughout the empire, since the lower classes are underrepresented in the archaeological record, and the same is true of indigenous provincials. Therefore, any surviving artifacts, including literary artifacts, should be analyzed in comparison with burial practices known from Africa in order to glean as much information as possible from this particular background of African Christianity.

Even with the scant material evidence, we can find indications of the pre-/non-Roman background affecting even Christian architecture. The remains of Christian basilicas across North Africa are decorated with many Punic "symbols of Ba'al/Saturn"[107] – so much so that Augustine admits how many African Christians assumed they were worshipping "Saturn" (i.e. the Punic god, Baal).[108] This brings us to the specific background of African religions.

African religions

The history of religion (to use our modern category) in North Africa can be summarized by listing the ancient Libyan deities (of which very little is known), followed by the Punic influence based in Carthage but spread throughout North Africa,[109] followed by Roman deities brought to North Africa after it was conquered by Rome, and then finally followed by Christianity and Islam. The problem with this sequential summary is that it gives the impression of one religion replacing the previous, like the proverbial billiard balls mentioned earlier. In reality, the worship of pre-Punic deities continued throughout the Punic and even the Roman periods.[110] To complicate matters further, there was much of what many would call syncretism between these varying religions. Even the way in which this syncretism occurred varied widely, but let us begin by explaining the phenomenon one ancient writer called *interpretatio Romana*.[111]

When studying classical mythology, it is common to speak of Greek deities under their Roman name and vice versa. For example, Poseidon is known as Neptune in Latin. The simple name translation, however, fails to account for the actual differences between the Greek and Latin deities. For example, in Greek mythology Poseidon is the god of both sea and land, whereas in later Latin writers Neptune is almost exclusively the god of the sea. Of course, this did not stop ancient Latin writers from explicitly claiming that their Neptune was the same god as Homer's Poseidon. The "interpretation" is valid because the Latin Neptune and the Greek Poseidon share so much in common. Modern scholars who wish to understand Neptune must explore the unique Roman aspects of this deity as well as the commonalities overlapping with the Greek god.

When a shrine to "Neptune" was discovered in North Africa at a great distance from the sea, the question arose as to how best to understand it. This "Neptune" was almost certainly not the Roman god of the sea, and with no evidence of Hellenistic influence in the area it was equally unlikely to have been thought of as the Greek god, Poseidon. Instead, the most plausible explanation is that this shrine was to a local deity believed to be the patron of the spring – a water god, like the Roman Neptune. When an inscription was made in Latin, the trade language of the region, the name Neptune was the obvious interpretation.

Many African deities, although mostly surviving under Roman names, still retain their pre-/non-Roman characteristics throughout the entire Roman period.[112] Therefore, any given deity in North Africa could be understood by both Romans and Africans in their own terms. Baal, the sky god, could easily be named Jupiter under Roman rule,[113] and both indigenous Africans and Roman colonists could worship at the same temple.[114] Just how many individuals in each group knew the differences is an open question. The educated elite most certainly knew that the Punic and Roman cults entailed different religious narratives. Sometimes there was a conscious attempt to syncretize the two, while at other times the apparent disjunction went unaddressed.

To be clear, while we speak of the exchange between the Greek/Roman deities to be on one level parallel with the Roman/African deities, we should also point out that there are differences between the two contexts. The major difference with African accommodation of Roman names for the gods and goddesses is that the African population had to do so in the aftermath of the Punic wars. While many Africans happily accommodated *Romanitas* by some form of syncretization of their deities with Roman deities, we should still assess how the ongoing cults to Punic and African deities could point to an ongoing African identity distinct (even if not opposed to) a Roman identity.

It also must be remembered that the interpretation of African deities into Roman names was not consistently applied across North Africa. More commonly, Baal Hammon, as one who blesses crops, could be named in Latin as Saturn (i.e. the Greek Kronos), the god of wheat. Shrines to "Saturn" were very prominent throughout North Africa, and these are generally taken by scholars to represent the ongoing devotion to Baal, only now in Latinized form.[115] We have already mentioned how names can indicate the African identity; here it is worth noting how scholars understand popular African names like Saturnus and Saturninus to reflect the ongoing cult of Baal/Saturn in the area.

The translations of African deities into Latin was by no means consistent. Sometimes Baal could be equated with the Roman sky god Jupiter, as mentioned on as just mentioned.[116] Hannibal took a vow to "Zeus" (i.e. Baal) to be the eternal enemy of Rome, and even if this anecdote is later legend, it still witnesses to the ancient practice of translating the names of Punic deities.[117] The inconsistent Romanization only further demonstrates that indigenous Africans did not think in terms of Roman mythologies. Instead, they were referring to their own deity, only using Latin.[118]

The same was true for the Punic goddess Tanit:[119] since she was Baal's consort, Tanit sometimes is recorded in Latin as either Juno or as Caelestis.[120] There may even be a connection to Ceres (cf. the Greek Demeter), since both the Punic Tanit and the Roman Ceres were fertility goddesses. In Africa alone can one find the worship of the "Cereres" (plural) due to the Punic influence (cf. the *Asheroth* of Phoenicia referenced throughout the Hebrew Bible).[121] Apuleius, who became a follower of the newly popular Egyptian cult to Isis, justifies his devotion to the goddess by explaining her to be the same as "Ceres," "Juno," and a whole array of other provincial fertility goddesses.[122]

Tanit in particular played a very important role in shaping African identity, both before and after the Roman conquest.[123] Dido herself reportedly brought her (i.e. Astarte) from Tyre when founding the city of Carthage. Therefore, she will be the patroness of the Punic city, often known in Roman times as Caelestis. Virgil, in his epic poem celebrating the founding of Rome, will portray "Juno" as the goddess attempting to undermine Aeneas because she knows that his heirs, the Romans, will destroy her beloved city of Carthage. Later, Hannibal is also said to be inflamed against the Romans by "Juno,"[124] for the oath he swore to hate the Romans was offered in the temple of Tanit.[125] When he later became a general, he commemorated his landing in Italy with an offering and inscription to "Juno" in the town of Lacinium, marking it with an inscription in both Greek (the language of southern coastal Italy at the time) and Punic.[126]

Another important figure for North African religious identity is Hercules. This name of course is itself a Latinization of the Greek demigod Heracles, which means the grace of "Hera" (= Juno in Latin). Even in Greek myth, Hercules has connections to Africa: in one of the famous twelve labors he had to cross the Libyan desert, and then he came to Atlas (i.e. the Atlas mountains of modern Morocco). The Pillars of Hercules, which he allegedly built to free Atlas from holding up the sky, mark the farthest western point of the Mediterranean in ancient thinking.[127] The Garden of the Hesperides, whence Hercules had to attain the golden apples, was believed to be the ancient Punic city of Lixus. There Hercules defeated the dragon that protected the garden, and the local river still winding around this site in Morocco became associated with the dragon's tail.[128] In North Africa, however, the deity inscribed with the Roman name Hercules was very different. He was worshipped first at Tyre and then at Carthage as the Phoenician god Melqart, and Melqart, although often equated with Hercules, had very distinct characteristics.[129] According to the Roman historian Livy, Hannibal claimed "Hercules" as his divine patron.[130]

Similarly, the Punic god Shadrapa often became identified with the Roman god of wine, Liber Pater (cf. Dionysus/Bacchus).[131] Liber Pater and Hercules offer an interesting case study since Septimius Severus was devoted to both. His temples and coinage illustrate how the African emperor of Rome did not attempt to choose between the Roman or the Punic forms of these deities. Instead, the population of his hometown Leptis Magna in Tripolitania could worship the Punic deities Melqart and Shadrapa, while his Roman constituency could likewise appreciate his support of Hercules and Liber Pater.[132] Septimius thereby functions as an elite member of Roman society in general and of his local African region in particular in that he embraces both Roman and non-Roman identities.[133]

Many elites of North Africa, like their Romanized deities, embodied (at least) two distinct social identities:[134] on one hand, they were descended from Africans (and again, it must be stipulated that this could mean Libyan, Punic, Mauretanian, or any other number of people groups in the area); on the other hand, they to some extent embraced *Romanitas*. That is, they likely exhibited any number or combination of the following actions: they spoke Latin, wore togas, attempted to rise in the societal rankings, and accepted official roles within the government (to name but a few examples). One expectation of elites throughout the Roman world was for them to sponsor public displays of loyalty. For example, senators would host games, festivals, and build public buildings and monuments. Each of these, it should be remembered, involved both religion and politics. The gods would have been invoked and sacrifices would have been offered at each of these events, including dedications of monuments and buildings. The political significance included the fact that Roman leaders were honored with all of these, most especially the emperor, and the local populace was appeased by the generosity of the patron sponsor. This system, therefore, incentivized the local elites to portray the deities in ways that were acceptable to both a Roman and an African audience.

Understanding these African deities, even if Romanized to varying degrees, is important for the following chapters because the Christian writers often referred to the local deities in their region, and more attention needs to be given to the many instances where North African Christians mention "Roman" deities to see if these deities also had an African identity.[135]

Even beyond the way these references to African deities may indicate an African identity, there is a larger question about how we should relate non-Roman cults to the arrival of Christianity. In the past, some scholars have explained the widespread and rapid acceptance of Christianity (and then later Islam) in Africa by way of highlighting the common Semitic background.[136] In other words, Punic is a Caananite religion, and when another Caananite religion (i.e. Christianity) arrives, it shares common motifs and values. If a Punic priest had someone show him the Hebrew alphabet, he would easily be able to understand much in a Christian Old Testament, since the two languages share much of the same semantic range. Augustine will use Punic words to explain passages from the Hebrew Bible to his audience (see examples in Chapters 7 and 8). Even so, we must use caution when making assumptions about such connections: this approach has been heavily criticized as a form of Orientalism, or a Eurocentric overgeneralization about Semitic groups.[137] While these criticisms are valid, it is worth noting the instances where the background of Punic deities may further inform our understanding of African Christian writers. Some of these instances will be discussed in the chapters that follow.

Another area in which the background of African religions can inform our study is in the way they came into conflict with Christianity. The early African sources on martyrdom can be read in light of the role the new elites played in Africa, since these elites often had the most to gain by maintaining the balance brought about by the *interpretatio Romana* of the various cults. Throughout the empire, Christianity often disrupted the role of elites in terms of local worship practices. For example, in the scene from Acts (19:23–27) the Christian message against idolatry resulted in a decline of Artemis worship in Ephesus. It was not the virgin priestesses nor the city officials who brought a charge against Paul's companions; it was the local silversmiths who had profited from selling goods for the worship practice. At the behest of these local elites, the city official had to intervene. In the post–New Testament martyr accounts, Christians are rarely persecuted at the initiative of Roman officials. In fact, when Pliny the Younger, a governor of the province of Bithynia-Pontus, wrote to the emperor Trajan for guidance in handling Christian trials, Trajan insisted that Pliny must "not apprehend [*conquirendi non sint*]" the Christians. Instead, "If indeed they should be brought before you," then Pliny must punish them – unless they sacrifice to the gods.[138] If government officials were not pursuing Christians, then who was "bringing" the Christians before provincial governors? In Africa the answer was often the new elites, whose status largely depended on their ability to appease both their local constituency and their Roman patrons through their religious rituals, via *interpretatio Romana*. Examples of this phenomenon can be found in the Christian martyrdoms, such as the *Acts of the Scillitan Martyrs* and the *Passion of Perpetua and Felicity*, which will be discussed below on pp. 87–98 (in Chapter 3).[139] A full study is needed that traces the developments of this phenomenon into later instances of persecution.

To repeat what was said by way of introduction, we should not let our discussion of "religion" be isolated from other spheres of ancient life, such as politics. The African religions have been identified here in order to compare how they contrasted with and yet were accommodated to the Roman deities. The encounter between the two regions' religious heritage often brings to light the political identities at play between Africans and Romans. Another area in which such identities can be seen is with the Africans' physical appearance.

African appearance

This last category of "appearance," like "art" (formerly known as "culture") on pgs. 56–59, is one used for a lack of a better term. As we explained in the opening of this chapter, we are trying to move away from race or even ethnicity and speak instead about identity. However, there several items that would normally be classified as ethnic identifiers, as are language and religion, only these have to do with appearances more than practices, and so are deemed "racial" or "ethnic" markers in popular parlance.[140] Again, it is worth remembering that in contemporary social scientific studies the concept of "race" has been rejected. Moreover, in the ancient sources the concept of "race" is something altogether different, not so much based on appearance, but more on a shared history and lineage. Even so, the ancient sources sometimes describe people's appearances, and they even do so by characterizing some people groups on the basis of their appearance.[141]

The Romans sometimes caricatured the Africans in terms of their appearance.[142] One of the minor poems of Pseudo-Virgil states, "She was his only help, African by race, her whole appearance proclaiming her native land."[143] The fact that someone could look at a woman and know by her *figura* that she was an *Afra* suggests that there were physical signifiers by which North Africans were recognized. For example, sometimes Roman sources referred to the skin color of Mauretanians, which was said to be halfway between lighter-skinned Italians and very dark-skinned Ethiopians.[144] In some instances, these Mauretanians, or "Moors" as they are sometimes called, are even described as "black-skinned [μελανόχροοι]."[145] Sometimes *Afer* (African) was even used by Romans as the equivalent of *Aethiops* (i.e. someone from Ethiopia, but sometimes someone who was black-skinned).[146] This, however, was usually due to a lack of familiarity with darker-skinned people.[147] While Africans were sometimes portrayed with distinct features in Roman art,[148] the literary sources tend to divide Africa generally between the Ethiopians to the south and Libyans to the north. This fits with the larger taxonomy used by Greeks and Romans wherein the dark-skinned Ethiopians from the far south were offset by the blond-haired and light-skinned Gauls to the far north. In between these two extremes could be found varying shades, with the Greeks and Romans holding the central place.[149] In short, the Greek and Roman sources were not consistent in their description of "Libyans."

Two examples from the second century CE help illustrate how Africans were viewed in terms of skin color. The first is Septimius Severus, whom modern scholars once believed to have been dark-skinned due to a sixth-century source, but this has been overturned by more recent studies.[150] Aside from one surviving painting of Septimius's family, wherein the emperor is depicted as darker skinned than his Syrian wife and their sons, there is no mention from Septimius's own time that comments on his appearance.[151] Therefore, even if we concluded that he was dark-skinned, it is noteworthy that the ancient sources do not identify him as such. In fact, Severus himself was once said to have been "troubled . . . by the [Ethiopian] man's ominous colour . . . black."[152]

The second example is found with Septimius Severus's rival, Clodius Albinus, who was also from North Africa.[153] According to one source, Clodius connected his name, Albinus, with an ancient Roman family, but the same source then explains that the name was due to his unusually white skin.[154] A letter from his father to a kinsman and proconsul of Africa, explains that the white skin was proof of the ancient ancestry of the Albini family. There is also an alleged letter from Marcus Aurelius describing Clodius as, "a native of Africa, but with little of the African about him [*Afro quidem homini se non multa ex Afris habenti*]."[155]

These examples from the second century serve as background of ethnic identifiers between Romans and Africans, and they illustrate how these demarcations could still be used at the time when Christianity arrived. It is also important to remember that such descriptions of appearance did not go away altogether, even after centuries of Roman colonization of Africa. Writing in Augustine's time, the Roman poet, Claudian, laments how certain noblewomen in Carthage were forced to marry Mauretanians and the result is "a hideous half-breed child" whose appearance "affrights its cradle."[156]

Similarly, in some poems written and collected in sixth-century Africa, one African woman is mocked because she has skin like an elephant and because "an aged ape gave birth to you in Africa when the world was young."[157] Another poet, in what has been called "localized xenophobia,"[158] describes a man named "Aegyptius" and his "blackness," for his "name which you can read befits an Ethiopian."[159] Despite the name and the claim that it belongs to an Ethiopian, the poem clearly refers to a Garamantean man (Garamanteans were another African people group from this area).[160] While we should not assume that all Africans could be so clearly differentiated from Romans by their physical appearance, when these physical characteristics are used to establish social identities, we should pay attention to them.

Other social boundaries were also formed between the Romans and the Africans by physical appearance. Ancient sources could also distinguish Africans by their unique clothing: Roman and Greek sources often portray Africans as nomadic barbarians wearing the "mantle" or the *pallium* instead of togas.[161] Strabo (c.64 BCE–c.24 CE), the Greek geographer, can claim, "I might almost say that . . . the Libyans in general, dress alike and are similar in all other respects."[162] Without an explanation as to its appearance, Valerius Maximus can refer to a "Punic cloak [*Punicoque sagulo*]," assuming the audience knows how Punics dressed.[163] Later, Septimius Severus will arrive in Rome and make the embarrassing mistake of wearing a *pallium* to a banquet, and so need to borrow a toga.[164] However, later in life, he returned to plain clothes with "scarcely any purple"; instead he preferred his "shaggy cloak."[165] Later, for the Vandal period, the "Mauritanians" wear only "a thick cloak and a rough shirt" and live in austere huts, while their foreign conquerors wear fine garments and indulge in extravagant pleasures.[166] While such descriptions of all Mauretanians are clearly stereotypes meant to depict the African people group as barbaric, the point remains that the toga is a symbol of *Romanitas* and local garb represents provincialism.

Many Africans accommodated Roman attire.[167] The encounter between the Romans and the other ethnic groups in the provinces resulted in a pressure on new elites to "become . . . Roman by adopting the Roman way of life, by speaking their language, by adopting their *politeia*."[168] Even so, those who by way of dress or otherwise acquired *Romanitas* also could retain a local identity.[169] As Walter Pohl clarifies, "Romanness, even for those who reached this goal, did not cancel regional and ethnic identities."[170]

In the earlier section on African politics, we heard Tertullian's remark about "Punichood" blushing before *Romanitas*. Tertullian delivered this remark in a work entitled *On the Cloak* (*De pallio*), in which he argues that his audience should abandon the toga and return to their indigenous clothing.[171] Most scholars have read this work as referring to a philosopher's cloak, not native attire, and this reading is justified by Tertullian's own statements wherein he likens his outfit to the Greek philosopher's cloak.[172] However, Tertullian also likens the *pallium* to the robes worn by priests in religious ceremonies, and hints at many other comparisons throughout the work. The various comparisons function by adding credibility to the *pallium*, but what all of the comparisons have in common is that they are not Roman, like the toga.[173] The clue to this is early in his treatise where, after reminding the Carthaginians how Rome destroyed their city, he offers to turn to other topics (*nunc aliunde res*) than *Punicitas* or *Romanitas*.[174] The overarching aim, however, is to convince his audience to abandon the Roman toga.

This reading of Tertullian's treatise does not negate his religious convictions; rather, it brings to light just how important dress and appearance is for Tertullian's theology. In what appears curious for a Christian writer, Tertullian devotes several treatises to attire and appearance.[175] Carly Daniel-Hughes has noted how Tertullian incorporates dress into his understanding of salvation itself.[176] Cyprian, the bishop of Carthage a generation after Tertullian, followed Tertullian's teachings and placed great emphasis on dress and appearance.[177] For both Tertullian and Cyprian, along with most ancient Christians, the notion of salvation is a communal one, and so we ought to take into account references to the social context, including references that call for a return to native garb.

At this point it should once again be stipulated that this difference between Africans and Romans along the lines of clothing in particular and appearance in general may be more the exception than the rule. We should not assume that all or even most Africans dressed or looked different than Romans. The point here is not to generalize how the Africans looked in their daily lives, but the opposite: to note the times where appearance can be used to establish the different social identities of Africans and Romans. When we come across these instances in our sources, we should attempt to understand how the sources may be stereotyping and/or maligning their opponents. To be sure, if one were to walk down the streets of any given city in Roman Africa, one would likely not be able to distinguish "natives" and "foreigners." Nevertheless, the social identities of native Africans and foreign Romans (for example) often do come into play in the sources – even the Christian sources, and these instances should not be neglected.

With these backgrounds and the way in which Africans could be identified and could identify themselves in mind, we can now begin to survey the ancient African Christians. When doing so, we will continue to ask what about these Christians was uniquely African. Sometimes, there is simply no evidence at all that African Christians distinguished themselves according to the categories of language, art, religion, and appearance. There are, however, what is perhaps a surprising number of times when they do.

Notes

1 Maureen A. Tilley, *The Bible in Christian North Africa: The Donatist World* (Minneapolis, MN: Fortress Press, 1997), 18.
2 (Grand Rapids, MI: Eerdmans, 1987). The phrase "world behind the text" is from Paul Ricoeur, who differentiated it from the "world within the text" and the "world in front of the text."
3 *On the Cloak* 4.1.
4 For an introduction to and sources for *Romanitas* see Dossey, *Peasant and Empire*, 41–48. Even so, the notion of "indigenous" does not mean "untouched by the outside world," for there probably never was such a mythic primitive people group. Instead, the term refers to the non-Roman aspect of any given topic. With African deities, for example, all of our evidence shows signs of syncretism: they are "Romanized" to some degree, but they nevertheless retain pre/non-Roman characteristics; see Alain Cadotte, *La romanisation des dieux: L'interpretatio romana en Afrique du Nord sous le Haut-Empire* (Religions in the Graeco-Roman World; Leiden: Brill, 2007), 6–7, and the discussion on pp. 59–63 on religion.
5 The following details are taken from Ramsay MacMullen, *Romanization in the Time of Augustus* (New Haven, CT: Yale University Press, 2000), 30–35.
6 For an overview of the history and sources of the "Libyo-Phoenicians," see Dossey, *Peasant and Empire*, 12–13.
7 The view championed in anthropology by Fredrik Barth, *Ethnic Groups and Boundaries* (1969), is discussed in chapter one, note 151.
8 For the surviving evidence, see James Noel Adams, *Bilingualism and the Latin Language* (Cambridge: Cambridge University Press, 2003), 200–245.
9 For one example in North Africa, see the excellent work of Modéran, *Les Maures*. More generally, see Stephen Mitchell and Geoffrey Greatrex (eds.), *Ethnicity and Culture in Late Antiquity* (London: Duckworth, 2000); Irad Malkin (ed.), *Ancient Perceptions of Greek Ethnicity* (Harvard, MA: Harvard University Press, 2001); and Jeremy McInerny (ed.), *A Companion to Ethnicity in the Ancient Mediterranean* (Oxford: Wiley Blackwell, 2014).
10 The view of social identity I am espousing here is not all that different from how ethnicity is understood in recent anthropological studies, especially those promoting the "constructivist" approach. This view speaks more in terms of ethnic *identity* than an essential *ethnicity*. See, for example, the essays in Kanchan Chandra (ed.), *Constructivist Theories of Ethnic Politics* (Oxford: Oxford University Press, 2012).
11 "Christianity and Local Culture," 93.
12 "Identity" has been contested as an analytic category. For example, Todd Berzon (in his review of Aaron P. Johnson, *Religion. . .*) recently used the criticisms of

Rogers Brubaker and Frederick Cooper (from a 2000 essay) to call this category into question. However, Berzon does not acknowledge that Brubaker and Cooper are lonely voices among social theorists who have thoroughly answered their concerns; see my review of the literature – including Brubaker and Cooper – in Wilhite, *Tertullian the African*, 37–40.

13 Social identity theory is being used with positive results in the field of early Christian studies: see J. Brian Tucker and Coleman A. Baker (eds.), *T&T Clark Handbook to Social Identity in the New Testament* (London: T&T Clark/Bloomsbury Publishing, 2014); and for a complete bibliography of current social scientific studies, see Seth J. Schwartz, Koen Luyckx, and Vivian L. Vignoles (eds.), *Handbook of Identity Theory and Research*, 2 vols. (New York: Springer, 2011). For my own synthesis of varying social scientific theories on identity, see Wilhite, *Tertullian the African* (2007); Wilhite, "Identity, Psychology, and the *Psychici*: Tertullian's 'Bishop of Bishops,'" *Interdisciplinary Journal for Research on Religion* (Fall 2009), Article 9: 1–26; and Wilhite, "Patristic Pastoral Exegesis: Cyprian's Biblical Hermeneutic of Identity," *Horizons in Biblical Theology* 32 (2010), 58–98.

14 See the study of Rebillard, *Christians and Their Many Identities in Late Antiquity*.

15 How individuals negotiate such overlap of identities in terms of hybridity has been the focus of Homi K. Bhabha, *The Location of Culture* (London: Routledge, 1994).

16 *Europe and the People Without History* (Berkeley, CA: University of California Press, 1982), 6.

17 For a helpful example from Greek and Egyptian encounter, see Tim Whitmarsh, "The Romance Between Greece and the East," in *The Romance Between Greece and the East*, ed. Tim Whitmarsh and Stuart Thomson (Cambridge: Cambridge University Press, 2013), 2–3. Other helpful essays along these lines can be found in Erich S. Gruen (ed.), *Cultural Identity in the Ancient Mediterranean* (Los Angeles: Getty Research Institute, 2011).

18 I.e. the studies of Laroui and Benabou, discussed in chapter one.

19 For the bibliography on the material remains in particular, see Dossey, *Peasant and Empire*, 211 n.36; and Burns, Jensen, et al., *Christianity in Roman Africa*. The early archaeologists of Africa often caused damage to ancient Christian sites, and therefore the material remains are not as well preserved as they should be. For example, many artifacts, including a Christian lamp, were lost in the uncovering of a Jewish burial site, with only a few drawings of the items surviving; see A. Delattre, *Gamart ou la nécropole juive de Carthage* (Lyon: Imprimerie Mougin-Rusand, 1895).

20 See Conant, *Staying Roman*; and further discussion in chapters nine, ten, and eleven.

21 E.g. the conflict between Septimius Severus from Lepcis Magna and Clodius Albinus from Hadrumetum. *The Augustan History: Clodius Albinus* 5, reports an oracle predicting that he would "establish the power of Rome (*Romanam magno*) . . . and scatter the Punics (*sternet Poenos*)," which Albinus interpreted as foretelling his victory over the Punic Septimius Severus. The problems with this source were noted in chapter one, but this source still provides examples of common caricatures available to writers in late antiquity.

22 *The Augustan History: Severus* 9: *ne videretur de civili triumphare victoria*.

23 See Pliny, *Natural History* 8.11: "Elephants are produced by Africa beyond the deserts of Sidra and by the country of the Moors [*Elephantos fert Africa ultra Syrticas solitudines et in Mauretania*]."

24 See one example in Michèle Blanchard-Lemée, Mongi Ennaïfer, Hédi Slim, and Latifa Slim, *Mosaics of Roman Africa: Floor Mosaics fFrom Tunisia*, trans. Kenneth D. Whitehead (London: British Museum Press, [orig. 1995] 1996), 19–22, who

examines representations of the goddess "Afra" (spirit of Africa) depicted with dreadlocks, "brunette-complexioned," "notably darker," and having "Negroid traits of the whole face." This image is from a mosaic in the El Jem Museum in Tunisia.

25 Other authors also mention elephants, but most often only when they discuss references to ivory in scripture.

26 *On the Death of the Persecutors* 16.

27 Pliny, *Natural History* 8.2; Plutarch, *Pompey* 14.

28 Plutarch, *Pompey* 14, says he captured these elephants from the African kings. Of course, Pompey later retreated to Africa and acquired the support of many Africans. Cf. Caesar, *The African War*, where many of the various people groups of North Africa sided with Caesar's opponents, willingly providing elephants for the battles.

29 See discussion in Bill Ashcroft, Gareth Griffiths, and Helen Tiffin, *The Empire Writes Back: Theory and Practice in Post-Colonial Literatures* (London: Routledge, 1989), 4.

30 E.g. aqueducts were added, a grid system was implemented, etc. See David Soren, Aïcha Ben Abed Ben Khader, and Hédi Slim, *Carthage: Uncovering the Mysteries and Splendors of Ancient Tunisia* (New York: Simon and Schuster, 1990).

31 See bibliography in Petr Kitzler, *From "Passio Perpetuae" to "Acta Perpetuae" Recontextualizing a Martyr Story in the Literature of the Early Church* (Berlin: De Gruyter, 2015), 16.

32 On "Rebuilding Punic Carthage" and on how Carthage shaped Roman identity, see Richard Miles, "Rivaling Rome: Carthage," in *Rome the Cosmopolis*, ed. Catharine Edwards and Greg Woolf (Cambridge: Cambridge University Press, 2006), 123–146. Miles provides examples like Cicero's *On the Commonwealth*, where in the final section he discusses Scipio Africanus and the destruction of Africa. Likewise, he discusses Silius Itallica's *Punica*; Statius's *Silvae*, which celebrates Hannibal's defeat; and Pliny's *Natural History*, which describes statues of Hannibal in Rome. I would add Propertius, *Elegies* 4.11, for Cornelia who swears by Rome's ancestors who defeated "Africa."

33 *Florida* 4.20 (my trans.): *provinciae nostrae magistra venerabilis . . . Africae Musa coelestis.* For Apuleius's African identity and context, see the collection of essays in Benjamin Todd Lee, Ellen D. Finkelpearl, and Luca Graverini (eds.), *Apuleius and Africa* (London: Routledge, 2014).

34 Miles, "Rivaling Rome," 134, comments: "[Apuleius'] proud claim . . . informs rather than contradicts the 'Punicity' of the city."

35 *On the Cloak* 1.1.

36 *On the Cloak* 1.3.

37 *On the Cloak* 2.1: *Sit nunc aliunde res, ne Poenicum inter Romanos aut erubescat aut doleat.* This and other passages lead L. E. Elliot-Binns, *The Beginnings of Western Christendom* (London: Lutterworth Press, 1948), 151, to conclude, "In [Tertullian] the characteristics of the African Church and of the Phoenician people, of whom he was so proud, are combined."

38 See discussion in Wilhite, *Tertullian the African*, 139–145.

39 Cf. Sallust, *The War With Cateline*, 10.

40 *City of God* 2.18. Of course, Augustine's "two cities" in this work are primarily that of earth and heaven, not Rome and Carthage. Nevertheless, the overtones of Augustine's commentary should not be ignored. He elsewhere (*City of God* 19.7) describes Rome as "the imperious city [which] has imposed not only a yoke but its language upon the subjugated nations as a societal peace . . . but this has come about by copious and extensive wars [*ut imperiosa civitas non solum iugum, verum etiam linguam suam domitis gentibus per pacem societatis inponeret . . . sed hoc quam multis et quam grandibus bellis*]." Ronald H. Bainton,

Christian Attitudes Toward War and Peace: A Historical Survey and Critical Re-Evaluation (New York: Abingdon, 1960), 91, comments, "Augustine was an African with a deep sense of the wrongs of the conquered." Also, see Augustine's critique of Roman historians: "who did not so much recount the Roman wars as they praised Roman imperialism" (*City of God* 3.19 [CCL 47: "*qui non tam narrare bella Romana quam Romanum imperium laudare*"]). For other examples of Augustine's surprisingly anti-Roman comments in this work, see Wilhite, "Augustine the African: Post-Colonial, Postcolonial and Post-Postcolonial Readings," *Journal of Postcolonial Theory and Theology* 5 (2014), 28–31.

41 Cf. Orosius, *History Against the Pagans* 4.23, who was a disciple of Augustine. Orosius, in turn, was a source for the later Arab writer, Ibn Khaldun, who documented North African history.

42 See, for example, throughout Appian, *The Punic Wars*.

43 See Farès Moussa, "Berber, Phoenicio-Punic, and Greek North Africa," in *The Oxford Handbook of African Archaeology*, ed. Peter Mitchell and Paul Lane (Oxford: Oxford University Press, 2013), 766; and Fergus Millar, *Rome, the Greek World, and the East*, ed. Hannah Cotton and Guy MacLean Rogers (Chapel Hill, NC: University of North Carolina Press, 2004), 2:255–256. The dating, however, is debatable; see Robert M. Kerr, *Latino-Punic Epigraphy: A Descriptive Study of the Inscriptions* (Tübingen: Mohr Siebeck, 2010), 21 n.23.

44 However, surviving parallel inscriptions of Libyan and Punic and even Libyan and Latin, have enabled some translation work: Karel Jongeling, *Late Punic Epigraphy: An Introduction to the Study of Neo-Punic and Latino-Punic Inscriptions* (Tübingen: Mohr Siebeck, 2005).

45 Even a distinct ethnicity: Modéran, *Les Maures*, 526–527. For discussion of the sources, see Mattingly and Hitchner, "Roman Africa," 195–213.

46 Zsuzsanna Várhelyi, "What Is the Evidence for the Survival of Punic Culture in Roman North Africa?," *Acta Antiqua Academiae Scientiarum Hungaricae* 38 (1998), 391–403; and Andrew Wilson, "Neo-Punic and Latin Inscriptions in Roman North Africa: Function and Display," in *Multilingualism in the Graeco-Roman Worlds*, ed. Alex Mullen and Patrick James (Cambridge: Cambridge University Press, 2012), 265–316.

47 *Apology* 98.8.

48 *The History of Wars* 4.10: πόλεις τε οἰκήσαντες πολλὰς ξύμπασαν Λιβύην μέχρι στηλῶν τῶν Ἡρακλείων ἔσχον, ἐνταῦθά τε καὶ ἐς ἐμὲ τῇ Φοινίκων φωνῇ χρώμενοι ᾤκηνται.

49 See Stephen Wilson, *The Means of Naming: A Social and Cultural History of Personal Naming in Western Europe* (London: University College London Press, 1998), 43–45, for common Latinized Punic names. Also, see Iiro Kajanto, "Peculiarities of Latin Nomenclature in North Africa," *Philologus* 108 (1964), 310–312, for the Punic influence.

50 "Libyans and Greeks in Rural Cyrenaica," *Quaderni di archeologia della Libya* 12 (1987), 382. These can be seen in Elisabeth Rosenbaum, *A Catalogue of Cyrenaican Portrait Sculpture* (London: Oxford University Press, 1960).

51 Birley, *The African Emperor*, 52.

52 See Ronald Syme, "Donatus and the Like," *Historia* 27 (4, 1978), 588–603. However, the statistical analysis is not without difficulty; see Yann Le Bohec, "L'onomastique de l'Afrique romaine sous le Haut-Empire et les cognomina dits 'Africains,'" *Pallas* 68 (2005), 217–239.

53 Braun, "Aux Origenes," 190; James B. Rives, *Religion and Authority in Roman Carthage From Augustus to Constantine* (Oxford: Clarendon Press, 1995), 223–224; Thomas J. Heffernan, *The Passion of Perpetua and Felicity* (Oxford: Oxford University Press, 2012), 281. Candida Moss, *Ancient Christian Martyrdom:*

Diverse Practices, Ideologies, and Traditions (New Haven, CT: Yale University Press, 2012), 123, finds them to have been "deeply embedded in Punic culture."

54 Stéphane Gsell, *Inscriptions latines de l'Algerie* (Paris: Librairie ancienne Honoré Champion, 1922), 1:239 #2534.

55 Mark Ellingsen, *The Richness of Augustine: His Contextual and Pastoral Theology* (Louisville, KY: John Knox, 2005), 9–10; Warren Thomas Smith, *Augustine: His Life and Thought* (Louisville, KY: John Knox, 1980), 11.

56 J. J. O'Meara, *The Young Augustine: An Introduction to the Confessions of St. Augustine* (London: Longman, 1980), 25. Also, while Patricius is a Latin name, the form of the name is more common in Africa than elsewhere in the empire (see Kajanto, "Peculiarities of Latin Nomenclature," 11–12).

57 Brown, *Augustine*, 63.

58 As I have argued elsewhere: Wilhite, "Augustine the African," 15–16.

59 Some of the following material is adapted from my earlier work, *Tertullian the African*, 126–130.

60 Anacharsis the Scythian is discussed at length in Herodotus, *Histories*, book 4 – the same book in which Herodotus discusses Libya.

61 *Letter to the Mother of Caesar* 5 (cited on p. 4 in chapter one). Fergus Millar, "Local Cultures in the Roman Empire: Libyan, Punic and Latin in Roman Africa," *Journal of Roman Studies* 58 (1968), 126–134, discusses "native" languages of Africa (Punic and Lybian) remaining throughout the Roman period. cf. Augustine, *City of God* 16.6, "For even in Africa we know several barbarous nations which have but one language [*Nam et in Africa barbaras gentes in una lingua plurimas novimus*]."

62 Edward Champlin, *Fronto and Antonine Rome* (Cambridge, MA: Harvard University Press, 1980), 16, comments:

> This contrast [between Fronto and the Graeco-Romans] suggests the key to what was truly "African" in the orator. Above all, Fronto was the learned man of his age, thoroughly familiar with both Greek and Latin culture and the standard-bearer of Latin letters. His only misfortune was that he was born neither Greek nor Roman, but African. . . . Considerable evidence suggests in the educated elite of Roman Africa a conscious suppression of the non-Latin heritage, a practice in marked contrast with that of the Hellenized East. The *lingua punica* was not a source of pride, most particularly in the late first and early second centuries, just when Africans were first beginning to penetrate the courts, the salons, and the senate of Rome.

> Cf. Koen Goudriaan, *Ethnicity in Ptolemaic Egypt* (Amsterdam: J.C. Gieben, 1988), for the example of Hellenistic Egypt where the tensions between the colonizer and the colonized created an ethnic awareness among the new Greek-speaking elites of Egypt.

63 Brock, *Studies in Fronto and His Age*.

64 *Apology* 24: *professus sum . . . Seminumidam et Semigaetulum . . . Non enim ubi prognatus, sed ut moratus quisque sit spectandum, nec qua regione, sed qua ratione vitam viuere inierit, consideratum est.* For the Gaetulians, see Strabo, *Geography* 17.3, in which they are said to reside across various parts of North Africa. Cf. Pliny, *Natural History* 5.1.17.

65 John Hilton, "Introduction," 126; ref. to *Florida* 9.6–7:

> This is especially true for me, since the reputation that I have already won and your kind confidence in me does not allow me to mouth anything I like off the top of my head. For who among you would forgive me for a single solecism? Who would allow me one ignorantly pronounced syllable? Who would permit me to jabber any wild and uncouth words like those that well up in the

mouth of the insane? Yet you easily forgive others for these same faults and quite justly so [*praesertim mihi, cui et ante parta existimatio et vestra de me benigna praesumptio nihil non quicquam sinit neglegenter ac de summo pectore hiscere. Quis enim vestrum mihi unum soloecismum ignoverit? Quis vel unam syllabam barbare pronuntiatam donaverit? Quis incondita et vitiosa verba temere quasi delirantibus oborientia permiserit blaterare? Que tamen aliis facile et same meritissimo ignoscitis*]

Also ref. to *The Augustan History: Severus* 19.9: *canorus voce, sed Afrum quiddam usque ad senectutem sonans.*

66 *Apology* 98.8–9 (trans. Butler, *The Apologia*, 151–152).

67 *The Augustan History: Severus* 19: *sed Afrum quiddam usque ad senectutem sonans.*

68 *Rome*, 132; ref. *The Augustan History: Severus* 15.7: *cum sua Leptitana ad eum venisset uix Latine loquens, ac de illa multum imperator erubesceret.*

69 *Silvae* 4.5.45–46: *non sermo Poenus, non habitus tibi / externa non mens: Italus, Italus.*

70 *Epitome de Caesaribus* 20.8 (trans. Millar, Fergus, Hannah Cotton, and Guy MacLean Rogers, *Rome, the Greek World, and the East* [Chapel Hill, NC: University of North Carolina Press, 2004], 2:258). For more details on the Punic aspects of Leptis Magna during the Roman period, see MacMullen, *Romanization*, 35–42.

71 *Passion of Perpetua* 2, for her birth; and 13.4 for her Greek.

72 Heffernan, *The Passion of Perpetua*, 151.

73 Augustine, *The Teacher* 13.44.

74 Augustine, *On Order* 2.17.45.

75 The view of Alexander Graham, *Roman Africa: An Outline of the History of the Roman Occupation of North Africa Based Chiefly Upon Inscriptions and Monumental Remains in that Country* (London: Longmans, Green, and Co., 1902), 301.

76 Richard Miles, "Communicating Culture, Identity and Power," in *Experiencing Rome: Culture, Identity and Power in the Roman Empire*, ed. Janet Huskinson (London: Routledge in association with the Open University, 2000), 58–59.

77 Sider, *Ancient Rhetoric*; Barnes, *Tertullian*; cf. Dunn, *Tertullian's* Adversus Iudaeos, 35–36.

78 E.g. in *The City of God* 8.12. For other examples of Apuleius's reception in Augustine and other African Christian writers (as well as non-Africans), see Julia Haig Gaisser, *The Fortunes of Apuleius and the Golden Ass: A Study in Transmission and Reception* (Princeton, NJ: Princeton University Press, 2008).

79 *Augustine*, 10–11.

80 Frend, *The Donatist Church*, looked to what he believed was a rise in "Berber" art at the same time as the ascendancy of the Donatist party. Frend's wider methodology, however, has been severely critiqued (see chapter seven). While a reductionistic approach where the religious convictions of the Donatists are eclipsed by the social aspects (as Frend at times seems to promote), Frend's basic hypothesis should be revisited, as has been recently argued by Rebillard, "William Hugh Clifford Frend (1916–2005)," 55–71.

81 Even the unique "Berber" mausoleums evince style borrowed from Egypt, Greece, and Rome; see Farès Moussa, "Berber, Phoenicio-Punic, and Greek North Africa," *The Oxford Handbook of African Archaeology*, ed. Peter Mitchell and Paul Lane (Oxford: Oxford University Press, 2013), 765–777.

82 Cf. Sallust, *The War with Jugurtha* 17.7, "Punic books [*libris Punicis*]." For discussion of the intra-African identity politics contained within these books, see Nabuko Kurita, "The '*Libri Punici*', King Hiempsal and the Numidians," *Kodai: Journal of Ancient History* 5 (1994), 37–46.

83 *Letter* 17.2. Conant, *Staying Roman*, 188, believes this statement testifies to Punic books still being written in Augustine's time.

84 *Florida* 20.10.

85 Gisela Ripoll, "Ceramics (West)," in *Late Antiquity: A Guide to the Postclassical World*, ed. G. W. Bowersock, Peter Brown, and Oleg Grabar (Cambridge, MA: Belknap Press, 1999), 368–369.

86 Dossey, *Peasant and Empire*.

87 See Anne Leone and Farès K. Moussa, "Roman Africa and the Sahara," in *The Oxford Handbook of African Archaeology*, ed. Peter Mitchell and Paul Lane (Oxford: Oxford University Press, 2013), 783; and Maria Eugenia Aubet, *The Phoenicians and the West: Politics, Colonies, and Trade*, 2nd ed. (Cambridge: Cambridge University Press, 2001), 315.

88 One example where the Punic practice can be securely identified as distinct from Roman is the controversial Tophet in Carthage. Since large numbers of the cremated remains of infants have been discovered here, and since the Phoenicians/Canaanites sacrificed their children in the biblical record, many believed this site was a place of child sacrifice. Scholars debate whether Carthaginians actually sacrificed their children or whether this represents an accusation from hostile sources; for bibliography, see Moussa, "Berber, Phoenicio-Punic, and Greek North Africa," 771. See where Tertullian reports how the Roman soldiers put a stop to this in his *patria*, or homeland, in *Apology* 9.

89 For pictures and examples, see Andrew Wilson, "Romanizing Baal: The Art of Saturn Worship in North Africa," in *Proceedings of the 8th International Colloquium on Problems of Roman Provincial Art, Zagreb 2003*, ed. M. Sanader, et al. (Zagreb: Opuscula archaeologica, 2005), 403–408. Wilson concludes (p. 408): "In some regions . . . Roman impact on the cult appears minimal . . . all that has changed is that they are now clothed and speak Latin." In more urban areas, however, a greater change in artistic style is apparent. For example, palm branches tend to be replaced by grapes. Palm branches, however, continue to appear in Christian artwork.

90 For more on the Romanization of Punic deities, see pgs. 59–63.

91 For general bibliography as well as an extended discussion of one unique set of these funerary monuments, see Jennifer P. Moore, *Cultural Identity in Roman Africa: The 'La Ghorfa' Stelae* (PhD thesis for McMaster University, 2000).

92 Statements made by apologists against funerary rites (e.g. Minucius Felix, *Octavius* 38), must be read critically since they are polemical statements against non-Christian practices, not descriptions of Christian ones.

93 The earliest African Christian funerary inscription is from 299 found in Satafis, Mauretania Sitifiensis (modern Ain-Kebira); see Eliezer Gonzalez, *The Fate of the Dead in Early Third Century North African Christianity: The Passion of Perpetua and Felicitas and Tertullian* (Tübingen: Mohr Siebeck, 2014), 132–134.

94 E.g. Eusebius, *Church History* 7.13.1–2, records Gallienus's decision to restore the cemeteries to the Christians, and the specific wording implies that these cemeteries were more than that, possibly places of worship.

95 For strictly Christian burial sites, see Decret, *Early Christianity*, 17.

96 See bibliography in Jane Merdinger, "Roman North Africa," in *Early Christianity in Contexts: An Exploration Across Cultures and Continents*, ed. William Tabbernee (Grand Rapids, MI: Baker, 2014), 235 and 242.

97 For the similarities between Libyan cult of the dead and the North African Christian practice, see Brett and Fentress, *The Berbers*, 35; D. J. Mattingly, *Tripolitania* (London: Routledge, 2003), 60; and Johannes Quasten, "'*Vetus Superstitio et nova Religio*': The Problem of *Refrigerium* in the Ancient Church of North Africa," *Harvard Theological Review* 33 (1940), 253–266.

98 Tertullian, *To Scapula* 3.1.

99   See Cyprian, *Letter* 12.2.1; and see discussion in Gonzalez, *The Fate of the Dead*, 135.

100 Cf. *Acta Purgationis Felicis* 5 (in Optatus of Milevis), for Christian prayer in cemeteries. Also cf. Augustin-Ferdinand Leynaud, *Les catacombs africaines: Sousse-Hadrumète* (Alger: Jules Carbonel, 1922). For extended discussion, see Burns, Jensen, et al., *Christianity in Roman Africa*, 491–517 (= chapter ten, "The End of Christian Life: Death and Burial").

101 Shaw, "The Passion of Perpetua," *Past and Present* 139 (1993), 320, for details. For debate and bibliography on the dating of Christian *refrigerium*, see Gonzalez, *The Fate of the Dead*, 134–139.

102 See details in Gonzalez, *The Fate of the Dead*, 135.

103 See *Confessions* 6.2.2 (my trans.) For the uniquely African background to Monica's practice, see discussion in Quasten, " '*Vetus Superstitio et nova Religio*,' " 258–259.

104 For specific references, see Quasten, " '*Vetus Superstitio et nova Religio*,' " 258–266.

105 Frend, *The Donatist Church*, 54–55.

106 Remains from the later centuries, however, are often built on earlier sites, such as what is thought to be the Basilica Maiorem in Carthage: although the building is from a later period, the fragments of an inscription to Perpetua and her fellow martyrs were found on the site. Scholars generally agree that it was the original burial/shrine to these Christian "ancestors [*maiorem*]." See details in Burns, Jensen, et al., *Christianity in Roman Africa*, 144–145.

107 John Kevin Coyle, "The Self-Identity of North African Christians," in *Augustinus Afer: saint Augustin, africanité et universalité*, ed. Pierre-Yves Fux, Jean-Michel Roessli, Otto Wermelinger (Fribourg: Editions Universitaires, 2003), 67.

108 E.g. Augustine, *Harmony of the Gospels* 1.30. It should be noted that Augustine goes to great lengths to show all of the competing and contradicting claims to "Saturn," namely among the Romans, Greeks, and the various philosophers (see 1.32–40).

109 Strabo, *Geography* 17.3.15, reports how Dido's "Phoenicians" possessed all the inhabitable land of North Africa. While certainly an exaggeration, the idea is correct that Punic influence can be found throughout North Africa (cf. Pliny, *Natural History* 5.1).

110 Pliny, *Natural History* 5.3.24, reports that the inhabitants of Byzacena were called "Libyophoenicians [*Libyphoenices*]." For Punic religion more generally, see Richard J. Clifford, "Phoenician Religion," *Bulletin of the American Schools of Oriental Research* 279 (1990): 55–64; Donald Harden, *The Phoenicians* (New York: Frederick A. Praeger Publishers, 1963); and Sabatino Moscati (ed.), *The Phoenicians* (New York: Rizzoli International Publications, 1999). Also, cf. Erich S. Gruen, *Rethinking the Other in Antiquity* (Princeton, NJ: Princeton University Press, 2011).

111 Tacitus, *Germania* 43.4. For a bibliography on this phenomenon, see Cadotte, *La romanisation*, 2–6.

112 Cadotte, *La romanisation*, 20, "of this African pantheon, we will see, retained the essentials of its personality – in spite of numerous centuries of Roman domination." (My trans.: "de ce panthéon africain qui, on le verra, a conservé l'essentiel de sa personnalité: malgré plusieurs siècles de domination romaine.")

113 Sometimes Punic sanctuaries were converted by the Romans into a temple to Jupiter – most famously the Byrsa Hill in Carthage. For the legendary founding of the Byrsa hill as a Punic shrine, see Appian, *The Punic Wars* 1.1.

114 Cadotte, *La romanisation*, 1, explains how Africa was "open to Romanitas but faithful to its own religious traditions." (My trans.: "ouverte à la romanité mais fidèle à ses traditions religieuses.")

115 The most extensive study is that of Marcel Leglay, *Saturne africain: Monuments*, 2 vols. (Paris: Arts et Métiers Graphiques, 1961, 1966); and Leglay, *Saturne africain: Histoire* (Paris: Arts et Métiers Graphiques, 1966); also see Wilson, "Romanizing Baal"; also, see Rebillard, "William Hugh Clifford Frend (1916–2005)," 68, for full bibliography, especially for critiques of earlier assumptions.

116 E.g. throughout Plautus's *The Little Carthaginian*, the Carthaginian characters pray to "Jupiter." Plautus, it should be noted, is a source that must be read critically. He demonstrates how Romans of his day would have understood the Punic enemy.

117 Cf. Polybius, *Histories* 3.11, reports the oath stated he would never befriend the Romans; Livy 21.1, has the oath swear eternal hatred. Also, see the invocation of "Zeus" (and others) in the treaty between Hannibal and Philip V of Macedonia against the Romans in Polybius, *Histories* 7.9.

118 Wilson, "Romanizing Baal," 407, further adds:

> the cult of Saturn appealed in particular to the middle and lower strata of society, and the relatively unsophisticated and repetitive nature of these monuments supports this view. Many of the dedicants carry African names, or Roman names commonly borne by North Africans.

119 Known as "Astarte" in Greek sources for Phoenicia; cf. Hebrew "Ashtoreth."

120 This is especially the case for literary references; e.g. Virgil, *Aeneid* 1.441–447 and Pliny, *Natural History* 6.36. In inscriptions, she is usually named "Caelestis" (e.g. *CIL* 3.993).

121 For bibliography and discussion of the Punic influence on the Cereres, see Emily Ann Hemelrijk, *Hidden Lives, Public Personae: Women and Civic Life in the Roman West* (Oxford: Oxford University Press, 2015), 58–69.

122 *Metamorphosis* 11.5.

123 Henry R. Hurst, *The Sanctuary of Tanit at Carthage in the Roman Period: A Reinterpretation* (JRA Supplement series 30; Portsmouth, RI: JRA, 1999).

124 Cf. Silius Italicus, *Punica* 1.38–69.

125 Cf. Silius Italicus, *Punica* 1.120–121.

126 Livy 28.46; cf. Polybius, *Histories* 3.33 and 3.56.

127 Strabo, *Geography* 3.5.5; cf. 3.5.7, for the relationship to the "Phoenicians [Φοινίκων]."

128 For background to Tingis and Lixus, see Strabo, *Geography* 17.3.2.

129 Herodotus, *Histories* 2.44.

130 Livy 21.21.

131 For inscriptions and bibliography, see Merdinger, "Roman North Africa," 258–259.

132 For the background of Tripolitania, and especially for the many surviving "Libyophoenician" material there, see Mattingly, *Tripolitania*.

133 As for patronage, see *The Augustan History: Severus* 24, where he claimed to have erected the Septizonium so that "his building should strike the eyes of those who came to Rome from Africa." For this discussion of Severus's use of Hercules/Melqart and Liber Pater/Shadrapa, I am indebted to Alexander Peck, who is working on this topic in his PhD thesis at the University of Warwick, under the supervision of Clare Rowan (also cf. Rowan, *Under Divine Auspices*).

134 For a full treatment, see Rives, *Religion and Authority in Roman Carthage*.

135 See Cadotte, *La romanisation*, 18, for comment and extensive list of examples.

136 E.g. Gilbert Charles-Picard, *Les religions de l'Afrique antique* (Paris: Plon, 1954); Leglay, *Saturne africain: Histoire*.

137 See recently, McCarty, "Transforming Religion."

138 *Letter* 10.98

139 See my analysis in Wilhite, *Tertullian the African*, 158–161.

140 The actual DNA of North Africans at this time is much more complex than the cultural construction of ethnic identity. The cross-polinization of populations across the Mediterranean is beyond the scope of this study. See, for example, the study by Lisa Matisoo-Smith, et al., "A European Mitochondrial Haplotype Identified in Ancient Phoenician Remains from Carthage, North Africa," *Plos One* 11 (5, 2016), e0155046; doi: 10.1371/journal.pone.0155046 [available online at www.researchgate.net/publication/303532575_A_European_Mito chondrial_Haplotype_Identified_in_Ancient_Phoenician_Remains_from_ Carthage_North_Africa].

141 Again, this was not the same notion we moderns have when speaking of genes and DNA. Jews, for example, were described in terms of a physical marker that set them apart as a people. However, that physical marker was circumcision, not something innate. For examples, see Walter Pohl, "Telling the Difference: Signs of Ethnic Identity," in *Strategies of Distinction: The Construction of Ethnic Communities, 300–800*, ed. Pohl and Helmut Reimitz (Leiden: Brill, 1998), 17–70.

142 The following paragraphs are adapted from my earlier work, *Tertullian the African*, 126–130.

143 *Moretum* 31–32: *erat unica custos, Afra genus, tota patriam testante figura*.

144 Frank M. Snowden, Jr., *Blacks in Antiquity: Ethiopians in the Greco-Roman Experience* (Cambridge, MA: The Belknap Press, 1970), 4; Lloyd J. Thompson, *Romans and Blacks* (London: Routledge Press, 1989), 61.

145 Procopius, *History of the Wars* 3.25, speaks of the Mauretanians as residing across Byzacena, Numidia, and Mauretania. For their appearance, see *History of the Wars* 4.13. cf. Pliny, *Natural History* 5.8.43, for the "Egyptians Libyans, and then the people called in Greek the White Ethiopians. Beyond these are the Ethiopians clans of the Nigritae [*Libyes Aegyptii, deinde Leucoe Aethiopes habitant. super eos Aethiopum gentes Nigritae*]" (LCL 352:250–251).

146 See Snowden, *Blacks in Antiquity*, 11, for examples.

147 Ibid.

148 For depictions in art, see Michèle Blanchard-Lemée, et al., *Mosaics of Roman Africa*, 19–22, who examines representations of the goddess Africa depicted with dreadlocks, "brunette-complexioned," "notably darker" and having "Negroid traits of the whole face." Janet Huskinson, "Looking for Culture, Identity and Power," in *Experiencing Rome: Culture, Identity and Power in the Roman Empire*, ed. Janet Huskinson (London: Routledge, 2000), 14, comments, "This is particularly interesting to note in the case of Africa, since the other mosaic image of her found in the house emphasizes more 'ethnic' features by giving her corkscrew curls, large eyes, and darker skin." Also, Eirean Marshall, "The Self and the Other in Cyenaica," in *Cultural Identity in the Roman Empire*, ed. Ray Laurence and Joanne Berry (London: Routledge, 1998), 49–63, lists examples of artistic depictions of Cyrenaeans depicting themselves and Romans with "Libyan features." Similarly, see Gilbert Charles-Picard and Colette Charles-Picard, *Daily Life in Carthage at the Time of Hannibal*, trans. A. E. Foster (London: Ruskin House, 1961), 129, for the archeological examinations of skeletons found at the site of the ancient city of Carthage and the discussion of a variety of somatic types with a majority of "African" or "Negro" types.

149 Snowden, *Blacks in Antiquity*, 171ff.; Thompson, *Romans and Blacks*, 100ff.

150 On Severus's "blackness," E.L. Jones, *Profiles in African Heritage* (Seattle: Frayn Printing Co., 1972), cited in Olivier Hekster and Nicholas Zair, *Rome and Its Empire, AD 193–284* (Edinburgh: Edinburgh University Press, 2008).

However, against this view, see Snowden, "Misconceptions about African Blacks in the Ancient Mediterranean World: Specialists and Afrocentrists," *Arion* 4 (3, 1997), 28–50.

151 Birley, *The African Emperor*, 36, "The muddled Antiochene chronicler John Malalas, four centuries later, says that Septimius was dark-skinned. There is not much chance of verifying this statement now (although one colour portrait has survived)." Birley's plate 16 is a gray-scaled version of this image, and it is an image where Severus is noticeably darker skinned than his eastern wife. It is also worth noting, how in this particular instance, his son's face, Geta, whose memory was condemned by his brother, was blackened with feces; see Peter Parsons, *City of the Sharp-Nosed Fish: Greek Lives in Roman Egypt* (London: Weidenfeld, 2007), 69. (I am indebted to AnneMarie Luijendijk who pointed me to this source).

152 *The Augustan History: Severus* 22.

153 *The Augustan History: Clodius Albinus* 1: "Now Clodius Albinus came of a noble family, but he was a native of Hadrumetum in Africa [*Fuit autem Clodius Albinus familia nobili, Hadrumetum tamen ex Africa*]"; cf. §12, where Septimius Severus described him as "A man from Africa, a native of Hadrumetum, who pretends to derive descent from the blood of the Ceionii [i.e. a Roman family] [*unum ex Afris et quidem Hadrumetinis, fingentem quod de Ceioniorum stemmate sanguinem duceret*]."

154 *The Augustan History: Clodius Albinus* 4.

155 *The Augustan History: Clodius Albinus* 10.

156 Claudian, *The War Against Gildo* lines 189 and 193: *Mauris . . . exterret cunabula discolor infans.*

157 Luxurius, *The Book of Epigrams* 15 (text in D. R. Shackleton Bailey, *Anthologia Latina* [Stuttgart: Teubner, 1982]: lines 5–7: *elephans . . . Mater simian quam creavit arvis/grandaeva in Libycis novo sub orbe*; trans. Morris Rosenblum, *A Latin Poet Among the Vandals* [New York: Columbia University Press, 1961], 120–121); cf. poem 43, where Garamantian girls are assumed to be ugly.

158 N. M. Kay, *Epigrams from the Anthologia Latina: Text, Translation, and Commentary* (London: Bloomsbury, 2006), 212.

159 *The Book of Epigrams* 172: *tenebras . . . quod legeris nomen convenit Aethiopi* (text/trans. N. M. Kay, *Epigrams from the Anthologia Latina*, 60/325); cf. *The Book of Epigrams* 179 (Kay), on Memnon, the Ethiopian king who fought with the Trojans; as well as *The Book of Epigrams* 173 (Kay), for more such descriptions of a Garamantean man.

160 Kay, *Epigrams*, 325.

161 Huskinson, "Looking for Culture," 8; and Marshall, "The Self and the Other in Cyenaica," 57, who cites examples.

162 Strabo, *Geography* 17.3.7.

163 *Memorable Doings and Sayings* 5.11.6.

164 *The Augustan History: Severus* 1: *Severus Africa oriundus.*

165 *The Augustan History: Severus* 19: *aliquid purpurae haberet . . . hirta chlamyde.*

166 Procopius, *History of the Wars* 4.6; cf. Corippus, *Iohannis* 2.134–137.

167 *The Augustan History: Clodius Albinus* 12, for Clodius's dress at an early age.

168 Edward van der Vliet, "The Romans and Us: Strabo's Geography and the Construction of Ethnicity," *Mnemosyne* 56 (3, 2003), 269; cf. John Hutchinson and Anthony D. Smith, "Concepts of Ethnicity: Introduction," in *Ethnicity*, ed. Hutchinson and Smith (Oxford: Oxford University Press, 1996), 10–11.

169 See Moore, *Cultural Identity in Roman Africa*, 296–263, for examples of funeral stelae for "indigenous" Africans who are depicted wearing togas. Likewise, the inscriptions at Lepcis Magna for a certain Annobal (i.e. "Hannibal") Tapapius Rufus contained both Latin and depictions of him in a toga, but also

were written in Punic and so "was far from a complete triumph of 'Roman' identity"; see Mattingly, *Imperialism, Power, and Identity: Experiencing the Roman Empire* (Princeton, NJ: Princeton University Press, 2011), 238–239.

170   "Introduction: Strategies of Distinction," in *Strategies of Distinction: The Construction of Ethnic Communities, 300–800*, ed. Walter Pohl and Helmut Reimitz (Leiden: Brill, 1998), 1.

171   *On the Cloak* 1.3.

172   *On the Cloak* 3.7, 4.1, 5.3, and cf. 6.1–2.

173   Alternatively, the toga is discredited by the many unseemly characters who wear it, such as "branded slaves" (*dediticios*), the "notoriously infamous" (*subverbustos*), "clowns" (*rupices*), "buffoons" (*scurras*), "rustics" (*paganos*), the "corpse-bearer" (*vespillo*), the "pimp" (*leno*) and the "gladiator-trainer" (*lanista*, 4.8).

174   *On the Cloak* 2.1.

175   *On the Apparel of Women, On the Cloak*, and *On the Veiling of Virgins*.

176   Carley Daniel-Hughes, *The Salvation of the Flesh in Tertullian of Carthage: Dressing for the Resurrection* (New York: Palgrave Macmillan, 2011).

177   E.g. *On the Veiling of Virgins*.

3 The earliest evidence of African Christianity

No one knows when Christianity first arrived in Africa. We find the story has already begun when we look at the first sources on Christianity, which date to around 180. In this chapter, we will present the possible origins of Christianity in Africa, and survey the earliest sources of Christianity, which range from 180 to 203 CE.

Although the earliest Christians in Africa left no records, there was almost certainly a Christian presence in the region by 150, if not sooner. In 180 a group of Christians from the town of Scilli were martyred, and the *Acts of the Scillitan Martyrs* records what purports to be the official court transcripts of their trial. The next Christian writing that survives belongs to Tertullian of Carthage, who began writing in the mid-190s. While we will devote the entirety of the next chapter to Tertullian, he will be an important source for the present discussion because he references the persecution that took place at the time of the Scillitan martyrs, as well as earlier instances of Christians who were put on trial for their faith. The next source for our knowledge of Christianity is a contemporary of Tertullian, and it is another martyrdom account. The *Passion of Perpetua and Felicity* narrate events from 203, and it provides another window into early African Christianity, since it is set in Carthage, and the martyrs are possibly from the town of Thuburbo Minus.[1]

Although these scattered sources cannot give us a complete picture of Christianity in Africa at this time, they do provide glimpses into these early Christian communities from various angles. Through these fleeting glimpses, scholars sketch a history of African Christianity's origins and early developments.[2] With this overview in place, we can now look into these sources more closely to see what can be learned about the earliest African Christians. After doing so, we will then inquire about the possible origins of Christianity in Africa. After outlining the possibilities, we can then turn to look at the two martyrdoms from this time more closely. Finally, we will end this chapter by asking what was uniquely African about these earliest African Christians.

Tertullian on the earliest African Christians

The earliest generations of African Christianity left no literary or archaeological evidence, which leaves scholars the task of making educated guesses about the origins and practices of those early Christians.[3] Such educated guesses are informed by the next generation of writings, such as the *Acts of the Scillitan Martyrs* and the *Passion of Perpetua and Felicity*. Before we turn to these sources, we can see what Tertullian of Carthage has to say about earlier Christians, even Christians who preceded these martyrdoms.

Around 197 Tertullian reports complaints from non-Christians about how many Christians there were in Carthage. He describes this non-Christian complaint as follows:

> Day after day, indeed, you groan over the increasing number of the Christians. Your constant cry is, that the state is beset by us; that Christians are in your fields, in your camps, in your islands. You grieve over it as a calamity, that each sex, every age – in short, every rank – is passing over from you to us.[4]

Later, in 212, he claimed Christians were the majority in the North African cities.[5] He then goes on to threaten that if all the Christians were to be tried and killed, all of Carthage and even all of Africa would be brought to its knees.[6] Given Tertullian's penchant for rhetorical flourish,[7] scholars do not take these claims at face value. Nevertheless, the Christian population likely had grown to some extent in order for Tertullian's claims to have some credibility with his audience.[8] The persecution of African Christians datable to the time of Tertullian's writing also lends credibility to the fact that some non-Christians felt the need to check the Christian population and influence in the region. Regardless of the size of the Christian population, Tertullian simply assumes that Christianity is well established in North Africa, and he does not attempt to hazard a guess as to how long ago Christianity first arrived there.[9] It was long enough that Tertullian can refer to his church's liturgy without explanation and even to how "the death of martyrs also is praised in song."[10] He, therefore, testifies to a well-established Christian community, one large enough to threaten a local governor with riot and developed enough to have its own liturgical tradition.

Tertullian points to previous Christians by way of naming their persecutors, and some of their gruesome deaths.[11] Tertullian first names Hilarianus, probably the same one mentioned in the *Passion of Perpetua and Felicity*.[12] These events date to 203, and so belong within Tertullian's own lifetime,[13] and Tertullian explicitly references Perpetua's vision (if not the text itself).[14]

Tertullian next claims Vigellius Saturninus was the "first here to use the sword [*gladium*] against us."[15] By "here," Tertullian could mean North Africans generally, since he contrasts this person with another Roman official from Cappadocia in the next sentence. This proconsul is likely a new elite from North Africa, since he has the theophoric name, Saturninus, common among Africans at this time but unusual for Romans.[16] Moreover, he is likely to be the same "Saturninus" mentioned in the *Acts of the Scillitan Martyrs*, which records the trial from 180. According to this document, these Scillitan Christians were executed "by the sword [*gladio*]."[17] While Tertullian cannot be proven to know the *Acts* themselves, his knowledge of the events must either be through written documents or oral tradition.

Tertullian then gives examples of prior officials who surprisingly acquitted Christians in the North African provinces.[18] One of them, Vespronius Candidus, is likely the same L. Vespronius Candidus Sallustius Sabinianus who commanded the III Augustan Legion in Numidia from around 174 to around 176, making him the default governor of the region.[19] In this case, then, no Christian martyrdom occurred in the 170s, but the event does testify to some Christian presence at that time even though no information is given as to the size or nature of this Christian presence.

We also have records of other martyrs, who must have been well known to the African Christian community at this time. Tertullian mentions a certain "Mavilus of Hadrumetum" who had been condemned "to the wild beasts," and he mentions this martyr almost as an afterthought, probably because he assumes that his audience (be it Scapula or otherwise) knows the events and so they need not be given in detail.[20] A similar instance occurs in the *Passion of Perpetua and Felicity*, and even though we will discuss this text more fully on pp. 87–89, it is worth mentioning one line here. Some previous martyrs are mentioned almost in passing: "Jucundus, Saturninus, and Artaxius, who were burnt alive in the same persecution, together with Quintus who had actually died as a martyr in prison [*Iocundum et Saturninum et Artaxium, qui eadem persecutione vivi arserunt, et Quintum, qui et ipse martyr in carcere exierat*]."[21] In reading this sentence, it is easy to imagine the final editor leaving it out altogether since it is almost a distraction from the action of the scene. Instead, these names and their mention in the text most likely had significance for the Christian audience, and so we can assume that their martyrdom was of some renown. At the same time, since the narrator prefaces the whole work by saying that new events are as inspired as old ones, it is also likely that these Christian martyrs died sometime prior to Perpetua and her companions.

We know of many other Christians' names only because they were recorded in ancient inscriptions. How many other martyrs and Christians from this period have left no trace in our historical record?[22] The few records that do survive likely represent the proverbial tip of the iceberg when it comes to how many other Christians must have resided in Africa in the second century.

In sum, the late second and early third century witnesses to a Christian presence in the late 170s, as well as corroborating the accounts of the Scillitan martyrs in 180 and Perpetua, Felicity, and their fellow martyrs in 203. We can now consider theories about the earliest African Christians that must have preceded the ones named in these earliest records. Although such theories require conjecture, they legitimately offer informed hypotheses regarding how and from where Christianity came to North Africa.

African Christian origins

Writing from Gaul around 190, Irenaeus of Lyon claims that every Christian church can trace its line of bishops back to the apostles.[23] This bold claim may have been true for Rome[24] or Irenaeus's hometown of Smyrna, but very few Christian churches from other cities have been able to produce such a list of bishops tracing back to the apostles. In a work attributed to Hippolytus of Rome (c.170–235), we find a list of the seventy disciples chosen by Christ (cf. Luke 10:1). Nineteenth on this list is Epaenetus, "bishop of Carthage."[25] Is it possible that the church in Carthage stems back to apostolic times?[26] Hippolytus himself cannot be used as evidence for this, since he does not seem to be a reliable source for events in Africa. He elsewhere describes Africans in general as gullible, especially in comparison with the Greeks.[27]

There is no evidence to corroborate such a first-century dating for Christianity in the African provinces.[28] Considering the various sources that do survive, including the archaeological remains, there is evidence of Christians spread through various smaller municipalities in Africa in the second half of the second century, such as Scilli, Hadrumetum,[29] possibly Thuburbo Minus,[30] and even Lambaesis[31]). There is possible archaeological evidence of Christianity dating from 238 in Tipasa, Mauretania, which is approximately 400 miles west of Carthage.[32] Although the Christian presence in Mauretania does not necessarily bear a direct connection with earlier Carthaginian Christianity, this evidence taken together with the multiple sites with a known Christian presence inland from Carthage adds to the general impression that Christianity spread quickly across North Africa, and this further substantiates the likelihood that Christians had been well established in some parts of Africa for at least a generation prior to these earliest known sources.

Tertullian, who knows Irenaeus's work, does not know the origins of his church in Carthage.[33] Since we cannot trace a line of succession from Tertullian's time (who never names a bishop of Carthage) back to a first bishop, historians must instead look to clues within the surviving evidence to see what possible ties there are to other regions, such as Rome, Greece, or even Palestine.

Although North African Christians used Latin, scholars have generally rejected Roman origins.[34] While the African Christians used Latin and this might at first glance suggest Italian origins, the church in Rome still used Greek at this time, and the use of Latin in Africa is simply the common language. This led W.H.C. Frend to comment on how Christianity in this context should be understood: "Roman Africa was ostensibly Latin, but beneath the outward form of latinisation, the population retained much of the religious and cultural heritage of Carthage."[35] There are also differences between African Christian practices and those found in Rome.[36] As one scholar put it, "The African church, while clearly aware of the Roman church and its policies, was quite independent: it was no mere Roman daughter-church."[37]

There is one passage in Tertullian worthy of discussion. In his *Prescript Against the Heretics*, Tertullian argues against all heretics, ostensibly. He must, however, have a more particular opponent in mind because he speaks about how "you" could check the cities near "you" that have ties to or at least a letter from an apostle, such as Corinth, Philippi, and Thessalonica.[38] This opponent apparently is in Greece, and this is even "close upon Italy." Therefore, "if you are near to Italy, you have Rome, where we too have an authority close at hand."[39] While in the past some scholars have looked at this line in Tertullian as evidence of a Roman origin, Tertullian's statement itself makes no such claim. Rome has apostolic authority, since Peter, Paul, and John all had been there.[40] Carthage, of course, can make no comparable claim, but Tertullian does go on to say that the church of Rome shares something in common with the African churches:[41] that commonality is the "Rule of Faith," a summary of orthodox teaching.[42] For Tertullian, as we shall see in the next chapter, the Roman church has no authority over the church in Carthage; instead, the two share a common faith and should work to share common Christian practices. The church of Rome, therefore, does not seem to have any direct influence over the churches in North Africa at this early phase. Instead, most scholars look to other sources of origin for African Christianity.

One alternative to Roman origins could be that Christianity first came to Africa from Judea.[43] The second Jewish war (132–135) resulted in all Jews being expelled from Jerusalem, and the region was renamed for the Jews' ancient enemy, the Philistines – the province will become *Syria Palestina*, or Palestine. This event fits within the possible time frame of the emergence of Christianity in Africa. Moreover, many scholars have seen an affinity with Jewish thought in early African Christian writings, such an emphasis on the Temple and the Levitical priesthood as a model for the church and its clergy. There is also a similar emphasis on holiness and ritual purity.

The problem for the Jewish origin hypothesis is lack of evidence. No evidence survives that places Jews in Carthage in or before the second century.[44] Soon thereafter funeral inscriptions can be found that clearly indicate a Jewish presence and even the existence of Jewish synagogues, which suggests that a Jewish community had been established at least a generation prior. Although later funerary records contain instances of Christians and Jews sharing burial sites, and Christians often borrowed Jewish symbols, such as the menorah, no direct contact between Jews and Christians can be established in the earliest generation of African Christianity. The only possible evidence of such contact is Tertullian's work, *Against the Jews*, which begins by reporting that a debate occurred between a convert to Judaism and a Christian. The historical incident, however, remains shrouded behind Tertullian's cryptic account, and it is clear to scholars that Tertullian's work goes on to offer what should be said in such a debate, but he offers no actual record of any arguments exchanged between Jews and Christians.[45] There must have been contact between the two groups, but the question is about how much influence one group actually had over another.[46] Furthermore, there is no evidence at all that links early African Christianity, or for that matter later African Judaism, with Jews from Palestine.

Another possible source of origin for Christianity in Africa is the Greek east.[47] There is some evidence of Greek usage among second-century African Christians.[48] Moreover, in the older view that Tertullian and Perpetua and her fellow martyrs were Montanists there was a clear tie with Phrygia in Asia Minor.[49] Even though Tertullian clearly knows of the Phrygian prophets, this connection is not sufficient to establish a source of origin.

With such little evidence, scholars will likely never be able to establish a clear line of descent from earlier Christians abroad to those in Africa. In fact Geoffrey Dunn is probably correct to say that we should assume a more complex alternative where competing forms of Christianity spread throughout North Africa.[50] In light of what evidence does survive, we can affirm two aspects about African Christianity, and these are two points that seem to stand in tension against one another.

The first item that can be affirmed about the earliest expression of African Christianity is that it was diverse and reflected some of the diversity of Christianity throughout the Mediterranean. While we will likely not be able to assert a clear line of succession from Palestinian Judaism or Greek Asia Minor, we should explore any possible points of contact. The evidence of Christianity in North Africa can be analyzed in comparison with Jewish sources, as well as Christian sources from outside of Africa for shared concepts and practices. Our theorizing should even take into account how wide ranging Christian belief could be at this time, and consider the influence of Christian groups outside of the mainstream, such as Valentinians (i.e. "Gnostics") and Kataphrygians (or "Montanists").[51] Christianity in North Africa in the second century was something of a melting pot, and we cannot assume that the churches were well organized under a hierarchy of bishops at this time (which is something that only clearly emerges in the third-century sources – see Chapter 5).

The second item that can be affirmed about the earliest expression of Christianity in Africa was that it was uniquely African. We will explore some of these unique expressions more fully at the end of this chapter after we have examined early martyrdoms from this period, but before doing so we should point out that at least some African Christians self-identified as Africans. There was even a community of African ex-patriots in Rome that worshipped separately as an African Christian church at the end of the second century.[52] This does not mean that these Christians were sectarian and resisted contact with Roman Christians. The church in Rome will even elect Victor as its bishop in 189, and Victor was African.[53] Nevertheless, this community remained distinct for unknown reasons. Was there a language barrier? Were there liturgical differences? Perhaps, such an "ethnic enclave" should not be surprising to us, since there was an African quarter in Rome for centuries prior to Christianity, where the Punic language was spoken and religion were practiced.[54] African Christians living in places such as Rome most likely had their African identity reinforced by Romans who would have categorized them by their *patria* or homeland.

The existence of an African church in Rome indicates that Christians from Africa did self-identify as Africans, even when living abroad and in the vicinity of other Christians. We will see more evidence of an African identity among second-century Christians when we look to the martyrdoms from this period. We will introduce the two martyrdoms in general, and then we can conclude the chapter by returning to the question of how the African context informs our understanding of these early African Christians.[55]

The Scillitan martyrs

Many scholars consider the surviving text of the *Acts of the Scillitan Martyrs* to be one of the most reliable *acta* from early Christianity.[56] Instead of a narrative that reports their suffering (i.e. like a *passio*, or martyrdom account), this text appears to be a copy of official court records, and with the exception of the last phrase ("for the name of Christ. Amen [*pro nomine Christi. amen*]," the text shows no definitive signs of Christian embellishment.[57] Even so, we should likely assume that this account has been revised by a Christian hand at some point after the events, for there do seem to be literary devices at play that would not be found in a court transcript.[58] This short text (= seventeen lines) tells of seven men and five women who refused to recant their Christianity, and as a result they were beheaded on orders of the proconsul of Africa.[59] The Scillitan martyrs, although beheaded as if Roman citizens, are generally recognized as lower-class members of society.[60]

Little is known about the town of Scilli. It was located 150 km west of Carthage and 60 km south of the coast, and it was the site of a marble quarry.[61] Nor is there explicit reference as to how or why the Scillitans were arrested. The trial took place in Carthage, where the proconsul of Africa presided.

Speratus is always listed first among the Christians, and he speaks on their behalf. The natural implication is that Speratus is their leader, but against this conclusion he is not given any clerical title, such as bishop, which is perhaps simply due to the nature of the document. When asked about certain items in their "chest [*capsa*]", Speratus answers, "Books and letters of a just man named Paul [*Libri et epistulae Pauli, viri iusti*]."[62] Here it is worth mentioning the possibility that these Christians were Marcionites.

Marcion came to Rome around 140 and taught a form of Christianity that rejected the Old Testament entirely. He allegedly only held to a shortened version of Luke's Gospel and to some of Paul's letters, and he composed a work known as *Antitheses* in which he contrasted Old and New Testament teachings. Could these Scillitan Christians be Marcionites? Given the similarity with Marcion's so-called canon (i.e. the *Antitheses*, the *Euangelion*, and the *Apostolikon*), it is no surprise that some might see in this brief account glimpses of a Marcionite community.[63]

This interpretation is an admittedly appealing one when taken on its own, for the Scillitans describe their God in terms of "mysterious simplicity [*mysterium simplicitatis*]," "whom no one has seen nor can see with their eyes [*quem nemo hominum vidit nec videre his oculis potest*]," for he is a God "who is in heaven [*qui est in caelis*]."[64] So far, Marcion's God could be in view. Alternatively, the limited scope of the *acta* requires caution on this matter; after all, the Christians simultaneously confess a God who should be "feared [*timorem*]"[65] because this God will judge and is concerned with justice,[66] which is uncharacteristic of Marcion's theology.[67]

The attempt, moreover, to move from the "books and letters of Paul" carried by the Scillitans to the canon attributed to Marcion retains a flawed assumption: it can no longer be assumed that a limited canon is unique to Marcion at this time. Instead, Marcion reflects a mid-second century phenomenon in Christianity where the canon as we know it did not yet exist and some Christian groups held to a smaller collection of Christian scriptures. Rather than appearing to be Marcionite, the Scillitan Christians appear to reflect a common mid-second century expression of African Christianity. The date of the trial is undoubtedly 180, but the material in this text assumes a pre-established Christian community in a village outside of Carthage. This rural Christian community appears to have a limited canon, and it bears no marks of a clearly organized hierarchy of clergy – although, to reiterate, we should not expect so much information from a short *acta*. We can also assume that Christians probably reached major metropolitan ports, like Carthage, before reaching inland towns like Scilli. This text from 180 certainly bears all the hallmarks of Christianity of a previous generation of Christians.[68] Therefore, it looks much like we would expect a Christian community to look from the mid-second century.

One curious aspect of this *acta* is the persecution itself. The image portrayed is of Christians who are not surprised by the pronouncement of their sentence, exemplified by their unanimous response, "Thanks be to God! [*Deo gratias*]."[69] As discussed on pp. 80–82, Tertullian knew of previous trials of Christians in North Africa, but he does not mention any previous Christian martyrdoms. There is no record of any widespread persecution in 180, neither throughout the empire nor in the region. The proconsul even offers the Christians thirty days to reconsider, but the Christians refuse.[70] The proconsul, it seems, reluctantly carries out the trial and even the sentencing, which implies that this persecution took place at someone else's behest.

Who then is responsible for the accusation and trial of these Christians? This is a question we will be able to answer better when we return to the question about what was uniquely African about these early African Christians. Before doing so, let us examine the other martyrdom from this time.

Perpetua, Felicity, and their fellow martyrs

There is arguably no text from the ancient world as mesmerizing and profound as the *Passion of Perpetua and Felicity*. The narrator gives an extended account of the incarceration, trial, torture, and execution of Perpetua and her fellow martyrs.[71] Like the account of the Scillitan martyrs, the witness of the *passio* is sufficiently contemporary to the events it portrays to be considered a credible source to most scholars.[72] However, the editing and even possible later redactions of the text should be given more attention.[73]

Perpetua and her companions were martyred on the 7th of March 203,[74] the birthday of Geta Caesar, Septimius Severus' son.[75] The trial likely took place in Carthage, and the description of the martyrs' death, condemned to the beasts, suggests that they were killed in the arena of Carthage, the ruins of which can still be visited today.

The text is one of the most memorable from all early Christian studies. Perpetua, from a noble family, the slaves Revocatus and Felicity, as well as Secundulus, Saturninus, and Saturus, were all arrested and placed in a dungeon. Perpetua and Felicity were both mothers: Perpetua's child was taken from her by her family; Felicity gave birth prematurely while in prison, which was in answer to prayer – otherwise she would not have been permitted to join the others in facing the beasts but would have had to face them with common criminals. Perpetua's father appears repeatedly, and his power over her weakens in each encounter as she draws nearer to her death. Despite the difference in slave and noble status, the Christians all kiss, a ritual of peace that embodies the ideal vision for the Christian community.

Perpetua experiences several visions, as does Saturus, and the editor celebrates "prophecies and new visions [*prophetias ita et visiones novas*]."[76] This emphasis on the work of the Spirit raises the question of Montanism in this text. While scholars have long debated this matter, it appears that a growing consensus rejects the label of Montanism for this martyrdom. Montanus, Priscilla, and Maximilla began prophesying around 170 in a part of Asia Minor known as Phrygia. They were opposed by many who saw their ecstatic prophecies as teaching novelty and not adhering to the authority of the bishops. What, then, does this Phrygian group have to do with our African martyrs?

In a recent study, Christoph Markschies explains how, despite visions and ongoing prophecies, the question about Montanism in this text has "essentially been posed incorrectly."[77] "Montanism" is itself an anachronistic label, for the adherents preferred "the New Prophecy" as a description of their movement. They were called the Kataphrygians by their opponents, and then later called Montanists on the assumption that movements are named for their founding leader, i.e. Montanus. The alleged Montanism found in North Africa differed in many ways from its Phrygian cousin, according to Markschies.

The two are so different, in fact, that they should be disassociated. In sum, there is "No 'Montanism light,' nor any cunningly concealed version of Montanism" to be found in the text.[78] This conclusion has been corroborated in another recent study by Eliezer Gonzalez, who asserts, "To view *Perpetua* as Montanistic is to distort and mask the proper historical setting of the text."[79] After reviewing the primary and secondary literature, Petr Kitzler has concluded, ". . . we can put this issue to rest by stating what again appears to be the current *communis opinio*: as a whole, the *Passio Perpetuae* is not a Montanist document."[80]

To be sure, scholars will continue to debate the alleged Montanist elements in this text,[81] and it should be emphasized that comparing North African Christianity to its Phrygian contemporaries is a helpful way to understand the various expressions of prophecy and visions for this period. The comparison, nevertheless, should not be made to say that Perpetua and her fellow martyrs were Montanists because they looked and acted like Montanists. It seems that in Carthage at this time visions and prophecies were an accepted part of the Christian faith.[82]

After Perpetua's own account of her experience in the prison, and after Saturus's vision is recorded, the narrator finishes the story by telling how the Christians died. In a gruesome scene, various animals attacked the Christians. There was so much blood the crowd jeered those in the arena by yelling, "Well washed! Well washed! [*Salvum lotum! salvum lotum!*]"[83] While this saying may have been a common expression before visiting the public baths in Roman Africa,[84] the narrator takes this to be a mockery of the Christian baptismal rite, only the jeer is accepted despite its malicious intent: martyrdom is a "second baptism" for early African Christians; it is a baptism in blood.[85] Perpetua, after being attacked by a cow – one of many allusions to her gender in the text,[86] is killed by a soldier, only his first strike missed and struck her collar bone. She then had to guide the sword to her own throat. "It was as though so great a woman, feared as she was by the unclean spirit, could not be dispatched unless she herself were willing."[87]

From this text we can glimpse more details about the church, or at least Perpetua's church, in Carthage at this time. First, along with the ongoing practice of ecstatic utterance and Christian prophecy that some historians label "primitive" (cf. *The Didache*, *The Shepherd of Hermas*, etc.), there is a clearly developed clergy at this time – something not detectable in the earlier and shorter *Acts of the Scillitan Martyrs*. This text mentions a bishop, a priest, deacons, catechumens and their teacher. Several Christian rituals appear in this text, such as the passing of the kiss, baptism, and the Agape meal. There may even be other liturgical elements embedded in one of the visions, such as the use of incense and candles. All in all, the depiction of

Christianity in this text fits with what we know of Carthaginian Christianity in Tertullian's writings, which will be explored further in the next chapter. Before turning to his writings, we can return to our question about what in these early African sources reflects the unique context of North Africa.

African Christianity in the late second and early third century

The uniquely African elements in the earliest generations of African Christians can be discussed along various lines.[88] To begin, we can look to Punic elements, such as individual names. The list of Scillitan martyrs includes Punic names.[89] This leads James Rives to state, "It is worth noting that several of these were typical African names: these people were not immigrants, but natives of the province who had converted to this new religion."[90] Similarly, Braun deduces from the Scillitans' names that they were native Punic.[91] The same can be said of many of the names found in the *Passion of Perpetua and Felicity*, such as Felicity, Saturus, and Saturninus.[92] The list of prior martyrs[93] also consists of "Romanized names, popular in Punic-speaking North Africa."[94]

In addition to their Punic names, there are certain traits, sometimes deemed "Semitic," that could point us to a Punic context. In his commentary on this martyrdom, Thomas Heffernan discusses the behavior of Perpetua's father, where he fell to the ground at her feet and wept.[95] Heffernan concludes, "[He] . . . does not behave like an elite Roman male. He overturns all our stereotypical understanding of the *paterfamilias*."[96] Heffernan then adds, "His behavior reminds one more of an ancient Jew than a Roman male." While some scholars believe that second and third century Carthaginian Christians had connections with local Jews, the thesis – as mentioned on p. 83 – lacks firm evidence and so the majority of recent scholars have rejected this claim.[97] Rather than looking for a Jewish prototype for Perpetua's father, we could consider the Punic context. In his telling of the fall of Carthage, the ancient historian Appian describes how the parents, including men, tore their hair, beat their breasts, and wept over their children's impending doom.[98] Here it is worth stipulating that the "African" elements noted for Perpetua's father must be held in tandem with, and not strictly opposed to, his depiction as a Roman. The text in fact seems to set him up as a typical Roman male with Perpetua expected to play the role of the dutiful Roman daughter. These expectations are then subverted when Perpetua in fact plays the more "masculine" role while her father steadily loses "power [*potestas*]" as defined by Roman law. This illustrates yet again that our subjects could be both Roman and African.

There are other hints in the martyrdom of ties with Carthage's Punic history. Walter Ameling offers a helpful suggestion about Perpetua's status as of "noble birth [*honeste nata*],"[99] which would normally indicate equestrian or senatorial status. Instead of belonging to these Roman classes,

Ameling suggests Perpetua's family was part of the indigenous elites in North Africa.[100] This hypothesis explains how the martyrdom's narrator can claim a "noble" status, while the Roman official can still condemn them to the beasts – something Roman law prohibits for the noble classes.[101]

Another Punic element in this text is found when the martyrs are first brought into the arena. The men are made to dress like priests of Saturn, and the women like the priestesses of Ceres.[102] These deities it should be remembered were popular in North Africa, but they are not simply Roman deities. By way of *interpretatio Romana* they represent Baal and Tanit.[103] This scene, therefore, becomes significant in more than a mere Christian-Pagan framework: here we see Roman officials making those who refuse to "sacrifice to the health of the emperors [*fac sacrum pro salute imperatorum*]" into Punic priests and priestesses.[104] Recalling the charge that human sacrifices were made to Baal in ancient Carthage, it is even more ironic that these Christians were made into human sacrifices as punishment. Here again, Heffernan notes the Punic element in this text:

> Another facet of traditional Roman religion and Christianity in North Africa is the likely persistence of earlier Punic cults and the rigorism associated with them. . . . One wonders whether the African Christians' willingness to seek martyrdom may not owe something to traditional practices of self-sacrifice associated with the cults of Baal/Saturn and Tanit/Juno Caelestis.[105]

This same scholar also mentions, "the extreme eschatological bent of the Carthaginian church, whose ideas on martyrdom may owe something to the indigenous religion and the practice of cultic killing to honor the deities of Baal and Tanit."[106]

There is another possible clue about the Punic background in this martyrdom. Also in regard to the mention of Saturn and Ceres in this account, Jan Bremmer points out a curious item in the passage: "Against all modern editions, the plural *Cereres*, instead of the singular *Cereris*, should be received in the text."[107] Perhaps this is a linguistic relic of the plural *Asheroth* from Phoenician/Punic religion and its parallel for the male form.[108] A relief from Maktar, a Punic town approximately ninety miles southeast of Carthage, retained a Latin inscription to *Cereres Punicae*.[109]

Other clues in this text indicate the social identities involved. Several authors note allusions to classical sources, such as Perpetua's narrative style when recording her dreams, which is reminiscent of Aeneas's own narration of the underworld wherein he sees Dido.[110] Aeneas and Dido, the reader will remember, were the legendary ancestors of Rome and Carthage respectively. Similarly, Heffernan comments on how the description of Dinocrates[111] resembles Virgil's description of "the Phoenician Dido with wounds still fresh."[112] Likewise, the African provenance comes into view again when Perpetua sees the golden apples, an allusion to the "African sisters," the

Hesperides.[113] This is in reference to one of the legendary labors of Hercules performed in Libya.[114]

More than simple use of allusion to Greco-Roman sources, some of these classical motifs can be seen in light of the Second Sophistic tendency to decenter and even subvert Rome's position in relation to provincials. For example, Sigrid Weigel sees the Roman heroine Lucretia as a prototype for Perpetua. Here, however, it must be remembered that Lucretia suffered at the hands of Rome's last king, which brought an end to Roman tyrants because Brutus swore he would "not let any of them or another to rule in Rome as king."[115] This entails "quasi-revolutionary manifestations" according to Weigel. Another example is when in reference to Perpetua's father's plea that she should "give up your pride [*depone animos*],"[116] Heffernan claims this same sentiment is found in Virgil's *Aeneid*.[117] To elaborate on Heffernan's observation, the reference in Virgil is to Turnus, who, like Perpetua, refuses to concede, but in Turnus's case he is resisting Aeneas, the legendary founder of Rome.

In light of these allusions to Carthage's Punic heritage, another item to consider is the martyrs' resistance to being placed within the rule and sphere of the Roman emperor. While this is to be expected of Christians undergoing persecution regardless of their region, some of the precise language used in these African texts categorizes the martyrs in political terms as much as religious ones.[118] We should, therefore, examine both the Christian/non-Christian identities at play, as well as the Roman/non-Roman identities.

Returning to the Scillitan martyrs, the proconsul presiding over their trial specifies that the Christians should swear by the "genius [*per genium*]" of the emperor and offer prayers for his health.[119] Speratus and the others refuse, knowing that to swear by or offer sacrifices to someone's *genius* is to acknowledge that person as a *dominus* or lord.[120] The Christian spokesperson responds to the proconsul's use of "lord [*domni*]"[121] for the emperor, insisting that he does obey the governing official and even pays taxes, and he then adds ambiguously, "I serve . . . my lord [*servio . . . domnum meum*]."[122] The proconsul begins with an invitation to recant: "If you return to your senses, you can obtain the pardon of our lord [*domni nostri*] the emperor."[123] The possessive pronoun, "our [*nostri*]," seems to be inclusive rather than exclusive, for two reasons.[124] First, the proconsul invites the twelve individuals to "return" not only to their "senses," but to a previous state of allegiance. Second, any proconsul would have assumed that the reign of the emperor extended throughout Africa Proconsularis, Tripolitania, Numidia and Mauretania, making anyone in the provinces able to claim him as "our lord [*domni nostri*]." Therefore, in the view of the proconsul the statement of "our lord" includes all those faithful to the emperor. The proconsul's words betray another indication of his inclusive social identity:

Saturninus the proconsul read his decision from a tablet: "Whereas Speratus, Nartzalus, Cittinus, Donata, Vestia, Secunda and the others have confessed that they have been living in accordance with the rites of the Christians, and whereas though given the opportunity to return to the usage of *the Romans* they have persevered in their obstinacy, they are hereby condemned to be executed by the sword."[125]

Saturninus's construction of outsiders falls along what we would see as religious identity, for he lists the six who "have been living in accordance with the rites of Christianity." However, the phrase, "usage of the Romans," also signifies a social identity that Saturninus does not, at least in this instance, place himself, and so we should explore further the social identity of this local official.[126]

The name of the proconsul also suggests African origin, and the use of the word "of the Romans [*Romanorum*]" in a way that suggests Saturninus does not place himself in that category both suggest that Saturninus was a new elite serving under the dual consulship of Praesens and Condianus.

With the Christians themselves, we also should note the multiple identities invoked in this account. The salient identity of the Scillitan martyrs is repeatedly shown to be that of Christian, as seen in the repeated declarations of "I am a Christian."[127] The individuals involved construct their identity according to the boundary between insiders and outsiders, being in this case the declaration of allegiance to Christ. This religious identity, however, does not rule other identities, especially in light of the Christian's next statement: "We have never done wrong . . . for we hold our own emperor in honour [*Numquam malefecimus . . . propter quod imperatorem nostrum observamus*]."[128] One could interpret this statement as indicative of the Christians' acceptance of the "pagan" emperor. Perhaps, Speratus is reflecting the understanding that Christians are to submit to governing authorities as established by God.[129] This approach does not seem to be primary in Speratus's reaction, however, given his later statement. When asked to swear "by the genius of our lord the emperor" (mentioned on p. 91), Speratus declares, "I do not recognize the empire of this world. . . . for I acknowledge my lord who is the emperor of kings and of all nations [*omnium gentium*]."[130] Speratus seems to have rejected Saturninus's attempt to apply an inclusive "our lord the emperor" to the Christians by responding with an exclusive "our own emperor."[131] Again, this is unsurprising given the opposition of Christian and non-Christian identities. In this case, however, there is more to the story.

When Saturninus misses this hint and continued to apply an inclusive first-person plural a second time, Speratus explicitly clarifies the opposition between the two groups. A natural reading of the social identity for Speratus seems on the surface to highlight the contrast between the "lord" of the Christians and the "lord" of the world. Such a conclusion, however, does not take into account the description Speratus gives of his lord as over "all nations [*omnium gentium*]," a phrase often used to describe the non-Roman peoples.[132] As indigenous Africans who could take on the broad social identity of "all nations [*omnium gentium*]" (i.e. non-Roman), the Scillitans also recognize the Romans and any supporters of Rome as outsiders in terms of social identity, as much as religion.[133]

Similar to the *Acts of the Scillitan Martyrs*, the *Passion of Perpetua and Felicity* holds clues as to the social identities of its subjects, which are specifically in contrast to Rome. Perpetua, Felicity, and the other martyrs are characterized "as one against a single foe, the Devil, aided by his minions the Romans."[134] Moreover, in two sections the narrator gives voice to the martyrs themselves in what purports to be autobiographical accounts of imprisonment. Listening to the voice of the narrator involves more than a simple observation of pronoun use in order to determine the social identities of the martyrs, as when, for example, the narrator can speak of the martyrs in the third person and still claim that "they" are part of the shared Christian identity.[135] The narrator's identity is primarily Christian in solidarity with the martyrs.[136] Other instances, however, indicate where the narrator invokes other social identities salient for the Christians.

Recalling the discussion on p. 62 about the role that Romanized elites played in Roman provinces in general and in North Africa in particular, we can detect the influence of African new elites in these martyrdom accounts. Scholars have offered a variety of theories to explain the persecution of Christians by Roman authorities.[137] Many suggest some legal basis for the persecution, and – although none still uphold the former view that Nero enacted specific legislation against the Christians – scholars do surmise that Christians could be convicted on the basis of laws pertaining to *collegia* or *superstitio*.[138] The majority of scholars, however, remain dissatisfied with legal explanations, because of the inconsistency of the persecutions.[139] Many, moreover, see in the Pliny/Trajan discourse a correction of Nero's actions, and as a result the procedures set forth by Trajan function as informal precedence for other provincial officers.[140] G.E.M. de Ste. Croix argues that Pliny's actions did not establish precedence "absolutely," but instead provided the provincial governors with the model by which to work, a model applied with great variance.[141]

While disputes continue over the legal basis of Roman actions toward Christians, most scholars recognize one factor that contributes to the inconsistent application of persecution: the demands of the local elites.[142] Commenting on the Pliny/Trajan correspondence, Wilken observes,

> Shortly after Pliny's arrival in the city, a group of local citizens approached him to complain about Christians living in the vicinity. What precisely the complaint was we do not know, but from several hints in the letter it is possible to infer that the charge was brought by local merchants, perhaps butchers and others engaged in the slaughter and sale of sacrificial meat. Business was poor because people were not making sacrifices. Towards the end of the letter, written after Pliny had dealt with the problem, he observed that the "flesh of sacrificial victims

is on sale everywhere, though up till recently scarcely anyone could be found to buy it."[143]

It appears that Trajan's directive, that Christians should not be sought out, was generally observed by provincial leaders, yet when the status quo of a certain demographic in the local population was challenged, as in the case of idols and sacrificial meat not selling, the Roman officials took action against the group causing the disturbance.[144]

In Africa, where new elites mediated religion between the Roman colonizers and the indigenous Africans in order to establish themselves in a special status in the eyes of both groups, any disturbance of the practice of the Romano-African sacrifices and rituals would have greatly threatened their position. Can we assume that Christians were not "sought out" by the Roman colonizers themselves, but by the new elites defending their special status? Could this explain the more violent tone of the attacks of the new elite such as Fronto and Apuleius on Christianity?[145]

Returning to the *Acts of the Scillitan Martyrs* in particular, Wypustek finds evidence of *superstitio* in the account of the Scillitan's trial: "If you return to your senses, you can obtain the pardon of our lord the emperor."[146] No mention, however, is made in the account of the Scillitan's trial of who brought the charges against the Christians. One clue may lie in the enigmatic exchange between the official and the Christian spokesperson: Saturninus says, "Cease to be of this persuasion"; Speratus responds, "It is an evil persuasion to commit murder, to bear false witness."[147] How does Speratus's response answer the proconsul?

Perhaps he declares that to deny being a Christian would "bear false witness." Yet, this does not explain what committing "murder" has to do with the line of questioning. The Scillitan Christian could have been indicating something about those who brought charges against him and the other Christians. That is, those local elites who accused the Christians are of the "evil persuasion to murder, to bear false witness" by alleging that the Christians were to blame for the decline in the worship of Roman-translated African gods.

The role of the elites can also be detected in the *Passion of Perpetua and Felicity*. The narrator's "Other" is evident in three passages of the account of the martyrs' trial and persecution. When the catechumens are confined to the dungeon, the narrator tells of the confrontation that occurred:

> While they were treated with more severity by the tribune, because, from the intimations of certain deceitful men, he feared lest they should be withdrawn from the prison by some sort of magic incantations, Perpetua answered to his face, and said, "Why do you not at least permit us to be refreshed, being as we are objectionable to the most noble Caesar, and having to fight on his birth-day? Or is it not your glory if we are brought forward fatter on that occasion?"[148]

The "certain deceitful men" have import for this section in terms of the portrayal of outsiders. The narrator, via Perpetua, portrays those who are influencing the arrest and treatment of the Christians as not only devious but treacherously allied with the Roman officials. The sarcasm of "the most noble Caesar [*nobilissimus Caesaris*]" and "your glory [*tua gloria*]" should not be missed in this passage. The account expresses more than antipathy between Christians and non-Christians; the passage intonates animosity specifically towards individuals – be they new elites or colonizers – in allegiance with "Caesar" and Rome.

For example, in the very next paragraph, the social identity of the narrator is distinguished ("We" vs. "They"). When describing the "last supper" of the martyrs, the narrator insists on redefining Roman colonizer phraseology:

> Moreover, on the day before, when in that last meal, which they call the free meal, they were partaking as far as they could, not of a free supper, but of an agape; with the same firmness they were uttering such words as these to the people, denouncing against them the judgment of the Lord, bearing witness to the felicity of their passion, laughing at the curiosity of the people who came together.[149]

What "they call [*vocant*]" the free meal, the narrator abrogates as an Agape feast, as if to say "in spite of the fact that it comes from the Romans."[150] The sentence resonates with the same tone towards the Romans as the previous paragraph, for "they" does not simply mean the non-Christians, but suggests Roman colonizers who have imported foreign phrases and terms. In this instance, rather than "certain deceitful men" who must be new elites or Roman colonizers, the "crowd [*populous*]" is portrayed as allied with the Romans, at least in the level of morbid curiosity. Later in the narrative, the crowd takes a clearer defined outsider role, especially in the final scenes.

During the account of the torture and killing of the Christians, the narrator again highlights the role of the *populus*. Revocatus, Saturninus, and Saturus enter the arena preaching to the crowd about the judgment of God that is to come. Only after the Christians rebuke the Roman official, however, does the narrator state, "At this the crowds became enraged and demanded that they be scourged before a line of gladiators [*ad hoc populus exasperatus flagellis eos vexari per ordinem venatorum postulavit*]."[151] The description of the local crowd in relation to the Roman officials brings to the forefront the question as to how the Christians were brought to trial in the first place.

Although the narrative tells that the new Christians "were apprehended [*apprehensi sunt*]," it does not report why or by whom.[152] If one can assume that Trajan's instructions not to seek out the Christians were heeded by Roman provincial leaders, then one must conclude that someone brought the accusation before the Roman officials. The narrator reports that Perpetua and her companions were treated harshly "because from the intimations of certain deceitful men, [the tribune] feared lest they should be withdrawn from the prison by some sort of magic incantations."[153] The label "deceitful men" parallels the *Acts of the Scillitan Martyrs*, wherein Speratus denounces those who "bear false witness" and strengthens the conclusion that the narrator is referring to those who "betrayed [*tradiderat*]" the North African Christians to the Roman officials.[154] Given that Perpetua's confrontation with the official in the next line calls into question the emperor himself, one wonders what part the most well-known and successful African new elite, Septimius Severus, played in the persecution of Christians.[155]

Scholars recognize the various indicators of Septimius Severus's views towards Christianity.[156] Some have highlighted the outbreak of persecutions that followed the emperor's visit to Egypt and declared that Septimius produced an edict launching an empire-wide persecution.[157] One ancient source refers to Severus's prohibition of Jewish and Christian proselytizing, and the issue has "become a matter of continuing dispute among scholars."[158] This account, however, may be of a "fictional nature" and the correlation of the emperor's visit and the outbreak of persecution could be coincidental.[159] The coincidence is repeated, however, when the birthday of Geta Severus, Septimius's son, is celebrated in Carthage on the same day as the torture and execution of Perpetua and her fellow martyrs.[160]

Moreover, beyond the chronological coincidence, historians have seen other factors that point towards the emperor's involvement in the persecution of Christians. Pointing to the Severan lawyer, Julius Paulus, who left commentary on legislation against the magicians, astrologers, and prophets, Wypustek argues that the law would have included Christians.[161] Even if the emperor himself did not initiate a persecution of Christians, we can see more than coincidence in these events. An important factor in interpreting the persecutions in North Africa that took place under Septimius's reign is the emperor's relationship to the new elite of Africa. Although in 197 Septimius executed twenty-nine senators with connections to North Africa upon the defeat of Albinus – a rival who was also from Africa – the emperor "also entrusted a high proportion of key provinces, with large armies attached, to men of African origin or connection."[162] Moreover, Raven notes that the indigenous African gods were prevalent during this time, even among the administration of the Roman armies.[163] The new elites, placed into such close proximity in status with the Romano-African emperor, could not afford to allow the Romano-African gods that played such a key role in establishing themselves as mediators between Romans and indigenous Africans to decline because of a new secretive and seemingly subversive religion.

Legacies and later trajectories

While the previous section proposed ways that the pre-/non-Roman heritage of Africa can be detected in the earliest African Christian sources, it remains to be seen how these earliest sources influenced later generations in a way that could be conceived as an "African school."[164] In discussing the earliest African Christian sources, it is important to see how the martyrs were cherished in later African Christian tradition and therefore function as heroes of this African tradition. They are the earliest ancestors, as it were, of African Christianity.[165]

The memory of the martyrs plays an important role in Christianity writ large, but the African Christians prove to be especially devoted to their heroes.[166] In other words, even though "Heroic martyr-acts . . . circulated widely" scholars have noted how "Africa was peculiarly productive" in this area.[167] Augustine himself once asked, "Is not Africa filled with the bodies of holy martyrs?"[168] Therefore, while there will be many unique features about African Christianity, and many more shared in common with wider Christianity, it is important to remember how these early martyrdoms shape the later African Christians who cherish their memory and attempt to emulate their acts.

This early African tradition can become more clearly classified as a "school" once it has a teacher, and so we should now turn to Tertullian of Carthage, the earliest Christian writer from this school. After discussing him at length in the next chapter, we will conclude that discussion by returning to this concept of an African school of thought and practice, and we will then summarize how Tertullian, Perpetua, and other Christians from the late second and early third century shaped some of the central values of the African Christian tradition.

Notes

1 *Passion of Perpetua* 2.1 (in the later Greek translation; cf. the *Acts Perpetua* A.1/B.1).

2 Earlier studies include Paul Monceaux, *Histoire littéraire de l'Afrique chrétienne depuis les origins jusqu'a l'invasion arabe*, vol. 1: *Tertullien et les origines* (Paris: Leroux, 1901); and for an introduction to the material, see Gilles Quispel, "African Christianity Before Minucius Felix and Tertullian," in *Gnostica, Judaica, Catholica: Collected Essays of Gilles Quispel*, ed. Johannes Oort (Leiden: E. J. Brill, 2008), 433–434.

3 See Paul Février, "Africa – Archeology," in *Encyclopedia of the Early Church*, ed. Angelo Di Berardino (Oxford: Oxford University Press, 1992), 1:16; and Jane Merdinger, "Roman North Africa," 223–243.

4 *To the Nations* 1.2 (trans. ANF 1); see Wilhite, *Tertullian the African*, 60–75, for the evidence that this text is directed towards Carthaginians (as opposed to his *Apology*, which assumes a Roman audience).

5 *To Scapula* 2.10: *pars paene maior ciuitatis cuiusque.*

6 *To Scapula* 5.2–3, where Tertullian pleads that Scapula would "Spare thyself, if not us poor Christians! Spare Carthage, if not thyself! Spare the province [*Parce ergo tibi, si non nobis. Parce Carthagini, si non tibi. Parce provinciae*]." (CCL 2; trans. ANF 3:106).

7 Cf. Tertullian, *Apology* 37.4–7, for similar claims about the whole empire. It is noteworthy that in this passage Tertullian begins with the example of the "Mauritanians [*Mauri*]" as rebels of Rome, followed by "enemies" from other regions. On Tertullian's rhetoric, see pp. 109–110 and 118–120 in chapter four.

8 Estimates have ranged up to 70,000 Christians in the second century. See bibliography and discussion in Rebillard, *Christians and Their Many Identities*, 10; and Heffernan, *The Passion of Perpetua*, 246, who concludes, "A more sober figure of perhaps fifteen hundred, assuming about 0.5 percent of a population of three hundred thousand, would be closer to the mark for the first decade of the third century." See additional figures and bibliography in Kitlzer, *From* Passio Perpetuae, 16.

9 Alternatively, he is comfortable calculating the age of the Marcionites (see his *Against Marcion* 1.19.2–3) as well as the years from Daniel to Christ (see *Against the Jews* 8).

10 *The Scorpian's Sting* 7.2 (ANF 3:639).

11 It is also noteworthy that the "death of the persecutors" theme will be recalled by later African writers, like Lactantius (see chapter six).

12 *Passion of Perpetua* 18.8. For details about this Hilarianus, see James Rives, "The Piety of a Persecutor," *Journal of Early Christian Studies* 4 (1, 1996), 1–25.

13 Later in *To Scapula* 4.5–6, Tertullian claims that Septimius "Severus" and his son, Marcus Aurelius Severus "Antonius," were favorable to Christians during their reign. The *Passion of Perpetua* 7.9, however, says the martyrs were killed as part of the games to honor Geta, Septimius Severus's other son.

14 See *On the Soul* 55.4. Some surmise that Tertullian edited the *Passion of Perpetua*; see extended discussion and bibliography in Rex D. Butler, *The New Prophecy & "New Visions": Evidence of Montanism in The Passion of Perpetua and Felicitas* (Patristic Monograph Series vol. 18; Washington: The Catholic University of America Press, 2006), 52–57. However, numerous studies have shown that this is highly unlikely; see bibliography and discussion in Petr Kitzler, *From "Passio Perpetuae,"* 17–19.

15 *To Scapula* 3.4.

16 See Tilley, "North Africa," in *The Cambridge History of Christianity*, ed. Margaret M. Mitchell, Frances M. Young, and K. Scott Bowie (Cambridge: Cambridge University Press, 2006), 1:384.

17 *Acts of the Scillitan Martyrs* 14.

18 Tertullian's statement in *To Scapula* 3.4 suggests Tertullian has direct knowledge of these other regions, only he does not identity his source(s). Later (*To Scapula* 4.8), Tertullian mentions Christian persecution happening in Mauretania, but again does not name his source for this information. His knowledge of these events, however reliable they may be, suggest that the Christians across Africa sought to remain in communication with one another.

19 Birley, "Persecutors and Martyrs in Tertullian's Africa," *Bulletin of the Institute of Archaeology of the University of London* 29 (1992), 37–68.

20 *To Scapula* 3.5. See discussion in Dunn, "Mavilus of Hadrumetum, African Proconsuls and Meiaeval Martyrologies," in *Studies in Latin Literature and Roman History*, vol. 12, ed. Carl Deroux (Collection Latomus 27; Brussels: Latomus, 2005), 433–446.

21 *Passion of Perpetua* 11.9.

22 See, for example, the map of the known martyr shrines, in Yvette Duval, *Loca sanctorum Africae: le culte des martyrs en Afrique du IVe au VIIe siecle* (Rome: École française de Rome, 1982), 1: xviii–ix. Another possible martyr to mention here is Namphamo, who is called the *archimartyr*, sometimes translated "protomartyr" or "first martyr," mentioned in Augustine, *Letters* 16 and 17 (discussed on p. 219 in chapter six).

23 *Against Heresies* 3.3.2. It is also of interest that Irenaeus claims there are churches in "Libya" (1.10.2), although this may be for rhetorical aims – he does not list any specific Christians there.

24 See his list in *Against Heresies* 3.3.3.
25 *On the Seventy Apostles* (ANF 5:255); cf. Rom. 16:5.
26 Cf. Acts 2:10, where the crowd at Pentecost included those from "the parts of Libya belonging to Cyrene." For other Biblical references to Carthage and even more generalized "Africa" (i.e. as the referent of Tarshish), see Edward Lipinski, *Iteneraria Phoenicia* (Orientala Lovaniensia Analecta; Leuven: Peeters, 2004), 253–260.
27 See the story of "Apsethus the Libyan" and how he duped "the Libyans" into believing he was a god by training parrots to say so. After a Greek trained a parrot to say otherwise, "the Libyans, coming together, all unanimously decided on burning Apsethus" (*The Refutation of All Heresies* 6.3 [ANF 5:75]).
28 Although one could make a case for Cyrenaica; see Oden, *The African Memory of Mark*; and Oden, *Early Libyan Christianity*.
29 Mentioned by Tertullian, *To Scapula* 3.5. Decret, *Early Christianity*, 11, claims the catacombs of Hadrumetum (modern Sousse, Tunisia) contain Christian burials dating to the 150s. Decret then concludes that Christians in Carthage likely predated those further south, and so he dates the first arrival of Christianity in Africa to a generation or more before 150; thus, he concludes there was "probably a church in Carthage before the end of the first century." Tilley, however, dates these to the mid-third century, following Leynaud, *Les catacombes africaines*, 11–15.
30 See Tabbernee, "Perpetua, Montanism, and Christian Ministry," *Perspectives in Religious Studies* 32 (2005), 424–427, for earlier bibliography and an argument against Thuburbo Minus as the provenance for Perpetua and her fellow martyrs; Heffernan, *The Passion of Perpetua*, 138, comes to the same conclusion. However, Walter Ameling, "*Femina Liberaliter Instituta* – Some Thoughts on a Martyr's Liberal Education," in *Perpetua's Passions*, ed. Jan N. Bremmer and Marco Formisano (Oxford: Oxford University Press, 2012), 82, contends that the information (found from the Greek version of the martyrdom) is reliable. Further details of these sources and their reliability are discussed on p. 87.
31 I.e. the base of the III Augustan Legion at the time Vespronius Candidus tried a Christian (mentioned in Tertullian, *To Scapula* 3.4; cf. Birley, "Persecutors and Martyrs in Tertullian's Africa," 44).
32 See bibliography in Jane Merdinger, "Before Augustine's Encounter with Emeritus: Early Mauretanian Donatism," *Studia Patristica* 70 (2013), 373. Tertullian, *To Scapula* 4.8, also mentions Christian persecution happening further west in Mauretania.
33 See *Prescript Against the Heretics* 36. Burns, Jensen, et al., *Christianity in Roman Africa*, 4, comment, "The African church . . . had no pretensions to a (legendary) apostolic foundation."
34 Cf. Augustine, *Letter* 185.4.17, "those churches from which the gospel came to Africa"; and *Letter* 52.2, "the Eastern churches, from which the gospel came to Africa [*orientalium ecclesiarum . . . unde euangelium in Africam venit*]." Other comments by Augustine have been catalogued in Monceaux, *Histoire littéraire de l'Afrique chrétienne*, 1:6–7. See discussion and bibliography in Barnes, *Tertullian*, 66–67.
35 Frend, "Heresy and Schism as Social and National Movements," in *Schism, Heresy and Religious Protest*, ed. Derek Baker (Cambridge: Cambridge University Press, 1972), 39.
36 David Rankin, *Tertullian and the Church* (Cambridge: Cambridge University Press, 1995), 16; Barnes, *Tertullian*, 66–67, and 275–276, on liturgical differences.
37 Burns, Jensen, et al., *Christianity in Roman Africa*, 4.

38 *Prescript Against the Heretics* 36.2.
39 *Prescript Against the Heretics* 36.2: *si autem Italiae adiaces, habes Romam unde nobis quoque auctoritas praesto est* (trans. slightly modified from T. H. Bindley, *On the Testimony of the Soul and On the 'Prescription' of Heretics* [London: SPCK, 1914], 84; cf. the Holme's trans. in ANF 3:260: "you are close upon Italy, you have Rome, from which there comes even into our own hands the very authority of apostles themselves.").
40 *Prescript Against the Heretics* 36.2.
41 *Prescript Against the Heretics* 36.4 (trans. Bindley, *On the Testimony of the Soul*, 85).
42 See discussion in Henri de Lubac, *The Christian Faith: An Essay on the Structure of the Apostles' Creed* (San Francisco, CA: Ignatius Press, 1986), 340–341.
43 For Jewish origins, see Daniélou, *The Origins*; Richard Patrick Crosland Hanson, "Notes on Tertullian's Interpretation of Scripture," *JTS* n.s. 12 (1961), 273–279; Frend, "Jews and Christians in Third Century Carthage," in *Paganisme, Judaïsme, Christianisme* (Paris: Éditions E. De Boccard, 1978), 185–194; reprinted in *Town and Country in the Early Christian Centuries* (London: Variorum, 1980); and Blake Leyerle, "Blood is Seed," *The Journal of Religion* 81 (1, 2001), 26–48. For Jews in North Africa generally, see Sarah Taieb-Carlen, *The Jews of North Africa: From Dido to De Gaulle*, trans. Amos Carlen (New York: University Press of America, 2010), esp. 1–22, for the pre-Islamic period.
44 Claudia Setzer, "The Jews in Carthage and Western North Africa, 66–235 CE," in *The Cambridge History of Judaism*, ed. W. D. Davies, et al. (Cambridge: Cambridge University Press, 1984), 69–70.
45 See Dunn, *Tertullian* (London: Routledge, 2004), 65. Extended bibliography and discussion can be found in Dunn, *Tertullian's* Adversus Iudaeos.
46 Dunn, *Tertullian*, 67.
47 For Greek, see Telfer, "The Origins of Christianity in Africa," 512–517; Barnes, *Tertullian*, 68–69; and Barnes, "Legislation Against the Christians," in *Church and State in the Early Church*, ed. Everett Ferguson (New York: Garland Publishing, 1993), 72.
48 Cf. *The Passion of Perpetua* 13.4, where Perpetua begins to speak Greek to the clergy (in Saturus's vision). Also, Tertullian wrote some works (not extant) in Greek: see *On Baptism* 15; *On the Military Crown* 6; *On the Veiling of Virgins* 1.
49 The arguments against understanding Perpetua and her fellow martyrs as Montanists will be given on pp. 87–89. For Tertullian, see chapter four.
50 Dunn, *Tertullian*, 14–15.
51 I have elsewhere argued that there is no credible evidence of Marcionite Christianity in Africa (see Wilhite, "Marcionites in Africa: What did Tertullian Know and When Did He Invent it?" *Perspectives in Religious Studies* 4 (2016), 437–452. The so-called Montanist threat, as will be shown on pp. 87–89, is by and large unconvincing to me, but Tertullian provides evidence that "New Prophecy" from Phrygia was known in Africa via literary texts. The Valentinians, however, seem to have posed a real threat to Tertullian and his community, and so at this point I think it must be assumed that there were Valentinian churches (or at least groups Tertullian could label "Valentinian" and "Gnostic") in the region.
52 Telfer, "The Origins of Christianity in Africa," 515:

     A large African colony established itself in Rome. . . . Victor's elevation to preside over the whole Roman Church is likely to have arisen from the fact that, by this time, there was a considerable Christian congregation in the African quarter.

     Also, cf. George La Piana, "The Roman Church at the End of the Second Century," *Harvard Theological Review* 18 (1925), 272–277.

53 *The Book of the Popes* 15: "Victor, of the nation of Africa" (my trans.); cf. Eusebius, *Church History* 5.22; Jerome, *Lives of Illustrious Men* 34 (cf.35)

54 See John Bert Lott, *The Neighborhoods of Augustan Rome* (Cambridge: Cambridge University Press, 2004), 22; cf. John Bert Lott, "Regions and Neighbourhoods," in *The Cambridge Companion to Ancient Rome*, ed. Paul Erdkamp (Cambridge: Cambridge University Press, 2013), 169; and Miles, *Carthage Must Be Destroyed*, 160; cf. Varro, *On the Latin Language* 5.132.159.

55 Some of the material that follows has been adapted from my earlier treatment of this text: Wilhite, *Tertullian the African Theologian: A Social Anthropological Reading of Tertullian's Identities* (PhD Thesis for the University of St. Andrews, 2006).

56 Barnes, "Legislation," 72; for introductory notes on the textual transmission, see Musurillo, "Introduction," in *The Acts of the Christian Martyrs*, ed. and trans. Musurillo (Oxford: Clarendon Press, 1972), xxii–xxiii.

57 The other possible sign of redaction is where one list of names only includes six martyrs (1; 14) and another includes twelve (16); see discussion in Musurillo, *The Acts*, xxii–xxiii. Nevertheless, the account does not have any embellishments one would expect if it belonged to a later hand.

58 See David L. Eastman, *Paul the Martyr: The Cult of the Apostle in the Latin West* (Atlanta: Society of Biblical Literature, 2011), 156–158; Moss, *Ancient Christian Martyrdom*, 125–129.

59 Stated to be on 17 July in Carthage during the consulship of C. Bruttius Praesens and Claudianus. On the proconsul, P. Vigellius Saturninus, see Tertullian, *To Scapula* 3.4.

60 Musurillo, *The Acts*, xxiii; Barnes, *Tertullian*, 63.

61 Serge Lancel, *Actes de la conference de Carthage en 411* (SC 373; Paris: Éditions du Cerf, 1972), 4:1456. The Conference of Carthage 411 records a bishop from Scilli (see *Gesta* 1.143 and 1.206). Also, cf. *The Martyrdom of Felix* (recording events from 303), for a martyrdom that has several parallels to the *Acts of the Scillitan Martyrs* and for "the highway called *Via Scillitanorum*" (31 [Musurillo, *The Acts*, 270–271]). There was also a basilica dedicated to the Scillitans (mentioned in Victor of Vita, *The History of the Vandal Persecution* 1.9; cf. Augustine, *Sermon* 155).

62 *Acts of the Scillitan Martyrs* 12–13.

63 See Richard I. Pervo, *The Making of Paul: Constructions of the Apostle in Early Christianity* (Minneapolis, MN: Fortress, 2010), 1, "these Christians could have been followers of Marcion"

64 *Acts of the Scillitan Martyrs* 4, 6, and 8.

65 *Acts of the Scillitan Martyrs* 9; cf. 8, *timeamus*.

66 Cf. *Acts of the Scillitan Martyrs* 11: *iusta*.

67 See Tertullian, *Against Marcion* 1.6.1: "we were aware that Marcion sets up unequal gods, the one a judge [*iudicem*], fierce and warlike, the other mild and peaceable, solely kind and supremely good." Tertullian here is probably dependent on Irenaeus, *Against Heresies* 1.27.1. For further discussion on Marcion's view of judgment, see Sebastian Moll, *The Arch-Heretic Marcion* (Wissenschaftliche Untersuchungen zum Neuen Testament 250; Tübingen: Mohr Siebeck, 2010), 49–54.

68 Burns, Jensen, et al., *Christianity in Roman Africa*, 4, suggests, "it would be reasonable to conjecture that some Christians had reached Africa a good half-century or more before the report of the Scillitan martyrs."

69 *Acts of the Scillitan Martyrs* 17.

70 *Acts of the Scillitan Martyrs* 13.

71 For bibliography, see William Tabbernee, *Montanist Inscriptions and Testimonia: Epigraphic Sources Illustrating the History of Montanism* (Patristics Monograph Series 16; Macon, GA: Mercer University Press, 1997), 55–60, and

108–110; and Gonzalez, *The Fate of the Dead*, 19–22. For the textual transmission, including comments on the Greek text, see Cecil M. Robeck, *Prophecy in Carthage: Perpetua, Tertullian, and Cyprian* (Cleveland: Pilgrim Press, 1992), 12–13; and Jan Bremmer, "The Motivation of Martyrs: Perpetua and the Palestinians," in *Religion im kulturellen Diskurs: Festschrift für Hans G. Kippenberg zu seinem 65. Geburtstag*, ed. Brigitte Luchesi and Kocku von Stuckrad (Berlin: De Gruyter, 2004), 535–536.

72   Kitzler, *From "Passio Perpetuae,"* 14–17.

73   Cf. Joyce E. Salisbury, *Perpetua's Passion: The Death and Memory of a Martyr* (London: Routledge, 1997), 113–114; Ross S. Kraemer and Shira L. Lander, "Perpetua and Felicitas," in *Early Christian World*, ed. P. F. Esler (London: Routledge, 2000), 2:1055–1058; and Kitzler, "*Passio Perpetuae* and *Actae Perpetuae*: Between Tradition and Innovation," *Listy Filologické* 130 (1–2 2007), 4.

74   However, Barnes, *Early Christian Hagiography and Roman History*, 305–306, has challenged the consensus dating and opted for 204.

75   *The Passion of Perpetua* 7.9. Heffernan, *The Passion of Perpetua*, 68–78, therefore concludes that Geta's title, "Caesar," in this text must require the text to be written before his brother Caracalla condemned him and his memory in 209. For details, see Kitzler, *From "Passio Perpetuae,"* 16–17.

76   *Passion of Perpetua* 1 (my trans.)

77   Christoph Markschies, "The *Passio Sanctarum Perpetuae et Felicitatis* and Montanism?", in *Perpetua's Passions: Multidisciplinary Approaches to the Passio Perpetuae et Felicitatis*, ed. Jan N. Bremmer and Marco Formisano (Oxford: Oxford University Press, 2012), 277.

78   Markschies, "The *Passio*," 290. It should be noted that Markschies does point to "Tertullian's form of the 'New Prophecy'" (284), and he finds the text indebted to the "seemingly slightly 'Montanist'" (287) views of Tertullian and his housechurch, "Which is not much" (288). For the problems with labeling Tertullian as Montanist in any way, see pp. 112–114. Markschies seems aware of these problems, for he concludes by highlighting acceptance of this martyrdom (and, I would add, Tertullian) by "the North African Christian majority Church" (290).

79   Gonzalez, *The Fate of the Dead*, 209.

80   Kitzler, *From "Passio Perpetuae,"* 34.

81   E.g. in his recent commentary, Heffernan, The Passion of Perpetua assumes the editor, if not the martyrs themselves, was Montanist.

82   More on Montanism at this time will be discussed in the next chapter with regards to Tertullian, including citations of numerous African Christian sources that affirm ongoing visions and prophecies.

83   *Passion of Perpetua* 21.2.

84   See the mosaic that reads "*salvom* [sic] *lavisse*" from Sabratha, discussed in Heffernan, *Perpetua*, 359; and for additional bibliography, see Paul A. Holloway, *Coping with Prejudice: 1 Peter in Social-Psychological Perspective* (Tübingen: Mohr Siebeck, 2009), 53–54 n.96.

85   *Passion of Perpetua* 21.2; Tertullian, *On Baptism* 16.

86   The later African writer, Arnobius, explains the sacrificial practice of the Romans: "the laws of sacrifice prescribe that like sexes should be slain to like, that is female victims to female, male to male gods" (*Against the Nations* 7.19 [ACW 499]).

87   *Passion of Perpetua* 21.10.

88   Some of the material that follows has been adapted from my earlier treatment of this text: Wilhite, *Tertullian the African Theologian*, 164, 177, 187–190.

89   Those of Nartzalus and Cintinus, according to Heffernan, *The Passion*, 282.

90   Rives, *Religion and Authority*, 223–224; likewise, Rankin, *Tertullian*, 11, affirms that the Scillitans come "from among the indigenous rural population"; cf. Tertullian *To Scapula* 3.4.

91 "Aux Orignes," 190, "d'origine punique."
92 On the names in the text, see Syme, "Donatus and the Like," 588–603.
93 *Passion of Perpetua* 11.9.
94 Heffernan, *The Passion*, 281.
95 *Passion of Perpetua* 5.5.
96 Heffernan, *The Passion*, 26. Alternatively, for this scene read as the father supplicating Perpetua in terms of Roman religion (i.e. she is a priestess), see J. den Boeft and Jan Bremmer, "Notiunculae Martyrologicae II," *Vigiliae Christianae* 36 (4, 1982): 383–402.
97 For bibliography, see Leyerle, "Blood Is Seed," who admits the evidence is lacking, but proceeds by way of comparing Tertullian's statements with Rabbinic statements.
98 See Appian, *The Punic Wars*, 77, 91 (LCL 2:528–529); also cf. 91–93, for various public displays of dismay and mourning. Also, Heffernan had earlier cited another comparison: "Augustine is *another African* male whose grief is not bounded by rules of decorum" (*The Passion*, 247, emphasis added; ref. to *Confessions* 4.4, 9.11–13). Another example is when Heffernan claims, "Carthaginian Christianity early on appears to have reified Judaism's understanding of blood." (*The Passion*, 361; ref. to 21.5). However, he had earlier credited this same thinking to Punic heritage (304).
99 *Passion of Perpetua* 2.1.
100 Ameling, "*Femina Liberaliter Instituta*," 82–84, specifically the *honestiore loco nata*, probably belonging to the *ordo decurionum*. Ameling accepts the statement in the Greek translation of the *Passio* and in both versions of the *Acta* that the martyrs were from Thuburbo Minus; see 83 n.25 for bibliography (however, cf. Tabbernee, "Perpetua, Montanism, and Christian Ministry,").
101 Ameling, "*Femina Liberaliter Instituta*," 88, also contests the notion that Perpetua knew Greek (cf. *Passion of Perpetua* 13.4). If Perpetua did not know Greek in any way, than her non-Roman aspects beg for further exploration in terms of her local identity.
102 *Passion of Perpetua* 18.4.
103 See Heffernan, *The Passion*, 326 and 331, for the Saturn/Baal and Ceres/Tanit motif. Cf. Tertullian, *The Scorpion's Sting* 7, "Saturn of the Africans."
104 *Passion of Perpetua* 6.3.
105 Heffernan, *The Passion*, 33 n.45.
106 Heffernan, *The Passion*, 304.
107 Jan Bremmer, "Felicitas: The Martyrdom of a Young African Woman," in *Perpetua's Passions*, ed. Jan N. Bremmer and Marco Formisano (Oxford: Oxford University Press, 2012), 47.
108 See the evidence for the cult of the Cereres in Africa in Hemelrijk, *Hidden Lives*, 58–69.
109 Paul L. MacKendrick, *The North African Stones Speak* (Chapel Hill, NC: University of North Carolina Press, 1980), 75.
110 Craig Williams, "Pepretua's Gender: A Latinist Reads the *Passio Perpetuae et Felicitatis*," in *Perpetua's Passions*, ed. Jan N. Bremmer and Marco Formisano (Oxford: Oxford University Press, 2012), 62.
111 *Passion of Perpetua* 7.7–8.
112 *Aeneid* 6.450; discussed in Heffernan, *The Passion*, 233.
113 *Passion of Perpetua* 10.8. See Hartmut Böhme, "The Conquest of the Real," in *Perpetua's Passions*, ed. Jan N. Bremmer and Marco Formisano, trans. Jeanne Riou (Oxford: Oxford University Press, 2012), 229 n.17.
114 Discussed on p. 61 in chapter two.
115 Sigrid Weigel, "Exemplum and Sacrifice," in *Perpetua's Passions*, ed. Jan N. Bremmer and Marco Formisano, trans. Joel Golb (Oxford: Oxford University Press, 2012), 193–194; ref. 1.59.1.

116   *Passion of Perpetua* 5.4.

117   Heffernan, *The Passion*, 189; ref. *Aeneid* 11.366.

118   Which, again, should not surprise us since there were no clearly demarcated spheres of politics and religion in the ancient world.

119   *Passion of Perpetua* 3 and 5.

120   Jane Gardner and Thomas Wiedemann, *The Roman Household: A Sourcebook* (London: Routledge, 1991), 32.

121   *Acts of the Scillitan Martyrs* 3 and 5.

122   *Acts of the Scillitan Martyrs* 6.

123   *Acts of the Scillitan Martyrs* 1.

124   Cf. Tertullian, *Against Praxeas* 11–12, for the importance of the inclusive first person plural pronoun.

125   *Acts of the Scillitan Martyrs* 14: *Saturninus proconsul decretum ex tabella recitauit: Speratum, Nartzalum, Cittinum, Donatam, Vestiam, Secundam, et ceteros ritu Christiano se uiuere confessos, quoniam oblata sibi facultate ad Romanorum morem redeundi obstinanter perseuerauerunt, gladio animaduerti placet* (emphasis added).

126   This reading is contrary to Musurillo's translation of section 3: "Saturninus the proconsul said: 'We too are a religious people, and our religion is a simple one [*Saturninus proconsul dixit: Et nos religiosi sumus et simplex est religio nostra*]." The use of "people" implies more than the Latin requires. Saturninus obviously wishes to place himself in the Roman group, i.e. the use of *nos*, but he does not claim to be of the same *homines*, *populus*, or *gens*. Moreover, the two passages illustrate an identity Saturninus could possess or discard at will.

127   *Acts of the Scillitan Martyrs* 9–13.

128   *Acts of the Scillitan Martyrs* 2.

129   E.g. Rom. 13:1–7; 1 Pet. 2:13–17. North African Christians could procure such a stance if they desired; e.g. Tertullian, *To Scapula* 1.3; *Apology* 30.

130   *Acts of the Scillitan Martyrs* 14. Robert F. Evans, *One and Holy: The Church in Latin Patristic Thought* (Church Historical series 92; London: SPCK, 1972), 5, deems this response "a clearly revolutionary spirit." Similarly, Rankin, *Tertullian*, 215. Cf. 1 Tim. 6:15; and Rev. 17:14, 19:16.

131   Musurillo evidently attempts to emphasize this aspect in Speratus' response by the translation "our own emperor" despite the absence of any emphasizing reflexive in the Latin.

132   E.g. Cicero, *On Divination* 1.11, 1.12, 1.36, 1.46, 1.84, 1.95; *Concerning the Response of the Soothsayers* 19; cited in Brian Krostenko, "Beyond (Dis)belief: Rhetorical Form and Religious Symbol in Cicero's *de Divinatione*," *Transactions of the American Philological Association* 130 (2000), 361. Similarly, in Minucius Felix, *Octavius* 6 and 8, Caecilianus declares the Romans worship the gods of *universarum gentium*, and *omnium gentium* are in agreement with Rome's religious/military superiority. cf. Tertullian, *To the Nations* 2.15.7, where *omne gente* is used in contrast with Rome. Also, see Tertullian, *Apology* 21.6, where in a chapter invoking explicitly Roman imagery, after mentioning Tiberius (21.1), Tertullian distinguishes how Christ chose "from every race, community and region [*ex omni iam gente et populo et loco*]." Elsewhere, Tertullian characterizes his opponent's argument, contrasting Rome (via Tiberius) and "all nations": "Marcion lays it down that there is one Christ who in the time of Tiberius was revealed by a god formerly unknown, for the salvation of all the nations [*Constituit Marcion alium esse Christum qui Tiberianis temporibus a deo quondam ignoto revelatus sit in salutem omnium gentium*]," (*Against Marcion.* 4.6.3). cf. *Against the Jews* 7.4: "universal nations" [*universae gentes*] in reference to the list from Acts 2:9–10 which includes "inhabitants of

the region of Africa which is beyond Cyrene [*regions Africae quae est trans Cyrenen inhabitants*]" and "Romans [*Romani*]." Tertullian can also use similar phraseology when distinguishing "all nations" from the Jews or Samaritans: *Against the Jews* 2.1; 9.20; and *Against Marcion* 4.16.11; 5.5.7.

133 In the same work he mentions the Scillitan persecution, Tertullian offers a similar statement that is framed as both religious and political: "We have no master – none but God" (*To Scapula* 5.4 [my trans.]: *Magistrum neminem habemus, nisi solum Deum*).

134 Tilley, *The Bible in Christian North Africa*, 43.

135 E.g. *Passion of Perpetua* 1.6 and 16.2–4.

136 See esp. the final paragraph.

137 Including the concern that persecution has been exaggerated in the accounts; see the discussion in Rebillard, "Popular Hatred Against Christians: The Case of North Africa in the Second and Third Centuries," *Archiv für Religionsgeschichte* 16 (1, 2015), 283–310.

138 On *institutum Neronianum*, see discussions in Musurillo, *The Acts*, lix; and Barnes, "Pagan Perceptions," 233. cf. Tertullian, *To the Nations* 1.7.9; Tacitus, *Annals* 15.44; and Suetonius, *Life of Nero* 16.2. For *collegia*, see Robert L. Wilken, *The Christians as the Romans Saw Them* (New Haven, CT: Yale University Press, 1984), 34–35; ref. Tertullian, *Apology* 39. For *superstitio*, L. F. Janssen, "'Superstitio' and the Persecution of the Christians," *Vigiliae Christianae* 33 (1979), 131–159, reprinted in *Church and State in the Early Church*, in the series *Studies in Early Christianity Series*, ed. Everett Ferguson (New York: Garland Publishing, Inc., 1993), 79–107; and in North Africa, Andrzej Wypustek, "Magic, Montanism, Perpetua, and the Severan Persecution," *Vigiliae Christianae* 51 (3, 1997): 276–297; Wypustek's arguments assume the *Passion of Perpetua* to be Montanist – a point denied in this study on pp. 87–89.

139 Janssen, "'Superstitio' and Persecution," 82.

140 Barnes, "Pagan Perceptions of Christianity," in *Early Christianity: Origins and Evolution to AD 600*, ed. Ian Hazlett (London: SPCK, 1991), 233; and Musurillo, *The Acts*, lxi–ii.

141 "Why Were the Christians Persecuted?" in *Church and State in the Early Church*, ed. Ferguson, 24. Also, Lucy Grig, *Making Martyrs in Late Antiquity* (London: Duckworth, 2004), 12.

142 Cf. Albert Henrichs, "Pagan Ritual and the Alleged Crime of the Early Christians: A Reconsideration," in *Kyriakon: Festschrift Johannes Quasten*, ed. Josef Andreas Jungmann and Patrick Granfield (Münster: Aschendorff, 1970), 21, who stresses the role of the elites over the plebs. For North Africa, see Christine Trevett, *Montanism: Gender, Authority and the New Prophecy* (Cambridge: Cambridge University Press, 1996), 69–70.

143 Wilken, *The Christians*, 15; ref. Pliny, *Letter* 10.96.10.

144 Musurillo, *The Acts*, lxi–lxii; who adds, "this would be particularly hard on the *humiliores* and the non-citizen classes (to which most Christians belonged before the *Constitutio Antoniana* of A.D. 212.)" cf. Acts 19:23–41.

145 See details in Wilhite, *Tertullian the African*, 52–55.

146 Wypustek, "Magic," 277; ref. *Acts of the Scillitan Martyrs* 2: *Potestis indulgentiam domni nostri imperatoris promereri, si ad bonam mentem redeatis.*

147 *Acts of the Scillitan Martyrs* 7: *Saturninus proconsul dixit ceteris: Desinite huius esse persuasionis. Speratus dixit: Mala est persuasio homicidium facere, falsum testimonium dicere.*

148 *Passion of Perpetua* 16.2–3: *cum tribunus castigatius eos castigaret, quia ex admonitionibus hominum vanissimorum verebatur ne subtraherentur de carcere incantationibus aliquibus magicis, in faciem ei Perpetua respondit:*

> *Quid utique non permittis nobis refrigerare noxiis nobilissimis, Caesaris sci-*
> *licet, et natali eiusdem pugnaturis? aut non tua gloria est, si pinguiores illo*
> *producamur?* (Wallis's trans.)

149 *Passion of Perpetua* 17.1: *Pridie quoque cum illam cenam ultimam quam lib-*
eram *vocant, quantum in ipsis erat, non cenam liberam sed agapem cenarent,*
eadem constantia ad populum verba iactabant, comminantes iudicium Dei,
contestantes passionis suae felicitatem, inridentes concurrentium curiositatem.
(Wallis's translation is again used over Musurillo, who translates *vocant*, "it is
called.")

150 It should be noted that the martyrs are in the Roman "military camp [*cas-*
trensem]" (*Passion of Perpetua* 7.9–10). On "abrogation" as a subversive
strategy often utilized by indigenous writers under colonization, see Ashcroft,
Griffiths, and Tiffin, *The Empire Writes Back*, 38–39.

151 *Passion of Perpetua* 18.7–9.

152 *Passion of Perpetua* 2.1.

153 *Passion of Perpetua* 16.2–4: *quia ex admonitionibus hominum vanissimorum*
verebatur ne subtraherentur de carcere incantationibus aliquibus magicis. The
English translation is that of R. E. Wallis, "The Passion of the Holy Martyrs
Perpetua and Felicitas" in *ANF* 3, as opposed to Musurillo who translates *hom-*
inum vanissimorum as "very foolish people" which neglects the self-serving
and dishonest insinuations of the phrase in this context.

154 *Passion of Perpetua* 4.5. For the pattern of local elites sponsoring festivals and
games in order to establish their own political identity, see Onno Van Nijf,
"Athletics, Festivals and Greek Identity in the Roman East," *Proceedings of*
the Cambridge Philological Society 45 (1999): 176–200. This could explain the
motive of local elites who "betrayed" Perpetua and the other Christians for the
celebration of Septimius Geta's birthday.

155 *Passion of Perpetua* 16.2–3:

> Perpetua spoke to him directly. "Why can you not even allow us to refresh
> ourselves properly? For we are the most distinguished of the condemned
> prisoners, seeing that we belong to the emperor; we are to fight on his very
> birthday. Would it not be to your credit if we were brought forth on the
> day in a healthier condition?" [*In faciem ei Perpetua respondit: Quid utique*
> *non permittis nobis refrigerare noxiis nobilissimis, Caesaris scilicet, et natali*
> *eiusdem pugnaturis? aut non tua gloria est, si pinguiores illo producamur?*]

> See discussion in W.H.C. Frend, "Open Questions Concerning the Christians
> and the Roman Empire in the Age of the Severi," *Journal of Theological Studies*
> n.s. 25 (2, 1974), 333–351.

156 For details, see Anne Daguet-Gagey, "Septime Sévère, un empereur persécuteur
des chrétiens?" *Revue des études augustiniennes* 47 (2001), 3–32.

157 Birley, *The African Emperor*, 135, rejects such a conclusion.

158 Wypustek, "Magic," 285; *The Augustan History: Severus* 17.1: "He forbade
conversion to Judaism under heavy penalties and enacted a similar law in
regard to the Christians." [*Iudaeos fieri sub graui poena vetuit. Idem etiam de*
Christianis sanxit.] Frend, "Open Questions," 340, argues there was such an
edict; Robeck, *Prophecy*, 11, concurs. Cf. Tert., *To Scapula* 4.5–6.

159 Birley, *The African Emperor*, 210; cf. his deduction from the chronological
coincidence in another instance (221): "While the Emperor and his party were
in Africa, the proconsul died. It may have been from natural causes. But the fact
that Plautinus was there at the time makes one wonder."

160 *Passion of Perpetua* 16.2–3; Birley, *The African Emperor*, 221, believes, "The
imperial party would have been otherwise occupied."

161 Wypustek, "Magic," 276; ref. Paulus, *The Sentences* 5.21.1–3, 5.23. It should be noted that this text is likely a later reworking of Paulus's original.

162 Rankin, "Tertullian and the Imperial Cult," *Studia Patristica* 34 (2001), 209; Rankin also discusses how "The author of the *Historia Augusta* even ventures that this 'murderer (*interfector*)' of so many of high estate 'was regarded by the Africans as a god' "; ref. *The Augustan History: Severus* 13.8–9: *ab Afris ut deus habetur.*

163 *Rome*, 145.

164 Burns, Jensen, et al., *Christianity in Roman Africa*, xlvi–xlvii. Their view is in some ways a retrieval of an earlier generation of scholars who broke down various regions, including the "African School"; e.g. John Fletcher Hurst, *History of the Christian Church* (New York: Eaton & Mains, 1897), 1:311.

165 For the *Passion of Perpetua*'s influence on later martyrdoms and writers in Africa, see Kitzler, *From* Passio Perpetuae; more generally, see Joseph Farrell, "The Canonization of Perpetua," in *Perpetua's Passions: Multidisciplinary Approaches to the Passio Perpetuae et Felicitatis*, ed. Jan N. Bremmer and Marco Formisano (Oxford: Oxford University Press, 2012), 300–320.

166 For the large list of known African martyrs, see Monceaux, *Histiore littéraire*, 3:536–551 (= appendix 2); and see Shaw, *Sacred Violence* 623 n.123. For African martyr accounts, see Jacqueline Amat, "Images du Martyre dans les Passions Africaines du IIIe Siècle," in *L'imaginaire religieux gréco-romain*, ed. Joël Thomas (Perpignan: Presses universitaires de Perpignan, 1994), 273–281; and Jéronimo Leal, *Actas Latinas de Mártires Africanos* (Fuentes Patrísticas 22; Madrid: Editorial Ciudad Nueva, 2009). For the material evidence of martyrs in Africa in the later period, see Duval, *Loca sanctorum Africae.*

167 Burns, Jensen, et al., *Christianity in Roman Africa*, 32.

168 *Letter* 78.3: *numquid non et Africa sanctorum martyrum corporibus plena est* (trans. WSA 2.1:306).

4 Tertullian

Tertullian is arguably the most misunderstood and yet most influential thinker from the whole Christian tradition. As the first Christian theologian to write in Latin, he veritably invented a new vocabulary that would shape the tradition that came after him. Therefore, his role in this Latin "western" tradition should be better appreciated. In addition to his role in this broader tradition, the influence of the unique African context also needs to be better understood in his writings.

For our present purposes, we especially want to consider him as a product of his local African context since this is an aspect of his life that has not been given sufficient consideration. Before singling out his African milieu, however, we need to provide an overview of his life and works. However, the central claim of this book is that North African Christians cannot be fully understood apart from their local context, and therefore even in our sections on Tertullian's life and works his context will come into view.

Tertullian's life

Tertullian must have been born around 160, but he first appears in the historical record in the 190s when he began producing several books. His writing career ends by 220 at the latest, and there is no evidence of when or how he died. In fact, outside of the information found in his own works, very little is known about his life at all.

Despite the fact that Tertullian is the first Christian to write in Latin, his legacy and reputation in modern theology is questionable at best. This is likely due to his supposed conversion to the Montanist heresy late in life – which is a claim that will require special attention in the discussion on pp. 112–114.[1] In addition to his alleged Montanism there have been several factual errors promulgated about Tertullian, and these have also marked Tertullian as less than desirable, even unacceptable for later theology. Thus, Tertullian is arguably the most misunderstood individual from all of Christian history. Therefore, in order to rectify our view of Tertullian, we should first begin by briefly sketching a picture of him in terms of how he is now understood by scholars – this is a picture that is vastly different than what most have been taught.

Many different depictions of Tertullian have emerged, several of which paint him in a very unpleasant light. While I do not intend to offer an *apologia*, a defense, of Tertullian's character, I do think that we must begin by making some clarifications and even some major corrections to what we know about Tertullian. To simplify this discussion, misunderstandings of Tertullian will be listed under six different misnomers, followed by a final title that is recommended as a replacement for the other six and that can serve as the starting point for future studies of Tertullian.

Tertullian the legalist

The first caricature of Tertullian we must dismiss is Tertullian the "legalist." Around a century after Tertullian's own lifetime, Eusebius of Caesarea claims that Tertullian was an expert in Roman law.[2] Added to Eusebius's claim is a list of Roman jurists discovered by historians, that is experts in Roman law, a list which includes a certain *Tertullianus*.[3] Some early modern scholars concluded that this must be the same Tertullian of Carthage, who was a convert to Christianity, and so he must have practiced jurisprudence in Rome before converting to the new faith and returning to his old home.

Theologians have been quick to identify Tertullian's doctrine as "legalistic": once a lawyer, always a lawyer. His theology and much of the Latin western tradition that inherited his vocabulary have been accused of retaining a legal framework that warps the true gospel of grace apart from the works of the law.[4]

As it turns out, these conclusions are unwarranted. Eusebius has been shown to exaggerate Tertullian's expertise in law so as to help his own argument about the illegality of persecution. Moreover, there is no evidence that Tertullian ever went to Rome. A close analysis of Tertullian's writings shows that he uses legal metaphors but does not have expertise in jurisprudence. Rather than being trained in law, Tertullian was trained in rhetoric. The last few decades of research have shown the benefit of analyzing Tertullian's works in light of the classical teachers of rhetoric, such as Aristotle, Cicero, and Quintillian.[5] Part of his education would have included discussion of laws (as well as many other subjects such as philosophy and poetry), but his aim was not to demonstrate legal proofs; his aim was to persuade.

Tertullian's rhetoric can include bitter attacks against his opponents, character attacks that disturb modern sensibilities. Marcion, for example, comes under fire from Tertullian for his heretical teachings, including the rejection of the Old Testament. Tertullian begins, however, with an attack, not on Marcion's doctrine, but on his *patria*, his homeland of Pontus, which was a region in northern Asia Minor known to ancient Greek and Roman writers as barbaric and nigh uninhabitable. Tertullian therefore launches into a tirade against Marcion, by way of Pontus:

> Even its situation would prevent you from reckoning Pontus hospitable: as though ashamed of its own barbarism it has set itself at a distance

from our more civilized waters. Strange tribes inhabit it – if indeed living in a wagon can be called inhabiting. . . . their sexual activity is promiscuous, and for the most part unhidden even when they hide it: they advertise it by hanging a quiver on the yoke of the wagon, so that none may inadvertently break in. . . . They carve up their fathers' corpses along with mutton, to gulp down at banquets. . . . Women also have lost the gentleness, along with the modesty, of their sex. They display their breasts, they do their house-work with battle-axes, they prefer fighting to matrimonial duty. There is sternness also in the climate – . . . rivers are no rivers, only ice: mountains are piled high up with snow: all is torpid, everything stark. . . . the only thing warm there is Savagery. . . . Even so, the most barbarous and melancholy thing about Pontus is that Marcion was born there.[6]

Tertullian's audience, he hopes, has already discounted Marcion. He must now simply demonstrate the uncivilized and unintelligent things Marcion teaches, for his audience is already predisposed to reject them along with this undesirable heretic. Tertullian's rhetorical aims and the way in which his opponents shape his argument in any given work will be discussed further in the following section.

To reiterate, Tertullian would be better understood as a classically trained rhetorician who could have argued cases, but whose expertise lies in the art of persuasion, not the interpretation of precedent. In other words, he is better understood in comparison with Fronto and Apuleius (African rhetoricians) than with Proculus or Gaius (Roman jurists). One last point of interest for the present study in regard to Tertullian and the legal profession: Ian Balfour has recently suggested that Tertullian may have been an expert in law, only the reason that his writings betray no substantial knowledge of Roman jurisprudence is that he was not an expert in Roman law. Instead, he knew Punic or Libyan law, which was enforced in North Africa whenever Roman laws did not apply.[7]

In sum, Tertullian, as a rhetorician instead of a jurist, did not set out to establish illegalities, but to reveal absurdities. Often, he speaks with hyperbole, sarcasm, and irony. In any given work, the reader must always read with a grain of salt to seek Tertullian's rhetorical aim, not just take his statements at face value. This brings us to the second caricature of Tertullian that must be rejected.

Tertullian the fideist

Tertullian has often been described as one who rejects philosophy, and along with that education, reason, and "culture" (usually ill-defined). In the place of these Tertullian clings to Biblicism and simplistic faith. Two famous quotes from Tertullian help establish this picture of him. In order to dismiss philosophy, he asks, "What indeed has Athens to do with Jerusalem?"[8] In another place, he defends the resurrection, by boldly affirming irrationality: "I believe it because it is absurd [*Credo quia absurdum*]."⁹ This Tertullian, it has been claimed, represents an unthinking approach to Christianity, wherein one can love the Lord with body, heart, and soul, but not with the mind. Christianity, in this posture, is "against culture," and so the faith becomes isolationist and abandons the real world for the utopian world to come.¹⁰

Here again, however, Tertullian has been grossly misread, and so we must distinguish Tertullian's own statements from how he was later understood. His statement about Athens and Jerusalem, when read in context, is clearly a rhetorical device used to prohibit specific heretical groups from twisting scripture to fit the philosophical systems of Plato and other Greek philosophers. Tertullian's wider body of writings, however, display a keen awareness and felicitous usage of Hellenistic philosophy. For Tertullian, all truth is God's Truth; and so when Tertullian finds the philosophers speaking the truth, he happily uses philosophy as a means of grace that can articulate the faith.

He can even reverse the order of the logic from 2 Tim. 3:16. This passage reads as follows, "All scripture is inspired by God and is useful for teaching, for reproof, for correction, and for training in righteousness." Given how flexible Latin sentence structure can be, Tertullian reverses the logic so that "every Scripture [*scripturam*] suitable for edification is divinely inspired."¹¹ Although Tertullian, like all Christians by this time, uses "scripture" as a technical term for sacred writings, the term has not lost its fundamental meaning as any writing. Thus, he can conclude that all "writing [*scripturam*]" which is useful for teaching – even writings by pre-Christian Greek philosophers! – is inspired. "What has Athens to do with Jerusalem?" This rhetorical question in fact has two possible answers. For Tertullian, Athens may not necessarily speak the language of Jerusalem, but Jerusalem can speak the language of Athens.

The other quote from Tertullian, "I believe it because it is absurd" is in fact not a quote from Tertullian. As it turns out, this is a mistranslation of what Tertullian actually said.¹² In arguing against those who find that Christ's resurrection is outrageously improbable, Tertullian points out how improbable it would be for someone to fabricate such an unlikely story. This strategy, further research has shown, is actually one recommended by Aristotle.¹³ Tertullian argues that the testimony is in fact incredible, and therefore should be considered plausible, since a false witness would never risk such an unbelievable tale. Tertullian's actual quote reads, "it is credible [not *I believe it*], because it is inept" or "amateurish [not *absurd*]."¹⁴

Rather than offering a mindless faith, Tertullian was very concerned that his Christian congregation be offered a holistic faith that even encompassed the life of the mind. This brings us to our third misunderstanding of Tertullian, which involves Tertullian's role in his congregation.

Tertullian the priest

Was Tertullian ordained? Jerome claims he was a priest,¹⁵ and most later tradition accepts Jerome's testimony. Modern scholars, however, have been unable to reconcile this claim with Tertullian's own statements where he denies that he is ordained.[16] Therefore, Tertullian the priest is rejected as a false construct. Even so, it is difficult to imagine that Tertullian would author the kind of works he did, many of which are clearly instructive for his Christian community, without having some formal role in that community.[17] Was he a catechist? A lay preacher? Cyprian will refer to him as a *magister*, a "chief" or possibly even "teacher."[18]

There are two historical possibilities that should be considered. The first is that in Tertullian's time, the Sunday morning Eucharist at which all Christians from the local municipality gathered was well established, but it was not the only liturgical expression of Christianity.[19] Christians were still meeting from house to house for the Agape meal in the evenings. A generation later, Cyprian will elevate the role of the Sunday morning Eucharist even to the point of discouraging evening Agape meals celebrated without the bishop. Later still, Augustine's church will pass canon law that prohibits Agape meals in the home, allowing Eucharist only in the basilica under the supervision of the bishop. When Tertullian speaks of "priestly" roles, he is clear that the head of every house can perform such roles, since he does so in the Agape meal. He also welcomes the proper order of the church's offices, so he stipulates that the bishop should baptize, but in the absence of a bishop or other clergy, any (male) believer can perform the baptism. Perhaps Tertullian's "priestly" office was merely that he was the head of a house-church.

The other possible leadership role Tertullian held was that of "lay elder."[20] The *seniores laici* were not ordained, but they did function as a governing body in the North African church. This group does not exist outside of North Africa, and so it already hints as to how Tertullian was indebted to his unique African context.[21] One scholar believes the office derived from the pre-Christian and even pre-Roman African societal structures, wherein local towns were governed by a council of local elders.[22] Even ancient Carthage was governed by a "council of elders" according to sources on the Punic wars.[23] Once again we see how difficult it is to understand Tertullian without considering his context. The next problematic description of Tertullian's life is that he became a Montanist.

Tertullian the Montanist

Probably the most debated aspect of Tertullian's life is the claim that he converted to Montanism late in life. For brevity's sake, I will summarize the scholarly debate to say that for the last forty years, scholars have rejected the notion that Tertullian left the true church of Carthage and joined a schismatic group called the Montanists. The so-called Montanists were from Phrygia, and only much later were named after their apparent leader, Montanus. Montanus along with two prophetesses, named Priscilla and Maximilla, allegedly placed the importance of ongoing prophecy over the scriptures and over the authority of the bishop. They were accused of many other deviant practices, but suffice it to say that Tertullian never met a Phrygian prophet in person and he knew of them only through their sayings, which were written down and distributed.[24]

Even so, Tertullian's use of the Phrygian prophets corresponds with a clear argument: he – like the Phrygians – will speak of "us" spiritual Christians in opposition to those "carnal" Christians. This, of course, is language that has been invoked since Paul, who described substandard Christians in terms of the "soul [*psyche*]," which is lower than the spirit and so oriented toward the flesh.[25] When Tertullian refers to his opponents as unspiritual he transliterates the Greek word for soul (*psyche*), calling them *psychici* or "the psychics." This appears to be a practice he learned after encountering the Phrygian prophecies. Apart from this terminological shift, however, Tertullian does not seem to have changed much in his actual practice of Christianity. The main development in his thought is arguably his disallowance of second marriages. This is usually attributed to his "Montanism." However, it should be noted that the Montanists were accused of forbidding marriage altogether and even promoting divorce, whereas Tertullian – like Paul – permitted marriage, even while advocating celibacy. William Tabbernee concludes "Tertullian's 'Montanist' views about marriage itself, as expressed in his treatise against Marcion, are totally consistent with what he had written earlier about the subject."[26] As for second marriages, Tertullian claims the "Paraclete" has revealed that second marriages were permitted, but the truly spiritual should discern the ideal of monogamy.[27] This revelation, however, appears to be from a local Carthaginian oracle, and not one of the Phrygian prophets.[28]

Regarding prophecy, Tertullian already believed in ongoing prophetic utterance and visions, as did Cyprian and others who came after him.[29] Apparently this is simply the practice of Carthaginian Christians at this time – as was seen in the *Passion of Perpetua* (discussed in Chapter 3). One scholar has even argued that the penchant for prophecy among African Christians can be traced to the Punic background, wherein Baal/Saturn primarily communicates to humans in dreams and visions.[30] Tertullian does defend "new prophecy," against an unnamed "bishop of bishops, the pontifex maximus," who is likely but not certainly the bishop of Rome.[31] This bishop had denounced the Phrygians and the practice of prophecy. Although he viciously attacked this bishop's decision, Tertullian never indicated that he left the Catholic church. At the most he belonged to what some scholars have called an *ecclesiola in ecclesia*, a little-church-group within the church, which valued ongoing prophecy.[32]

I remain, however, unconvinced by what is admittedly the majority view. There is no reference explicit or otherwise to an *ecclesiola in ecclesia* in Tertullian's works.[33] Tertullian was simply in good standing with his Carthaginian Christian community, and his embrace of ongoing prophetic utterances seemed to have been not only tolerated but welcomed by

Christians in Carthage.[34] Moreover, Tertullian's earlier or "pre-Montanist" writings actually show that Tertullian was already committed to the mindset and practices that in his later works are labeled "Montanist."

Tertullian's alleged conversion to Montanism has especially proven problematic for his legacy. As I have already stated, Tertullian's alleged Montanism caused later theologians to avoid his teachings. It should be noted, however, that before Jerome, who in 394 was the first to accuse Tertullian of being a Montanist, Tertullian was widely read and appreciated, as even Jerome admits.[35] Jerome, it seems, influenced Augustine, who thereafter spoke of Tertullian as a Montanist, as would most who belonged to the western/Augustinian tradition that followed.[36] Jerome and Augustine, however, had the luxury of seeing Montanism as a schismatic sect, clearly distinct from the Catholic party in the fourth century. Such clear boundaries were not the case in Tertullian's day. Even Cyprian, one generation after Tertullian, who became famous for tolerating no schism, read Tertullian every day. When asking for Tertullian's books, he would say to his assistant, "Give me the master."[37] Tertullian in fact was not denounced as a heretic in his own time and his influence has greatly impacted those who came after him. While Montanus, Priscilla, and Maximilla certainly functioned as sources for his thought, we should not overestimate their influence. In fact, there is a curious irony here in that Tertullian defends prophetesses like Priscilla and Maximilla, and yet he is also remembered as someone who hated women, which brings us to our fifth caricature of Tertullian.

Tertullian the misogynist

Perhaps more than any other church father, Tertullian has been criticized for his stance on women. Tertullian infamously appears in feminist discussions of early Christian history as a quintessential example of misogyny and patriarchy in the guise of authoritative doctrine.[38] Here again, Tertullian himself offers some memorable quotes that seem to merit this description of him. In the opening of one his works addressed to women in his congregation, he says to women – all women – "You are each an Eve!" When reading this passage, you can almost see him wagging his finger at them as he shouts, "You are the Devil's gateway!"[39]

Alternatively, it should be noted that many scholars have returned to Tertullian's views on women to find the reading in the previous paragraph superficial.[40] One scholar notes how Tertullian's statements against women, like the one cited in the previous paragraph, "are frequently cited as proof of Tertullian's irredeemable misogyny and used to condemn him, function more like modern sound bites, and they may obscure the full spectrum of his thought on the role of women in the Church."[41] In a more circumspect interpretation, Heffernan concludes, "Tertullian's attitude toward women is complex."[42]

To attempt a balanced view, we should acknowledge the tension found in Tertullian's writing when it comes to women. To put it simply (and anachronistically), Tertullian was no feminist. Of course, he should be judged according to the standard of his own day and time; and yet, while it is important to understand Tertullian according to the standards of his own time, it still has to be acknowledged that Tertullian's rhetoric, if not his underlying sentiment, is often violent when it comes to women.[43]

With that important caveat in place, we can note how Tertullian at several points promotes women's voices, including the Phrygian "Montanists" mentioned on in the previous section, as well as a woman in his own congregation who prophesies during the liturgical service.[44] Arguably, statements that appear to be overbearing toward women, such as his instruction on how they should dress, could be understood as his attempt to liberate women in his congregation from the cultural trappings of Roman society, such as the ornamental coiffure and expensive dress expected in society at that time.[45] This last point about Roman expectations brings me to my next caricature of Tertullian.

Tertullian the Roman

Tertullian wrote in Latin, and his father – according to Jerome – was "a proconsular centurion [*centurione proconsulari*]."[46] This easily allows for modern scholars to see Tertullian as thoroughly Romanized, and so he has even been dubbed "The Father of Latin Theology."[47] Let me be clear by first affirming that Tertullian should be awarded such an accolade, since he is the first Latin Christian writer, and since his writings significantly impact the later Latin tradition. Furthermore, Tertullian should be understood as fully integrated into Roman society; he likely belonged to a family of some status and he received an excellent education in classical Greco-Roman sources.[48] However, to label Tertullian as Romanized risks reifying his thought and missing a significant aspect of his writings. Tertullian himself actually coined the term *Romanitas*, but he did so while mocking Roman-ness, implying that he (at least at times) rejected a Roman identity.[49]

Concerning his father's office as a "proconsular centurion," Timothy David Barnes investigated this description in 1971 and determined there was no such office in the ancient world.[50] Jerome, Barnes demonstrated, had in fact read a corrupted copy of Tertullian's *Apology*, where Tertullian discussed how, "Children were openly sacrificed in Africa to Saturn as lately as the proconsulship of Tiberius . . . as the soldiers of our country [*patriae nostrae*] still can testify who did that very work for that proconsul."[51] Rather than reading "our country [*patriae nostrae*]" as is given here, Jerome must have understood Tertullian to be speaking about his "father [*patri*]," which is in fact a scribal error found in one surviving manuscript. So then, rather than concluding that Tertullian's father was a soldier, scholars today believe that Tertullian was claiming the country of Africa, where children were sacrificed to Saturn (i.e. the Punic Baal) as his *patria*, his native homeland.

In fact, out of all of the usual items listed for Tertullian's life (like those given here in this list) the one sure fact from which scholars can seek to understand him is that Tertullian lived in and wrote from Carthage. Let us, therefore, look at what Carthage and North Africa mean for our understanding of Tertullian.

Tertullian the African

With this last label, we shift from caricatures to historically reliable information. It is understandable that previous generations of westerners have read Tertullian as a Roman. In order to understand Tertullian in context, however, we must allow that Romanization, like any colonization, does not mean that the powerful empire imposes its will on passive subjects. Instead, local indigenous individuals and groups had their own agency; their responses could range from resistance to acceptance, including manifold ways of negotiating these two extremes. As discussed on p. 51 in Chapter 2, a famous maxim from the period of the British empire is to refer to someone who was from, for example, India as "more English than the English." Such a person, of course, still remains thoroughly Indian as well. Perhaps we should consider the possibility that Tertullian was in some ways more "Roman than the Romans," while in other ways he remained thoroughly African.

In one of his works, Tertullian gives his own full name as *Septimius Tertullianus*.[52] This Latin name appears to have all of the hallmarks of a classical Roman name; the *gentilicium*, or family name, is in fact shared with the emperor of Rome at this time, Septimius Severus. Historians, however, have always known that this emperor in fact represents the kind of African identity I am describing: Septimius Severus was from Leptis Magna in modern Libya, and his family, the Septimii, was an old Punic family that did not speak Latin well.[53] Tertullian's Roman-sounding name, therefore, may say as much about what is not Roman in his heritage as it does about what is Romanized.

Tertullian, as it turns out, is remembered in the earliest reference to him not by his Romanized name, but simply as *Tertullianus Afer*, Tertullian the African.[54] What then was "African" about Tertullian? Before answering this question directly, Tertullian's works need to be introduced.

Works and teachings

Tertullian's works often defy precise genres. Even so, a helpful taxonomy is to think of his writings in the following four categories.

1   Apologetics – works written ostensibly to non-Christians in which he defends Christian practice, often by way of attacking non-Christian actions.[55] Christians were being persecuted, and Tertullian offers multifaceted responses, even including his claim that Christians love their

persecutors and do not wish them to receive divine retribution for their unjust actions.[56] Tertullian is not the first to offer such a defense of the faith, but he develops the works of earlier writers like Justin Martyr in unique ways. Situated at the beginning of Christian Latin thinking, he is even the first to argue for concepts like "human rights [*humani iuris*]" and religious liberty.[57]

2 Exhortations – works written to those within the Christian community about doctrine and practice. Tertullian addresses numerous problems that Christians faced, such as how to avoid idolatry in all its pervasive expressions in Roman society, as well as how to dress, how to pray, how to face persecution, and how to view marriage.[58] Whereas the apologetic treatises speak to an outsider/non-Christian audience, these treatises speak directly to insiders, that is, Christians within his community.

3 Polemics – works written to those he views as outside of his Christian community, namely the heretics. Many items of faith must be rightly understood, such as baptism, the human soul, the incarnation, and the resurrection, and often specific opponents are named, such as Hermogenes, Valentinus, and Marcion.[59] While modern scholarship has taken a more circumspect view of these groups, considering them different forms of "Christianities," Tertullian held to Irenaeus's view wherein these were once Christians who deviated from the faith. Therefore, they are not outsiders in the same way as the "idolators," and yet they are no longer insiders.

4 Polemical exhortations – for lack of a better category, these works are written to those who Tertullian admits are still within the orthodox Christian community, and yet whose teachings threaten true Christian faith and so must be challenged. Four works in particular display Tertullian's felt need to attack "the psychics" (discussed on pp. 112–114 as part of his so-called Montanism), and they respectively insist on the need for a correct understanding of the uniqueness of the three divine persons, the importance of fasting, the preference of widowhood over second marriages, and modesty in general.[60]

Although his works have been categorized here in terms of how they relate to insiders and outsiders, there is still a question as to how Tertullian's works were actually delivered to his intended audience. As with most apologists, Tertullian's apologetic works were likely intended for his fellow believers. The non-Christians addressed in the work are part of a fictive audience. By hearing how Tertullian would address outsiders, those Christians within Tertullian's community would be taught how they could answer charges brought by their non-Christian neighbors. Whether the same is true for his polemical works is highly debatable. Did Tertullian publish his work for his opponents to read? Or were these also works delivered to his own community to teach them why his opponents were wrong?

Even if we accept that Tertullian's works were for his own Christian community, how should we imagine that they were delivered to his audience? Were they first speeches? For now, this must remain an open question. What is clear is just how much Tertullian shaped his arguments in accordance with his training as a rhetorician. In attempting to understand any of these writings, the modern reader must recognize how thoroughly rhetorical Tertullian is in his argumentation. Tertullian studied the best of classical rhetoric, such as can be found in Aristotle, Cicero, and Quintillian, and he employed their tactics of persuasion without hesitation.

Often, his precise stance on a given issue can be puzzling since he takes the opposite position in different works in order to suit his specific aims in those works.[61] For example, Mary remained a virgin although she married, so that she serves as an example to virgins in Carthage who refused to dress like a married woman. And yet, Mary did not remain a virgin if it helps to disprove those heretics who think Christ's flesh was immaterial and therefore did not damage her hymen.[62] Similarly,

> If an opponent [i.e. Marcion] denied that some requirement in the Hebrew Scriptures still applied because it had been replaced by the new covenant of Jesus, he could argue for the continuing relevance of the old because Jesus had come to fulfill not abolish the old. Yet, equally, on other occasions [i.e. *Against the Jews*], could he argue the exact opposite by appealing to more supersessionist passages of the New Testament.[63]

Another example is where the human soul has its own "corporeality," when debating the Valentinians who make the soul indistinguishable from God's own substance. In another work, however, Tertullian insists that the soul is not material/bodily, because he must reject Hermogenes's idea that the soul cannot participate at all in God, who is immaterial and spiritual.[64]

One last example of Tertullian's rhetorical doublespeak pertains specifically to the context of Roman Africa. When writing to Scapula, the proconsul of Africa in 212, Tertullian describes how benign the Christians are in their threat to the Roman Empire. After pointing out how no Christians joined the armed rebellions of recent years, he states:

> A Christian is enemy to none, least of all to the Emperor of Rome, whom he knows to be appointed by his God, and so cannot but love and honour; and whose well-being moreover, he must needs desire, with that of the empire over which he reigns so long as the world shall stand – for so long as that shall Rome continue.[65]

This open letter, however, must be compared to his earliest apologetic work, *To the Nations*, written to local Carthaginians, not to the Roman persecutors themselves.[66] In that earlier work, he mocks the notion that the

Romans' gods have given them dominion over the world, and then ends with a claim to know the end of Rome that is to come:

> at last almost universal dominion has accrued to the Romans. It is the fortune of the times that has thus constantly shaken kingdoms with revolution. Inquire who has ordained these changes in the times. It is the same (great Being) who dispenses kingdoms, and has now put the supremacy of them into the hands of the Romans, very much as if the tribute of many nations were after its exaction amassed in one (vast) coffer. *What He has determined concerning it, they know who are the nearest to Him.*[67]

Obviously, such menacing and thinly veiled threats of Rome's apocalyptic end are not things that would be well received by Scapula, and so Tertullian omits such talk and tailors his argument to his audience when writing to him. Deciding Tertullian's "real" views on Rome is no easy task given such rhetorical dexterity. In short, Tertullian's theology is notoriously difficult to decipher.[68]

One helpful approach to interpreting Tertullian in such moments is to inquire into his rhetorical aim. Tertullian often aims to persuade his audience to take a given course of action, such as to dress modestly and to avoid gross displays of wealth.[69] In order to persuade the audience, Tertullian then deploys a series of arguments. Examples include how ambition caused the fall of humanity, fallen angels taught metallurgy, precious jewels are associated with dragons, and – one of my personal favorites – an argument from the created order: if God wanted people to wear purple clothes, God would have made purple sheep! If any of these individual arguments fails to convince, any one of the others hurled at the audience might. Tertullian, we can safely assume, does not actually find wool dying to be a sinful act; instead, his rhetoric utilizes every possible argument that might convince his audience.

Tertullian also displays his rhetorical gifts in his use of extended metaphor. The teacher he opposes in *On Baptism* belongs to the Cainites, who were thought to be a Gnostic sect. This teacher has opposed the practice of water baptism, and so Tertullian likens her to a "viper" who prefers dry places. The metaphor ties together the specific teaching against water, the negative connotation of a snake, the infamous belief among certain Gnostic sects that the Serpent in Genesis is in fact the hero, not the villain. Alternatively, the Christians, who like water (i.e. with baptism), are actually little "fish," which invokes the famous acronym from early Christianity where the Greek word *ICHTUS* (ΙΧΘΥΣ) stands for "*Jesus Christ, God's Son, the Savior.*" Tertullian's ability to interweave multiple allusions is best seen in his use of classical Greek and Roman sources. His use of literary and philosophical works demonstrate a high level of education and training.

Sometimes, as we have seen, Tertullian's rhetoric can include bitter attacks against his opponents, character attacks that disturb modern sensibilities. Marcion, for example, comes under fire from Tertullian for his heretical teachings, including the rejection of the Old Testament. Tertullian begins, however, with an attack, not on Marcion's doctrine, but on his homeland of Pontus, which was known to ancient Greek and Roman writers as barbaric and nigh uninhabitable (cited on pp. 109–110). After such a vivid and repulsive picture of Marcion's *patria*, Tertullian's audience, he hopes, has already discredited Marcion. He must now simply demonstrate the uncivilized and unintelligent things Marcion teaches, for his audience is already predisposed to reject them as such.

Even when attacking orthodox Christians (i.e. in his polemical exhortations, mentioned on p. 117), Tertullian can be ruthless. The "bishop of bishops" has absolved adultery for those already within the church. While Tertullian cannot attack this bishop's character directly[70] as he did with Marcion, he can challenge the validity of such action, likening this bishop's church to the temple needing to be cleansed by Jesus:

> O edict, on which cannot be inscribed, "Good deed!" And where shall this liberality be posted up? . . . But it is in the church that this (edict) is read, and in the church that it is pronounced; and (the church) is a virgin! Far, far from Christ's betrothed be such a proclamation! She, the true, the modest, the saintly, shall be free from stain even of her ears. She has none to whom to make such a promise; and if she have had, she does not make it; since even the earthly temple of God can sooner have been called by the Lord a "den of robbers," than of adulterers and fornicators.[71]

Whereas at first glance this looks to be an outright rejection of this bishop and his church, recent scholars have found that Tertullian still locates himself within this church. After all, "She" is still Christ's betrothed. Tertullian utilizes this tone much like he did against Marcion: the audience is likely caught up in a fit of *pathos* and cannot accept such a disgrace to be permitted in their church – and they have not yet even heard the arguments. It is worth reiterating how this form of argumentation makes Tertullian's works very difficult to retrieve in terms of a theological contribution for later and even modern discussions. However, his rhetorical style is in no way insurmountable. He, in fact, shaped much of the later theological terms, if not theological trajectories altogether, and so his works deserve further study. In such future studies, any given statement found in Tertullian will need to be triangulated with his stated rhetorical purpose and located within the constellation of his whole corpus.

One central theme that drives Tertullian's thought is his concern with idolatry. While this theme is especially manifested in his apologetic works, the concern with idolatry also affects his view of Christian discipline. In terms of the "world," Tertullian, like Paul before him and Augustine after him, thinks of this sphere as the political order opposed to Christ's new order,[72] and this world surrounding the Christians is filled with demons.[73] Because African Christians "should be in the world [*saeculo*] but are not of it" (which is not a direct quote from scripture, as is commonly thought, but a maxim that originates with Tertullian),[74] one of the chief concerns is to protect the boundary between the two. The importance of holiness and purity continues to be a theme among the generations of African Christians that follow, and even when the empire supports Christianity, the relationship between the church and the *saeculum*, or world, will remain an ongoing concern.[75]

Tertullian's concern with holiness and discipline reflects his view of the spiritual battles taking place in the world. Spiritual forces of evil underlie the visible world, and going to places like the circus or the theatre, not to mention pagan shrines, can result in the Christian being "contaminated" by evil spirits.[76] The sacrifices and rituals offered by the non-Christian in virtually every arena of life invoke demons whose presence is a physical threat to the Christian who comes into contact with them. Tertullian on the one hand is a dualist in that he views the spiritual reality as distinct and higher than the material reality. On the other hand, Tertullian is very much a materialist because there is no distance between the spiritual and the material spheres: the spiritual pervades the material; the spiritual beings themselves even have their own kind of "corporeality."[77] Just as idols are merely wood and stone that do not feel, but can be inhabited by demons who work through them, so Christian practices and even tangible Christian items, like baptismal water[78] and women's jewelry, are at risk of being contaminated by evil spirits. Conversely, just as Christ "clothed" himself in humanity, humans should also "clothe" themselves properly.[79]

The concerns to dress modestly (as in *On Modesty*), live a life of self-renunciation and fasting (*On Fasting*), and abstain from sexual lust (*On Monogamy*) are all part of the Christian "discipline," which is required to keep Christians from being contaminated by the evil spirits who tempt the flesh to lust.[80] This dualist-yet-materialist outlook stems from a participatory ontology: the spiritual can participate in the things of the flesh, and vice versa – something that the so-called Gnostic form of Christianity denied.

The concern about participating in or contracting the contagion of idolatry and its affect on the Christian community will be hallmarks of many later African Christians, as will be seen with Cyprian and then later with the Donatists. Since Christians were periodically required to make sacrifices to the Roman gods, this threat of contagion was perceived as an imminent threat, and so Christians were expected to live their life in constant preparation for martyrdom.

The tradition of North Africa is sometimes known as the "Church of the Martyrs," and this mentality is evident in Tertullian more so than any other. He exhorts Christians to share their witness boldly, despite the risk involved. Here is Tertullian's defiant statement to his persecutors:

> Go on then with zeal, you good presidents, you will stand higher with the people if you sacrifice the Christians at their wish, kill us, torture us, condemn us, grind us to dust; your injustice is the proof that we are innocent. Therefore God allows that we thus suffer. . . . Nor does your cruelty, however exquisite, avail you; it is rather a temptation to us. The more often we are mown down by you, the more in number we grow; the blood of Christians is seed. . . . For who that contemplates it, is not excited to inquire what is at the bottom of it? who, after inquiry, does not embrace our doctrines? and when he has embraced them, desires not to suffer that he may become partaker of the fullness of God's grace . . .? . . . when we are condemned by you, we are acquitted by the Highest.[81]

These words are sometimes difficult to read today, since we are once again seeing Christian martyrs being made in North Africa. In Tertullian's day, he and his fellow African Christians believed that the "world [*saeculum*]" had declared war on his church, and its demonic powers threatened Christians who were unprepared because they did not adhere to the strict discipline the church teaches. This explains why Christians must avoid the games – the spectacles of Rome – because sacrifices are made as part of those ceremonies, which turns spectators into idolaters. Instead of risking the contagion of demons at the spectacles, Tertullian calls his fellow believers to prepare to be *in* the spectacles as sacrifices – not to the Roman deities – but to the true God.[82] He exhorts his audience, "Ye Servants of God, about to draw near to God, that you may make solemn consecration of yourselves to Him, seek well to understand the condition of faith, the reasons of the Truth, the laws of Christian Discipline."[83] Despite how much is asked of Christians in making this sacrifice, Tertullian offers the vision of the future hope as consolation and encouragement:

> But what a spectacle is that fast-approaching advent of our Lord, now owned by all, now highly exalted, now a triumphant One! What that exultation of the angelic hosts! What the glory of the rising saints! What the kingdom of the just thereafter! What the city New Jerusalem![84]

Tertullian the African

Now that Tertullian and his works have been introduced, we can return to his context and ask what in his writings display an African identity. What was "African" about Tertullianus Afer? This is a question to which I have devoted an entire monograph to try to answer, so I will not repeat that lengthy study at present.[85] Instead, I will offer three brief anecdotes that provide glimpses into this aspect of Tertullian's life and writings.

First, Tertullian's self-awareness as an African comes to the forefront of his argument in his work *On the Cloak*. Let me first stipulate that this "cloak," or *pallium,* is not yet the episcopal vestment known in later church tradition, although it is interesting to reflect on how the Christian bishop's pallium actually has its roots in pre-Christian African tradition. Tertullian's pallium is very different from what we envision today.

The *pallium* is a simple cloak contrasted with the Roman toga. Most modern commentators have concluded that Tertullian exchanged the toga for the cloak of the philosopher, as Justin Martyr did before him. Tertullian knows Justin Martyr's works, and he no doubt welcomes the comparison, but there is much more going on with Tertullian's wardrobe. Tertullian explicitly makes the comparison with a philosopher's cloak in this work, and he points out how this pallium is "Greek to a degree."[86] He also compares his *pallium* with the robes worn by pagan priests, and to other similar simple gowns.

All of these various comparisons, however, come after Tertullian stipulates his rhetorical aim in this work, and so it is worth taking a moment to hear his argument. In the opening lines of his treatise, Tertullian introduces his work by saying,

> Men of Carthage, ever princes of Africa, ennobled by ancient memories, blest with modern felicities, I rejoice that times are so prosperous with you that you have leisure to spend and pleasure to find in criticising dress. These are the "piping times of peace" and plenty. Blessings rain from the empire and from the sky.[87]

In these opening lines, Tertullian sets the tone for the treatise as one of bitter sarcasm, reacting both to those "criticising dress" and those who receive the blessings "from the empire."[88]

Tertullian then counters his critics in Carthage, "the first men of Africa [*principe . . . Africae*]" for how they too once wore the same pallium: "Still, you too of old time wore your garments – your tunics – of another shape,"[89] and he then contrasts the toga with the "pallium . . . which used to be worn by all ranks and conditions among you."[90] The Carthaginians, he goes on to say, have forgotten this native garb because they have donned the Roman toga instead. Tertullian then reminds them how the battering ram was invented by Carthage – but was later forgotten by Carthaginians. This memory lapse proved fatal in the Punic wars, for as Tertullian painfully reminds them, the battering ram eventually was used by Rome to destroy Carthage. So now, he says, the *pallium*, which was the traditional and ancient dress of Africa, has become unrecognized by Carthaginians.[91] Much like what we saw with the references to Virgil's *Aeneid* in the *Passion of Perpetua and Felicity*, there is a literary allusion in Tertullian's statement that refers to the ancient Punic past of Carthage. Vincent Hunink comments on this passage to say, "One may argue, however, that the quotation of Vergil is more than just decorative, as it adds to the speaker's obvious intention of appealing to nationalistic feelings of his audience."[92] After Tertullian's discussion of Carthage's shameful past defeats, the tension reaches a sufficient level of discomfort so that Tertullian finally agrees to abate the intensity of his rhetoric: "Draw we now our material from some other source, lest Punichood either blush or else grieve in the midst of Romans."[93]

His audience is Romanized; in fact, he describes them as especially "in the way of dress . . . precocious in Romanizing."[94] At this point, it is worth asking: what does this Romanizing have to do with Christianity? In fact, Tertullian throughout this treatise has yet to make any single reference to Christianity. It is not until the very last line that he finally speaks poetically to the *pallium* itself to say: "Rejoice, O Pallium, and exult! . . . you have now become a Christian's gown!"[95] While this strange ending has caused some to conclude that Tertullian originally wrote this treatise before his conversion and then added the final line later, such a reading has not convinced the majority of scholars.[96] If Tertullian originally wrote this work from a Christian perspective, he suppresses this identity until his conclusion in order to speak as an African to Africans about their need to distinguish themselves from another group, the Romans.

A second glimpse into how Tertullian's African identity shaped his thought can be found in one citation of scripture in particular. In one of his many theological debates, Tertullian claims that his opponents will be condemned at the final judgment for their mistakes. To support his claim, he cites this saying of Jesus:

> The queen of the South will rise up at the judgment with this generation and condemn it, for she came from the ends of the earth to hear the wisdom of Solomon, and behold, something greater than Solomon is here.[97]

Tertullian, however, quotes only the first half of this statement, apparently from memory, and when he does so, he replaces "the queen of the south" so that the verse reads, "There will arise a queen of *Carthage*." This is undoubtedly a reference to Dido, the founding queen of Carthage. Tertullian goes on to recount the famous story found in the Roman poet, Virgil. In Virgil's *Aeneid*, Dido, the queen of Carthage, fell in love with Aeneas, who travelled from the fallen city of Troy to Italy, where he would establish the new Roman race. When Aeneas leaves Dido, she is overcome with grief and commits suicide on a funeral pyre. Tertullian, however, preserves a different version of the story, which historians believe was a local version with a significant difference from the Roman account.[98] In Tertullian's telling, Aeneas's advances were unwanted, and when he tried to force himself upon Dido, she committed suicide in order to protect her chastity and her city's honor. The reader will remember that Tertullian claimed Africa as his *patria*, or homeland. Tertullian's substitution of "the queen of the south" with "the queen of Carthage" demonstrates just how affected he was by his homeland and its heritage.

It is worth noting here that, later in North African Christian history, both the Donatists and Augustine will substitute "Carthage" or even "Africa" for the word "south" in the scriptures.[99] What to make of this practice, of course, requires further discussion, but for our purpose in this study, suffice it to say that this habit – consciously or otherwise – illustrates how ingrained an African identity was for these African Christians.

A third and final example can illustrate how Tertullian's African identity shaped his thinking, even on things he had to say about Christianity.[100] In one of his earliest works, Tertullian wrote a letter to Christians in prison who were awaiting martyrdom. The addressees are all women, and so after offering several paragraphs of encouragement and exhortation, Tertullian offers a list of previous heroes and heroines who have given their lives in a noble death. This list, however, is not what we would expect. Rather than listing previous Christian martyrs, Tertullian offers a litany of individuals from classical Greek and Roman sources.

One might suspect that Tertullian is limited by the lack of Christian examples of martyrdom available at the time, and he must, therefore, draw from non-Christian heroes to present acts of bravery in the face of torture and death.[101] Does Tertullian not know of the Scillitan martyrs who died in North Africa around 180, or about Perpetua, Felicity, and their fellow martyrs who died in 203? He is likely writing earlier than 203 and he perhaps does not yet know of the Scillitans,[102] but surely he does know about the beheading of Paul, the martyrdom of Peter, and the stoning of Stephen,[103] not to mention the crucifixion of Jesus. None of these men, however, are offered as examples to the martyrs. Perhaps, given what we know about the socio-political landscape of the time, we can elaborate on the "martyrs" Tertullian does name.

Even accepting that Tertullian preferred classical sources, the list is somewhat mystifying to modern scholars, because half of the examples given are said to have "a mental disease [*morbus . . . animi*]" and so the rationale behind the list is not readily apparent.

Tertullian's passage, however, does become clear once one reads it in light of his context: writing from Africa under a time of both Roman political colonization and religious persecution, the examples he gives can easily be categorized in their relation to Rome. All five of the men listed are Roman heroes, but they are all deemed "insane." The women heroines, however, are all truly virtuous – and remember Tertullian is writing to women martyrs. He lists the five women examples as follows:

1   Lucretia, who was raped by the last prince of Rome; her suicide brought about the end of the Roman monarchy.

2 and 3   Dido and Hasdrubal's wife, both Carthaginian heroines who died to preserve Carthage's honor from Roman men.

4   Cleopatra, whom Tertullian says died "that she might not fall into the hands of her enemy"[104] – the 'enemy' of course, being Caesar Octavian Augustus, the archetypal Roman.

5   Leaena, who is said to have chewed off her own tongue, denying
         the possibility of betraying her "confederates [*coniuratos*]."[105]

All five of these heroines represent acts of solidarity against tyranny, and all
but Leaena's act were in direct resistance to Rome.[106] While we should in
no way discount or downplay the religious conviction Tertullian assumes in
this work, we should likewise not overlook the social identities he invokes
in this treatise.

This brief treatment of Tertullian's African identity has only been able
to provide examples of how his non-Roman identity can be detected in his
writings. Much more work needs to be done to explore how his context and
heritage shaped his thought. In an attempt to highlight an often-neglected
aspect of Tertullian, I have focused largely on his African identity, especially in this section. Many other avenues of study, however, offer valuable
insights into Tertullian, and these should not be neglected or eclipsed by
the emphasis being given here. Understanding Tertullian in light of Stoicism
or classical rhetoric (both discussed on p. 111), for example, has proven
invaluable in recent scholarly studies. These topics need not be mutually
exclusive. This can especially be seen in the case of Tertullian's Christianity.
His own theology is an immensely important topic, since he stands at the
head of a Latin Christian tradition. Tertullian certainly writes first and fore-
most as a Christian under persecution. His writings, however, also betray
how indebted he is as an African to his own non-Roman heritage.[107] It is
hoped that future studies can further explore both his African heritage and
his impact on later Christian history. Before concluding this chapter on Tertullian, we can briefly discuss how Tertullian and his fellow Christians from
this time shaped the African tradition that followed.

Legacy and later trajectories

We ended Chapter 3 by mentioning how one recent group of scholars have
concluded,

> Like the disciples of Origen, though in a radically different way, these
> African theologians formed a school. Whereas those Greeks focused
> their concern with salvation on the nature of the Godhead and its mani-
> festation in Christ, these Latins worried about the adequacy of human
> organizations and ministers to mediate the divine life.[108]

In other words, "African Christianity developed a distinct and distinguished
school of theology."[109] What was taught within said school? These authors
continue:

> African theology focused on the role of the church as the medium of
> Christ's salvific work and therefore on the church's holiness and the

efficacy of its rituals. Concern over the qualifications of the ministers for discharging their offices drove conflicts over the practices of congregations. . . . Thus the preoccupation with the nature and role of the church as the continuing presence of Christ on earth resulted in the development of a distinctive African theology that regularly puzzled and even alarmed Christians in Italy and Gaul. Yet it became the dominant theology of Western Christianity.[110]

The characteristics of the African school listed here can be detected even in the earliest sources discussed in this chapter.

The importance of the church can even be seen in the earliest African martyrdoms. Although the word church (*ecclesia*) does not appear in the *Acts of the Scillitan Martyrs*, it is clear that the text itself is preserved for liturgical usage. The *Passion of Perpetua and Felicity* explicitly begins and ends by celebrating how the martyrs exhibit the gifts of the Spirit, given "for the good of the Church [*ad instrumentum Ecclesiae*]."[111] Tertullian will likewise celebrate the church as "Mother," which is not entirely unique, but it is a concept that he shapes in a unique way that will form an important axiom for later African Christians.[112]

The early African Christian sources depict the church in opposition to the evil forces of the world.[113] This theme, of course, is also found in non-African Christian sources, but it is one that takes on a special prominence in these sources. As we have seen, the boundary between the various identities at play in these texts is in fact porous: Africans are Roman in a sense, and Christians are in the world. These early Christian texts, however, record a church that is striving to establish a firm boundary between itself and outsiders. The role of baptism, then, is already of utmost importance: Perpetua and her fellow martyrs must be baptized in the dungeon, even though they will soon be baptized in blood; likewise, Tertullian sees baptism as necessary for salvation, and he even clarifies that *the* church's baptism is the only one that counts – heretical baptism is no baptism at all.[114] This view of heretical baptism will become a prominent point of debate between Cyprian and the bishop of Rome, and then later between the Donatists and the "Catholic" party.

Just as baptism, as an entry into the church, becomes an important doctrine, so one's continuation in the church is of utmost importance. The "most blessed [*beatissimi*]" state is that of martyrdom,[115] and so Tertullian insists that Christians should prefer the dungeon to the world. In fact, the world itself is a prison, and so the incarcerated Christians have left a prison as much as they have entered one.[116] The prison and the world remain under the domain of the devil, whose relationship with the ostensible head of state, the emperor, is only insinuated.[117] Christians, therefore, are called to give their lives in the "battle [*congressi*]" and "war [*bellum*]" against their enemy.[118] Tertullian is not the first to use military language to describe Christianity (cf. Eph. 6:11–17), and the duality between the world and the church is a tension felt throughout Christian history. The African school, nevertheless, continues to use these motifs with special vehemence in succeeding generations.

Because African Christians "should be in the world [*saeculo*], but are not of it,"[119] one of the chief concerns expressed by them is protecting the boundary between the two. The importance of holiness and purity continues to be a theme in the generations that follow, and even when the empire supports Christianity, the relationship between the church and "the world [*saeculum*]" will continue to be an ongoing concern for African Christians.

Along with this church/world opposition, there is a concern in these early African sources with those who handed the Christians over to the Roman officials (discussed on pp. 93–96). In the *Passion of Perpetua and Felicity*, Saturus was not originally arrested with the other Christians, but he "handed himself over [*se . . . tradiderat*]" to the officials.[120] It should be noted that surrendering oneself for martyrdom is frequently denounced by early Christian writers. This statement in the text, therefore, has even more credibility as a historical datum because of the criterion of embarrassment. The narrator evidently does not see Saturus's action as problematic, probably because Saturus was the teacher of these catechumens and so he should be with them for their baptism – of water and of blood. Perpetua and her fellow martyrs were especially celebrated in later African Christianity. What impact did this depiction of martyrdom have on those later Christians? Much later, some in the African Christian tradition (i.e. the Donatists) will even be accused of excessive zeal for martyrdom: they allegedly sought out martyrdom from Roman soldiers, and they would even commit suicide and claim it was martyrdom.[121] Although these accusations are likely exaggerated, they do indicate the value of martyrdom for those in the African school. Any who would "hand over" the martyrs, the scriptures, or any other sacred items of the church will be deemed a *traditor* (literally "one who hands over," but eventually a "traitor"), and the problem of *traditores* will be at the heart of the Donatist controversy.[122]

We can now turn to the rest of the third-century African school to see how these characteristics found among the earliest African Christians and in Tertullian developed even further in writers like Cyprian.

Notes

1 See Andrew McGowan, "Tertullian and the 'Heretical' Origins of the 'Orthodox' Trinity," *Journal of Early Christian Studies* 14 (4, 2006), 437–457.
2 *Church History* 2.2.4: "a man well versed in the laws of the Romans, and in other respects of high repute, and one of those especially distinguished in Rome" (trans. NPNF[2] 1:106).
3 Barnes, *Tertullian*, 22–29.
4 For example, this was the view of T. F. Torrence, *Theological Dialogue* 1:91–107, cited and discussed in Jason Robert Radcliff, *Thomas F. Torrance and the*

Church Fathers: A Reformed Evangelical and Ecumenical Reconstruction of the Patristic Tradition (Cambridge: James Clarke & Co., 2015), 180.

5 See esp. Sider, *Ancient Rhetoric and the Art of Tertullian*; and Fredouille, *Tertullien et la conversion de la culture antique*. Tertullian seems to follow Quintillian most closely. It is of interest for the present study that Quintillian himself listed "Domitian the African" and Julius Africanus (son of the general who defeated the Carthaginians) as esteemed orators. Unfortunately, very little is known about Domitian, whom Quintillian claims was the "most excellent [*praestantissimi*]" orator (*The Orator's Education* 10.1.118).

6 *Against Marcion* 1.1.3–4 (Evans' trans., slightly modified).

7 Ian Balfour, "Tertullian and Roman Law: What Do We (not) Know?", *Studia Patristica* (forthcoming). Cf. Strabo, *Geography* 17.3.24, who mentions how some provinces, including "Libya," were permitted to keep their "ancestral laws [πατρίους νόμους]" (LCL 267:212–213).

8 *Prescript Against the Heretics* 7.9: *Quid ergo Athenis et Hierosolymis?*

9 Cf. *On the Flesh of Christ* 5.

10 H. Richard Niebuhr, *Christ and Culture* (New York: Harper & Brothers, 1951).

11 *On the Apparel of Women* 1.3.3.

12 Pierre Bühler, "Tertullian: The Teacher of the *credo quia absurdum*," in *Kierkegaard and the Patristic and Medieval Traditions*, ed. Jon Stewart (Aldershot, England: Ashgate, 2008), 136.

13 See James Moffatt, "Aristotle and Tertullian," *Journal of Theological Studies* 17 (1915–1916), 170–171; and Robert D. Sider, "Credo quia absurdum?" *Classical World* 73 (1980), 417–419. Also, see Fredouille, *Tertullien*, 326–337.

14 *On the Flesh of Christ* 5: *credibile est, quia ineptum est.*

15 *Lives of Illustrious Men* 53.

16 *Apology* 18.4; 50.15; *On Penance* 1.1; *To Scapula* 5.5; *On the Resurrection of the Flesh* 59.3; *On Patience* 1.1.

17 Rebillard, *Christians*, 10, still believes he was a presbyter, based on *On the Soul* 9.4.

18 In Jerome, *Lives of Illustrious Men* 53.

19 See Burns, Jensen, et al., *Christianity in Roman Africa*, 233–293, for primary texts and discussion for the following paragraph.

20 Tabbernee, *Fake Prophecy and Polluted Sacraments: Ecclesiastical and Imperial Reactions to Montanism* (Leiden: Brill, 2007),131, believes that Tertullian was both the head of a house-church and a lay elder.

21 It must be admitted, however, that the evidence for the *seniores laici* in Tertullian's time is at best limited: see possible references in *Apology* 39.4–5 and *Passion of Perpetua* 12.

22 Brent D. Shaw, "The Elders of Christian Africa," in *Mélanges offerts à R.P. Etienne Gareau* (Numéro spéciale de cahiers des études anciennes; Ottowa: Editions de l'Université d'Ottowa, 1982), 207–226; and Shaw, "The Structure of the Local Society in the Early Maghrib: the Elders," *The Maghreb Review* 16 (1–2 1991), 18–54 (both essays reprinted in Shaw, *Rulers, Nomads and Christians in Roman North Africa* [Aldershot: Variorum, 1995]).

23 Eve MacDonald, *Hannibal: A Hellenistic Life* (New Haven, CT: Yale University Press, 2015), 19. Also, cf. Aristotle, *Politics* 2.8, for the constitution of Carthage and the role of the "Council of Elders [γερουσίαν]."

24 See Gerald Bray, *Holiness and the Will of God: Perspectives on the Theology of Tertullian* (London: Marshall, Morgan, and Scott, 1979), 10–11; and William Tabbernee, *Prophets and Gravestones: An Imaginative History of Montanists and Other Early Christians* (Peabody, MA: Hendrickson Publishers, 2009), 94; for more general bibliography on Tertullian's "Montanism," see Wilhite, "Tertullian and the Spirit of Prophecy," in *Tertullian and Paul*, ed. Todd D. Still and David E. Wilhite (London: T&T Clark, 2013), 45–50.

25 Key Pauline passages include Rom. 7:14, 15:27, 1 Cor. 3:1–3, 9:11, 2 Cor. 1:12, 10:14. The label, however, is not limited to Pauline texts; cf. 1 Pet., 2:11, Jude 1:23; and 2 Clem. 14.

26 *Fake Prophecy*, 151.

27 Cf. *Against Marcion* 1.19.4; *Exhortation to Chastity* 8–9.

28 *On Fasting* 1.3 should not be forced to say more than it does; *On Monogamy* never mentions the Phrygian prophets, but only speaks of Jesus's "new prophecy" in reference to Matt. 19:8–9.

29 E.g. Cyprian, *Letter* 39.1.2; cf. Pontius, *Life of Cyprian* 12; *Martyrdom of Montanus and Lucius* 5, 7–8, 11, 21; *Martyrdom of Marian and James* 5–8, 11; Arnobius (cited in Jerome, *Chronicle* 327); the *Martyrdom of Maximian and Isaac* 8–9; *Martyrdom of Marculus* 10; Victor of Vita, *History of the Vandal Persecution* 2.18–22; many others in Carthage during the Byzantine reconquest (according to Procopius, *History of the Wars* 3.21). Also, see Dossey, *Peasant and Empire*, 289 n.118, who finds prophecy to continue among the Donatists, especially the women, as evidenced by references in the anonymous Donatist sermons (cf. a similar report, not discussed by Dossey, in Procopius, *History of the Wars* 4.8, about the Mauretanian women who opposed the Byzantines). The question of prophecy and "Montanists" also raises an issue that deserves further attention: the Donatists were often labeled "Montanists" in the sources. Sometimes, this is a confusion over their title *Montenses* ("hill-dwellers" in Optatus, *Against the Donatists* 2.4.3–5). There may, however, be more connections between these two historically distinct groups (see further discussion on pp. 204–205 in chapter seven).

30 Michael Bland Simmons, *Universal Salvation in Late Antiquity: Porphyry of Tyre and the Pagan-Christian Debate* (Oxford: Oxford University Press, 2015), 58.

31 See argument and earlier bibliography in Wilhite, "Identity, Psychology, and the *Psychici*: Tertullian's 'Bishop of Bishops,' " 1–26.

32 Douglas Powell, "Tertullianists and Cataphrygians," *Vigiliae Christianae* 29 (1975), 33–54; and Rankin, *Tertullian and the Church*.

33 L. J. van der Lof, "The Plebs of the *Psychici*: Are the *Psychici* of De Monogomia Fellow-Catholics of Tertullian?" in *Eulogia: Mélanges offerts à Antoon A.R. Bastiaensen à l'occasion de son soixante-cinquième anniversaire*, ed. G.J.M. Bartelink, A. Hilhorst, and C. H. Kneepkens (Steenbrugis: In Abbatia S. Petri, 1991), 353–363. Tabbernee, *Fake Prophecies*, 66, suggests that what scholars consider an *ecclesiola in ecclesia* may have simply been a house-church – but he stresses that Tertullian mentions no "Montanist church" nor "Montanist clergy." Along these lines, Rebillard, *Christians*, 10, denies a monepiscopate in pre-Cyprianic North Africa. Aside from a certain Optatus (mentioned in *The Passion of Perpetua* 13.6), and Agrippinus (mentioned by Cyprian, *Letter* 71.4.1), there is no bishop named, and there is never an attempt to construct a list of episcopal succession. "Thus, it is more likely that there were several Christian organizations that were independent, though sharing a common sense of belonging to the church" (Rebillard, *Christians*, 10). Along these lines, Allen Brent, *Hippolytus and the Roman Church in the Third Century* (Lieden: Brill, 1995), 454–457, thinks Pontian (r.231–235) was the first monarchical bishop of Rome; cf. Brent's views on the late development of the monepiscopate in Carthage in Brent, *Cyprian and Roman Carthage*, esp. 250–289.

34 I have elsewhere argued against any notion that Tertullian belonged to a faction within the Carthaginian church on the grounds that Tertullian's opponents are not in Carthage: Wilhite, "Identity, Psychology, and the *Psychici*"; and Wilhite, *Tertullian the African*. Tabbernee, *Fake Prophecy*, 66–67, surveys the Carthaginian possibilities.

35 For Tertullian's positive reception before Jerome, see Eusebius, *Church History* 2.2.4; Lactantius, *The Divine Institutes* 5.1; 5.4; Optatus, *Against the Donatists* 1.9; Jerome, *Chronicle* 16.23–24 (PL 27); and Augustine, *Letter* 27*.3. More generally, for citations (credited or otherwise) of Tertullian, see the lengthy collection in the table of CCL 1, and discussions in Jérôme Lagouanere and Sabine Fialon (eds.), *Tertullianus Afer: Tertullien et la literature chrétienne d'Afrique (IIe-Vie siècles)* (Instrumenta Patristica et Mediaevalia 70; Turnhout: Brepols, 2015).

36 Augustine certainly knows Jerome's work from at least as early as 395 (*Letter* 28), and he in all likelihood read Tertullian in light of Jerome's claims in *On Illustrious Men*, which was completed in 394. Therefore, Augustine's Tertullian is the heretic outlined by Jerome, and so he always reads Tertullian as a "Cataphrygian" or Montanist. Writing in 414, Augustine, *On the Excellence of Widowhood* 4.6 (trans. WSA 1/9:116), states, "This is what led in particular to the growth of the Cataphrygian and Novatianist heresies, swollen by the noisy, mindless puffing of Tertullian [*hinc enim maxime cataphrygarum ac novatianorum haereses tumuerunt, quas buccis sonantibus, non sapientibus etiam tertullianus inflavit*]"; cf. 5.6 (trans. WSA 1/9:117): "Otherwise, we shall condemn even first marriages, which not even the Cataphrygians or the Novatianists, or their most eloquent instructor Tertullian dared to say were dishonorable [*alioquin etiam primas nuptias condemnabimus, quas nec cataphryges nec novatiani nec disertissimus eorum astipulator tertullianus turpes ausus est dicere*]." Also, see where Augustine, *Against Adversaries of the Law and the Prophets* 2.9.32 (written c.418), addresses Tertullian's rejection of second marriages, but with no elaboration. Augustine does, however, cite Tertullian favorably when denouncing idolatry (*City of God* 7.1; cf. Tertullian, *Apology* 13.2/*To the Nations* 2.9.5); after doing so, he immediately begins to attack the Roman gods in particular (7.2).

37 Reported in Jerome, *The Lives of Illustrious Men* 53 (trans. NPNF[2] 3).

38 For a general introduction and bibliography to feminist readings of Christian origins up to Tertullian's period, see Elizabeth A. Castelli, "Heteroglossia, Hermeneutics, and History: A Review Essay of Recent Feminist Studies of Early Christianity," *Journal of Feminist Studies in Religion* 10 (Fall 1994), 73–98.

39 *On the Apparel of Women* 1.1.1–2.

40 Defenses (or at least nuanced readings) of Tertullian include F. Forrester Church, "Sex and Salvation in Tertullian," *Harvard Theological Review* 68 (1975), 83–101; Suzanne Heine, *Women and Early Christianity* (London: SCM Press, 1987), 28; Karen Jo Torjesen, "Tertullian's 'Political Ecclesiology' and Women's Leadership," *Studia patristica* 21 (Louvain: Peeters, 1989), 277–282; Elizabeth Carnelly, "Tertullian and Feminism," *Theology* 92 (1989), 31–35; Marie Turcan, "Être femme selon Tertullien," *Vita Latina* 119 (September 1990), 15–21; and Daniel L. Hoffman, *The Status of Women and Gnosticism in Ireneaus and Tertullian* (Studies in Women and Religion 36; Lewiston, NY: E. Mellen Press, 1995), 148.

41 Heffernan, *The Passion of Perpetua*, 40.

42 *The Passion of Perpetua*, 40. Heffernan then helpfully reviews the evidence in Tertullian (p. 41).

43 Examples include his treatment of the Cainite teacher, who he calls a female "viper," in *On Baptism* 1.

44 *On the Soul* 9.

45 *On the Apparel of Women* 1 and 2 (see esp. 2.4.1–2 for this interpretation).

46 *Chronicle* 16.23–24 (PL 27; my trans.); cf. *The Lives of Illustrious Men* 53 (trans. NPNF[2] 3:373, "proconsul or centurion").

47 S. L. Greenslade, *Early Latin Theology* (London: SCM Press, 1956), 23; cf. Osborn, *Tertullian: First Theologian of the West*.

48 Schöllgen, *Ecclesia Sordida?* 184, concludes that he would have been of equestrian status.
49 *On the Cloak* (discussed on pp. 66 and 132).
50 Barnes, *Tertullian*.
51 *Apology* 9.2 (trans. ANF 3:24–25): *Infantes penes Africam Saturno immolabantur palam usque ad proconsulatum Tiberii . . . teste militia patriae nostrae, quae id ipsum munus illi proconsuli functa est.*
52 *On the Veiling of Virgins* 17.9.
53 See chapter two, p. 55, for the references.
54 *Chronicle* 16.23–24.
55 *To the Nations* (early 197), *Apology* (later in 197), and *To Scapula* (212); cf. *On the Cloak* (date uncertain; perhaps 205).
56 *To Scapula* 1.
57 *To Scapula* 2.2. What Tertullian meant by "rights," of course, needs further analysis since he certainly did not think in terms of modern subjective rights. I am indebted to Robert Wilken for pointing out the role Tertullian played in later thinkers on this subject.
58 *On Idolatry* (196), *On the Shows* (196), *To the Martyrs* (197), *To the Wife* (198), *On Prayer* (198), *On Penance* (198), *On Patience* (198), *On the Apparel of Women* (205, but book 2 possibly written in 196), *On the Military Crown* (208), *Exhortation to Chastity* (209), and *On Fleeing Persecution* (209).
59 *On Baptism* (198), *Testimony on the Soul* (198), *Prescript Against the Heretics* (203), *Against Hermogenes* (204), *The Scorpian's Sting* (204), *On the Flesh of Christ* (206), *Against the Valentinians* (207), *On the Soul* (207), *On the Resurrection of the Flesh* (207), and *Against Marcion* (208, but written in stages). Cf. *Against the Jews* (197).
60 *Against Praxeas, On Fasting, On Monogomy,* and *On Modesty* (all likely written in 210). Other works are often deemed "Montanist." For the list of Montanist characteristics of different treatises, see Barnes, *Tertullian*, 43–44.
61 This is a skill taught in the rhetorical schools (e.g. Cicero, *To Gaius Herennius: On the Theory of Public Speaking* 2.2).
62 Cf. *On the Veiling of Virgins* 6 and *On the Flesh of Christ* 23. See discussion in Otten, "Tertullian's Rhetoric of Redemption: Flesh and Embodiment in *De carne Christi* and *De resurrectione mortuorum*," *Studia Patristica* 65 (2013), 331–348; and Dunn, "Rhetoric and Tertullian: A Response," *Studia Patristica* 65 (2013), 349–356.
63 Geoffrey D. Dunn, "Tertullian, Paul, and the Nation of Israel," in *Tertullian and Paul*, ed. Todd D. Still and David E. Wilhite (London: T&T Clark, 2013), 97.
64 Cf. *Against Valentinus* and *Against Hermogenes*; also see his *On the Soul*. Because Tertullian uses Stoic thought, he is normally read as believing in a corporeal soul. This needs much more careful nuance, however, because for Tertullian "corporeal" does not mean tangible or material.
65 *To Scapula* 2.6.
66 As was *To Scapula* and ostensibly even *Apology* 1.1, "Rulers of the Roman Empire [*Romani imperii antistites*]."
67 *To the Nations* 2.17.18–19 (emphasis added).
68 The last major treatment of Tertullian's theology is Robert E. Roberts, *The Theology of Tertullian* (London: Epworth Press, 1924); however, see the helpful study by Osborne, *Tertullian: First Theologian of the West*, whose focus on Tertullian's philosophy has done much to repair this problem. Also, recommended are Frédéric Chapot, *Virtus veritatis: Langage et vérité dans l'Oeuvre de Tertullien* (Paris: Etudes augustiniennes, 2009); and sections throughout Burns, Jensen, et al., *Christianity in Roman Africa*.
69 *On the Apparel of Women*.

70 Although see *On Modesty* 21–22.
71 *On Modesty* 1.7–9 (trans. ANF1).
72 E.g. *To the Martyrs* 2, 5; *Apology* 5.2, 18.2, 20.1–2; 26.1; 42.2.
73 *On the Shows* 8.9.
74 Tertullian, *To the Martyrs* 2.5 (my trans.): *sitis in saeculo, qui extra saeculum estis.*
75 Cf. Lactantius (discussed in chapter six) and Augustine's *City of God* (discussed in chapter eight).
76 *On the Shows* 8.10, "even the places themselves, we maintain, become defiled. The polluted things pollute us [*et ipsa loca contaminari altercati sumus: de contaminatis contaminamur*]."
77 This does not mean tangible materiality, something misunderstood by Augustine in his criticisms of Tertullian. See, for example, Augustine, *On Heresies* 86. For full treatment of Augustine's reception of Tertullian, see Chapot, "Tertullian," in *Augustine Through the Ages*, ed. Allan Fitzgerald (Grand Rapids, MI: Eerdmans, 1999), 822–824.
78 However, Tertullian's understanding of the Spirit's participation in the baptismal waters themselves is layered and complex; see *On Baptism* 4–7.
79 See *On Baptism* 13, where, after celebrating Christ's birth, death, and resurrection (i.e. in an incarnate body) he speaks of "a certain clothing for the faith which had previously been naked [*vestimentum quodammodo fidei quae retro erat nuda*]" (my trans.) In this instance he is speaking of baptism (i.e. a clothing of oneself in Christ; see Gal. 3:27), but he elsewhere insists that real clothes also must be affected by one's faith: Christian virtue should "flow out from the soul to the clothes [*emanet ab animo in habitum*]" (*On the Apparel of Women* 2.13.3 [my trans.]).
80 On the demonic contagion in these, see examples in *On Modesty* 9.8–15; *On Fasting* 2.3, 2.5, 8.3. On discipline, see examples in *On Modesty* 1.5, 10.9; *On Fasting* 1.2, 6.2; and *On Monogamy* 2.1–3.
81 *Apology* 50.12–16 (ANF 3 trans. slightly altered).
82 The sacrificial role of the martyrs can be found in earlier writers like Ignatius (e.g. *To the Romans* 2).
83 *On the Shows* 1.1.
84 *On the Shows* 30.1.
85 Much of the following material has been adapted from my *Tertullian the African* (2007).
86 *On the Cloak* 4.1 (trans. ANF 4:8).
87 *On the Cloak* 1.1: *Principes semper Africae, viri Carthaginenses, vetustate nobiles, novitate felices, gaudeo vos tam prosperos temporum, cum ita vacat ac iuvat habitus denotare: pacis haec et annonae et otia: ab imperio et a caelo bene est* (text in Vincent Hunink, *Tertullian, De Pallio: A Commentary* ([Amsterdam: J.C. Gieben, 2005]; trans. ANF 4:5).
88 Hunink, *Tertullian*, 68:

> The text shows a remarkable contrast between the local African culture (of Carthage and other towns), and the Roman culture that has become dominant in the whole world. . . . the contrast with Rome is further sharpened by rather sinister references to its history.

89 *On the Cloak* 1.1: *Tamen et vobis habitus aliter olim, tunicae fuere.*
90 *On the Cloak* 1.1: *et si quid praeterea condicio uel dignitas uel temporalitas vestit; pallium tamen generaliter, vestrum.* Hunink, *Tertullian*, 71, comments, "The contrast between 'Carthage' and 'Rome' still remains implicit here." Later, Hunink adds (84), "The speaker drives home his point by expressly repeating the Carthaginian origin of the old *pallium*."

91 *On the Cloak* 1.3; with reference to Virgil, *Aeneid* 1.14, 3.415.
92 Hunink, *Tertullian*, 87.
93 *On the Cloak* 2.1: *Sit nunc aliunde res, ne Poenicum inter Romanos aut erubescat aut doleat.* This and other passages lead L. E. Elliot-Binns, *The Beginnings of Western Christendom* (London: Lutterworth Press, 1948), 151, to conclude, "In [Tertullian] the characteristics of the African Church and of the Phoenician people, of whom he was so proud, are combined."
94 *On the Cloak* 1.2: *de habitu . . . Romanum praecoca.* For the toga as a common symbol of Roman power, see Virgil, *Aeneid* 1.282, "The Romans, lords of the world, and the nation of the toga [*Romanos, rerum dominus, gentemque togatam*]." This passage is quoted by Martial in his allusion to Domitian, *Epigrammaton* 14.124: "He that gave the stars to his great father makes the Romans lords of the world and people of the gown [*Romanos rerum dominos gentemque togatam ille facit, magno qui dedit astra patri*]."
95 *On the Cloak* 6.2: *Gaude, pallium, et exsulta! . . . ex quo Christianum vestire coepisti* (my trans.)
96 Bray, *Holiness and the Will of God*, 8; and see discussion in Hunink, *Tertullian*, 10.
97 Matt. 12:42/Luke 11:31 (ESV).
98 Church, "Sex and Salvation," 97 n. 59.
99 See details in chapters seven and eight.
100 See where he brags of how far the gospel has spread, even into "Africa . . . [to] the Gaetulians and the many territories of the Moors" (*Against the Jews* 7.4 [trans. Dunn, *Tertullian*, 79]).
101 Sider, *Ancient Rhetoric*, 117–118; and Tilley, "The Passion of Perpetua and Felicity," in *Searching the Scriptures*, vol. 2 *A Feminist Commentary*, ed. Elisabeth Schüssler Fiorenza (New York: Crossroad, 1994), 845. cf. Fannius, who wrote down all the crimes and victims of Nero (see Pliny, *Letter* 5.5).
102 See *To Scapula* 3.4, where Tertullian names the proconsul under whom the Scillitans were persecuted. In *On the Soul* 55, he names Perpetua. Both are typically dated later than *To the Martyrs*.
103 He knows Acts, and even cites the Pentecost passage of how "those inhabiting parts of Africa beyond Cyrene" heard the gospel (*Against the Jews* 7.4; ref. Acts 2:10).
104 *To the Martyrs* 4.6: *ne in manus inimici perveniret.*
105 *To the Martyrs* 4.7.
106 On Lucretia, see Ovid, *The Book of Days* 2.807, where Sextus Tarquinus is portrayed as saying, "Resistance is vain . . . I'll rob thee of honour and life [*nil agis eripiam . . . per crimina vitam*]"; cf. Ovid's own retort (2.811–812), "Why victor dost thou joy? This victory will ruin thee. Alack, how dear a single night did cost thy kingdom! [*quid, victor, gaudes? haec te victoria perdet. heu quanto regnis nox stetit una tuis!*]" The incident is credited with the establishment of the end of the Roman monarchy. See also Valerius Maximus, *Memorable Doings and Sayings* 6.1.1, for one of his thirteen examples of "modesty [*pudicitia*]":

> Lucretia, model of Roman chastity, whose manly spirit by Fortune's malignant error was allotted a woman's body, was forcibly raped by Sex. Tarquinius, son of king Superbus. In a family council, after bitterly bemoaning her injury, she killed herself with a sword she had brought concealed in her clothing and by so courageous a death gave the Roman people reason to change the authority of kings for that of Consuls [*Dux Romanae pudicitiae Lucretia, cuius virilis animus maligno errore fortunae muliebre corpus sortitus est, a Sex. Tarquinio regis Superbi filio per vim stuprum pati coacta, cum grauissimis uerbis iniuriam suam in concilio necessariorum*

deplorasset, ferro se, quod ueste tectum adtulerat, interemit causamque tam animoso interitu imperium consulare pro regio permutandi populo Romano praebuit].

Lucretia is the only one on Valerius's list who is mentioned by Tertullian. Cf. Florus, *The Epitome of Roman History* 1.3, for Lucretia viewed as *pudicitia* by the gods, and Hans-Friedrich Mueller, " *Vita, Pudicitia, Libertas*: Juno, Gender, and Religious Politics in Valerius Maximus," *Transactions of the American Philological Association* 128 (1998), 228n.19, and 227n.17, for "germane to religious ritual." Susan Dixon, *Reading Roman Women: Sources, Genres, and Real Life* (London: Duckworth, 2000), 46, describes Lucretia as "the embodiment of the prime virtues of the Roman matron." Additionally, Barbette Stanley Spaeth, *The Roman Goddess Ceres* (Austin, TX: University of Texas Press, 1996), 115, says Lucretia was the Roman heroine antithetical to Dido because of her chastity. As for Cleopatra, the claim that she resisted Rome is somewhat dubious given her allegiance to Antony; it is a distinction, however, that Tertullian the rhetorician did not need to acknowledge. For "tyranny," see the account of Leaena by Pliny, *Natural History* 7.23, where she "refused to betray tyrannicides" [*non indicavit tyrannicides*]."

107 Michael Bland Simmons, *Arnobius of Sicca: Religious Conflict and Competition in the Age of Diocletian* (Oxford: Clarendon Press, 1995), 201, finds that Tertullian (like Arnobius after him) used characteristics of Punic Baal to describe the Christian God.

108 Burns, Jensen, et al., *Christianity in Roman Africa*, xlvi–xlvii. Cf. Arthur Cleveland Coxe, *Institutes of Christian History: An Introduction to Historic Reading and Study* (Chicago: A.C. McClurg and Company, 1887), 59, who spoke of the "Punic school," beginning with Tertullian and Cyprian, and continuing with later African writers like Arnobius, Lactantius, and Augustine.

109 Burns, Jensen, et al., *Christianity in Roman Africa*, xlvii.

110 Burns, Jensen, et al., *Christianity in Roman Africa*, xlviii.

111 *Passion of Perpetua* 1.5; cf. 21.11, *in aedificationem Ecclesiae*.

112 See Rankin, *Tertullian*, 79–82.

113 Cf. Minucius Felix, *Octavius* 26–27.

114 *On Baptism* 15.2; *On Modesty* 19.5.

115 *Passion of Perpetua* 21.11.

116 *To the Martyrs* 2.

117 Tertullian, *To the Martyrs* 1.4; *Passion of Perpetua* 20.1 (cf. 4.4, 4.7, 10.6).

118 Tertullian, *To the Martyrs* 1.4–5.

119 Tertullian, *To the Martyrs* 2.5 (cited on p. 121).

120 *Passion of Perpetua* 4.5.

121 See chapter seven.

122 For the Donatist use of the *Passion of Perpetua*, see Kitzler, *From "Passio Perpetuae,"* 106–109.

5 Cyprian and the later third century

It is in the third century that African Christians more explicitly claim their own tradition, and in so doing they add to and develop what has been called the "African school." Sources from the third century provide many different windows into African Christianity. In the following chapter we will examine many different kinds of sources, such as dialogues, treatises, letters, inscriptions, and more martyrdoms. It is important that we attempt to hear each source on its own terms, and yet at the same time we will find certain themes running throughout this century, such as the need to defend the faith from non-Christian attack. In addition to hearing these diverse concerns, we will note how these Christians often display a specifically African identity. Let us begin with one African whose text is set in Rome.

Minucius Felix

Sometime after Tertullian, Minucius Felix wrote one surviving text, known as the *Octavius*.[1] This text's survival is somewhat of a historical accident: it was mistakenly included as the "eighth" (Latin = *octavus*) book of a later African writer.[2] Octavius is in fact the main character in the work. Virtually nothing is known about the author, who appears in the work as one of the characters and the narrator.[3] The consensus view is that he is from Cirta in North Africa.[4] Inscriptions survive from this town (modern Constantine, Algeria) that name a local magistrate, Q. Caecilius Natalis, and that are dated to 210. This is remarkable since (the same?) "Caecilius Natalis" serves as one of the dialogue partners in the work.[5] In the dialogue, Caecilius refers to "our friend of Cirta [*Cirtensis nostri*],"[6] who later in the work is identified as "Fronto."[7] This of course is the famous rhetorician from Cirta, Marcus Cornelius Fronto, who became senator in Rome and a patron to his hometown in Africa.[8] In addition to the connection with Cirta in particular, there are connections with this text and other parts of Africa. An inscription naming a certain "Octavius Januarius" survives from Saldae (modern Béjaïa, Algeria, west of Cirta on the coast).[9] Likewise, the (same person's?) name, Minucius Felix,[10] survives in inscriptions from Tebessa (southeast of Cirta)[11] and Carthage.[12]

The main character, Octavius, is commemorated in the opening, for he has recently died. Minucius Felix, the narrator and witness of the dialogue, recalls their past life in which they had an intimate relationship.[13] Then, when they both converted from the "darkness into the light," Octavius did not "reject me as a companion [*non respuit comitem*]."[14] This may be more than a relationship of comrades: since Octavius is older and described in the role of a teacher, he may have been a mentor or tutor to Minucius Felix. Even in their new faith, he outpaced Minucius Felix, and as evidence of this, the dialogue is recalled where Caecilius was converted by Octavius's arguments.

Despite the African provenance of the main characters, the dialogue itself is set in Ostia, the port town near Rome. Octavius goes to Rome on business, after which the group of friends (including Minucius and Caecilius) walk down to the sea, and after bathing walk along the shore.[15] As they pass a statue of Serapis, Caecilius gestures a sign of reverence. Serapis, it should be noted, was an Egyptian deity who had been accommodated by the Greeks and then made popular around the empire. Septimius Severus even began to depict himself as Serapis in official imperial imagery as a way of taking on an identity beyond his provincial African background.[16] Caecilius's action, therefore, should not be considered exclusively as a religious gesture. It may be a form of embracing an identity that transcends Caecilius's African background. In response to Caecilius's gesture, Octavius remarked how such a "superstition" should be corrected among friends. They then walk by a group of boys competing for who could skip stones the furthest, which seems to be a metaphor for the contest to follow among these African friends. The real contest occurs when Caecilius demands that Octavius debate him about the appropriateness of worshipping the gods.

It should be clarified that the primary identities in this debate are those of Christian and non-Christian. The repeated statements about "your" practices are explicitly generalized, offering examples of non-Christian practices from various regions. This generalized dialogue, however, also includes many instances where the local and even African identities are invoked, and since these have received less attention in most discussions, they will be highlighted in what follows.

As Caecilius begins the debate, he focuses on "local gods."[17] Although the diverse provinces differ in which god they worship, they are all right to respect their ancestral traditions. The list of examples is curious, however, in that no mention is made of Africa. Instead, the focus ends with Rome's practice:

> the Eleusinians [worship] Ceres, the Phrygians the Great Mother, the Epidaurians Aesculapius, the Chaldaeans Bel, the Syrians Astarte, the Taurians Diana, the Gauls Mercury, the Romans one and all. Thus it is that their power and authority has embraced the circuit of the whole world.[18]

Later, Caecilius will repeat how "the commonwealth of Rome is protected and adored" by the gods.[19]

After acknowledging how certain philosophers reject the civic gods, Caecilius insists that most "atheists" belong to "a gang . . . of discredited and proscribed desperadoes."[20] They prefer illicit orgies, according to Caecilius, whose specific claims echo Tertullian's *Apology* and who reports all of the rumors and accusations about Christians.[21] Caecilius does not give credit to Tertullian (who let us remember is being cited by the author, Minucius Felix), but instead claims to have learned all this from Fronto, "our friend from Cirta."[22] Of the Christian God, furthermore, "Rome has no knowledge."[23] In fact, Caecilius asks, "Have not the Romans without your God empire and rule, do they not enjoy the whole world, and lord it over you?"[24]

Caecilius offers a pragmatic reason for worshipping the gods: those who do not, experience the consequences. In an extended list of examples from classical sources, he also mentions two instances that merit attention: "the fleet of Claudius and Junius, not in action against the Carthaginians, but in disastrous wreck; and did not Trasimene run red with blood of Romans because Flaminius despised the auguries?"[25] Claudius and Junius were consuls of Rome during the first Punic war, but they eschewed the traditional sacred rites and were respectively defeated in battle and drowned in a storm. The Roman consul Flaminius also ignored the gods' omens and then lost in a one-sided battle against Hannibal.[26] We should not make too much of these examples from the Punic war, since they are embedded in a much longer list. Moreover, the characters in this dialogue may have felt no sympathy with the Carthaginians from the Punic war, since their homeland of Numidia in fact sided with Rome against Hannibal.[27] Nevertheless, these examples do belong to a lengthy list of elements within this text that are peculiar to Africa. Octavius, for example, later responds to this statement: he admits that these leaders neglected to sacrifice, but other Roman leaders, like Regulus, did so and still lost to the Carthaginians in the first Punic war.[28] It is difficult, therefore, to imagine that these two examples invoked by Caecilius did not evoke an awareness of social identity since these are Africans who have come to Rome.

In short, Caecilius's primary argument is a practical one: worshipping the gods benefits the worshipper. His primary example is Rome, whose conquest of the world is credited to the gods.[29]

Octavius begins his response by calling attention to the order of the heavens and earth.[30] He even recites how various provinces are cared for by providence: namely, Britain, Egypt, Mesopotamia, and India.[31] As with Caecilius's list, Octavius omits any mention of Africa, as if they (or perhaps their audience) were standing in Africa looking abroad. Also like Caecilius, Octavius then draws the focus to Rome. Unlike Caecilius, however, Octavius does not speak of Rome's glory, but instead he mocks its heritage, referring to the "twins fighting for kingship over a few shepherds and a hut" – which are of course Romulus and Remus and the poor hilltops that will become the city of Rome.[32]

Octavius will later refer to these twins again. In response to the charge that Christians have inappropriate relations with their "brothers," Octavius quips, "you recognize no tie of brotherhood, except indeed for fratricidal murder."[33] The "you" here is ambiguous and could refer to "you non-Christians" or "you Romans." The latter is certainly emphasized since in this same passage, Octavius, as Tertullian had done with the toga, rejects the symbols of *Romanitas*, such as "your official titles and purples [*honores vestros et purpuras*]."[34] Perhaps the ambiguity is intentional, so that it insinuates Caecilius as having become Romanized, which is slandered as fratricidal, in addition to the primary opposition between Christian and non-Christian.

After Romulus and Remus, Octavius mentions the "Wars waged between son-in-law and father-in-law spread over the whole world," which refers to the civil war between Pompey and Julius Caesar.[35] Octavius returns to this civil war later, remembering how Caesar went "into Africa" to defeat his enemy.[36] Later in his argument, he will also contrast Roman heroes, namely Mucius Scaevola, Manius Aquilius, and Marcus Atilius Regulus.[37] The Christians display more courage and undergo more tortures than these failed Roman leaders, the last of whom died in Carthage during the first Punic war. These Roman heroes are the same ones that Tertullian discredited in *To the Martyrs*.[38]

Octavius then changes the subject from Rome to the nature of God. After emphasizing the reason for Christians' rejection of idolatry,[39] Octavius attacks polytheism[40] and idolatry[41] as foolish. Although the argument is dominated by classical Roman imagery of the gods, and even by examples from various provinces, Octavius again makes a very pointed reference to "Your own Jupiter himself sometimes stands beardless, at others portrayed with a beard; under the name of Hammon, he has horns."[42] This is a reference to Baal Hammon, the Punic god worshipped across North Africa, sometimes under the Romanized name of "Jupiter."[43] The translation "horns," while a natural read, should be informed by the many statues of Baal Hammon that survive where he wears a tall cornucopia-like crown,[44] an item sometimes described with the same term used by Octavius.[45] He later makes a similar statement about Juno, who is sometimes to be associated with the "Carthaginian [*Poenai*, i.e. Punic]" Tanit.[46] We should not make too much of such statements, since the dialogue lists many non-African deities as well. But these examples do show how the text can invoke the Punic background of these characters.

After he has turned from the general discussion of the gods, Octavius addresses Caecilius's specific claim that the gods have blessed Rome. Octavius returns to Caecilius's claims about "auspices and auguries," which at first glance appear to be directed toward non-Christian practice in general. The translator of the Loeb edition fails to include the adjective *Romana*, but it should be noted that Octavius is specifically targeting "*Roman* auspices and auguries [*auspicia et auguria Romana*]."[47] Octavius then counters Caecilius's argument with a very lengthy and negative assessment of Rome's origins and history. After doing so, he targets Roman imperialism, describing Rome's imperialism much more negatively than his opponent had done:

> Thenceforward it becomes the practice of all succeeding kings and leaders to dispossess neighbours of their territory, to overthrow adjoining states with their temples and their altars, to drive them into captivity, to wax fat on losses inflicted, and crimes committed. All that the Romans hold, occupy and possess is the spoil of outrage; their temples are all of loot, drawn from the ruin of cities, the plunder of gods and the slaughter of priests.[48]

Rather than seeing Rome's success as a gift of the gods as Caecilius had done, Octavius faults Rome for capturing so many peoples and plundering their temples. After this focus on Rome, Octavius then defends Christians of the rumors spread about them.[49]

One of the accusations made against Christians is that they eat babies. Octavius turns this accusation against the non-Christians, arguing that no one could believe such atrocities actually occurred unless that person was willing to practice them.[50] Who would sacrifice babies? Octavius insists that it is the non-Christians ("you [*vos*]") who do so by exposing infants, sometimes even strangling unwanted babies, and through abortion. The precedent is by Saturn himself who "devoured [*voravit*]" his children, a reference to the Greco-Roman myth of Cronos/Saturn.[51] The Roman Saturn, however, has been identified by this time with Punic Baal, and so Octavius can add how "in some parts of Africa infants were sacrificed to him."[52] Octavius even adds a very specific description about how the children were sacrificed, which may reflect local knowledge of this past event. This specific African example is followed by others from Egypt, Gaul, and once again Rome. The evidence against the Christians is said to be fabricated; these rumors are fabricated by individuals like "your own Fronto," who as mentioned on p. 4 was also from Cirta.[53]

When addressing the relationship of Christians to Jews, Octavius recommends that Caecilius read the primary sources, if not the Jewish scriptures, then Josephus, "or, if you prefer Romans, consult Antonius Julianus."[54] In other words, the opponents in this work are not only non-Christians; they are Roman non-Christians, whose identity stands in contrast to the African Christians. After then reviewing some of the Christians' teachings and virtues, Octavius concludes, and Caecilius himself is convinced and converted.[55]

In sum, Minucius Felix's work pits the Christian and non-Christian against each other in debate, but this debate is carried out by Africans who must also negotiate the pressure to align with Rome and its gods. Within this work, Minucius Felix (or "Octavius"), offers standard Christian theology, describing the divine attributes as would Justin Martyr or any Christian apologist.[56] Beyond these general Christian tenets, it is tempting to see the influence of African and specifically Punic understanding of God in some of these statements. For example, knowing that Baal Hammon (already mentioned in this text) was the sky god who ruled the world with his lightning and wind,[57] it is arguable that these attributes are reflected in Octavius's proof that one God is sovereign:

> herein is the ground of our belief that we can perceive him, though we cannot see. For in his works, and in the motions of the universe, we behold his ever-present energy; in the thunder and the lightning, in the thunderbolt or the clear sky. It is no cause for wonder if you see not God; wind and storm drive, toss, disorder all things, yet the eyes see not wind and storm.[58]

While the direct indebtedness to Punic thought could not be proven with the limited evidence available, it is worth exploring the possible connections between Punic religion and African Christian teachings, especially since scholars have made such connections for later African writers who read Minucius Felix, such as Arnobius and Lactantius (who will be discussed in Chapter 6). For now, we can turn to another African Christian who may have similar ties to a Punic background.

Cyprian

With Cyprian we turn to a figure who gives us more information about his context, beliefs, and practices than any of his predecessors.[59] Cyprian's works are numerous, and the surviving collection of eighty-two of his letters is unprecedented for this time, and so we can find many details in these personal correspondences that would otherwise not be known.[60] As bishop of Carthage during a decade that witnessed extreme persecution from non-Christians as well as numerous controversies within Christianity, Cyprian spoke to many important issues and thereby provides us with a picture of the North African church at this time. Cyprian operated at the hub of a vast network of bishops, a network that was primarily in the African provinces and then secondarily connected to other regions around the Mediterranean.

His deacon, Pontius, wrote a *Life* about Cyprian – in fact, it is the first *Vita* written about a Christian, which is itself noteworthy: "Out of Africa also came the first Christian biography."[61] Although Cyprian never mentions Pontius, Pontius claims to have been with Cyprian in his last days and to have witnessed his death.[62] Pontius neglects to tell us anything about Cyprian's birth and early life – which is very unusual for the genre. Because he was well educated[63] Cyprian must come from a wealthy family, and scholars estimate that he was born sometime around the beginning of the third century. Given his high level of education and his wealthy background, it is reasonable to assume that Cyprian is thoroughly Romanized. His literary and administrative skills become apparent after he becomes a Christian leader in Carthage. After discussing his life and writings, we will return to the question of his Carthaginian and African identity, which can be detected in addition to his *Romanitas*.

Cyprian's wealth, or "almost all" of it, was given to the poor around 246 when he converted to Christianity.[64] He then devoted himself to scripture and a life of strict Christian practice.[65] Almost immediately, according to Pontius, Cyprian was made a bishop,[66] something that Pontius has to admit goes against the normal Christian practice (cf. 1 Tim. 3:6).[67] Not everyone approved of him, however, for there was some controversy when he was elected bishop (c.248).[68]

Early in the 250s, a major plague occurred in Carthage and elsewhere in the empire. The event left countless people dying in the streets and numerous bodies unburied because everyone "fled to avoid contagion"[69] – that is, everyone but the Christians, whom Cyprian instructed to care for those in need, even non-Christians. In his work *On Mortality*, Cyprian describes the symptoms vividly.[70] In keeping with Tertullian's rejection of the Roman toga, Cyprian rejects the Roman funeral gown (*atras vestes*) for his community, because even those who die in the plague are already wear their "white robes [*indumenta alba*]" in heaven.[71]

Cyprian also emphasized charity. In his *On Works and Almsgiving*, he insists that Christ's mandate to give one's possessions to the poor (see Luke 12:33) applies to all Christians. In another instance, when some Numidian Christians were captured by "barbarians [*barbarorum*]," Cyprian collects a very sizable sum (100,000 sesterces) to ransom them.[72] Several times during his episcopacy, Cyprian instructs the clergy in Carthage to release church funds to the poor. His work endeared him to many in his church, although several controversies would result in several groups opposing him as well. Before turning to these controversies, we need to understand the persecution that functioned as the background to all three controversies.

Persecution

In 250 the new emperor, Decius, attempted to unite a troubled empire by having all citizens offer sacrifices on its behalf.[73] While this was not intended as a persecution of Christians exclusively, they were certainly the most affected group in the empire.[74] Decius, however, died the next year in battle[75] which brought a swift end to his order to sacrifice. Although the persecution had been short lived, it had made a significant impact on Christianity, especially in North Africa, because of the way it caused divisions among the churches.

Decius required that each person sacrifice in front of witnesses and receive a certificate of proof, a *libellus*. Altars were placed on the capitol for sacrifice, and five local officials in Carthage were to witness the sacrifice and sign the *libellus*.[76] Any who did not were put on trial by the local magistrate. If they continued to resist the edict, they were then sent to a second trial before the proconsul. Between these trials, the prisoners would have been imprisoned and even tortured. Although the sentence from the proconsul would have been exile,[77] many died from the torture and were celebrated by their fellow Christians as martyrs.[78]

In addition to the martyrs, there was another group known as the "confessors."[79] They had made their "confession" of Christ and so had already become a "witness": the Greek word *martys* means witness, but it early on came to signify those who had died bearing witness to Christ (cf. Rev. 6:9). These confessors, however, were not (yet) killed, and so they were classified differently, but because of their courage and endurance of persecution they were elevated to priestly status, at least unofficially, in the eyes of some Christians.

Those who offered the sacrifice were seen as apostates, ones who denied the faith. They were called "the lapsed [*lapsi*]," because they "fell" from grace. This group consisted of those who had actually sacrificed, also known as "the sacrificers [*sacrificati*]," and those who through bribery or other means obtained their *libellus*, and so were known as the *libellatici*.[80] Although they had not actually been contaminated by idols, these *libellatici* were still considered apostate because they had become false witnesses instead of martyrs.[81] A very large number of Christians in Carthage seemed to have fallen into this group, perhaps even the majority.[82]

During this persecution, Cyprian went into hiding. Scholars once believed that there must have been an earlier edict targeting bishops, but this is no longer the accepted view. Instead, it is believed that there was some sort of local outbreak of hostility because of the "pagans" or "foreign peoples (*gentilium*)"[83] in Carthage at which Cyprian was the center.[84] He went into voluntary exile[85] to an undisclosed location, and kept in communication through letters to his clergy.[86] Many criticized Cyprian for his exile at this time, claiming instead that he had fled persecution.[87] A generation before, Tertullian had forbidden such an act of cowardice.[88] Of course, Cyprian and his supporters did not view his actions in this way. In fact, Cyprian encouraged other Christians to do the same in order to avoid the risk of apostasy.[89] He responds to his critics by saying that those who did not flee chose to remain only in order to protect their property from being seized – in sum, they loved their money more than Christ.[90]

It does appear that the lower classes were less affected by Decius's edict. The group known as the *stantes* were those who never apostatized but did so by avoiding arrest and torture.[91] These were simply Christians who did not flee, but neither presented themselves at the forum and yet escaped notice of the officials.[92] Cyprian faced a controversy when the lapsed, including both *sacrificati* and *libellatici*, wanted to be readmitted into communion with the faithful.

Controversies

Three major controversies troubled Cyprian during his reign as bishop of Carthage. These controversies are outlined separately in what follows for the sake of convenience, while in actuality there would have been significant overlap in the chronology of events. They are all three related, and the problems all stem from the persecution mentioned in the previous section.

The first controversy is known as the Laxist controversy. When the lapsed Christians asked to be readmitted into communion with the faithful, Cyprian denied them forgiveness. To be sure, as a bishop who stood in the line of apostles, Cyprian believed he had the keys to "bind and loose," that is to condemn and to pardon sins.[93] The sin of apostasy, however, was one that he believed could not be forgiven on earth, since Jesus himself had stipulated, "but whoever denies me before others, I also will deny before my Father in heaven" (Matt. 10:33). Unless the lapsed were willing to confess Jesus on earth – and likely be martyred – Cyprian was in no position to give them assurance of their salvation.[94]

Some of the lapsed approached the confessors in prison, and asked them to intercede with Christ. Some of these confessors, moreover, suffered so severely that they would soon die and be directly in Christ's presence (cf. Rev. 6:9). With a promise in hand from these confessors, the lapsed insisted that Cyprian should now grant them readmission to communion. Although Cyprian remained firm in his stance,[95] other clergy agreed to grant forgiveness and communion to the lapsed.[96] Cyprian deemed this action by some of the clergy as direct opposition to him as bishop and to the true church in communion with him, an act which he ultimately regarded as schism.[97] He would label them the Laxists, those who were too "loose" and quick to forgive.[98]

To clarify, Cyprian's rigorist stance was not absolute. He believed that the lapsed could spend their life in a state of penance, hoping that Christ would have mercy on them despite their failures. He even agreed to grant communion on their death beds. In other words, Cyprian's opposition to the Laxists was a stance he took in the middle of the persecution: he insisted that to act rashly and grant communion was unwise since the persecution prevented him and his fellow bishops from gathering in a council to decide collectively how to respond to the lapsed. When given the opportunity to do so, Cyprian's fellow bishops preferred a more moderate position wherein the lapsed could be forgiven after three years of penance. Later, after Gallus became emperor in 252 many feared that another persecution was imminent,[99] and so another council of African bishops meeting under Cyprian agreed to grant forgiveness to all the lapsed who had remained in penance under supervision of the true church[100] – the true church, that is, as defined in opposition to the Laxist false church.

Meanwhile, in Rome a second controversy emerged that would mirror what Cyprian faced in Carthage, the Rigorist controversy. Cornelius had recently become bishop of Rome, and he too had to face the question about re-admitting lapsed Christians. Unlike Cyprian's initial rigorist stance, Cornelius was more lenient and granted forgiveness. This angered some in Rome, including some confessors, and so a group there denounced Cornelius and appointed Novatian as the new bishop.[101] Both Cornelius and Novatian wrote to request support from bishops in other cities. When Cyprian received an appeal from both to be recognized, he faced a dilemma: support Cornelius, who was seen as a Laxist, or support Novatian, who was understood to be a schismatic. Cyprian eventually decided that Cornelius was the rightly elected bishop, and therefore he denounced Novatian as a schismatic. Novatianists even established a church in Carthage, and so Cyprian was rivaled by a Laxist and a Rigorist bishop.

Later, a third controversy emerged from the first two, the baptismal controversy. In Carthage, some Christians conceded that the Laxist church was a false church, and they wished to join Cyprian's true church. Some had even been baptized by the Laxists. Cyprian, in consultation with a council of African bishops, decided that such Christians needed to be "rebaptized," or at least that is what his opponents labeled his action. Cyprian himself stipulated that those coming from the Laxist (and Novatianist) party had not been baptized at all: a false church has only a false baptism, and so converts to the true church must receive the true baptism – a view held by Tertullian.[102] In Rome, the new bishop, Stephen, faced the same question, but came to the opposite answer: there is only "one baptism" (Eph. 4:5), and so the act could not be repeated. Any who came from a Novatianist church to Stephen's true church merely had to repent for their schism and receive the laying on of hands.

When Cyprian and Stephen realized their opposing views, a lengthy letter-writing campaign began. Each tried to convince the other, but to no avail. Each held councils in their region and received the support of their fellow bishops, in Africa and Italy respectively. They even wrote further abroad, such as to Egypt and to other bishops in the east for support. Stephen excommunicated Cyprian, and when Cyprian claimed the full support of the African church, Stephen excommunicated all of Africa. When Cyprian gained the support of the eastern bishops, Stephen excommunicated all of the east as well.[103] This controversy ended only because both Cyprian and Stephen died during the final persecution of this decade.[104]

When Valerian became emperor in 257, he revived the pressure on Christians.[105] He especially targeted the clergy, for several bishops died under his edict.[106] We also know of other bishops and laypersons persecuted at this time, such as those in Numidia who were sent to work in the mines, which was essentially a death sentence.[107]

In 257 Cyprian was tried and exiled to the port town of Curubis.[108] This was a Punic port city elevated to colonial status under Augustus. It retained, however, its "Punic influence" and "Punic governments," including "its old Punic assembly, senate, and *sufetes*."[109] The next year Valerian ordered all

Christian clergy to be killed, and so Cyprian was brought back to Carthage and beheaded on the 14th of September. Pontius notes that Cyprian was the first African bishop to be martyred,[110] and later African Christians thought of him as *the* bishop, martyr, and saint of their tradition.

His works and teachings

Cyprian wrote numerous tracts.[111] Although some appear to be pastoral advice applicable for any place and time,[112] many of these can be shown to have been responses to events in North Africa, such as the persecution and the schisms.[113] The majority of his works directly address ecclesiology, since the definition of the church and its practices had come into question from these events.

While in hiding, Cyprian wrote *On the Lapsed* and possibly also wrote *On the Unity of the Church* at the same time.[114] He insisted that the persecution itself was a test for the church, to see who were the true Christians. Even the schism of the Laxists was a test instigated by the devil, for true Christians could not leave the true church. In fact, Cyprian's conclusion became a famous maxim for later ecclesiology: *extra ecclesiam nulla salus*, "Outside the church, there is no salvation." This belief meant that his response to the baptismal controversy was predictable: since there is no salvation outside the true church, the sanctifying rituals of schismatic false churches were in fact not salvific at all.

To speak of "true church" for Cyprian was a tautology. There is only one church, and therefore any rival church body is a false church. A schism is usually defined as a division within a church, as opposed to a heresy, which is a false teaching that breaks from the tradition of the true church. For Cyprian, however, these distinctions are purely formal: any schism is heresy, and vice versa. There cannot be a schism within the true church, for like Christ's seamless robe that could not be divided, the church cannot be rent in two. Only false churches can arise to rival the true church. This is why the unity of the church is so emphasized.

At the civic level, Cyprian's church appears to have been well organized under his rule as bishop. While many congregations met in various locations around Carthage, Cyprian supervised them all and could appoint and even excommunicate the priests who served each congregation.[115] Since priests had the potential to disobey their bishop, Cyprian warned Christians to cleave to the one true bishop as the only one who could guarantee unity within the church. Any local gathering not approved by the bishop constituted a false church.

Like Tertullian before him, Cyprian's view of baptism reflected a fear of contagion from idolatry. The candidate must first be exorcised of demons, but then the baptism washed away all such contagion so that the new believer could join in communion with the church without contaminating others in the church. Therefore, when the lapsed had contact with idols, they could no longer be permitted into communion. The lapsed had con-tracted contagion from the evil spirits. One "cannot partake of the table of the Lord and the table of demons" (1 Cor. 10:21).

Cyprian even reported instances where lapsed Christians attempted to partake in his church's communion, but the demons within them revealed what had happened. One man became mute, and a certain woman bit off her own tongue.[116] During the persecution, a baby had been left with a non-Christian nurse who took her to a sacrifice. After participating in the demonic sacrifice, the child then could not bear to be in the presence of Cyprian's Eucharist: when the parents, who did not know of the nurse's actions, brought the baby to church, it fell into a fit of convulsing and vom-ited up the wine.[117] A similar scene occurred with an older girl, who was able to confess her crime after the incident.[118] Another woman had sacrificed to the Roman gods, and she tried to touch the Eucharistic bread, but instead it burst into flames.[119] Similarly, a man who had sacrificed then attempted to receive communion, but the bread turned to ash in his hand.[120] This again explains why Cyprian took the Laxist controversy so seriously, and why in the later baptismal controversy he had to determine whether someone had received a true baptism. The contagion of idolatry was seen as a real threat to his community.

The avoidance of demonic idols was counterbalanced by an attempt to imitate Christ in every way.[121] Although he made concessions for those who lapsed, Cyprian held to a rigorist view of the faith in which every Christian should be a martyr, one who gives witness even unto death.[122] Although some were not martyred in the arena, every Christian could receive martyrdom status by dying to self and giving themselves sacrificially to others.[123] Even in the midst of the Laxist and the Rigorist controversies, Cyprian remembered that the true battle was with "the world [*saeculum*]."[124] Cyprian's view of the world in this and other works is heavily indebted to the African tradition that came before him, as found in the writings of Tertullian and Minucius Felix, and it will be repeated and expounded by later African writers, such as Augustine. Because he is within the stream of African Christian tradition, it is worth exploring this aspect of his identity further. Let us now look fur-ther at what can be considered African about Cyprianus Afer, Cyprian the African.[125]

Cyprian the African

With Cyprian it has to be admitted that we find much less data about his African identity in his works, especially when compared to Tertullian before him and the Donatists and Augustine who come after him. It is possible that Cyprian did not see himself as African, but as a Christian who was from a thoroughly Romanized context.[126] Or, perhaps, since Cyprian's surviving writings largely focus on controversies that brought him into direct con-flict with Christians in Rome. Perhaps, Cyprian chose not to highlight his

African identity because the differences between the African and Roman traditions were already causing enough tension. He would naturally want to focus on the unity of the church universal, even if he was defending his African tradition. Whatever the reason, the limited amount of material in Cyprian's writings about any African identity means that we must limit our conclusions and not overstate our case. Even so, we can examine certain items in his works that do suggest an African self-identity.

In the past, scholars often identified African Christians in stereotypical terms.[127] Edward Gibbon described Cyprian's dispute with the bishop of Rome as a "Punic war . . . carried on without any effusion of blood."[128] Later, in even more harsh generalizations about Punic Africans, Philip Schaff commented on Cyprian's temperament:

> Strange that this most powerful defender of old catholic orthodoxy and the teacher of the high-churchly Cyprian, should have been a schismatic and an antagonist of Rome. But he had in his constitution the tropical fervor and acerbity of the Punic character, and that bold spirit of independence in which his native city of Carthage once resisted, through more than a hundred years' war, the rising power of the seven-hilled city on the Tiber. He truly represents the African church, in which similar antagonism continued to reveal itself, not only among the Donatists, but even among the leading advocates of Catholicism.[129]

Contrasted with these negative portrayals of Cyprian's *Punicitas*, there were numerous references to Cyprian as an African by abolitionist writers in the late nineteenth century, who wished to reclaim a positive "African" tradition.[130] While these modern descriptions of Cyprian tell us virtually nothing about how he was understood in his own time, there is a comparison of statements about Cyprian that were made much closer to Cyprian himself.

Augustine, whose Africanity will be discussed later, once had to defend "Punic names" in his region of Africa. As part of his response, he states, "After all, even the blessed Cyprian was Punic [*Poenus*]."[131] How does Augustine know that Cyprian was Punic? To my knowledge, nothing in Cyprian's extant oeuvre would indicate this explicitly. It is possible that Augustine simply uses the label to describe Cyprian in the same way as the Italian who used it to describe Augustine – it is merely a rhetorical device. No one would deny Cyprian's authority,[132] and therefore if Augustine can claim Cyprian was Punic the accusation that Augustine was Punic loses its effect. However, it is equally possible that Augustine had heard of Cyprian's Punic identity from the Donatists, many of whom only spoke Punic, and all of whom claimed to be heirs to Cyprian. If so, then Augustine conveniently recalled this fact when countering a different party, the Pelagians of Italy.

It should also be considered that in the third and fourth century, "Catholic" writers assumed that "African" bishops were Punic.[133] For example,

Prudentius, who died in the early fifth century, wrote a poem in which he praised Cyprian:

> The Punic land bore Cyprian to give lustre to the whole earth every-where; that was the home he came from, but he was to be the glory and the teacher of the world. As martyr he belongs to his native country, but by his love and speech he is ours. His blood rests in Africa, but his tongue is potent everywhere.[134]

Similarly, when speaking generally about the languages of different regions, Pacian, the bishop of Barcelona (d.391), mentions Punic in his list: "You ought then to accuse a one taught in Latin for speaking Latin, and a Greek for speaking Greek, a Parthian for speaking Parthian, a Punic for speaking Punic [*Punice Poenum*]."[135] Pacian makes his statement in a let-ter disputing Novatianism in which he cites Cyprian. Did he have evidence that Cyprian spoke Punic? Or did he merely assume so? Pacian's successor attended the council of Serdica in 343, and Donatus of Carthage (leader of the Donatist party – see p. 195, in Chapter 7) attended the same council.[136] Did he learn that Carthaginian bishops like Donatus and maybe Cyprian before him spoke Punic? Or did he learn from Donatus himself that Cyprian was (at least remembered as) Punic? As mentioned on p. 147, the evidence from Cyprian himself is simply not able to answer this question, and so these claims from the fourth century do not provide solid evidence of Cypri-an's identity.

While there is no clear evidence from Cyprian's own time to suggest he spoke Punic, he does seem to be aware of and even accused of aligning with the local populace against Rome. In what is normally taken to be a standard apologetic work, wherein a Christian answers the accusations of a non-Christian, Cyprian responds to one accusation in particular: Demetrian, a local elite who had frequently debated Cyprian in person, accuses Cyprian and his fellow Christians for the problems in the "world [*mundo*]."[137] These problems include famines, droughts, and all sorts of natural disasters. Chris-tians are also blamed for the recent "incursion by an enemy [*hostem . . . exurgure*]."[138] Cyprian responds by saying that peace would not be pos-sible for Demetrian's crowd even without this enemy because "you" create enough strife "among your toga-clad selves [*inter ipsas togas*]."[139] Cyprian contrasts Demetrian's group with the "barbarians [*barbaris*]," and then he turns the table on his accuser to claim that the reason the famine is occurring is because Demetrian's fellow toga wearers have oppressed the needy and robbed the starving. No further clues exist to identify who the "barbarian" enemy is in this exchange, but around this time there were nomadic tribes invading the coastal cities of Africa.[140] Cyprian, of course, does not condone or even identify with any barbarian group, for he had to ransom Christians who were captured by them. Demetrian, however, does seem to identify Christians in general and Cyprian in particular with this (or at least some) group of African barbarians. Was this because some Christians sided with a military uprising against Rome at this time? There will be some instances where this happens in the fourth century among the Donatists, but there is not enough evidence in the third century to decide. Cyprian, while not identifying with such military resistance, does distance himself from those wearing the toga, even when he and his fellow Christians are accused of supporting the enemy of Rome.[141] Pontius even remembers Cyprian's clothing for being distinct: although his statement is ambiguous and could imply elite "vestments [*vestitus*]," Pontius's emphasis seems to be on Cyprian's humility in dress.[142]

We mentioned on p. 147 that Jerome calls our author "Cyprian the African." While we know very little about Cyprian's early life and background, we can find some clues in his own name. The standard giving of his name is "Thascius Caecilius Cyprianus." This, however, is a historical construction from several sources, not a standardized tripartite Roman name. In an official public notice posted in Carthage by the Roman officials, he was named "Caecilus Cyprianus." This proper Latin name would naturally be used in public records. Is this an indication that Cyprian comes from a Latin family? Not necessarily. Jerome also tells us that Cyprian took the name Caecilius from a mentor.[143] This adopted name, therefore, tells us little about Cyprian's pre-Christian family and life. What about the name Thascius?

In the heading of one of his own letters, we read that he is named "Cyprian, who is also called Thascius [*Cyprianus qui et Thascius*]."[144] In the account of his martyrdom, thought to have been written soon after his death, this name is also mentioned: "You are Thascius, who is also called Cyprian? [*tu es Thascius qui et Cyprianus?*]."[145] Likewise, in telling of Cyprian's death, Pontius states, "Suddenly, a rumor which spread throughout Carthage grew, to the effect that Thascius [Cyprian] had been brought forth. Everyone knew him. . . . From all sides the people flocked to the scene."[146] This suggests that "Thascius" (the editor adds "Cyprian" in brackets for the modern reader's sake) was the name by which Cyprian was known locally among the "people [*plebs*]."[147] Because this name appears to be how Cyprian was known to the populace, some scholars have deduced that Thascius was Cyprian's "Punic nickname."[148]

Returning to Cyprian's self-introduction as "Cyprian, who is also Thascius," G. W. Clarke noted how unusual such a formula is for Cyprian. It must be that Puppianus's letter (to which Cyprian is responding) used a similar style: "Puppianus had grandly flaunted his own distinguished family names (belonging as he did in all likelihood to a wealthy and locally eminent senatorial family)."[149] Clarke adds that Cyprian's *agnomen*, Thascius, "is of unknown derivation, in origin presumed (vaguely) 'Punic' or 'Libyan.'"[150] Clarke finally notes how Cyprian was known as Thascius in the *Acta* and *Vita* among the people, and so "this was the name by which he was popularly known."[151] Perhaps the association of the name "Thascius" with the African people explains a curiosity in a later text known as the *Gelasian*

Decree (mid-sixth century). The author, Pseudo-Gelasius, lists "heretics or schismatics" whose works are deemed "apocryphal."[152] Although this author lists "the works of the blessed Caecilius Cyprian, martyr and bishop of Carthage" among those celebrated as "saints" who support the church, it also lists as "apocryphal" the writings of "Thascius Cyprian" in a list that includes other Africans such as Lactantius, Commodian, Arnobius, Tyconius, and Donatus.[153] As we saw with Pacian on p. 149, it appears that Cyprian, especially "Thascius," was remembered in Rome as affiliated with an African tradition, if not the Donatist schism.[154]

In addition to these later witnesses and in addition to what can be gleaned from Cyprian's name, we can find elements of an African identity in Cyprian's own writings. In the same letter where Cyprian gives us his name as "Thascius," he attacks Puppianus for claiming to be bishop. There can only be one rightly appointed bishop, just as "Bees have a queen bee and cattle a leader."[155] This analogy to one leader of a hive or herd is in fact an allusion to an earlier African Christian writer. Minucius Felix had earlier argued against polytheism, insisting that there can only be one God, just as "The bees have one king; the flocks one leader; among the herds there is one ruler."[156] One sentence prior, Minucius Felix had also referenced Romulus and Remus: one had to kill the other, because "so great an empire could not receive two rulers," which of course is sarcastic for Minucius Felix – murder is not required, except in the practice of Romans. It is noteworthy that Cyprian, or more precisely, "Thascius," remembered this statement when countering Puppianus. Although he does not need to comment on the founding of Rome in his own letter, Thascius of Carthage easily remembers such a line when discussing the need for one leader in an African congregation against this rival bishop.

Aside from an explicit African identity, we can see much in Cyprian's writings that is unique to his African church. We have already mentioned the unique baptismal theology of Africa.[157] It should be stipulated that in Cyprian's time, the bishops of Iberia, Gaul, Asia Minor, and Egypt all agreed with Cyprian, making this a more ecumenical practice than a uniquely African one. Nevertheless, the bishops with Cyprian, namely, those from "the provinces of Africa, Numidia, and Mauritania," worked with a clear self-awareness that their practice was true to their African heritage and distinct from that of Italy.[158] Cyprian had earlier referred to his fellow colleagues as "the bishops appointed here in Africa" when writing to the Roman bishop Cornelius, with whom he was on good terms.[159] Moreover, less than a century later, when the ecumenical consensus sides against "rebaptism" of heretics,[160] the majority of Africans will continue to hold to their own tradition.[161] What other teachings did Cyprian offer that reflect a uniquely African context?

Cyprian did make much of how the clergy, especially the bishop, functioned as the "priest." This is not, however, the New Testament "elder [*presbyter*]" for Cyprian, but the Old Testament priest who offers the sacrifice, the *sacerdos* to use his Latin term. Along with this understanding of the clergy's function, Cyprian made much in his writings about Christ's own sacrifice and the call for Christians to imitate him in sacrificing their own lives. This led Berhard Lang to comment,

> The way Cyprian and, later, Augustine defined sacrifice, is quite unlike Jesus' understanding. In fact, it constitutes a real innovation, if not revolution, in Christian thought. Unlike Jesus, Cyprian took his idea of sacrifice not from traditional low-key animal sacrifice, but from that most qualified form of offering: human sacrifice. . . . How could theologians like Cyprian and Augustine discover and appreciate the value and meaning of human sacrifice? If an answer is to be ventured at all, then it must be the following one: as North Africans, they lived close to and participated in the Semitic mentality, which they encountered both in their Punic neighborhood and, of course, in the Bible. Child sacrifice remained a conspicuous feature of Punic ritual down to the third century CE.[162]

While Lang's claim requires further study before it can be substantiated, it is worth exploring further what in Cyprian's thought reflects his Punic or African context.

Cyprian inherited a distinct African ecclesiology from his predecessors, and he further shaped that ecclesiology for future generations of African Christians. One aspect of his ecclesiology that is unique to Africa is the independent nature of every locale and every bishop.[163] We mentioned on p. 145 how Stephen excommunicated Cyprian, the African churches, and the churches of the east. Cyprian never responded in kind. This is likely because Cyprian and Stephen were operating with a different understanding of what is a church and who can excommunicate another from the church.

Both Italian and African bishops will strive to practice their faith in harmony with other bishops in their region and abroad, and they will meet in regional councils and communicate via letters in order to discern what kind of practice meets this standard of unity.[164] These regions even organized themselves so that communication flowed through the primate or metropolitan – that is, the bishop of the largest and most influential city. Despite his central role in the communication and administration of the African church, Cyprian did not claim authority over Africa. For example, Cyprian believed that apostates should not be granted forgiveness until the end of their life, but he deferred to the view of his colleagues when they met at the council of Carthage and decided to grant forgiveness after only three years of penance. This decision to defer, however, was something he made without any coercion. Cyprian chose to align his practice with the other bishops in the region. Apparently, no council could make him do so. In his correspondence with other bishops, both in Africa and abroad, Cyprian insisted that no bishop could tell another what to do. All bishops should ideally come to an agreement, but if they could not, none had the right to dictate actions to another. Every bishop, no matter where he presided, was an heir to Peter and therefore had the keys.[165] At the height of the baptismal controversy, after Stephen had denounced the African bishops for not accepting heretical baptism, Cyprian and eighty-six other bishops prefaced their reasons for their view of baptism with the caveat about the independence of each bishop:

> For neither does any of us set himself up as a bishop of bishops, nor by tyrannical terror does any compel his colleague to the necessity of obedience; since every bishop, according to the allowance of his liberty and power, has his own proper right of judgment, and can no more be judged by another than he himself can judge another. But let us all wait for the judgment of our Lord Jesus Christ, who is the only one that has the power both of preferring us in the government of His Church, and of judging us in our conduct there.[166]

This could well be dubbed the Cyprianic doctrine of the bishop. Although all bishops should be in accord, no bishop can excommunicate another. What would this even mean for one bishop to excommunicate another? When a bishop excommunicates a congregant, he literally bars the person from the communion table, since he – or his delegated priest – stands at the table and governs who can receive. I imagine Stephen's declaration that Cyprian was excommunicated evoked little to no response from Cyprian, except perhaps to cause him to shrug apoplectically. Why would Cyprian be receiving communion from Stephen's table anyway?

As churches continue to multiply in North Africa after Cyprian's time, this insistence on local autonomy will remain in place. In other regions, Christianity will develop more of a hierarchical system wherein rural towns and villages will be governed only by a *chorepiscopus* (something like a sub-bishop) or a priest who operated under the authority of the nearest bishop of a major city. In North Africa, however, the end of the third and the beginning of the fourth century will witness numerous bishoprics established, even in the smallest of municipalities.[167] Therefore, the bishop's role in Africa remains more of a local shepherd and less of an administrator within a larger hierarchy.[168]

The Cyprianic model of the episcopacy did not negate the value placed on unity with the larger church. Cyprian contended that the bishop should always operate in consultation and harmony with his "colleagues," and this model of collegiality where local councils met and distributed their decisions abroad for other councils to consult continued for generations that followed in North Africa.

This form of ecclesiology could be described as a bottom-up or grassroots approach: when gathering in a local council, the aim was to determine what had been the tradition in that locale or region; it was uncertain how this would be handled when another region held to a different tradition. In Cyprian's time, he and his African colleagues were well aware that their tradition differed from the Italian, and they disapproved of what they deemed a wrong practice in Italy, but they nevertheless permitted such divergent traditions within the wider worldwide communion of churches. A few generations later, when Constantine enables a worldwide council of bishops, most of Christianity will assume that such local discrepancies were to be minimized, at least when it came to key doctrines (such as Christology) and practices (such as baptism). Many in North Africa, however, will disagree, which brings us to the Donatist controversy.

While Cyprian will be widely read and respected,[169] his memory will be especially cherished in Africa: when he died, "Africa wept."[170] For example, nineteen of Augustine's sermons survive in which he preached on the memory of Cyprian, and he would have had to preach many more such sermons since Cyprian's feast day was celebrated every year. Closer to Cyprian's own time, we have Pontius's *Life* of Cyprian, as well as an *Acts* of his trial and death that is distributed soon after the events.[171] Two churches were built to honor Cyprian in Carthage: the *Mensa Cypriani* or Table of Cyprian was built over the site where Cyprian was martyred, and the *Memoria Cypriani* or Memory of Cyprian was built over the site of his burial. Augustine's mother will flee to this last basilica to pray when her son leaves Carthage.[172] Cyprian's legacy will also inspire a large Pseudo-Cyprianic body of literature, and the Donatist controversy will largely revolve around who can claim to be heir to Cyprian's teaching.[173] He was venerated throughout the Christian period in Africa; centuries later, in the early ninth century – after the Arab expansion into Africa – the Muslim Caliph, Haroun al-Rashid (d.809), will offer Cyprian's relics to Charlemagne as a gift.[174]

Cyprian was not alone in facing martyrdom at this time. Prudentius reports a large number of Christians in Carthage were martyred on the same day.[175] A text written contemporaneously to Cyprian shows that the tension between Christians and "idolators" was high at this time.

We can now turn to other texts from the later third century. In so doing, we will see more glimpses of the African Christian community at this time, as well as the growing self-awareness of the African Christian tradition.

That Idols Are Not Gods (*Quod idola dii non sint*)

The text once attributed to Cyprian, *That Idols Are not Gods*, is now generally considered anonymous.[176] Even if it is not authentically Cyprian, it appears to be North African (and it is certainly anti-Roman). The dating, if Cyprian is not the author, is commonly said to be fourth century because it appears to depend on Lactantius (d.325), but Loon sufficiently demonstrates that Lactantius could be dependent on this text (not vice versa). While Cyprian is most likely not the author, the work should be dated to the later half of the third century. It certainly mirrors the kinds of treatises seen earlier in this century (e.g. Tertullian, *To Scapula*; Minucius Felix, *Octavius*; and Cyprian, *To Demetrian*).

The text gives very little data about the occasion of its writing. The first paragraph immediately launches into an attack on the "god whom the common people worship."[177] Specific examples of different peoples and their gods are then offered, including the Mauretanians, who "manifestly worship kings."[178] After this generic listing of many provinces and deities, the author turns to "the Romans."[179] Their "indigenous gods" are denigrated, such as the deified Romulus whose reprehensible acts of perjury, rape, and murder are rehearsed.[180] Aeneas likewise is remembered, but as one who introduced foreign (i.e. Trojan) gods "among the Romans." Rome's claim to divine favor is rejected, for kingdoms rise and fall by chance. Rome's founding and the founding of the Republic are said to be disgraceful. Then, Rome's heroes, such as Regulus, Paulus, and Caius, are discredited since the Roman gods could not help them. These are all tropes seen in earlier African writers.[181]

Demons haunt all idols and therefore plague all who worship them.[182] Contrasted with the multitude of idols, the true God is one.[183] Unlike this divine unity, all human government is characterized by disputes and disunity, while in fact only Roman examples are provided, like Romulus and Remus, and Pompey and Caesar – another argument found in earlier African writers.[184]

The legacy of this monotheism is credited to the Jews, although the author must explain how they fell into their own idolatry and received God's wrath as a result.[185] Their idolatry explains why they rejected Jesus, but this later rejection is explicitly a result of the blindness of turning to idols. When telling how the Jewish leaders rejected Jesus, this author shifts the blame to the Romans, or at least to "Pontius Pilate, who was then the procurator of Syria on behalf of the Romans."[186]

Christ, of course, is said to have been victorious in his resurrection and ascension, and he will come again "for the punishment of the devil and to the judgment of the human race."[187] Despite how some are still tortured in this author's community for their confession of Christ, Christ is claimed as the true "general [*ducem*]," "emperor [*principem*]," and "founder [*auctorem*]."[188]

This text, like earlier African writings going back to the earliest martyrdoms, depicts a community unwilling to align itself politically with Rome and its leaders. While this is to be expected of a Christian community undergoing persecution, the text explicitly couches its argument in direct opposition to Rome and its symbols of pride.

Commodian

Another author who should be mentioned when discussing third-century Christian Africa is the writer known as Commodian. He is mentioned only by two later sources, Gennadius (died c.495) and Pseudo-Gelasius (early to mid sixth-century). Gennadius claims he was a convert to Christianity and that he followed "Tertullian, Lactantius, and Papias" in teachings such as "voluntary poverty [*voluntariae paupertatis*]."[189] Just how Gennadius knows that Commodian uses these three writers is unclear. He probably makes an assumption about Papias, who was an early second-century writer who famously espoused "chiliasm," the belief in a literal millennial reign of Christ,[190] which Commodian also teaches.[191] The other two alleged sources, Tertullian and Lactantius, lead scholars to conclude that Commodian was African. Furthermore, in the "Gelasian Decree," Pseudo-Gelasius simply lists Commodian among the "apocryphal" authors, meaning that his writings are not accepted because they derive from "heretics or schismatics." This list includes the expected apocryphal gospels and writings of heretics, and then even writers like Tertullian, Lactantius, Cyprian ("Thascius Cyprianus"), Arnobius, and Tyconius – all of whom are African writers.[192]

Apart from these later witnesses, scholars must use the material within Commodian's own writings to date this author and to locate him in a certain context. Commodian wrote two treatises, *The Instructions* and *The Apologetic Song Against the Jews and Against the Nations* (or more simply, *Song Against Two Peoples*).[193] The author knows Cyprian's conflict with Felicissimus, and so a third-century date has been offered.[194] It must also be stipulated, however, that the text may reflect a much later period: some have detected sentiments from the Donatist controversy, and so this author could be writing as late as the fifth century.[195] I have elected to discuss Commodian here, since his apologetic work echoes what can be found in Minucius Felix, Cyprian, and the anonymous work *That Idols Are not Gods*, but this does not mean that the texts could not speak to a fourth or fifth century context as well. If it does belong to the later period, then this text illustrates how the African school continued to draw from earlier apologetic treatises and continued to articulate an anti-Roman sentiment.

This author provides his own name, but in a cryptic way. In his *Instructions*, each stanza uses an acrostic. For example, the fourth stanza discusses Saturn – and this is certainly describing the Roman Saturn. Each line of this stanza begins with letters that spell out "SATURNUS." Likewise, the fifth stanza describes "JUPPITER," with each line beginning with one of the letters from this Roman god's name. In the last line of the work, the author states, "the curiosity of the learned men shall find my name in this."[196] For this same last stanza, the heading is "NOMEN GASEI," which has perplexed scholars. The word *gasei* is not a Latin word, and there has been no agreement on how to understand it. This is where one would expect the *nomen poetae*, the name of the poet, and so all kinds of emendations have been suggested. Some have even conjectured that the word is "of Semitic origins and signifies a poet."[197] Perhaps the "Semitic" word could be found in the Punic/Phoenician language, instead of Hebrew, but to my knowledge no one has explored this possibility. The letters from *NOMEN GASEI*, it turns out, are not used in this last stanza, but there is still an acrostic. The beginning letter from each line spell "ISTIRHC SVCIDNEM SVNAIDOM-MOC," which appears to be nonsense until one reads it backwards so that it says, *Commodianus Mendicus Christi*, "Commodian, the Poor in Christ."

While most scholars interested in Commodian have studied his eschatology and his interpretation of scripture, it is worth considering how he might reflect a uniquely African perspective. In addition to the external clues, there are statements in Commodian's work that suggest to scholars that he belongs to the African tradition. One primary example is found where Commodian discusses the impending time of the Antichrist:

> Then, doubtless, the world shall be finished when he shall appear. He himself shall divide the globe into three ruling powers, when, moreover, Nero shall be raised up from hell, Elias shall first come to seal the beloved ones; at which things the region of Africa and the northern nation, the whole earth on all sides, for seven years shall tremble. But Elias shall occupy the half of the time, Nero shall occupy half. Then the whore Babylon, being reduced to ashes, its embers shall thence advance to Jerusalem; and the Latin conqueror shall then say, I am Christ, whom ye always pray to.[198]

The "whore of Babylon" here is clearly Rome, and this is to be expected from any Christian in the early centuries, given the book of Revelation.[199] What is unique is how Commodian divides "the northern nation," which is Rome and which can be called "northern" only from the perspective of "the region of Africa."[200]

Commodian's other work is against "two peoples," the Jews and the Gentiles. This second group is generally unbelievers, as can be seen from the author's reading of all of the evil empires of the Old Testament. Egypt, Babylon, and Persia (to name but a few) in fact appear to be types of the one truly evil empire, Rome. Rome "rejoices while the whole earth groans."[201] This rejoicing will be short lived, according to Commodian, who in his own turn rejoices that her "tyrants"[202] are being judged and that "in the end Rome will burn."[203] Some of the statements from this work prove to be so anti-Roman that it led a past generation of scholars to insist that the work was Donatist.[204] It has now been demonstrated, however, that even references to the apocalyptic doom of Rome at the hand of the "Goths" could belong to the mid-third century.[205] Furthermore, we have shown that third-century authors like Tertullian, Minucius Felix, Cyprian, and the anonymous author of *That Idols Are not Gods*, can all express their eschatology in terms that focus on Rome. This is not unusual for a Christian from any context, but these authors' self-awareness of being "from the region of Africa," along with their indebtedness to their predecessors in what has been called "the African school," further substantiates the fact that authors like Commodian wrote with an African self-identity, something that especially emerges in contrast to Rome.

This African identity that arose in direct opposition to Romans can also be found in other texts from the third century. In a few surviving martyrdoms, we can see additional glimpses of the Christian community in Africa at this time.

Late third-century martyrdoms

While we know that many African Christians died as martyrs during the third century, there are few surviving texts that record martyrs who came after Cyprian. One of these texts is the *Martyrdom of Montanus and Lucius*.[206] This account records events in Carthage from 259, and although all such martyrdoms are open to critical assessment this one is generally considered reliable.[207] The main body (sections 1–11) purports to be a letter written by the Christians in prison awaiting martyrdom. The narrator takes over, much like the *Passion of Perpetua and Felicity*, in order to conclude the text.

A riot (*tumultum*) of some sort erupted in Carthage that resulted in the arrest and persecution of eight Christians, including Lucius and Montanus.[208] Just what caused this riot, and why the Christians would be implicated in it, is never explained. The local official originally tried to burn the Christians, but the fire miraculously failed, as with the "three youths" from the book of Daniel.[209] As with Commodian, the reading of the three Hebrews persecuted by Babylon likely implies a typology of Rome for the author of this text. The events are peppered with military, even revolutionary, imagery: later in the text the Christians are likened to the Maccabees.[210]

The military imagery is clearly metaphorical, for it is complemented by a series of dreams that ensures the prisoners that their confession will be victorious over "the devil."[211] The prisoners also receive encouragement from Cyprian himself, who appears to them in a vision.[212] The martyrs themselves give speeches at the end of their life, and the narrator closes with a eulogy to their faith.

Another martyrdom from this time is the *Martyrdom of Marian and James*, which reports events from a rural village outside of Cirta in Numidia.[213] This account allows Marian and James to take center stage, but there were many other martyrs, as witnessed by the "enormous pile of slaughtered bodies."[214] Despite this and other details that may be more exaggeration than strict historicity, this text is generally considered a reliable witness to the events.[215] Most of the details reflect what is already known about this period from Cyprian and other sources. James is said to have been tortured, and so a "confessor," during the Decian persecution, while in this Valerian persecution the clergy in particular was targeted.[216]

As with the *Martyrdom of Montanus and Lucius*, Cyprian appears in a vision to encourage Marian and James.[217] Later, the Christians experience visions before their deaths, such as "horses in the sky of show-white brilliance, on which rode young men in white garments."[218] The "white rider" of Revelation (6:2) is often noted here by commentators, but it is difficult to understand why there are multiple horses and riders in this martyrdom. If we knew more about the Numidian religion, we might find parallels in this text.[219]

As with all martyrdoms from North Africa, the theme is one of "battle" with the world.[220] For unexplained reasons, an unusually large band of soldiers arrested Marian and James and took them to Cirta.[221] Several others had been arrested, who were unknown to Marian and James's group, but who turned out to be Christian as well.[222] It is tempting to see the aftermath of the Gordians' revolt (see discussion in Chapter 1) in the background of these events: in the African regions where a weakened military had resulted in political destabilization, any dissident group was likely being dealt with swiftly. Does this sweep of the countryside imply that the Christians consisted of indigenous Africans, a group that may have harbored anti-Roman sentiments at this time? No evidence directly links the political backdrop with the Christian material at this time, and so we should probably assume that after the Decian and the Valerian persecutions many Christians would have been targeted regardless of any potential political threat.

As in the earlier African martyrdoms, the new elites in Africa seem to have played a role in the arrest of these Christians: the "magistrates of Cirta" are deemed "priests of the Devil."[223] One of the Christians, Aemilian, was of equestrian rank, and since this is notable, we can probably assume that the others were from the lower classes.[224] He reported a conversation with a non-Christian that tells us more about the social identities involved.[225] Musurillo translates *gentilis* as "pagan," which is natural since Christians commonly referred to "gentiles" in this way. The Latin word, however, often implied that someone was non-Roman, and this text could therefore single out this individual as non-Christian or African, or it could be an intentional play on words meant to suggest both to the audience. The man is Aemilian's "brother in the flesh,"[226] but this does not seem to imply they shared an earthly father. Instead, this likely means a kinsman, or someone from the same people group. After answering several of his questions about heavenly reward, Aemilian – for no obvious reason in the dialogue – cites Jesus' statement about the camel and the eye of the needle and how impossible it is for "a rich man to enter the kingdom of heaven."[227] This exchange suggests that Aemilian's kinsman is a fellow African, but one who belongs to the new elite class. The narrator faults the new elites as a group for their role in the incarceration and torture of Christians, who are understood to be from the lower classes of African society – with Aemilian being the notable exception – and suspected of threatening the social order.

These two martyr accounts, taken together with the material in Cyprian's time and the numerous examples of martyr shrines found in the archaeological records, testify to an African Christian community that identifies itself over and against a persecuting empire. While this is true for Christianity at large at this time, the specific social identity of Africans oppressed by Romans is prominent in the sources. Furthermore, this opposition of an African identity to Roman outsiders will continue to be reflected in the Christian material from the fourth century, to which we can now turn.

Notes

1 Text LCL 250; cf. Bernhard Kytzler, *M. Minuci Felicis Octavius* (Bibliotheca scriptorum Graecorum et Romanorum Teubneriana; Leipzig: B. G. Teubner Verlagsgesellschaft, 1982); and ACW 39.
2 Arnobius, *Against the Nations* (see p. 176 in chapter six for details)
3 Jerome, *Lives of Illustrious Men* 58, claims he was an advocate of Rome, but this may be a misreading of *Octavius* 4, where Minucius Felix is asked to arbitrate the dialogue set near Rome, and/or Lactantius, *The Divine Institutes* 5.1, where Minucius Felix is said to be known by other lawyers.
4 Lactantius, *The Divine Institutes* 5.1, lists him with other African authors.
5 CIL 8.6996, 8.7094, 8.7095, 8.7096, 8.7097, 8.7098.
6 *Octavius* 10.
7 *Octavius* 31.
8 Discussed in chapters one and two.
9 CIL 8.8962: *OCT[AVIUS] IAN[UARIUS]*.
10 Named "Marcus" in the text itself (*Octavius* 3). Cf. Jerome, *Lives of Illustrious Men* 58, only knows him as Minucius Felix.
11 CIL 8.1964, but as "*L. (= Lucius?) MINUCI FELIX.*"
12 CIL 8.1249: *MINUCIUS FELIX SACERDOS SATURNI.*
13 *Octavius* 1, "he was at once sole confidant of my affections, and my partner in wanderings from truth [*solus in amoribus conscius, ipse socius in erroribus*]."
14 *Octavius* 1: *de tenebrarum . . . in lucem.*
15 *Octavius* 2.
16 Tim Whitmarsh, "Thinking Local," in *Local Knowledge and Microidentities in the Imperial Greek World*, ed. Tim Whitmarsh (Cambridge: Cambridge University Press, 2010), 11.
17 *Octavius* 6: *deos colere municipes.* Of course, local deities were often transported to various locales throughout the empire, but this phenomenon does not affect the point being made here.
18 *Octavius* 6: *Eleusinios Cererem, Phrygas Matrem, Epidaurios Aesculapium, Chaldaeos Belum, Astarten Syros, Dianam Tauros, Gallos Mercurium, universa Romanos. Sic eorum potestas et auctoritas totius orbis ambitus occupavit.*
19 *Octavius* 7: *Romana civitas et protegitur et ornatur.*
20 *Octavius* 8: *homines, inquam, deploratae, inlicitae ac desperatae factionis.*
21 *Octavius* 9; cf. Tertullian, *Apology* 9.
22 Fronto's work against Christians, if he ever did produce such a work, has not survived.
23 *Octavius* 10: *non . . . Romana . . . noverunt.*
24 *Octavius* 12: *Nonne Romani sine vestro deo imperant regnant, fruuntur orbe toto vestrique dominantur?*
25 *Octavius* 7: *Claudi et Iuni non proelium in Poenos, sed ferale naufragium est, et ut Trasimenus Romanorum sanguine et maior esset et decolor, sprevit auguria Flaminius.*
26 See Livy 22.1–6; Cicero, *On Divination* 1.35.
27 Then again, Octavius mentions Juba, king of the "Mauretanians [*Mauri*]" (*Octavius* 21), and speaks of them as outsiders.
28 *Octavius* 26.

29 Caecilius ends as follows, "And now, what says our brave Octavius, of the good old Plautine stock, prince of bakers but last and least of philosophers? [*Ecquid ad haec" ait "audet Octavius, homo Plautinae prosapiae, ut pistorum praecipuus, ita postremus philosophorum?*]" (*Octavius* 14). The Loeb editor notes:

> No good explanation of the personal allusion is forthcoming. Plautus, the Roman comedian, is said to have worked in a mill, and he uses the word *pistor* of those engaged in the milling and baking industries. It is quite possible that Octavius had been in some way connected with the trade, and that this accounts for the turn of pleasantry. Attempts at emendation have been made – such as istorum, Christianorum, ictorum – but none of them seems happy, and all eliminate the alliterative p. Jokes are not intended for posterity.

Perhaps the "alliterative p" could be retained if Octavius was of "*Punicae prosapiae.*"

30 *Octavius* 17.
31 *Octavius* 18.
32 *Octavius* 18: *Ob pastorum et casae regnum de geminis.*
33 *Octavius* 31: *[Vos nec adgnoscits] nec fratres vos nisi sane ad parricidium recognoscitis.*
34 *Octavius* 31; cf. 37.
35 *Octavius* 18: *Generi et soceri bella toto orbe diffusa sunt.* The statement includes a quote from Lucan, *On the Civil War* 1.line 110.
36 *Octavius* 26: *in Africa.*
37 *Octavius* 37.
38 Discussed at the end of chapter four.
39 *Octavius* 18–20.
40 *Octavius* 18–21, the "gods" were in fact human kings (etc.) who were venerated after their death.
41 *Octavius* 22–24.
42 *Octavius* 23: *ipse Iuppiter vester modo inberbis statuitur, modo barbatus locatur; et cum Hammon dicitur, habet cornua.*
43 Discussed in chapter two.
44 For the ubiquity and importance of the cornucopia in Punic Africa, see Simmons, *Arnobius*, 184–187. Also, see Corippus, *Iohannis* 2.109–111.
45 For example, see the statue from Sousse, Tunisia, discussed in H.H. Scullard, "Carthage and Rome," in *The Cambridge Ancient History*, vol. 7 part 2: *The Rise of Rome to 220 B.C.*, 2nd ed., ed. F. W. Wallbank, et al. (Cambridge: Cambridge University Press, 1970), 514; and Charles-Picard and Charles-Picard, *Daily Life in Carthage*, 76. For *cornu* as describing a crested helmet or headdress, see Virgil, *Aeneid* 12.89, "cornua cristae" (LCL 64:306); and Livy 27.33, "alterum cornu galeae" (LCL 367:342–343).
46 *Octavius* 25.
47 *Octavius* 26 (LCL 250:392 with my trans., emph. added; cf. p. 393).
48 *Octavius* 25: *Iam finitimos agro pellere, civitates proximas evertere cum templis et altaribus, captos cogere, damnis alienis et suis sceleribus adolescere cum Romulo regibus ceteris et posteris ducibus disciplina communis est. Ita quicquid Romani tenent, colunt, possident, audaciae praeda est: templa omnia de manubiis, id est de ruinis urbium, de spoliis deorum, de caedibus sacerdotum.*
49 *Octavius* 28–30.
50 *Octavius* 30, "None can believe it, but one capable of the crime [*Nemo hoc potest credere nisi qui possit audere*]."
51 *Octavius* 30.
52 *Octavius* 30: *Africae partibus . . . infantes immolabantur.*

53 *Octavius* 31: *tuus Fronto.*
54 *Octavius* 33: *vel, si Romanis magis gaudes, Antoni Iuliani.*
55 *Octavius* 39–40.
56 E.g. *Octavius* 18, 20, 32–33.
57 J. A. Ilevbare, *Carthage, Rome, and the Berbers: A Study of Social Evolution in Ancient North Africa* (Ibadan, Nigeria: Ibadan University Press, 1981), 126.
58 *Octavius* 32: *ex hoc deum credimus, quod eum sentire possumus, videre non possumus. In operibus enim eius et in mundi omnibus motibus virtutem eius semper praesentem aspicimus, cum tonat, fulgurat, fulminat, cum serenat. Nec mireris, si deum non vides: vento et flatibus omnia impelluntur, vibrantur, agitantur, et sub oculis tamen non venit ventus et flatus.*
59 Helpful introductions to Cyprian and the literature about him include Henk Bakker, Paul van Geest, and Hans van Loon, "Introduction: Cyprian's Statute and Influence," in *Cyprian of Carthage: Studies in His Life, Language, and Thought*, ed. Henk Bakker, Paul van Geest, and Hans van Loon (Leuven: Peeters, 2010), 1–27.
60 For his letters, see text in CCL 3B-C; and trans. in ACW 43, 44, 46, 47. Not all of these letters were by Cyprian; some were to him and others were from a council at which he presided.
61 Burns, Jensen, et al., *Christianity in Roman Africa*, 32. For Pontius's *Life of Cyprian*, see text in CSEL 3, and trans. in FC 15.
62 The only mention of Pontius is from Jerome, *The Lives of Illustrious Men* 68.
63 *Life of Cyprian* 2. Pontius, in fact, tells us little to nothing about Cyprian not already known from Cyprian's own works, which makes this text somewhat suspect. The consensus of scholars, however, accept Pontius's work as reliable.
64 Pontius, *Life of Cyprian* 2. Jerome, *The Lives of Illustrious Men* 67, claims Cyprian gave it "all [*omnem*]" to the poor.
65 *Life of Cyprian* 2.7. More will be said on his wealth, for he continued to give from his personal funds to the poor after he becomes bishop (see Clarke, *The Letters of St. Cyprian*, 1:186 n. 9 and n. 10; and 1:201 n.11. He may have inherited more wealth after his conversion to Christianity; see *Life of Cyprian* 4.
66 See discussion in Dunn, *Cyprian and the Bishops of Rome: Questions of Papal Primacy in the Early Church* (Strathfield: St Pauls, 2007), 20–23.
67 *Life of Cyprian* 3. For the possible connection between Cyprian's distribution of wealth to Cyprian's appointment as bishop, see Charles A. Bobertz, *Cyprian of Carthage as Patron: A Social Historical Study of the Role of the Bishop in the Ancient Christian Community of North Africa* (PhD Dissertation for Yale University, 1988).
68 *Life of Cyprian* 5.
69 *Life of Cyprian* 9.
70 Esp. §14.
71 *On Mortality* 20.
72 *Letter* 62.2.2; see details in Clarke, *The Letters of St. Cyprian*, 3:277–280 and 3:283.
73 It should be noted that some persecution preceded Cyprian's episcopacy; writing in 251, he mentions three martyrs who died in the previous generation of one local family: *Letter* 39.1.1, Celerinus's grandmother Celerina and uncles Laurentinus and Egnatius. For possible dates, see Barnes, *Tertullian*, 157–158; and Rebillard, *Christians*, 47.
74 The view that Decius intentionally persecuted Christians is as old as Lactantius, *On the Death of the Persecutors* 4. See Brent, *Cyprian and Roman Carthage*, 117–192, for discussion and bibliography about whether Christians were targeted.
75 See Lactantius's description in *On the Death of the Persecutors* 4: "nor could he be honoured with the rites of sepulture, but, stripped and naked, he lay to

be devoured by wild beasts and birds, – a fit end for the enemy of God." This African writer will be discussed further in chapter six.

76 Cyprian, *Letter* 43.3.1
77 For exiled Christians, see *Letters* 21.4.1; 30.8.1; 55.13.2; 66.7.2.
78 See Rebillard, *Christians*, 48.
79 For confessors in prison, see *Letters* 6; 10; 13. Rebillard, *Christians*, 53, cites Clarke, *The Letters of St. Cyprian* (ACW 43), 1:259; and Elio Lo Cascio, "Una possibile testimonianza sul valore dell' *antoninianus* negli anni di Decio?" in *Consuetudinis Amor: Fragments d'histoire romaine (IIe-VIe siècles) offerts à Jean-Pierre Callu*, ed. François Chausson and Étienne Wolff (Rome: L'Erma di Bretschneider, 2003), [299–309] 300–302, who estimate approximately fifty confessors.
80 Cyprian, *On the Lapsed* 27–28; *Letters* 20.2.2 and 55.14.1. On earlier Christians bribing to avoid persecution, see Tertullian, *On Fleeing Persecution* 5.3, 12–14. Similarly, some Christians bribed the guards in order to visit Perpetua and her compatriots in prison (*Passion of Perpetua* 3.7).
81 Recent studies have explored how these "lapsed" Christians must have understood their own actions: Brent, *Cyprian and Roman Carthage*, 228–240 and Rebillard, *Christians*, 47–60; cf. Cyprian, *Letter* 55.13–14, for their various claims.
82 See the bibliography in Rebillard, *Christians*, 50 and 103 n.29. The evidence is found in Cyprian, *Letters* 11.1.2 and further details in Clarke, *The Letters* 1:240 n.3.
83 *Letter* 7.1 (Clarke, *The Letters* 1.67). For *gens/gentiles* as "foreign peoples" in Tertullian, see Wilhite, *Tertullian the African*, 64 n.108 and discussion in chapter four.
84 *Letters* 7.1 and 20.1.2; cf. 59.6.1; and see discussion in Rebillard, *Christians*, 49.
85 See his defense in *Letter* 20.
86 For the known clergy in Carthage at this time, see Clarke, *Letters* 1:39–44.
87 *Letter* 7; cf. *Letters* 8 and 20, for the correspondence with Rome about his fleeing from Carthage.
88 Tertullian, *On Fleeing Persecution*.
89 *On the Lapsed* 3 and 10, with reference to Matt. 10:23; cf. Tertullian, *On Fleeing Persecution* 6.1–7, for an earlier rejection of such an interpretation of this passage. Rebillard, *Christians*, 52, points out that no mention is made in Cyprian's letters of other Christians who took this option.
90 *On the Lapsed* 12.
91 G.E.M. de Ste. Croix, "Aspects of the Great Persecution," *Harvard Theological Review* 47 (1954), 96–100.
92 See the reference to numerous people belonging to this group in *On the Lapsed* 2. They seem to consist mostly of the poor (12.2.2; 14.2.1).
93 Cf. Matt. 16:18–19, cited in *Letter* 33.1.1.
94 Although Cyprian can continue to cite Matt. 10:33 after he compromises and reconciles the lapsed in *To Fortunatus* 5, the citation comes in a litany of verses that encourage martyrdom, which is the whole aim of the treatise.
95 Brent, *Cyprian and Roman Carthage*, 262–286, argues that Cyprian differed from earlier Christian tradition by disallowing the confessors to pardon sins. His argument primarily rests on *The Apostolic Tradition* 9, which he locates in Rome in the early second century. I would stipulate that the Roman practice in this text need not have been the norm in Cyprian's Carthage.
96 The formation of this party is often viewed as more complex and drawing from the presbyters who had earlier opposed Cyprian's appointment as bishop. See discussion and bibliography in Dunn, *Cyprian and the Bishops of Rome*, 30.
97 Geoffrey D. Dunn, "Heresy and Schism According to Cyprian of Carthage," *Journal of Theological Studies* 55 (2, 2004), 551–574.

98 Felicissimus becomes the leader or at least spokesman of the Laxists early in this controversy; see Cyprian, *Letter* 2.
99 That this persecution never came about, see Clarke, *The Letters*, 3:4–17. It should be noted that Lactantius is silent about Gallus.
100 For the council of spring 252, see *Letter* 57.
101 For a more in-depth discussion of Novatian, including his correspondence with Cyprian, see James Papandrea, *Novatian: On the Trinity, Letters to Cyprian of Carthage, Ethical Treatises* (Corpus Christianorum in Translation 22; Turnhout: Brepols, 2015); and Papandrea, *The Trinitarian Theology of Novatian of Rome: A Study in Third-Century Orthodoxy* (Lewiston, NY: Edwin Mellen Press, 2008).
102 Tertullian, *On Baptism* 15.2.
103 See details in Cyprian, *Letter* 75 (= Firmilian of Caesarea's letter to Cyprian).
104 For an attempt to understand this baptismal controversy for the sake of later generations of Christians (even contemporary ones), see J. Jayakiran Sebastian, *"baptisma unum in ecclesia sancta": A Theological Appraisal of the Baptismal Controversy in the Work and the Writings of Cyprian of Carthage* (Hamburg: Lottbeck Jensen, 1997).
105 See a unique papyrus from this date that attests to the targeting of Christians in at least some areas: P.Oxy 3035 (available online at www.csad.ox.ac.uk/POxy/ papyri/vol42/pages/3035.htm).
106 Stephen (2 August 257), Sixtus of Rome (6 August 258), and Cyprian (14 September 258). cf. Eusebius, *Church History* 7.11.10, for Dionysius of Alexandria (et al.) exiled to Libya at this time.
107 See Cyprian, *Letters* 76–79. For the known martyrs at this time, see the list in Graeme (and Burns and Jensen), *Christianity in Roman Africa*, 25. They are found in the *Pass. Mont. et Luc.*
108 Pontius, *Life of Cyprian* 12.
109 MacMullen, *Romanization*, 36. Also, see M'hamed-Hassine Fantar, "Death and Transfiguration: Punic Culture after 146," in *A Companion to the Punic Wars*, ed. Dexter Hoyos (West Sussex: Wiley Blackwell, 2015), 455. For Punic inscriptions in Curubis, see Kerr, *Latino-Punic Epigraphy*, 15.
110 *Life of Cyprian* 19.
111 See Pontius, *Life* 7.
112 E.g. *On the Dress of Virgins, On the Lord's Prayer, On Works and Almsgiving, On the Good of Patience*, and *On Jealousy and Envy*.
113 C.F.A. Borchardt, "Cyprian on Patience," *Studiae historiae ecclesiasticae* 18 (1992), 17–26.
114 This latter work famously has two manuscript traditions, which affect the dating. The consensus of scholars now follow Maurice Bévenot, *St. Cyprian's De Unitate chap. 4 in the Light of the Manuscripts* (Analecta Gregoriana, 11; Rome: Gregorian University, 1937); and Bévenot, "'Hi qui sacrificaverunt': A Significant Variant in Saint Cyprian's *De Unitate*," *Journal of Theological Studies* n.s. 5 (1954), 68–72, who argues that both editions come from Cyprian himself: one was written in the early period, and then he edited the work in a later controversy. The earlier edition could be dated even earlier than Bévenot first thought; see Clarke, *The Letters of Saint Cyprian*, 2:302; and Bobertz, "The Historical Context of Cyprian's *De Unitate*," *Journal of Theological Studies* 5 (1990), 107–111.
115 This likely reflects an economic phenomenon where bishops were patrons, but priests were clients paid from the church's funds; see Alistair Stewart-Sykes, "Ordination Rites and Patronage Systems," *Vigiliae Christianae* 56 (2002), 115–119. For discussion and bibliography on patronage and Cyprian's role as

bishop in particular, see Geoffrey Dunn, "The White Crown of Works: Cyprian's Early Pastoral Ministry of Almsgiving in Carthage," *Church History* 73 (4, 2004), 715–740.

116 *On the Lapsed* 24.

117 *On the Lapsed* 25.

118 *On the Lapsed* 26.

119 *On the Lapsed* 26.

120 *On the Lapsed* 26.

121 Simone Deléani, *Christum sequi: Etude d'un thème dans l'oeuvre de saint Cyprien* (Paris: Etudes augustiniennes, 1979).

122 See *To Fortunatus*.

123 *On the Good of Patience, On Works and Almsgiving*, and *On Mortality*.

124 *To Demetrian*, esp. 18–19. See also the points made by Evers, *Church, Cities, and People*, 65–68.

125 As he is called by Jerome, *Lives of Illustrious Men* 67.

126 Brent, *Cyprian and Roman Carthage*, demonstrates Cyprian's ongoing reliance on his Roman education and thoroughly treats Cyprian's responses to the Roman presence in Carthage.

127 As discussed on pp. 7–8, in chapter one.

128 *The History of the Decline and Fall of the Roman Empire* (New York: Harper Brothers, 1879), 1:562.

129 *History of the Christian Church*, 2:822. Also, see his comment on Cyprian's statement about sexual sins among the church's virgins (*Letter* 61.3 in ANF 5:357–358 n.2556 [= *Ep.* 4 in Clarke]): "This abomination may have lingered in Africa much longer than elsewhere among the Punic converts from Canaanite manners."

130 See the portraits of the "African" Hannibal and Cyprian in an abolitionist poster from 1836 (= fig. 4.1 in Margaret Malamud, "Black Minerva: Antiquity in Antebellum African American History," in *African Athena: New Agendas*, ed. Daniel Orrells, Gurminder K. Bhambra, and Tessa Roynon [Oxford: Oxford University Press, 2011], 83).

131 *Incomplete Works Against Julian* 6.18 (CSEL 85.2: *Noli istum Poenum . . . spernere. Non enim quia te Apulia genuit, ideo Poenos vincendos existimes gente, quos non potes mente. Poenas potius fuge, non Poenos; nam disputatores Poenos non potes fugere, quamdiu te delectat in tua virtute confidere, et beatus enim Cyprianus Poenus fuit.*); cf. 6.23. Miles Hollingworth, *Saint Augustine of Hippo: An Intellectual Biography* (Oxford: Oxford University Press, 2013), 52, comments on this passage to say that "Augustine effectively played the race card."

132 Cf. *Sermon* 310.1

133 See more on this in chapters six and seven.

134 *Crowns of Martyrdom* 13 (LCL 398:328–329): *Punica terra tulit, quo splendeat omne quidquid usquam est, inde domo Cyprianum, sed decus orbis et magistrum. Est proprius patriae martyr, sed amore et ore noster. Incubat in Libya sanguis, sed ubique lingua pollet.*

135 Pacian, *Letter* 2.4.3 (cf. the trans. in FC 17:330, "a Carthaginian for speaking Punic").

136 Augustine, *Letter* 44.3.6; *Against Cresconius* 3.34.38.

137 *To Demetrian* 1. For "world," see throughout the treatise.

138 *To Demetrian* 10 (my trans.)

139 *To Demetrian* 10 (my trans.)

140 *Letter* 62.2.2; see details in Clarke, *The Letters of St. Cyprian of Carthage*, 3:277–280 and 3:283.

141 In addition to this passage, see *On Mortality* 9, and compare Tertullian's treatment of the toga discussed in chapter four.

142 *Life of Cyprian* 6.3. See discussion in Vincent Hunink, "St. Cyprian: A Christian and Roman Gentlemen," in *Cyprian of Carthage: Studies in His Life, Language and Thought*, ed. Henk Bakker, Paul van Geest, and Hans van Loon (Leuven: Peeters, 2010), 37. It should be noted that Hunink sees this portrayal of Cyprian as specifically "Roman"; however, he also allows that the other "faces" of Cyprian are present in the sources, and "still more *personae*" can be found with further study (41).

143 *Lives of Illustrious Men* 67; which may merely be based on the similarity of this mentor's name ("Caecilianus" in Pontius, *Life of Cyprian* 4) and his own ("Caecilius" in *Letter* 66.4).

144 *Letter* 66.6.

145 *Acts of Cyprian* 3.3; cf. 4.3.

146 *Life of Cyprian* 15.3.

147 *Life of Cyprian* 15.5.

148 Michael von Albrecht and Gareth L. Schmeling, *A History of Roman Literature: From Livius Andronicus to Boethius*, rev. ed. (Leiden: Brill, 1997), 2:1568.

149 Clarke, *The Letters of St. Cyprian of Carthage*, 3:323.

150 Ibid.

151 Ibid.

152 Text in Ernst von Dobschütz, *Das "Decretum Gelasianum de libris recipiendis et non recipiendis"* (Texte und Untersuchungen 38.4; Leipzig: J. C. Hinrichs, 1912).

153 It should be noted that many non-African writers are listed as well. The question posed here is why these writers are listed among other apocryphal writers.

154 If there is any historic connection between the extant *Gelasian Decree* and Pope Gelasius (r.492–496) himself, then this information about Cyprian becomes even more important since Gelasius was said to have been "from the African nation [*natione Afer*]"; see *The Book of the Popes* 51.1 (Duchesne, *Le Liber pontificalis*, 1:255; trans. Louise Roepes Loomis, *The Book of the Popes (Liber Pontificalis)* [New York: Columbia University Press, 1916], 1:110; cf. the translation of Davis, *The Book of Pontiffs*, 44, "born in Africa").

155 *Letter* 66.6.

156 *Octavian* 15.7.

157 It should be noted that there must have been some diversity on this practice within North Africa. Not all African bishops would have attended the councils under Cyprian. The anonymous *Treatise on Rebaptism* may represent an opposing view to Cyprian in Africa (Text in CSEL 3; trans. in ANF 5:667–678; for the dating, see bibliography in Burns, Jensen, et al., *Christianity in Roman Africa*, 191). That this work was written in Africa, however, is merely a conjecture made from the theological dispute with Cyprian. This conjecture ignores the possibility that someone outside Africa (such as in Rome) could have opposed Cyprian. Recently, Brent, *Cyprian and Roman Carthage*, 297, has argued that it represents Stephen's views, "if not written by Cyprian himself." In fact, I would note that nothing in the text positively identifies Africa as its provenance. Conversely, there may even be pro-Roman statements that link the text with Cyprian's opponents. For example, the text calls Peter the "leader and first of the apostles" or even the "general and emperor of the apostles [*Petro ipso duce ac principe apostolorum*]" (*On Rebaptism* 9). This is very different from the way Cyprian spoke of Peter, even before his dispute with Stephen (e.g. *Letter* 59.14.1).

158 *Sentences of the Eighty Seven Bishops*. cf. Dunn, *Cyprian*, 6, "What is an interesting fact is that most of our information concerns not just the relationship

between the two bishops [of Rome and Carthage] but the relationships between the African bishops and the Italian bishops."

159 *Letter* 59.14.2: *episcoporum in Africa constitutorum.*
160 First at Arles (314) and then the Council of Nicaea (325).
161 Even the baptisteries of North Africa are uniquely shaped and decorated (see details and bibliography in Tabbernee, *Early Christianity in Contexts*, 237).
162 Bernhard Lang, *Sacred Games: A History of Christian Worship* (New Haven, CT: Yale University Press, 1997), 265.
163 See Dunn, *Cyprian and the Bishops of Rome*. What is more, each bishop is selected by and answers to his local congregation; see, for example, *Letter* 67.3.2–5.2. It is noteworthy that this practice continued in North Africa in later centuries, while in other regions the bishops developed more hierarchichal relationships. Carthage, as the metropolitan see, did govern councils, as did primates for each province in Africa. For these later developments, see Robert A. Markus, "Carthage – Prima Justiniana – Ravenna: An Aspect of Justinian's Kirchenpolitik," *Byzantion: Revue international des etudes byzantines* 49 (1979), 227–302, reprinted in Markus, *From Augustine to Gregory the Great: History and Christianity in Late Antiquity* (London: Variorum, 1983); and Markus, "Country Bishops in Byzantine Africa," in *The Church in Town and Country*, ed. Derek Baker (Oxford: Ecclesiastical History Society and Blackwell, 1979), 1–15, reprinted in Markus, *From Augustine to Gregory the Great: History and Christianity in Late Antiquity* (London: Variorum, 1983).
164 For details on all known African councils (dating from 220 to 646), see Jean-Louis Maier, *L'Episcopat de l'Afrique romaine, vandale et byzantine* (Rome: Institut Suisse de Rome, 1973), 17–91. Maier also provides details of all known bishops from ancient Africa (*L'Episcopat*, 249–446, in alphabetical order; cf. 95–248 for each diocese).
165 *Letter* 33.1.1.
166 *The Sentences of the Eighty-Seven Bishops* (ANF 5:565).
167 See Dossey, *Peasant and Empire*.
168 This begins to shift in the time of Constantine in Africa, even though it happens at a slower pace than elsewhere.
169 For the celebration of the *Cypriana* throughout the empire, see Procopius, *History of Wars* 3.20 (LCL 81:168–169).
170 Prudentius, *Crowns of Marytrdom* 13: *maesta Africa* (LCL 398:336–337).
171 A Donatist version also survives; see Tilley, *Donatist Martyr Stories*, 1–5.
172 *Confessions* 5.8.15. Because of Augustine's description, this basilica can be identified today with relative certainty as the St. Monique church, whose ruins still overlook the ancient port of Carthage.
173 See especially Augustine's *On Baptism*, where he has to counter the Donatists' claim that they are the heirs to Cyprian's teachings. The large corpus of Pseudo-Cyprianic material (including both forged and misattributed works) are listed in CPL 51, 57, 58, 59, 60, 61, 62, 64, 65, 67, 75, 76, 722, and 2276. For Donatist claims to Cyprian, see Matthew Alan Gaumer, "Dealing with the Donatist Church: Augustine of Hippo's Nuanced Claim to the Authority of Cyprian of Carthage," in *Cyprian of Carthage*, ed. Henk Bakker, Paul van Geest, and Hans van Loon (Leuven: Peeters, 2010), 181–201.
174 These relics can still be seen in Kornelimünster, Germany.
175 *Crowns of Martyrdom* 13; cf. Augustine, *Sermon* 306, who says they were in Utica.
176 Text in CSEL 3.1; trans. ANF 5. For a recent defense of Cyprianic authorship, see Hans van Loon, "Cyprian's Christology and the Authenticity of *Quod idola dii non sint*," in *Cyprian of Carthage*, ed. Henk Bakker, Paul van Geest, and Hans van Loon (Leuven: Peeters, 2010), 127–142. However, most have

remained unconvinced and continue to cite Eberhard Heck, "Pseudo-Cyprian, *Quod idola dii non sint* und Laktanz, *Epitome diuinarum institutionum*," in *Panchaia: Festschrift für Klaus Thraede*, ed. Manfred Wacht (Jahrbuch für Antike und Christentum Ergänzungsband 22; Münster: Aschendorffsche Verlagsbuchhandlung, 1922), 148–155.

177 *That Idols Are not Gods* 1: *Deos . . . quos colit vulgus.*

178 *That Idols Are not Gods* 2: *Mauri vero manifeste reges colunt.*

179 *That Idols Are not Gods* 4: *Romanis.*

180 *That Idols Are not Gods* 4: *vernaculos*; cf. §5.

181 *That Idols Are not Gods* 5.

182 *That Idols Are not Gods* 6–7.

183 *That Idols Are not Gods* 8.

184 Cf. Minucius Felix, *Octavius* 15.6; Cyprian, *Letter* 66.6 (discussed on p. 151).

185 *That Idols Are not Gods* 10–12.

186 *That Idols Are not Gods* 13: *Pontio Pilato, qui tunc ex parte Romana Syriam procurabat.*

187 *That Idols Are not Gods* 14: *ad poenam diaboli et ad censuram generis humani.*

188 *That Idols Are not Gods* 15 (my trans.; cf. ANF 5:468–469).

189 *Lives of Illustrious Men* 15.

190 Cf. how Eusebius derides the same view in Papias: Eusebius, *Church History* 3.39 (= *Fragments of Papias* 3.12, in Michael Holmes [ed./trans.], *The Apostolic Fathers*, 3rd ed. (Grand Rapids, MI: Baker, 2007], 738–739).

191 E.g. *Instructions* 2.2 and 2.39 (= *Instructions* 43 and 80 in ANF 4:211 and 218).

192 Discussed on p. 151 regarding Cyprian.

193 Text in CCL 15. The first has been translated in ANF 4:203–218, but the second to my knowledge has not been translated into English.

194 See *The Instructions* 2.2–6; 2.21; 2.25.

195 See bibliography in Quasten, *Patrology* (Westminster, MD: Christian Classics, 1986 [orig. 1950]), 4:259; and Thomas S. Burns, *Barbarians Within the Gates of Rome: A Study of Roman Military Policy and the Barbarians, Ca. 375–425 A.D.* (Bloomington, IN: Indiana University Press, 1994), 365 n.33. Brisson, *Autonomisme et et christianisme*, contended for the later dating, and many scholars follow his views.

196 *Instructions* 2.39: *Curiositas docti inveniet nomen in isto.*

197 Quasten, *Patrology*, 4:260, who provides an additional bibliography.

198 *Instructions* 1.41 (trans. = *Instructions* 41 in ANF 4:211).

199 Rev. 17:1–6.

200 This phrase about Africa is not in all the manuscripts (see CSEL 15:54).

201 *Song Against Two Peoples* 921–922: *Haec quidem gaudebat, sed tota terra gemebat* (my trans.)

202 *Song Against Two Peoples* 924: *tyranni.*

203 *Song Against Two Peoples* 925: *in finem fumante roma* (my trans.)

204 E.g. Brisson, *Autonomisme* (cited in n.195 of this chapter). Also, cf. Lactantius, *On the Death of the Persecutors* 38.

205 Cf. *Song Against Two Peoples* 810; and see Burns, *Barbarians Within the Gates*, 365 n.33.

206 The text and translation is available in Musurillo, *The Acts of the Christian Martyrs*, 214–239; however, better studies of the manuscripts have since been produced. I will use the text from François Dolbeau, "La Passion des saints Lucius et Montanus: Histoire et édition du texte," *Revue des etudes augustiniennes* 29 (1983), 39–82. Translations are my own.

207 See Rebillard, *Christians*, 55–56, for bibliography.

208 *The Martyrdom of Montanus and Lucius* 2.

209 *The Martyrdom of Montanus and Lucius* 3: *tributs pueris.*

210 Cf. Cyprian, *To Fortunatus* 11.
211 *The Martyrdom of Montanus and Lucius* 5, 7–8.
212 *The Martyrdom of Montanus and Lucius* 11, 21.
213 Text/trans.: Musurillo, *The Acts of the Christian Martyrs*, 194–213.
214 *Martyrdom of Marian and James* 12.3: *inmensam stragem corporum cumulus*.
215 See Barnes, *Early Christian Hagiography and Roman History* (Tübingen: Mohr Siebeck, 2010), 94–95, for discussion; and Rebillard, *Christians*, 55–56, for bibliography.
216 Cf. *Martyrdom of Marian and James* 5 and 2. James was a deacon and Marian was a lector.
217 *Martyrdom of Marian and James* 6–7.
218 *Martyrdom of Marian and James* 12.5: *equi desuper niveo colore candentes, quibus veherentur iuvenes candidati* (Musurillo 210–211).
219 Cicero briefly reports how King Masinissa of Numidia worshipped the sun and other heavenly beings: Masinissa "turning his eyes up to heaven, he uttered these words: 'I thank thee, O supreme Sun, and ye other heavenly beings' [*ad caelum et: Grates, inquit, tibi ago, summe Sol, vobisque, reliqui caelites*]" (*The Republic* 6.9 [LCL 213:260–261]).
220 *Martyrdom of Marian and James* 1.3 (and throughout): *praelium* (Musurillo 194–195). Cf. Juvenal, *Satires* 14.161–162, for this term as referring to the Punic wars: "the Punic battles [*Punica . . . proelia*]."
221 *Martyrdom of Marian and James* 4.
222 *Martyrdom of Marian and James* 4.8.
223 *Martyrdom of Marian and James* 5.1: *Cirtensium magistratibus . . . diaboli sacerdotibus*.
224 *Martyrdom of Marian and James* 5.8.
225 *Martyrdom of Marian and James* 8.2.
226 *Martyrdom of Marian and James* 8.2.
227 *Martyrdom of Marian and James* 8.2.

6 The early fourth century in Africa

As we turn to the fourth century, we see a shift from a persecuting empire to a Christian empire, and this shift makes an enormous impact on Christianity. While this impact is felt throughout all fourth-century Christianity, the dynamics in Africa are quite unique. The growing involvement in Christian affairs by the emperor affects the Christian churches in Africa specifically in regards to the Donatist schism. This controversy will be treated in full in Chapter 7, but it must be mentioned here in order to avoid a common shortcoming in historians' treatment of North African Christian history. Too often, some of the African writers from this century are divorced entirely from the North African Christian context. This is understandable, since Arnobius predates the Donatist schism, and since neither Arnobius nor Lactantius offer any direct comment on it. I contend, however, that they need to be relocated to their African homeland and understood in light of the events and dynamics of this context. While it is not until Donatus himself is bishop (after 314) that Africans will explicitly ask "what has the emperor to do with the church?"[1] writers like Arnobius and Lactantius nevertheless can be found asking a similar question in their statements about Christianity and empire. While the Donatist controversy must be treated separately for the sake of space and logical presentation, that controversy will be referenced repeatedly in what follows.

The Donatist controversy can be summarized in terms of two parties that divided in North Africa regarding who was the rightful bishop of Carthage. A schism occurred in North Africa between those who believed that Caecilian was rightly appointed as the bishop of Carthage and others who believed that he was unfit. Around 313 the two sides appealed to the new Christian emperor, Constantine, and Constantine sided with Caecilian's party. The dissenting group was labelled the Donatist party because they eventually appointed Donatus as their bishop in Carthage. This controversy especially focused on the aftermath of the persecutions from the early fourth century under the emperor Diocletian.

Diocletian's influence on the empire was immense. It will, therefore, be helpful to recount some of his important initiatives and their impact on African Christianity. Recalling the failed attempts of emperors in Cyprian's time to unite and strengthen the empire by requiring everyone to sacrifice to the Roman gods, it is important to remember how the mid–third century witnessed continued political chaos and civil war. Not until Diocletian ascended to power in 284 did the empire begin to re-establish a centralized and unified power structure. Because of the fragmented state of the provinces, Diocletian established a system of shared power: he appointed Maximian as co-emperor, and then later appointed Constantius and Galerius as "Caesars," which ranked just below the two "Augusti." This structure of four leaders came to be known as the tetrarchy, and it eventually re-established Rome's power in the various provinces, including Africa where Maximian led a campaign against "African tribes" in 297.[2] This new power structure allowed various regions of the empire to be governed in various ways. In Africa, the Christian sources record some of the specific reactions to Diocletian's new initiatives.

Christian records from the early fourth century

The Roman military in Africa had been enlisting new recruits at this time, and a record survives of one Christian, named Maximilian, who refused to be conscripted.[3] The event took place in Theveste, Numidia, once the base of the III Augustan Legion. Despite Maximilian's protests, the proconsul insisted, "Serve [*milita*], or you will die."[4] Refusing the Roman military signet, Maximilian declares, "I will not serve this world [*non milito saeculo*], but only my God."[5]

Maximilian's refusal is generally assumed to be for the same reason given by Christians throughout the empire.[6] That is, military service involves sacrifices to idols and killing. However, the proconsul references the tetrarchy by name, claiming that "there are soldiers who are Christian" who protect the Augusti and Caesars.[7] In response, Maximilian deferentially refuses to comment on those Christians serving the tetrarchs: "they know what is best for them." Then, Maximilian adds, "I cannot do wrong [*malam*]." When questioned further about the evil allegedly committed by the army, Maximilian pointedly declares, "*You* know what they do."[8] The text never elaborates on what appears to be assumed knowledge about the military's wrongdoings. The intended audience, we may assume, knew what these military crimes were. Were these examples of military excesses in Africa during Maximian's African campaign?[9] Or was it simply the fact that the Roman legions were fighting local African peoples?[10] Maximilian's martyrdom, it must be admitted, does not provide enough information to answer these questions with any degree of certainty. The account simply ends by reporting how a certain Pompeiana obtained Maxmilian's body and buried it in Carthage next to Cyprian.

There is one possible explanation of the reference to "evils" committed by the Roman army in this text. According to one later writer named Eucherius of Lyons (bishop c.434–450), an entire legion of soldiers refused Maximian's command to sacrifice before a battle against the Gauls around 287.[11] In return, Maximian killed the entire legion. At least one of these soldiers, Maurice, was remembered as "an African," but more specifically the legion came from Thebes, Egypt. Historians find it incredible that an entire legion consisted of Christians, and so this account is usually deemed hagiographical and unreliable.[12] Even so, while the entire account is likely legend, many historians believe it contains the memory of real historical events.[13] In this vein of thought, D. F. O'Reilly argues that the legion was "Theban," but it consisted of a large number of soldiers from Mauretania as well.[14] The memory of Maximian's massacre of Africans could explain the response of Maximilian in 295 to being conscripted to fight in Maximian's African campaign.

A more reliable event occurred in 303 in Milan that also indicates how Maximian was viewed in Africa. Victor Maurus, or Victor "the Moor," was a praetorian guard, but he refused to sacrifice to the Roman gods and was therefore killed on Maximian's orders.[15] While the details of Victor's life and death belong to later accounts, Ambrose serves as a witness to his martyrdom, in that he promoted Victor's veneration. Similarly, Nabor and Felix were venerated in Milan as martyrs. They were also Mauretanians who had served under Maximian, but then refused to sacrifice and so were tortured and killed. Ambrose celebrated all three of these saints as "Moors by race [*Mauri genus*]," in one of his hymns.[16]

Taken together, then, the reports of Maurice, Victor, and other martyrs, establish a pattern wherein African Christians refuse military service, and Maximian has them killed for their resistance.[17] Returning to the martyr Maximilian, his resistance to the Roman army may have involved an awareness of this pattern. In fact, the *Acts of Maximilian* displays such a clear anti-Roman sentiment that some historians have questioned its authenticity, assuming it must belong to a later period, perhaps even belonging to the Donatist party.[18] The Donatist account of the martyrs Maxima, Donatilla, and Secunda records how the emperors Maximian and Gelerius ordered Christians "in the province" (i.e. Africa) to sacrifice, and there are indications that indigenous Africans were especially targeted.[19]

As for emperor Maximian himself, after celebrating his victories in Africa with a triumphal march into Carthage (298), the co-emperor returned to Rome in 299. Historians know very little about the state of the African provinces in the aftermath of Maximian's campaign.[20] Most turn their attention back to developments in the other members of the tetrarchy.

The other Augustus, Diocletian, deserves credit for strengthening the empire both in terms of military victories against opponents and in terms of political strategy within his borders. One tactic for solidifying the internal unity of the empire was to require all citizens to sacrifice to the Roman deities. For Christians who rejected all such acts as idolatry, this requirement was untenable. For Diocletian, this act supported his general aims with the larger populace, and the Diocletian reforms are remembered as successful in restoring the empire to a position of strength.

In 305 the tetrarchy experienced a changing of the guard. Diocletian and Maximian both abdicated their positions and retired. In their place, Constantius and Galerius were both promoted to the rank of Augusti. In turn, Maximinus – Maximian's nephew – and Severus were appointed as new Caesars. This new tetrarchy, however, did not hold the peace for long.

The next year, Maxentius – Maximian's son – rebelled and declared himself emperor. By then, Constantius had died; Severus took his place as Augustus, and then the caesarship went to Constantius's son, Constantine. Severus attacked the rebel Maxentius, but most of his troops defected to Maxentius's side, and so Maxentius took control of the city of Rome. Maximian himself eventually made enemies of his own son and of Constantine, and committed suicide.

Maxentius's rebellion famously came to an end. Constantine, after seeing a vision that led him to Christianity, defeated Maxentius at the battle of the Milvian bridge in 312. By then Licinius had been appointed as co-emperor, and the two Augusti would jointly rule the empire until 314 when the two engaged in civil war. Constantine eventually defeated Licinius in 324 and became the sole ruler of the Roman Empire.

Constantine is often credited with the so-called Edict of Milan (313), which legalized Christianity and officially ended persecution. For this, he is celebrated by writers like Eusebius of Caesarea and remembered as a saint by later generations. Constantine's reception in Africa, however, was mixed and at best lukewarm. Those belonging to the Donatist party will of course criticize Constantine after he sides with the so-called Catholic party. Even those not associated with Donatism, however, offer little to no celebration like that found in other sources. Instead, writers like Lactantius write about Constantine as they would any other "good" emperor who lifted persecution – as will be shown on pp. 185–187. Perhaps this can be explained by the living memory of martyrs who were tortured and killed under the tetrarchy.

One such martyr is Felix, who was bishop of Thibiuca and who died in 303.[21] Diocletian and Maximian's edict included a requirement that the scriptures should be handed over and destroyed.[22] In searching for these sacred writings, a Roman official questioned the "local elders [*seniores plebis*]," the "priest Asper [*Aprum presbyterum*]," and two "readers [*lectores*]."[23] In what was surely an embarrassing moment, the priest singled out the bishop, Felix, as holding the scriptures.[24] When Felix was apprehended, he and the magistrate argued over the validity of the emperors' orders – Felix, of course, believed God's authority was higher. Felix was then sent to Carthage, where he was incarcerated and ultimately beheaded. This martyrdom, beyond its locale, shows several signs of indebtedness to the African Christian tradition: the local elders (mentioned on p. 112), a likely dependence on Tertullian,[25] and the fact that Felix was buried on the *Via Scillitanorum*, which was certainly an allusion to the Scillitan martyrs.[26]

Another martyrdom from this time is the *Martyrdom of Crispina*, which records events from 305.[27] Crispina was from Thagora (= Taoura, Algeria), but her trial took place in Theveste – the same place as Maximilian's (see on p. 171). As with Felix, the event was occasioned by "the law of our lords the emperors," which is an expression echoing the *Acts of the Scillitan Martyrs*, and which explicitly refers to Diocletian and Maximian.[28] Crispina refuses to sacrifice to the gods, or more precisely, to "the gods of Rome."[29] The proconsul attempts to persuade her by claiming that "all of Africa [*omnis Africa*]" has sacrificed, but Crispina refuses lest she is contaminated (*polluatur*) by demonic idols.[30] This concern with contagion echoes the controversies from Cyprian's time, and it will be reflected again in the Donatist controversy, where those who sacrificed and/or handed over the scriptures are seen as a risk that pollutes rest of the Christian community.

Another aspect of this martyrdom is important for understanding the theology of African Christians at this time: Crispina repeatedly rejects the Roman deities and insists instead on worshipping the one, true God.[31] This highest God "who is in heaven"[32] will be the focus of Arnobius and Lactantius: instead of the pantheon of false gods, Christians insist on the one and only God, or the God in the highest, or even the highest God. This theology, it will be shown, was adopted by Constantine himself, perhaps at the behest of Lactantius.[33] Before his conversion to Christianity, Constantine claimed to serve Sol Invictus (the sun, i.e. the highest heavenly being), and after his conversion Constantine will continue to use the iconography of Sol Invictus as imagery acceptable to both Christians and non-Christians alike. The proconsul who tried Crispina, however, refers to all the gods of Rome. When he sentences her to death, Crispina thanks her God that she has been set "free from [the proconsul's] hands."[34]

While it is possible that the memory of these three martyrs (not to mention others lost to the historical records)[35] produced a lukewarm reception of Constantine due to a general Christian sentiment towards Rome's role in persecution, this explanation is unsatisfactory. Christians in the eastern provinces experienced equal amounts of persecution, and even more martyrs died for the faith there than in Africa. We should, therefore, look to other factors to explain this unreceptive posture towards Constantine. I suggest that the history and heritage of African Christianity, which included a trend of explicit antipathy to Rome – in terms of the Punic heritage, the Christian apologetic, and now even the Cyprianic schism with Stephen – provides a backdrop to understanding the response of fourth-century African Christians.

To demonstrate such a claim, which is difficult with the limited amount of sources, we would expect to find evidence of a specifically African identity opposed to the Roman identity.[36] One possible place where this surfaces is in the sources on one individual who links the previous martyrs under the Diocletian persecution to the later Donatist controversy under Constantine: Anulinus, the proconsul of Carthage.

In his *Church History*, Eusebius of Caesarea records the celebrated "Edict of Milan," in which Constantine and Galerius granted religious freedom to "the Christians and all others."[37] Curiously, he immediately attaches another letter to the proconsul Anulinus, explaining that this freedom is in fact granted only to "the Catholic Church."[38] The next document Eusebius records is from Constantine to Pope Miltiades in Rome, in which Constantine summons a council to hear the case against Caecilian (i.e. regarding the Donatist controversy).[39] Constantine tells Miltiades that the documents of the case have also been sent to him (although Eusebius does not record these), and these same documents were collected by none other than Anulinus. Anulinus's letter is later cited in full by Augustine, who also references the documents collected by Anulinus.[40] It is clear in the letter itself that Anulinus has already sided with Caecilian by the time he has sent this dossier.

In Eusebius's next document, Constantine addresses Chrestus, bishop of Syracuse, telling him of the schism in Africa, and he summons him to Arles for a larger council on the matter.[41] Another letter is appended in which Constantine writes to Caecilian himself.[42] This letter dates to a time after the Roman council under Miltiades and after the Council of Arles (314); Constantine knows that the schism has continued in Africa, only now he describes the Donatist party in most unfavorable terms:

> And since I have learned that certain people of unstable mentality are eager to lead the laity of the most holy catholic church astray by foul inducements, know that when they were here I instructed Anulinus, the proconsul, and also Patricius, the vicar of the prefects, that especially in this matter they are not to overlook such incidents. Therefore, if you observe any such men persisting in this madness, you must not hesitate to bring this matter before the aforementioned judges.[43]

To recap, Anulinus is the one responsible for sending the evidence against the Donatists to Rome, and he is the proconsul to whom Caecilian should send the schismatic Donatists. Here, it is important to remember that Anulinus himself presided over the trial, torture, and execution of the African martyrs during the reign of Maximian and Diocletian.[44] Many African Christians would have seen the continuity between Diocletian's persecution of Christians and Constantine's actions against the Donatists, especially since Anulinus enforced both.

In the last document Eusebius offers in this collection, Constantine writes to Anulinus himself. The emperor instructs the proconsul to grant tax exemptions only to the "Catholic" party in Africa, since it "conferred the greatest good fortune on the Roman name."[45] It should be no surprise, then, that the Donatists retained an identity as a church persecuted by Rome. It should be further recognized that Rome's persecution was carried out by none other than Anulinus, and so the so-called Donatist party continued to resist the authority of Anulinus even after Constantine. Constantine commissioned Anulinus to side with the Caecilianist party, which supported the "Roman name." The records about Anulinus illustrate how this "Roman name" was opposed by African Christians, both before and after

Constantine's conversion and the pre-Constantinian martyrdoms influenced the resistance to Constantine's involvement in the African church's affairs.[46]

Before turning exclusively to the most vehement opponents of Constantine (i.e. the "Donatists," discussed in Chapter 7), and even before turning to Lactantius who describes Constantine in much less glowing terms than has often been assumed, let us begin by examining a pre-Constantinian author, Arnobius, whose apologetic against the Roman gods in some ways can be seen to anticipate, if not influence, the theology of Constantine himself as well as later African Christians.

Arnobius of Sicca

We know very little about Arnobius.[47] He was from Sicca (modern El Kef, Tunisia),[48] and he taught rhetoric during the reign of Diocletian. At the time of his writing, Arnobius had "recently" converted from worshipping gods made out of material elements such as "elephant bones."[49] He converted to Christianity after experiencing a dream of some sort, but his bishop remained suspicious of the former rhetorician who had previously been outspoken against Christianity.[50] Arnobius, therefore, wrote his only known work, *Against the Nations*, to prove his sincerity.[51]

The occasion for Arnobius's work is stated to be recent disasters blamed on Christians.[52] These include famine and a "deficiency of grain."[53] It is worth remembering at this point how Africa was the grain supply for Rome, and a frequent tactic in the many rebellions against Rome was to halt the grain supply. Why are Christians being blamed for the lack of grain in the Roman Empire?

The common accusation found in Christian apologists is that Christians tempt people to abandon worship of the traditional gods, and these gods in turn cease to bless the crops. This generic accusation, however, does not seem to explain Arnobius's argument. He is certainly willing to counter it with explicit political criticism:

> If in any one state whatever they have caused many to die with hunger, through disgust at our name, why have they in the same state made wealthier, nay, very rich, by the high price of corn, not only men not of our body, but even Christians themselves?[54]

In this case, he is blaming the rulers for the imbalance of wealth resulting in the sale of grain.[55]

In the same passage, Arnobius answers the claim that the gods are punishing humans for failure to placate them. When doing so, he describes specific people groups in Africa:

> If among the Gaetuli and the Tinguitani they sent dryness and aridity on the crops on account of this circumstance, why did they in that very

year give the most bountiful harvest to the Moors and the Nomads, when a similar religion had its abode in these regions as well?[56]

For Arnobius, therefore, the argument can easily invoke local African identities, and these identities – while not monolithic – can even be placed in opposition to the rulers of Rome, about which we will say more on pp. 178–181.

His work, *Against the Nations*, begins with this accusation against Christians in Africa, and it then turns to a series of topics. Although Jerome thought Arnobius's work lacked organization,[57] Arnobius did have a distinct outline for his seven books. In answer to the accusation that Christians are to blame for the lack of grain, Arnobius reviews historical examples of natural disasters from before the time of Christianity. The false gods are faulted for not preventing these disasters, and the one true God is shown to be superior (book 1); Christ is superior to the philosophers, especially their view of the human soul as immortal (book 2); the nations' gods are then shown to be human creations (book 3); the idolaters are shown to actually insult the gods, and their views of the abstract and lesser known gods are ridiculed (book 4); the myths and mystery cults are denounced (book 5); the temples and ceremonies are shown to be improper for divinity (book 6); and finally, an assortment of details about idolatry in general are mocked, which ends with a very specific attack on Roman gods and Roman history (book 7).

Arnobian theology

As a new convert, Arnobius's teachings represent an undeveloped theology. In some ways, this makes him even more interesting because he represents Christian doctrine as it was first learned by an African at this time. His emphasis is unsurprisingly not on the earthly life of Jesus (a name never used by Arnobius).[58] While Christ performed miracles, and suffered and died, Arnobius aims to show how Christ as the one true God surpasses the false gods, which are modeled on the human image. Arnobius anticipates Augustine's pessimistic view of human sinfulness: human evil is not a result of human free will, but is something natural to humans.[59] He at one point even concedes to the Platonists that humans are imperfect compared to a perfect God, and thus a lesser being may have been their maker.[60]

Arnobius's view of God is mostly articulated as a negation. An idol is *not* God. The true God, in fact, can*not* be depicted with idols. Furthermore, the one true God is *not* material, *not* visible, *not* tangible (etc.). Alternatively, when offering a positive statement about God, Arnobius simply speaks of God as the greatest, highest, most perfect (etc.); God is the king and lord of heaven.[61] As part of this argument about God's true nature as "the highest," Arnobius allows for an ambiguity between absolute monotheism (there is only one God) and a form of monolatry (worship only one of the gods). If other gods exist, it would be like having one king, whose subordinates are honored when he is honored.[62] Likewise, if there are other gods, they would be honored by worship of "the First God . . . the Father of things and the Lord, the Establisher and Governor of all things."[63] At times, Arnobius does deny that the false gods actually exist – yet he also repeatedly finds the best character traits of the gods to be things that he can accommodate as the Christian view of God. The habit of accommodating characteristics from other gods is itself something that Arnobius finds his non-Christian audience doing:

> you maintain that Liber, Apollo, the sun are but one divinity multiplied by three names . . . if it is true that the sun is the same as Liber and the same as Apollo, it follows that in "the nature of things" there is no one such as Apollo or Liber.[64]

This statement is in reference to the practice of *interpretatio Romana*; the various names of the gods refer to one entity. Although Arnobius insists that the false gods do not exist, he can also claim that whenever one worships the "highest" true God one is worshipping the Christian God.[65] Later, Arnobius's student, Lactantius, will hold a similar theology of the "highest" God, and Lactantius's views can be seen even in Constantine's early statements (discussed on p. 174).

While Arnobius's view of God is primarily derived from Christian tradition, and although he constantly compares this God with false gods from throughout the empire, Arnobius's theology also reflects his local, African context. Michael Simmons provides several parallels between African views of Saturn found in epigraphic sources and Arnobius's theology, which leads him to conclude, "Saturnian theology may have influenced his understanding of the Christian God."[66] Simmons reviews how Arnobius mocks Saturn, only to accommodate all of the best qualities of Saturn into the Christian view of God. By "Saturn," of course, Arnobius is referring to the Punic Baal, only now fully synthesized with the Latin deity via *interpretatio Romana*.[67] For example, when speaking of how some worship the Sun as the highest God (which Arnobius trumps by speaking of the sun's Creator),[68] Simmons contends that this does not reflect Plato's *Timaeus,* as others have said of Arnobius.[69] Instead, Arnobius's views have "another origin," namely the "conceptual parallel with ideas found in Saturnian theology."[70] Again, the tension lies in how Arnobius uses "Saturnian theology" to describe the Christian God, but he does so in direct competition with Saturn's preeminent place for his African audience. Simmons' point allows us to turn now to more items found in Arnobius that reflect his African context.

What was African about Arnobius?

Later in the fourth century, Jerome offers advice about how to read certain Christian authors:

> I think Origen ought at times to be read for his learning, in the same manner that we treat Tertullian and Novatus, Arnobius and Apollinarius,

and a number of ecclesiastical writers both in Greek and Latin: we should choose out the good in them and shun what is contrary.[71]

What could be "contrary" about Arnobius? Although he celebrates that Arnobius's work *Against the Nations* can be found "everywhere,"[72] elsewhere Jerome reports that Arnobius was especially respected in Africa.[73] Tertullian, Novatus, and Apollinaris all were remembered as turning to heresies late in their life, but no hint of this occurs with Arnobius. When using later standards, there are certain unorthodox teachings found in Arnobius,[74] and so these could be what Jerome had in mind, and yet this does not seem to place Arnobius into the same heretical status as the other writers Jerome mentions. Did Jerome know or suspect that he sided with some African heresy, such as Donatism? Unfortunately, there is simply no way to answer this question because there is no additional evidence. While nothing ties Arnobius to the later Donatist controversy, there is evidence of Arnobius having an explicitly African identity.

Many statements in his work *Against the Nations* reflect Arnobius's African identity. W.H.C. Frend observed these and remarked,

> [Arnobius displayed] a liking for Judaistic exclusivity of North African Christianity that made him call his seven books of apologetic "Contra Gentes", i.e. against "the outsiders" or "nations" of the Hebrew psalmist (Ps. xcvi.5). His final book, written after the outbreak of the Great Persecution ended on a strongly anti-Roman note (*Contra Gentes* vii.51).[75]

Frend's assumption that African Christianity belongs to Jewish origins is an outdated scholarly opinion.[76] He correctly detects, however, "a strongly anti-Roman note" that is likewise reflected in other African Christian sources from this time.[77]

The anti-Roman statements in Arnobius echo the tactics used by earlier apologetic writers, especially those from North Africa.[78] Like those earlier African writers, Arnobius mocks Rome's sordid history: the Trojans (i.e. Roman ancestors) are faulted for the Trojan war (1.6); Romulus's ruthless demise is recounted (1.41); Aeneas's divine mother, Venus, is accused of promiscuity (4.27); and several of Rome's heroes are frequently invoked, but in acerbic tones.[79] As with the earlier African apologists, Arnobius likely took these examples from Livy, and so on the one hand he should be understood as a member of the Roman Empire trained in classical Roman sources. On the other hand, his interpretation of these sources reflects an antagonism towards Rome's political power and follows in the pattern of the African school wherein others have used these same tactics.

Throughout the work, Arnobius returns to the fact that he is specifically speaking to Romans (at least rhetorically – he may be speaking more *about* them).[80] More generally, Rome is faulted for its imperialism: "Did we, forsooth, urge the deities into frenzy, so that the Romans lately, like some swollen torrent, overthrew all nations, and swept them beneath the flood?"[81] In a similar vein, Arnobius criticizes how,

> Tyrants and your kings, who, putting away all fear of the gods, plunder and pillage the treasuries of temples; who by proscription, banishment, and slaughter, strip the state of its nobles? who, with licentious violence, undermine and wrest away the chastity of matrons and maidens,- these men you name *indigites* and *divi;* and you worship with couches, altars, temples, and other service, and by celebrating their games and birthdays, those whom it was fitting that you should assail with keenest hatred.[82]

In other words, the Roman "tyrants" insult the gods when they conquer foreign lands and plunder the temples.

Using a different line of argument, Arnobius references how non-Christians admit the gods are portrayed in mere human form. In response, he offers a hypothetical situation in which animals worshipped humans by depicting them as animals, which obviously would be an insult to the humans. The insult is specifically aimed at Roman history: Arnobius imagines "the founder of Rome, Romulus, . . . with an ass's face, the revered Pompilius with that of a dog," and "under the image of a pig were written Cato's or Marcus Cicero's name."[83] This kind of rhetoric, which would have been insulting and unconvincing to Romans, would likely have been humorous and compelling to Arnobius's African audience.

The anti-Romanism, of course, may be due to a Christian identity opposed to the pagan persecutors. Arnobius certainly would affirm that the Christian identity is at the forefront of his argument: for example, he celebrates how "in Rome herself, the mistress of the world" there are those who have accepted Christian teaching.[84] This statement, however, betrays two points: the first is that Arnobius still uses the Roman identity as the primary "other" or opponent.[85] Does this by default mark his own identity as not-Roman and African? Second, Arnobius's compliment is not without backhandedness, since Rome is "the mistress [*dominam*]" and in light of his previously cited statements this should be read as bitter sarcasm. In all likelihood, his audience is not strictly Roman.

One clue about Arnobius's intended audience can be found when he speaks against the "new men [*novis . . . viris*]."[86] Scholars of intellectual history have generally understood this statement as an attack against the followers of the philosopher Porphyry.[87] While it is beyond argument that Arnobius engages Porphyry and "New Philosophers,"[88] we need not exclude other possible targets in addition to the Porphyrians. The philosophers attacking Christianity in general across the Mediterranean would likely have called to Arnobius's mind local examples who instigated the arrest and trials of African Christians. Perhaps Arnobius, like Tertullian and other African apologists before him, is countering the new elites of North Africa. McCracken translates this phrase as "upstarts," and while Arnobius is attacking the idea that the soul is divine in this passage, he does so to critique those who are "deceived by what promises us vain hopes . . . carried away by an extravagant opinion of themselves, namely that souls are immortal, very near in degree of rank to the Lord and Ruler of Creation."[89] Assuming that he writes to an African audience, which he aims to persuade, this would explain why Arnobius devotes his last book to so much anti-Roman rhetoric. Just as he describes his God in Punic characteristics in order to appeal to his African audience (as discussed in the previous section), he villainizes Rome in his conclusion, making allies with an African audience against a common enemy, even while critiquing many new African elites who have aligned themselves with Rome.

There are additional statements in Arnobius's works that specifically represent an African context. For example, he refers to Saturn (i.e. Latinized Baal) as the "guardian of the countryside [*custos ruris*]," reflecting a Libyo-Punic understanding.[90] Likewise, he can refer to specific marble quarries found in Africa.[91] When debating the alleged novelty of the Christian religion, Arnobius compares it to the Roman religion. While the founding of Rome itself is admittedly ancient, Arnobius points out all of the recent religious imports to Rome, such as Egyptian deities and how "Punic Hannibal" had introduced the mother goddess to Italy.[92] At the end of his work, Arnobius returns to Hannibal in what seems to be a forced example of someone whose destiny was not controlled by stone idols.[93] This reference, however, is not forced at all, when Arnobius is understood as writing to fellow Africans.

In sum, Arnobius was an African whose African context shaped his Christian apologetic. He was widely read, especially in Africa, and his influence can be further seen in the works of his pupil, Lactantius, to whom we may now turn.

Lactantius

Lactantius was a student of Arnobius,[94] and despite his larger body of writings we know little more about the student than we do the teacher.[95] Despite the obscurity of his past, however, we do know that he rose to prominence.

Lactantius studied in Sicca under Arnobius before being invited to the new capitol of the eastern empire, Nicomedia, to teach rhetoric sometime around 300.[96] Under Diocletian's persecution, he resigned his post, but then around 314 Constantine hired Lactantius to teach his first-born son, Crispus.[97] His role with Crispus is a curious detail, since later Constantine killed his own son for unknown reasons – perhaps a personal betrayal.[98] While it is tempting to look for a connection between Crispus's death in 326 and Lactantius's in 325,[99] there is simply no record at all about how Lactantius died. One source records that he was extremely poor, but it gives no explanation as to why this would be the case for someone with an elite teaching position who had served two emperors.[100]

Works and teachings

Six works of Lactantius survive, along with fragments of his letters quoted in later writers.[101] In all his works, Lactantius displays his skill as a writer and a rhetorician, and he writes as one well-versed in classical literature.[102] Early modern scholars often refer to him as the Christian Cicero.

In some ways, his *On the Death of the Persecutors* parallels other church historians, like Eusebius, only Lactantius focuses on the emperors who persecuted Christians, not the Christians themselves. His remaining works focus on Christian teachings, but these teachings also continue the apologetic tradition wherein the faith is defended from and contrasted with the non-Christian religions of the empire.[103]

One of his surviving works stands apart as difficult to determine in terms of its rhetorical aims: his treatise, *On the Phoenix*, is in praise of the extraordinary bird. Although it is generally read as an allegory and assumed to have both theological and political implications, the author never exits the allegory to offer any interpretation.[104] The mystical bird, the *Phoenice*, returns to the east, or more precisely to Syria. Because of this bird's death and resurrection there, Syria is named "Phoenicia."[105] Phoenicia, of course, is the ancestral home of the "Punic" peoples in North Africa, an awareness that other North African Christians explicitly referenced.[106]

In regard to his teachings, Lactantius held several unique tenets. He differed from his predecessor, Arnobius, in that he viewed humanity in very positive terms.[107] Similarly, whereas Arnobius emphasized the transcendence of the God of heaven, Lactantius offered a correction to those who thought of God as so distant that he did not intervene in human affairs.[108] Whereas the philosopher's god may be so abstract as to be impersonal and even inactive, Lactantius's active God is both transcendent and still rules the world. Michael Simmons thinks that Lactantius, like his teacher Arnobius and Tertullian before him, describes God in characteristics of Punic Baal in order to compete with "Saturn's" popularity in Africa at the time.[109]

Any disorder in the world resulted from a lesser being produced by God who was jealous of God's offspring, the Son.[110] Humans should restore order to this world politically. Lactantius rejects the idea found in Cicero's *Republic* (as argued by Carneades) that all humans and governments act in self-interest and that civic law should be based on such self-interest. Instead, the "natural" justice stems from one God creating humans as a brotherhood.[111] This view of one true justice as opposed to local civic justices of self-interest largely anticipates Augustine's "two cities," and although he has been overshadowed by Augustine, Lactantius represents a largely untapped resource for those interested in political theology.[112]

It is likely that Lactantius's view of God influenced Constantine. Before his conversion, Constantine worshipped *Sol Invictus*, the Unconquerable Sun, as the highest, most powerful God. Lactantius's apologetic works continue Arnobius's practice of speaking of "the most high God" and, wherever possible, finding common theology with non-Christian philosophers and even poets. The sincerity of Constantine's conversion has been questioned in modern times because – among other things – he continued to use *Sol Invictus* and other non-Christian imagery in his official imperial propaganda. Instead of viewing such a practice as hypocrisy, we should probably see Constantine as carrying out Arnobius's and Lactantius's theological program of abstracting the highest gods of "paganism" and identifying them with the one true God of Christianity.[113]

In the end, God's true justice and the earthly governments will clash in a battle that will result in the defeat of all evil. Since God created the world in six "days," and since a thousand years is as one day with the Lord (cf. Psalm 89.4/90.4), history will culminate in a 7,000-year epoch in which Christ will reign victorious.[114] It is clear that Lactantius is following the book of Revelation (especially chapters 17–20), and so it is no surprise that Lactantius depicts the fall of Rome.[115] It is, however, noteworthy how Lactantius views Rome's role in history: the Syballine oracles predicted Rome's fall in ages past,[116] but Rome truly became a force of conquest after "Carthage was removed," for it was after the Punic wars that Rome "stretched forth her hands toward the whole world on land and sea."[117] This awareness of Carthage's role raises the question about whether Lactantius showed any self-awareness of being an African.

What was African about Lactantius?

There are a few things about Lactantius that point to his African identity. Reminiscent of Cyprian's name and its implications for his African heritage,[118] Lactantius's name may provide us with clues about his own background. In the manuscripts, his works are introduced as written by "L. Caelius Firmianus who is also called Lactantius [*qui et Lactantius*]." Lactantius, however, is an odd name in Latin, since it comes from the root word, *lactans*, to nurse. Early modern scholars looked instead to "a Semitic source. The root LQT makes possible the Punic form of LaQTaN, 'he whose occupation is gleaning': the latinised form Lactantius suited the African onomatology of the time."[119] Admittedly, this is limited and questionable evidence, but Lactantius's name, coupled with his provenance, is enough for some scholars to conclude that he "was of Punic descent."[120] These clues require further exploration as to how Lactantius's African identity may be detected in his writings.

In trying to discern how Lactantius's African background is reflected in his writings, we are limited to his surviving works. Jerome mentions a work entitled *The Banquet*, written "as a young man in Africa," and an *Itinerary* that records his travels "from Africa" to Nicomedia.[121] We would certainly learn much to answer our question if these texts were available, since their ties to Africa were explicit enough to be noted by Jerome.

In most of Lactantius's extant writings his identity is that of a Christian, set against the idolatrous identity of non-Christians. The non-Christians, however, are more precisely the Romans – as with previous African writers. Since he can at times speak of both "Greeks" and "Romans" as outsiders, it is tempting to conclude that he primarily sees himself as African.[122] We cannot, however, rush to this conclusion, because Lactantius's many works display instances where he can include himself within the Roman Empire and the Roman way of life.[123] Even so, given that provincials could see themselves as both Roman and non-Roman, it is no surprise that early modern scholars read these kinds of statements and concluded that Lactantius spoke "native Punic."[124]

Like the African apologists who preceded him, Lactantius penned numerous anti-Roman statements.[125] Some of these are relatively benign notes of history, such as when Valerian's capture by the Persians allows Lactantius to contrast how "the Roman name was a sport and mockery for the barbarians."[126] The moral of the story is that "Romans should not place too much confidence in their strength."[127] Similarly, Lactantius criticized Diocletian's unjust tax system, which favored the rich and divided the provinces.[128] Up to this point, Lactantius's posture could be held by a Christian from any province. Nevertheless, like his African predecessors, his apology is not simply against "paganism" in general; he specifically targets Roman practice: "I come now to the religious belief proper to the Romans."[129] After this statement, Lactantius's rhetoric turns vitriolic toward Roman history, and therein we can detect more about his own identity.

When describing Rome's founders, Lactantius claims Romulus's mother was in fact a prostitute, not the wolf of legend, and much of Rome's ancient history embodies this essentially adulterous character trait.[130] When Lactantius describes Saturn's lineage, he does not report the common Roman version wherein Saturn was once resident and king of Latium. Instead, Lactantius knows that Saturn comes originally from Mesopotamia.[131] In other words, Lactantius primarily thinks of the Phoenician Saturn (i.e. Baal), also popular in Africa. Later, Lactantius can mock the Italian myth of Saturn: since he was originally the Phoenician god of the skies, it is laughable that he was "expelled" (from heaven? or Mesopotamia?) and sent to Latium.[132] Another famous Roman mocked by Lactantius is Cato, who ended his senate speeches with the cry, "Carthage must be destroyed!"[133] Lactantius finds him to have been confused in his understanding of both the Stoics and Caesar, which is why he committed suicide in shame.[134] Lactantius openly derides the symbols of Rome, such as "the purple robes and axes [*fasces*], so that they might rule over those they would strike with terror and fear."[135] Likewise, Roman heros such as Regulus are also mocked.[136] All of these statements, it should be noted, can be found in previous African apologists.

Just as Lactantius makes explicitly anti-Roman statements, in doing so he at times betrays a specifically African identity. For example, he derides the title "Africanus" given to conquerors of Africa: Hercules was "a sort of Africanus among the gods" and he was "befouled with outrages, adulteries, and lusts."[137] In reviewing ancient writers, Lactantius regrets that Apuleius of Madauros is sometimes omitted.[138] Lactantius makes this statement when reviewing other North Africans he admires, including Minucius Felix, Tertullian, Cyprian, the pre-Christian poet Terence, and even Aeneas's statement to Dido.[139] In the cosmic battle between good and evil, the world was divided into four quadrants, and the "south and east" belong to God, while the north and west belong to the devil.[140]

It may be telling that in his work *On the Death of the Persecutors*, Lactantius records Licinius's edict,[141] not the more famous version recorded in Eusebius, which is credited to Constantine and Licinius.[142] Perhaps, since Lactantius came from Africa, he refused to credit Constantine, who had worked so closely through Anulinus. In the rest of the work, he credits Licinius for putting to death the rest of the family members of past persecutors. Then, he concludes with a cryptic warning: "I thought it proper to commit them to writing exactly as they happened, lest the memory of events so important should perish, and lest any future historian of the persecutors should corrupt the truth."[143] The current peace is then celebrated, and the final sentence addresses "Donatus," to whom the whole work is dedicated:

> and do you, above all others, my best beloved Donatus, who so well deserve to be heard, implore the Lord that it would please Him propitiously and mercifully to continue His pity towards His servants, to protect His people from the machinations and assaults of the devil, and to guard the now flourishing churches in perpetual felicity [*perpetuam quietem*].[144]

Whereas Eusebius moved immediately from the so-called Edict of Milan to the documents against the Donatist party and then to the wickedness of Licinius, Lactantius elects to cite Licinius's version of the edict of toleration and then celebrates Licinius's actions, followed immediately by a warning against any future persecutor of Christians. "Donatus" and others are to celebrate the peace given by Licinius – not Constantine!

Another clue as to the African context is where this same Donatus is said to have suffered persecution: "Not if I had a hundred tongues and a hundred mouths and a voice of iron, could I comprehend all the forms of their crimes, could I get through all the names of the punishments."[145] This eloquent way of saying that Donatus's sufferings are indescribable turns out to be a quote from Virgil's *Aeneid*.[146] When Virgil makes this statement, he is describing the lower regions of Hades, just paragraphs after encountering Dido of Carthage. This is comparable to something Lactantius says in his *On God's Workmanship*: therein, a certain Demetrianus is advised with another quote from the *Aeneid*.[147] In this instance, Virgil's statement is directing Aeneas to honor the Carthaginian "Juno" above all others. While these literary allusions are admittedly cryptic, it is at the very least curious that Lactantius cites Virgil's statements about Carthaginian symbols.

Finally, Lactantius adds one more classical reference when he celebrates Donatus's endurance during the persecution: "How pleasing was that spectacle to God when He beheld you as victor, not bringing under subjection to your chariot white horses or huge elephants, but, best of all, the very triumphant ones themselves."[148] The reader will remember that Roman generals celebrated their triumphal march by riding on a chariot pulled by white horses, and once Pompey attempted to celebrate his victories in Africa by hitching his chariot to elephants.[149] Here, Lactantius claims that Donatus's actions have outpaced the Roman practice, even a specific time when a Roman coopted the symbol of Africa.[150]

As for the recipient of this work named by Lactantius, historians generally assume that this Donatus is not the one for whom the Donatist party was named. Even so, it is tempting to see a cryptic reference in Lactantius's statement. Remembering his work, *On the Phoenix*, which is an unexplained allegory about the mystical bird from Phoenicia, we know that Lactantius is capable of writing such cryptic messages. Timothy David Barnes thinks that Lactantius does refer to the Donatist schism elsewhere, but it must be admitted that this is debatable.[151] Even if Barnes is incorrect and Lactantius does not explicitly reference the Donatist schism, it is difficult to imagine that Lactantius would not have known about the controversy in his homeland. If so, then a reference to a "Donatus," in which he rehearses the "Deaths of the Persecutors," could have implications for how the emperor handles the Donatist controversy. This work was written soon after Constantine's conversion, and this would be in the same time period (314–317) when Constantine began to seize Donatist church property[152] – the same actions previously ordered by Diocletian against all Christians.[153] This work, written while Licinius is still a defender of Christianity, credits the eastern emperor, not Constantine, with the "Edict of Milan." After this – again, cryptically – Lactantius states, "Of the adversaries of God there still remained one, whose overthrow and end I am now to relate."[154] Who is the one remaining persecutor? Diocletian has just died, so it could be Maxentius[155] or even Daia Maximinus.[156] Daia's death is recounted,[157] and then all the remaining heirs of past emperors die, all at the hand of Licinius.[158] Throughout this narrative of the end of the persecutors, no further mention is made of Constantine – a silence that may be deafening. In fact, on a rereading of this text, Constantine is never mentioned favorably in the whole work.[159] The reporting of Constantine's activities is always cold and factual, noting how "the Romans" or "the Senate" name him "Maximus."[160] Before we can decide how to interpret Lactantius's view of Constantine, we should examine his view of Maximian.

In Africa, Maximian (as discussed at the beginning of this chapter) was especially remembered for his persecution of African Christians. This same sentiment is found in Lactantius. After first mentioning how Maximian received and carried out orders to persecute the Christians, Lactantius directs his praise to "Donatus" who endured these trials (discussed in the previous two paragraphs).[161] Later, after recounting the various developments within the tetrarchy, Lactantius recounts Maximian's death. Because he twice betrayed Constantine and tried to kill him, Maximian was forced to commit suicide by hanging himself. Curiously, when caught, Maximian stood like "hard flint standing there or a Marpesian rock," which is another quote from Virgil's *Aeneid*, a statement that originally described Dido when Aeneas encountered her in the underworld.[162] Likewise, when describing the hanging, Lactantius cites Virgil's description of Amata's suicide (Amata was the queen of the Latins defeated by Aeneas). In the final passage of the work, Lactantius celebrates how God killed Diocletian and Maximian.[163] As with the first time he mentioned Maximian, Lactantius immediately follows the reference with a direct address to "Donatus." Maximian, along with all of the persecutors, is denounced. Meanwhile, Donatus is told to pray so that God will "ward off all the snares and attacks of the devil from His people, so that the Church may flourish and be guarded by perpetual peace."[164] Lactantius, although writing after 313, still expects further persecution.

The one affirmation of Constantine's actions occurs when Lactantius reports how he first came to power and re-established the Christian church properties.[165] This reference to restoring church property would have been an acute juxtaposition to Constantine's seizing of Donatist basilicas in 314, when this text was written. Although the text is ambiguous (or possibly intentionally cryptic), the aim here may be to persuade Constantine to abandon any persecution of African Christians.[166] Did Constantine head Lactantius's warning? We know that in 317 Constantine turned his attention away from the controversy in Africa and left the Donatists alone.

More can be said about Lactantius's view of Constantine. Not only is there no positive celebration of Constantine in *On the Death of the Persecutors*, but there is also virtually no affirmation of the new emperor throughout all of Lactantius's works. The possible exception is in *The Divine Institutes*, but this requires further explanation. The work survives in two forms, one having additional passages in praise of Constantine. Modern scholars have debated whether these additional passages were later deleted in some manuscripts (because they also contained questionable doctrine), or whether these were later interpolations to an originally shorter text. Eberhard Heck has convinced most scholars that both versions came from Lactantius himself, with the additions about Constantine added around 324.[167]

To be clear, the argument I am forwarding does not require that Lactantius never favorably mentioned Constantine.[168] On the one hand, perhaps Heck is correct, and Lactantius later came to see Constantine in a more Eusebian light as the defender of the faith. This, however, would have been (coincidentally?) after Constantine left the Donatists to themselves. On the other hand, if Heck is wrong,[169] than it is even more alarming that Lactantius never offered praise for Constantine.

In the undisputed text of *Divine Institutes*, written in Africa around 309, Lactantius has clear warnings for the "Romans" (see p. 184 in this book), specifically "evil princes [*mali principes*]" and "unjust persecutors [*inius-tissimi persecutores*]" that "contrive against us."[170] The entire work ends with further warnings: after again citing the African poet Terence, who says "there has to be flogging; shackles must be worn,"[171] Lactantius declares, "Let no one trust in riches, in public office, even in royal power."[172] Finally, Lactantius concludes with an exhortation to serve God, "while the spirit controls these members," which itself is another quote from Virgil's *Aeneid* wherein Aeneas has just betrayed Dido, the queen of Carthage.[173]

In sum, Lactantius writes as an African, and we should consider how his context informs his writings whenever we study him. His value for historians is undeniable, since he provides much information on the era of Diocletian. Without minimizing how Lactantius belongs to the wider context of the Roman Empire, we can also recognize his uniquely African viewpoint. Most Christians from the fourth and fifth centuries came to accept the conclusion of Eusebius of Caesarea: Constantine, and the Roman emperors since Constantine's conversion to Christianity, are establishing God's kingdom on earth. God sent them; we owe them our allegiance. Lactantius, writing just before Eusebius, and then Augustine, writing a century later, both represent a more ambiguous stance. Lactantius never praised Constantine to the extent that Eusebius would (if at all); and Augustine – after the fall of Rome to the Visigoths in 410 – insisted that the Christian's citizenship is ultimately in the City of God. It will be up to later African Christians to develop this view of the church's independence from the secular powers in ways that shape medieval Christendom.[174] The view of Augustine and these later writers will be discussed further in the chapters that follow, after we turn to another scene in the African church at this time, the Donatist controversy.

Notes

1 Donatus's works do not survive, but he is quoted by Optatus, *Against the Donatists* 3.3: *Quid est imperiori cum ecclesia?* This question appears to echo Tertullian, *Prescript Against the Heretics* 7.9, "what indeed has Athens to do with Jerusalem? [*Quid ergo Athenis et Hierosolymis?*]"

2 Barnes, *Constantine and Eusebius* (Cambridge, MA: Harvard University Press, 1981), 16. Cf. Aurelius Victor, *The Book of the Caesars* 39.22; and it is worth noting here that Aurelius Victor was himself African (see details in (H. W. Bird, *Sextus Aurelius Victor: A Historiographical Study* [Liverpool: F. Cairns, 1984]).

3 *The Acts of Maximilian* (text and trans. in Musurillo, *The Acts of the Christian Martyrs*, 244–249). It should be noted that many of the martyrdoms reporting events from this time period are of debatable dates. They may reflect later tradition about this time period rather than eyewitness accounts (as will be discussed in more detail in chapter seven). Nevertheless, they can still be used here to establish my argument about how these events were perceived by (at least some) African Christians.

4 *Acts of Maximilian* 2.1.

5 Ibid.

6 More specifically, the text is indebted to Tertullian's *On the Military Crown*.

7 *Acts of Maximilian* 2.9.

8 *Acts of Maximilian* 2.10 (emphasis added).

9 Lactantius, *On the Death of the Persecutors* 8.5, speaks of Maximian's violation of young men and women, but this is a general accusation of "wherever he went."

10 Lactantius, *On the Death of the Persecutors* 8.2, claims that Maximian was prone toward "evil [*ad male*]," and then tells how he squandered the wealth of "Africa and Spain" (8.3).

11 For Eucherius, see John M. Pepino, *St. Eucherius of Lyons: Rhetorical Adaptaion of Message to Intended Audience in the Fifth Century Provence* (PhD dissertation for Catholic University of America, 2009).

12 The text of the *Passion of the Martyrs at Agaune* is in CSEL 31:165–173. See details in Peter Murray, Linda Murray, and Tom Devonshire Jones, *The Oxford Dictionary of Christian Art and Architecture*, 2nd ed. (Oxford: Oxford University Press, 2013), 363.

13 E.g. Frend, *Martyrdom and Persecution in the Early Church: A Study of a Conflict from the Maccabees to Donatus* (Oxford: Blackwell, 1965), 360. Even David Woods, "The Origin of the Legend of Saint Maurice and the Theban Legion," *Journal of Ecclesiastical History* 45 (1994), 385–395, insists that historians can find historical elements behind the legend, only he disagrees with Frend and locates these elements to a later decade.

14 D. F. O'Reilly, "The Theban Legion of St. Maurice," *Vigiliae Christianae* 32 (1978), 195–207.

15 See details in Gillian Vallance Mackie, *Early Christian Chapels in the West: Decoration, Function and Patronage* (Toronto: University of Toronto Press, 2003), 117.

16 See A. S. Walpole, *Early Latin Hymns* (Hildesheim: Georg Olms, 2004), 84.

17 Decades later Maximian will still be remembered as a "tyrant" in Numidia; see Optatus, *Against the Donatists* 1.16–18 and discussion in Barnes, "Beginnings of Donatism," *Journal of Theological Studies* 26 (1, 1975), 13–22.

18 See Paolo Siniscalco, "Maximilian," in *Encyclopedia of Ancient Christianity*, ed. Angelo Di Berardino (Downers Grove: Intervarsity Press, 2014), 2:744, for bibliography of scholars who doubt the authenticity of the text.

19 See *Acts of the Abitinian Martyrs* 2 and *Martyrdom of Maxima, Donatilla, and Secunda* 1. In this last account, the proconsul asks, "Are you Christians or pagans?" If this were historically accurate, the proconsul could not have meant "non-Christian" when using the term "pagan," but instead would have mean one from the rural regions (cf. *Theodosian Code* 7.21.2) or even one opposed to the military (cf. Justinian, *Body of Civil Laws: Code* 3.28.37). The statement by "Campitana" is also likely not an individual, but a reference to the "rustics" (see notes in Tilley, *Donatist Martyr Stories*, 19).

20 More generally, see Patricia Southern, *The Roman Empire from Severus to Constantine*, 2nd ed. (London: Routledge, 2015), 231–238.

21 *Martyrdom of Felix* (Text/trans.: Musurillo, *The Acts of the Christian Martyrs*, 266–271).

22 *Martyrdom of Felix* 1, *libros deificos*, 1; cf. 15, *scripturas deificas*.

23 *Martyrdom of Felix* 1 (my trans.) cf. Musurillo, *The Acts of the Christian Martyrs*, 266–267, translates this first phrase to say "the elders of the Christian community," a translation that seems to assume the *seniores laici*. While I concur that this group is the likely referent, the text itself is ambiguous and could refer to the local non-Christian elders of the community; see Shaw, "The Elders of Christian Africa," 207–226; and Shaw, "The Structure of the Local Society in the Early Maghrib: the Elders," 18–54.

24 *Martyrdom of Felix* 5.

25 Cf. *Martyrdom of Felix* 22; and Tertullian, *On the Military Crown* 4.

26 *Martyrdom of Felix* 31. Cf. the *Martyrdom of Maxima, Donatilla, and Secunda* 4.

27 Text/trans.: Musurillo, *The Acts of the Christian Martyrs*, 302–309.

28   *Martyrdom of Crispina* 1.1: *legem dominorum nostrorum principum*; cf. 1.3:
     dominis nostris Diocletiano et Maximiano; and 2.4: *domini nostril invictissimi
     Caesares*. See *Acts of the Scillitan Martyrs* 1, 5 (discussed in chapter three). Like
     the Scillitans, Crispina insists that her lord (*domini mei*) is other than the Roman
     emperor (*Martyrdom of Crispina* 1.6).
29   *Martyrdom of Crispina* 1.4: *deorum Romanorum*; cf. 2.1: *diis Romanorum*; 2.4:
     religionem Romanam; and 3.1: *diis nostris*.
30   *Martyrdom of Crispina* 2.4.
31   *Martyrdom of Crispina* 1.3–4; 1.6–7; 2.3; 3.3.
32   *Martyrdom of Crispina* 2.2.
33   For more on Lactantius's role in relation to other influences such as Porphyry,
     see Elizabeth DePalma Digeser, *The Making of a Christian Empire: Lactantius
     and Rome* (Ithaca, NY: Cornell University Press, 2000); and Jeremy M. Schott,
     Christianity, Empire, and the Making of Religion in Late Antiquity (Philadel-
     phia: University of Pennsylvania Press, 2008).
34   *Martyrdom of Crispina* 4.2: *de manibus tuis . . . liberare* (Musurillo 306–307). Cf.
     Arnobius, who describes martyrdom as liberation (e.g. in 2.77: *liberatio . . . libertatis*).
35   An indication of these is the sheer number of otherwise unknown martyrs com-
     memorated in inscriptions across Mauretania that date to the 300s (see Duval,
     Loca sanctorum Africae, 717–724).
36   See earlier discussion in chapter two.
37   Eusebius, *Church History* 10.5.4 (trans. Paul L. Maier, *Eusebius: The Church
     History* [Grand Rapids, MI: Kregel Publications, 2007], 360).
38   Eusebius, *Church History* 10.5.16 (trans. NPNF[2] 1:380).
39   Eusebius, *Church History* 10.5.18–20.
40   *Letter* 88.
41   Eusebius, *Church History* 10.5.21–24.
42   Eusebius, *Church History* 10.6.1–4.
43   Eusebius, *Church History* 10.5.4.
44   e.g. *Martyrdom of Felix* 26–29; *Martyrdom of Crispina* 1–4; cf. Optatus, *Against
     the Donatists* 3.8.3.
45   Eusebius, *Church History* 10.7.1.
46   Anulinus is also faulted in the Donatist *Martyrdom of Maxima, Donatilla, and
     Secunda* and the *Acts of the Abitinian Martyrs*.
47   For a bibliography, see Oliver Nicholson, "Arnobius and Lactantius," in *The
     Cambridge History of Early Christian Literature*, ed. Young, Ayres and Louth
     (Cambridge: Cambridge University Press, 2004), 259–265; and Simmons, *Uni-
     versal Salvation in Late Antiquity*, 53–63.
48   Cf. the "Punic women [*Punicae feminarum*]" in Sicca who served at the temple of
     "Venus," mentioned in Valerius Maximus, *Memorable Doings and Sayings* 2.6.15.
49   *Against the Nations* 1.39.
50   Jerome, *Chronicle* 327.
51   Text in CSEL 4; trans. ACW 87.
52   *Against the Nations* 1.1. This, of course, is not a new accusation: cf. Tertullian,
     Apology 30; *Against the Nations* 1.9; *To Scapula* 3; Cyprian, *To Demetrian*.
53   *Against the Nations* 1.3 and 1.9.
54   *Against the Nations* 1.16; cf. Lactantius, *On the Death of the Persecutors* 23,
     who describes Rome's unjust taxation of the provinces and its inhumane way of
     enforcing taxation.
55   If so, this would target Maximian in particular. Cf. Lactantius, *On the Death of
     the Persecutors*, 8.3, who faults Maximian for squandering the wealth of "Africa
     and Spain [*Africa vel Hispania*]."
56   *Against the Nations* 1.16. Also, see the "Moors"/*Mauri* (1.36), the Psylli (2.32),
     and the Garamentes (6.5). The Psylli was a nomadic group in North Africa,

known for their ability to cure snakebites. Lucan mentions them when speaking of how Cato was lost "in Africa" (*The Civil War* 9).

57 *Letter* 58.10.
58 See specifics in Simmons, *Arnobius*, 19–21.
59 E.g. *Against the Nations* 2.33. When Augustine forwards this view, he develops a clear distinction between human nature as it was created by God and human nature after the fall.
60 *Against the Nations* 2.7. The reference is to Plato's view of a "demiurge" that made the lower realm with its imperfections; see, for example, *Phaedrus*.
61 E.g. *Against the Nations* 1.31; cf. 6.3.
62 *Against the Nations* 3.3.
63 *Against the Nations* 3.2: *deus primus . . . pater rerum ac dominus, constitutor moderator que cunctorum.*
64 *Against the Nations* 3.33; cf. 3.34 on Diana, Ceres, and Luna.
65 E.g. *Against the Nations* 2.72, for the Greek philosophers.
66 Simmons, *Arnobius*, 16.
67 Simmons, *Arnobius*, 194. Simmons is following Leglay, *Saturne africain*.
68 *Against the Nations* 1.29.
69 Simmons, *Arnobius*, 196.
70 Simmons, *Arnobius*, 197.
71 *Letter* 62.2.
72 *Lives of Illustrious Men* 79.
73 *Chronicle* 327.
74 E.g. God may not have made humans directly (discussed on p. 177).
75 Frend, "Prelude to the Great Persecution: The Propaganda War," *Journal of Ecclesiastical History* 38 (1, 1987), 14.
76 As discussed on pp. 83–84 in chapter three.
77 Nicholson, "*Civitas Quae Adhuc Sustentat Omnia*: Lactantius and the City of Rome," in *The Limits of Ancient Christianity: Essays on Late Antique Thought and Culture in Honor of R. A. Markus* (ed. William E. Klingshirn and Mark Wessey; Ann Arbor: University of Michigan Press, 1999), 14–15, reads Arnobius as respecting Rome's past. I would concede that Arnobius speaks of Rome's past virtues, but even Nicholson denies that this is classical antiquarianism: instead, it is "effective strategy" to critique contemporary Rome.
78 Cf. Tertullian, *Apology* 24; and *That Idols Are Not Gods* 2.
79 E.g. *Against the Nations* 4.1, on Hercules, Romulus, Aesculapius, Liber, Aeneas.
80 E.g. in the middle of the work (*Against the Nations* 4.4), Arnobius addresses this group to clarify, "We would ask you, and you above all, O Romans, lords and princes of the world, whether you think that . . ."
81 *Against the Nations* 1.6.
82 *Against the Nations* 1.64.
83 *Against the Nations* 2.73.
84 *Against the Nations* 2.12.
85 Similarly, see *Against the Nations* 5.8, where Varro is "that famous Roman . . . writing on the race of the Roman people." This further demonstrates that Christian/non-Christian is not the only set of identities in play. Another set of identities must be Roman/provincial (see 5.24 and 6.11), if not Roman/Punic (2.73 and 7.50).
86 *Against the Nations* 2.15.
87 See Simmons, *Arnobius*, 11 n.72, for a bibliography.
88 See Simmons, *Universalism*, 53–56, for the primary texts.
89 *Against the Nations* 2.15: *nihil quod nobis polliceatur spes cassas, . . . et inmoderata sui opinione sublatis, animas immortales esse, domino rerum ac principi gradu proximas dignitatis.*

90 Oliver Nicholson, "*Civitas Quae Adhuc Sustentat Omnia,*"15, with ref. to *Against the Nations* 6.12. This passage also contains references to Jupiter Hammon, which deserve further attention in light of the potential Libyan associations.

91 *Against the Nations* 2.40.

92 *Against the Nations* 2.73 (my trans): *Hannibal Poenus.*

93 *Against the Nations* 7.50.

94 See Jerome, *Lives of Illustrious Men* 80. For analysis of the literary relationship between Arnobius and Lactantius, see Hugo Koch, "Zu Arnobius und Lactantius," *Philologus* 80 (1925), 467–472; and cf. George E. McCracken, *Arnobius of Sicca: The Case Against the Pagans Volume 1* (ACW 87; Westminster, MD: Newman Press, 1978), 12–15, 48–51.

95 For a bibliography see Nicholson, "Arnobius and Lactantius," 259–265; and Simmons, *Universal Salvation,* 64.

96 See Lactantius, *Divine Institutes* 5.2.2.

97 Jerome, *On Illustrious Men* 80.

98 Writing well after the events, Zosimus, *New History* 2.29, claims Crispus had an affair with his stepmother.

99 Jerome, *Lives of Illustrious Men* 80, connects the two, but with no elaboration.

100 Jerome, *Chronicle* 2330.

101 The texts can be found in CSEL 19 and 27. Translations available in ANF 7 and FC 49, 54.

102 See Robert Maxwell Ogilvie, *The Library of Lactantius* (Oxford: Clarendon Press, 1978); and Jackson Bryce, *The Library of Lactantius* (New York: Harvard University Press, 1974).

103 *On God's Workmanship, The Divine Institutes, The Epitome of the Divine Institutes,* and *On the Wrath of God.*

104 See Jackson Bryce, "*De Ave Phoenice* and the Religious Policy of Constantine the Great," *Studia Patristica* 19 (1989), 13–19.

105 Cf. Mary Francis McDonald, *Lactantius: Minor Works* (FC 54; Washington, DC: Catholic University of America Press, 1965), 215.

106 E.g. Optatus, *Against the Donatists* 3.3.10–13; Augustine, *Incomplete Explanation of the Epistle to the Romans* 13.3; cf. Augustine, *Sermon* 24; and Psalm 83.7/82.8.

107 *On God's Workmanship.*

108 *On the Wrath of God.*

109 *Arnobius,* 201.

110 *The Divine Institutes* 2.8.

111 *Divine Institutes* 5.14–17.

112 See Digeser, *The Making of a Christian Empire.*

113 For introduction to this debate, see Peter Leithart, *Defending Constantine: The Twilight of an Empire and the Dawn of Christendom* (Downers Grove, IL: InterVarsity, 2010).

114 See esp. *Divine Institutes* 7.14.7–17.

115 *Divine Institutes* 25; cf. 6.9.

116 See Nicholson, "*Civitas Quae Adhuc Sustentat Omnia,*" 16, with ref. to *Divine Institutes* 1.6.7–16.

117 *Divine Institutes* 7.15.15. (FC 49:514).

118 See discussion on pp. 150–151 in chapter five.

119 N. Orloff, "Notes," *Journal of Theological Studies* 2 (1901), 418.

120 James Westfall Thompson and Bernard J. Holm, *A History of Historical Writing: From the Earliest Times to the End of the Seventeenth Century* (New York: Macmillan, 1942), 1:127.

121 *Lives of Illustrious Men* 80: *eius symposium, quod adulescentulus scripsit africae, et* Ὁδοιπορικόν *de africa usque nicomediam* (trans. NPNF² 3:378).

122 See *On the Wrath of God* 11.

123 E.g. *On the Wrath of God* 22, where "the Greeks" are contrasted with "our own writers [*nostrorum*]," Varro and Fenestella.

124 Orloff, "Notes," 418.

125 As with Arnobius, Nicholson, "*Civitas Quae Adhuc Sustentat Omnia*," 20, concludes that Lactantius retains a respect for Rome. I would contend that (a) individuals can hold both pro-imperial and anti-imperial statements in light of postcolonial analysis; even so, I find that (b) the "respect" for Rome found in Lactantius likely reflects an accommodation of classical assumptions about Rome rhetorically leveraged by Lactantius.

126 *On the Death of the Persecutors* 5.

127 *On the Death of the Persecutors* 5.

128 *On the Death of the Persecutors* 7 and 23.

129 *The Divine Institutes* 20.

130 *The Divine Institutes* 1.20.

131 *The Divine Institutes* 1.23.

132 *The Divine Institutes* 5.5.

133 Cited on p. 1, in chapter one; see Pliny, Natural History 15.20; Plutarch, Marcus Cato 27.

134 *The Divine Institutes* 3.18.

135 *The Divine Institutes* 5.6.

136 *The Divine Institutes* 5.13.

137 *The Divine Institutes* 9.

138 *The Divine Institutes* 5.3.

139 *The Divine Institutes* 5.1, 5.4, and 5.9.

140 *The Divine Institutes* 2.9.

141 Lactantius, *On the Death of the Persecutors*, 48. Although the text itself is explicitly from "Constantine and Licinius," Lactantius introduces the letter as by Licinius alone. Lactantius then devotes the rest of his work to Licinius, not mentioning Constantine again.

142 Eusebius, *Church History* 10.5.2–14.

143 Lactantius, *On the Death of the Persecutors* 52 (ANF 7:322).

144 Lactantius, *On the Death of the Persecutors* 52 (ANF 7:322).

145 Lactantius, *On the Death of the Persecutors* 16.

146 6.625–627.

147 *On God's Workmanship* 1, with ref. to Virgil, *Aeneid* 3.436.

148 Lactantius, *On the Death of the Persecutors* 16.

149 The sources and details are given on p. 139 in chapter two.

150 It is worth noting how Cyprian's martyrdom, which was one of the most celebrated in Africa, describes his entry as a "triumph" (*Acts of Cyprian* 5).

151 *Constantine and Eusebius*, 291, note 96, with ref. to *The Divine Institutes* 4.30. The passage in question, however, references specifically doctrinal disputes ("that it was impossible or not fitting for a God to enclose Himself in the womb of a woman"), and Lactantius names the Montanists, Novatians, Valentinians, Marcionites, and "Anthropians." I find no reference to the Donatists themselves (as heretics, or otherwise) in this passage.

152 See details on p. 200 in chapter seven.

153 For Diocletian's actions, see Lactantius, *On the Death of the Persecutors* 12 and 15.

154 *On the Death of the Persecutors* 43: *Unus iam supererat de adversariis Dei, cuius nunc exitum ruinam que subnectam.*

155 *On the Death of the Persecutors* 44.

156 *On the Death of the Persecutors* 45–47.

157 *On the Death of the Persecutors* 49.

158 *On the Death of the Persecutors* 50–51.

159 However, his father is mentioned as esteemed: Constantius is "worthy to hold command of the whole world alone [*dingus que qui solus orbem teneret*]" (*On*

the Death of the Persecutors 8.7). However, Constantius did allow the Christian churches to be destroyed (15).

160 I should probably note his statements about how Constantine was a "most holy youth [*sanctissimus adulescens*]," and of "the most deserving rank [*fastigio dignissimus*]" and loved by his soldiers, but these are not affirmations in Christian terms (*On the Death of the Persecutors* 18.10). These are factual reports of how Constantine was seen by his contemporaries. Compare the English translations, which concur with this point: "a most upright young man and very worthy of that high rank" (FC 54:159); and "a young man of very great worth, and well meriting the high station of Caesar" (ANF 7:308).

161 *On the Death of the Persecutors* 15–16.

162 *On the Death of the Persecutors* 30, with reference to *Aeneid* 6.471.

163 *On the Death of the Persecutors* 52.

164 *On the Death of the Persecutors* 52.

165 *On the Death of the Persecutors* 24.9: "When he took control, Constantine Augustus did nothing until he returned the Christians to their religion and their God. This was his first sanction of the restoration of the holy religion [*Suscepto imperio Constantinus Augustus nihil egit prius quam Christianos cultui ac deo suo reddere. Haec fuit prima eius sanctio sanctae religionis restitutae*]." According to Barnes, *Constantine and Eusebius*, 291, this statement is evidence that Lactantius regarded Constantine as "the protector of Christianity from the day of his ascension in 306." Instead, I find this statement much less enthusiastic, especially since there is no other statement endorsing Constantine in Lactantius's corpus (excepting the possible late additions in his *Divine Institutes*).

166 Barnes, "Lactantius and Constantine," 41–43, traces how Lactantius differs from Constantine's official propaganda when describing Constantine's former allies in the tetrarchy.

167 Heck, *Die dualistischen Zusätze und die Kaiseranreden bei Lactantius* (Heidelberg: Winter, 1972). See details in Quasten, *Patrology*, 2:397–398; and more recent bibliography, in Barnes, *Constantine and Eusebius*, 291.

168 See discussions about dating Lactantius's works as they relate to Constantine's actions in Elizabeth DePalma Digeser, "Lactantius and Constantine's Letter to Arles: Dating the *Divine Institutes*," *Journal of Early Christian Studies* 2 (1994), 33–52; and Barnes, "Monotheists All?" *Phoenix* 55 (1/2 2001), 142–162. This would establish Lactantius as influencing Constantine's theology and actions regarding church decisions. I do not disagree with the line of influence from Lactantius to Constantine, but I am not convinced that the additions are authentic to Lactantius. Even if they are accepted, I am not convinced that they reflect a sincere pro-Constantinian sentiment in Lactantius, given the rest of the tenor of his works.

169 See his more recent considerations in Heck, "Constantin und Lactanz in Trier-Chronologisches," *Historia: Zeitschrift für Alte Geschichte* 58 (1, 2009), 118–130.

170 *The Divine Institutes* 5.23.

171 *The Divine Institutes* 7.27, with reference to Terence, *Phormio* 2.1.19.

172 *The Divine Institutes* 7.27.

173 *The Divine Institutes* 7.27, with reference to Virginl, *Aeneid* 4.336.

174 See Kate Cooper, "Marriage, Law, and Christian Rhetoric in Vandal Africa," in *North Africa Under Byzantium and Early Islam*, ed. Susan T. Stevens and Jonathan P. Conant (Washington, DC: Dumbarton Oaks, 2016), 237–249.

7   The Donatist controversy

In many ways, the Donatist controversy is the part of African Christian history that is best documented and most commonly treated as uniquely African. Nevertheless, scholars have wide-ranging views as to how best to interpret this controversy and how to understand the relationship of Donatists to their African background. In what follows, we will discuss the events that took place in this controversy, as well as the various Donatists and Donatist sources known to us, and then reassess how we interpret Donatism in light of the African background and as part of the African Christian tradition.

Identifying Donatists

The Donatist controversy emerged in the wake of Diocletian's persecution.[1] In response to various lapsed clergy, Christians in Africa debated how to reconcile them, and they disagreed as to whether the lapsed could serve again as ministers. When the bishop of Carthage died (c.312),[2] many Christians contested the validity of his successor, Caecilian, claiming that he had been ordained by one who had lapsed and therefore had been contaminated with idolatry. Caecilian's opponents elected Majorinus. Majorinus died soon after his appointment, and then Donatus was appointed as the rival bishop to Caecilian.[3] Thus, the Donatist party was said to have formed a schism over and against their opponents, the "Catholics." These immediate events first need to be placed in the larger story of Christianity in North Africa going back at least to the time of Cyprian.

Cyprian's disagreement with Stephen of Rome was never truly resolved. Both died and the controversy died with them. Both parties during the Donatist controversy claimed to be heirs to Cyprian, but a consensus of scholars today find that the "Donatists" have a better claim to his legacy.[4] Jean-Paul Brisson even concluded that this party could very well have been labeled "Cyprianism" instead of "Donatism."[5]

The name of this party and its claim to the African heritage deserve a brief explanation. The label "Donatist" was meant to identify this party as a schismatic group. Its opponents claimed to be the "Catholic" party, that is, the party in communion with the "universal" church.[6] Historians, however, cannot accept such labels uncritically. Both parties at the time claimed to be "Catholic," and no Donatist called him/herself a "Donatist." Despite the widespread agreement among historians that the label "Donatist" carries an inherent bias as well as historical inaccuracy, no plausible alternative has emerged.

Brent Shaw once argued that the category "Donatist" should be replaced with the simple label "African," since this party represented the traditional African teaching.[7] Later, however, Shaw revised this view and opted for the description of this party as "the dissident Christian community."[8] Shaw's reluctance to continue with the category of "African" likely reflects the concerns of his Princeton colleague, Peter Brown, who criticized a certain understanding of the Donatists as an indigenous social movement.[9] Brown rejected this trend among some modern scholars because it portrayed the Donatists as insincere in their religious beliefs: they merely cloaked their revolutionary and social concerns in the Christian religion. Brown's critique is valid, and many others have joined him, especially in rejecting extreme versions of this theory wherein the Donatists are some sort of nationalist or even Marxist movement.[10] Nevertheless, without accepting such an extreme form of the indigenous theory that is anachronistic and reductionistic in its understanding of the Donatists, there is a need to revisit how the Donatists saw themselves as "African." At the end of this chapter, we will return to this question more fully. For now, however, it needs to be mentioned because in the attempt to find acceptable categories, it seems that the "Donatist" and even the "dissident" label would have been unacceptable to those individuals. They simply understood themselves as Christian, and as the Christian church representing the traditional African teaching.

While Shaw's initial suggestion to label this party as "African" avoids certain problems, it nevertheless presents additional difficulties of its own. First, the opponents would still be labeled "Catholic," unless a valid replacement is found. Also, many in the so-called Catholic party would also see themselves as "African" and claim to be holding to the traditional African teaching. One solution is to keep the label "Donatist," as the party under the bishop Donatus, and then use the alternative label "Caecilianist" for the party under the bishop Caecilian. While neither party would have accepted these terms (for neither saw itself as a schismatic party), the use of these categories at least treats both sides equally, privileging neither as the "Catholic." In what follows, I will use the labels of Donatist and Caecilianist for the sake of convenience, but at the conclusion of the chapter, we will return to the identity of the Donatist party, and examine in particular what makes the Donatist party African.

The beginning of the schism

As we have already seen in Chapter 6's treatment of early fourth-century martyrdoms, Diocletian's edict required everyone in the empire to sacrifice.[11]

The clergy were especially targeted, and they were commanded to "hand over [*traditor*]" the scriptures and other sacred items of the church. Any who did so were deemed *traditores*, a Latin word that only comes to mean "traitors" at this time. Their betrayal and their contact with idolatry means that they had contracted a demonic contagion, and so they could not be readmitted into the church without penance. Furthermore, any clergy who wish to return must be demoted to the laity.

All those involved agreed with these facts as they have been summarized thus far. The disagreement arose as to how to handle clergy whose contagion was unknown at the time they performed a sacramental act. Was the sacrament still valid, or was it contaminated? One bishop, named Felix of Abthugni (modern Henchir es-Souar, Tunisia), allegedly handed over the scriptures, and he became an important test case.

Felix came to Carthage after the bishop Mensurius died, in order to take part in the ceremony for the newly elected bishop, Caecilian. The consecration of a bishop of Carthage impacted the whole of North Africa, since he ranked first in any regional council. When bishops from Numidia arrived, they were surprised to find that the process had been rushed and completed without them.[12] Even more surprising, one of the bishops who did perform the laying on of hands was this Felix, whom they claimed was a *traditor*. Caecilian conceded this point, only stipulating that the Numidians should then appoint him properly.[13] They, however, refused, insisting his ordination was contaminated, and they instead appointed Majorinus as bishop.

The additional details about this initial disagreement are mired in sources that favor one party or the other.[14] While the surviving sources are predominantly from the Caecilianist party, these sources do preserve a large number of quotes from the Donatists themselves. These reports, of course, must be read critically, but scholars do find much reliable information about what the Donatists believed and said. The two major sources for our discussion are Optatus of Milevis (or "Optatus the African"[15]) and Augustine of Hippo. Augustine will be treated more fully in Chapter 8, but his role in the Donatist controversy is very important and so he will be cited throughout this chapter. Optatus wrote in 363 (and later updated his work around 384) in response to the Donatist bishop of Carthage at the time, who had reclaimed the ancient basilicas in Carthage for his party.[16] Both Optatus and Augustine preserve a number of letters, transcripts of court proceedings, and other documents, which will be introduced and cited in the following discussion. With these sources in place, therefore, we can proceed to hearing each party's accusations against its opponents.

The Caecilianist sources raised several accusations. First, they claimed, a "seditious woman [*feminam factiosam*]" named Lucilla sought revenge on Caecilian, because he had rebuked her during the liturgy for kissing a relic.[17] When given the chance, she sponsored the opposition party. The opportunity arose when Mensurius died, which brings us to the second accusation. Two Carthaginian presbyters, Botrus and Caelestius, "lusted for the appointment [*ordinari cupientes*]," and so arranged that Mensurius's successor be chosen immediately, without waiting for the Numidians to arrive.[18] They were disappointed when Caecilian was chosen instead of them. This simultaneously explains the lack of procedure in Caecilian's election and the reason that some clergy immediately seceded from him. The third accusation was that the church's belongings had at an earlier time been entrusted to the Carthaginian "elders." These "lay elders [*seniores laici*]," distinct from presbyters and other clergy, were unique to North Africa, and consisted of respected men in the congregation.[19] By the time the list of these items was given to Caecilian, the elders had allegedly sold them for their own gain.[20] These three parties – the rebuked woman, the disgruntled priests, and the greedy elders – joined together in rejecting Caecilian, and so they convinced the Numidian bishops to appoint a rival. These Numidian bishops, furthermore, were eager to do so, since they themselves were in fact *traditores*. They had met in an earlier council, led by Secundus of Tigisus, and discovered that many of them had handed over the scriptures.[21] In coming to Carthage, they fabricated the evidence that Felix, who had ordained Caecilian, betrayed the scriptures so as to divert attention away from their wrongdoing.[22] The schismatic party met and appointed Majorinus, who was "of Lucilla's house [*domesticus Lucillae*]."[23] Of course, this was the version of events from the perspective of the Caecilianists. The Donatists had their own version of the story.

The Donatist party had their own set of accusations against the Caecilianists. In addition to the claim that Felix of Abthugni was a *traditor*, they even claim that Caecilian himself "betrayed" the church with "whips and lashes," when as a deacon he prevented Christians from bringing food and water to their fellow believers in prison who awaited martyrdom.[24] In fact, Donatists will repeatedly accuse Caecilian as taking an active part in the persecution of other Christians, something that may be related to his support from the proconsul, Anulinus (discussed in Chapter 6).[25] Beyond these specific accusations, the Donatists generally claimed that all Caecilianists had contracted the contagion by their communion with those who had contact with idols, and so they refuse to remain in communion with them.

Beyond these accusations, there are several items that indicate that a majority of the Christians in Carthage sided with the Donatist party.[26] While Optatus will portray a basilica filled with the Carthaginian Christians who sided with Caecilian, Augustine later admits that a "multitude [*multitudinem*]" of the "people [*plebem*] sided with the Numidians and their appointment of Majorinus.[27] Also, when Constantine sends two bishops "to Africa [*ad Africam*] . . . in order to pronounce where is the catholic church,"[28] they return after forty days of disruption by the Donatist party, deciding the church was spread throughout the world. Such a theological affirmation masks the fact that the Donatist party in Carthage was large enough to decide "where" the church was located: the true church was where the rightful bishop, Donatus, presided.[29]

Both parties, therefore, claim a majority: the Donatists represent the majority of African Christianity,[30] while the Caecilianists claim the majority of the overseas churches support them. As one sources has it, "The whole world rejoices over catholic unity, *except for the African party*."[31] These two party identities, the African and the imperial, arguably define each side throughout the schism. There is, however, a significant caveat to this point, since the Donatists allegedly were the first to appeal to Caesar.

Appeals to Constantine

It is said that the Donatists first appealed to Constantine.[32] Later, Donatus asked, "What has the emperor to do with the church?"[33] But whenever the leaders of the Caecilianists encountered such an anti-imperial sentiment among Donatists, they were quick to remind the Donatists of this first appeal. For their part, the Caecilianists, like many Christians outside of Africa, came to the conclusion that "there is no-one higher than the Emperor save God himself."[34]

In 313 the emperor summoned a council in Rome under Miltiades, which decided in favor of Caecilian.[35] The emperor's surviving correspondence suggests that he – informed by the proconsul Anulinus – had already sided with Caecilian even before any hearings.[36] The Donatists appealed a second time, and Constantine ordered a larger council in Arles in 314. This council also sided with Caecilian, but the bishops' stated reasons are worth reviewing.

The records from the council (see esp. canon 14) mentioned neither Caecilian or Majorinus, but simply decided that a cleric ordained by a *traditor* still retains a valid ordination. When explicitly addressing "the Africans" (canon 9), the question was not about the rightful bishop, but about rebaptism. This of course related to the older debate between Cyprian and Stephen, having nothing to do with the controversy in Carthage. Again, in their letter from the council to the bishop of Rome, the bishops report:

> Now as to Africa, we decided that they should use their own custom of rebaptizing in such a way that, if any heretic comes to the church, they should ask what his creed is: and if they see that he was baptized in the name of Father and Son and Holy Ghost, they should merely lay hands upon him.[37]

In other words, these bishops in Gaul confirmed the teaching of Stephen, implicitly rejecting the past view of Cyprian, which was still held by the majority of "Africans." It is no surprise, therefore, that the Donatists refused to accept this council's authority. Because Caecilian and his party were willing to capitulate to the non-African tradition and accept schismatic baptism, they "thereby gained the approval of the whole Catholic communion outside Africa."[38]

After these failed appeals, the Donatists persisted in their rejection of Caecilian, and so in 317 Constantine took action and seized their basilicas. The Donatists likely understood this action as a return to Diocletian's persecution, for he seized and even destroyed Christian churches. In Carthage a large group of Donatists gathered in their basilica, resisting the imperial force attempting to confiscate the building. The Roman soldiers enforced Constantine's order with violence, resulting in several deaths.[39] Outside of Carthage, it is unclear what (if any) actions were taken to seize the Donatist basilicas.[40] The Donatists interpreted this violent government intervention in the controversy as outright persecution of the church. This action proved to them that the Caecilianists were in league with evil, while the party of Donatus represented the true church: the true church always "endures persecution, it never persecutes [*quae persecutionem patitur, non quae facit*]."[41]

Then, in 321, Constantine stopped repressing the Donatists,[42] an action that has been given little to no explanation.[43] The size and influence of the Donatists leads Barnes to conclude that Donatism "dominated the African church" at this time.[44] Perhaps Constantine saw North Africa as a lost cause. In his letter to the Caecilianists, Constantine blamed the schism on the madness of a few and defers vengeance to God (cf. Rom. 12.19), thereby requiring patience from the Caecilianists.[45] Eusebius only reports that "insanity" had taken over "in Africa."[46]

As a better explanation of Constantine's decision regarding the Donatists, I would like to suggest that Constantine did not ignore the schism; instead, he viewed it as part of a wider problem, the so-called Arianism of the east.[47] When Eusebius narrates the beginning of schism in Alexandria, he says it spread throughout "Egypt and Libya"; in other words "all Libya" was affected.[48] Eusebius then records Constantine's letter to Alexander and Arius, bemoaning how "all of Africa" has succumbed to this "insanity."[49] Most historians believe that Caecilian attended the Council of Nicaea in 325 as Carthage's representative. In addition to Arianism, the Melitian schism in Alexandria mirrored the Donatist controversy in many ways.[50] From the perspective of Constantine, all of these controversies originating in "Egypt and Libya" likely appeared to be deriving from a common source and were in need of a common solution. The solution would be to summon a worldwide council, the Council of Nicaea.

Jerome also connected Donatism to Arianism, claiming that Donatus himself wrote a subordinationist work entitled *On the Holy Spirit*.[51] Donatus was connected to the Council of Serdica in 343, which would have further tied his party to the Arian controversy.[52] Another possible connection can be found in Athanasius's *Letter to the Africans*, which attempts to convince the bishops there of the need to defend Nicaea's formula against any compromises, implying that at least some in Africa needed convincing.[53]

In fact, a quick survey of the late fourth century discovers a number of sources that refer to the Donatists' alliance with the so-called Arian party,[54] but scholars have generally ignored these because of Augustine's acceptance of Donatist theology as orthodox.[55] Augustine argued that Donatists were schismatic, not heretical, and therefore even if the laws against heretics were to be applied to them, they should be reconciled to his "Catholic" church. However, even Augustine acknowledged that some Donatists taught subordinationism, only he claimed they did so to court the "Goths [*Gothos*]," who at that time were invading the provinces. As will be discussed in Chapter 9, the Vandals in particular were invading North Africa, and they espoused some form of subordinationism.[56]

Constantine's treatment of Arianism did differ from his initial treatment of Donatism: bishops who rejected the creed of Nicaea were exiled (although no churches were confiscated), and even this approach was ameliorated soon thereafter so that any Arian sympathizers were reconciled to the rest of the church (much to the chagrin of the pro-Nicene writers of the time). This discrepancy, however, likely is due to the fact that Constantine's earlier tactics against the Donatists only worsened the problem. When he turned to an empirewide controversy, he adapted his approach, and he even left the Donatist party alone. These apparent ties between Donatism and Arianism would help explain why Constantine left the Donatists in peace: he focused on what he saw was a larger problem. This peace in Africa continued under the next rulers, Constantine's sons, until the mid-fourth century.[57]

Escalation of violence and persecution

Around 347, two violent forces collided in the Donatist controversy. The emperor Constans sent Paul and Macarius as "agents of unity . . . [who] used harsh measures."[58] Optatus claimed this was a mission of charity; the Roman officials were to distribute funds to the poor.[59] The Donatist leaders viewed these charitable gifts as bribes. One Donatist leader, also named Donatus, who was the bishop of Bagaia, reportedly recruited the other violent force in this conflict, the Circumcellions.[60]

The Circumcellions, according to the Caecilianist sources, were armed groups of Donatists who would attack any of their enemies, including Roman soldiers. This group reportedly preferred to identify itself as *Agonistici*, usually translated as "fighters."[61] Modern historians have debated how best to understand this group, with options including nomadic monks, migrant workers, and freedom fighters.[62]

Part of the difficulty for historians is that the sources for the Circumcellions all stem from Caecilianists and so cannot be taken at face value. The earliest source on the Circumcellions is worth citing at length:

> the other Donatus, bishop of that city [of Bagaia], desiring to raise an impediment to unity and an obstacle to the arrival of the aforesaid persons [Paul and Macarius], sent heralds through the neighbouring places and all the market-towns, calling the disaffected circumcellions

[*circumcelliones agonisticos*] by name with an invitation to assembly at an appointed place.[63]

At this point it is worth noting how the name itself has proven impossible to translate adequately. The word *agonistici* recalls those who fought in the public games (*agon*, the contest), but the word is also related to *agonia*, a "victim," which is why Edwards – whose translation is given here – uses "*disaffected* circumcellions."

Likewise, the word *Circumelliones* itself is difficult to define, since it is a combination of two Latin terms: *circum*-[64] and *cellae* (i.e. "those who go around the store-houses"). Just what this group does is further explained by Optatus:

> the records of debts had lost their force, no creditor at that time had the freedom to enforce payment, all were terrified by the letters of those who boasted that they had been leaders of the saints; and if there was any delay in obeying their behests, a raging multitude suddenly flew to their aid, and, as terror went before them, besieged the creditors with dangers, so that those who should have had suitors on account of their loans were forced into groveling prayers through fear of death. Each one hastened to write off even his greatest debts, and reckoned it gain if he escaped injury at their hands. Even the safest journeys could not take place, because masters, thrown out of their vehicles, ran in servile fashion before their own retainers, who were sitting in their masters' place.[65]

This paragraph has been used to interpret the Circumcellions as a social (and even socialist) movement with little real ties to the religious convictions of the larger Donatist party. Augustine makes one statement about how (at least one group of) Circumcellions needed a translator because they spoke Punic.[66] As mentioned on the previous page, with Donatists in general, theories that dismiss the religious conviction of the Circumcellions risk being too reductionistic. With so little evidence about this group, and with all of the evidence coming from the Caecilianist sources, as scholars we have to admit how little we know about this group.

I would suggest that Augustine knows of Circumcellions from earlier sources such as Optatus. He then interprets any violent mob as "Circumcellions." His view, however, is too simplistic for our historical analysis: African communities, like most of the ancient world, had a long history of mob violence,[67] and furthermore the Caecilianists were known to carry out mob violence themselves.[68] Whenever his Donatist opponents accuse his party of being "Macarians" and resorting to imperial violence, Augustine responds to say that the Donatists have their own violent enforcers, the Circumcellions. This rhetorical reply, however, tells us little about the Circumcellions themselves. Augustine even admits elsewhere that the Donatists deny any ties to such violent mobs[69] – instead, these were simply local commoners disgruntled with the Roman/Caecilianist leaders.

These two violent forces, the Circumcellions (however defined) and those with Paul and Macarius (armed soldiers) collided in an event of which the details are largely lost. We do know that many were injured and some were killed, something the Donatists complained about for decades.[70] Donatists likened the actions of Macarius to those of Anulinus from a previous generation,[71] and so Macarius inaugurated another period of persecution for the Donatists. In this period the Donatists ceased to call their opponents Caecilianists, and instead referred to them as Macarians.[72]

The memory of persecution under Macarius also continued among the Donatists because of several martyrdoms that recounted the trials faced at the time. *The Martyrdom of Maximian and Isaac* tells of two martyrs who died in 347 in Numidia.[73] In the same year, Marculus was executed under the "two beasts" Paul and Macarius, and he was memorialized both in a surviving martyrdom account and in an inscription at a basilica in El Ksar el Kebir, Algeria.[74] In addition to these deaths, many Donatists were exiled during this time, something likened to Christ himself when he and his family had to flee from Herod to Egypt.[75] Donatus himself died in exile in 355 and so was considered a martyr.[76]

Donatus's long reign as bishop of Carthage provided stability for his party, and this stability continued under the next bishop, Parmenian, who served almost as long (355–392). Parmenian is a "pilgrim [*peregrinus*]," according to one source, which has led some historians to think he was from Gaul or Iberia.[77] However, this is by no means certain; Brent Shaw denies that the term necessarily meant "not African."[78] Parmenian by all accounts led his party well, and his (now lost) works must have been influential, since the Caecilianists had to write major works in response to them.[79] Parmenian's tenure witnessed not only stability, but an extended period where the Donatists gained ground in their claim to be the "Catholic" party in Africa – they were even recognized as such by local officials.[80] The Caecilianists even admitted to being the minority party "in Africa" at this time.[81]

When Julian – who would be deemed "the Apostate" because he returned to polytheism – became emperor, he allowed Christian groups previously deemed heretical to reclaim their basilicas. The Donatists did so often it seems by force – some Caecilianists were killed defending their basilica.[82] While this benefited Donatists in the short term, later Caecilianists will use the link between Donatists and "the Apostate" in a propaganda war. Also, the Roman stance against "rebaptism" will again be enforced when Christian emperors come back to power after Julian.[83] Toward the end of Parmenian's life, there were signs of the Donatist party's fragmentation, and this eventually led to opportunities for the Caecilianists to regain control of North Africa.

Donatist diversity and decline

The Donatist party from the beginning included much diversity.[84] This has led Maureen Tilley to conclude that we should "study not just Donatism but Donatisms."[85] To do so, more analysis needs to be devoted to how any given individual or church identified itself in this controversy, since none would have declared themselves "Donatists" or "Caecilianists." In all likelihood, a Christian traveling through Africa would likely not initially be able to identify any difference between the two communities. This seems to have occurred in the late fourth century when Melania and Pinianus, a married couple who had elected to practice celibacy and moved to Africa to establish monasteries, arrived and permitted both Caecilianist and Donatist Christians on their estate – much to the chagrin of Augustine's party.[86]

What seems to have united the Donatist party was that it opposed Caecilian's ordination and believed that any who were in communion with him would have contracted the contagion of idolatry. Just how many cities and towns would have included both a Donatist and a Caecilianist basilica governed by rival bishops is not at all clear in the early period of the controversy. We can assume that Christians across Africa practiced their faith with as much diversity as any other province. Without major controversy over these differences, the differences simply do not get noted in the surviving sources. It is not until the late fourth century that more of this diversity comes to light, as some factions break from the Donatist party.

A relatively early schism from within the Donatist party was the Rogatist controversy. Rogatus and a small number of bishops broke away from the Donatists, allegedly because of the violent excesses of the Circumcellions. Although relatively small,[87] they remained even up to Augustine's time.[88]

When speaking of the diversity and breadth of the Donatist party, we should consider how the Donatists viewed the church of Rome in particular. The emphasis on communion with overseas churches may be reflected in the fact that the Donatist party established its own church and bishop in Rome. Most scholars believe that the Donatists established a rival bishop in Rome so that they could lay equal claim to Rome's authority as the true church descended from Peter. Such a view, however, is likely too reliant on Optatus's own assumptions: after arguing for Caecilianist superiority by showing they had Peter's shrine (i.e. in Rome), he mentions how a certain Victor of Garba was sent from Africa to Rome as bishop.[89] Optatus observes how Victor had no predecessor, and thus has no valid claim to Peter, as does the rightful bishop of Rome.[90] It should be noted, however, that Optatus never states that the Donatist party made such a claim. Instead, he acknowledges how Victor went to Rome to pastor a small flock of "Africans and sojourners."[91] These are expatriates living on the edge of Rome, probably in the African quarter, as was previously discussed in Chapter 3.[92]

Caecilianists call the Donatists in Rome *Montenses* or "mountain men" because they met in a cave in one of the hills around Rome.[93] This label seems to have created confusion in the sources with the "Montanists" (who were discussed in Chapters 3 and 4) and this alleged link between the two groups deserves further study. For example, Filastrius, an Italian bishop from this time (c.384), believes the "Montanists" are rebaptizers who have populated

"Africa" with their heresy.[94] The earlier anonymous author describes the Monatists with characteristics that will later be attributed to Donatists, such as suicidal tendencies.[95] In the *Theodosian Code*, "rebaptism" in general is outlawed in imperial edicts from the fifth century, but it names only "the Donatists," the "Montanists [*Montanistarum*]," and the Novatianists.[96] It should be noted that the Novatianists (who here seem to be *exempla nega-tiva* from the past) and the Donatists share a rigorist stance on rebaptism. The "Montantists" mentioned in this law are likely the Donatists in Rome, i.e. the *Montenses*.[97]

As for the Donatists' attempt to establish their own bishop of Rome, there is no evidence that the Donatists claimed this bishop of Africans in Rome to be a successor of Peter – or, for that matter, whether the bishop of Rome even could claim such a succession as unique since Cyprian had insisted that all bishops were successors to Peter. Instead, the Donatist bishop of Rome ranked below the bishop of Carthage at the conference of 411.[98] In addition, there may have been other Donatist communities outside of Africa, but the evidence is very slight.[99]

We know very few details about this Donatist church in Rome. Augustine lists the successors of Peter in Rome, and then states, "But the Donatists unexpectedly sent an ordained priest from Africa; he presided over a few Africans in Rome and originated the name of the Montenses or Cutzupits."[100] He also reports that this Roman-Donatist community experienced its own internal schism around 378.[101] It does not appear that the Donatists them-selves viewed this community as one that could trace a succession back to Peter, and therefore it likely was not truly seen by the Donatists as a replace-ment of the original Roman church.

We should also note here the curious ties that the bishops of Rome had with Africa at the outbreak of the schism. According to a sixth-century source, Pope Miltiades (r.311–314), who presided over the first case against the Donatists in 313 (see p. 199), was also "of the nation of Africa [*natione Afer*]."[102] His successor, Silvanus (r.314–335), was "of the nation of Rome,"[103] but Constantine gave him numerous estates as sources of income for the church of Rome, including many across "the regions of Africa (*partes Africae*)."[104] Rome's role, in short, is unclear for Donatists, which is likely due to the decentralized nature of Donatism.

Another way in which the diversity within Donatism can be seen is in the various internal schisms. Substantial fragmenting occurred under Par-menian's successor, Primian. He angered many from his own party in and around Carthage, which resulted in the Maximianist schism that had sev-eral dozen bishops supporting Maximian instead of Primian as the bishop of Carthage. Primian, however, in 394 gathered 310 bishops in a council to support him. Eventually, the Maximianists were reconciled to Primian. Those who did rejoin Primian's party were accepted with no rebaptism or additional purification. Augustine repeatedly used this readmittance of Maximianists as evidence that Donatists were inconsistent: they required rebaptism for schismatic Caecilianists, but not schismatic Maximianists. We have no Donatist account of how this apparent discrepancy in practice was reconciled, but it is likely that the Donatists viewed the Caecilianists as contaminated with idolatry because of their communion with apostate *traditores*, whereas the repentant schismatic did not contract any such contagion and therefore needed no rebaptism.[105] We also hear of other groups that represent diversity within Donatism about which we know very little, such as the Urbanists and the Donatists among the Arzuges.[106]

Further diverse elements within Donatism can be seen in individual writers. Tyconius was an influential author and interpreter of scripture (even Augustine admired him), but Parmenian excommunicated him in 385.[107] He allegedly spoke too emphatically about the need for the church to be universal, and this suggested to some that the Donatist party must reunite with the wider church of the empire. Nevertheless, even after his excommunication Tyconius refused to join the Caecilianist party. An opposite story is another Donatist leader named Petilian. Petilian was raised by "Catholics" but allegedly forced to convert to Donatism.[108] Afterward, he not only continued in the Donatist party, he began to publish tracts defending it and became one of its leading advocates.[109] When speaking of Petilian's ordination and of the anointing with oil, Augustine pauses to note how the Hebrew word for "chrism" is a close cognate to the Punic word for anointing – apparently Augustine associated Petilian with "the Phoenician language [*Punicae linguae*]."[110]

Another defender of the Donatist party was Cresconius, a grammarian about whom virtually nothing else is known.[111] How many others like Cresconius defended Donatism, only without meriting a response from Augustine and therefore disappeared from our records? In addition to these few individuals whose names and works survive because of their opponents' responses to them, there are numerous sermons and treatises that have now been recognized as Donatist. These mostly survive because of misattribution to other writers, but they illustrate further how many different voices could speak from and for the Donatist party.[112]

Finally, there are numerous Donatists named by others whose works do not survive, and there are also many anonymous works that have survived by an accident of history for which we have little context.[113] All of these various authors and works should be incorporated in the study of Donatism in order to allow the diversity of voices from within this movement to be better heard.

Other individual writers are known from sources that mention them, but unfortunately their works do not survive. For example, Vitellius the African wrote three known works: *Why the Servants of God Are Hated by the World*, *Against the Nations*, and *On Ecclesiastical Procedure*. When reporting about Vitellius's works, Gennadius complains that "we" (i.e. Catholics/Caecilianists) are listed as persecutors. He also notes how *Against the Nations* is in fact directed against his party, which suggests that Vitellius saw the Caecilianists as foreigners.[114]

One last issue that illustrates some of the diversity across Donatism and helps inform our understanding of Donatists in the late fourth century is the accusation that Donatists supported the rebellions of Firmus and Gildo (discussed earlier in Chapter 1). Caecilianists claimed that Firmus's revolt (372) included Donatist support, but these accusations may be exaggerations, or even a confusing of indigenous Africans supporting Firmus with Donatists (who were often indigenous Africans; see more on this on pp. 217–225).[115] In his later rebellion (395–398), Gildo, the leader the Romans called "a second Hannibal,"[116] gathered an enormous federation of indigenous African groups, so that – even accounting for rhetorical exaggeration – Augustine's reports about the Donatists would likely have been easily accepted.[117]

The general accusation that the Donatists writ large supported Gildo has been rejected by historians today.[118] After all, in the time of Firmus and Gildo, Donatists could claim to be the "Catholic" party in Africa, and they often won the favor of local governing officials.[119] However, if one moves beyond generalizations about all Donatists, then one can find evidence of some Donatists supporting Gildo, such as Optatus, the bishop of Thamugadi (= modern Timgad, Algeria), who allegedly organized the Circumcellions to support Gildo.[120] After Gildo's swift defeat, Optatus died in prison, and his successor, Gaudentius, in turn did not threaten military violence against the Roman official, but he did threaten (in 419) to set his own basilica on fire, along with him and his congregants in it, if the edict to unify with the Caecilianists was enforced.[121] The association between Donatists and violent uprisings (real or fictional) contributed further to the decline in Donatist power, because the Caecilianist party used this to appeal to the emperors in the early fifth century.

Once again it should be remembered that this section on Donatist diversity still suffers from the constraints of the category of "Donatism." In Chapter 6, we criticized the tendency to read Lactantius and other fourth-century writers apart from the African context and controversies. Here, we should point out that other fourth-century writers from Africa show no signs of belonging to the "Donatist party," but they should still be understood as part of the African tradition, which drew on the same sources and themes as the Donatists. For example, while no ancient source claims Augustine's mother, Monica, was a Donatist, modern scholars have made this conclusion based on how distinct her Christianity was in comparison to that found in Milan.[122] Another comparison like this could be made with Marius Victorinus.

The African writer Marius Victorinus converted to Christianity late in life.[123] Before his conversion, he established himself as one of the leading intellectuals of his time.[124] He was appointed Rhetor, the official teacher of rhetoric, in Rome, and he was even honored with a statue in Trajan's Forum.[125] His public career ended after his conversion, but only when Julian "the Apostate" came to power in 363 and declared all Christians be removed from public office.[126]

His surviving writings range from technical books on rhetoric[127] to works on philosophy.[128] We also know from Augustine that Victorinus translated many Greek works into Latin.[129] As far as strictly Christian writings, Victorinus wrote several important – but often overlooked – works that address the Arian controversy.[130] In his *Against Arius*, he shows a keen awareness of the various voices that objected to the council of Nicaea.[131] The main voice, however, from the Arian side is a certain "Candidus," who was, along with his two letters, fabricated by Victorinus in order to express the Arian viewpoint as a foil.[132] The primary concern, according to Victorinus, has to do with God "generating" the Son, which would imply change in God, a theme also addressed in his *On the Generation of the Divine Word*.[133] Candidus claims that the Son cannot be the "same substance" as the Father (i.e. the language from the Creed of Nicaea) because God is beyond all categories such as "substance," a point with which Victorinus in fact agrees. Victorinus's theology aligns with, and was likely influenced by, the earlier fourth-century writers (discussed in chapter six) who described God in Punic terms as "the highest" and "over the heavens." In fact, if we remember the earliest sources of African theology we can see this theme very early.[134] To be sure, Victorinus is equally influenced by Neoplatonism, but this ability to push the language of God beyond all abstraction is not new to the African Christian tradition, as it can be found in writers like Tertullian.[135] Even though God is "beyond being," when speaking of the divine "being" or "essence" one must include the Son, and therefore Nicaea's language of "same-substance" must be confessed by Christians, as Victorinus argues in his *The Necessity of Accepting the Homoousion*.[136] With the Son equally divine with the Father, Victorinus also presses the same language for the Spirit. He expressed his Trinitarian teachings in three surviving hymns, which again show signs of indebtedness to the early African tradition.[137] One last set of writings by Victorinus are commentaries on Paul's letters.[138] Of these, only his commentaries on Galatians and Ephesians survive in full, and all but the first sixteen verses survive for his commentary on Philippians.[139] In these works, Victorinus was not only the first African writer to author commentaries on scripture, but he was also the first Latin writer to do so.

Victorinus's conversion to Christianity inspired none other than Augustine. When considering his own conversion, Augustine sought a fellow African intellectual named Simplicianus.[140] Upon discovering that Augustine had been reading "Platonist books," Simplicianus expressed relief that he had read the Latin translations made by Victorinus, because "the writings of other philosophers [were] works full of fallacies and dishonesty."[141] At this point, Augustine is relaying the story told by Simplicianus, and therein Simplicianus (and Augustine) report how Victorinus converted from idolatry, but particularly from the "gods Rome had once vanquished, but now worshipped."[142] The account is embellished with a quote from Virgil's *Aeneid*. The scene from Virgil is telling because it is from the description of Aeneas's new shield, on which is the all the history and destiny of Rome.[143]

Simplicanus's report goes on to describe Rome in very incendiary terms: Rome is the "Babylon" full of "demon-worshipers . . . not yet felled by the Lord."[144] Of course, an initial reading of this story in Augustine's *Confessions* finds the contrast to between a Christian identity and a "pagan" one. However, after his baptism, Augustine relays that "Rome stood amazed."[145] After this Augustine shifts to another encounter, this time with "Ponticianus . . . an African he was our compatriot."[146] While we need not diminish the centrality of Christian identity in this account, clearly Augustine remembers the importance of Victorinus's (and his own) African identity as well.

As for his self-identity as an African, Victorinus left few clues in his surviving writings, but this is mostly due to the specific aims with which he wrote. He did once speak of both "the Latins" and "the Greeks"[147] as if he did not belong to either group, which possibly hints at his African identity. Curiously, outside of Africa few knew and received Victorinus and his works. Even Jerome, who knows him as an "African by birth,"[148] also claims he was ignorant of the scriptures[149] and so was clearly not familiar with (or for some reason distrusted) Victorinus's commentaries. Perhaps, as we have seen with other writers like "Thascius Cyprian" and Arnobius, the fourth-century controversy left many African Christians suspect in the eyes of those from other regions.[150]

Another African writer from this time is known only from his surviving "Tractates" or sermons.[151] Zeno became bishop of Verona, Italy around 362 and served until his death around 370, but from internal clues in his sermons historians agree that he was from Africa. Given his locale, it is no surprise that he occupies himself with other topics and makes no mention of the Donatist controversy. At the same time, it should be noted that even if Zeno had stayed in Africa, his sermons would likely not record much in terms of "Donatism." This is a period in Donatist history when there was relatively little outside pressure on the Donatist party, and so African Christians would not normally have even thought of themselves in terms of such a party. Their local church may be identified as Donatist in the eyes of modern historians, but the local Christians at the time likely thought of it simply as their church, or even as "the Catholic church" in Verona or whatever town they happened to worship. Zeno's surviving works reflect a local pastor addressing traditional Christian themes, with no comment upon wider controversies such as Donatism. One possible instance where Donatist practice arises is when Zeno chastises his congregants for too excessive feasts in the cemeteries – a practice that Ambrose will later censure Augustine's mother for doing, which leads modern scholars to think of her as Donatist.[152] If this is a Donatist practice taking place in his church, Zeno opposes it (or at least its excesses). Even so, we have repeatedly shown that Donatists were diverse, and so this does not speak to whether Zeno or his audience belongs to such a label.

Zeno does indicate his indebtedness to the African Christian tradition in several of his sermons.[153] He famously celebrated the martyr Archadius, who died in Caesarea Mauretania.[154] He especially prefers to cite Tertullian, Cyprian, and Lactantius, and he even shows signs of indebtedness to the non-Christian African writer, Apuleius. His scripture usage and translation also matches that of the African tradition. While some claim that Zeno's African background is irrelevant to understanding him,[155] we contend that gaining a better appreciation of his heritage and indebtedness to the African tradition may help us better understand this bishop's surviving sermons. To be sure, much like Victorinus, we need not deny how conversant Zeno is in the wider Roman context, but his background should also be considered when studying this often overlooked bishop from Africa.

Another African writer from this time is Julius Quintus Hilarianus. Very little is know about Hilarianus, but his work *On the Duration of the World* indicates that he was writing around 397.[156] In this work, he calculated the ages of the world according to the major biblical epochs, and he concluded that the apocalypse would occur in the year 500.[157] This sort of millenarianism was once thought to have been an exclusively Donatist eschatology, since most other Christians by this time had altered their apocalyptic expectations in light of Constantine's conversion.[158] However, this view has been shown to be incorrect because many Christians around the Mediterranean retained their ancient expectation in Christ's millennial reign and at the same time not all Donatists held this as a central tenet of the faith.[159] Hilarianus's only other surviving work is entitled *On the Day and Month of Easter*, in which he attempts to explain the proper formula for calculating Easter in light of the Jewish Passover.[160] Earlier African Christians had also faced this problem,[161] but the controversy was not restricted to Africa.

Once again, the point is not to identify a given writer with Donatism, but to broaden our scope from the false construct of Donatism to looking at African Christianity at this time in all its diversity. When we do think of a Donatist party that opposed the Caecilianists, then we can return to instances when these identities arose as the two parties clashed. Although Donatists had gained a majority status by the late fourth century, and although they were often able to practice their faith with no external pressure, the tide would turn against them at the end of the fourth century and in the beginning of the fifth.

The end of Donatism?

When the two parties in North Africa did clash it was violent. The violence of some Donatists came to the attention of the Roman officials by way of legal appeals for protection made by Caecilianists. In 403 a Donatist convert to the Caecilianist party was beaten, dunked in mud, and wrapped in weeds as an act of public humiliation.[162] The same year, Maximian, the Caecilianist bishop of Bagai, was severely beaten after the Donatists took his basilica by force. The bishop had hidden under the altar, which in North Africa stood in the center of the sanctuary, not within the apse.[163]

He nevertheless was seized, beaten, and stabbed in the groin, before being thrown into "excrement [*stercoris*]."[164] Maximian would survive and go to Ravenna to plead the case of his party.[165] Not long after (in 409), Possidius, the bishop of Calama, went to Ravenna personally to appeal to the emperor to intervene: a violent mob had attacked his basilica, killing some of the clergy and severely beating Possidius himself.

In response, a series of imperial laws were enforced against the Donatists. By this time, heretics were no longer tolerated in the empire, and so the Caecilianists worked to be identified as the "Catholic" party and in turn label the Donatists as the schismatics against which heretical laws should be applied. The use of legal sanctions required a special proceeding, the Conference of Carthage in 411.[166]

The western emperor, Honorius, summoned a conference in Carthage meant to settle the Donatist controversy. Apparently the imperial support of the Caecilianists was not fully known in all of Africa.[167] Although the emperor's representative, Marcellinus, and the Caecilianist party assumed the Donatists were on trial for forming a schismatic church, the so-called Donatists objected from the outset to this label, insisting they were simply "the true bishops of our Lord Jesus Christ [*Episcopos . . . veritatis Christi domini nostri*]" in Africa.[168] The proceedings themselves provide historians with a unique opportunity to hear the Donatist side, because special care was taken to record the interactions verbatim.[169]

The Roman official presiding over this conference, Marcellinus, required all bishops from both parties to attend. Each side sent representatives to the proceedings, and while the Caecilianists sent a small number, the Donatists arrived with all 285 of their bishops. This number, they claimed, was not even fully representative of their party because many were unable to make the journey from distant parts of Africa. The total number of Donatist bishops, they claimed, was more than 400.[170] Since the stated aim of the conference was to identify who was the "Catholic" party, the Donatists' claim to be the majority church in Africa could not go unanswered. The Caecilianists responded by bringing all of their bishops to the procedures as well, but they numbered only 266 – less than the Donatists. The proceedings halted until more Caecilianist bishops could be found, which brought their party's number up to 286 – now a majority, and they too claimed to have more than 400 bishops total, only some of theirs could not make the journey either.

The proceedings record disputes between the two parties at every step. The Donatists challenged the validity of their opponents because they knew of instances where Caecilianists had named someone a bishop of a place where that person had never visited, much less pastored.[171] Once all were present, the Donatists refused to sit.[172] After all, Christ stood before Pilate, and the scriptures commanded that one not sit in the presence of sinners (Psalm 1:1). The Caecilianists had committed specific sins: Petilian, the Donatist bishop of Carthage, claimed that his party's bishops were appointed to each diocese through traditional means, while his opponents, the Caecilianists, had been placed as bishops in most places by force.[173]

Next, roll was called, and this gave both sides the chance to claim that they were the rightful bishop of their municipality. As each Caecilianist bishop presented himself to the conference, his Donatist opponent could respond. Each side took the opportunity to claim to be the rightful bishop, sometimes the only bishop, in the diocese.[174] The Donatists would often respond by saying things like "He's lying," "but he has only one parishioner!," or "I don't even recognize this man."[175] The Caecilianists responded by mocking the Donatists as bishops only of backwoods and rural towns, not in major cities.[176] In response, the Donatists conceded that the Caecilianists had large basilicas in the urban centers, but they mocked those basilicas for being empty of any parishioners.[177]

Despite the elaborate posturing by both sides, the outcome of the conference was predetermined: the Caecilianists were to be declared the Catholic party, and the Donatists were to be forced to hand over all of their church properties and unify with the Caecilianists. After extensive arguments from both sides, the conference ended as expected.

Here we should note how 411 was once seen as marking the "end" of Donatism. Although evidence was known of later Donatist activity, these were either dismissed as the last gasps of the movement or even as simple errors where dissenting groups were misidentified as Donatists. Augustine claimed that the conference of 411 effectively ended Donatism.[178] However, his works reveal that (at least some) Donatists did continue to resist the emperor's command to unify with the Caecilianists.[179] Even after Augustine's death in 430, a large body of literature continued to testify to Donatist activity.[180]

The most recent studies of Donatism have begun to take seriously how long Donatism lingered in North Africa.[181] The paradigm will be important here: on one hand, if Donatism was a schismatic group originating in the early fourth century and then defeated in the early fifth, then the primary sources are read in such a way as to see Donatism as the anomaly; on the other hand, if Donatism is in fact the traditional expression of Christianity in North Africa, and the Caecilianists gained "Catholic" status only because of their ties to Rome and to the emperor, then it is the Caecilianists who must be said to disappear in the early fifth century when the Vandals take over North Africa and persecute the pro-Nicene Christians. Neither paradigm does sufficient justice to the complexity of the actual events and people involved. Nevertheless, we can no longer assume that Donatism merely ended sometime after 411. All of this can be seen in the way that Augustine is read in relation to the Donatist controversy.[182]

In Augustine's perspective, "Donatus wanted to claim all of Africa [*nam Donatus tunc volebat Africam totam obtinere*]."[183] However, this tells us more about how Augustine viewed the schism than about what Donatus actually wanted or did: Donatus did not need to obtain all of Africa; the majority of Africa recognized him from the outset. The Donatists were simply the churches of North Africa, and these churches continued to be the majority in Augustine's time, as he sometimes admits.[184] It is Augustine's party that will need to establish new churches in order to obtain Africa and claim to be the Catholic party. As Peter Brown puts it:

> From 393 onwards, Augustine and his colleagues took the offensive against the Donatist church. They had good reason to do so. In Hippo, the Catholics were in a minority . . . For Donatism, not Catholicism, was the established church of Numidia."[185]

In response, Augustine worked tirelessly, "day and night [*diebus ac noctibus*]," to correct the Donatists.[186] Ultimately, Augustine decided, the Donatists must be coerced with whatever force necessary, since Christ commands his followers to "compel them to come in" (Luke 14.23).[187] Despite belonging to the minority party in Africa, Augustine – following the logic of the earlier writer, Optatis of Milevis – argued vehemently that his party was *the* Catholic/majority party when considered on a worldwide scale. Fortunately for Augustine, he could easily persuade Christians outside Africa, since – as he admits – few outside Africa knew of or understood the Donatist controversy.[188]

Robert A. Markus explains why the paradigm about Donatism matters for our understanding of the history and theology of the controversy:

> Donatism was no new creation. It was the representative in the fourth century of an older African theological tradition with deep roots in its characteristic religious mentality. . . . Donatism was, quite simply, the continuation of the old African Christian tradition in the post-Constantinian world. It was the world that had changed, not African Christianity.[189]

Later, Markus adds, "It is the catholic church of Optatus and Augustine, between Constantine and the disappearance of Roman rule in 430, that constitutes the anomaly in African Christianity."[190] Markus's view echoes that of Peter Brown, who acknowledged that Donatism was not a "movement" at all: it was Augustine's party that had to establish itself in North Africa.[191] Even when it did so, the Donatist party did not disappear; instead, "In Augustine's writings and sermons, from 405 to 409, and after 411, we can catch glimpses of a great church driven underground."[192] The potential ties between the "Donatist" party per se (or better, traditional African Christianity) and the later periods will be explored further in the chapters that follow. For now, it is simply important to note that when historians write about Donatist history, they can continue until as late as the year 1159.[193]

Even so, the label of "Donatism" may be part of why historians struggle to agree on what counts as evidence of Donatism after 411. Brent Shaw argues,

> If, as has been argued, the so-called "Donatists" never existed except insofar as the Catholic Church, backed by the power of the Roman state, was able to label and to define them, then, logically, when the latter no longer had the authority and the sheer force to keep that definition alive, no more "Donatists" would exist. Rather, the traditional Christians of north Africa would continue to exist as *they* always had.[194]

This brings us back to the problems with labeling this party as "Donatist." The category itself can control how historians read the evidence. If we, instead, viewed this party as the traditional church in Africa, rivaled by a party that had the support of both the Roman church and the Roman emperor, then much will need to be reconsidered in our history for this period.[195]

The following chapters will continue to review African Christianity in later historical periods. In doing so, we will return to the question of the survival of "Donatism," only with a more nuanced understanding of the Christians who were given this label.

Reassessing Donatist characteristics

Apart from the history of the Donatist controversy, the Donatists should be understood in terms of some specific characteristics. Too often, unfortunately, these "Donatist characteristics" are simply repetitions of Caecilianist rhetoric. In actual reality, the two parties were largely indistinguishable in faith and practice. For example, Pinianus and Melania, who were mentioned on p. 204, famously practiced lives of celibacy. When they moved from Rome to Africa in 408 to establish monasteries, they did not see enough of a distinction between Donatists and Caecilianists to exclude one or the other – much to Augustine's chagrin. In other words, the two parties had much in common: both held to Christian orthodoxy in terms of their teaching; both referred to themselves as "Catholic"; both cried "Praise be to God [*Deo laudes!*]" and both cried "Thanks be to God [*Deo gratias!*]";[196] both valued martyrdom; both parties "purged" the basilicas reclaimed from their opponents; both sides had "Circumcellions" (i.e. violent mobs); and both used wooden clubs during riots.[197] There was even a time when Donatists and Caecilianists intermarried and interacted in almost all aspects of society.[198] Nevertheless, there are differences between Donatists and Caecilianists in some of the sources.

The point of debate between Donatists and Caecilianists hinged on whether Caecilian was rightly ordained or whether he had been contaminated by idols when a *traditor* laid hands on him at his ordination. Interestingly, both parties agree that such an act would have invalidated Caecilian's ordination (it is not until Augustine that anyone suggests the contagion would not have spread to Caecilian). The debate was whether such contagion had actually occurred. Nevertheless, through the writing of Optatus of Milevis and Augustine of Hippo the Donatist party becomes associated with concern about a "pure" church. Such a concern, according to Optatus and Augustine, is hypocritical, since Donatists and even Donatist bishops committed mortal sins, such as murder. The Donatists likely never understood themselves as the sinless church nor their clergy as the sinless class of Christians. Instead, they claimed – like Cyprian – to be free from the contagion of idolatry. This contagion (apparently) was tangible, for they (allegedly) destroyed or at least scraped and purified the altars and churches when they confiscated them from Caecilianists.[199] Of course, this again stems from Caecilianist sources, and therefore, while it is probable that some Donatists carried out such acts, we cannot assume that all did so. One anonymous Donatus sermon celebrates how a basilica was reclaimed from the Caecilianists.[200] No mention is made of the need to purge the church or its adornments. Instead, it simply celebrates the martyrs who are commemorated in the sacred space, and denounces Caecilian himself for betraying the martyrs.

The value placed on martyrdom is itself another Donatist characteristic. As already mentioned, both Donatists and Caecilianists valued martyrdom and venerated saints who died for their faith. The Donatists, however, were said to place excessive value on martyrdom. The first way that this overemphasis occurred was in the veneration of martyrs at their shrines: the Donatists celebrated the martyrs by having feasts, and these feasts often included drunken excess.[201] Moreover, anyone who died for their faith could be considered a martyr – but some church leaders believed this needed to be regulated. The Caecilianist Council of Carthage under Gratus in 348 ruled that only the church could declare someone a martyr, which indicates that Donatists recognized many more.[202] When Optatus recalls the origins of the schism, he tells of how Caecilian rebuked Lucilla for kissing a martyr's bone before partaking in the Eucharist, adding "if, that is, he was a martyr."[203] Around the same time that Optatus narrates this account, Augustine and his mother arrived in Milan, where Ambrose rebuked Monica for her practice of feasting at the shrines of saints. Rebecca Moore comments on this scene:

> Monnica's piety and practice seem to reflect the African Christianity that Augustine subsequently tried to replace with catholic, or Romanized, Christianity. . . . Although Monnica complied with Caecilianist Christianity – a minority church movement that rejected the Donatists' insistence on the rebaptism of those whose sins required it – she continued her North African traditions until Ambrose admonished her to stop.[204]

The difference between Caecilianists and Donatists in their veneration of martyrs is one of degree: the Caecilianists continue to honor the saints, but they attempt to curtail the excesses they detect in the Donatist practices.

Another way in which the Donatist emphasis on martyrdom appeared excessive to Caecilianists is in their alleged willingness to commit suicide in order to claim martyr status. Here again, we are dependent on Caecilianist sources for all of these claims about Donatist views on martyrdom, and while there may be some basis for them, they nevertheless cannot be accepted uncritically. According to the Caecilianists, the Donatists in general and the Circumcellions in particular[205] were so eager to attain martyr status that they would provoke Caecilianists and "pagans" to attack them[206] or even throw themselves off cliffs.[207] This accusation, it should be noted, is generally accepted as accurate by historians. I suspect, however, that this point needs to be significantly nuanced, if not revised altogether. First, the Caecilianist sources never record firsthand information; they always speak in generalizations when discussing Donatist and Circumcellion suicides. Brent Shaw reviews the evidence of Donatist suicides but lists no specific instances, other than Gaudentius, who barricaded himself in his basilica to defend it, and Donatus of Mutagenna, who allegedly threw himself down a well.[208] Augustine himself even states that Donatus of Mutagenna was insane, and so he cannot represent a typical "Donatist" act. Gaudentius's actions also have nothing to do with Donatist zeal for martyrdom; Ambrose of Milan carried out a similar action in order to prevent a basilica from being taken by the Arians. Perhaps, "Donatists" do not identify themselves with suicide-martyrdom at all. Instead, they display a zeal for the faith, and so are willing to sacrifice their own lives *if necessary* (as is common in early Christianity). Their opponents used rhetorical license to exaggerate this zeal. Furthermore, there are instances of Donatists thrown from cliffs, but these were not suicides; Roman soldiers carried out such acts (perhaps mocking the Donatists' reputation for suicide in this fashion).[209] The closest example to suicide would be the virgin Victoria, who threw herself from a cliff.[210] This, however, was not attempted martyrdom; Victoria preferred death to forced marriage to a non-believer. What is more, the account reports how God miraculously saved Victoria from death. Finally, more study should be done on the potential links between this accusation and the African history, which includes a long list of tragic heroes and heroines who committed suicide rather than submit to Rome (e.g. Dido, Hannibal, Hasdrubal's wife, Gordian, Firmus, and Gildo).[211] It would have been very easy to persuade Roman officials that Africans (i.e. Donatists) were prone to suicidal resistance.

One practice that does differentiate Donatists from Caecilianists was the act of "rebaptism." Of course, the Donatists, like Cyprian before them, did not see this act as *rebaptiz*ing: if someone came from a false church (now including the Caecilianists), then the sacraments performed in that false church were also false. As already mentioned on p. 199, the Caecilianists accommodated the Roman practice of accepting heretical baptism and required only the confession of sin and the laying on of hands. Augustine debated the merits of this practice against the Donatists, and in so doing he struggled to explain the previous African tradition. At one point, he will claim that the later council of Arles corrects the earlier councils in Africa under Agrippinus and Cyprian.[212] Knowing that this appeal to an overseas council likely persuaded few, Augustine can later argue the opposite: that Agrippinus and Cyprian's councils should not have overturned previous tradition where heretical baptism was accepted in Africa (by some).[213]

While Cyprian could claim that all the churches of the east agreed with his African tradition, by Augustine's time the tide had turned and the majority of churches (or at least those churches sanctioned by the emperors) repudiated "rebaptism" by accepting the sacrament performed by schismatic groups.[214] This placed the Donatists in Africa in the position of explaining their idiosyncratic practice.

The Donatists defended their practice of "rebaptizing" as the ancient tradition of the African church, and they in turn had to denounce the practice of the overseas churches. Augustine repeatedly mocked "The sect of Donatus . . . found only in Africa [*pars autem Donati in solis Afris*]."[215] The Donatists were "frogs croaking from the swamp, 'We are the only Christians!' "[216] "How can they claim," asks Augustine in his *Letter to the Catholics*, that "Africa alone [*Africam . . . solam*] remained for Christ?"[217]

Here again, the Caecilianist accusation needs to be nuanced in our understanding. Some Donatists did assume that overseas churches were true churches – much like Cyprian's treatment of Stephen and the Italians. Maureen Tilley summarizes it well:

> The Donatists did not claim that there were no orthodox churches outside of North Africa. . . . They merely stated that it was their opinion that those in communion with the Catholics of North Africa were in communion with the wrong party.[218]

When the Donatists faced the claim by Augustine and his party that all the world stood against the Donatists, the Donatists easily answered by claiming to be the remnant church.[219] Jesus himself had prophesied that many would fall away before the end (Matt. 24:4–14; Luke 17:22–37). Therefore, while the Donatists did come to understand themselves as the righteous remnant, this self-understanding is secondary to their attempt to defend their African tradition.[220]

In addition to the African theological tradition, there are certain elements that connect the Donatists to the African context and history. Before concluding this chapter, therefore, these connections need to be reviewed.

What was African about the Donatists?

Because many sources on Donatism indicate certain indigenous characteristics, some modern historians concluded that the Donatists were "nationalist" in some way. This way of interpreting the Donatists, however, has been shown to be misguided.[221] "Nationalism," of course, is a modern phenomenon that should not be read back into the fourth-century sources. Also, since many Donatists (allegedly) appealed to the emperor and later utilized the Roman legal system, there has been a reaction among historians to attempt to understand the Donatists to be as Romanized as the Caecilianists. The only difference between the two according to this second school of thought is the difference in theology. I suggest that both the extremes of reading the Donatists (purely nationalist or purely religious) fails to do justice to the Donatist party. While we can no longer think of all Donatists as forming an anti-Roman resistance movement, we can explore instances where a uniquely African identity surfaces for some Donatists.[222] In the following section, I will introduce three areas where we can find the African heritage and identity as important for the Donatists: Donatists and the Punic language, Donatists and African identity, and Donatists in conflict with Romans. These three areas do not exhaust all there is to say on the subject. On the contrary, they are offered here as areas that need to be further studied.

Donatists and the Punic language

The first area where the Donatists' ties to an indigenous African identity can be found is in the use of the Punic language. Augustine struggled to find enough ministers who could communicate with the Punic-speaking population in the area around his city of Hippo: "the preaching of the gospel suffers much in our territories for the lack of Punic language [*Punicae linguae*]."[223] It must be remembered that most of these rural villages already had clergy, and we can assume they were Punic-speaking clergy: they were the Donatist bishops that Augustine aims to rival and ultimately replace with Caecilianist bishops. Augustine elsewhere explained how a neighboring town, Fussula, was predominantly Donatist, and so he "looked for someone apt and suitable for that place, who was also trained in the Punic language."[224] The town of Theognetus, near Fussala, also spoke "the Punic tongue"; in this instance the entire populace rejected the Caecilianist Numidian primate and "not even a single nun remained" on the side of Augustine's party.[225] Likewise, Christians in Calama and Mappala, or at least those in Donatist churches, needed Augustine's works translated into Punic.[226] Apparently, this was true of the whole of what Augustine calls "our territories [*in nostris regionibus*]."[227] Similarly, Augustine reports how the Circumcellions needed a "Punic interpreter."[228]

The Punic language among (some) Donatists certainly indicates something more than a simple language barrier. The (in)famous cry of the Donatists, "God be praised [*Deo laudes*]," and other similar phrases derive from "Ba'al-Saturnine formulae" in that they were originally found in "Punic paganism."[229] If Punic language is an indicator that some Donatists could be identified in terms of a Punic social identity,[230] then this heightens the attention that should be paid to the Donatists' claim to the African herit-age and ancestry. Augustine at one point bemoaned how entrenched the Donatists were in their ancestral line: despite showing a Donatist man evi-dence that his church was in error, the Donatist stubbornly replied, "What my parents were, I am too."[231]

Of course, Augustine himself can be labeled "Punic," as will be discussed in Chapter 8. So then we must conclude that for Augustine being Punic did not necessarily imply one was also Donatist.[232] Augustine can refer to Punic generically as "the African language [*lingua Afra*]."[233] There are, nev-ertheless, two references to Punic that are particularly illuminating for our present study.

Early in his ministry (c.390), Augustine responded to a non-Christian, named Maximus of Madauros, who mocked Christians for worship-ping martyrs.[234] In particular, Maximus mocks the "Punic names [*Punica nomina*]" of the martyrs.[235] In response, Augustine defends *Punicitas*:

> As an African man, writing to Africans, and even as one abiding in Africa, you could not have forgotten yourself and thought of Punic names as flawed. . . . Should this language be disapproved by you, you must deny that in Punic books produced by very educated men many wise teachings have been recorded; you must regret that you were born here, for this land is the still-warm cradle of the Punic language itself. . . . You disrespect and snub Punic names to such an extent, it is as if you had surrendered to the Roman altars.[236]

Augustine himself, therefore, can – at least in this instance – pit the Punic and Roman identities against each other, and he does so by defending the Punic heritage.[237] So while it is safe to assume that some in Augustine's party also spoke and read Punic,[238] there is still an important point to be made about these Punic martyrs.

Augustine's own relationship with these martyrs is ambiguous, at best. He concludes the same letter to Maximus by clarifying the rites involved with the named martyr shrines in Madauros. In response to Maximus's claim that Christians worship these Punic martyrs as pagans worship their local deities, Augustine does not – as contemporary theologians might expect – explain the differentiation for Catholics between worship and veneration.[239] Instead, Augustine insists that "Catholics" neither worship nor adore these saints at all, implying that it is the Donatists who do so. Augustine then faults Maximus for not asking the Catholic party about these martyrs, since there is a Catholic church in Madauros. This conclusion is supported by J. H. Baxter's 1924 article, which argued that the martyrs were not "proto-martyrs," as has been commonly thought in the past, but they were Donatists persecuted under Macarius.[240]

In addition to Augustine linking Punic-named martyrs to Donatists, there is another important instance where Augustine identifies Donatists by their

Punic language. In his earliest anti-Pelagian work, Augustine applauds how appropriate it is that in his region of North Africa, certain Christians call baptism "salvation [*salutem*]" and call the sacramental body of Christ "life [*vitam*]."[241] To which Christians in particular is Augustine referring? He simply calls them the "Punic Christians [*Punici christiani*]."[242] While he nowhere explains to Pelagius that these Punic Christians are Donatists – after all, Augustine elsewhere notes how most overseas Christians have not even heard of the Donatist controversy[243] – he does refer to the Punic Christians in this passage as a distinct group, using the third person plural, never the first person. Therefore, if these are not Augustine's fellow Caecilianists, then the phrase "Punic Christians" is arguably Augustine's gloss for the Donatist party.

Donatists and African identity

A second area where the Donatists can be understood as African is when they explicitly use an African identity. One unique expression of an explicitly African social identity found among Donatists is their use of scriptures about "the south."[244] Augustine reports how the "Donatists" interpret "that passage where it is written, 'Where do you pasture your flocks, where do you make them lie down in the south?' "[245] This reference is to Song of Songs 1.7, which reads (in the modern translation):

> I am black, and beautiful, O daughters of Jerusalem, like the tents of Kedar, like the curtains of Solomon. . . . Tell me, you whom my soul loves, where you pastor your flock, where you make it lie down at noon.[246]

The word for "noon" used in the Latin is *in meridie*, the time in the day when the sun is most southward, and so by common usage it becomes a synonym for the south. The Donatists claim to be God's flock referenced in Song of Songs, which rests "in the south" (i.e. south of Rome).[247] In response, Augustine mocks the poor geographical logic:

> If in that passage "south" should be interpreted as Africa where the sect of Donatus is found, because it is under a hotter region of the sky, the Maximianists will surpass all of you, since their schism arose in Byzacena and Tripoli. But the Arzuges quarrel with them and claim that it rather refers to them. Mauretania Caesariensis, nonetheless, is closer to the western than to the southern part; since it does not want to be called Africa, how will it boast of being called "the south"?[248]

Augustine's tactic is to redefine the concept of the south: it is not a region, it is a relative descriptor, and the Maximianists in Byzacena and the Arzuges further along the outposts of the southern provinces have a better claim to being this flock. Augustine's observation, of course, is precisely the claim the Donatists are making: the concept of "south" is a relative term, and they are southern relative in particular to the Romans.[249]

Augustine intentionally argues against the Donatists practice of equating being southern with being African, but in other places Augustine cites and even accepts this practice. In one sermon, Augustine deviates from his focus on Ezekiel to expound on other passages about shepherds, including the Shepherd and the flock of Song of Songs.[250] Augustine laments how the "heretics" misread the passage, so that "the noonday or south means Africa."[251] Augustine this time capitulates, "let the noonday or south be Africa, Africa be the noonday," only he insists that his party is also "in Africa." Next, Augustine turns to another passage in which the Donatists exchange the word "south," this time for "the *Afric*": Habakkuk 3:3, in our modern translations reads, "God came from Teman," which is a southern city of Edom. The Latin word used in Augustine's text was *Afric*, that is the *Afer ventus*, or south wind.[252] The Donatist interpreter cited by Augustine, however, uses this text to identify his party, "the African."

In addition to the reference to the "South" in Song of Songs, and the *Africus* of Habakkuk, Augustine cites one more passage used by the Donatists, referencing Simon the Cyrene in the Gospel of Mark (15:21). Augustine quotes his opponents as saying: "A Cyrenaean . . . is an African. That's why [Simon the Cyrene] was the one who was compelled to carry the cross."[253] Augustine proceeds to parse the provinces so that Cyrenaica, along with all of Pentapolis and Libya, belongs to the eastern provinces, and not properly to Africa. Nevertheless, for our present purposes, Augustine still provides evidence that (at least some) Donatists identified themselves as African. This self-identity enables Donatists to claim all references to the "south," since their primary opponents were to the north, that is Rome and Ravenna.

With this set of evidence, it must also be stipulated that Augustine's party could equally claim to be "African":[254] "We too are Africans," he says to his Donatist counterparts.[255] In 420 Consentius writes from Iberia to Augustine. He complains of how some of his fellow bishops refuse to expel a heretical group there, and they claim "the African bishops" as precedent since they did not expel the Donatists.[256] However, even in this same letter Consentius can later revert to calling the Donatists simply by the term "the Africans."[257] Consentius illustrates how easy it was to identify the Donatists in terms of a regional social identity, and Augustine's other references evince how some Donatists explicitly pitted their African identity in the south against their enemies from Rome to the north.

Donatists and conflict with Romans

The third and last area listed here in which the Donatists exhibit an African identity is in scenes of violent conflict. The Donatists oppose the Caecilianists aligned with Roman officials, and the language used to explain these violent encounters tell us something about the identities involved. The first scene to consider is a riot that took place in Calama in 408. This case involved "pagans," not Donatists, but it sets the stage for other clashes of the kind. A local official from Calama named Nectarius wrote to Augustine, pleading for the people of his "homeland [*patria*]."[258] In his response Augustine shifts the focus from the earthly *patria* to the heavenly one, and chastises Nectarius for loving only the earthly.[259] Augustine then shifts to another *patria* altogether, Italy, and he does so by quoting a line from Virgil: "in the case of your fatherland so much of the men by whom that land flourished as of the wars by which it burned, in fact, not just with wars, but with flames."[260] This exchange is telling for our approach in that Augustine's response should be analyzed according to its rhetorical content and aims, for he rhetorically alludes to the social identities involved.

In the *Aeneid,* "that land [*terra illa*]" is explicitly "Italy [*Itala*]," but the scene is when Juno drove the local populace to rebel against the newly arrived progenitors of Rome.[261] We can assume that Nectarius gets the point;[262] he likely also associated the "burning" with Rome's other major conquest, the burning of Carthage in the third Punic war (an event famously celebrated throughout Virgil's *Aeneid*). Augustine seems to drive the point home, for he says "not only did it burn, it blazed,"[263] and he then makes a somewhat forced allusion to Cato.[264] This, of course, is the Cato who ended his senatorial speeches by crying, "Carthage must be destroyed!"

The reference to Virgil's scene is also poignant in its mention of Juno. In Virgil's narrative, Juno is the one who drove the locals to revolt against the Romans, and Juno it will be remembered preferred Carthage and the Punics throughout the *Aeneid*. Even more poignant for our purposes, this Juno is to be understood, via *interpretatio Romana,*[265] as Tanit, the most popular goddess of Punic Africa.[266] Augustine has Punic religion in view, as further evidenced by his reference to human sacrifice in the next paragraph.[267] In sum, when reading Augustine's descriptions in light of the social identities contested in Calama, one finds that the mob is depicted as rural, anti-Roman, and Punic.

In this scene, those who attacked the church in Calama were a Punic mob. One question remains: why did this "pagan" mob attack the "Catholic" church only? Why did it not also attack the Donatist basilica? While no certain answer can be given with our limited evidence, the event could easily be explained if we understood the Donatists to be fellow indigenous Punics, while the mob viewed the Catholics in Calama as outsiders. Making a differing point, Erika Hermanowicz studies this scene and concludes, "The elites . . . They were protecting their own."[268]

A second scene is comparable to the Calama riot, but it took place earlier (399) in the town of Sufes. Again, Augustine reports how a "pagan" mob was involved, but this time they killed sixty Christians. Once again, we could ask whether any Donatists were targeted in this riot. We know of a Donatist presence in Sufes,[269] but we are again given no direct statement about Donatists in this incident. Two clues from Augustine's letter suggest that this scene involves Punic and Roman identities. The first is Augustine's explicit charge: "Among you the laws of Rome have been buried . . . There is certainly no respect and no reverence for the emperors."[270] In addition to the charge that the city's population is anti-Roman, Augustine refers to the statue of "Hercules" that the Christians destroyed. Even more poignantly, Augustine reports how the city describes the deity: "For if you should say this is 'your Hercules' [*nam si vestrum Herculem dixeritis*]," after which Augustine offers to buy another statue. It is probable that the specific claim to Hercules is not to the Roman Hercules at all, but to Melqart, who was often named "Hercules" in Romanized towns of Punic heritage. Here, then, is a second instance where Augustine's party is attacked by locals for its ties to *Romanitas*. The Donatists, it seems, were left unscathed in such encounters.

A third scene of violent conflict occurs in Carthage.[271] Augustine tells of how a mob of Caecilianists cheered the "shaving" of Hercules beard; that is, a statue from the temple of Hercules was defaced in response to a local official who had agreed to have the statue's beard gilded.[272] Augustine attempts to preach to this crowd, which interrupted his sermon by chanting, "As was done in Rome, so also in Carthage [*Quomodo Roma, sic et Carthago!*]"[273] In other words, the recent edict of emperor Honorius against pagan worship should also be enforced in Carthage. The simple categories of pagan and Christian, however, fail to account for all of the surviving evidence. As in Sufes, this scene in Carthage is in all likelihood in reference to the Punic cult of Melqart under the Romanized name of Hercules.[274] Augustine clearly recognizes the tension between the pro- and anti-Roman sentiment, because he reminds his audience of how veneration of "Roman" gods has also ceased.[275]

Augustine seems to be pointing out how the Romans were as equally guilty in their paganism as the Carthaginians. However, the crowd, let us remember, had been chanting the 83rd Psalm in this service: this Psalm is a prayer against the Phoenician peoples in general and it names the city of Tyre in particular.[276] Augustine explicitly identifies Tyre with Punic identity in another work, his unfinished commentary on Romans: "For the Canaanite [in Matt. 15] is a Punic woman from the region of Tyre."[277] It must be remembered that just as Troy was the mother city of Rome, Tyre was the ancestral city of Carthage, and so a hymn calling for the fall of Tyre and her gods seems more than coincidental on the day the Carthaginian statue of Melqart was violated (by Caecilianists?), with the act being celebrated by Caecilianists. Prior to Augustine, Optatus had also identified Carthage with Tyre, only he did so in regards to Donatus in particular: rather than calling him bishop, the "people [*populi*]" always refer to their leader as Donatus of Carthage.[278] Optatus insists that Donatus's title should be "the prince of Tyre," which is in reference to the Old Testament prophecy against the prince of Tyre (see Ezek. 28:2), but it works only because Tyre is the mother of all Punic cities, especially Carthage (see Isa. 23.1).[279] Augustine's Caecilianist audience during the riot in Carthage repeats what seems to be a common trope against the indigenous population: they are Punics/Phoenicians. For a third instance, we have a scene where Caecilianist Christians in particular claim an allegiance with Rome, while the local populace (albeit not Donatist per se) is identified as Punic and indigenous.

Other scenes should be read in the same light as the three mentioned earlier. For example, around 420 a "turbulent mob" in Caesarea demanded Bishop Honorius be transferred from Cartenna in Mauretania to be installed as their bishop, despite the objection from prior canon law.[280] Both Caesarea[281] and Cartenna were Donatist strongholds.[282] Although some in Caesarea wrote to Augustine for his protection, they and Augustine both fear that the case will be taken to the imperial court, and the mob will be deemed "heretics."[283] What kind of heretics remains unstated, but surely the charge of Donatism is the most likely candidate. Perhaps, Augustine fears that the provincial "people, and especially the poor [*illi autem et maxime pauperes*]"[284] are all too easily identified as Donatists because so many Donatists belonged to the provincial populace.

Another scene is the violent attacks on Caecilianists in Bagai (discussed in the previous section): the Donatists there, Augustine says, believe the church is "in Africa alone [*in sola Africa*],"[285] which is an important claim for social identity. Augustine admits that the Caecilianists were "surpassed by their great numbers" by the Donatists.[286] Augustine will describe this Donatist mob in terms of "savagery [*saeviendo*]."[287] It should be noted that Erica Hermanowicz has argued persuasively that the Donatists did not aim to kill in this or other similar attacks; instead, they aimed to humiliate.[288] This would have been especially humiliating for Maximian, since Roman nobility, now including Caecilianist bishops, were exempted from corporal punishment. In response, Maximian, who survived the event, traveled to Ravenna and appealed to the emperor, an action that Augustine apparently needed to justify. Augustine likens Maximian's actions to Paul's from Acts 22–23, where "he" (ambiguously now) "did not hesitate to appeal to Roman laws, declaring himself to be a Roman citizen, since it was not permitted to flog Roman citizens."[289] Unlike Paul's time, the now-Christian emperor of Augustine's day will issue edicts that enforce "unity," but Augustine proceeds to explain how in some areas in Africa the locals still resist.[290] Evidently, some local officials unenthusiastically carried out the emperor's edicts even in the final years before the Vandal invasion.[291] Is this not an instance where Roman interference clashed with indigenous loyalty? In other words, the Caecilianist party understood itself and was understood by the Donatists to be distinctly sided with Rome.

Let us briefly conclude this section by pressing beyond the immediate evidence, and looking to what may be broader patterns among the Donatists. Let us assume for the moment that some Donatists retain a local/non-Roman identity. Some harbor resentment and even engage in open resistance to Roman interference in local affairs. This would explain the connection between (some) Donatists and Firmus and Gildo. This same assumption would help explain the ease with which the Vandals invaded North Africa.[292] It is worth remembering that in the same letter in which he describes the local scenes of violence, Augustine acknowledged how (some) Donatists in his day attempted to court the Arian invaders of the empire.[293] These specific scenes and these larger instances of local uprisings, therefore, do have a part to play in our understanding of the Donatists. Many spoke Punic and in various ways identified themselves explicitly as Africans.

Conclusions and caveats

While in this chapter I have focused on the African context and identities of the Donatists (especially in the last section), it needs to be repeated that this has been emphasized in order to fill a gap in current discussions of Donatism. The points raised here should not be overstated to say that all Donatists thought of themselves as African or held anti-Roman sentiments. As mentioned on pp. 203–210, the Donatists were diverse, and so we cannot assume that any one characteristic applies equally to all Donatists. Many Donatists appealed to the Roman legal system and courted the favor of the Roman officials. Many – it is safe to assume – would have understood themselves as Roman and as full participants in the Roman Empire.

Likewise, in attempting to highlight the Donatists' African heritage and identity, we should not in turn assume that the Caecilianists were somehow not African. Some Caecilianists did articulate their African identity (e.g. Augustine, who will be treated more fully in Chapter 8), and we can assume that many more would have if given the opportunity. I have suggested a pattern wherein Donatists tend to identity themselves as defending the African tradition and the Caecilianists tend to align themselves with Rome, but this pattern must be tested on a case-by-case basis.

The Donatists also further developed their self-identity in terms of a unique African Christian tradition. As Matthew Gaumer claims:

> North Africans maintained a distinguished theological tradition that set them apart from the world as God's elect, the adopted *collecta* of Israel. At the same time, their Catholic counterparts were creating ever stronger bonds with the Roman Empire, resulting in such extreme changes such as using coercive techniques to demand conformity to the Catholic Church.[294]

This pattern of identifying oneself as aligned with or distanced from Rome requires much further study in terms of Christian tradition. While it likely should not be seen as the definitive element in Donatism, it deserves to be considered in any attempt to understand this controversy.

At this point, it is still unclear what percentage (or whether percentages can even be estimated) or how many from each party would explicitly align themselves in these regional terms. The examples reviewed here may not sufficiently represent the demographics of Africa at this time. Nevertheless, it has been argued here that we should understand the Donatist controversy in light of the African context and consider the identities invoked in regional terms. It is hoped that additional studies along these lines will help us understand this controversy better in the future.

Now that we have covered the Donatist controversy, we can narrow our focus to one particularly influential person involved in it. The Donatist controversy predated Augustine by many decades, but it spanned the whole period of his life. Therefore, we had to interact with his works throughout this present chapter. Next, we can consider Augustine more fully on his own terms.

Notes

1 For a review of the secondary literature on Donatism, see John Whitehouse, "The Scholarship of the Donatist Controversy," in *The Donatist Schism: Controversy and Contexts*, ed. Richard Miles (Liverpool: Liverpool University Press, 2016), 34–53.

2 There is debate on the dating, with many recent historians moving the schism back to c.308. See A. R. Birley, "Some Notes on the Donatist schism," *Libyan Studies* 18 (1987), 30–31, for bibliography.

3 There was a later dispute as to which Donatus was first involved in the controversy; on the alleged distinction between Donatus of Carthage and Donatus of Casae Nigrae, a distinction both Donatists and Catholics claimed at the conference of 411, see Barnes, "The Beginnings of Donatism," 16.

4 For a bibliography and opposition to this consensus about Donatists' exclusive claims to the a unified/Cyprianic African tradition, see Jane Merdinger, "In League With the Devil? Donatist and Catholic Perspectives on Pre-Baptismal Exsufflation," in *The Uniquely African Controversy: Studies on Donatist Christianity*, ed. Anthony Dupont, Matthew Gaumer, and M. Lamberigts (Leuven: Peeters, 2014), 153–178. For Augustine's use of Cyprian, Matthew Alan Gaumer, *Augustine's Cyprian: Authority in Roman Africa* (Leuven: Brill, 2016).

5 *Autonomisme et christianime*, 181, "le nom de cyprianisme."

6 See, for example, Augustine, *On Baptism, Against the Donatists* 1.4.5.

7 "African Christianity." Similarly, Peter Iver Kaufman, "Donatism Revisited: Moderates and Militants in Late Antique North Africa," *Journal of Late Antiquity* (2009), 131–142, esp. 138–139, used "African secessionists" instead of Donatists, seeing the group as under and even reacting to "Roman occupation."

8 Shaw, *Sacred Violence*, 5–6.

9 Brown, "Christianity and Local Culture in Late Roman Africa," 85–95.

10 See full treatment in Wilhite, "Were the 'Donatists' a National or Social Movement in Disguise? Reframing the Question," in *Studia Patristica* (forthcoming).

11 Or simply offer incense; see Arnobius, *Against the Nations* 7.26.

12 Optatus of Milevis, *Against the Donatists* 1.18.

13 Optatus of Milevis, *Against the Donatists* 1.19.

14 The following material is adapted from Wilhite, "Donatism in Carthage Until 411," in *Religion in Carthage*, ed. Jane Merdinger (Leiden: Brill, forthcoming).

15 Jerome, *The Lives of Illustrious Men* 110.
16 For the archaeological and literary records of these basilicas and for the debate between Optatus and his opponent, see Wilhite, "True Church or True Basilica? Parmenian's Ecclesiology Revisited," *Journal of Early Christian Studies* 22 (3, 2014), 399–436.
17 Optatus, *Against the Donatists* 1.16. The Donatists' excessive enthusiasm for martyrs and their shrines will be a recurring theme in Caecilianist sources (see discussion on p. 215).
18 Optatus, *Against the Donatists* 1.18.
19 See Pier Giovanni Caron, "Les 'seniores laici' de l'Église africaine," *Revue international des Droits de l'Antiquité* 6 (1951), 7–22; Frend, "*Seniores laici* and the Origins of the Church in North Africa," 280–284; Shaw "The Elders of Christian Africa," 207–226; Shaw, "The Structure of Local Society in the Early Maghrib," 18–54; and Burns, Jensen, et al., *Christianity in Roman Africa*, 392–396.
20 Optatus, *Against the Donatists* 1.18
21 See the Council of Cirta 304 as reported in Optatus, *Against the Donatists* 1.13 and his appendix 1 (= *Gesta apud Zenophilum*). Barnes, *Early Christian Hagiography*, 135–136, doubts the veracity of this document.
22 Optatus, *Against the Donatists* 1.14.
23 Optatus, *Against the Donatists* 1.19.
24 *Acts of the Abitinian Martyrs* 20. This text, however, while claiming to be a contemporary account, has been challenged as Donatist propaganda from a much later period; see Alan Dearn, "The Abitinian Martyrs and the Outbreak of the Donatist Schism," *Journal of Ecclesiastical History* 55 (1, 2004), 1–18.
25 E.g. *A Sermon on the Passion of Saints Donatus and Advocatus* 4 and 8. Eusebius, *Church History* 10.5.18, records Constantine's letter to Miltiades in which Caecilian is accused of "many" charges.
26 See John Whitehouse, "The Course of the Donatist Schism in Late Roman North Africa," in *The Donatist Schism: Controversy and Contexts*, ed. Richard Miles (Liverpool: Liverpool University Press, 2016), 17.
27 Cf. Optatus, *Against the Donatists* 1.19.3 and Augustine, *Letter* 43.5.14.
28 *Against the Donatists* 1.26.1; cf. Mireille Labrousse, *Optat de Milèv: Contre les Donatistes* (Paris: Éditions du Cerf, 1996), 412:229 n.2, for other theories on the bishops' purpose in Africa.
29 As to the implication that they controlled the cathedral and other basilicas, see Wilhite, "True Church or True Basilica?", 399–436.
30 For example, Donatus presided over a council in Carthage (336) with 270 bishops attending from across North Africa.
31 Optatus, *Against the Donatists* 3.9.1: *Gaudet totus orbis de unitate catholica praeter partem Africae* (Edwards 77, but with translation modified and emphasis added).
32 However, Barnes, "The Beginnings of Donatism," 20–21, argues that the document (in Optatus, *Against the Donatists* 1.22) has been misunderstood (and often mistranslated): instead of appealing for secular judges, the Donatists were requesting bishops from Gaul who were experiencing no schism and thus were impartial: *Petimus ut de Gallia nobis iudices dari praecipiat pietas tua* (Optatus, *Against the Donatists* 1.22). As further evidence, Barnes cites the fact that Constantine himself interpreted the letter as such and summoned the synod of Arles.
33 Optatus, *Against the Donatists* 3.3.3: *Quid est imperatori cum ecclesia?* Cf. Tertullian, *Prescript Against the Heretics* 7.9, "What has the academy to do with the church? [*Quid academiae et ecclesiae?*]"
34 Optatus, *Against the Donatists* 3.3.9: *super imperatorem non sit nisi solus Deus.*
35 According to a sixth-century source, Miltiades was also "of the nation of Africa (*natione Afer*)"; see *Book of the Popes*, 33 (Duchesne, *Liber pontificalis*,

1.168; my trans.) Curiously, this source mentions the Manichaeans, but not the Donatists.

36 E.g. Eusebius, *Church History* 10.7.1–2, reports tax exemption to clergy within Caecilian's party. See Frend, *The Donatist Church*, 146, for this reading. For the primary sources about the use of imperial laws throughout the Donatist controversy, see Noel Lenski, "Imperial Legislation and the Donatist Controversy: From Constantine to Honorius," in *The Donatist Schism: Controversy and Contexts*, ed. Richard Miles (Liverpool: Liverpool University Press, 2016), 166–219.

37 Optatus, *Against the Donatists*, appendix 4 (trans. Edwards 188). Optatus also indicates that rebaptism was the concern for Macarius in 347 (see *Against the Donatists* 3.2.1).

38 Burns, Jensen, et al., *Christianity in Roman Africa*, 195–196. Augustine, *Letter* 43.7.20, says that another council in Rome was summoned, but Caecilian did not attend. Curiously, Caecilian was detained in Milan, while Donatus was allowed to return (Optatus, *Against the Donatists* 1.26).

39 *A Sermon on the Passion of Saints Donatus and Advocatus* 6–8; 11–13.

40 There is later evidence (c.329) that Donatists conflicted with the Caecilianists over their basilicas. See appendix 10 in Optatus, *Against the Donatists* and an inscription (*CIL* 8.215.17) discussed in Frend, *The Donatist Church*, 163.

41 *Conference of Carthage 411* 3.258 line3–4 (CCL 149A:243).

42 For the decree of 5 May, 321, and sources, see Frend, *The Donatist Church*, 161.

43 Perhaps Constantine simply turned his attention to Licinius; see Barnes, *Constantine and Eusebius*, 60.

44 Barnes, *Constantine and Eusebius*, 61.

45 Optatus, *Against the Donatists*, appendix 9.

46 *Life of Constantine* 1.45.

47 The category of "Arianism" suffers from similar problems as "Donatism." See the discussion in Wilhite, *The Gospel According to Heretics: Discovering Orthodoxy through Early Christological Conflicts* (Grand Rapids, MI: Baker Press, 2015), 105–128. For bibliography on Donatist ties to Arianism, see Burns, Jensen, et al., *Christianity in Roman Africa*, 58 n.127.

48 *Life of Constantine* 2.61–62.

49 *Life of Constantine* 2.66 and 2.68.

50 *Life of Constantine* 2.72. Similarly, the Donatists appeared to mirror the Novatianists or "Cathari," according to Epiphanius, *Panarion* 59.13.6. Likewise, Eusebius, *Church History* 6.42.1, calls the Novatians "Cathari," while *The Book of the Popes* 21, claims Novatus was "from Africa (*ex Africa*)" (Mommsen, *Le liber pontificalis* 1:148).

51 *Lives of Illustrious Men* 93; cf. Augustine, *On Heresies* 69.

52 Augustine, *Letter* 44.3.6; *To Cresconius* 3.34.38.

53 Athanasius, *To the Africans*.

54 E.g. Sozomen, *Church History* 4.15; Epiphanius, *Panarion* 59.13.7; Theodoret of Cyrrhus, *Compendium of Heretical Accounts* 4.6.

55 E.g. *On Heresies* 69.1.

56 Augustine, *Letter* 185.1.1. See further discussion on pp. 249, 258, 267, and 269–70.

57 Constans, whom the Nicene party lauded for suppressing the "Arians," would be remembered by the Donatists as a persecutor (e.g. *Martyrdom of Marculus* 3).

58 Optatus, *Against the Donatists* 3.1.1: *operariis unitatis multa quidem aspere gesta sunt*.

59 Optatus, *Against the Donatists* 3.3.

60 Optatus, *Against the Donatists* 3.4.

61 Augustine, *Expositions on the Psalms* 132.6; with reference 2 Tim. 4.7.

62 For scholarly interpretations of the Circumcellions, see Shaw, *Sacred Violence*, 660–674, 828–839; and Anna Leone, *The End of the Pagan City: Religion,*

Economy, and Urbanism in Late Antique North Africa (Oxford: Oxford University Press, 2013), 14–18. Bruno Pottier, "*Circumcelliones*, Rural Society and Communal Violence in Late Antique North Africa," in *The Donatist Schism: Controversy and Contexts*, ed. Richard Miles (Liverpool: Liverpool University Press, 2016), 142–165, has recently attempted to revive the argument that the Circumcellions were a form of nomadic monks.

63 Optatus, *Against the Donatists* 3.4.2 (Edwards 68).

64 Cf. O. R. Vassall-Phillips, *The Work of St. Optatus* (London: Longmans, Green, and Co., 1917), who translates the phrase as "fighting *dervishes*"!

65 Optatus, *Against the Donatists* 3.4.3–4.

66 *Letter* 108.5.14.

67 E.g. Herodotus, *Histories* 4.180; cf. Augustine, *On Christian Doctrine* 4.24.53.

68 E.g. Augustine, *Letter* 50; *Sermon* 24.

69 After citing Augustine's report that the Donatists disavow any connection to the Circumcellions (namely, *Against the Letter of Parmenian* 1.2.17, 1.24–26; *Against Cresconius the Grammarian* 3.49.54), Frend, *The Donatist Church*, 172, doubts the authenticity of the Donatists' claim, saying they did so "conveniently." Also, see Optatus, *Against the Donatists* 3.4.5, who admits that the rest of the Donatist bishops requested that local officials squelch the Circumcellions.

70 Optatus, *Against the Donatists* 3.4.12. Also, see Petilian's claim that the Roman officials responsible died violently as punishment from God (in Augustine, *Against the Letters of Petilian* 2.209; cf. Lactantius, *On the Death of the Persecutors*).

71 See Optatus, *Against the Donatists* 3.8.3.

72 Augustine, *Against the Letters of Petilian* 2.39.92; 2.92.208; *Letters* 49.3; 87.10.

73 Text and translation in Maier, *Le dossier*, 1:259–275 and Tilley, *Donatist Martyr Stories*, 63–75.

74 *Martyrdom of Marculus* 3. Text and translation in Maier, *Le dossier*, 1:277–291 and Tilley, *Donatist Martyr Stories*, 78–87. For the monument, see MacKendrick, *The North African Stones Speak*, 267.

75 See the theologizing of this in the anonymous *Sermo in natali sanctorum innocentium* (in *PLS* 1:289–294). For discussion, see Tilley, *The Bible in Christian North Africa*, 86–89.

76 Augustine, *Brief Meeting with the Donatists* 16.20.

77 Optatus, *Against the Donatists* 1.5; 3.3. Monceaux, *Histoire littéraire*, 5:221.

78 *Sacred Violence*, 108–109.

79 I.e. Optatus's *Against the Donatists* (which may have been originally titled, *Contra Parmenianum*); and Augustine's *Against the Letter of Parmenian*. For his other "books" and "songs," see Augustine, *On Heresy* 43.

80 For their legal status, see Erika T. Hermanowicz, *Possidius of Calama: A Study of the North African Episcopate at the Time of Augustine* (Oxford: Oxford University Press, 2008), 126–129. For specific developments, see Wilhite, "Donatism in Carthage Until 411."

81 Optatus, *Against the Donatists* 7.1.2.

82 Optatus, *Against the Donatists* 2.16–21; 6.1–8.

83 *Theodosian Code* 16.6.1.

84 Merdinger, "Before Augustine's Encounter With Emeritus," 371–379, argues this for Mauretania in particular. More generally, see a helpful review of the sources in Jesse Hoover, *The Contours of Donatism: Theological and Ideological Diversity in Fourth-Century North Africa* (MA thesis for Baylor University, 2008).

85 Tilley, "Redefining Donatism: Moving Forward," *Augustinian Studies* 42 (1, 2011), 25.

86 See details in Barnes, *Early Christian Hagiography*, 249–256.

87 See Augustine, *Letter* 93.43, for a council of 270 Donatist bishops.
88 See Frend, *The Donatist Church*, 197–199.
89 *Against the Donatists* 2.4.
90 Cf. Gennadius, *The Lives of Illustrious Men* 5, who claims Optatus as a source for a certain Macrobius being elevated to bishop of Rome for the Donatist party.
91 *Against the Donatists* 2.4.3: *Afri et peregrini* (my trans.); cf. 1 Pet. 2:11: *advenas et peregrinos* (Vulg.).
92 *Against the Donatists* 2.4.3–5.
93 See Frend, *The Donatist Church*, 164.
94 *Book of Various Heresies* 83.
95 In Eusebius, *Church History* 5.16.13–15.
96 See *Theodosian Code* 16.6.3–5 and 16.6.6.1.
97 Cf. *Theodosian Code* 16.5.43.
98 E.g. *Conference of Carthage 411* 1.149 (CCL 149A:127).
99 For "the house of one woman in Iberia [*in Hispaniam domui unius mulieris*]," see Augustine, *Against the Letters of Petilian* 2.109.247.
100 *Letter* 53.2; cf. Augustine, *Letter to the Catholics* 3.6.
101 Augustine, *Expositions on the Psalms* 36.2.20; and see Frend, *The Donatist Church*, 206–207.
102 *The Book of the Popes*, 33 (my trans.) Curiously, this source mentions the Manichaeans, but not the Donatist controversy.
103 *The Book of the Popes*, 34 (my trans.)
104 *The Book of the Popes*, 34 (my trans.)
105 This suggestion and further discussion of Cyprian's precedence in this debate can be found in Burns, Jensen, et al., *Christianity in Roman Africa*, 200.
106 The Urbanists (see Augustine, *Against Cresconius the Grammarian*, 4.60.73) were in certain parts of Numidia, while the Arzuges (see Augustine, *Letter* 93.8.24) were in Byzacena and Tripolitania.
107 See Augustine, *On Christian Doctrine* 3.30.42; *Against the Letter of Parmenian* 1.1.1. For Tyconius's non-extant works, see Gennadius, *The Lives of Illustrious Men* 18. Tyconius's commentary on Romans has been reconstructed by Roger Gryson (in CCL 107A).
108 According to Augustine, *Sermon to the People of the Church of Caesarea* 8.
109 See Augustine's response in *Against the Letters of Petilian* and *Concerning the One Baptism, Against Petilian*. Petilian was also one of seven leading spokespersons for the Donatists at the Conference of Carthage (411).
110 *Against the Letters of Petilian* 2.105.239.
111 See Augustine's *Against Cresconium, a Donatist Grammarian*.
112 These include a *Compendium* that consisted of several works, such as the *Book of the Genealogist* (*Liber genealogus*) known in many recensions (see Richard Rouse and Charles McNelis, "North African Literary Activity: A Cyprian Fragment, the Stichometric Lists and a Donatist Compendium," *Revue d'histoire des textes* 30 [2000], 189–238); and the numerous anonymous sermons now identified as Donatist (see Dossey, *Peasant and Empire*, 164–167; and Shaw, *Sacred Violence*, 843–849). These sermons, however, have raised a number of questions about how or whether to identify them as Donatist; for a detailed discussion, see Tilley, "Donatist Sermons," in *Preaching in the Latin Patristic Era: Sermons, Preachers, Audiences*, ed. Anthony Dupont, Shari Boodts, Gert Partoens, Johan Leemans (Leiden: Brill, forthcoming); and Shari Boodts and Nicholas de Maeyer, "The *Collectio Armamentarii* (Paris, Bibliothèque de l'Arsenal 175): *Status questionis* and New Avenues of Research," in *Praedicatio Patrum: Studies on Preaching in Late Antique North Africa*, ed. Gert Partoens, Anthony Dupont, Shari Boodts, Mathijs Lamberigts (Instrumenta Patristica et Mediaevalia; Turnhout: Brepols, forthcoming).

113 E.g. those listed by Gennadius; see discussion in Dossey, *Peasant and Empire*, 163–164.
114 Gennadius, *The Lives of Illustrious Men* 4. Admittedly, "nations" could refer to "gentiles" or unbelievers. However, the geographic reference should not be dismissed without further consideration of the context.
115 For primary sources, see Frend, *The Donatist Church*, 197–199. Tengström, *Donatisten und Katholiken*, 79–83, finds the Caecilianist accusations exaggerated.
116 Claudian, *On the Consulship of Stilicho* 3.pref. Also, see where Claudian (in *The War Against Gildo*) describes all of Africa as governed by "the Moors [*Mauri*]," likens Gildo to "Punic" Hannibal (lines 81ff.), recalls the triumph of Aeneas (lines 129ff.), and celebrates how "Africa shall serve Rome, and Rome alone [*soli famulabitur Africa Romae*]" (line 207). This whole poem, it should be noted, is an invective that describes Africa in general and Carthage in particular as barbarian, overheated, and full of half-breeds.
117 Esp. in Claudian, *The War Against Gildo*; see discussion and additional sources for Gildo in Geoffrey Grimshaw Willis, *Saint Augustine and the Donatist Controversy* (London: SPCK, 2005), 21–23.
118 See Kaufman, "Donatism Revisited," 137, for bibliography.
119 See details in Wilhite, "Donatism in Carthage Until 411."
120 Augustine makes this claim numerous times in his works. However, as with Donatist support for Firmus, Tengström, *Donatisten und Katholiken*, 84–90, finds Augustine's claims to be exaggerated. Cf. Claudian, *The War Against Gildo*; and Orosius, *A History Against the Pagans* 7.36, who only mention Gildo's party as consisting of indigenous Africans, not Donatists per se.
121 See Augustine's *Against Gaudentius*.
122 See Frend, "The Family of Augustine: A Microcosm of Religious Change in North Africa," in *Atti del Congresso internazionale su S. Agostino nel XVI centenario della conversione (Roma, 15–20 settembre 1986) I* (Studia Ephemeridis "Augustinianum," 24 Rome, 1987), 140, reprinted in *Archaeology and History in the Study of Early Christianity* (London: Variorum, 1988); and more recently, Rebecca Moore, "O Mother, Where Art Thou? In Search of Saint Monnica," in *Feminist Interpretations of Augustine*, ed. Judith C. Stark (University Park, PA: Pennsylvania State University Press, 2007), 159. Monica will be discussed further on pp. 241, 243, and 250–251 in chapter eight.
123 For details, see Stephen Andrew Cooper, *Marius Victorinus' Commentary on Galatians: Introduction, Translation, and Notes* (Oxford early Christian studies; Oxford: Oxford University Press, 2005), 16–40 (= "The Life and Times of Marius Victorinus"). An additional bibliography can be found in Thomas Riesenweber, *C. Marius Victorinus, Commenta in Ciceronis rhetorica: Prolegomena und kritischer Kommentar*, vol. 1 (Berlin: De Gruyter, 2015).
124 Augustine, *On Christian Doctrine* 2.40.61, praised Victorinus, along with Cyprian, Lactantius, Optatus, and Hilary for accommodating material from the pre-Christian philosophers, much like Moses and the Israelites plundered the Egyptians.
125 Jerome, *Chronicle* 2370 (354); and Augustine, *Confessions* 8.2.3.
126 Augustine, *Confessions* 8.5.10.
127 *The Art of Grammar* (which survives only partially; see Hellfried Dahlmann, *Zur Ars Grammatica des Marius Victorinus* [Akademie der Wissenschaften und der Literatur; Wiesbaden: Steiner, 1970]) and *Explanations on Cicero's Rhetoric* (CCL 132). Also, there is a work no longer attributed to Victorinus, but which is considered to be of African origin: *On Physics* (PL 8:1295–1310). It is not strictly philosophical, in that it speaks to specifically Christian and biblical themes.

128 *On Definitions* (preserved as [Pseudo-]Boethius; see PL 64).

129 *Confessions* 8.2.3

130 For his theological contributions, see Richard Patrick Crosland Hanson, *The Search for the Christian Doctrine of God: The Arian Controversy, 318–381* (Edinburgh: T&T Clark, 1988), 531–556.

131 Text in CSEL 83.1:54–277; trans. in FC 69:89–303. See discussion and bibliography in John Voelker, "Marius Victorinus' Exegetical Arguments for Nicene Definition in *Adversus Arium*," *Studia Patristica* 38 (2001), 496–502.

132 See details in Arkadiusz Baron, "Candidus: Marius Victorinus' Fictitious Friend and His Doctrine of the 'Logos,'" *Theological Research* 1 (2013), 79–94.

133 Text in CSEL 83.1:15–48; trans. in FC 69:45–88.

134 E.g. the Scillitan martyrs speak of God in terms of "mysterious simplicity [*mysterium simplicitatis*]" (4), "whom no one has seen nor can see with their eyes [*quem nemo hominum vidit nec videre his oculis potest*]" (6), for he is a God "who is in heaven [*qui est in caelis*]" (8).

135 Tertullian ridiculed Marcion for placing his "alien God" (i.e. not the God of the Old Testament) in a "higher heaven." He insists that such a claim requires this other heaven to be bigger than God, which leads to absurdity. Tertullian can speak of God as "in heaven" but also as the creator of heaven itself and therefore "over heaven." See his *Against Marcion*.

136 Text in CSEL 83.1: 278–284; trans. in FC 69:305–311. Also, see the commentary in Pierre Hadot and Paul Henry, SC 68, 69.

137 *Hymns on the Trinity* (text in CSEL 83.1:285–305; trans. FC 69:315–335). His indebtedness to Tertullian's Trinitarian thought can be seen in his use of "Paraclete" for the Holy Spirit and the analogies of spring/river/pool and root/branch/fruit (e.g. Victorinus, *Hymn* 3 and Tertullian, *Against Praxeas* 8).

138 CSEL 83.2. The commentary on Galatians has been translated in Cooper, *Marius Victorinus' Commentary on Galatians*.

139 His various statements in these suggest that he also wrote commentaries on Romans and 1 and 2 Corinthians.

140 See his *Confessions* 8.2.3.

141 *Confessions* 8.2.3.

142 *Confessions* 8.2.3.

143 *Aeneid* 8.819–820.

144 *Confessions* 8.2.4.

145 *Confessions* 8.2.4.

146 *Confessions* 8.6.14.

147 See in *Against Arius* (e.g. FC 69:209).

148 Jerome, *The Lives of Illustrious Men* 101.

149 Jerome, *Commentary on Galatians*, pref.

150 This trend will continue into the Byzantine era, as witnessed by the letters of Pope Gregory (see chapter ten).

151 Text in CCL 22; trans. of some sermons available in Gordon P. Jeanes, *The Day Has Come!: Easter and Baptism in Zeno of Verona* (Collegeville, MN: Liturgical Press, 1995).

152 For discussion, see Jeanes, *The Day Has Come!*, 136, who dismisses any possible connection with Donatism.

153 See details and bibliography in F. E. Vokes, "Zeno of Verona, Apuleius, and Africa," in *Studia Patristica* 8.2 (1966), 130–131.

154 See *Sermon* 1.39 and 2.6.

155 Vokes, "Zeno of Verona, Apuleius and Africa," *Studia Patristica* 8/2 (1966) (Texte und Untersuchengen 93), 132–134, calls his African identity into question because none of these items prove an African background.

156 Text PL 13:1097–1106. See details in Pierre de Labriolle, *The History and Literature of Christianity: From Tertullian to Boethius*, trans. Herbert Wilson (London: Routledge, 2013; orig. 1924), 301–302.

157 See details and discussion in Brian Daley, *The Hope of the Early Church: A Handbook of Patristic Eschatology* (Cambridge: Cambridge University Press, 1991), 127.

158 James T. Palmer, *The Apocalypse in the Early Middle Ages* (Cambridge: Cambridge University Press, 2014), 45, describes African Christianity from this time as "a fundamentalism which embraced millenarianism."

159 See Hoover, *The Donatist Church in an Apocalyptic Age* (PhD dissertation for Baylor University Press, 2015).

160 Text PL 13:1106–1114.

161 See Pseudo-Cyprian, *On the Calculation of Easter* (in CSEL 3.3:248–269), written in 243. This work, however, may not be of African origin. See translation and comments in George Ogg, *The Pseudo-Cyprianic De pascha computus* (London: SPCK, 1955).

162 Augustine *Letter* 88.6; *Against Cresconius, the Grammarian* 3.48.53.

163 See Burns, Jensen, et al., *Christianity in Roman Africa*, 288.

164 Augustine, *Against Cresconius, the Grammarian* 3.43.47; *Letter* 185.7.27, believes they attemped to kill Maximian – a view usually repeated uncritically by scholars. However, Hermanowicz, *Possidius*, 138–142, argues convincingly that the Donatists aimed to humiliate, not kill.

165 For additional details, see Hermanowicz, *Possidius*, 149.

166 For the secondary literature on this conference, as well as insightful commentary, see Neil McLynn, "The Conference of Carthage Reconsidered," in *The Donatist Schism: Controversy and Contexts*, ed. Richard Miles (Liverpool: Liverpool University Press, 2016), 220–248.

167 See Augustine, *Letter* 88.10: "in order that it may be shown to those who do not know it that it has already been brought to an end [*ut eis, qui nesciunt, iam finita monstretur*]."

168 *Conference of Carthage 411* 2.10 (CCL 149A:163).

169 Text in CCL 149A (and cf. the text and French translation in SC 194, 195, and 224).

170 See details in Shaw, "African Christianity," 27.

171 *Conference of Carthage 411* 1.61.

172 E.g. *Conference of Carthage 411* 2.4. See discussion of the legal reasons in Tilley, "Dilatory Donatists or Procrastinating Catholics," 7–19.

173 *Conference of Carthage 411* 1.165.

174 For the numbers of sees with competing or single bishops, see Dossey, *Peasant and Empire*, 128–129.

175 Examples cited and translated in Shaw, "African Christianity," 29.

176 *Conference of Carthage 4111.181–182*.

177 It should be noted that both sides' accusations were polemical and exaggerated.

178 E.g. *Letter* 28*.1.

179 For a list of Augustine's anti-Donatist works written after 411, see Gaumer, "'*Ad Africam visitare sepulchrum sancti Cypriani*': Concerning the Indelible Donatist Character of North African Christianity, 411–1159 CE" in *Religion in Carthage*, ed. Jane Merdinger (Leiden: Brill, forthcoming).

180 See the second volume of Maier, *Le Dossier*; and Gaumer, "*Ad Africam.*"

181 See Stanisław Adamiak, "When did Donatist Christianity End?" in *The Uniquely African Controversy: Studies on Donatist Christianity*, ed. Anthony Dupont, Matthew Gaumer, and M. Lamberigts (Leuven: Peeters, 2014), 211–236.

182 For dating and discussion of Augustine's anti-Donatist works, see Éric Rebillard, "Augustine in Controversy with the Donatists before 411," in *The*

Donatist Schism: Controversy and Contexts, ed. Richard Miles (Liverpool: Liverpool University Press, 2016), 297–316.

183 *Psalm against the Donatist Party* 101.

184 E.g. *Sermon to the People of the Church at Caesarea* 8, regarding Constantine; and *Against Cresconius, the Grammarian* 3.56.62, regarding Carthage. Also see Augustine, *Against the Letters of Petilian* 2.84.184, for the control the Donatists have over Numidian society in particular. Also see, Optatus, *Against Parmenian* 7.1; and Possidius, *Life* 7. Frend, *The Donatist Church*, 211, counts approximately 420 Donatist episcopal sees, when adding the council of Bagai and the Maximianists and other splinter groups from Donatism.

185 *Augustine*, 222. Gaumer, "The Evolution of Donatist Theology," 183, adds, "North African Christians who, in line with their tradition, were growing apart from the secular world against a minority who saw the future of the church at peace with the temporal regime."

186 Possidius, *Life* 9.

187 E.g. Augustine, *Letter* 93.2.5 and 185.6.24.

188 *Letter* 87.5, speaking specifically of Eastern Christians. We should not, however, think of African Christians as being isolated altogether. Two inscriptions claim that pieces of the cross of Christ had been sent to them from Jerusalem: CIL 8.20600: DE LIGNV CRVCIS (dated to 359); and CIL VIII.2.9255: SANCTO LIGNO CRVCIS CHRISTI (dated to around 370). What is more plausible is that outsiders would not have know whether any given bishop and local church was "Donatist" or "Catholic," since both parties would have used the latter title.

189 "Christianity and Dissent in Roman North Africa: Changing Perspectives in Recent Work," in *Schism, Heresy, and Religious Protest*, edited by Derek Baker (Cambridge: Cambridge University Press, 1972), 28–29.

190 "Christianity and Dissent," 35.

191 Brown, "Religious Dissent in the Later Roman Empire: The Case of North Africa" *History* 48 (1963), 282–305, repr. in *Religion and Society in the Age of Augustine* (1972), 301–331; and "Religious Coercion in the Later Roman Empire: The Case of North Africa," *JRS* 58 (1968), 85–95.

192 Brown, *Augustine*, 335.

193 E.g. Matthew Gaumer, "'*Ad Africam visitare sepulchrum sancti Cypriani*': Concerning the Indelible Donatist Character of North African Christianity, 411–1159 CE" in *Religion in Carthage*, ed. Jane Merdinger (forthcoming).

194 "African Christianity," 33.

195 Tilley, "Redefining Donatism," 22, called for a reassessment of Donatism with this regional identity in mind: "In many ways Donatism represented the ancestral heritage of North Africa and Augustine represented an Italian imposition." In support of this view, Augustine himself concedes that the Donatist party is the older within Africa (see, for example, *On Baptism, Against the Donatists* 1.15.23).

196 Although *Deo laudes* is assumed to be a common Donatist slogan, this can be found among Caecilianists. Alternatively, the expression *Deo gratias* can be found in Donatist sources.

197 The primary sources and discussion can be found in Shaw, *Sacred Violence*, esp. 173 and 515 (on basilicas), 241 and 710 (on circumcellions/gangs), 420–421 (on orthodoxy), 469 (on the cry *Deo Laudes!*; cf. 622), 678 (for wooden clubs), 790–791 (on the "hyper-value" placed on martyrdom).

198 Augustine, *Letter* 33.5. It should be noted that Augustine speaks of tension in such marriages.

199 For total destruction of altars, etc., see Optatus, *Against the Donatists* 6.1. For the purging of altars, etc., see Optatus, *Against the Donatists* 6.6.

200 *Sermon on the Martyrdoms of Donatus and Advocatus* (text Maier, *Le dossier*, 1:198–211; trans. Tilley, *Donatist Martyr Stories*, 50–62).

201 Although Augustine also complains of members of his congregation involved in such practices (e.g. *Letter* 22.3). Perhaps, we should see this as more "African" than "Donatist." Even so, the Donatists shaped their identity through the martyr narratives as opposed to the imperially aligned Caecilianists; see Alan Dearn, "Donatist Martyrs, Stories and Attitudes," in *The Donatist Schism: Controversy and Contexts*, ed. Richard Miles (Liverpool: Liverpool University Press, 2016), 70–100.

202 It also may indicate that many Caecilianists were drawn to this practice as well. As discussed on pp. 58, 97, 98n22, African Christians memorialized numerous martyrs.

203 *Against the Donatists* 1.16.1: *sic tamen martyris.*

204 Moore, "O Mother, Where Art Thou?", 159. On Monica's Donatist background, see James J. O'Donnell, *Augustine: A New Biography* (San Francisco: HarperCollins, 2005), 55. Also, cf. Augustine's cousin, Severinus, who belonged to the Donatist party (*Letter* 52).

205 See Optatus, *Against the Donatists* 3.4.8, for the "false desire for martyrdom [*cupiditate falsi martyrii*]" among the Circumcellions.

206 Augustine, *Letter* 185.3.12.

207 On "crazy cliff jumpers [*insania praecipitatos*]," see the Council of Carthage 348 (CCL 149:4). Maureen Tilley, "African Asceticism: The Donatist Heritage," in *The Uniquely African Controversy: Studies on Donatist Christianity*, ed. Anthony Dupont, Matthew Gaumer, and M. Lamberigts (Leuven: Peeters, 2014), 135, points out that this accusation has been made against Christians long before the Donatist controversy (see Tertullian, *To Scapula* 5).

208 *Sacred Violence*, 623–625 and 721–770.

209 E.g. Maximian and Isaac's bodies were cast into the sea in *Martyrdom of Maximian and Isaac* 12–16; Marculus's body was thrown over a cliff in *Martyrdom of Marculus* 11 (cf. Optatus, *Against the Donatists* 3.6; Augustine, *Tractates on the Gospel According to Saint John* 11.15; *Answers to the Letters of Petilian, the Donatist* 2.14.32; 2.20.46; and *Against Cresconius the Grammarian* 3.49.54).

210 *Acts of the Abitinian Martyrs* 17. Similarly, Secunda "threw herself down [*praecipitavit*]" from a balcony, but she did so to follow Maxima and Donatilla and she landed unharmed (*Martyrdom of Maxima, Donatilla, and Secunda* 4).

211 Another possible African source to be considered is Apuleius's story of how Psyche was carried down from a cliff by Zephyr, the west wind (see *Metamorphosis* 4.35). I am indebted to Erika Hermanowicz for suggesting this comparison.

212 *On Baptism* 2.3.4: "the earlier are often corrected by those which follow them."

213 *On Baptism* 2.8.13–12.9.14.

214 See both the Council of Arles (314) and Nicaea (325). Nicaea did require rebaptism for the followers of Paul of Samosata, a matter – I take it – that had to do with their faulty theological understanding of the Triune formula.

215 *Letter* 53.2.

216 Augustine, *Expositions of the Psalms* 95.11: *clamant ranae de palude: Nos soli sumus christiani.*

217 *Expositions of the Psalms* 95.17.43; cf. 17.44.

218 Tilley, "Dilatory Donatists," 17.

219 See Tilley, "Sustaining Donatist Self-Identity," 21–35.

220 See the study of Hoover, *The Donatist Church in an Apocalyptic Age*.

221 See discussion of the secondary literature on p. 32 in the final section of chapter one.

222 Rebillard, "William Hugh Clifford Frend," 71.

223 *Letter* 84.2. On Punic as distinct from Berber/Libyan in Augustine, see bibliography in Millar, "Local Cultures," 130.

224 *Letter* 209.3. Cf. *Letter* 20*.3, "Hence I believed it useful to present for ordination the man who was there, because I had heard that he also knew the Punic language [*quia et linguam Punicam scire audieram, ordinandum ut offerrem utilem credidi*]." Later in this same letter, Augustine reveals that the Donatists are in the majority in the region (20*.27).

225 *Letter* 20*.21.

226 *Letter* 66.2.

227 *Letter* 84.2 (WSA 2.1:341, following the corrected text). This refers ostensibly to the town of Siniti, where Lucillus was appointed the Catholic bishop, since he could speak the native language; see discussion in Mandouze, *Prosopographie chrétienne du Pas-Empire*, 1:650; and cf. *City of God* 22.8.11. Also see *On Heresies* 87, for a Punic village near Hippo (*rusticana in campo nostro, id est Hipponiensi*).

228 *Letter* 108.14. Of course, the Donatist bishop, who had returned from exile in 409, apparently needed an interpreter to speak to the Circumcellions.

229 Coyle, "The Self-Identity of North African Christians," 67.

230 Modéran, *Les Maures*, 526–527.

231 *Expositions on the Psalms* 54.20.

232 Cf. *On Heresies* 87.

233 *Expositions of the Psalms* 44.24.

234 *Letter* 16.

235 *Letter* 17.2.

236 *Letter* 17.2 (my trans.): *neque enim usque adeo teipsum obliuisci potuisses, ut homo Afer scribens Afris, cum simus utrique in Africa constituti, Punica nomina exagitanda existimares . . . . quae lingua si inprobatur abs te, nega Punicis libris, ut a viris doctissimis proditur, multa sapienter esse mandata memoriae; paeniteat te certe ibi natum, ubi huius linguae cunabula recalent. . . . et tamen Punica nomina tamquam nimium Romanorum altaribus deditus contemnis ac despicis.* See discussion of this passage in Shaw, "Who are You?", 528–529. "Punicitas," it is worth noting, was coined by Tertullian, along with "Romanitas" (see *On the Cloak* 2.1).

237 For thirty-two Punic names found in inscriptions in Madauros, see Joseph Mesnage, *Romanisation de l'Afrique* (Paris: B. Beauchesne, 1913), 117. Numerous other examples can be given throughout the African provinces (see *Corpus Inscriptionum Semiticarum* volume 1 (= *Inscriptiones Phoenicias continens*), as well as the multiple volumes of CIL 8.

238 The complete loss of Punic literature may be due to a steady decline in the use of the Punic language (as is generally assumed), but there is another factor to consider. The only known campaign against a body of literature in North Africa was during the Diocletian persecution, when the Christian writings or "scriptures" were seized and destroyed. Much like the total devastation of the pre-Constantinian archaeological record of Christian churches, this destruction of books could explain the loss of Punic literature, if the African Christians were seen as tied to the local Punic population. Such a conjecture, of course, needs further study to know whether or not it is testable given the surviving records from this time.

239 A differentiation found as early as *Martyrdom of Polycarp* 17.3.

240 J. H. Baxter, "The Martyrs of Madaura," *Journal of Theological Studies* (October 1924), 21–37. For more recent bibliography, see Tabbernee, *Early Christianity*, 234–235, who concurs with Baxter's conclusion, calling them "Punic saints."

241 *On the Merits and Forgiveness of Sins and Infant Baptism* 1.24.34.

242 The full quote: *On the Merits and Forgiveness of Sins and Infant Baptism* 1.24.34: "Punic Christians are perfectly correct in calling baptism 'salvation' and in calling the sacrament of Christ's body 'life' [*optime Punici christiani baptismum ipsum nihil aliud quam salutem et sacramentum corporis Christi nihil aliud quam uitam uocant*]." (WSA 1.20:54). Brown, *Augustine*, 269, translates this first phrase, "the African Christians are best."

243 *Epistle to the Catholics* 16.40.

244 In what follows, I am indebted to the work of Hoover, *The Donatist Church*, who analyzes the Donatists' use of certain scripture passages in comparison with Christian usage from outside Africa in order to better understand Donatist ecclesiology and eschatology.

245 *Letter* 93.8.24.

246 Song of Songs 1:5–7 (NRSV).

247 Anthony Dupont and Matteo Dalvit, "From a Martyrological '*Tabernacula Pastorum*' Towards a Geographical '*In Meridie*': Augustine's Representation and Refutation of the Donatist Exegesis of Sg. 1, 6–7," *Revue d'histoire ecclésiastique* 109 (1–2 2014), 5–34 (see esp. 24), argue that Augustine misrepresents the Donatists; they said the true church resides "in the south" not "only in the south."

248 *Letter* 93.8.24 (WSA 2.1:393; correcting "eastern" with "western" for *occidentali*).

249 Cf. Tertullian, *On Monogamy* 17.2, who replaces "south" (ref. Matt. 12.42) with "Carthage"; and Augustine, *City of God* 16.21; 16.38, who can also make "African" and "southern" synonymous. Apparently, this practice was common among African Christians.

250 Song 1:7, cited in *Letter* 46.36.

251 *Letter* 46.37.

252 Cf. Corippus, *Iohannis* 7.323. It is noteworthy that Jerome's *Vulgate* chose the equivalent phrase *ab austro*, to indicate the synonymous term for the south wind, the *auster*. Also, of historical interest for this essay, the *phoenicias* was the Greek term for the south wind, since it blew from the south(east) of Greece, from Phoenicia. One can still see the Windrose in Dougga that inscribed with the word *Africus*, marking the direction of the south wind.

253 *Sermon* 46.41.

254 It is this fact that prompted Brent Shaw to cease from referring to the "African" and "Catholic" parties: cf. his earlier essay "African Christianity," 5–34, with his later work, *Sacred Violence*, esp. 5–6, where he prefers "dissident Christian community."

255 *Sermon* 162A.12, which only further indicates that some believed the Donatists to have had an exclusive claim to Africa.

256 *Letter* 11*.25.

257 *Letter* 11*.26

> So too, there is a great difference between the Spaniards, who tremble in fear when caught in sacrilege, and the Africans, who even boast stubbornly in their schism. In the same way the Priscillianists, who are truly worthy of every execration and of a different abomination, undoubtedly differ from the Donatists who, by the character of their crime, are cruel and violent.

258 In Augustine, *Letter* 90.

259 *Letter* 91.1.1; cf. 104.

260 *Letter* 91.2: *nos in vestra patria non tam experti sumus, quibus floruit terra illa viris, quam "quibus arserit armis."*

261 Virgil, *Aeneid* 7.643–644: "with what manhood even then did kindly Italy bloom; what armed forces kindled her to flame [*quibus Itala iam tum floruerit terra alma viris, quibus arserit armis*]" (LCL 64:46–47).

262 It is noteworthy that "Libya" is referenced in the litany of peoples who mustered against the Trojans in this scene (*Aeneid* 7.718). For Nectarius's attempt to abrogate this remark, see Augustine, *Letter* 104.1.2; Augustine, however, insists on it (104.4.17).

263 My trans.

264 *Letter* 91.4, after first recommending "the citizen" Cicero. Later (*Letter* 104.2.6), Augustine references two other examples that beg for further elaboration from a postcolonial paradigm. First, he mentions Cincinnatus's plow (which he exchanged for a Roman toga so that he could squelch a rural rebellion against Rome, according to Livy 3.26). Second, he commends Fabricius, who denounced the consul Rufinus for extravagant living (acc. to Livy [per.] 14; cf. Cicero, *On the Orator* 2.76.268).

265 On *interpretatio Romana* generally, see 59–63 in chapter two. On this passage in Augustine, see Leone, *The End of the Pagan City*, 16, following Leglay, *Saturne africain* 1:491–492, who believes the rural Donatist bishops replaced the priests of Baal Hammon/Saturn. This enabled Donatism to remain strong, whereas the "Latin-oriented Christianity" of the Caecilianist party struggled in pre-411 North Africa.

266 In *Letter* 104.5, Augustine references a silver statue, which may have been comparable to the silver statue of Tanit mentioned a in third-century inscription in Dougga (see Paul L. MacKendrick, *The North African Stones Speak*, 69). See Claude Lepelley, *Les cités de l'Afrique romaine au bas-empire* (Paris: Études augustiniennes, 1979), 2:97–101, 100, for Calama's Punic religion; Hermanowicz, *Possidius*, 164 n.24, concurs with Lepelley and interprets the event reported in Augustine accordingly.

267 *Letter* 91.5. Ahmed Ferjaoui, "Le témoignage de Tertullien sur le sacrifice d'enfants à Saturne à la lumière des données ostéologiques du sanctuaire de Henchir el-Hami (Tunisie)," *Rivista di Studi Fenici* 40 (2012), 245–250, finds the material remains to support Tertullian's claim (*Apol.* 9.2–6) that child sacrifice continued to occur in Carthage in the second century, after which time Baal Hammon was still worshipped, only via a Romanized cult.

268 *Possidius*, 164.

269 *Conference of Carthage 411*, 1.142, 1.187, 1.215.

270 *Letter 50: apud vos Romanae sepultae sunt leges . . . imperatorum certe nulla veneratio nec timor.*

271 On possible dates, see Rebillard, "Late Antique Limits of Christianness: North Africa in the Age of Augustine," *Group Identity and Religious Individuality in Late Antiquity*, ed. Rebillard and Jorg Rupke (Washington: CUA Press, 2015), 309.

272 See discussion in Shaw, *Sacred Violence*, 230–231.

273 *Sermon* 24.6 (my trans.; cf. WSA 3.2:77).

274 Shaw, *Sacred Violence*, 230. For images of Punic Melqart with a lion skin and other Greco-Roman elements, see Corinne Bonnet, "Le culte de Melqart à Carthage: Un cas de conservatisme religieux," *Religio Phoenicia: Acta colloquii Namurcensis habiti diebus 14 et 15 mensis Decembris anni 1984*, ed. Corinne Bonnet, Edward Lipiński, and Patrick Marchetti (Namur: Société des études classiques, 1986), 218–221.

275 *Sermon* 24.6: "Roman gods, Roman gods – so if, I say, the Roman gods have disappeared from Rome, why should they stay here? [*dii Romani, dii Romani, si ergo, inquam, dii Romani Romae defecerunt, hic quare remanserunt?*]" (WSA 3.2:78). The editor of the WSA comments:

> There is a marked ambivalence about this whole passage. On the one hand there is the sentiment of the Roman citizen, calling on the people of Carthage to do what Rome, "the head of the nations," had done. But on the other hand,

and rather more heartfelt, I think, is the African's resentment at having been imposed on so long by Roman gods: a nationalist sentiment which Augustine clearly shared with his audience. That the gods were in fact Roman in names only will appear when we consider the case of Hercules in particular.

276 Psalm 83.7/82.8.
277 *Incomplete Explanation of the Epistle to the Romans* 13.3: *Chananaea enim, hoc est Punica mulier de finibus Tyri.* For discussion, see Gillian Clark, "Pastoral Care: Town and Country in Late-Antique Preaching," in *Urban Centers and Rural Contexts in Late Antiquity*, ed. Thomas S. Burns and John Eadie (East Lansing, MI: Michigan State University Press, 2001), 268. Also, cf. *Letter to the Catholics* 16.42; for Dido's fleeing Tyre to found Carthage, see Augustine, *Exposition of the Psalms* 47.6. Before Augustine, see Optatus, *Against the Donatists* 3.3, where Donatus as "the prince of Carthage" is allegorically read as the prince of Tyre from Ezek. 28.2; and Prudentius, *Crown of Martyrdom* 13, where he speaks of "Tyrian Carthage [*Tyriae Carthaginis*]."
278 *Against the Donatists* 3.3.13.
279 *Against the Donatists* 3.3.10–13.
280 Augustine, *Letter* 22*.6.
281 See, e.g., Augustine, *Proceedings With Emeritus*.
282 See, e.g., Augustine, *Letter* 87.10; 93.21–22.
283 *Letter* 22*.9–10.
284 *Letter* 22*.7.
285 *Letter* 185.1.3.
286 *Letter* 185.7.27: *ingenti multitudine superabant.*
287 *Letter* 185.7.27; cf. 104.4.13, "*saevientium.*"
288 *Possidius*, 138–142.
289 *Letter* 185.7.28: *Romanas etiam leges inplorare minime dubitavit civem Romanum se esse proclamans, quos tunc affligi verberibus non licebat.*
290 *Letter* 185.7.30.
291 See Hermanowicz, *Possidius*, 154. More generally, see Jill Harries, *Law and Empire in Late Antiquity* (Cambridge: Cambridge University Press, 1999), 53–59.
292 See further discussion on pp. 266–272 in chapter nine.
293 *Letter* 185.1.1.
294 Matthew Alan Gaumer, "The Evolution of Donatist Theology as Response to a Changing Late Antique Milieu," *Augustiniana* 58 (3–4 2008), 203. For this self-identity as the remnant or *collecta* of the faithful left in the world, see Tilley, "Sustaining Donatist Self-Identity."

8 Augustine the African

One cannot overstate the influence of Augustine. His thought affects virtually all fields of western thought, ranging from philosophy to psychology, from music to poetry, and from prayer to sexuality. Some of his works, like the *Confessions* and *The City of God,* remain best sellers today, and through them he continues to influence contemporary thought and practice.

Augustine's influence truly transcended his North African context, and yet he should not be read entirely apart from his context. In what follows, we will offer an introduction to Augustine's life, works, and teachings. Then, we will focus on ways in which his African background can be detected in his works. As with the chapters that have gone before, this artificial separation between the ancient writer and his African identity is merely for the sake of convenience. Since this last aspect of Augustine has been too often neglected, it will be given special attention in the latter part of this chapter. It is hoped that future studies can further integrate the man and the context that shaped him.

Augustine's life and legacy

We know more about Augustine's life than any other individual from ancient Africa, if not from all late antiquity. His *Confessions* wherein he tells of his own journey, and his later *Retractions* (as his title is usually translated) wherein he recounts all of his writings and their occasions, as well as his numerous letters and sermons, provide a wealth of data about him and the events of his lifetime. Furthermore, one of his closest mentees, Possidius, wrote a *Life* that helps provide further details and interpretations about Augustine and the controversies he faced.

Born on November 13, 354 in Thagaste (modern Souk Ahras, Algeria), Augustine came from a family with moderate means. His father, Patricius, held the office of one of the civic officials,[1] and he ensured Augustine received a good education,[2] first in his hometown and then in the nearby city of Madauros. Patricius was not baptized until the end of his life, when Augustine was still only seventeen, and Augustine remembers him as unfaithful and violent.[3]

Augustine's mother, Monica, was a drunkard early in her life, but before Augustine was born, she had become a person of devout faith.[4] Her devotion to Augustine, at times overbearing, is famously recalled in his *Confessions*, and she no doubt had a significant impact on his life well into his adulthood.

Augustine's birth family also included a brother, Navigius, and an unnamed sister. Both of them apparently remained close to Augustine, for they each followed him in establishing monastic communities in North Africa.[5]

Monica brought Augustine to the church to be initiated into the Christian life. The rite of initiation included several ritual acts, such as exorcism, anointing with oil, and being salted. Monica, however, withheld the last acts of initiation, baptism and the laying on of hands.[6] Those events would come much later in his life. Before his own devotion to the Christian faith, Augustine tells of going astray, both morally and philosophically.

As a youth, he was sexually promiscuous, and he would speak of how forbidden fruit constantly tempted him.[7] He once stole pears, primarily for no other reason than to enjoy the scandal of doing wrong, and he later pondered this "fallen" state of his soul. By the age of nineteen, he had moved to Carthage to study rhetoric – the most promising career path for someone of his stature. There, he also took a concubine, who bore him a son, Adeodatus. At this time, he also began reading philosophical works like Cicero's *Hortensius*, and found that in comparison with such works the Bible was barbaric and uncultured. While searching for a more philosophically sound religion, he encountered the Manicheans.

Mani and his followers believed in two eternal powers, the Good God of Light and the evil power of darkness. The material world resulted from the war between these two powers, and in this world of flux the countless emissions of Light became mired in various bodies. The "elect" Manicheans sought to release the droplets of Light in various ways, which ultimately meant their own soul would escape the body and ascend back to the realm of Light. Augustine followed this sect for approximately nine years, until he became dissatisfied with their claim to explain the evil in the world.

He began teaching rhetoric to others, first in Thagaste (375), then Carthage (376), and next in Rome (383). Then, Augustine became the *magister rhetoricae*, the Professor of Rhetoric, in the western capital, Milan. In this prestigious post he interacted with those close to the emperor, and the majority of this elite circle was by this time Christian. It is no surprise, therefore, that Augustine began to reconsider Christianity at this time. His acceptance of Christian teachings, however, did not happen immediately.

He still kept his concubine, but now his mother considered her unfit for a man of Augustine's status. The unnamed lover was sent back to Africa, where she vowed never to know a man again.[8] Monica arranged a marriage for Augustine, but the betrothed was only ten, and so he took another concubine for the two years of waiting that would ensue.

Augustine continued to read Cicero and other philosophers. Cicero offered Augustine an example of someone who synthesized various philosophical traditions: he took seriously the brand of skepticism popular in some circles, while also incorporating Stoicism. In addition to these competing philosophical schools, Cicero also insisted that citizens should honor the civic gods – something neither skeptics nor Stoics championed. Augustine followed Cicero's example, only he would incorporate a "new Platonism" to the Christian faith.

The Neoplatonists, like Plotinus and Porphyry (who had lived for some time in Carthage),[9] retrieved some of the positive aspects of Plato's teachings that had been overlooked in what is called "middle Platonism." The Neoplatonists accepted the goodness of the material order: it was not bad/evil; instead, it was good, only on a sliding scale of goodness. It was fallen, perhaps, but necessarily so because nothing is as good as God. Some things are better than others, and therefore there is only pure Goodness and various levels of less goodness. This pure Goodness they could call God, or the One. Everything else should aspire to be oriented toward and in a right relationship with the Good.

While the original teachers of Neoplatonism were non-Christians (in the case of Porphyry, anti-Christian), several of Augustine's predecessors found this philosophy compatible with Christianity. Marius Victorinus (discussed in Chapter 7) not only translated Neoplatonic treatises into Latin, but he also used Neoplatonic teachings to explain the Christian faith. Similarly, when Augustine attended Christian services in Milan, he found the bishop, Ambrose, allegorizing the scriptures and using Neoplatonic philosophy to explain them. In these teachers, Augustine found that Christianity could be credible both philosophically and socially.

Augustine received baptism in April of 387. His internal struggle to make this decision became famous through his retelling of it in his *Confessions*. Augustine observed others who abandoned public life and devoted themselves to Christian piety. The most famous example is Anthony of the Egyptian desert, but he also recalled fellow Africans who had made such a decision, such as Marius Victorinus. Unlike these venerable predecessors, Augustine found it difficult, if not impossible, to quit his old way of living. He envisioned his two former lovers, named "Vanity" and "Frivolity," beside him seducing him to stay. Against these two, he saw Lady Continence beckoning him to her side.[10] After hearing children's voices chanting from some distance, "Take up and read, take up and read [*Tolle, lege, tolle, lege*]," Augustine opened the scriptures to a passage from Romans:

> Let us live honorably as in the day, not in reveling and drunkenness, not in debauchery and licentiousness, not in quarreling and jealousy. Instead, put on the Lord Jesus Christ, and make no provision for the flesh, to gratify its desires.[11]

Augustine's "conversion" was as much to a life of celibacy and asceticism as it was a conversion to Christianity itself. He saw the ascetic life as the highest ideal of the Christian faith. Augustine resigned his teaching post, ended the relationship with his concubine, broke the engagement arranged by Monica, and retreated to the nearby village of Cassiciacum to begin his life of contemplation and devotion. During this short time, he began writing from a Christian viewpoint.[12] After his baptism in Milan (April 25, 387 – Easter), he and his mother began their travel back to their hometown in Africa. En route, they both experienced a vision of bliss while at the port town of Ostia, Italy.[13] Monica sadly died after this event, but Augustine continued on to Thagaste, where he intended to form a monastic community.

A few years later, while recruiting members of his community, Augustine travelled to the nearby city of Hippo Regius. The Caecilianist bishop, Valerius, had no priest serving with him, and so he convinced his congregation to appoint one while Augustine was in town. The crowd seized Augustine and demanded his ordination, which he claimed went against his objections and tears.[14] Even in this new role, Augustine continued his plans to establish a monastery, and Valerius gave him the bishop's house in Hippo so that those who wished to share "all things in common" could live together without owning any property individually.[15] Sadly, around this time, Augustine's only son, Adeodatus, and his friend, Nebridius, both died.

As priest in Hippo (391–395), Augustine experienced controversy. Valerius had already given Augustine much more authority than is normally allowed to priests in Africa,[16] and one of Augustine's acts was to curtail the feasts for the martyrs.[17] These feasts were very popular with African Christians, especially those in the Donatist party. The Donatists from the beginning opposed Augustine, claiming he was still a Manichean. The primate of Numidia, Megalius of Calama, initially distrusted Augustine: he opposed Augustine's appointment as bishop in 395, because he feared him to still be Manichaean and because he had been accused of using a love potion on a certain woman.[18] Although Megalius reportedly changed his mind and accepted Augustine,[19] the Donatists continued to use Megalius's letter to discredit the Caecilianist bishop of Hippo.

Many of Augustine's works at this time were devoted to refuting both the Manicheans and the Donatists, but he also had to address other matters. He wrote letters extensively, many of which survive, and he also began collecting his own sermons. His works and teachings will be discussed further in the following section, but suffice it to say that Augustine masterfully juggled his many roles as bishop. In addition to the weekly liturgy and preaching, he served as judge for Christian cases, as host for Christians traveling through Hippo, and as the public voice of his "Catholic" form of Christianity, which had to contest opponents through debates and writings.

Another controversy that arose around this time had to do with a monk from the British Isles named Pelagius. After traveling to Rome, Pelagius criticized the hypocritical Christians he met there, and he insisted that God wants humans to use their free will to obey Christ's teachings. Augustine argued that Pelagius's view of the will as "free" did not sufficiently account for how the will was "fallen" and in need of God's intervening grace.

In 410, the unthinkable occurred. The supposedly eternal city, Rome, fell to the Visigoths. In response, Augustine began writing *City of God*, which outlined how Christians have citizenship both in the earthly city and the heavenly city, but it is only the last one that will endure.

Late in life, Augustine continued his struggle against Donatists and Pelagians, but the ongoing presence of the "barbaric tribes" that threatened the empire revived another theological challenge. Groups like the Visigoths and Vandals who operated outside of the strict control of the Byzantine empire continued to teach forms of "Arianism," which had been denounced in the previous century.[20] One group of Arian opponents in particular, the Vandals, invaded North Africa in the twilight of Augustine's life.

In 429 the Vandals invaded Mauretania from Iberia. The next year they besieged the city of Hippo while Augustine lay dying in his monastery. After three months of siege, with the penitential Psalms hung around his room, Augustine died (August 28, 430). A few weeks later the invitation to attend the Council of Ephesus (431) arrived, where Pelagius would be condemned in what would later be known as the Third Ecumenical Council.[21] Eleven months after his death, the city of Hippo fell and was looted by the Vandal invaders.

Augustine's body was buried in Hippo, but sometime in the late fifth or early sixth century it was moved to Sardinia.[22] Later still, his body was relocated to the cathedral in Pavia, Italy. In 1695, workers on this cathedral discovered a hidden collection of bones, and the pope eventually declared them to be the relics of Saint Augustine. When the French occupied Algeria in the 1830s, they attempted to re-establish Christianity in North Africa. They built a new cathedral in Annaba (the site of ancient Hippo) and later sent one of Augustine's bones there, which still can be viewed in the Basilique Saint Augustin. Although his bones were temporarily lost, Augustine's influence in the Latin west continued to be significant through his teachings. After reviewing these, we – like Augustine's relics – will return to his African context.

Augustine's works and teachings

Isidore of Seville (c.560–636) famously quipped that anyone who claimed to have read all of Augustine's writings was a liar.[23] While Isidore's comments addressed how impossible it is to find all of Augustine's works, modern readers cite it to bemoan the time needed to work through all of Augustine's works. In what follows, not all of Augustine's works can even be listed.[24] Instead, various kinds of his writings will be briefly surveyed and a few important examples will be discussed in order to get a glimpse into Augustine's teachings, for which he later became famous.

Soon after his conversion, Augustine wrote a series of works that explored philosophical matters from a Christian perspective.[25] While he never abandoned his philosophical commitments altogether, these works involved a time when Augustine allowed Neoplatonism, Stoicism, and other influences to guide his understanding. His later works show a progression where his reading of scripture begins to trump the philosophers.[26]

As a priest and bishop, Augustine wrote many practical works teaching about how to practice the faith.[27] Similarly, he had much to say to Christian ministers responsible for teaching others,[28] and his many commentaries written throughout his life fall into this category as well.[29] Also in this pastoral vein, Augustine worked to establish monasticism in North Africa, and several of his surviving works addressed the proper way to live the ascetic life.[30] Unlike the eastern tendency to distance monastic communities from the church (e.g. one is in the desert, one is in the city), Augustine placed the monastery geographically and theologically within the local church. Just as the church was within the world and a sign to the world of a higher calling, so the monastery was within the church and a sign to the church of its highest ideal.

Many of Augustine's works function to demarcate true Christianity from false forms, and thereby he vigorously sought to formulate correct doctrines.[31] As he says in his *Confessions*, "The rejection of heretics brings into relief what your Church holds and what sound doctrine maintains."[32] In fact, most of Augustine's unique teachings emerge from debates with opponents whom he deemed heretical, and his teachings can best be understood in terms of what they reject as much as what they posit. In this way, Augustine (like all theologians) was very much a product of his environment, and yet (unlike most theologians) he established precedent for later generations through his careful engagement with the issues of his day.

Augustine devoted much of his early ministry to disputing the Manicheans. Because they viewed evil as co-eternal with goodness, Augustine devoted much of his attention to answering the question, *Unde malum?*, "Whence came evil?" Like the Neoplatonists, Augustine rejected that evil existed at all; in fact, "evil" is non-existence. Of course, he acknowledged that people call things evil, but in reality there is only Goodness and various levels of less-good. A human will that has turned from God could rightly be called "evil" because it is causing harm, but here again it is the deprivation of good (*privatio boni*), not a truly evil substance that was created by another or that is co-eternal with God. The human will is made good by God, but it can turn "evil" by falling away from God.

The analogy for this view of good and evil would be light and darkness. God did not say, "Let there be darkness." There is no such thing as darkness; darkness is no thing, or nothing. The word "darkness" is in reference to an absence of light. There is only light, and lesser shades of brightness until one reaches no light at all, nothing.

The other major teaching that Augustine embraced in response to the Manicheans is the absolute distinction between God and the world.[33]

Whereas the Manicheans believed that parts of God were enmeshed in the world, Augustine found the biblical account of *creatio ex nihilo*, "creation from nothing," to require a different view: God created the world; the world is created. Even the human soul is categorically and ontologically different from God. Although this human soul is *like* God (in that it is spiritual, not material), the soul is not *part of* God. The human soul, like God, has intelligence and volition, and so it can choose to *participate* in God's qualities; that is, the soul can freely choose to be just, loving, and merciful, but its ultimate goal is not to escape the flesh to do so, as the Manicheans taught.

Augustine was uncertain about the soul's origin. Origen of Alexandria, like many pre-Christian philosophers, believed that souls pre-existed in a heavenly state before turning from God and thereby falling into bodies. Augustine entertained this idea, but admitted that it did not have a biblical basis – at least not without significant allegorizing. On the one hand, the goodness of human bodies had to be defended against the Manicheans and in light of the Genesis account. On the other hand, Augustine could not accept that souls were generated materially in the same way that bodies were, a teaching known as "traducianism." The third and last option remaining was to believe that God created individual souls within bodies that were materially generated. Augustine was never satisfied with this answer either, because it appeared that God unjustly implanted an innocent soul into a sin-filled body. Although he never came to a firm conclusion on this matter, he did continue to insist on the goodness of created bodies and the justness of God's punishment to those born into original sin.

Augustine's view of punishment and bodies also affected his view of the resurrection. A strict Neoplatonist would have taught that souls who contemplated the Good would escape their body and unite themselves to the One, while souls who turned from the good would fall into nothingness and be annihilated. Although Augustine was very Neoplatonic in his thinking, his Biblicism checked this way of thinking, especially in terms of eschatology. In the resurrection, both just and wicked souls would be reunited with their bodies. The wicked would be cast into hell for everlasting torment while the just would enjoy God's reign forever. Augustine did have concerns that an overemphasis on the material resurrection was untenable. The notion of a literal banquet feast seemed to him too simplistic. Alternatively, he could not deny the materiality of the resurrection, like the Manicheans had done. Instead, he believed that our material bodies would be spiritualized in some mysterious way in the presence of the glory of God.[34]

Augustine's other major opponents from his early career were the Donatists.[35] Much was said of them in Chapter 7, but here we need to revisit this group from Augustine's perspective. Augustine returned to Africa to find the Donatists as the majority party who clung to their African heritage at the expense of the worldwide ("Catholic") communion of Christians. Early in his ministerial career, he even wrote a "pop" song to try to counter the Donatist influence.[36] Their African heritage, of course, was the teachings of Cyprian, who had earlier insisted that a false church could not offer true sacraments. Augustine described the Donatists as obsessed with being the "Pure Church," which was hypocritical since their churches were filled with sinners. The concern for sacramental purity needed correcting: Augustine, like many outside Africa at the time, argued that true baptism could be offered by schismatic and heretical churches. His solution was to liken the sacrament of baptism to a military tattoo, which could not be removed even if one became a deserter. Donatists received the mark of baptism, but if they stayed in schism they were deserters and the baptism counted toward their condemnation, not their salvation.

The Donatists, of course, rejected Augustine's interpretation, and so he called upon government officials to use physical force to "compel" (Luke 14:23) the Donatists into the true church. This affirmation of violence was defended by likening a government official to a father. A father must discipline unruly children, and a government official must discipline schismatics and heretics under his jurisdiction. This way of sanctioning violence corresponds to Augustine's foundational assumptions about what would later be called Just War Theory: just as a father must protect his children, so a ruler must protect his citizens from invaders. The violence is justifiable.

Augustine's other major opponents were the Pelagians.[37] In response to Pelagius's emphasis on human works, Augustine began to emphasize divine grace. Only by grace could a person follow Christ's teachings. The will, while free to choose all sorts of sins, is fallen and cannot will itself back to God (after all, it is the will itself that is broken). In this way of thinking, all do not respond positively to the Christian message, because God does not extend saving grace to all. This last point, known as "single predestination," sounded to many like blaming God for the condemnation of the lost. Instead, Augustine insisted that Adam and Eve were created free, and it was they who freely willed to rebel against God. This original sin of Adam means that all humans, who were once "in Adam" (cf. 1 Cor. 15:22; Rom. 5:12), are now guilty of this original sin and are worthy of condemnation. Not all are condemned, however, because God graciously redeems some.

As proof that God elects individuals to salvation, Augustine turned to the practice of infant baptism. By this time in Christian history, even Pelagians permitted the baptism of infants, and as part of the ritual, the infants (through their sponsors) are asked to repent from sin. For Augustine, this practice proved that all descendants of Adam and Eve were born into this state of original sin, and they merely add their own volitional sins to this state after they grow older. The inescapable conclusion of such a view is that unbaptized infants go to hell, and this was a conclusion that Augustine accepted as valid. Furthermore, Augustine continued to follow the logic of his views and concluded that those who truly are elect can never fall from grace absolutely. The perseverance of the saints was assured by God's grace as much as their initial call to repentance and baptism was an act of God's grace.

One additional point should be made about Augustine's view of grace, and this point moves us directly to Augustine's view of God. For Augustine, "grace [*gratia*]" is that which God gives. What does God give? God gives God's own self to his chosen ones. That is to say, God pours the Spirit into the heart of the elect. This act of Love, which for Augustine is often synonymous with Grace, means the Spirit of God can be named Love, or Grace, or Gift, much like the Son of God can be named God's Word, or Truth, or Wisdom. Since the Spirit of God is the Love of God, Augustine reads "love" in scripture (and elsewhere) as referring to Love himself (cf. 1 John 4:16), just as truth in scripture (and elsewhere) can refer to Truth himself (cf. John 14:6). While this practice can be found in earlier writers, Augustine uses this understanding of God's Truth and Spirit to formulate the doctrine of the Trinity in a way that is both more elaborate and more precise than any of his predecessors.

In his *On the Trinity*, Augustine would explain the orthodox teaching by use of scripture and philosophical precision. At one point in this work, he aims to use the most abstract concepts possible in order to do justice to how we think of the transcendent God. This transcendent God, nevertheless, is also known specifically as Father, Son, and Spirit, and so Augustine explained how three different entities could be one in essence. While a few examples from nature offer analogies, the only true "image" of the Triune God is the human, namely the human soul or mind. In what later became known as the psychological analogy[38] for the Trinity, Augustine described a mind that knows itself and loves itself.[39]

In said analogy there is mind, knowledge, and love, which correspond to the Father, the Son, and the Spirit. Of course, this risks prioritizing the Father, but Augustine insists that the priority is a logical one, not a chronological one (as the Arians teach), since the Son and Spirit are co-eternal with the Father. Furthermore, Augustine's analogy reflects how scriptures speaks of "God" (= Father) and the "Word" (= Son) and "Breath" (= Spirit).[40] If, however, in this analogy Knowledge and Love still seem somehow inferior to Mind, Augustine can peer deeper into the human soul to further demonstrate how they are in essence the mind itself: the substance of one's mind is memory.[41]

In this iteration of the analogy, the memory cannot function as such without the understanding of said memory nor the will to understand said memory (admittedly, a very different psychology than how we are taught in modernity). In sum, the three entities of memory, understanding, and will are essentially one, because the understanding in view is the understanding *of the memory* and the will in view is the will *to understand the memory*. The understanding is not some other thing; it is the understanding of the memory itself, or the memory itself (understood). Likewise, the will to understand the memory is not something else altogether; it is the will to understand the memory itself, or the memory itself (willingly understood). To be sure, this is abstract and perhaps unconvincing on its own terms, but it offered a rationale and a defense in answer to the lingering Arian question: how can three entities be one God?[42] Three entities can be one in essence with God's image (the human soul), and so this can be true with God. Augustine's Arian opponents were likely never convinced, but he offered his own party the basic blueprint for thinking about the Trinity, a blueprint that will be used in the west throughout the middle ages and into modern times.

More than any other writer from antiquity, Augustine worked to shape his perception and legacy. He wrote his own *Confessions,* which autobiographically recounted his early life and conversion. In many of his sermons[43] and in many more of his letters,[44] Augustine defends himself and corrects misunderstandings about his actions and teachings. Often when he would publicly debate an opponent, he would write a "digest" of the debate that summarized the event for an audience who might have heard rumors. Late in life he wrote his *Retractions,* which reviewed all of his works to date and offered their proper interpretations. He inspired, if not commissioned, his disciple Possidius to pen the *Life* of Augustine, which was written from a very sympathetic viewpoint. None of these things should be taken to mean that Augustine was narcissistic or somehow misguided in his concern about his own reception. If anything, it further displays his genius, for Augustine knew that a Christian thinker could be lauded one day and then denounced the next. Origen of Alexandria, for example, had been villainized by many, and in Augustine's time Jerome himself had fallen from grace partly because he had been labeled an Origenist. Augustine worked to ensure that he would not fall into the same mistake Jerome had by letting his reputation be tarnished.

Early in Augustine's ministerial career, Jerome and Augustine had entered into a famous dispute over Jerome's use of the Hebrew texts as well as some of his interpretive decisions, and in letters exchanged between the two one can see how Augustine wrote with the public opinion in mind. The actual debate began because Augustine believed the Septuagint (the pre-Christian translation of the Hebrew scriptures into Greek) was divinely inspired while the Hebrew texts used by Jews in his day had been corrupted. Jerome, therefore, wrongly used the Hebrew texts for his Latin translation, the Vulgate.

Augustine did not always oppose Jerome. For example, the two of them became allies against the Pelagians. Another dispute arose over the Christian view of marriage, and in this case Augustine sided with Jerome against Jovinian, who claimed that the reward for celibacy is no greater than the reward for marriage.[45] Augustine disagreed, however, with Jerome in that he still insisted that marriage was "good," even after the time of Christ. Augustine had to concede that even within marriage and even for the purpose of procreation sex was sinful, because it always included lust. Nevertheless, he stipulated that this kind of sin was venial (= forgivable), unlike fornication and adultery, which are mortal sins requiring public penance. Therefore, marriage itself was good, even if sex – since the fall – was tainted by lust.

While much more could be said about Augustine's writings and teachings, this brief survey at least points to the breadth and depth of his thinking. As mentioned in the opening of this chapter, Augustine's writings will influence later Christianity, especially in the west, in innumerable ways. Since he had moved from Africa to Italy and then back, he wrote explicitly for and on behalf of the worldwide church as he understood it, and his concern with Christianity writ large meant that he had to address questions that Christians would face from all parts of the empire and questions that would affect generations to come. Without detracting from Augustine's universal concerns and influence, Augustine should also be studied in terms of his African heritage and in regard to how he saw himself as an African, for he also wrote explicitly in response to events in Africa and with an explicitly African identity. We can now turn back to his African context to find ways in which his African identity can be detected in his writings.

What was African about Augustine?

Augustine, like previous individuals discussed in this book, can be understood as both thoroughly Romanized and as distinctly African. His indebtedness to Greco-Roman thought and practice is widely known, and so here we need to isolate specific points about Augustine that could be considered African, since these are less widely known and often overlooked altogether.[46] These specific points will be listed in terms of his family background, times when he is identified as an African by others, and times when Augustine identifies himself as African.

Augustine's African background

We can begin with Augustine's immediate family and its background. Augustine described the region of his birth as one where most people speak "Punic" and with only the urban centers knowing Latin.[47] As for his father, Patricius appears to have been a typical African[48] elite who tried to ascend the status ladder of the Roman social hierarchy. He was mildly successful,[49] becoming a member of the local *curia*,[50] and he made every effort to capitalize on his social connections and attach his son to the local African patrons better connected with Roman nobility.[51] Such a practice is consistent with earlier African elites, such as Fronto and Apuleius who invoked *hospitii iura* (the rights of friends) in order to further themselves and fellow Africans in Roman society.[52] Patricius's name may derive, via *interpretatio Romana*, from the African deity known as "Liber Pater" (i.e. equivalent to Dionysos/Bacchus).[53] If Augustine's mother, Monica, comes from an indigenous background – and the consensus of scholars now assumes she did – then the very fact that Patricius would marry her suggests that he was not Roman, given the studies of marriage in Roman Africa that have found intermarriage to be rare.[54] Looking through a postcolonial lens, Patricius appears as an African who trained his son to pursue *Romanitas*.

Augustine's mother seems to be less a woman of the Roman world and more an indigenous African. It was her husband and her son who entered into the pursuit of *Romanitas*. Augustine once commented on how difficult it would be for her to speak Latin without an accent,[55] which she apparently never tried to do.[56] This is reminiscent of Septimius Severus, who was the first African emperor and who was embarrassed by his sister's African accent.[57] Rebecca Moore comments:

> Monnica's piety and practice seem to reflect the African Christianity that Augustine subsequently tried to replace with Catholic, or Romanized, Christianity. . . . Although Monnica complied with Caecilianist Christianity – a minority church movement that rejected the Donatists' insistence on the rebaptism of those whose sins required it – she continued her North African traditions until Ambrose admonished her to stop.[58]

Moore refers to what is a growing consensus view among scholars: Monica came from a so-called Donatist background.[59] As discussed in Chapter 7, many Donatists displayed uniquely African/non-Roman traits, such as speaking Punic. Augustine himself relays how Monica retained certain aspects of Christianity that were from "her own local practice."[60] Even Monica's name, which likely derived from the Libyan god, Mon, indicates her indigenous background while suggesting no attempt at *interpretatio Romana*.[61] Taking account of both of Augustine's parents, Patricius signifies Augustine's new elite identity, striving for *Romanitas*, while Monica signifies a more indigenous identity. Augustine will retain both throughout his life.[62]

Another member of Augustine's family, his only son, Adeodatus, also provides information about Augustine's background. This name, according to Peter Brown, was an instance of *interpretatio Romana* from the Punic name, Iatanbaal.[63] Brown's source for this is I. Kajanto's *Onomastic Studies in the Early Christian Inscriptions of Rome and Carthage*, wherein Kajanto demonstrates the common occurrence of this name. Were Adeodatus to be a translation of the less-common yet more literal rendering of Hannibal (Punic = gift of God; cf. Latin "*a-Deo-datus*"), then even more of an indigenous identity could be inferred in that to name one's child after the great antagonist of Rome and defender of Carthage would be a blatant display of African pride. If we assumed a pattern from Augustine's parents to his common-law marriage, then Adeodatus is a name given to suit both the mother's indigenous sympathies and Augustine's pursuit of *Romanitas*. Augustine related how he and Adeodatus both spoke Punic, but not as well as others.[64] Perhaps, both of them learned Punic from their mothers, who continued to speak the indigenous language to their sons, despite their fathers' preference for the Roman language.

Accusations about Augustine's identity

In addition to his family's background, Augustine's African identity can be seen in the way he was identified by others. One example occurred in the famous correspondence between our author and Jerome. Augustine pressed Jerome to explain his preference of the Hebrew text over the Septuagint, and Jerome curtly responded that he does not wish to enter into further discussion. Jerome likens himself to a retired veteran who prefers a life of quietude. He then warns Augustine, "If, however, you assiduously hammer me to engage, then I remind you of that historical event where Quintus Maximus in his patience shattered Hannibal in his youthful pride."[65] By likening Augustine to Hannibal, who was defeated by Quintus Maximus, Jerome evokes the Punic wars and Africa's tragic hero, in effect demarcating Augustine as an overzealous African. Augustine does not explicitly address Jerome's allusion, but the rhetorical point would certainly not have been missed, especially since Augustine had earlier written to Jerome explicitly speaking on behalf of "all the African churches."[66]

In a less famous exchange between Augustine and a Manichaean named Secundinus, the two exchange typical rhetorical jabs. Secundinus, who styles himself a "Roman," attacks Augustine's "Punic" ancestry and – like Jerome – calls Augustine "Hannibal."[67] This derogatory accusation of *Punicitas* will be hurled at Augustine in a later period of his life as well.

In Chapter 7 we saw how Augustine mocked the Donatists for their provincialism. Although they were found only in Africa, the Donatists in Augustine's view were "frogs croaking from the swamp, 'We are the only Christians!' "[68] Ironically, this same charge will be returned on Augustine himself when he attacks Pelagius.[69] In what has been called a fit of "nationalist, if not racist" polemics[70] Julian of Eclanum claims Augustine imposed a peculiarly African teaching on the Catholic church.[71] Specifically, Julian accuses Augustine of both "Numidian stubbornness" and "Punic reasonings," and he therefore labels Augustine "the Punic Aristotle."[72]

Augustine delays his direct response to his identification as a Punic African until late in book six of his *Incomplete Work Against Julian*, and then his strategy is to embrace the descriptor only so he can immediately extend the designation "Punic" to other church fathers whom Julian would have not been able to dismiss:

> Wish not to disparage this "Punic." . . . Even given the fact that Italy birthed you, it still remains that you think the Punics are bested by your blood-line, when in reality they have not been bested by your brain-power. Flee not the "Punic" but the penal. For you cannot avoid Punic respondents so long as you adore your own power. After all, even the blessed Cyprian was Punic.[73]

Mark Ellingson comments on this passage:

> Thus we can authoritatively rule out the possibility of his having an Italian ethnic background. . . . Is it not time for the academic community in

general to take a hard look at the possibility of Augustine's ethnic Berber background and how that might affect the way that we interpret him?[74]

The exact ethnic identity in Julian's accusation is less important for this current discussion than is the fact that Julian is able to use this label for Augustine without explanation. It was apparently a common one for Africans in general, if not Augustine in particular.

In responding to Julian's charge of provincialism, Augustine echoes earlier African elites who could not deny their African *patria* and so instead rhetorically appealed to so-called barbarians such as Anacharsis the Scythian who, the Africans Fronto and Apuleius both insisted, was wiser than the Greeks.[75] The practice of labeling Augustine "Punic" or African, however, is not limited to Augustine's opponents.

Late in Augustine's life, a fellow African and soon-to-be bishop of Carthage, Quodvultdeus, requested Augustine's instructions, which he poetically called, "African bread isolated from any foreign flavors."[76] Quodvultdeus's imagery alludes to the fact that Africa had become the breadbasket of the Roman Empire. Quodvultdeus' request for "African bread" that remains in Africa is meant to compliment Augustine, because Augustine's fellow Africans desire this bread "pure of any foreign [= Roman?] flavors."

These examples suffice to demonstrate that Augustine was perceived, by at least some, to be African of Punic descent. To be sure, many others – probably including Augustine himself – perceived Augustine in more strictly Roman terms, but it must be repeated that a Roman identity need not exclude an African self-identity altogether. The last set of examples illustrate how Augustine identified himself.

Self-identifying as an African

In his treatise on providence, Augustine admitted that he spoke Latin with an accent, a habit that "annoyed the Italians."[77] He somewhat ambiguously suggests elsewhere that Latin was his first language,[78] and yet his admission here that he spoke the *lingua Romana* with a provincial, if not African, accent is reminiscent of Apuleius in the second century. In defining his speech as one free from barbarisms, Apuleius stated:

> For who among you would forgive me for a single solecism? Who would allow me one ignorantly pronounced syllable? Who would permit me to jabber any wild and uncouth words like those that well up in the mouth of the insane?"[79]

In a chapter entitled "Augustine the African," O'Donnell explains how the new elites of Africa struggled to transcend their Africanity and to assume *Romanitas*, which required their speech to be "more Roman than the Romans."[80]

Augustine also remembers how in his early life he was trained to weep about the story of Dido and Aeneas.[81] Peter Brown calls this tale "a very African interlude in the life of the upright founder of Rome."[82] Similarly, regarding the account in the *Confessions* where Augustine forsook his mother in Carthage and sailed to Rome, O'Donnell interprets Augustine's jilting of Monica under the Aeneas/Dido motif:

> The most remarkable scene, as she weeps on the shore at Carthage while her son sails off, abandoning her for Italy, is dramatically inscribed into the literary tradition, with Augustine suddenly becoming Aeneas abandoning Dido. We can all connect the dots of that story.[83]

If we follow O'Donnell's "connecting of the dots," then the young Aeneas-like Augustine who pursues a career as a rhetor in Rome must do so by forsaking his African mother/-land in pursuit of *Romanitas*.

Augustine's pursuit of *Romanitas*, however, does not negate his self-identity as an African. In responding to Maximus of Madauros, who had denigrated the indigenous heritage of North Africa, Augustine insists,

> As an African man, writing to Africans, and even as one abiding in Africa, you could not have forgotten yourself and thought of Punic names as flawed. . . . Should this language be disapproved by you, you must deny that in Punic books produced by very educated men many wise teachings have been recorded; you must regret that you were born here, for this land is the still-warm cradle of the Punic language itself. . . . You disrespect and snub Punic names to such an extent, it is as if you had surrendered to the Roman altars.[84]

Not only has Augustine chastised Maximus's betrayal of his *Punicitas*, he shrewdly counters these sentiments by deeming them "Roman," apparently the unspoken motivation behind Maximus's words. By labeling his opponent's sentiments as Roman, Augustine may be scoring points with an African audience.

Around the same time – and in a friendlier letter – Augustine encourages Bishop Aurelius of Carthage. Through their joint labor, Augustine prays, God may heal "the African church," a reference to their attempt to defeat the Donatist party.[85] Augustine must also explain to Aurelius how the current bishop of Hippo is not indigenous to the region, but "even if he were African," he could be no more effective because of his prudence.[86]

Later, around 412, in answering concerns raised by Marcellinus, a magistrate in Carthage, Augustine addresses the comparison of Christ with other magicians, such as Apollonius and Apuleius. Augustine responds, "It is best to speak of Apuleius, who is known as an African among us Africans."[87] After embracing this African identity shared by all three men (i.e. Augustine, Marcellinus, and Apuleius), Augustine touches upon the embarrassing failure of Apuleius's attempt to transcend his Africanity and attain the prestige of *Romanitas*: "Not only did [Apuleius] never attain a governorship, he never even attained any sort of powerful public office, despite all his magical arts, his noble birth place, higher education, and being gifted with great eloquence."[88] Although Augustine also acknowledges in this same paragraph that Apuleius was the "priest of the province [*sacerdos provinciae*]" (i.e. Africa), Augustine nevertheless mocks Apuleius's failed attempt to attain a prestigious governmental office in the Roman Empire, a mockery that arises only after the fall of Rome at a time when Augustine begins to formulate his Two Cities paradigm in his *City of God*.[89] Rome is no longer the idealized city – a point to which we will return shortly.

Late in his career, Augustine exchanged letters with Hesychius, the bishop of Dalmatia.[90] Hesychius had assumed that the end of the world was imminent because "the Gospel of Christ has infiltrated every place."[91] Hesychius names the Roman Empire as the vehicle for the spreading of the gospel, a common assumption since Eusebius. Augustine responds with a lengthy letter refuting these assumptions, especially about Rome. First, Augustine knows that the gospel has not been preached "everywhere": "For among us here in Africa there are uncounted barbarian nations among whom the Gospel is still yet to be preached."[92] Augustine's "among us [*apud nos*]," is explicitly in reference to "us Africans," and his self-identity arises in direct response to the Dalmatian bishop's claim about the Roman Empire. This exchange illustrates how Africa consisted of numerous people groups, but an overarching African identity arises in opposition to a Roman identity. Regarding the Roman Empire, Augustine adds, "For the Lord swore an oath to Abraham that all nations, not just the Romans, would be of his seed."[93] It is also worth noting that in this same paragraph, Augustine broaches the twin subjects of the Roman slave trade in and subjugation of the African province – a problem he also addressed in another letter.

Late in Augustine's career, he wrote to a friend residing in Italy and reported:

> There are so many (who in common lingo are called) slave peddlers, that they are depleting the greater part of our population and even a large number of our freeborn, exporting those who are sold into provinces across the Mediterranean.[94]

Augustine then clarified his concern: "that Africa is not completely emptied of its own natives."[95] Augustine in this example at no point refers to himself as an African or as a native, yet his sympathy with the indigenous population and his frustration with the trade laws of the empire is evident in his hope that Alypius will sway the imperial court to take action on behalf of Africans.

While these examples all require further attention to contextual concerns, they do demonstrate how Augustine understood himself as an African. While such a conclusion may seem trivial, the point needs to be clarified in Augustinian scholarship that has not yet come to terms with Augustine's African heritage. Gerald Bonner, for example, devotes considerable attention to Augustine's ethnicity and concludes, "In determining a man's race, culture is a more significant factor than blood; and nowhere do we find Augustine thinking of himself as anything other than a Latin-speaking Roman."[96] This statement, while likely born out of a valid concern to avoid mistakes of a previous generation of scholars (discussed in Chapter 1), is no longer tenable since the examples provided here exhibit multiple instances of "Augustine thinking of himself as . . . other than a Latin-speaking Roman."

In a similar vein of thought, Johannes van Oort, after reviewing the evidence suggesting that Augustine's parents were of African descent, asserts:

> Yet all of this does not tell us very much. Even if Augustine's mother and perhaps also Patricius were Berbers, it is still true that they manifested themselves in a typically Roman fashion. . . . [Augustine] belongs to the West European cultural sphere.[97]

The picture, however, is not so simple, for van Oort next qualifies his understanding of Augustine to admit that "his writings display an unmistakably African chauvinism."[98] One instance of this Roman/African tension that van Oort does acknowledge is in Augustine's *City of God*:

> This work, so influential in world history, was written by a Roman from Africa. Was his attitude towards the Empire different from that of its citizens elsewhere? Could there have been in him the same permeating element of hostility towards Rome that was undeniably present among Berbers and Phoenicians? These questions merit further consideration.[99]

The need for "further consideration" is one that can especially be undertaken by seeing Augustine as a product of both Rome and Africa, and these two identities can even help illuminate his works, as van Oort rightly states. While we cannot review all of his works to see these identities in the limited space allowed in this chapter, it is worth taking van Oort's selected treatise as a case study.

In his *City of God*, Augustine answers the claim that wars are necessary. Suddenly, he launches into what seems to be an unrelated tirade on Rome: "the imperious city has imposed not only a yoke but its language upon the subjugated nations as a societal peace . . . but this has come about by copious and extensive wars."[100] Roland H. Bainton comments on this passage to say, "Augustine was an African with a deep sense of the wrongs of the conquered."[101] Augustine attacks the so-called civilizing mission of Rome, which had been celebrated by Roman writers, but which the African bishop finds unjustifiable.[102] Thus far in this work Augustine has avoided direct conflict with the fallen city, only casually inserting his African perspective into the discussion, such as when he uses "Africa" as a synonym for "south,"[103] and only occasionally betraying pro-African sentiments, such as when he complains about the Roman sources for the Punic war, "who did not so much recount the Roman wars as they praised Roman rule."[104] There is, however, another motif in this treatise where Augustine's antagonism toward Rome can be found.

Throughout the work, Augustine aggressively denigrates the traditional heroes of Rome – repeating many of the standard lines found in earlier African apologists. The following list is a veritable who's-who of Rome's glorious past, yet in Augustine's treatment these individuals are sardonically maligned. The "she-wolf" that suckled Romulus and Remus was a euphemism for a prostitute;[105] Aeneas's mother was an adulteress;[106] and Lucretia – the virgin whose chastity founded the Roman Republic – is said to have actually enjoyed her rape by the Roman prince, Sextus Tarquinius.[107] On this last point, Brown comments, "[To Romans,] the *controversia*, in which he piles on innuendoes against the chastity of Lucretia, would have appeared in singularly bad taste."[108] Additionally, Augustine more than once mocks the death of Regulus, who by all Roman accounts was a pious patriot who died for Rome's security.[109] Likewise, Scipio Africanus, whose title was awarded for defeating the Carthaginians, and whose era is celebrated by Sallust as the golden age of Rome, is sarcastically referred to by Augustine as "the great," and is mocked for his late-life exile from Rome, the irony of which is itself too great for Augustine to pass over in silence.[110] Similarly, Caesar Augustus, celebrated by Virgil as the pinnacle of Rome's history, where it is said that he was destined by the fates to rule the world, is said by Augustine "to have stolen all freedom from the Romans."[111] These examples of Augustine's anti-Roman sentiment require more analysis than can be fully offered here. Nevertheless, they illustrate how a rereading of Augustine's works with attention to his African identity helps bring to light certain themes.

Augustine after the fall of Rome, like Lactantius before Constantine's conversion, sees Rome as having a temporary role in history. The future judgment of the world, however, will be especially severe for Rome. Augustine's positive evaluation of Rome and what we would call the classical Roman heritage is counterbalanced by Augustine's African identity, which entailed a critical assessment of Rome as well.

In a recent "intellectual biography," Miles Hollingworth notes how Augustine's context informed his own understanding: "Clearly the more telling consideration is the question of self-identity. In his writings, Augustine leaves information to how conscious he was of his African heritage; and to standing out as one."[112] Perhaps more than any other figure from history, Augustine's writings and legacy leave us with an image of an incredibly complex individual. Therefore, no one aspect of Augustine should become so important in our interpretation of him that it eclipses other sides of his persona. This is especially true of his African identity.[113] Hopefully, the focus offered here on Augustine's African identity has helped to supplement previous studies. In addition to everything else we can say about him, he belongs within the larger story of Christianity in Africa. We can now turn to another major episode in that history. It is one that begins one year prior to Augustine's death: the Vandal invasion.

Notes

1 Possidius, *Life* 1.
2 *Against the Academics* 2.1.3.
3 *Confessions* 9.9.19.
4 *Confessions* 9.8.18.
5 *Confessions* 9.9.22; Possidius, *Life* 26.
6 In Augustine's time, parents could baptize infants who were in mortal danger, but it was still the norm to receive baptism later in one's life.
7 *Confessions* 2.3.5–6.
8 *Confessions* 6.15.25.
9 See sources in Simmons, *Universal Salvation*, 300 n.14.
10 *Confessions* 8.11.27.
11 Romans 13:13–14 (NRSV).
12 See his works known as the Cassiciacum Dialogues; cf. the entry by Joanne McWilliam in *Augustine Through the Ages*, for details.
13 *Confessions* 9.10.25.
14 Possidius, *Life* 4.
15 *Sermon* 355.2, with ref. to Acts 4:32.
16 Possidius, *Life* 5.
17 See details in Brown, *Augustine*, 202.
18 See Augustine, *To Cresconius* 4.64.79; and *Against the Letters of Petilian* 3.16.19.
19 *Against the Letters of Petilian* 3.16.19; Possidius, *Life* 8.
20 For details, see William A. Sumruld, *Augustine and the Arians: The Bishop of Hippo's Encounters With Ulfilan Arianism* (London: Associated University Presses, 1994). The label "Arianism" is problematic, much like "Donatism." This will be treated in more detail in chapter nine, but for convenience we will keep this label presently since it is the one Augustine himself used.
21 Liberatus of Carthage, *A Short Report on the Nestorian and Eutychian Controversies* 4.17 (text E. Schwartz (ed.), ACO tome 2: *Concilium Vniversal Chalcedonense*, vol. 5: *Collectio Sangermanensis* [Berlin: De Gruyter 1936], 103).
22 See Harold S. Stone, "Cult of Augustine's Body," in *Augustine Through the Ages*, ed. Allan Fitzgerald (Grand Rapids, MI: Eerdmans, 1999), 256–259, for further details.
23 For this and other readers of Augustine from this time period, see John J. Contreni, "Early Carolingian Era," and Joseph F. Kelly, "Late Carolingian Era," in *Augustine Through the Ages*, ed. Allan Fitzgerald (Grand Rapids, MI: Eerdmans, 1999), 124–132.
24 The beginner can find all of the details in Allan Fitzgerald, *Augustine Through the Ages* (Grand Rapids, MI: Eerdmans, 1999).
25 These include *Against the Skeptics*, *On the Happy Life*, *On Order*, *The Soliloquies*, *On Music*, *On the Greatness of the Soul*, and *The Teacher*.
26 For bibliography and debate over Neoplatonism in Augustine's thought, see Jean-Luc Marion, *In the Self's Place: The Approach of Saint Augustine*, trans. Jeffrey L. Kosky (Stanford, CA: Stanford University Press, 2012), 3–4 and

Augustine the African 259

passim; Marion finds Augustine's alleged Neoplatonism to be an exaggeration by modern historians of religion.

27 E.g. *On Faith and the Creed, On the Christian Struggle, On the Creed to Catechumens, Enchiridion/Handbook on Faith, Hope, and Love, Responses to Januarius, On the Divination of Demons, On the Value of Fasting, On Seeing God, On Faith and Works, On the Presence of God, On Patience, On Adulterous Marriages, On Lying, Against Lying, On the Care of the Dead,* and *On Eight Questions From Dulcitius.*

28 Such as *On Christian Doctrine* and *On the Instruction of Beginners.*

29 Including *To Simplicianus, Explanations of the Psalms, Questions on the Gospels, Questions on the Heptateuch, Sayings in the Heptateuch, On the Agreement of the Evangelists, Tractates on the Gospel According to Saint John, Tractates on the First Letter of John,* and *On Eight Questions From the Old Testament.*

30 *On the Work of Monks, On the Good of Widowhood, On Continence, The Rule: A Rebuke, The Rule: Monastic Order,* and *The Rule: Precepts.*

31 E.g. *On Heresies* and *Tractate Against the Jews.*

32 *Confessions* 7.19.25.

33 For an introduction, see J. Kevin Coyle, "Anti-Manichean Works," in *Augustine Through the Ages,* ed. Allan Fitzgerald (Grand Rapids, MI: Eerdmans, 1999), 39–41.

34 E.g. *City of God* 22.

35 For an introduction, see Tilley, "Anti-Donatist Works," in *Augustine Through the Ages,* ed. Allan Fitzgerald (Grand Rapids, MI: Eerdmans, 1999), 34–39.

36 *Psalm Against the Donatist Party;* see Geert van Reyn, "Hippo's Got Talent: Augustine's *Psalmus contra partem Donati* as Pop(ular) Song," in *The Uniquely African Controversy: Studies on Donatist Christianity,* ed. Anthony Dupont, Matthew Alan Gaumer, and Matthijs Lamberigts (Leuven: Peeters, 2015), 251–268.

37 For an introduction, see Gerald Bonner, "Anti-Pelagian Works," in *Augustine Through the Ages s,* ed. Allan Fitzgerald (Grand Rapids, MI: Eerdmans, 1999), 41–47.

38 I.e. the "psyche," from the Greek word for soul, *psychē.*

39 *On the Trinity,* book 9.

40 In the ancient languages, "spirit" literally means wind or breath.

41 *On the Trinity,* book 10.

42 For an introduction, see Michel R. Barnes, "Anti-Arian Works," in *Augustine Through the Ages,* ed. Allan Fitzgerald (Grand Rapids, MI: Eerdmans, 1999), 31–34.

43 For translations of his sermons, see WSA 3.1–11; and see his *Expositions on the Psalms* in WSA 3.15–20. For the critical editions, see entry in *Augustine Through the Ages.*

44 For translations of his letters, see WSA 2.1–4. For the critical editions, see entry in *Augustine Through the Ages.*

45 *On the Good of Marriage* and *On Holy Virginity.*

46 In the following section I use material first published as Wilhite, "Augustine the African: Post-colonial, Postcolonial and Post-postcolonial Readings," *Journal of Postcolonial Theory and Theology* 5 (2014), 1–34; repr./trans. in *Mayéutica* 41 (2015), 53–75. In addition to the postcolonial view of "hybridity," one can now also analyze Augustine in terms of *mestizaje;* see Justo L. González, *The Mestizo Augustine: A Theologian Between Two Cultures* (Downers Grove, IL: IVP Academic, 2016); unfortunately, I did not obtain my copy of González's work in time to allow for a thorough interaction in the following section. González's lack of interaction with secondary literature causes problems at several points, such

as his belief that Augustine referred to "Libyan" language (rather than Punic) – a now outdated view. Despite the many instances like this where he makes factual mistakes, González's theoretical approach is a welcome one.

47 For a description of the neighboring villages of Thagaste, see *Letter* 108.5.14; *Letter* 209.2–3. For the region surrounding Hippo, see *Letter* 105.2.3–4, *Letter* 209.3, and *Ten Homilies on the Epistle of John to the Parthians* 2.3, where Augustine explains, "they speak Punic, that is, African [*dicant . . . punicam, id est, afram*]."

48 O'Meara, *The Young Augustine*, 25, concludes that Patricius was "a native Numidian."

49 Cf. *Confessions* 2.3.5, for Patricius's class status. Also, in *Sermon* 356.3, Augustine tells of the poor attire provided by his father.

50 Possidius, *Life* 1.

51 *Against the Academics* 2.1.3.

52 Gardner and Wiedemann, *The Roman Household*, 176; ref. Fronto, *On the Loss of his Grandson* 1.3; and Apuleius, *Apologia* 94–95.

53 See Rives, *Religion and Authority in Roman Carthage*, 129 and passim; and Rives, *Religion in the Roman Empire* (London: Blackwell, 2007), 71–73.

54 O'Meara, *The Young Augustine*, 28. On marriage in North Africa, see especially, David Cherry, "Marriage and Acculturation in Roman Algeria," *Classical Philology* 92 (1, 1997) 71–83, where he finds the marriages between "Roman(ized) and un-Romanized" uncommon; and more generally in North Africa, Cherry, *Frontier and Society in Roman North Africa*, 101–140 (= chapter four, "Husbands and Wives in the Frontier Zone").

55 *On Order* 2.17.45; mentioned on p. 55.

56 For a bibliography and discussion of Monica's role in the Cassiacum dialogues, see Laurie Douglass, "Voice Re-Cast: Augustine's Use of Conversion in *De ordine* and the *Confessions*," *Augustinian Studies* 27 (1996): 39–54.

57 *The Augustan History: Severus* 15.7: *cum sua Leptitana ad eum venisset uix Latine loquens, ac de illa multum imperator erubesceret*; Cf. 19.9: *canorus voce, sed Afrum quiddam usque ad senectutem sonans.*

58 Moore, "O Mother, Where Art Thou?", 159.

59 O'Donnell, *Augustine*, 55. See also Augustine's cousin, Severinus (*Letter* 52), who was Donatist; Frend, "The Family of Augustine," 140.

60 Gerald Bonner, *St Augustine of Hippo: Life and Controversies* (Norwich: Canterbury Press, 2002), 75; ref. *Confessions* 6.2.2.

61 Frend, *The Donatist Church*, 230.

62 This view of Augustine, I would contend, is more helpful than strictly seeing Augustine as a "Berber" (e.g. René Pottier, *Saint Augustin le Berbère*, [Paris: Publications techniques et artistiques, 1945]). See Ellingsen, *The Richness of Augustine*, 8, who perceives a consensus of scholars now agreeing that Augustine was "of mixed racial background." Also, see André Mandouze, "Cloture de la session d'Alger," in *Augustinus Afer: saint Augustin, africanité et universalité*, ed. Pierre-Yves Fux, Jean-Michel Roessli, Otto Wermelinger (Fribourg: Editions Universitaires, 2003), 386, who offers relfections on how best to speak of Augustine's "Africanité." As to why Augustine later converted to Caecelianist/ Catholic Christianity, as opposed to Donatist, Frend, "The Family of Augustine," 150, concludes:

> Donatism involved a break with the intellectual pagan heritage and the substitution of the Bible for the Classics. . . . Both Manichaeism and Catholicism in North Africa expressed a greater degree of continuity with the pagan-classical past, and were vastly more attractive to Augustine and his friends.

Similarly, O'Donnell, *Augustine*, 49, suggests that Augustine embraced Catholicism after his encounter with Faustus: "The Manichee Faustus, originally from

Milevis, was what Augustine could have become; a well-educated man who fell among the Manichees and knew success among them and scorn everywhere else."

63 Brown, *Augustine* (1967), 63. However, Frend, "The Family of Augustine," 150, simply reads this as a Christian appellation. What, precisely, is "Christ-centred" about the name, Frend does not explain.

64 *The Teacher* 13.44.

65 Augustine, *Letter* 72.3: *ne, si me ad scribendum freqenter inpuleris, illius recorder historiae, quod Hannibalem iuveniliter exultantem Quintus Maximus patientia sua fregerit* (my trans.); cf. Livy 22.12–18. Also, see Augustine, *Letter* 75.4.18, where Jerome attacking Augustine's flock for being provincial calls them "ignorant commoners [*inperitorum plebeculam*]."

66 *Letter* 28.2: *omnis Africanarum ecclesiarum* (my trans.)

67 Secundinus, *Letter* 2, claims Augustine belongs to the "Punic peoples [*Punicae gentes*]," and in *Letter* 3, Augustine is again attacked for his Punic ties to Hannibal. Augustine counters Secundinus's claim to *Romanitas* in a mocking tone (*Against Secundus* 19) and addresses the Punic question by shifting from a geographical to a theological matter (*Against Secundus* 25).

68 Augustine, *Expositions of the Psalms* 95.11: *clamant ranae de palude: Nos soli sumus christiani.*

69 Pelagius was initially found innocent by an eastern council, and then after his trial was moved west many Italian bishops still defended his views. While Augustine did have support outside of Africa, most famously the bishop of Rome, one can see how easily his views could be labeled as an African tradition and not part of the Catholic/ecumenical teachings of the church.

70 Josef Lössl, "Augustine, 'Pelagianism,' Julian of Aeclanum and Modern Scholarship," *Zeitschrift für antikes Christentum* 11 (1, 2007), 143.

71 For further discussion of this exchange, see Mathijs Lamberigts, "The Italian Julian of Aeclanum about the African Augustine of Hippo," in *Augustinus Afer: saint Augustin, africanité et universalité*, ed. Pierre-Yves Fux, Jean-Michel Roessli, Otto Wermelinger (Fribourg: Editions Universitaires, 2003), 83–93.

72 *Incomplete Work Against Julian* 1.16: *Numidae induruisse* (my trans.); 1.72: *Punicae dialexeos*; and 3.199, *Aristoteles Poenorum*.

73 *Against Julian* 6.18, *Noli istum Poenum . . . spernere. Non enim quia te Apulia genuit, ideo Poenos uincendos existimes gente, quos non potes mente. Poenas potius fuge, non Poenos; nam disputatores Poenos non potes fugere, quamdiu te delectat in tua virtute confidere, et beatus enim Cyprianus Poenus fuit*; cf. 6.23.

74 *The Richness of Augustine*, 10.

75 Fronto, *Letter* 5; Apuleius, *Apology* 24.

76 *Letter* 223.3: *sequestratis saporibus peregrinis . . . panem Afrum.*

77 *On Order* 2.17.45: *Itali exagitant*. Also see discussion in Brown, "Christianity and Local Culture," 85–95.

78 *Confessions* 1.14.23.

79 *Florida* 9.6–7: *Quis enim uestrum mihi unum soloecismum ignoverit? Quis uel unam syllabam barbare pronuntiatam donaverit? Quis incondita et vitiosa verba temere quasi delirantibus oborientia permiserit blaterare?* (text in Paul Vallette, *Apulée: Apologie, Florides* [Collection des universités de France; Paris: Les belles lettres, 2002]; trans. in John Hilton, *Apuleius: Rhetorical Works*, ed. Stephen J. Harrison [Oxford: Oxford University Press, 2001]). See Hilton, "Introduction," 126, for Apuleius's first language being Punic.

80 O'Donnell, *Augustine* (Boston: G. K. Hall, 1985), 2, in his chapter entitled, "Augustine the African." See also Mandouze, "Clôture de la session d'Alger," 386, who claims that Augustine on occasion acted "plus romain que les Romains."

81 *Confessiones* 1.8.20.

82 *Augustine*, 23.

83 *Augustine*, 55.

84 *Letter* 17.2: *neque enim usque adeo teipsum oblivisci potuisses, ut homo Afer scribens Afris, cum simus utrique in Africa constituti, Punica nomina exagitanda existimares . . . . quae lingua si inprobatur abs te, nega Punicis libris, ut a viris doctissimis proditur, multa sapienter esse mandata memoriae; paeniteat te certe ibi natum, ubi huius linguae cunabula recalent. . . . et tamen Punica nomina tamquam nimium Romanorum altaribus deditus contemnis ac despicis* (my trans.)

85 *Letter* 22.2: *Africana ecclesia.* F.L. Cross, "History and Fiction in the African Canons," *Journal of Theological Studies* 12 (1961), 229, reads this statement as evidence of Augustine's own hopes of revivifying the church throughout Numidia.

86 *Letter* 22.4: *etiam si Afer esset.*

87 *Letter* 138.4.19: *Apuleius enim, ut de illo potissimum loquamur, qui nobis Afris Afer est notior.*

88 *Letter* 138.4.19: *non dico ad regnum sed ne ad aliquam quidem iudiciarum rei publicae potestatem cum omnibus suis magicis aribus potuit pervenire honesto patriae suae loco natus et liberaliter educatus magnaque praeditus eloquentia.* The reference to Apuleius's *honesto patriae suae loco natus*, Madaurus, is probably a rhetorical play on words: Apuleius's social location by birth was prestigious, but his geographical place of birth, while provincial, is the same region that Augustine is from and which the recipient of this letter governs; see Harrison, *Apuleius*, 1–6.

89 Earlier in this letter (138.3.16–17) Augustine answers those who blame Christians for the fall of Rome. Just prior to his discussion of Apuleius (138.4.18), Augustine issues a vitriolic attack on Roman religion in particular, as opposed to "pagan" religion in general.

90 *Letters* 197, 198, and 199, the dating of which belong somewhere between 419 and 427.

91 *Letter* 198.6: *ubique . . . evangelium Christi pentravit.*

92 *Letter* 199.46: *sunt enim apud nos, hoc est in Africa barbarae innumerabiles gentes, in quibus nondum esse pradicatum evangelium ex his.*

93 *Letter* 199.47: *Non enim Romanos sed omnes gentes dominus semini Abrahae media quoque iuratione promisit*; with reference to Gen. 22:16–18; 26:3–4.

94 *Letter* 10*.2: *Tanta est eorum qui uulgo mangones vocantur in Africa multitudo, ut eam ex magna parte humano genere exhauriant transferendo quos mercantur in provincias transmarinas et paene omnes liberos.*

95 *Letter* 10*.5: *ut Africa suis non amplius evacuetur indigenis.* The Roman/African binary opposition is not so clear-cut, however, because Augustine can still speak of the "barbarians," by whom he may mean the Circumcellions, whose marauding is less of a threat, given the Roman armies; cf. *Letter* 220.

96 *Augustine* (2002), 32.

97 Johannes van Oort, *Jerusalem and Babylon: A Study into Augustine's City of God and the Sources of His Doctrine of the Two Cities* (Supplements to Vigiliae Christianae 14; Leiden: E. J. Brill, 1991), 19.

98 *Jerusalem and Babylon*, 20. Van Oort also stipulates, "In short, he was a civilized African as we can imagine one to be in the Late Roman period" (21). What an "uncivilized African" would have looked like, van Oort leaves undefined.

99 Van Oort, *Jerusalem and Babylon*, 20; also see the statement in Van Oort, *Jerusalem and Babylon*, 21.

100 *City of God* 19.7: *ut imperiosa uiuitas non solum iugum, verum etiam linguam suam domitis gentibus per pacem societatis inponeret . . . sed hoc quam multis et quam grandibus bellis* (my trans.).

101 *Christian Attitudes Toward War and Peace*, 91, and see 96. In his next sentence Bainton notes how Augustine "was at the same time a Roman, speaking Latin not Punic."

102 Examples of Roman writers include Pliny, *Natural History* 3.5.39–40 and Virgil, *Aeneid* 6.851–853. For further discussion on this motif, see Richard Hingley, *Globalizing Roman Culture: Unity, Diversity and Empire* (London: Routledge, 2005), 49–71; and the various essays in Craige B. Champion (ed.), *Roman Imperialism: Readings and Sources* (Oxford: Blackwell, 2004).

103 E.g. *City of God* 16.21; 16.38.

104 *City of God* 3.19: *qui non tam narrare bella Romana quam Romanum imperium laudare.*

105 *City of God* 18.21.

106 *City of God* 3.3.

107 *City of God* 1.19. See Livy 1.57–60. cf. Cicero, *The Republic* 2.46; *On Ends* 2.66. For full review of primary sources, ancient rhetorical uses, and Augustine's treatment, see Dennis Trout, "Re-Textualizing Lucretia: Cultural Subversion in the City of God," *Journal of Early Christian Studies* 2 (1, 1994), 53–70.

108 *Augustine*, 309.

109 *City of God* 3.20; cf. 1.15; 1.24.

110 *City of God* 3.21.

111 *City of God* 3.21: *libertatem omni modo extorsisse Romanis* (my trans.) It is also worth noting that in this paragraph, Augustine in effect blames the fall of Rome on Rome's cruel victory over Carthage in the Punic wars.

112 *Saint Augustine of Hippo*, 52.

113 González's (*Mestizo Augustine*, 17–18), use of the concept *mestizaje* is more helpful than the postcolonial concept of "hybridity" in that the two poles are themselves understood as having their own "mixed" and complex state:

> In the case of Augustine, his mestizaje is not simply the encounter between the African and the Roman. Inasmuch as he is an African, he also reflects the mestizo reality of the region, where even before the arrival of the Romans there was a mixture and clash of views and traditions that were Berber or Libyan with others of Punic or Carthaginian origin. And on the Roman side, it is best not to speak of a Roman culture, but rather of a Greco-Roman one, for the Romanitas Augustine knew was to a great degree also Greek. In any case, mestizaje with all its complexities was a constant presence in the life and thought of Augustine as it is also among most of humanity.

9 The Vandal era of African Christianity

The Vandal era of North African history lasted approximately a hundred years (429–534). The Vandals took control of Africa from the "Roman" emperor,[1] which was the first time that Africa functioned independently of Rome since the Punic wars. The "Byzantines" later reconquered the land and ruled Africa again until the Arab expansion in the late sixth and early seventh centuries.

The Vandal period is in many ways typical of the western empire at this time, in that the empire had entered into what later historians misnamed the "Dark Ages." Many "barbarians" ruled various provinces, and so the Vandal era should be studied in light of this wider phenomenon. When studying this period, historians must account for both the radical changes that took place and also for the large amount of continuity that remained in local societies. The various provinces of the western empire had new rulers, but everyday life would have largely gone on unchanged. The same is true for Africa. While being mindful of the similarities between Africa and other regions at this time, the particular events in Africa and the unique social context of this region should also be explored.[2] In what follows, the general chronology of events will be introduced, followed by a discussion of some of the African writers from this time.[3]

The Vandal invasion of Africa

In 429, King Geiseric led his Vandals from Iberia into Africa. This band of 80,000 quickly moved across Mauretania, and while they would have only had around 20,000 fighting men, they easily besieged and conquered many Roman cities throughout Numidia by 430.[4]

From the vantage point of the Romanized Africans, the Vandals were brutal: Augustine's biographer, Possidius, reports that the Vandals burned and plundered the African provinces.[5] Modern scholars, however, have abandoned the old depiction of them as ruthlessly destructive (thus the modern concept of "vandalism"). Possidius, for example, is known to have grossly exaggerated; he even claims that only three churches (at Carthage, Cirta, and Hippo) survived the invasion.[6] The Vandals came to rule North

Africa, not destroy its resources. When it came to the churches, the Vandals replaced the "Catholic" bishops and clergy with their own.[7] When Geiseric took control of Carthage, many lost their property and were forced to flee,[8] including all the "Catholic" clergy who were exiled.[9] Just how much devastation occurred more generally during the initial invasion is difficult to assess.

One Christian writer from Gaul, Salvian (c.400–c.495), explained the fall of Carthage as part of the judgment of God on the wider empire. In his work *On the Government of God*,[10] Salvian faulted Christians for their moral failures, and he claimed that as punishment for their sins God used the foreign invaders to persecute the Christians. Meanwhile, across the empire, he believed local populations were embracing the "barbarians" as liberators from Rome's unjust rule.[11]

When discussing Africa and Carthage in particular, Salvian offers both positive and negative assessments. On the positive side, Salvian believes Africa is "the soul [*animam*] of the republic."[12] However, on the negative side, Salvian especially decries the lust and sinfulness of the people of Carthage as well as all of Africa. While Geiseric and his army besieged Carthage, the Christians in Carthage "went mad in the circuses and reveled in the theatres."[13] Salvian believed this state to be a reversion to Africa's pre-Roman times, which were both barbaric and ungodly:

> Who does not know that all Africa always burned with the obscene resinous tree of lust? . . . Who does not know that almost all Africans are unchaste, with the exception, perhaps, of those converted to God, that is, those changed by faith and religion? . . . It is so infrequent and unheard of that an African is not unchaste as it is novel and customary than an African is not an African.[14]

The city of Carthage itself should have been an exception, because the Romans conquered it and civilized it, according to Salvian. He describes it as "a Rome in Africa."[15] Nevertheless, according to Salvian, Carthage had sadly become typical of all so-called civilized cities by this time in that it was full of wickedness and vice.

For Salvian, this sad moral state was true both of Christians and non-Christians, and it applied both to the Romans in Africa as well as the native Africans: "The Africans, who formerly were never able to conquer the Romans in power and greatness, have now surpassed them in impurity . . . what I have said the Africans were . . . the Romans, their masters, were."[16] Salvian also sees this distinction between the Romans and the native Africans in terms of the native religion with respect to "Celestis, that demon of the Africans" (i.e. the Punic Tanit) who was still worshipped in this time period, even by those who claimed to be Christians.[17] These false-Christian "Africans" especially harbored a "hate for the monks"[18] in that they would violently oppose any foreign clergy appointed in Carthage.[19] In contrast to the population of Carthage, the Vandal conquerors appeared to Salvian to be morally superior, especially in that they stopped Carthaginian men from dressing in "effeminate" attire.[20] Whether Salvian ever visited Carthage or had firsthand information about the events of the Vandal invasion is debatable, and so he is not necessarily a reliable source. Even so, he does provide historians with one perception of Christianity in Carthage at this time. Edward Gibbon thought Geiseric right to put an end to the "voluptuous people," that is, the Carthaginians, for their "unnatural lusts" were due to their "Punic faith," which is to say, their "faithless character."[21] This modern bias, however, forgets that Salvian rebuked both Punic and Roman practices. Even so, the point remains that the Roman and the indigenous populations were seen to be distinct at this time.

Apart from Salvian's theological claims about divine retribution, it is difficult to explain how such a relatively small number of Vandals could have landed on African shores and moved so swiftly, given the presence of the Roman army in Africa at the time. Ancient sources claimed that Boniface, the Roman commander of Africa who had fallen out of favor with the imperial family, may have invited the Vandals to come support him.[22] When Boniface regained political favor and disinvited the Vandals, they were disinclined to acquiesce. In all likelihood, this claim that Boniface is to blame was probably an attempt to explain why Boniface did not oppose the Vandals more immediately and successfully.[23] The chronology does not fit neatly into other known events: Boniface by this time had been restored to good graces with the emperor, although, if he had been the one to invite Geiseric to Africa, it may have been too late to rescind the offer. Procopius, although speaking of raids sometime after the initial Vandal invasion of Africa, claims that Geiseric won over the allegiance of all "the Moors [Μαυρουσίων]."[24] What is known, is that the Vandals entered Africa largely unopposed, and they conquered the region in swift fashion.

Vandals, Catholics, and Donatists

The change of political affairs affected the Christians of North Africa. At this same time, two leading opponents of the Donatists died. Augustine died in 430 while the Vandals besieged Hippo. Likewise, in Carthage Aurelius died, and his successor Capreolus was prevented from attending the ecumenical Council of Ephesus (431) "on account of the Vandal attacks on the African regions."[25] His letter to the council was read aloud and entered into the records of the meeting.[26] He also wrote to the emperor Theodosius II to announce Augustine's death. A third letter by Capreolus is known wherein he wrote to two Iberian Christians, Vitalis and Constantius, to explain the errors of Nestorianism – a heresy that taught that the Word of God indwelled the person of Jesus as a distinct entity.

In 437 Capreolus was succeeded by Quodvultdeus.[27] Before becoming bishop, Quodvultdeus had been a deacon and an admirer of Augustine. As mentioned in Chapter 8, Quodvultdeus once wrote to the bishop of Hippo, requesting Augustine's teachings, which he poetically deemed "African bread isolated from any foreign flavors."[28] Quodvultdeus's imagery alludes to the fact that Africa had become the breadbasket of the Roman Empire. In response, Augustine devoted his work *On Heresies* to Quodvultdeus. The name "Quodvultdeus" means "What God Wills" in Latin, and is thus a "Latinized Punic theonym."[29]

Twelve of Quodvultdeus's sermons survive. Three sermons on the creed were delivered while he was still a priest, and they provide a glimpse into the lives of African Christians at this time.[30] His audience spoke Latin, but many would have come from the "Punic-speaking and Berber-speaking" population.[31] Furthermore, "their culture was largely Roman provincial. . . . Yet the cultural air they breathed was distinctively Punic, particularly in traditions and religion."[32] Echoing earlier African Christian writers and apologists, Quodvultdeus calls for his audience to reject Roman theatres and games. In replacement of Jupiter and Juno (= Baal and Tanit?), they should heed Christ and Mary.[33] It is tempting to see Tanit, the "Face of Baal," in the background of Quodvultdeus's explanation of how Moses saw God "face to face" (Exod. 33:11) and yet no one can see God's face and live (Exod. 33:23). Quodvultdeus immediately resolves this tension by turning to how God was revealed through a "woman" who remains a "virgin."[34] In addition to non-Christian temptations, Quodvultdeus is concerned in this sermon with the "Arians" and with "rebaptism."[35] The mention of rebaptism raises the question of the Donatists in this period, to which we will return on p. 269. For now, suffice it to say that Quodvultdeus has both the Vandals and the Donatists in mind.[36]

Two of the sermons attributed to Quodvultdeus are entitled *The Barbaric Age*, and they describe the judgment of God come on the world in the form of the Vandal invasion. After recalling the calamity, Quodvultdeus cries out as if his homeland is no longer recognizable, "Where is Africa, which has become a garden of pleasures for the whole world?"[37] This judgment, he believes, should fall especially on the heretics, namely the Pelagians and the Vandals.[38] After recalling several righteous examples from the Old Testament, Quodvultdeus contrasts them with his own time: "on the contrary, what evils have we not performed?"[39] Next he proceeds to say how "we" have human sacrifice, which seems to be a reference to the ancient Punic practice.[40] Despite this illicit past, his audience can also look to great examples, "the martyrs who have conquered the world," such as Perpetua and Felicity.[41] To conclude his sermon, the bishop echoes a common concern among African Christians about the "contagion" of heresy, only – unlike previous generations – it is the specific heresy of the Arians.[42]

Soon after becoming bishop, Quodvultdeus was exiled in 439, along with many other clergy.[43] One African source describes the event as "penal exile [*poenali exilio*],"[44] which Jonathan Conant concludes was "a pun on *poena*, 'punishment,' and *Poenus*, 'Carthaginian' or 'Punic.'"[45] While in exile Quodvultdeus wrote *The Book of Promises and Prophecies of God*, which traces God's work throughout history through select passages of scripture.[46] Therein, Quodvultdeus calculates the end of the world to be 510, and the current events are harbingers of the impending doom. He also recalls how "Caelestis" had always been worshipped in Carthage, and when the Romans arrived the emperor Marcus Aurelius dedicated a temple to this goddess, who had come to represent all the feminine deities.[47] Earlier, Apuleius had described Tanit in the same way,[48] and one can see in Quodvultdeus's description a clear reference to the ongoing worship of the Punic goddess. Quodvultdeus adds the interesting event where the earlier bishop of Carthage, Aurelius, had converted Tanit's temple to a Christian basilica. Thomas Finn notes how the Tanit-Caelestis cult's popularity can be seen in Quodvultdeus's need to replace this "virgin and ever fruitful mother" with both Mary and the church.[49]

In terms of the indigenous African population, even the Vandal bishop in Carthage seems to have been drawn from the Punic population.[50] At the same time, it should also be clarified that the "Catholic" party does not necessarily exclude indigenous African Christians. Those whom he lists as martyred by the Vandals includes Punic or indigenous names.[51]

After Quodvultdeus's exile and death (c.453) the Vandal king did not at first permit his replacement in Carthage. It was not until around 455 that the next bishop, Deogratias, finally filled this vacancy. Outside of Carthage, many other churches were also forbidden from having their own bishop.[52] Of course, these vacancies refer to times when the "Catholic" party did not have a bishop in Carthage. We know the Vandals appointed their own bishop, and there likely would have even been a continuing underground Donatist presence.

We have few records from this time, and those that survive are primarily from the "Catholic" perspective.[53] The main source for the Vandal period of North Africa is Victor of Vita, who wrote *A History of the Vandal Persecution*.[54] Little is known of Victor himself, but he speaks of the Carthaginians exiled by the Vandals around 482, and his work was probably written a few years later. Although he writes at this later date, he begins with the events from the initial Vandal incursion in the 430s. While scholars have acknowledged Victor's lack of objectivity, they have still relied on him for facts about this period and the Vandal "persecution." This reliance has recently been questioned because Victor was not only biased, but he also wrote decades after the initial Vandal invasion and at a time when the "persecution" had become much more intense. He too easily read the events and ethos from his time back into the 430s. Furthermore, Victor's account assumed something that historians now have called into question: the claim to being "persecuted."[55]

The Vandal conquest certainly included violence and plunder, but were these acts especially imposed against "Catholics" as a form of persecution for their faith? To answer this question, we must first account for the legal precedent for "persecution." Prior to the Vandal period, both Donatists and Caecilianists attempted to use political and sometimes physical force against their opponents. Whichever side successfully applied this force was labeled as a "persecutor," and those being "persecuted" could claim the moral high ground. Just when it seemed the Caecilianist party had permanently secured its position as the legitimate party, and not simply the temporary usurpers who persecuted the righteous remnant (as the Donatists claimed), the Vandals conquered North Africa and began "persecuting" the Caecilianists with the same legal tactics earlier used against the Donatists.[56]

In addition to this legal precedent, the Vandal "persecution" needs to be seen in light of the political landscape. The ongoing presence of the "Catholic" church, with its affinities with churches throughout the Roman Empire, posed a political threat to Vandal rule, and therefore the Vandal suppression of "Catholics" in Africa was driven by political concerns as much as doctrinal ones.[57] While this change in scholarly perspective in no way denies the actual physical force used against the Donatists by the Caecilianists, or against the "Catholics" by the Vandals, it does remove the bias involved in speaking about persecutors, and instead acknowledges how the various parties at this time used the same tactics to claim legitimacy.[58]

We cannot be sure how the Donatists viewed the Vandals.[59] As mentioned in Chapter 7, we know the Donatists continued into the Vandal era.[60] For example, an inscription on a church in Ala Miliaria (Benian, Algeria) is later than 434, and it mentioned the *traditores* – a hallmark Donatist concern.[61] Another possible source for the ongoing presence of Donatists in Africa comes from Alexandria. Writing probably after 431 "to the Bishops who are in Libya and Pentapolis" Cyril, the bishop and patriarch of Alexandria (r.412–444), addresses how to reconcile "lapsed" Christians.[62] Thus, "Libya" (which most likely only refers in this case to eastern Libya, near Egypt) is continuing to debate the problem of readmitting the lapsed, even after the end of the so-called Donatist controversy. The question arises as to how those Christians that later historians would label "Donatists" viewed their new rulers.

Often the question of the Donatists in the Vandal era is considered in terms of doctrine. The Vandals held to a form of "Arianism,"[63] in which the Son is less divine than the Father. These Vandal "heretics" allegedly persecuted the "Catholic" party for their Trinitarian teaching.[64] It is traditionally assumed that any remnants of Donatism united with the Caecilianists when faced with this common enemy. For example, the (Catholic?) bishop of Ala Miliaria – a town mentioned in the last paragraph for its evidence of ongoing Donatism – was exiled in 484 for not submitting to Arianism.[65] However, one surviving Donatist work gives a clue as to how (at least some) Donatists viewed the Vandals. In an anonymous work entitled the *Liber genealogus* ("The Genealogist Book") the number 666 from Revelation is explained as referring to the name "Geiseric [*Gensericus*]."[66] This reference, however, dating from 438, is not found in the later "Donatist" edition of the work, which dates from 455.[67] This change can only tell us so much, since we do not know how much such a revision represents a positive view of the Vandals. The author may have simply thought the remark ill-advised under the new reign. Alternatively, it may represent a shift among Donatists: instead of seeing the new invaders as a force of evil, the Vandals represent a valid authority in Africa. Also around this time, an African bishop named Asclepius wrote one book against the Arians and another against "the Donatists,"[68] which suggests the ongoing presence of both parties as enemies of Asclepius's "Catholic" party. In the late fifth century, a certain Nicasius was described as a Donatist who "came over" to the Vandal kings.[69] The distinctly Donatist presence was still known at the beginning of the sixth century, for some "Donatists [*Donatistarum*]" had arrived in Gaul from Africa wanting to be accepted into the church there.[70] Likewise, the debates of the early sixth century spoke of the Donatists in the present tense, as if they were still a distinct group in North Africa.[71]

In Chapter 7 the possible connections between the Donatists and Arianism were outlined for the early period of the Donatist controversy. With the arrival of the Vandal form of Arianism in Africa, another commonality needs to be discussed. The Vandals, like the Donatists, did not accept the validity of schismatic/heretical baptism, and so they – according to their opponents – required "rebaptism."[72] While this likely further solidified the difference between Vandal Christianity and the "Catholic" party in Africa, it likely also blurred the boundary between the Donatists and the Vandals both within Africa and from the perspective of those outside Africa. In past decades, some scholars claimed the Vandals conquered North Africa so quickly because they were aided by the Circumcellions, but this same school of thought labels the Circumcellions as an indigenous and/or proletariat group with Donatist religion as a mere facade.[73] More recently, Leslie Dossey shows evidence for conversions to Arianism among Africans ("*Africani*") – possibly Donatist Africans – an occurrence that continued much later than is usually acknowledged.[74] Likewise, Éric Fournier thinks that the Vandal practice of rebaptizing African Catholics was "an instance where Vandals were attempting to ground their policy in local tradition,"[75] that is, Donatist tradition. As an alternative to the assumption that Catholics and Donatists united against a common Arian enemy, Fournier thinks the Vandals and Donatists united against the common "Catholic" enemy. The evidence has most recently been reviewed by Robin Whelan, who concludes, "The Catholics and Donatists cannot straightforwardly be mapped onto the new parties, and many aspects of the new contest were different. Yet much can still be gained by keeping these earlier African ecclesiastical politics in mind."[76]

In sum, it must be admitted that the evidence for either theory (Donatist/Catholic alliance or Donatist/Arian alliance) is slight. This question requires more attention from scholars, and the question will likely be determined by deciding which theory makes the most sense of the evidence. Furthermore, we should not assume that all Donatists reacted to the Vandals in the same way. As mentioned in Chapter 7, the Donatist movement represents a wide diversity of individuals and groups, and so we cannot be certain how any given Donatist would have responded to new challenges, such as the Vandals' teachings. We can, however, see glimpses of resistance to Vandal Arianism in the sermons preached at this time, or at least the "Catholic" sermons of Victor's party. He reports how any reference to an evil ruler from the Old Testament, such as Pharaoh or Nebuchadnezzar, was taken as code for the Vandal king[77] – a practice that we can assume was not new to North African sermons, and that certainly continued after the Vandal period.[78]

This question of Donatist-Vandal relations illustrates how little we know from this period. Another example of the limits to our knowledge can be found when we look at women's roles in the church at this time. One mosaic discovered in Augustine's city of Hippo dates to is devoted to a certain "Guilia Runa."[79] This otherwise unknown Christian woman from the early Vandal period is called a "priestess [*presbyterissa*]."[80] It is tempting to conclude that this inscription reflects some sort of Vandal influence, but then again no other Vandal "priestesses" are known – for that matter, no other use of this term can be found in all Latin writings or inscriptions. J. Kevin Coyle, therefore, thinks the term belongs among the many other examples of African Christians (or at least Donatist Christians) who adopted "Ba'al-Saturnine formulae" from "Punic paganism."[81]

This example of a unique local expression raises another item to be considered: how did the local population view the Vandals? It is certain that the Vandals moved swiftly across North Africa and conquered the area with relatively little resistance. "Vandals cannot have formed more than five per cent of the total [population of Africa]."[82] How did the local populace view the new invaders? Some historians have suggested that the oppressed peoples of Africa, including the Donatists, welcomed the Vandals as liberators from Roman oppressors.[83] One could add to this discussion that Boniface, the count who allegedly invited the Vandals into Africa, was himself most likely of "African origin," since his name is "a translation of a Semitic (Punic) name."[84] Part of the difficulty with answering this question is that we cannot think of local Africans at this time (or any other) as monolithic. The wealthier and more Romanized citizens certainly bemoaned the Vandal presence, for they lost their lands and were driven into exile, or worse. Victor of Vita claimed the Mauretanians aided the Vandals against the "Catholics," and then later Procopius tells how the Mauretanians offered allegiance to both the Vandals and the Romans, but then sided with the winners.[85] Since this label of "Mauretanians" is itself generic, even Victor can report diverse views within such a group. Most of the times that Victor mentions the Mauretanians, it is to label them as barbarians who aided the Vandals. They took "Catholic" Christians as slaves from the Vandals. There is one instance where a large group of these exiled and enslaved Catholics converted an entire group of Mauretanian "pagans" from an inland region of Mauretania (= modern Béni Mansour, Algeria).[86] The Christians who converted this group then sent word to Rome, or at least a "Roman city," to request that clergy be sent to administer baptism.[87] So while the "Catholic" party in Africa does not exclude the indigenous population, it did see itself as aligned especially with Rome. Many "Catholics" fled Africa during the Vandal period and went to Rome and other western provinces across the Mediterranean. Alternatively, despite the harsh persecution, some "Catholics" stayed in Africa.[88] As with previous eras, the "Africans" of this time could range in how they identified themselves. Many continued in a very Romanized form of life, while still retaining distinctly African identities and perhaps even embracing the new Vandal rule.[89]

Vandal expansion of power

The eastern emperor, Theodosius II, in Constantinople and the western emperor, Valentinian III, were both powerless to stop the Vandals in Africa (like other groups in the western provinces), and in 435, Trigetius, Rome's representative in Africa, signed a treaty with the Vandal king, granting him control of Numidia.[90] The treaty did not, however, last long, and by 439 Carthage had fallen to Geiseric.[91] In the chronicles written by Roman writers from this era, the fall of Carthage represented an epic event:

> It is almost as if the reader is being shown Hannibal's Carthage resurrected: first the city is given back its walls and then, less than twenty years later, *Carthage* throws off Roman rule. . . . Indeed, if we look back over earlier entries devoted to the country, the theme of African restiveness seems to run through the majority.[92]

Next, the Vandals – with the help of Carthaginian ships, we must assume – raided the northern Mediterranean coastline and took control of Sicily. Because the Roman Empire was detained fighting Huns and Persians, it could not stop Geiseric. Therefore, another treaty was reached in 442, granting the Vandal king control of Africa Proconsularis, Byzacena, Numdia, and Tripolitania. After further complications in the relations between the emperor and the various *foederati*, or allies, Geiseric took advantage and raided the northern Mediterranean, even sacking the city of Rome itself in 455. Sidonius described these events in terms of a new "Punic war."[93] Such a description likely says more about Sidonius's rhetorical skill than the actual ethnicity of the Vandal raiders, and yet the ability of the Vandals to navigate the seas must have been due to the Punic population of Africa.[94] In fact, some Vandal coins used Punic imagery, which may have been meant to "evoke the idea of a new Carthaginian empire."[95] The booty from this raid made Geiseric extremely wealthy and he retreated to Carthage, where he and his heirs reigned unmolested for many years thereafter.

While the early Vandal period is now understood more in terms of conquest than persecution, the later phase of Vandal rule included an intentional shift to a policy of targeting "heretics." The Vandals, as mentioned
on p. 269, saw themselves as carrying out the laws against the heretics set by
their Roman predecessors. Like the Roman governors from Augustine's era,
the new Vandal king Huneric, Geiseric's son and heir, began persecuting
Manicheans when he took the throne in 477.[96] At the request of the eastern emperor Zeno and the western empress-regent Placidia, Huneric also
allowed the Catholic/Nicene party to appoint its own bishop, for another
lengthy vacancy had occurred when Deogratias died (c.457). In 481 Eugenius was elected bishop of Carthage. From his name and because Zeno himself had sent emissaries to Carthage for this election, it could be deduced
that Eugenius was himself from the Greek east and so represents a foreign
form of Christianity in Africa.[97]

In 484 Huneric summoned "bishops from the whole of Africa"[98] to
Carthage for a council that repeated the pattern of the Donatist and Caecilianist conference of 411. Although Victor failed to record the number
who responded, one document from this trial lists 466 "Catholic" bishops.[99]
This time, the Vandal Arians and the African "Catholics" met to determine
which party represented the true church. The answer was predetermined
by the Vandal king, who denounced the "Homousians" (as the Vandals
called the "Catholics" because of their support for the Nicene creed, which
defined the Son as of the "same-substance [*homoousios*]" with the Father).[100]
Eugenius of Carthage accused the Vandals of being a church found "in the
African provinces alone," an accusation made against the Donatists in
Augustine's time.[101] Eugenius asked Huneric to summon bishops from all
over the world, "in particular the Roman church, which is the head of all
the churches"[102] – a statement that adds to the impression of the "Catholic"
party in Africa as one which identifies itself particularly with Rome.

The conference of 484, furthermore, was not only predetermined in
its outcome, but it was also a ruse: while the pro-Nicene bishops were in
Carthage, Huneric had already sent out notice that their basilicas and church
property were to be handed over to the Vandals.[103] According to the Vandal
king, however, this decision came after the "homousians" refused to cooperate at the council.[104] After this conference, all "Catholics" were forced to
be "rebaptized."[105] Further actions were taken to ensure a "unity" between
the homoean/Arian party and the homousian/Nicene party, just as the edicts
of unity in Augustine's time had done between the Caecilianists and the
Donatists.[106] Despite this official policy, the persecution at this time mostly
focused on the area around Carthage.[107] Even with this limited scope, the
Vandals handed 4,966 Nicene/Catholics to "the Moors," who took them to
the desert.[108]

Huneric not only targeted Nicene/Catholics, but he also distrusted other
Vandals. Out of fear that other claimants to Geiseric's throne might challenge him, Huneric killed several members of the royal family. At this time

he even had a Vandal patriarch, Jucundus, burned, because he was seen as subversive.[109] It is possible that Jucundus's native identity is detectable in two ways. His name, while not exclusive to North Africa, was one associated with previous African martyrs and may have even had a Punic background.[110] Moreover, when Victor first mentions Jucundus, he counsels Geiseric not to kill one of the Nicene/Catholics because "the Romans will begin to preach that he is a martyr."[111] Whether he was Vandal or a native African (or both), Jucundus certainly considered the "Romans" as outsiders. Of course, the same can be said of "Catholics" like Victor: after listing many Latin writers, he specifies the last in this prestigious list as "our Augustine [*noster . . . Augustinus*],"[112] and he next insists that the "barbarians" (i.e. the Vandals) are known by their envy of "the Romans."[113] Therefore, like Jucundus, Victor may consider himself non-Roman, but the difference is that Jucundus sees the Romans as enemies while Victor sees them as allies. This can be seen in the way that Victor alludes to a scene from Virgil's *Aeneid*. Unlike previous African writers who portrayed Aeneas negatively, Victor likened the Vandals who persecuted the "Catholics" to Mezentius, who persecuted Aeneas.[114] Aeneas (the founder of Rome) and Victor's party (associated with Rome) both are the righteous ones under persecution.

A similar view can be found in the writings of Dracontius. Blossus Emilius Dracontius served as a jurist under the proconsul of Carthage during the late fifth century. He wrote in praise of a foreign ruler (either the emperor Zeno or a rival Vandal ruler), and so he was imprisoned. He later wrote *Satisfaction*,[115] wherein he pleaded guilty to the new Vandal king, Gunthamund (so dated between 484–496). He also wrote *On the Praises of God*,[116] which explains the grace of God in the created world (book one)[117] and God's ongoing acts of grace after the fall (book two). Dracontius then proceeds (book three) to encourage the reader to accept God's grace through the use of both biblical and non-Christian examples of virtue. These non-Christian examples are especially from Roman history. More use of these examples can be found in his *Romulea*, which are short poems on various mythic figures, especially Roman mythic figures.[118]

How many other Africans shared Victor's and Dracontius's view of Roman history cannot be known with the scarcity of sources from this time. We know of one Mauretanian named Masuna, who went by the title, "King of the Mauretanians and the Romans,"[119] which would have been a title given in direct opposition to the Vandal claim, the kings of "the Vandals and the Alans." As was seen in the earlier Roman period of North Africa, the indigenous identity of someone like a Mauretanian was not mutually exclusive with a Roman identity.[120] One especially memorable case comes in the person of Pope Gelasius, who reigned at this time (492–496). One source reports that Gelasius was "by nationality an African [*natione Afer*],"[121] and yet the pope can describe himself as "Roman born [*Romanus natus*]."[122] Apparently, as we have seen so often throughout this book, one's local identity (African) need not be antithetical to a larger imperial identity (Roman).[123]

After Huneric's death in 484, his son, Gunthamund, was more tolerant of Nicene Christianity. At this time some Catholics who had been "rebaptized" by the Vandals asked to be readmitted into the Catholic church. In 487 a special conference was held in Rome under Pope Felix I at which four African bishops attended. The council decided that "lapsed" Christians would be readmitted to the faith, despite some in Carthage who protested.[124]

Gunthamund's tolerance was short lived, for upon his death in 496 he was succeeded by Thrasamund, his younger brother. Thrasamund once again persecuted Catholic Christians while simultaneously offering economic incentives to Catholics who converted.[125] During this time, Pope Symmachus (r.498–514) was remembered for giving alms to the exiles coming from Africa.[126] The bishop of Carthage, Eugenius, was exiled in 496, and the "Catholic" see of Carthage would not have a bishop again until 523 when Bonifacius was elected.[127]

One bishop exiled by Thrasamund at this time (c.502) was Fulgentius of Ruspe.[128] The details about Fulgentius come from Ferrandus, *Life of Fulgentius*, written to commemorate the man who meant so much to "the peoples of Africa."[129] Fulgentius came from a Carthaginian senatorial family, whose property had been seized by the Vandals. Fulgentius's parents moved to Thelepte in Byzacena (= modern Medinet-el-Kedima, Tunisia), and his mother insisted that he be given a proper education since he had to "survive among the Africans."[130] Fulgentius, apparently, belonged to a very Romanized family who identified themselves as distinctly non-African.[131]

When "a horde of barbarians"[132] raided Byzacena, Fulgentius and his monastic community fled the region, only to encounter an "Arian" priest named Felix, who was also "by race a barbarian."[133] This Felix, it seems, did not belong to the same "barbarians" who raided Byzacena, for they were identified by Ferrandus as Mauretanians.[134] Felix had Fulgentius beaten and sent away. In response, Fulgentius planned to leave Africa and join a monastic community in Egypt, until he learned that he would be unwelcome due to another schism taking place there.[135] Fulgentius, therefore, returned to his monastery in Africa, and he soon became the bishop of Ruspe, a town on the coast of Byzacena.[136] The appointment of Catholic bishops, however, had been forbidden by Thrasamund, and so Fulgentius was exiled and his see was left vacant. He was sent to Sardinia along with all the Catholic bishops of Africa, which according to one source numbered just over sixty at this time.[137]

Around 515, Thrasamund summoned Fulgentius back to Carthage for a debate, which according to Ferrandus, Fulgentius won decisively.[138] Thrasamund then sent Fulgentius back to Sardinia, but when Thrasamund died in 523, his successor, Hilderic, allowed Fulgentius to return. Fulgentius wrote many works, mostly dealing with doctrinal concerns, such as Arianism and Pelagianism.[139] In his surviving eight sermons Fulgentius practiced the common style known as *sermo humilis*, because most of his audience would have spoken Latin only as a second language to their native Punic.[140]

Moreover, despite his identity being connected especially to Roman aristocracy, Fulgentius writes explicitly within the African Catholic tradition: he defends Augustinian thinking throughout his works, and at times cites African writers such as Cyprian and Optatus of Milevis by name.[141] Because of his literary skills and theological acumen, Fulgentius served as a leading spokesperson of the Catholic party in North Africa, until he died in 533 from an illness.

Thrasamund represents the last Vandal who subjugated the Nicenes, and his efforts abated late in his reign. Hilderic succeeded Thrasamund as king in 523, and he permitted Fulgentius and all the "Catholics" to return from exile. They appointed their own bishop of Carthage, an office vacant since Eugenius's death in 505, and then convened a council to re-establish the structure and organization of the Catholic hierarchy in Africa.[142]

The end of the Vandal kingdom

In the early sixth century, the Vandal opposition to "Catholic" Christianity was waning, along with Vandal control of Africa. Instead of a significant external threat, the Vandal kingdom experienced problems from within Africa. Mauretanian groups began to take control of areas to the west. Geiseric's fourth successor, Hilderic, was unpopular among his own people: his cousin, Gelimer, arrested him and ruled in his place. One of the reasons Hilderic had become unpopular was his close ties to the Byzantine emperor, and in response to Gelimer's usurpation Justinian led his Byzantine armies to reconquer Africa in 534.

Some glimpses of the late Vandal period can be seen in the poems known as the *Anthologia Latina*, which were written in Africa and collected around 532.[143] As opposed to Victor's depiction of devastation and destruction, these poems portray the ongoing luxuries of the period, such as the baths, circuses, and plush villas. Although modern commentators will criticize the skill of these writings, many poets in the collection praise the Roman literary tradition and see themselves as carrying on the Latin poetic legacy. Even so, these poets could still identify "Romans and Tyrians [i.e. Punics]" in their audience, as if they were two distinct groups.[144] When mocking an old woman, one poem invokes uniquely African imagery: after mocking her skin as like an "elephant," the speaker tells her, "an aged ape gave birth to you in Africa when the world was young."[145] Another poem in this collection addresses a man from the Arzyges.[146] "The point of the designation here is to show that the would-be poet is a native African, and therefore to be regarded as unromanised"; this attitude furthermore represents "localized xenophobia" common in the collection.[147] For example, a man named "Aegyptius" serves as the target of another poem, which focuses on his "blackness," for his "name which you can read befits an Ethiopian."[148] Despite the name and the claim that it belongs to an Ethiopian, the poem clearly refers to a Garamantean.[149] Many poets in this collection offer what

John N. Stark, Jr. called "a form of racial profiling and racist thinking expressed through skin colour prejudices against blacks."[150] In our present discussion, we have attempted to replace "race" and even "ethnicity" with the concept of identity, but Stark's point is correct in that many of the poems in this collection identify the local population along the lines of physical appearance. The trope against "black help" in a poem against the mythical king Memnon may offer us a clue about this theme.[151] Memnon of Ethiopia had aided Priam in the Trojan war but then died fighting Achilles. This poem's allusion to that scene may be a warning against Romans forming an allegiance with the Garamanteans.[152] The reason such a reading seems likely is that the poems, more than simply presenting a depiction of ethnic boundaries, present the characters as divided along political and social lines.

The social descriptions in these poems include the division between Romans and Africans. The poet refers to the "Punic realm" of "the Tyrians" which has been conquered by the twins of Ilia (i.e. Romulus and Remus).[153] Furthermore, Romulus is praised for murdering his brother, since it resulted in the founding of Rome.[154] Likewise, another poem praises Troy: "deservedly does your posthumous daughter [i.e. Rome] rule."[155] One poem, alternatively, insults the Vandal government officials for their abuse of propertied citizens.[156] These sentiments suggest that at least some Roman Africans viewed themselves as conquerors of the indigenous Africans, albeit a conquest now interrupted by the Vandal kings. This Roman group surely welcomed the fall of the Vandal line.

The end of the Vandal era occurred suddenly. In retrospect, historians today find little to no record of the Vandal presence in North Africa. The literary records indicate that the Vandals took over basilicas rather than built their own. Some archaeological remains confirm this, such as when funeral inscriptions are devoted to individuals with Germanic names.[157] These names occurred next to traditional Roman and even Punic names, which illustrates how the Vandals successfully embedded themselves within the Romano-African society. The longer the Vandals ruled in Africa, the more we can assume they became indistinguishable from the local population.[158] By the 480s, Victor could say "their number is small and feeble."[159]

Even given this evidence for Vandal acculturation, the Vandals may have still been easily distinguished as an ethnic group in North Africa: one report tells how the Vandals continued to wear a distinct style of dress and looked different from the locals.[160] This once again raises the question of how the indigenous Africans viewed the Vandals.[161] We have mentioned the numerous times that Mauretanians are named by Victor as allied with the Vandals. Victor's terminology is not precise as "the Mauretanians" includes a wide array of African people groups.[162] Victor also reports a curious vision of a Christian in his party who saw the Faustus Basilica (used as the Catholic cathedral at this time) being threatened by "Ethiopians."[163] Victor also expresses the hope felt among his party when someone had a vision of a tree rising large enough to "cover almost all Africa with its shade."[164] This hope, however, was false, because the vision concludes with this tree being knocked down by a donkey.

As a minority ruling class, the Vandal defeat by the Byzantine rule meant that they were easily replaced. Vandal African society in many ways was in continuity with the previous Roman era. Likewise, when the eastern emperor re-established control over Africa, Byzantine Africa kept much intact from previous eras. One of the most distinct differences between the two was the religious shift of the rulers. The larger population, unfortunately, remains mostly hidden to the historian. There are, nevertheless, a few glimpses of this population's religious identity. Victor reports that the basilicas devoted to the Scillitans, Perpetua and Felicity, and Cyprian continued to be popular at this time. The Vandals in fact commandeered these basilicas for themselves (as they did with all basilicas within the city of Carthage).[165] These same holy sites would be reclaimed and remodeled by the Byzantine rulers when they reconquered North Africa from the Vandals.[166] Curiously, one source from this time claims the "bishops of Africa" wrote to Pope Boniface II (r.530–532), submitting themselves to the Roman see.[167]

In sum, the Vandal presence in North Africa added additional complexity to the landscape. Our categories of Roman and African, Caecilianist and Donatist, Orthodox and heretical, do not sufficiently explain how individuals and groups identified and aligned themselves. This complex array of social and doctrinal possibilities continues into the Byzantine reconquest of North Africa, to which we can now turn.

Notes

1 The eastern capital was by then in Constantinople, but still self-styled "Roman." The same is true of the western capital at the time in Ravenna, which governed Africa.

2 As argued by A. H. Merrills, "Introduction: Vandals, Romans and Berbers: Understanding Late Antique North Africa," in *Vandals, Romans and Berbers: New Perspectives on Late Antique North Africa*, ed. A. H. Merrills (Aldershot, UK: Ashgate, 2004), 7. Other important studies include articles in *L'antiquité tardive* 10–11 (2002–2003); and other essays in Merrills, *Vandals, Romans, and Berbers*.

3 For more extensive discussion, see Serge Lancel and Paul Mattei, *Pax et Concordia: chrétiens des premiers siècles en Algérie (IIIe-VIIe siècles)* (Paris: Marsa, 2003), 99–115.

4 The numbers are originally reported by Victor of Vita, *History of the Vandal Persecution* 1.2; and Procopius, *History of the Wars* 3.5.18–19. For discussion of the primary texts and their meaning, see Walter Goffart, *Barbarians and Romans, A.D. 418–584: The Techniques of Accommodation* (Princeton, NJ: Princeton University Press, 1980), 231–234. See estimates and details in Peter Heather, *The Fall of the Roman Empire: A New History of Rome and the Barbarians* (Oxford: Oxford University Press, 2006), 267–272; and Andreas Schwarzc, "The Settlement of the Vandals in North Africa," in *Vandals, Romans and Berbers: New Perspectives on Late Antique North Africa*, ed. A. H. Merrills (Aldershot, UK: Ashgate, 2004), 50–51.

5 *Life of Augustine* 28; and cf. Quodvultdeus, *The Barbaric Age* 2. Regarding this last source, Thomas Macy Finn, *Quodvultdeus of Carthage: The Creedal Homilies. Conversion in Fifth-Century North Africa* (ACW 60; New York: The Newman Press, 2004), 3, comments, "Echoing in Quodvultdeus' homilies, especially in *De tempore barbarico* 1 and in the ears of his audience, were those ancient words of the first Cato: *Delenda est Carthago* [Carthage must be destroyed]" (cf. chapters one and two in this volume for Cato's words).

6 *Life* 29. Also, Éric Fournier, *Victor of Vita and the Vandal "Persecution": Interpreting Exile in Late Antiquity* (PhD dissertation for the University of California, Santa Barbara, 2008), 136–137; and Fournier, "Rebaptism as a Ritual of Cultural Integration in Vandal Africa," in *Shifting Cultural Frontiers in Late Antiquity*, ed. David Brakke, Deborah Deliyannis, and Edward Watts (Burlington, VT: Ashgate, 2012), 243–254, has demonstrated that Possidius is dependent on Augustine (*Letter* 228.5), who spoke in general terms of what the Vandals could do. Possidius and others after him take Augustine's description as actual occurrences. If one were to accept Possidius at face value (cf. Victor, *History of the Vandal Persecution* 3.67, who claims Africa lost "all" true churches), then his statement would have to imply that only three "Catholic" (i.e. Caecilianist) churches survive, while the rest of the Christians known in later sources would have been Donatist and/or Vandal. Perhaps by coincidence, this situation appears to be the case in the time of Pope Gregory VII (r.1073–1085). In his surviving letters (see especially *Letters* 3.19, 3.20, and 3.21), he reports how Africa no longer has the necessary minimum of three bishops to consecrate a new bishop (discussed on p. 333 in chapter eleven). By that time, Cirta had been destroyed by the Arab conquest, and so Gregory writes only to Hippo and Carthage. However, Gregory knows of other Christians in Africa, but these refuse communion with the Christians (of his party?) in Carthage.

7 See Hydatius, *Chronicle* 110 (439 CE). On the conversions to Vandal Christianity, see Danuta Shanzer, "Intentions and Audiences: History, Hagiography, Martyrdom, and Confession in Victor of Vita's *Historia Persecutionis*," in *Vandals, Romans and Berbers: New Perspectives on Late Antique North Africa*, ed. A. H. Merrills (Aldershot, UK: Ashgate, 2004), 285–290.

8 E.g. Celestiacus, one of the *curiales* of Carthage, befriended by Theodoret of Cyrrhus. For primary sources and discussion, see Pauline Allen and Bronwen Neil, *Crisis Management in Late Antiquity (410–590 CE): A Survey of the Evidence from Episcopal Letters* (Supplements to Vigiliae Christianae 121; Leiden: Brill, 2013), 61–66.

9 See Hydatius, *Chronicle* 110 (439 CE). The archaeological remains indicate that the Catholics built or were given their own basilicas. Sometimes, as in Sufetula, the Vandal, Catholic, and Donatist basilicas stood next to each other; see MacKendrick, *The North African Stones Speak*, 104–107.

10 Text in G. Lagarrigue, SC 176, 220 (1971, 1975); trans. Jeremiah H. O'Sullivan, *The Writings of Salvian, the Presbyter (FC* 173; Washington, Catholic University of America Press [orig. 1947] 2008). Salvian began writing this work in 439 when Carthage fell, just as Augustine had written *The City of God* in response to the sacking of Rome.

11 *On the Government of God* 5.5.

12 *On the Government of God* 6.68. See discussion of this passage in Susanna Elm, "New Romans: Salvian of Marseilles *On the Governance of God*," *Journal of Early Christian Study* 25 (1 2017), 1–28.

13 *On the Government of God* 6.12: *insaniebat in circis, luxuriabat in theatris.* Curiously, he elsewhere credits the Carthaginian church as founded by the apostles (cf. *On the Government of God* 7.68–69 and 7.79).

14 *On the Government of God* 7.16.65–66: *quis nescit Africam totam obscenis libidinum taedis semper arsisse, non ut terram ac sedem hominum? . . . quis non omnes omnino Afros generaliter impudicos sciat nisi ad deum forte conversos, id est fide ac religione mutatos? . . . Tam infrequens enim est hoc et inusitatum, impudicum non esse Afrum, quam nouum et inauditum Afrum non esse Afrum.*

15 *On the Government of God* 7.16.67: *in Africano . . . quasi Romam.*

16 *On the Government of God* 7.17.77: *Romanis, quos quidem Afri, quia nequaquam olim vincere imperio ac sublimitate valuerunt . . . impuritate vicerunt. quod dicimus nos fuisse Afros . . . dominos eorum esse Romanos.*

17 *On the Government of God* 8.2.9: *Caelestem illam . . . Afrorum daemonem.* O'Sullivan comments (n.6), "This is the Goddess Tanit." Salvian also knows of Carthage's Punic heritage as the heir to Tyre, and so he reads the prophecy against the king of Tyre (Ezek. 28) as directed against Carthage (see *On the Government of God* 7.58–61; and discussion in Elm, "New Romans."

18 *On the Government of God* 8.4.19: *in monachis . . . Afrorum probatur odium.*

19 *On the Government of God* 8.4–5.

20 *On the Government of God* 7.18–23.

21 *The Decline and Fall of the Roman Empire*, 3:381.

22 For sources and discussion, see Guy Halsall, *Barbarian Migrations and the Roman West, 376–568* (Cambridge: Cambridge University Press, 2007), 240–241.

23 However, Jeroen W. P. Wijnendaele, *The Last of the Romans: Bonifatius— Warlord and Comes Africae* (London: Bloomsbury, 2015), 75, finds the story about Boniface plausible.

24 *History of the Wars* 3.4.22.

25 Liberatus of Carthage, *A Short Report on the Nestorian and Eutychian Controversies* 4.18: *propter impetus Vandalorum Africanas regiones* (ACO 2.5:103; my trans.).

26 For his letters, see PL 53; cf. ACO 1.1.2:61.

27 For details about Quodvultdeus and especially for bibliography on his authorship of some works, see van Slyke, *Quodvultdeus of Carthage*. It is worth noting that in his review of van Slyke in the *Journal of Ecclesiastical Studies*, Frend faulted van Slyke for not sufficiently accounting for "the prime cause of the collapse of Roman Africa and the Catholic Church [in Africa], the uprising of sections of the native population and slave revolts recorded by Quodvultdeus himself in his sermon *De tempore barbarico.*"

28 Augustine, *Letter* 223.3: *sequestratis saporibus peregrinis . . . panem Afrum* (my trans.); cf. *Letter* 221, and Victor, *History of the Vandal Persecution* 1.19–21.

29 Finn, *Quodvultdeus of Carthage*, 2.

30 See Burns, Jensen, et al., *Christianity in Roman Africa*, 68.

31 Finn, *Quodvultdeus of Carthage*, 9, who follows Lancel, *Carthage*, 436–438.

32 Finn, *Quodvultdeus of Carthage*, 9.

33 *First Homily on the Creed* 2.1–13.

34 *Third Homily on the Creed*, 3.13. Similarly, the theme "the face of the Lord [*facies domini*]" is a trope in *On the Barbaric Age II*, 2, only this time with no reference to Mary.

35 E.g. *First Homily on the Creed* 12.7–8.

36 Finn, *Quodvultdeus of Carthage*, 111 n.84.

37 *On the Barbaric Age II*, 5: *ubi est africa, quae toto mundo fuit velut hortus deliciarum?* (my trans.)

38 *On the Barbaric Age I*, 3.

39 *On the Barbaric Age I*, 4: *contrario quae mala non fecimus?* (my trans.)

40 Cf. *On the Barbaric Age II*, 3.

41 *On the Barbaric Age I*, 5: *Vicerunt martyres mundum* (my trans.); and *On the Barbaric Age II*, 12.

42 *On the Barbaric Age I*, 10: *pestem* (my trans.)

43 Victor, *History of the Vandal Persecution* 1.15; Quodvultdeus, *Temp.* 11–12.

44 Victor, *History of the Vandal Persecution* 1.16.

45 *Staying Roman*, 67 n.1.

46 Text in Réné Braun, CCL 60 (1976). This text was (mis-)attributed to Prosper of Aquitane, and not all scholars accept Quodvultdeus as author; see bibliography in Michael P. McHugh, "Quodvultdeus," *Augustine through the Ages: An Encyclopedia*, ed. Allan D. Fitzgerald, et al. (Grand Rapids, MI: Eerdmans, 1999), 693–694.

47 *The Book of Promises and Prophecies of God* 3.38.

48 *Metamorphosis* 11.5.

49 Finn, *Quodvultdeus of Carthage*, 15.

50 For Jucundus, see Victor, *History of the Vandal Persecution* 1.19; 2.13; for the name Jocundus as Punic, see Heffernan, *The Passion of Perpetua and Felicity*, 54–55; cf. *Passion of Perpetua* 11.9.

51 E.g. Saturianus (1.30), Felix (1.46), Mascula (1.47), Saturus (1.48), and Laetus (2.52; cf. Lindley Richard Dean, *A Study of the Cognomina of Soldiers in the Roman Legions* [PhD dissertation for Princeton University, 1916], 114; cf. Gruen, *Rethinking the Other in Antiquity*, 137).

52 Victor, *History of the Vandal Persecution* 1.23.

53 The thirteen surviving literary references and the seven surviving inscriptions are conveniently listed in Gaumer, *"Ad Africa vistare sepulchrum sancti Cypriani,"* (forthcoming). Also, see the recent review of the evidence in Jonathan Conant, "Donatism in the Fifth and Sixth Centuries," in *The Donatist Schism: Controversy and Contexts*, ed. Richard Miles (Liverpool: Liverpool University Press, 2016), 345–361. Cf. the *Carthaginian Computus of 455*, which attempts to calculate Easter in comparison to the Jewish calendar, and which mentions "King Geiseric [*regis Geiserici*]" (PL 59:145A) and so must be of African origin; this text gives no indication of its theological affinities (see further details in Alden A. Mosshammer, *The Easter Computus and the Origins of the Christian Era* [Oxford: Oxford University Press, 2008], 217–219).

54 Text in Serge Lancel, *Victor de Vita: Histoire de la persecution vandale en Afrique* (Paris: les Belles Lettres, 2002); translation in John Moorehead, *Victor of Vita: History of the Vandal Persecution* (Translated Texts for Historians 10; Liverpool: Liverpool University Press, 1992).

55 Fournier, *Victor of Vita*, 119–163, reconstructs this period of Vandal history without using Victor, and finds that other sources such as Hydatius are more nuanced and do not simply identify the Vandals as persecutors. More recently, Fournier, "The Vandal Conquest of North Africa: Origins of a Historiographical Persona," *Journal of Ecclesiastical History* (forthcoming), has traced the descriptions of Augustine to the later fifth century writers dependent on him; these later writers use Augustine's description as a way to characterize all Vandal actions as "persecution" of "Catholic" Christians.

56 A large portion of the persecution involved the seizing of property, much like the Caecilianist/Catholic tactic against the Donatists (see chapter seven). For further details, see Modéran, *Les Vandales et l'Empire romain*, ed. Michel-Yves Perrin (Arles: Éditions Errance, 2014), 167–180.

57 Jonathan K. Parsons, *The African Catholic Church Under the Vandals, 429–533* (PhD thesis for the University of London, 1994).

58 See this idea more fully treated in Fournier, *Victor of Vita*.

59 For an introduction to the sources and debates, see Robin Whelan, "African Controversy: The Inheritance of the Donatist Schism in Vandal Africa," *Journal of Ecclesiastical History* 65 (3, 2014), 504–521.

60 Despite Quodvultdeus's claim that the Donatists (and the Manichaeans) were already defeated; see *On the Flood* 5 (= Homily 7; CCL 60:415). Quodvultdeus

does not mention the Donatists elsewhere, even when listing contemporary heresies; e.g. *Against Five Heresies* 1 (= *Homily 10*) and *The Book of Promises and Prophecies of God* 2.6; discussed in Adamiak, "When did Donatist Christianity End?", 216–217.

61 See details in Adamiak, "When did Donatist Christianity End?", 213.

62 *Letter* 79 (see translation in John I. McEnerney, *St Cyril of Alexandria: Letters 51–110* ([Washington, DC: Catholic University of America Press, [orig. 1987] 2007]).

63 As with the discussion of "Donatism" (and its alleged links with "Arianism") in chapter seven, the improper label "Arianism" will be used here for the sake of convenience. The Vandal form of subordinationism had little to no connection with Arius, the presbyter from Alexandria. For a summary of the issues involved in this label, see Christoph Markschies, "The Religion of the Late Antiquity Vandals: Arianism or Catholicism?" trans. Karl-Axel Hansson, in *The True Story of the Vandals*, ed. Pontus Hultén, et al. (Varnamo: Museum Vandalorum, 2001), 87–97.

64 For the early attack on churches, see Possidius, *Life of Augustine* 28; Victor of Vita 1.4–9, 15–16, 41–42, 51; and Hydatius, *Chronicle* 110 (439 CE).

65 For details of this bishop, named Mensius, see Courtois, *Les Vandales et L'Afrique*, 92.

66 *Liber genealogus* 616 and 618; see Conant, *Staying Roman*, 171, for details.

67 See discussion in Tilley, *The Bible in Christian North Africa*, 153.

68 Gennadius, *On Illustrious Men* 74. He was also "famous for his extemporaneous teaching."

69 Victor, *History of the Vandal Persecution* 3.71. Even if the majority of scholars are correct to say that this passage was not original to Victor, the fact that someone added this statement about a Donatist is still an indication that Donatists (or at least one) supported the Vandals.

70 Avitus of Vienne, *Letter* 24 (*PL* 59:240).

71 See Robert B. Eno, *Fulgentius: Selected Works* (FC 95; 1997), 389 and 407, for the debate between Fastidiosus and Fulgentius.

72 Cf. Augustine, *Letter* 185.1.1.

73 See bibliography and criticisms in Merrils and Miles, *The Vandals*, 20–26.

74 "The Last Days of Vandal Africa: An Arian Commentary on Job and its Historical Context," *Journal of Theological Studies* n.s. 54 (2003), 60–138, esp. 111–112.

75 *Victor of Vita*, 121.

76 "Arianism in Africa," in *Arianism: Roman Heresy and Barbarian Creed*, ed. Guido M. Berndt and Roland Steinacher (London: Routledge, 2016), 250–251.

77 Victor, *History of the Vandal Persecution* 1.22.

78 See examples in Thomas S. Ferguson, *Visita nos: Reception, Rhetoric, and Prayer in a North African Monastery* (New York: Peter Lang, 1999), 15; and see Dossey, "Last Days of Vandal Africa" (cited above in n.74).

79 AE (1953), 107.

80 For a photo and brief introduction, see Kevin Madigan and Carolyn Osiek, *Ordained Women in the Early Church: A Documentary History* (Baltimore, MD: Johns Hopkins University Press, 2005), 197.

81 "The Self-Identity of North African Christians," 67.

82 Raven, *Rome in Africa*, 198.

83 See bibliography in Stanslaw Adamiak, "When did Donatist Christianity End?" in *The Uniquely African Controversy: Studies on Donatist Christianity*, ed. Anthony Dupont, Matthew Gaumer, and M. Lamberigts (Leuven: Peeters, 2014), 214 n.9. Alternatively, Modéran, *Les Vandales*, 101–115, argues that the Roman army in Africa had been steadily depleted up to the time of the Vandal invasion.

84 Wijnendaele, *The Last of the Romans*, 30.
85 *History of the Wars* 3.25.
86 Victor, *History of the Vandal Persecution* 1.35–38.
87 Victor, *History of the Vandal Persecution* 1.37: *civitas Romana*. Moorhead's translation strikes me as forced.
88 In addition to Victor's record, there were four African bishops in attendance at the Council of Chalcedon (451); see Burns, Jensen, et al., *Christianity in Roman Africa*, 58. For the poets in the *Anthologia Latina* (which will be discussed on pp. 276–277) as "spokesmen for the concerns of the Romano-African lay elite," see Richard Miles, "The *Anthologia Latina* and the Creation of a Secular Space in Vandal Carthage," *Antiquite Tardive: revue internationale d'histoire et d'archeologie* 13 (2005), 305–320.
89 See Conant, *Staying Roman*, 186–195.
90 Procopius, *History of the Wars* 3.4.13–15.
91 See details in Procopius, *History of the Wars* 3.4.15; and Hydatius, *Chronicle* 107 (439 CE).
92 Steven Muhlberger, *The Fifth-Century Chroniclers: Prosper, Hydatius, and the Gallic Chronicler of 452* (Leeds: Francis Cairns Ltd., 1990), 178. See further discussion of this theme in Miles, "Rivaling Rome," 123–146.
93 According to Merrills and Miles, *The Vandals*, 118.
94 Raven, *Rome in Africa*, 199.
95 A. D. Lee, *From Rome to Byzantium AD 363 to 565: The Transformation of Ancient Rome* (Edinburgh: Edinburgh University Press, 2013), 185; cf. Merrills and Miles, *Vandals*, 73.
96 Victor, *History of the Vandal Persecution* 2.1.
97 Christian Courtois, *Victor de Vita et son oeuvre* (Algiers: Imprimerie Officielle du gouvernement général de l'Algérie, 1954), 21–22.
98 Victor, *History of the Vandal Persecution* 2.52.
99 On the one document from this trial which lists 466 Homoousian/Catholic bishops (the *Notitia provinciarum et civitatum Africae*), see Courtois, *Victor de Vita*, 91–100, who finds its numbering unreliable. For the text, see CSEL 7:117–134; and Maier, *L'Episcopat*, 85–91.
100 Victor, *History of the Vandal Persecution* 2.39; cf. 3.1 for more on the contested title "Catholic."
101 Eugenius's letter is quoted in Victor, *History of the Vandal Persecution* 2.41–42, quote from 2.41: *non specialis provinciarum Africanarum*.
102 In Victor, *History of the Vandal Persecution* 2.43: *praecipue ecclesia Romana, quae caput est omnium ecclesiarum.*
103 Victor, *History of the Vandal Persecution* 3.2.
104 Victor, *History of the Vandal Persecution* 3.7.
105 Victor, *History of the Vandal Persecution* 3.46–51.
106 See details in Fournier, *Victor of Vita*, 253–263.
107 The scholar who has done the most to study this question is Yves Modéran. See especially *Les Maures*; full bibliography for Modéran's many contributions can be found in Modéran, *Les Vandales*. Bibliography for other pertinent works can be found in Fournier, *Victor of Vita*, 218 n.13.
108 Victor, *History of the Vandal Persecution* 2.26–37.
109 Victor, *History of the Vandal Persecution* 2.13. cf. 1.44.
110 Heffernan, *The Passion of Perpetua and Felicity*, 55.
111 *History of the Vandal Persecution* 1.44: *incipient eum Romani martyrem praedicare.*
112 *History of the Vandal Persecution* 3.61.
113 *History of the Vandal Persecution* 3.62.

114 *History of the Vandal Persecution* 3.63, with reference to Virgil, *Aeneid* 8.481–487.

115 Dracontius's works (with a French translation) can be found in Claude Moussy, Colette Camus, Jean Bouquet, and Étienne Wolff (ed./trans.), *Dracontius: Oeuvres*, 4 vols. (Paris : Les Belles Lettres, 1985–1996); trans. in M. St. Margaret, *Dracontii Satisfactio with Introduction, Text, Translation, and Commentary* (PhD Dissertation for the University of Pennsylvania, 1936).

116 Translation partially available in James F. Irwin, *Liber I Draconitii de Laudibus Dei with Introduction, Text, Translation, and Commentary* (PhD dissertation for the University of Pennsylvania, 1942).

117 Including the curious claim that "Africa" is known for its "dragons [*dracones*]" (*On the Praises of God* 1.313–314). Is this a play on the poet's own name? He also references the "phoenix [*Phoenicis*]" (*On the Praises of God* 1.653), which in earlier African writers sometimes was a symbol of Phoenicia.

118 See a bibliography and discussion in Andrew H. Merrills, "The Perils of Panegyric: The Lost Poem of Dracontius and its Consequences," in *Vandals, Romans and Berbers: New Perspectives on Late Antique North Africa*, ed. Andrew H. Merrills (Aldershot, UK: Ashgate, 2004), 145–162.

119 CIL 8.9835: "REG MASVNAE GEN MAVR ET ROMANOR" (my trans.)

120 Andy Blackhurst, "The House of Nubel: Rebels or Players?" in *Vandals, Romans and Berbers: New Perspectives on Late Antique North Africa*, ed. Andrew H. Merrills (Aldershot, UK: Ashgate, 2004), 59, emphasizes "the interface between, on the one hand, Roman culture and military organization, and, on the other, the native communities, which simultaneously posed a potential threat to Roman order." Conant, *Staying Roman*, 2 and passim, has helpfully analyzed the "fracturing of Roman identity" for the Vandal and Byzantine periods of North Africa.

121 *The Book of the Popes* 51.1 (Duchesne, *Le Liber pontificalis*, 1:255; trans. Loomis, *The Book of the Popes*, 1:110; cf. the translation of Davis, *The Book of Pontiffs*, 44, "born in Africa").

122 *Letter* 12.1 (text in Andreas Thiel, *Epistolae romanorum pontificum genuinae* [Braunsberg: Edward Peter, 1868] 1; trans. Bronwen Neil and Pauline Allen, *The Letters of Gelasius I (492–496): Pastor and Micro-Manager of the Church of Rome* [Turnhout: Brepols, 2014], 73).

123 However, see Conant, *Staying Roman*, 83 n.65, who concludes that Gelasius's statement about being born Roman "probably only signifies that . . . he was born in imperial territory before it came under barbarian control." See further discussion in Neil and Allen, *The Letters of Gelasius I*, 5–8 (= the section "An African Pope?"), who conclude that Gelasius was from Africa, but a Roman citizen. They add that Gelasius governed differently than his predecessors in Rome, and because he was indebted to Augustine they comment on how this difference "may be properly attributed to his African origins" (7).

124 Burns, Jensen, et al., *Christianity in Roman Africa*, 73.

125 See Procopius, *History of the Wars* 3.8.

126 *The Book of the Popes* 53.

127 Curiously, *The Book of the Popes*, 54, claims "Africa" had been without a bishop for seventy-four years.

128 For further bibliography on Fulgentius, see Modéran, "Fulgence de Ruspe," in *Encyclopédie berbère* (Peeters, 1998), 2939–2944.

129 Ferrandus, *Life of Fulgentius* prologue: *populos Africanos*. It should be noted that the attribution of this text to Ferrandus is disputed. Ferrandus was a deacon in Carthage who died around 546; cf. Fulgentius, *Letters* 11–14. Fulgentius's treatises, sermons, and letters are available in CCL 91 and 91a. For a bibliography on Fulgentius, see Conrad Leyser, " 'A Wall Protecting the City':

Conflict and Authority in the *Life of Fulgentius of Ruspe*," in *Foundations of Power and Conflicts of Authority in Late-Antique Monasticism*, ed. A. Camplani and G. Filoramo (Leuven: Peeters, 2007), 175–192. For a chronology of his life, see Modéran, "La chronologie de la vie de saint Fulgence de Ruspe et ses incidences sur l'historire de l'AFrique vandale," *Melanges de l'Ecole francaise de Rome antiquite* 105 (1993), 135–188.

130   Ferrandus, *Life of Fulgentius* 1: *victurus inter Afros* (my trans.; cf. FC 95:7, "to live among the Africans").

131   For Fulgentius's high standing among the aristocracy of Rome, see especially his letters (text CCL 91; some are available in trans. in FC 126); discussed in Susan Stevens, "The Circle of Bishop Fulgentius," *Traditio* 38 (1982), 327–341.

132   Ferrandus, *Life of Fulgentius* 5: *barbaricae multitudinis*.

133   Ferrandus, *Life of Fulgentius* 6: *natione barbarus*.

134   Ferrandus, *Life of Fulgentius* 6: *Mauri* (cf. FC 95:17, "the Moors").

135   Ferrandus, *Life of Fulgentius* 8. The Acacian schism was a debate over Leo's *Tome* and the teaching that Christ had two natures; Egypt, along with many in the east, rejected it in favor of "Monophysitism." This will be discussed further in chapter ten.

136   Ferrandus, *Life of Fulgentius* 14.

137   Ferrandus, *Life of Fulgentius* 18. See also Fulgentius, *Letter to Thrasamund*.

138   Ferrandus, *Life of Fulgentius* 20–21.

139   For an introduction and bibliography on Fulgentius's theology and works, see Francis X. Gumerlock, *Fulgentius of Ruspe on the Saving Will of God: The Development of a Sixth-Century African Bishop's Interpretation of 1 Timothy 2:4 During the Semi-Pelagian Controversy* (Lewiston, NY: Edwin Mellen Press, 2009).

140   Thomas S. Ferguson, "Fulgentius of Ruspe," in *Biographical Dictionary of Christian Theologians*, ed. Patrick W. Carey and Joseph T. Lienhard (Westport, CT: Greenwood Press, 2000), 204.

141   E.g. *Letter to Euthymius, On the Forgiveness of Sins* 1.21.1; and *Letter to Monimus* 2.13.3.

142   Council of Carthage (February 525).

143   The text is available in D. R. Shackleton Bailey, *Anthologia Latina* (Stuttgart: Teubner, 1982). Two selections of poems available in English are Morris Rosenblum, *A Latin Poet Among the Vandals* (New York: Columbia University Press, 1961); and N. M. Kay, *Epigrams From the Anthologia Latina: Text, Translation, and Commentary* (London: Bloomsbury, 2006). The numbering of each editor is noted in citations that follow.

144   E.g. Luxurius, *The Book of Epigrams* 3, line 8: *Romulidas et Tyrias* (my trans.; cf. Rosenblum 112–113; cf. *The Book of Epigrams* 43 in Rosenblum and 214 in Bailey). Cf. *The Book of Epigrams* 1, 4, 5, and 6 (Bailey 2–6), on Aeneas and Dido, and many others poems focus on Aeneas. The most significant recasting of Dido occurs in *Epigram* 71 (Bailey 67–75), which is a letter from Dido to Aeneas; see discussion of the sources and how Dido differs from these sources in Scott McGill, "Rewriting Dido: Ovid, Virgil, and the *Epistula Didonis ad Aeneam (AL 71 SB), Classica et mediaevalia* 60 (2009), 177–199.

145   Luxurius, *The Book of Epigrams* 15, lines 5–7: *elephans . . . Mater simian quam creavit arvis / grandaeva in Libycis novo sub orbe* (Rosenblum 120–121); cf. *The Book of Epigrams* 43, where Garamantian girls are assumed to be ugly.

146   *The Book of Epigrams* 120 (Kay 49).

147   Kay, *Epigrams*, 212.

148   *The Book of Epigrams* 172: *tenebras . . . quod legeris nomen convenit Aethiopi* (Kay 60 and trans. on 325). Cf. *The Book of Epigrams* 179 (Kay), on Memnon Cf. *The Book of Epigrams* 173 (Kay), for more such descriptions of a Garamantean man.

149 Kay, *Epigrams*, 325–325.
150 John N. Starks, Jr., "Was Black Beautiful in Vandal Africa?" in *African Athena: New Agendas, Classical Presences*, ed. Daniel Orrells, Gurminder K. Bhambra, and Tessa Roynon (Oxford: Oxford University Press, 2011), 239.
151 *The Book of Epigrams* 179: *nigrum . . . auxilium* (Kay 62 and trans. on 339).
152 *The Book of Epigrams* 185 (Kay) celebrates how the elephant, though deadly, can be conquered. I would suggest that this too could be a fable for the political and military conquest of Africa (for the elephant as a symbol of Africa in late antiquity, see my discussion on pp. 50–51 in chapter two).
153 E.g. Luxurius, *The Book of Epigrams* 91, line 8: *Punica regna . . . Tyrios* (my trans.; cf. Rosenblum 164–165).
154 Luxurius, *The Book of Epigrams* 39 (Rosenblum). Similarly, Mucius Scaevola is praised in *The Book of Epigrams* 144 (Kay).
155 *The Book of Epigrams* 151: *merito tua postuma regnat* (Kay 56 and trans. 287).
156 Luxurius, *The Book of Epigrams* 55–56.
157 See examples in Burns, Jensen, et al., *Christianity in Roman Africa*, 95–97.
158 Schwarcz, "The Settlement of the Vandals in North Africa," 57, states, "And they [the Vandals] were, sooner or later, indistinguishable from the Roman provincials of Africa in their costume and habits." Schwarcz does not discuss how "Roman" the "Roman provincials of Africa" were at this time, nor any non-Roman elements of the local population.
159 *History of the Vandal Persecution* 1.2: *exiguus et infirmus*.
160 Victor, *History of the Vandal Persecution* 2.8, the "barbarian clothes [*habitu barbaro*]" of the Vandals; cf. 2.9 on how the Vandals "saw a woman or man who looked like one of their race [*videntes feminam vel masculum in specie suae gentis*]." Cf. Procopius, *History of the Wars* 3.2 (lines 4–6), for the appearance of the Vandals (and all Germanic peoples).
161 Procopius, *History of Wars* 3.5–7, tells of the Mauretanians who stood with Gellimer until his surrender.
162 On this point, see the discussion and illustrations of uniquely indigenous archaeological structures in Alan Rushworth, "From Arzuges to Rustamids: State Formation and Regional Identity in the Pre-Saharan Zone," in *Vandals, Romans and Berbers: New Perspectives on Late Antique North Africa*, ed. Andrew H. Merrills (Aldershot, UK: Ashgate, 2004), 77–98.
163 *History of the Vandal Persecution* 2.18: *Aethiopibus*.
164 *History of the Vandal Persecution* 2.21: *omnem paene Africam opacabat*.
165 *History of the Vandal Persecution* 1.9; cf. 1.15–16.
166 For discussion of specific sites and how "the Byzantine rulers seem to have been at pains to conciliate their African subjects," see W.H.C. Frend, "From Donatist Opposition to Byzantine Loyalism: The Cult of Martyrs in North Africa 350–650," in *Vandals, Romans and Berbers: New Perspectives on Late Antique North Africa*, ed. Andrew H. Merrills (Aldershot, UK: Ashgate, 2004), 259–269 (quotation from 265).
167 *The Book of the Popes* 58: *ab Afris episcopis*.

10 The late Byzantine era in Africa

"Africa is one of the most neglected subjects in modern scholarship on late antiquity and early Byzantium. Neither exactly Byzantine nor exactly western."[1] This observation by Averil Cameron, the highly esteemed historian of Byzantine history, points both to the gap remaining in our understanding of African history from this era and to the need to study Africa as a unique context. Furthermore, this portion of African Christianity's history needs to be resituated within the story of African Christianity in general since the main subjects understood themselves as belonging to the African tradition that had come before them.

In order to address these needs, we will first begin with a brief review of where Africa fits within the wider events of the Roman Empire at this time. From that vantage point we will then be able to narrow our focus on events and perspectives in Africa. Following this discussion, we will turn to the Three Chapters controversy, since some of the most prominent voices involved come from Africa. The next major scene arises when Pope Gregory the Great gets involved in African affairs and in so doing meets some resistance from the African bishops. Finally, we will discuss Maximus the Confessor, who comes to Africa and interacts with the local Christians, and from there addresses another controversy spreading throughout the empire. In all these sections we will rehearse the history and the development of Christian thought, and while doing so we will also note times where the African identities of those involved can be detected in the sources.

Justinian's reconquest of Africa

In 527 Justinian was crowned emperor in Constantinople, and his reign marked a turn in history in that he restored much of the former power of the empire. He made peace with the Persians to his east, and he reconquered much of the Latin west. Most importantly for our purposes, the emperor reclaimed North Africa when he sent his general, Belisarius, in 533 to defeat the Vandals.

Belisarius swiftly defeated Gelimer, the Vandal king, but this Byzantine "conquest," or Roman "reconquest," of Africa needs to be qualified in several ways. First, the rulers known to history as "the Byzantines" in fact described themselves and were seen by their enemies as "the Romans."[2] This identity even affected the reconquest of Africa since the leading official of the reconquest sternly warned his troops not to plunder the native Carthaginians, for "all the Libyans had been Romans in earlier times."[3] Elsewhere, this same source speaks to what the Libyans were before they were "Roman," for "the barbarian Moors" were "a Phoenician race."[4] The local Carthaginians allegedly viewed the Roman reconquest as a divine intervention and a fulfillment to a prophecy. It was said that Saint Cyprian himself would have vengeance on the Vandals, and in what appeared to be fulfillment of this prophecy, his feast day, the *Cypriana*, occurred immediately after Belisarius reclaimed Carthage.[5]

While this interpretation was the view of those who benefited from the new "Roman" rule, others must have seen things differently. Leslie Dossey concluded, "More than the Vandal occupation, the Byzantine 'liberation,' had all the marks of outside imperialism."[6] Before the Byzantines took control of Africa, the African provinces had been able to rule their own affairs by their own laws, as evidenced by Justinian's complaint about the matter.[7] Rather than assuming that one interpretation of the new imperial presence dominated, we should probably assume that Africans held to various views. To quote Cameron again:

> on the one hand the Byzantines, presenting themselves as the restorers of Roman rule, probably seemed unconvincingly eastern to the Roman Africans, yet on the other, the arrival of eastern refugees and the leading role played in North Africa in the early seventh century by Greek-speaking monks seem to have been accepted without difficulty.[8]

Adding to Cameron's last point, the African churches were expected to reorganize to match the Byzantine style of a hierarchy of bishops. However, rather than doing so according to the eastern pattern, certain duties that the Byzantines expected of the clergy were in fact assigned to the lay elder of the African Christians, which appears to be a remnant of the "lay elders [*seniores laici*]" native to Africa (discussed in previous chapters).[9]

Another important qualification to make here is that the conquest of the Vandals did not entail a full conquest of non-Vandal Africa. Gelimar and his Mauretanian allies surrendered after a lengthy siege,[10] but the Romans would spend the next fifteen years dealing with other local groups, and several sporadic uprisings occurred throughout the sixth and seventh centuries. The Roman armies did not entirely restore the African provinces to their pre-Vandal condition. Instead, the emperor in Constantinople now ruled over the regions that had been controlled by the Vandals, but these regions had shrunk during Geiseric's reign. Various people groups, especially among the Mauretanians, gained much independence from the center of power in

Carthage, whether that was a Vandal king or a governor representing the eastern emperor. Burns and Jensen (et al.) describe this era by saying,

> Despite their reinstatement, the African Catholic bishops soon learned that their Byzantine liberators were actually a new set of elite colonial rulers who kept largely to themselves and controlled both military and civil affairs. Thus, their joy at the defeat of the Vandals soon turned toward dismay, especially since the last of the Vandal kings, Gelimer, may have been more tolerant than their new ruler in Constantinople proved to be.[11]

In the decades following Belisarius's campaign, a series of uprising occurred in Africa in which Mauretanian groups join with the remaining Vandals and various other "rebels" such as deserters and runaway slaves.[12] In the middle of narrating these indigenous uprisings, Procopius pauses to explain the ethnic origin of the various "Mauretanians": these are the people from "Phoenicia" who were driven out of their land by Joshua, the leader of the Hebrews, and they still speak the "Phoenician tongue."[13] While Procopius is likely dependent on stereotypes from earlier authors and so his statements cannot be taken at face value, he at least records what must have been the common "Roman" view of the "Libyan" peoples. Furthermore, he even claims that there is evidence of this self-identity among the Africans, for he records an inscription from Africa that reads, "We are they who fled from before the face of Joshua, the robber, the son of Nun."[14] In other words, at least some of the indigenous population of Africa understood themselves as the same Phoenician people group that is mentioned in the Old Testament.

Procopius's reports have to be considered to some extent reliable, because he did go to Africa along with Belisarius's retinue to document the wars, even if his agenda is to positively portray Justinian's actions. Alternatively, his public praise of the emperor in his *History of Wars* is notoriously offset by his *Secret History*. In the latter work, he tells of how much destruction the Byzantine reconquest brought about in Africa:

> For in the first place, Libya, which attains to so large dimensions, has been so thoroughly ruined that for the traveller who makes a long journey it is no easy matter, as well as being a noteworthy fact, to meet a human being. . . . And as for the Libyans, those who formerly lived in the cities, those who tilled the soil, and those who toiled at the labours of the sea – all of which I had the fortune to witness with my own eyes – how could any man estimate the multitude of them? And still more numerous than these were the Moors there, all of whom were in the end destroyed together with their wives and offspring.[15]

Procopius's description of widespread massacre and deserted roads is generally considered to be dramatic exaggeration (he next claims Italy was even more deserted). Nevertheless, his claim that the emperor's policies in Africa were abusive and oppressive may have some merit to them. In particular, he claims,

> administering Libya with full licence, [so that Justinian] might swallow it up and thus make plunder of the whole of it. At any rate he immediately sent out assessors of the land and imposed certain most cruel taxes which had not existed before. And he laid hold of the estates, whichever were best. And he excluded the Arians from the sacraments which they observed. Also he was tardy in the payment of his military forces, and in other ways became a grievance to the soldiers. From these causes arose the insurrections which resulted in great destruction.[16]

Whether or not Procopius is correct to blame the emperor's abuses for the local African uprisings, he at least represents one writer who found there to be a clear dividing line between "the Libyans" and the new Byzantine presence.[17] Procopius's viewpoint as an outsider can be compared with surviving material from those who wrote from Africa itself.

Another writer, named Fulgentius, wrote from Africa at this time, and like Procopius he explicitly invoked ties to ancient history – only this time he largely differed in his interpretation of the common story of Aeneas and his time with Dido in Africa. As for the identity of this author, many historians conclude that this Fulgentius the Mythographer was a different author than Fulgentius of Ruspe discussed in Chapter 9.[18] This later Fulgentius likely wrote in the early sixth century from Carthage, which can be deduced from his surviving works.[19]

Fulgentius has intrigued modern historians both for what he did with classical mythology and with Roman history. Throughout his *Mythologies*, Fulgentius exposed pagan myths as from the "lying Greeks [*mandacis Greciae*]."[20] Nevertheless, he did defend one myth: in his *Explanation of Virgilian Continence*, Fulgentius explained Virgil's intentions, claiming that the Roman author never meant to write a literal tale, but instead wrote an allegory of the soul's journey. Virgil's account of Rome's story, however, is almost entirely ignored by Fulgentius: the last six books, dealing with Rome's wars – including the Punic wars – received very little attention.[21] Emily Alibu explained:

> In denying the Roman myth Fulgentius was mounting an attack on the center of pagan culture and its heroic ideals. . . . At the very least he estranged himself from traditional Roman religion while endorsing a new world view, a new concept of the heroic."[22]

Early modern readers were largely appalled by how Fulgentius deconstructed the Greek and Roman heroes, leaving only weak allegorical interpretations of morality. Fulgentius's rejection of Roman heroism, however, belongs to the line of previous African apologists going back to Tertullian. Despite this African tradition, not everyone reads Fulgentius in such a light. Gregory Hays insists:

> If Fulgentius can be said to have an African identity at all, it is not racial, cultural or linguistic in nature, but literary – an identity shaped not under the blazing heat of "le sol africain" but by the midnight oil of the study.[23]

While Hays may be correct about how indebted Fulgentius is to the wider classical literary tradition, his remark is an odd statement to make after reviewing the instances when Fulgentius refers to himself as a "Libyan."[24] From what has been surveyed thus far in this book, it would be better to say that someone like Fulgentius can embrace the wider Mediterranean traditions while also retaining an African identity.

In contrast to Fulgentius, some African writers from this time distanced themselves from any indigenous identity and instead aligned themselves explicitly with the "Romans." One writer at this time, Flavius Cresconius Corippus, celebrated Justinian's conquest of Africa. In a work called *Iohannis*, or *John*, he recounts the conquests of John Troglita, the Byzantine general sent to Africa by Justinian to squelch the indigenous uprisings there.[25]

Corippus was apparently from Africa near Carthage. One surviving manuscript names him as an "African school teacher [*Africanus Grammaticus*]."[26] Corippus describes his previous profession as being in the "countryside [*rura*],"[27] and then in the same passage he admits that his poor pronunciation may discredit his work, which may indicate that Latin was not his native tongue.[28] Nevertheless, he hopes "Carthage may rejoice. . . . Even as my rustic Muse contends with the Muses of Rome."[29] While Coripus refers to the muses and other "pagan" deities in his work, he clearly writes as a Christian. This reference to the literary inspiration of a muse is telling because "Corippus saw himself as Justinian's Vergil."[30] The reader will remember that Virgil's *Aeneid* featured Dido's Carthage and all of Africa as something to be conquered by Aeneas and his descendants. Corippus, likewise, celebrates the "mighty Aeneas [*magnum Aeneam*]," but he goes on to claim that John Troglita was "superior to Aeneas [*Aeneam superat*]."[31] John, in Corippus's account, claims to fulfill the demands of Cato, who for so long had demanded that Carthage must be destroyed.[32]

Throughout his work, Corippus's celebration of Roman virtue is sharply contrasted with the indigenous African groups who opposed them.[33] Then, beyond these moral assessments, Corippus contrasts the Romans and the Africans in terms of skin color, which for him symbolizes good and evil: when John's fleet sails toward Africa, a fallen angel appeared to them, which Corippus describes as "Akin to darkness, its face seemed Moorish."[34] Later, when describing the captives defeated by the Byzantine soldiers, he states, "Nor were all the captives of the same color. There sat a woman, horrid to behold, the same color as her black children. They were like the young of crows."[35] He describes them derogatorily as backwards in terms of attire, wearing peculiarly African clothes.[36] He can generalize about the "Punic people [*Poenorum*]"[37] across Africa, and Corippus describes the various Mauretanians as worshipping Punic deities.[38] These statements indicate that Corippus understood himself as a Roman in terms of social identity, and his contrast between the Romans or Latins on the one hand and the Africans or Libyans on the other peppers the entire work.[39] Furthermore, his positive appraisal of the emperors and the Byzantine conquest of Africa is likely because Corippus had been a landowner outside of Carthage, and so his economic and political interests belong to the "civilized" empire as opposed to the "barbarians."[40] In sum, his poem celebrates how the Byzantines were able to "restore Africa to its Roman destiny."[41] While Corippus's account is important for history, it must be remembered that he is writing some time after these events and for the purpose of winning the emperor's favor.[42] It is now clear that a hostile source like Corippus cannot be used to generalize about all "Moors." For example, while the Punic language and religion did continue among some groups, many other Mauretanian groups were Christianized by this time.[43]

Despite his lack of objectivity, Corippus does report the difficulties and setbacks that John Troglita faced in his prolonged attempt to reclaim North Africa, and these events can be corroborated with other sources. Several of these "Mauretanian" groups, some mounted on camels,[44] gained control of vast regions of North Africa. It should also be noted that despite his negative assessment of the Mauretanians and his ability to generalize about them (as discussed in the previous paragraph), Corippus in fact documents many diverse groups and practices within this generalized people. His material, therefore, helps to corroborate and inform the reports from other Byzantine sources about the local resistance to Byzantine rule in Africa.[45]

Repeated uprisings occurred in 546, wherein indigenous African groups aligned with one another and with remaining Vandals to oppose the Byzantines. Despite his initial success against the indigenous army, John's troops were soon defeated by a very large alliance. The various indigenous groups used guerilla tactics, which placed the Roman armies at a continuous disadvantage. The Romans were lured further south away from their supplies and into regions with less water, which led to their defeat. John had to retreat to Carthage and amass another army, but once again his troops were outnumbered. Thanks to support from some Mauretanians who sided with John, the Byzantine armies finally forced a major battle in which they killed the leaders of the uprisings. With their leaders dead, the African armies dispersed, which resulted in a period of peace that followed.

The Byzantine period also brought about changes for the churches in Africa.[46] The Vandal party now became the recipients of "persecution" in that the full pressure of the Roman laws against heretics were now applied to them – these were the same legal tactics used by the Caecilianist/Catholic party against the Donatists, which were then used by the Vandals against the Nicene/Catholic party.[47] Justinian revised the laws so that they applied to all "Arians, Donatists, Jews, and others" who do not belong to the emperor's religion.[48] All of these persons may repent and join the emperor's church, but those who have been "rebaptized" are not to be trusted in military "service [*militiam*]."[49] Furthermore, Justinian gave the basilicas used by the Vandals back to the Nicene/Catholic party, now led by Reparatus, bishop of Carthage, who presided over the "council of all Africa."[50]

In concrete terms, changes can even be detected in the architecture of this time: the style of construction known as *opus Africanum* originated in Carthage during the Punic period,[51] and builders in Africa continued to use this technique throughout the Roman and even Vandal period.[52] The Byzantine rulers abandoned this method when they built new edifices. The Byzantines rebuilt the walls of Carthage, added new basilicas, monasteries, and other public buildings.[53]

Another way in which the change in political power impacted Christians in Africa at this time was in the re-implementation of local church councils. From 523 until 646, records survive of intermittent councils of the "Catholic" church in Africa. The subject matter and attendance varied widely, but these records indicate an ongoing vibrant community that continued to strive to articulate its faith in response to the contemporary circumstances. A general council met in Carthage in February 525, but with only sixty-one bishops.

François Decret comments on why so few attended this council, "many of the independent-minded bishops of Byzacena and Numidia were not eager to meet with their colleagues from Proconsularis, including the primate of Carthage."[54] Decret's suggestion seems to be that many bishops from this region were "independent-minded" because they belonged to the indigenous tradition stemming back to the Donatists. It must be admitted that such a claim is conjectural, and the political situation and the potential danger when traveling may be a better explanation for the low attendance at this council.

In 534 Reparatus of Carthage presided over a council with 220 bishops. The next year a council met to decide on the admittance of those who came from the Vandal party. These were to be accepted, but Vandal clergy would be demoted to the laity. Such a stance differs from the previous practice in Africa wherein Donatist clergy who joined the Caecilianist/Catholic party retained their status. Burns and Jensen (et al.) view this shift as reflective of how the North African Catholic party grew more closely aligned with the Roman church, as would be expected since so many of the African Catholic bishops had been exiled to Italy and Sicily during Vandal persecutions.[55] Again, this explanation is plausible, but it should be noted that the shift in practice could also reflect a consistent theological commitment: in Augustine's era, the Donatists were accepted as Trinitarian, while the Vandals were Arians who denied the full divinity of the Son and so were not truly baptized into the name of the three divine persons.

Regardless of the explanation, these councils and the African churches' posture toward the church of Rome once again raises the question of the African and especially the Donatist tradition.[56] As will be discussed in the following paragraph, in the late sixth century the church of Rome will express concerns about the ongoing presence of "Donatists" in Africa. Were the Donatists still active as a distinct party in North Africa in the early fifth century? Unfortunately, no evidence survives that can clearly answer this question. The literary texts from the period of the Byzantine reconquest of North Africa are entirely silent about Donatism, and while there is much archaeological material to suggest an ongoing Donatist presence during this period, such artifacts are notoriously difficult to date precisely. The question about Donatism in these decades simply lies beyond the scope of strict historical proof. Instead, historians must hypothesize about this gap in our knowledge. One could assume that no African Christians retained a Donatist self-identity in this period since there is no evidence to demonstrate such self-identification. This hypothesis, however, is an argument from silence, and misplaces the burden of proof. An alternative is to argue from the political landscape of the previous century. The Vandals controlled the areas around Carthage and the coastline, but many regions where Donatism was strongest, such as both provinces of Mauretania, were left to themselves. Even when the Byzantines reconquered North Africa, they had little to no control over these inland and western regions. Therefore, we should assume that the Donatist party in these regions continued to thrive. It must be repeated that such a conclusion is conjecture, but such is the case for all attempts to speak of African Christianity in the regions beyond imperial control at this time.

A final paradigm to consider is the one discussed in Chapter 9. If we conclude that Donatists were simply the majority of Christians in Africa who would have understood themselves as holding to their own African Christian tradition, then the label "Donatist" veritably disappears when the "Catholic" (i.e. Caecilianist) party is driven out by the Vandals. All of these options have weaknesses, but rather than letting any objections to a given paradigm dismiss it altogether, we should assume that the situation in Africa at this time was complex, and so our reading of the identities involved will have to weigh the evidence carefully in light of various theories.

While it is tempting to limit our history to the known facts, a broad history of North African Christianity like the one I am giving here cannot ignore the question of the ongoing presence of Donatists at this time, since the "Donatists" will appear to resurface in our sources later in the sixth century. We will discuss those sources later in this chapter, but for now we can return to what is known about the African churches at this time. While we must leave aside the question of Donatism in the first half of the sixth century, we can explore how the African churches refused to submit to the "Roman" theological influence. With the reconquest of North Africa by the "Romans" from Constantinople, the African church was expected to adopt the Greek practice of each metropolitan bishop answering directly to the emperor, as opposed to deciding matters in regional synods.[57] This foreign view of church authority likely fostered the African bishops' resistance to the emperor's interference in their affairs. Such resistance to foreign authority can be seen in the Three Chapters controversy, to which we can now turn.

The African Three Chapters controversy

The Three Chapters controversy largely involves events outside of Africa. Nevertheless, in the worldwide Christian debate that occurred in the mid-sixth century, African voices came to the forefront as voices of opposition. Robert Markus bemoaned how no study has been devoted to the African writers in this controversy, which takes into account "the long history of African dissent."[58] In what follows, we can draw on this long history and see these dissenting voices as belonging to their own African Christian tradition. Before reviewing these African writers, however, we need to summarize the controversy.[59]

A century prior to our period, Christians across the empire debated how best to understand the incarnation. Nestorius of Constantinople (patriarch from 428 to 431) preferred to refer to Mary as "Mother of Christ [*Christotokos*]," rather than say she was the "mother of God [*Theotokos*]." He insisted that Christ's human nature should be seen as distinct from his divinity, and therefore Mary should be said to have birthed his humanity – but she is not the mother of God/divinity. Nestorius's enemies, however, heard him to teach two distinct persons in Christ: Jesus the human and God the Son. This teaching ("Nestorianism") was condemned at the council of Ephesus in 431, but Nestorius's supporters claimed he was never given a fair hearing. After much controversy, another ecumenical council met in Chalcedon in 451 to settle the dispute: the natures of Christ must be kept distinct, but Christ must be understood as one person.[60] This alleged settlement, however, met with ongoing opposition from Nestorius's opponents. Cyril of Alexandria had opposed Nestorius in 431, and his defenders – especially in Egypt – rejected Chalcedon's decision and instead declared that Christ had one nature. The two-nature theory of Chalcedon, it was feared, would inevitably lead back into the two-person thinking of Nestorius. One emperor, Zeno, issued a statement in 482 that attempted to resolve the issue by forbidding anyone from saying "one nature" or "two natures."[61] This was addressed especially to the Alexandrians, and those in "Libya" (probably referring to the parts of Africa near Egypt and under the jurisdiction of the Patriarch of Alexandria). Suffice it to say that neither party found Zeno's solution satisfactory.

The two sides continued to be at odds until the time of Justinian, which brings us back to the time period under discussion in this chapter. One of Justinian's aims was to unite Christianity in the empire. In order to appease the so-called Monophysites (*mono-* = one; *physis* = nature), or "one-nature" followers of Cyril, Justinian condemned the "three chapters." By Three Chapters, historians mean the works of three earlier Christian leaders who attacked Cyril: Theodore of Mopsuestia, Theodoret of Cyrrhus, and Ibas of Eddssa.

Theodore of Mopsuestia (350–428) had taught Nestorius, and his writings were found to contain the same "Nestorian" error. Since he had died before the council of Ephesus, that council had denounced a creed by him but left his legacy intact. However, Justinian condemned both Theodore and his writings.

Justinian also targeted Theodoret of Cyrrhus (c.393–460). Theodoret's views largely aligned with Nestorius, but he insisted that there were not two persons in Christ. Instead, he insisted that the two-natures view of the incarnation protected the divinity of Christ, since Christ was said to suffer and die (both ungodly acts because God is impassible and immortal). In turn, Theodoret held that Cyril's emphasis on the one Christ suffering created problems: if the Word of God could suffer and die in the incarnation, then the Word is less than divine (because God is impassible and immortal). This attack on Cyril made Theodoret suspect, and he had to defend himself at the Council of Chalcedon. However, because Theodoret denounced Nestorius, the council deemed him orthodox.

The third of these writers that came under scrutiny was Ibas of Edessa (d.457). As bishop of Edessa (= modern Şanlıurfa, Turkey), Ibas attempted to reconcile the Cyrilian and Nestorian parties. He even helped to convince Cyril to sign the "Formula of Reunion" in 433 in which Christ is said to have "two natures." After Cyril's death, a letter by Ibas in which he criticized Cyril was found and distributed by those who wished to condemn Ibas as a Nestorian. After Ibas was found innocent in a trial in Tyre in 449, Dioscorus, Cyril's successor in Alexandria, formed another council at Ephesus in the same year. There, although absent, Ibas was condemned by the council, but Pope Leo and many others denounced this council as a "Robber synod" for its improper procedures and its use of violent force. At Chalcedon, Ibas and others denounced at Dioscorus's council defended themselves. Ibas was found to be orthodox after he denounced Nestorius as a heretic, and the council restored him to his office in Edessa.

Despite the fact that Theodore, Theodoret, and Ibas had all died in good standing, the Cyrilian/Monophysite party continued to insist that their works, especially their criticisms of Cyril, led to Nestorianism. In 543, in an attempt to appease the Cyrilian party, Justinian issued a declaration denouncing Theodore and all his works, Theodoret's works against Cyril, and Ibas's letter against Cyril. In other words, these three "chapters" or bodies of writings, and apparently their authors, were condemned as heretical.

By condemning the Three Chapters, Justinian attempted to appease the Cyrilian party, but his actions in turn upset the Chalcedonian party. Since Theodore had not been condemned in his own lifetime, and since Theodoret and Ibas had both been affirmed as orthodox at the Council of Chalcedon, the emperor's actions against the three appeared to be a direct rejection of Chalcedon's authority.

In Rome, Pope Vigilius opposed Justinian's actions. In 545 the emperor summoned the pope to Constantinople, but once there the pope refused to sign the condemnation. When presented with Latin translations of the Three Chapters (for he was unable to read Greek), Vigilius did write a *Iudicatum* or "Judgment" against the Three Chapters in 548. However, he soon retracted the statement when he found how many of his western bishops disapproved. Justinian detained Vigilius in the eastern capital until he agreed to relent. The emperor summoned another council in order to support his decision, and so at the second Council of Constantinople (553) the Three Chapters were denounced as Nestorian. Vigilius refused to attend the council, and only after a six-month imprisonment did he finally agree to join the emperor and the council in condemning the Three Chapters. The statement issued by the council went out of its way to cite African sources in particular, such as when the council stated,

> Moreover, several letters of Augustine of sacred memory, who was particularly outstanding among the African bishops were read in which he indicates that it is correct to condemn heretics even after their death. Other most reverend bishops of Africa have also observed this church custom.[62]

Despite this council's claim about previous Africans, many African Christians at the time viewed such actions as a betrayal of Chalcedon.

Two Roman deacons had written to the church of Carthage, requesting a statement on the Three Chapters controversy. A Carthaginian deacon named Ferrandus wrote back vehemently supporting Theodore, Theodoret, and Ibas, and he denounced the emperor's interference in theological matters.[63] This is likely the same author of the *Life of Fulgentius* (discussed in Chapter 9), and if so, then Ferrandus would have been in exile with Fulgentius and the other bishops during the late Vandal persecution. Two of his letters to Fulgentius survive, the first of which has to do with a certain "slave . . . an adolescent in age, an Ethiopian in color."[64] This young catechumen was dying and unable to answer the baptismal questions for himself, and yet he had been baptized anyway. What was the state of the man's salvation? Fulgentius confirmed Ferrandus for this course of action, and affirmed that the man's faith confirms his salvation. In another letter, Ferrandus asked questions about the incarnation and about the trinity.[65] This training in orthodoxy and especially in African tradition[66] prepared Ferrandus for the later Three Chapters controversy, which entailed both one's understanding of the incarnation and how earlier tradition is to be received. Ferrandus emphasized the importance of a council for dogmatic decisions, arguing how Ibas's letter had been read – and not condemned – at Chalcedon.

Ferrandus's main work is a collection of earlier canons from African councils.[67] According to African conciliar decisions (and Ferrandus assumes this reflects a truth for the church writ large), the emperor should not be the arbiter of church affairs.[68] No emperor or later council could overturn the earlier tradition. Even though individual bishops could appeal directly to the bishop of Rome,[69] even the bishop of Rome must honor the councils. Ferrandus's arguments aligned with a council meeting in Carthage in 550, and the bishops there decided to excommunicate Pope Vigilius for his support of the emperor.[70]

Justinian summoned the bishop of Carthage at this time, Reparatus, to Constantinople. There he – unlike Vigilius – remained firmly opposed to Justinian's actions. Justinian had Reparatus convicted for treason, claiming he had supported an uprising in Africa.[71] Reparatus was sent into exile where he later died. When his successor was appointed in Carthage, the Byzantine army had to install him under armed protection, and when the locals protested, the soldiers drove them away violently.[72] Another bishop, Victor of Tunnuna, supported Reparatus and so was also sent into exile. Victor added to Prosper of Aquitaine's *Chronicle*, continuing it until 567, and he did so with the perspective of one who opposed Justinian's condemnation of the Three Chapters.[73]

Another African bishop from this time was Verecundus of Junca, a city in the southern province of Byzacena. Verecundus's writings apparently reflect widespread disapproval of Justinian's actions. Because of his part in the 550 Council of Carthage, Justinian summoned Verecundus to Constantinople, where the African bishop supported Vigilius in his attempt to resist Justinian's condemnation of the Three Chapters. He, Vigilius, and others with them fled Constantinople across the Bosphorus to Chalcedon and took sanctuary in the basilica of Saint Euphemia, where the Council of Chalcedon (451) had allegedly received a miraculous sign of affirmation from the saint. Verecundus died there in 552, but he left behind three known works that affirm Chalcedonian theology in opposition to Justinian's position. The first is a collection of extracts from the Council of Chalcedon itself.[74] Another of his surviving works is a poem entitled, *On Penitential Satisfaction*, written in a Latin that modern scholars deem poor quality.[75] He also wrote an exegetical commentary on the canticles from the Old Testament.[76]

Along with Reparatus and Verecundus, Justinian summoned Primasius, bishop of Hadrumetum, to Constantinople. Primasius wrote a work on heresies that has not survived, but his commentary on the book of Revelation is extant. In his commentary, Primasius declared that the "Donatists ought not to brag [*donatistae hinc extolli non debent*]," implying that this party still existed in Primasius's day – or at least a group appearing to Primasius as Donatist.[77] In fact, Primasius's work in a sense rescues Tyconius's method of interpreting Revelation, in that Tyconius (who originally belonged to the Donatists) is credited with proper exegetical method; Primasius disagrees with him only in terms of the groups referenced by the prophecy of

John.[78] Tyconius thought that the apocalypse depicted the Donatist church against the world, whereas Primasius believed the battle was between his own (Chalcedonian? African?) party and the world. As for his opposition to Justinian, Primasius later relented when the opportunity to become primate of Byzacena became available. Because he conceded to Justinian's request, Primasius was permitted to return home. Once there, however, his fellow African bishops condemned him for this compromise.[79]

Another African Christian in Constantinople at the time was Facundus, the bishop of Hermionem (also in Byzacena).[80] Even before Vigilius arrived in Rome, Facundus refused to compromise with Justinian's actions.[81] Later, he denounced anyone willing to follow the emperor as abandoning the true faith taught at Chalcedon, including Vigilius, Vigilius's successor, Pelagius, and Primasius.[82] In order to avoid arrest, Facundus went into hiding.[83] Even after Justinian's death, when his adopted son, Justin II, turned his attention away from the Three Chapters controversy, Facundus continued to defend Theodore, Theodoret, and Ibas, and he attacked those who had supported Justinian's campaign against them.[84] In his work, *Defense of the Three Chapters*, Facundus argues along several lines: First, the actions taken at Chalcedon cannot be overturned, which becomes an extended argument about the trustworthiness of tradition. Even if previous church fathers erred according to later standards, they cannot be condemned postmortem because they were condoned in their own time. To give an example, he draws on his own African tradition: Cyprian taught rebaptism in his own time, but no one would condemn him.[85] The essence of heresy, therefore, is not error, but unwillingness to reform from error when confronted with an ecumenical council – an argument that echoes Augustine.[86] Facundus also faults the emperor: the emperor should not meddle in church affairs.[87] Beyond arguing this as a general principle (which would echo the Donatist tradition in North Africa), Facundus specifically questions Justinian's motives. The emperor cared more about uniting his fragmented empire than he cared about true doctrine. Finally, Facundus offers criteria for determining a truly ecumenical council, which is an argument he expanded in his next work, *Epistle on the Catholic Faith*.[88]

Because Facundus depicts the church as resisting the political power of the empire, Robert Markus concludes that the African bishop reflected his African Christian tradition. In particular, Markus comments, "We can glimpse behind Facundus's words a vision of the secular world not so very far removed from that of Tertullian's."[89] Markus elsewhere adds that Facundus's remarks are "reminiscent of Tertullian and Donatus."[90] While Markus's reading may be valid, we should not forget that Facundus's stance applied specifically to the Three Chapters controversy; he was no Donatist.[91] In fact, he vehemently argued against this accusation in this work *Against Mocian*.[92] Mocian had accused the African opponents of Rome of being Donatist, but Facundus rejected such an accusation and yet still continued his attack against the emperor.

Another dissenting voice from Africa can be found in Pontianus, bishop of Thenae in Byzacena. Around 554 he wrote a letter to the emperor insisting that one cannot condemn the dead. Therein, he humbly explains how he and his fellow bishops ("we among the Africans [*nos in Africanis*]") received copies of the Three Chapters and did find errors in them, but he fears that the emperor's actions would undermine Chalcedon.[93]

Soon after Pontianus's work, a deacon of Carthage named Liberatus[94] wrote a history of the controversy stemming back to Nestorius himself and culminating in Justinian's Council of Constantinople (553).[95] This history is a heavily biased account of Justinian's actions. Liberatus argues against Monophysites from the time of Eutyches to his own contemporaries by drawing from his own African tradition: he is indebted to earlier African writers, and he even uses Tertullian's argument (from *Prescript Against Heretics*), stipulating that certain parties do not have the right to appeal to the church's scripture and tradition.[96] Furthermore, Liberatus denounced the African clergy who were supporting and supported by Justinian because they received bribes.[97]

It should be noted that Africans were not unanimous in their critique of Justinian. A certain Junillus Africanus served in Constantinople as quaestor for Justinian. The report about him in Procopius is entirely negative: in addition to his questionable business practices,

> Junilus, a Libyan, . . . did understand Latin, yet, as far as Greek was concerned, he had neither attended an elementary school, nor was he able to pronounce the language itself in the Greek manner (indeed, on many occasions when he tried hard to speak a Greek word, he won the ridicule of his assistants).[98]

Others in Africa, however, had a more positive view of him. Junillus devoted a work to Primasius, the bishop of Hadrumetum, on the interpretation of scripture.[99] Primasius had visited Constantinople in the "interests of [his own] province [*provinciae . . . utilitas*]" (i.e. Byzacena, if not Africa more generally) and while there he asked if one of the Greek authors had devoted a treatise to biblical interpretation. Junillus in turn found the works of Paul of Nisibis and adapted them into the work sent to Primasius.[100] Junillus's version takes the form of a dialogue between a teacher and his disciple, and it reviews many important questions about how best to interpret the scriptures. Junillus makes no comparison with Tyconius's earlier treatise, which even Augustine praised, but Primasius knew Tyconius's work and so the request for additional guides to biblical interpretation may be an attempt to compare the eastern thinkers with Primasius's own African tradition.[101] It is worth noting that in the same work, Junillus took the opportunity to argue how God sanctioned earthly rulers.[102]

When Justinian died in 565, his successor, Justin II, turned his attention away from theological matters to the wars with the Persians and the

Lombards. This left the ongoing opposition to Justinian's actions able to regain ground. Throughout the controversy the African bishops refused to accept the theological decisions of the emperor in Constantinople in the Three Chapters controversy. Instead, they sided with the bishop of Rome. This Roman allegiance, however, was short-lived. Only while Pope Vigilius agreed with their traditional view did the African bishops support the Roman church. When the pope finally approved the emperor's decision, the African church displayed its independence – a long tradition in North African Christianity.[103]

Once again, it is tempting to connect these dissenting African Christians with the Donatist party. Eno does so, with a caveat about the theology involved: "There is no direct continuity of teaching of course, but there is a considerable similarity of tone."[104] Eno is certainly correct that the Africans differed theologically with the "Donatists" when it came to issues such as rebaptism. Nevertheless, even in their own time these African Christians will be deemed "Donatist," something Frend helps to explain, "Their opponents denounced this attitude as 'Donatist,' but this was only literary invective. The falsity of the charge, however, should not blind the historian to the Donatist character of the stirrings in the reconquered Numidian countryside."[105] While there is too little evidence to link the theological dissenters opposing Justinian to the indigenous groups opposing Roman rule, these scholars do rightly note the explicit ties with these African Christians and earlier African Christian tradition. This self-understanding deserves further attention in future studies about the Three Chapters controversy. For now, suffice it to say that the middle of the sixth century witnessed a vigorous display of theological reflection on Christian tradition writ large, as well as the local African Christian heritage.

This local African tradition will again come into conflict with the practice of Christians overseas when Gregory the Great discovers "Donatist" practices still taking place in Africa. We can now turn to the end of the sixth century to discuss the controversy that occurred during Gregory's papacy.

Gregory the Great

In 590 Gregory became bishop of Rome, and his program of organizing and expanding the church under his jurisdiction helped earn him the title "the Great [*Magnus*]" in the memory of later Christians. Gregory's family had served in public office in Rome, and Gregory, who was born in the city, had been groomed for public office as well. After beginning his political career, however, he retreated from public service in order to lead a monastic life modeled after the teachings of Benedict (who, in turn, had appropriated much from Augustine). It was with great reluctance that Gregory finally agreed to leave the cloister and return to Rome, this time as its bishop.

The bishop of Rome's authority had steadily increased in the west. Whereas the bishop of Rome had always been given the highest place of prestige in the church, Pope Leo had earlier gained more official power for the papacy, functioning as patriarch over the entire west and even claiming primacy over the entire church.[106] Gregory followed Leo's lead and used his political training to form the western church into a well-organized hierarchy. Although earlier African Christians – like Tertullian, Cyprian, and the Donatists – had assumed that the bishop of Rome's jurisdiction did not stretch over their own provinces, the Caecilianist/Catholic party and later the anti-Arian/Catholic Christians would depend on the bishop of Rome for support. The Three Chapters controversy revealed how African Christians still reserved the right to criticize the pope, but as a last resort and assuming that having the bishop of Rome's support and approval was the ideal state of the African church. When Pope Gregory came to rule over the Roman church, he at times directed his attention toward Africa.[107]

Around 590 Gregory the Great writes a series of letters about "Donatists" who rebaptized "Catholics" in Africa. Before turning to Gregory's letters, we should note how historians interpret the pope's statements today. While some modern scholars think Gregory was misinformed, others believe that Donatism continued throughout the Vandal and into the Byzantine period.[108] Furthermore, historians debate whether the references to Donatists in this century (which have been catalogued in this present study) constitute a reliable record of actual Donatists or are simply rhetorical depictions of African dissenters deemed "Donatist." In addition to the references to Donatists given so far in this chapter, there are material remains that archaeologists have found that point to an ongoing Donatist party. Several inscriptions from the Byzantine era include the theme of "unity [*unititas*]" and reference to "one baptism [*unum baptisma*]," which suggests a rival communion that rebaptizes.[109] These, however, could refer to an ongoing Arian/Vandal form of Christianity, and so no single piece of evidence can count as undeniable proof either for or against a Donatist presence.[110]

Even beyond the particular references to Donatism, there is an argument for the ongoing existence of a Donatist form of Christianity that is worth revisiting once more in light of Gregory's references to Donatism. Whereas the momentous council of Carthage in 411 did bring the Donatist claims to legitimacy to an end in the eyes of the empire, we have already recounted in previous chapters how Donatists became an underground church that left clear traces of its ongoing survival. In the fourth and early fifth century, the Donatists were strongest in Numidia and Mauretania. Then, when the Vandals had virtually no control over these areas, all evidence of (both for and against) Donatism largely disappeared from the records for these areas. Which is more plausible: that Donatism naturally died out in these and other areas or that these areas allowed Donatism to flourish, perhaps even without the need for the ongoing identity of "Donatist"? Burns and Jensen and their collaborators conclude that the Donatists developed strategies against the Caecilianist/Catholics that helped them survive the Vandal persecution, especially since most Donatists resided in territories outside of Vandal control. These scholars add, "The tenacity of this ethnically African movement [i.e. Donatism] perhaps demonstrates a continued disaffection of the native population from a Catholic, Romanized hierarchy as well as from foreign secular authorities."[111] This debate, which cannot be resolved here, is important to keep in mind when reading the sources referring to Donatists at this time. Let us then return to Gregory's letters to see what can be learned about African Christianity at the turn of the seventh century.

In 591 Gregory writes to Gennadius, the exarch of Africa,[112] asking him to oppose "the adversaries of the Catholic Church."[113] In particular, Gregory wants Gennadius to take action in "resisting the Donatists."[114] The Donatist threat derived explicitly from Numidia, where a council had been held to appoint a new primate. The Numidian Christians did not award seniority to the largest imperial city in the province, something known as a "metropolitan," but instead they declared the highest ranking bishop their primate, no matter where he presided.

It is telling that in a letter written almost at the same time, Gregory describes Gennadius's victories in Africa in terms that recall ancient Rome's civilizing mission:

> [regarding the] wars you frequently rush into, not from a desire to pour out men's blood, but for the sake of extending the republic's domain, in which we see the worship of God, so that the name of Christ spread in every direction through the subject nations.[115]

Clearly, Gregory writes to the exarch of Africa with a clear sense of how the Romans rule over Africans. The historical background to this sentiment is the ongoing rebellions from Mauretanian groups in the latter half of the seventh century.[116] Some of these groups gained major victories over Roman forces around 570.[117] When the new emperor, Tiberius II, appointed Gennadius to Africa, the general led successful campaigns against the native rebels. Gregory congratulates Gennadius on this success, and in addition to this political statement, Gregory clearly understands Christianity in Africa as divided between "Roman" and local allegiances so that the African Christians outside of the "Catholic" canonical practice are "Donatists." It should be noted that Gennadius's successes were not long lasting: in 593 he had to retreat into Carthage because of defeats by the Mauretanians, who had raided most of the African provinces.

In another letter written at the same time, Gregory speaks directly to "all the bishops of Numidia"[118] about their local custom.[119] In this letter Gregory agrees to condone the practice of appointing the senior bishop as primate, only he warns against accepting those who came "from the Donatists."[120] His claim about the Donatists requires further scrutiny.

If Gregory's letter accurately recorded a practice of Numidian bishops accepting Donatists, then we have evidence of both an ongoing Donatist presence and of a tendency for (some) African "Catholics" to accept said Donatists. Such a reading of Gregory, however, is not without problems. It may be that Gregory was misinformed about "Donatists." He may have assumed that any dissident group and/or any "rebaptizers" would be Donatists, and such an assumption would be based on earlier caricatures and not firsthand information about African Christians. Therefore, Gregory's letters must be read critically.

Gregory did receive firsthand information about the Numidian Christians from a certain Hilary, through whom the Numidians communicated with the bishop of Rome. Even so, this communication was directed toward Gregory's predecessor, Pelagius II, and not Gregory himself, so there is still the real possibility of Gregory's being misinformed. Then again, Gregory continues to use Hilary to communicate with the Numidian bishops, as seen in another letter written at this same time.[121]

In this next letter Gregory tells of reports from two deacons in Numidia who accuse their bishop, Argentius of Lamigenum, of accepting bribes from "Donatists" and promoting those Donatists to a church office.[122] Gregory orders a local council be held to investigate the matter. No record survives to indicate whether or not Gregory's orders were carried out in Africa. It is likely that they were not.

The next summer Gregory issues a letter related to another matter. The manuscripts of this letter differ slightly in terms of who Gregory addresses: most record this letter simply to "all [*universis*]," but many editors correct this to read "all the eastern bishops," while some even have the unlikely addition of "the bishops throughout Iberia."[123,124] In short, the stated audience is unknowable for this letter. The aim of the letter, however, is clear: it is "concerning the three chapters."[125] Gregory defends Rome's historic position, going back to Vigilius, in condemning the Three Chapters. He then insists that anyone still reluctant to accept the decision of "the royal city [*in urbe regia*]" should repent and return to the "mother Church."[126] It is curious that editors have not considered the southern and African bishops as recipients of the letter, since it was African writers who were the most outspoken against Pope Vigilius and Emperor Justinian (see pp. 295–301). In this letter Gregory cites no scripture nor any council or decree; his only citation in the whole letter is from Cyprian,[127] and this in fact is the only time Gregory cites Cyprian in all of his letters. This unique citation of the former bishop of Carthage may have been an intentional use of African tradition against any remnant African Christians who still objected to the Roman church's support of the denunciation of the Three Chapters. This conclusion, however, is admittedly tenuous because many regions retained factions that broke with Rome over this issue.[128]

There are two other letters from this same month (July 592) that demonstrate that Gregory had African Christianity in view as a major concern. One is to a bishop in southern Italy (Squillacium) named John. Gregory warns him about ordaining various sorts of sinners and criminals, and he then insists:

> On no account accept Africans indiscriminately, nor unknown strangers, who want to be ordained. For some of the Africans are in fact

Manicheans, other rebaptized, and most foreigners in fact, even when
established in the minor orders, have often been proved to have had
pretensions of higher honors.[129]

This clearly shows Gregory's distrust of the African church.

In a second letter written in that same month Gregory writes to a certain
Columbus. Columbus was a bishop in Numidia (but his city is not known).
He writes because another bishop in Numidia, Maximian of Pudentia,
allegedly accepted a bribe from the Donatists and allowed a Donatist to be
appointed as a bishop.[130] Gregory then refers to the previous year's controversy in Numidia, where he had opposed the local custom of allowing the
primate to go to the senior bishop: "the Catholic faith prohibited this from
continuing and persisting, even if an earlier use might have permitted it."[131]
Gregory then further explains:

> Moreover we have learnt from the report of letter that the Donatist her-
> esy is spreading each day, because of their sins, and large crowds, given
> license through venality, are being baptized again by the Donatists, after
> having had a Catholic baptism.[132]

Here again historians cannot know for certain whether Gregory's letters
accurately relay facts about an ongoing Donatist party, or whether Gregory
assumed that any "rebaptizers" in Africa were "Donatists." He did remain
in ongoing communication with others in Africa, such as Dominic, bishop
of Carthage, at this time.[133] Although their ongoing correspondence demonstrates Dominic's alliance with Gregory, the bishop of Carthage did insist at
the beginning of their relationship that he had certain "ecclesiastical privi-
leges" that the bishop of Rome could not supersede.[134]

One year later Gregory again writes to Columbus, praising him for his
commitment to "Saint Peter, the prince of the apostles."[135] In turn, Gregory
warns Columbus about the "primate of your synod," which is a reference
to Adeodatus.[136] The cause for concern is that ordination is being given to
those who are too young. Gregory repeats this concern in a letter written at
the same time to Adeodatus himself, and he advises Adeodatus to consult
with Columbus in every decision.[137] Whatever actions Adeodatus took, his
fellow Numidian bishops did not approve, for they remove him from office,
as known from Gregory's letter to the primate of Byzacium, Crementius.[138]
Only a few months later, Gregory wrote again to Gennadius, the exarch of
Africa. Apparently the bishops in Africa had not heeded Gregory's advice,
for the pope had to ask the exarch to intervene in "Numidia, [since] many
things are being committed contrary to the way of the Fathers and the stat-
utes of the canons."[139] Once again, Gregory recommended Columbus as an
advisor.

One year later, Gregory's concerns have only grown, and in a letter to
the praetorian prefect in Africa, Pantaleo, he decries "the audacity of the
Donatists" who "rebaptize" Catholics.[140] At this time Gregory also writes

a letter to the new primate of Numidia, Victor, and addresses a letter sharing these concerns to Columbus as well. Therein, Gregory repeats the same
claims and recommends a council be held to deal specifically with Donatism
and rebaptism.[141] In Carthage, Bishop Dominic presided over a council
dealing with unnamed "heretics," which in all likelihood is in reference to
Gregory's concern with Donatism, but there are few firm details known
from this council.[142]

Two years later Gregory writes back to Columbus, again insisting the
Donatist problem be addressed. A bishop named Peter arrived in Rome and
asked for the pope to intervene in his case, where he had been removed from
office. Gregory refers Peter back to Columbus asking to him to judge the
case. Gregory then tells of reports that "Catholic" Christians allow members of their household to be baptized by "Donatists."[143] Columbus should
forbid this, and anyone who continues in the practice should be "cut off
totally from the clergy."[144] Two months after this letter to Columbus, Gregory writes three more letters about the problem in Numidia. To the exarch
Gennadius, Gregory (who is obviously frustrated) complains that Gennadius has not sent a certain bishop from Numidia named Paul to Rome.[145]
The "Donatists" persecuted Paul, and Gennadius – not the primate –
excommunicated him. In a letter to Dominic, Gregory encourages him to
continue in piety and thanks him for recent gifts, but makes no mention of
the Donatists.[146] In a third letter Gregory, writes to Emperor Maurice, asking him to enforce the anti-heretical laws against the "Donatists" because
the problems are growing in "the province of Africa."[147]

Gregory writes again to Columbus two months later, indicating that
the same problems continue in Numidia. In doing so, Gregory addresses
Columbus's complaint: "that you suffer the enmity of many men, because
we contact you quite frequently with our letters."[148] Apparently, Gregory
has been both ignored and denigrated in Numidia, and Columbus's association with the pope has brought enmity from his fellow African bishops.[149]

Gregory's next letter about problems in Africa arrives the next year
(597), when he advises Dominic of Carthage about monks who refuse to
remain under the authority of a cloistered abbot but instead leave, "wan-
dering wherever they want to go."[150] While these monks likely should not
be identified with the Circumcellions of earlier Donatism, they likely do
represent a different understanding of monastic orders than the bishop of
Rome condones.

Another year later and the pope continues to work on behalf of the
bishop Paul, as evidenced by three letters sent to Numidian bishops on
his behalf asking for further investigation into his case.[151] Later that same
year (July 598), Gregory writes to Dominic of Carthage. In addition to
general encouragement and expressions of Christian affection, Gregory
claims Roman origins for Christianity's arrival in "the African regions."[152]
It should be remembered that earlier Christians, such as Tertullian, did not
know of a connection to an apostolic see. Gregory, who likely believes his

claim is historically accurate, certainly mentions this indebtedness of Africa to Rome in his letter to Dominic for rhetorical reasons.

Another two years pass and Gregory once again writes about the problems in Numidia. A terrible plague has spread through many "parts of Africa," and he writes to share his prayers and encouragement.[153] Two months later, writing to Innocent, the praetorian prefect of Africa, Gregory speaks in general terms about reports of where "the African judges [i.e. the bishops] are guilty of many violent acts in their areas and many other deeds contrary to customary edicts"[154] Again, Gregory acknowledges the local customs, but wishes for the African bishops to align with his Roman tradition. It seems that they never comply. The result of Paul's case, for which Gregory expended so much energy, is not known. As late as 602, Gregory continues to involve himself in African church affairs,[155] but then he turns his attention elsewhere and the controversy between the pope and Numidia disappears from the historical record.

Gregory's view of African Christians and his inability to enforce decisions in Africa have elicited many comments from scholars, and so we should return to the question with which we began this section.[156] Does Gregory provide reliable information about Donatism and African Christianity? Robert Markus states, "The change of Gregory's tone over the years needs no comment. He had come to accept the limits on the range of his influence which he could do nothing to remove."[157] Markus elsewhere describes what he thinks was the real "Donatist" element Gregory faced: "What Gregory interpreted as Donatism was nothing more and nothing less than the African Church's traditional sense of autonomy re-asserting itself."[158] John R. C. Martin further establishes Markus's argument by noting how independent the African, and especially the Numidian, bishops were: "The appeal cases reveal that while both the North African church and imperial administrators might pay the pope a nominal courtesy, he was in practice powerless to act on any matter without their support. And the evidence is that they regarded such matters as their own internal affair."[159] Markus, however, has even more to say about the nature of this African independent spirit. For him, the true Donatists merged with the Catholics at the onset of the Vandal invasion[160] (a premise shown to be problematic in Chapter 9). He concludes, therefore, that the late sixth-century expression of independence from Rome's ecclesiastical jurisdiction is due to the "rise of the Berber [i.e. Mauretanian] kingdoms . . . what Gregory knew as 'Donatism' was in fact a non-Roman, Berber Christianity."[161] Jonathan Conant concurs with Markus up to a point, "the African church was an essentially conservative institution that instinctively rejected what it saw as encroachments on its prerogatives from external authorities such as the emperor in Constantinople and the Pope in Rome."[162] He hastens to add, however, that "this did not equate to a rejection of the empire – nor indeed of the papacy – as such." Conant rejects any idea of the African "church acting as a nationalistic organ uncertain as to the benefits of Byzantine rule."[163] Instead, Conant finds the African church in Gregory's time, although independent and of a "fourth-century attitude," to be fully integrated into the empire.

Given the focus of this present study, it is tempting to concur with Markus about the indigenous makeup of these independent African bishops. After all, Markus cannot be blamed for seeing Gregory's opponents in Africa in line with African Christianity's previous history: their "dissent comes to a sharp focus at two points on which we may almost be tempted to speak of an African orthodoxy: the Emperor's place in the Church, and the autonomy of provincial churches in the face of Rome."[164] Against this view, it must be admitted that Markus's argument draws too sharp of a dividing line between the Roman and the "Berber," and we should instead acknowledge how many of the recipients of Gregory's letters likely understood themselves as full participants in the political, economic, and public affairs of the empire.[165] Conant's point is well taken, but even here more can be said.[166] As has been shown in the earlier periods of African Christian history, to be "Roman" does not necessarily imply that one is somehow "not African." While we need not go so far as Markus and see an indigenous "Berber" ethnicity at the root of the controversy with Pope Gregory, we should take into account the identity and self-understanding of the African bishops.

In short, Gregory's exchange with the African bishops represents another scene where the bishop of Rome disputed with and failed to convince African Christians. We should not attempt to make too much of this pattern, since we have an equally important record of African Christians attempting to remain in communion with Rome. What Gregory's correspondence does indicate is that the African Christians still operated with a strong sense of independence. They need not agree with the pope or the emperor, something that can be found in the next scene in the story of African Christianity when Maximus the Confessor comes to Carthage.

Maximus the Confessor

The next major scene witnessed in the sources of North African Christianity occurred twenty-two years after Pope Gregory's death when Maximus the Confessor arrived in Carthage. Maximus (c.580–662) had to flee from a new threat raging in the east, and with Carthage as his new base of operations he continued to combat his opponents in Constantinople. The African bishops, as we shall see, supported him in his efforts.

Little is known of Maximus's early life.[167] Later accounts tell how he was born in Palestine, but scholars discount these sources today. He rose to a high rank in Emperor Heraclius's government, but at some point Maximus abandoned his career and joined a monastery across the Bosphorus from Constantinople. This move, however, would not last because the Persians conquered the region and forced many, including Maximus, to flee.

In 626 Maximus fled to what he called in a letter to the Byzantine general in North Africa "the region of the Africans,"[168] where he both influenced[169] and was influenced[170] by the Christians there. One source went so far as to claim that Maximus "led astray the whole of Africa, and there was no one who disputed with them in Africa."[171] Although this source is hostile to Maximus and late, other sources corroborate this point about the strong support Maximus received from the African bishops.[172]

Around the same time, Maximus's theological friend and ally, Sophronius, also came to Africa.[173] Sophronius, like Maximus, was a monk who had become embroiled in the theological controversies of his day, and he would later play a crucial role in the Monophysite controversy when appointed patriarch of Jerusalem.[174]

In essence, the controversy at this time was an extension of the Three Chapters controversy from the previous century. As part of an ongoing effort to appease the so-called Monophysite Christians, Sergius, the patriarch of Constantinople (610–638), attempted a compromise by claiming that Christ had two natures but one "energy." The emperor Heraclius (r.610–641) attempted to use this formula to reunite the Dyophysites and Monophysites.

Heraclius himself (as discussed in Chapter 1) began his ascendancy to power from Africa. His father, Heraclius the elder, had served as exarch of Africa, but he then opposed the emperor Phocas. Although some, like George of Pisidia, in a work entitled *On Heraclius's Return from Africa*, praised the new emperor, others must have seen his action as a usurpation of power.[175] Heraclius faced numerous political challenges in his early reign, and the possibility of uniting the Christian churches with Sergius's new formula must have been appealing.

Heraclius appointed patriarchs of Antioch and Alexandria who supported the formula, and along with Sergius, the pope in Rome added his approval.[176] When Sophronius became the patriarch of Jerusalem, he adamantly opposed Sergius's formula as a capitulation to monophysitism. Sophronius instead insisted that Christ had two energies corresponding to his two natures: a human and a divine.[177] This alternative was at least partially compelling.

Sergius and his supporters conceded to Sophronius's objections, and so they offered a revised hypothesis. Rather than speaking of "energy," Christ's two natures were said to be united in his one "will" (Greek: *thelēma*). This view, later known as "monothelitism" (i.e. "mono" or one + *thelēma* or will), quickly gained the support of Rome, Constantinople, Alexandria, and Antioch. Sophronius, however, died in 638. With Jerusalem now under Muslim rule, the Christian community was not able to appoint a successor for decades.[178] The only voice left, therefore, to challenge the monothelite form of monophysitism was Maximus, who remained in Africa where he had been tutored by Sophronius.

Not long after this, because of other scandals taking place in the emperor's court, another pilgrim arrived in Carthage: Pyrrhus, the patriarch of Constantinople. After Heraclius's death, Pyrrhus had been accused of plotting against Heraclius's son, and so he was exiled to Africa. While there, he agreed to debate Maximus.[179] Maximus insisted that Christ must have two wills that correspond to his two natures and two energies. After an extended debate, Pyrrhus allegedly conceded to Maximus, and so went to Rome and gained the support of Pope Theodore I, who also held to a dyothelite, or two-will, Christology.

It is worth noting here that Theodore of Rome himself had come to his view because of the council of the African bishops who had opposed the attempts of the emperor Heraclius to enforce monoenergist and then monothelite Christology.[180] Fortunatus, who was bishop of Carthage at the time, disagreed with Maximus, but it seems that he was unique in doing so, for he was denounced by a council of African bishops in 646 and removed from office. His successor, Victor, would support the dyothelite position, and other primates in Africa at the time held regional councils that did the same: namely, Columbus of Numidia, Stephen of Byzacena, and Reparatus of Mauritania. The African bishops then sent letters to Theodore of Rome and to the emperor in Constantinople, stating their firm stance on dyothelite Christology.[181] Many African bishops even went to Rome, and at least one, Victorianus of Uzalis (modern El Alia, Tunisia), participated in the Lateran Council of 649, where the Monothelites were anathematized.

For leading in this action, Theodore's successor, Pope Martin I, was accused of treason and arrested. More than strictly theological treachery, Martin's treason was said to be his political collaboration with Gregory, the exarch of Africa.[182] Exarch Gregory, as was mentioned in Chapter 1 and as will be discussed further in Chapter 11, had declared himself emperor – not of Rome, but of Africa, making Africa independent from Rome.

Maximus likewise was arrested for treason,[183] and exiled.[184] At the trial, a soldier testified about how Maximus had advised the general in Africa to withhold troops and not to aid the emperor against the Arab incursions: Maximus allegedly stated, "God did not approve lending aid to the Roman Empire during the reign of Heraclius and his kin."[185] While this is likely unfounded rumor, it nevertheless represents how the Roman officials in Constantinople likely would have viewed Maximus and other dissenters in North Africa. For his crimes, Maximus's tongue was cut out and one of his hands was cut off, and although he did not die until later, he earned the title "Confessor."

Later, Pyrrhus returned to Constantinople, where he reverted to his Monothelite teachings and was eventually accepted back as the patriarch in 654. The emperor's opponents, however, were influential enough to continue the debate until 680, when the third Council of Constantinople met and declared Monothelites heretics. Because of the incursion of Muslims into North Africa (see Chapter 11) none of the African bishops attended the council. Although neither Maximus nor the African bishops were mentioned in the proceedings, their view won the day.[186]

The Monothelite controversy marks the last literary evidence of African Christianity. Christianity in Africa did survive for some time after the region was conquered by the Arab empire, and the evidence for its survival will be reviewed in Chapter 11. For now, we can simply observe how the evidence from the time of Maximus the Confessor depicts African Christianity as fiercely independent of Rome and Constantinople, as has been the case in so many earlier periods of its history.

Conclusions about Byzantine Africa

In the Byzantine period, African Christians became even more entangled in the debates and politics of the empire, while at the same time the empire lost even more of its control over the region. This paradox speaks to the theme repeated throughout this book regarding the diverse and complex social setting of this region. When the Byzantines reclaimed Africa from the Vandals, they acquired the loyalty of much of the local populace while also alienating others in Africa. The former group largely identified themselves within the Roman heritage of the past, while the latter group's voices disappear from our record, with only caricatures remaining of them in the literature of their opponents. Where do the Christians fit into this picture? As with the general population, African Christians simultaneously engaged in the wider empire and contested and resisted the foreign traditions that differed from their own cherished African Christian legacy.

When compared to earlier African Christian history discussed in previous chapters, we see much of the same patterns in the Byzantine era. Robert Markus (whose other views were discussed in detail on pp. 307–308) surveys the surviving evidence from the last centuries of African Christianity:

> the persistence and volume of dissent throughout the history of African Christianity is striking enough to prompt the historian to seek an underlying thread behind the changing forms. The Church of Tertullian and Cyprian, the Church of Donatus and Parmenian, the Church of Ferrandus and Facundus, are all stamped with a common character; and some of its features are to be discerned even in the Church of Augustine and Aurelius. It is a character with a vitality which made itself felt again in the seventh century, when the opposition to monothelitism, rallied around Maximus, had its mainstay in the African Church. But the days of imperial rule in Africa were numbered. Within half a century of the African rebellion against Constans II (645), a rebellion with wide popular support, especially among the Berber tribes, Africa was in Arab hands.[187]

The pattern Markus sees in African Christianity at this time is certainly remarkable, and yet we once again should express some caution about his depiction. Many African Christians would have understood themselves as full participants in the Roman political and ecclesiastical systems. For some, this was a clear alternative to the explicit anti-Roman stance of these sixth-century literary sources. For many others, they would have likely seen no contradiction between their belonging to the Roman systems and their allegiance to their local African traditions.

Now that this history has been surveyed, we can turn to the disappearance of ancient African Christianity from our sources. This disappearance began with the spread of the Arab conquerors into North Africa, and so it is to this final chapter and to the final remnants of evidence about ancient African Christianity that we can now turn.

Notes

1 Averil Cameron, "The Byzantine Reconquest of North Africa and the Impact of Greek Culture," *Graeco-Arabica* 5 (1993), 153; reprinted in Cameron, *Changing Cultures in Early Byzantium* (Aldershot, UK: Variorum, 1996).

2 E.g. Procopius, *History of the Wars* 3.19: Ῥωμαῖοι.

3 Procopius, *History of the Wars* 3.20: Λίβυας γὰρ ἅπαντας Ῥωμαίους τὸ ἀνέκαθεν ὄντας.

4 Procopius, *Buildings* 6.3: Μαυρούσιοί τε βάρβαροι . . . Φοινικικὸν ἔθνος. It should be noted that all of book six in this work is devoted to Egypt and Africa.

5 Procopius, *History of the Wars* 3.21.

6 Dossey, *Peasant and Empire*, 26.

7 *Justinian's Novels* Appendix 9.

8 Averil Cameron, "Byzantine Africa: The Literary Evidence," in *Excavations at Carthage* vol. 7, ed. John H. Humphrey (Ann Arbor: University of Michigan, 1982), 32.

9 See Tilley, "The Collapse of a Collegial Church: North African Christianity on the Eve of Islam," *Theological Studies* 62 (1, 2001), 15.

10 Procopius, *History of the Wars* 4.7.

11 *Christianity in Roman Africa*, 77.

12 Procopius, *History of the Wars* 4.8–13 and 4.19–28, on the Mauretanians. For a mutiny of "Arian" soldiers in the Roman army, see 4.14–17.

13 Procopius, *History of the Wars* 4.10. Although these groups included Latin and even Punic names, they were primarily Mauretanians in linguistic/ethnic terms; see Conant, *Staying Roman*, 293–294; further details are found throughout his chapter "The Moorish Alternative" (pp. 252–305).

14 Procopius, *History of the Wars* 4.10: Ἡμεῖς ἐσμεν οἱ φυγόντες ἀπὸ προσώπου Ἰησοῦ τοῦ λῃστοῦ υἱοῦ Ναυῆ. Procopius also notes other "nations . . . in Libya [ἔθνη ἐν Λιβύῃ]" who predate the Punic population.

15 *Secret History* 18: Λιβύη μὲν γὰρ ἐς τοσοῦτον διήκουσα μέτρον οὕτως ἀπόλωλεν ὥστε ὁδὸν ἰόντι πολλὴν ἀνδρὶ ἐντυχεῖν χαλεπόν τε καὶ λόγου ἄξιον εἶναι . . . . Λιβύων δὲ τῶν ἐν ταῖς πόλεσιν ᾠκημένων τὰ πρότερα καὶ γῆν γεωργούντων ἐργασίαν τε τὴν κατὰ θάλασσαν ἐργαζομένων, ὅπερ μοι αὐτόπτῃ ἐπὶ πλεῖστον γεγονέναι τετύχηκε, πῶς ἄν τις τὸ πλῆθος διαριθμεῖσθαι ἱκανὸς εἴη τῶν πάντων ἀνθρώπων; τούτων δὲ πολλῷ ἔτι πλείους Μαυρούσιοι ἦσαν ἐνταῦθα, οἷς δὴ ἅπασι ξύν τε 8γυναιξὶ καὶ γόνῳ διεφθάρθαι ξυνέβη.

16 *Secret History* 18: κατ᾽ ἐξουσίαν Λιβύην καταπιὼν ὅλην λῄζεται. Τιμητὰς ἀμέλει τῆς γῆς εὐθὺς ἔπεμπε καὶ φόρους ἐπετίθει πικροτάτους τινὰς οὐ πρότερον ὄντας. καὶ τῶν χωρίων προσεποιεῖτο, εἴ τι ἄριστον ἦν. καὶ Ἀρειανοὺς τῶν ἐν σφίσιν αὐτοῖς μυστηρίων εἶργε. καὶ ταῖς στρατιωτικαῖς δυνάμεσιν ὑπερήμερος ἦν, καὶ ἄλλως τοῖς

στρατιώταις ἐγεγόνει βαρύς. ἐξ ὧν αἱ στάσεις φυόμεναι τετελευτήκασιν εἰς ὄλεθρον μέγαν.

17 For other dividing lines, such as dress and appearance, see Conant, *Staying Roman*, 263–273.

18 See Gregory Hays, "Date and Identity of the Mythographer Fulgentius," *Journal of Medieval Latin* 13 (2003), 163–252.

19 Namely, *The Mythologies*; *The Explanation of Virgilian Continence*; *The Explanation of Obsolete Words*; and *On the Ages of the World and of Man*. Texts in Rudolf Helm, *Fulgentii Opera* (Leipzig, 1898; reprint. Stutgart, 1970); and a heavily criticized translation is available by Leslie George Whitebread, *Fulgentius the Mythographer* (Columbus, OH: Ohio State University Press, 1971).

20 *Mythologies* prol.11.

21 *Explanation of Virgilian Continence* 103.13–107.4.

22 Emily Albu, "Disarming Aeneas: Fulgentius on *Arms and the Man*," in *The Power of Religion in Late Antiquity*, ed. Andrew Cain and Noel Lenski (Farnham, UK: Ashgate, 2009), 28.

23 "'*Romuleis Libicisque Litteris*': Fulgentius and the 'Vandal Renaissance,'" in *Vandals, Romans and Berbers: New Perspectives on Late Antique North Africa*, ed. Andrew H. Merrills (Aldershot, UK: Ashgate, 2004), 107.

24 "*Romuleis Libicisque Litteris*," 104.

25 Text in Jacob Diggle and F.R.D. Goodyear, *Flavii Cresconii Corippi Iohannidos seu De Bellis Libycis LIbri VIII* (Cambridge: Cambridge University Press, 1970). Trans.: George W. Shea, *The Iohannis or De Bellis Libycis of Flavius Cresconius Corippus* (Studies in Classics 7; Lewiston: Edwin Mellen, 1998). See discussion in Cameron, "Byzantine Africa: The Literary Evidence," 29–62.

26 The *Codex Matritensis*, discussed in Shea, *The Iohannis*, 3.

27 *Iohannis*, pref.25. . . 28.

28 Also, cf. *Iohannis* 2.24–27.

29 *Iohannis* pref.35–37.

30 Shea, *The Iohannis*, 2.

31 *Iohannis* pref.7 and 15; cf. 1.159–196. Similarly, Corippus interprets the murder of Remus by Romulus to have been necessary to establish a single monarchy; Remus's blood was a necessary sacrifice for Rome (*Iohannis* 4.88–96).

32 *Iohannis* 6.340.

33 Cf. *Iohannis* 1.27–47; 1.500–581. Likewise, after moving to Constantinople, Corippus celebrated the new emperor, Justin II (r.565–574), in his work, *In Praise of the Younger Justin*; see Averil Cameron, *Flavius Cresconius Corippus: In laudem Iustini Augusti minoris* (*In Praise of Justin II*) (London: Athlone, Press, 1976), for text, translation, and commentary.

34 *Iohannis* 1.244–245: *cognate tenebris / Maura videbatur facies nigroque colore*. Later (2.137), the Mauretanians are said to have "black feet [*sub nigra calctur*]."

35 *Iohannis* 6.92–94: *nec color ipse fuit captivis omnibus unus. / concolor illa sedet cum nigris horrida natis, / corvorum veluti*.

36 Corippus, *Iohannis* 2.134–137; cf. *The Augustan History: Severus* 19; and Procopius, *History of the Wars* 4.6.

37 *Iohannis* 3.277; cf. 4.86; 7.504; 7.218; 7.553; 8.577. He also describes Carthage in particular as a "Tyrean city [*Tyriam . . . urbem*]" (7.150) and as "Sidonean" (cf. 3.19; 3.280; 6.63; 6.223; 7.195).

38 E.g. *Iohannis* 4.85–86, on "Punic altars [*penates Poenorum*]"; and *Iohannis* 2.109–111, on Baal Hammon, or "horned Ammon [*corniger Ammon*]," who is also referenced in 3.81–82; 6.147–190; 7.515–536; 8.304; cf. Minucius Felix, *Octavius* 23 (discussed in chapter five). There is also mention of the indigenous Mauretanian god, Gurzil, son of Hammon (*Iohannis* 5.22–39; 6.119; 8.304), and then in a later section several indigenous gods are recounted as worshipped

by the various peoples mustered against John – one group even worships "Jupiter" (= Baal?) with human sacrifices (8.300–315). For the archaeological corroboration of Libyo-Punic religions being practiced at this time, see discussion and bibliography in Mark A. Handley, "Disputing the End of African Christianity," in *Vandals, Romans, and Berbers: New Perspectives on Late Antique North Africa*, ed. A. H. Merrills (Aldershot, UK: Ashgate, 2004), 297.

39   It should also be noted that Corippus repeatedly lists the many different "tribes" of "Africans"/"Mauretanians," showing that he is aware of the diversity within this larger category.

40   See Shea, *The* Iohannis, 4.

41   *Iohannis* 4.234: *potuit Libyam Romanis reddere.*

42   Therefore, historians tend to trust Procopius's account more. Corripus's later work *In Praise of Justin II* focuses on the new emperor's actions in Constantinople, and so scarcely refers to Africa. E.g. *In Praise of Justin II* 1.pref., where he explains, "Why should I speak of the peoples of Libya and the battles in Syrtis already covered in my writings?" (Cameron, *Flavius Cresconius Corippus*, 34 and 85); cf. 1.18–19, on an earlier successful prefect of Africa; and 1.285–287, where the conquest of the Vandals and Libya is actually mentioned as depicted in an embroidery honoring Justinian.

43   Conant, *Staying Roman*, 267–269.

44   E.g. Corripus, *Iohannis* 5.352; 6.194; 6.511.

45   Cameron, "Byzantine Africa," 36.

46   For details, see Lancel and Mattei, *Pax et Concordia*, 99–115.

47   On the law against Vandals in Africa, see Justinian's *Body of Civil Law: New Law* 37 (="On the African Church").

48   *Body of Civil Law: New Law* 37.5: *neque Arianis neque Donatistis nec Iudaeis nec aliis* (my trans.). See also material in Maier, *Le dossier du Donatisme* 2:324–334. The reference to Donatism here is taken by Stanisław Adamiak ("When did Donatist Christianity End?" 217) to refer to an ongoing reality of a separate Donatist party, not simply a "perfunctory formula."

49   *Body of Civil Law: New Law* 37.7: *rebaptizatos . . . militiam* (my trans.)

50   *Body of Civil Law: New Law* 37.1: *concilo totius Africae* (my trans.)

51   Jean-Pierre Adam, *Roman Building: Material and Techniques* (London: Routledge, 2005), 233.

52   See Burns, Jensen, et al., *Christianity in Roman Africa*, 97, for its importance in dating to the pre-Byzantine period.

53   Burns, Jensen, et al., *Christianity in Roman Africa*, 76. One can see in the remains of a house in Utica (in modern Tunisia) where three different historical layers of flooring have been unearthed, which nicely illustrates how the various centuries and empires built upon the previous ones.

54   *Early Christianity in North Africa*, 195.

55   *Christianity in Roman Africa*, 78.

56   See Conant, "Donatism in the Fifth and Sixth Centuries," 345–361; and Gaumer, "*Ad Africa vistare sepulchrum sancti Cypriani.*" Around this time, Cassiodorus made numerous references to the Donatists. He wrote, however, from Constantinople, and he was dependent on Augustine. Therefore, his references do not necessarily constitute evidence of a distinct Donatist party at this time. For an argument that Cassiodorus should be read as evidence of Donatism, see Adamiak, "When did Donatist Christianity End?" 220–222; and P.G. Walsh, *Cassiodorus: Explanation of the Psalms* (ACW 51; New York: Paulist Press, 1990), 11.

57   Cf. Cameron, "Byzantine Africa," 45, on the Greek patterns of leadership and influence.

58   Markus, "Reflections on Religious Dissent," 144–149.

59   For a general introduction see Wilhite, *The Gospel According to Heretics*, 145–168; and for a more detailed treatment, see Michael Maas, *Exegesis and Empire*

in the Early Byzantine Mediterranean: Junilius Africanus and the Instituta Regularia Divinae Legis *(Studien und Texte zu Antike und Christentum* 17; Tubingen: Mohr Siebeck, 2003), 42–64.

60 What is known as the hypostatic union articulated in the Chalcedonian Definition.

61 Zeno's *Henoticon* can be found in Evagrius, *Church History* 3.14.

62 *Sentence Against the "Three Chapters":* Sed etiam Augustini religiosae memoriae qui inter Africanos episcopos splenduit, diversae epistolae rictatae sunt, significantes quod oportet haereticos et post mortem anathematizari. Talem autem ecclesiasticam traditionem, et alii Africani reverendissimi episcope servaverunt. For the sessions of this council, see from Richard Price, *The Acts of the Council of Constantinople of 553,* 2 vols. (Liverpool: Liverpool University Press, 2009).

63 *Letter* 6. The text of his letters is in CCL 90:359–362, 385–387. In addition to his letters, he authored a collection of ecclesiastical canons that included prior decisions from both Greek and African councils; the text is in CCL 149:284–311. For discussion of Ferrandus, see R. B. Eno, "Ferrandus and Facundus on Doctrinal Authority," *Studia patristica* 15, ed. E. A. Livingstone (Berlin, 1984), 291–296.

64 *Letter* 1: *famulus . . . adolescens, colore Aethiops* (= 11.2 in Fulgentius's collection; CCL 91:360).

65 *Letter* 2 (= 13 in Fulgentius's collection; CCL 91:385–387).

66 Fulgentius's response includes both numerous explanations of scriptural passages as well as reference to Augustine's teachings (see *Letter* 12.24–26 [CCL 91:378–381]; 14.16–18 [CCL 91:403–408]; 14.27–34 [CCL 91:419–428]; 14.46 [CCL 91:442]). Also, Ferrandus specifically references the church's teaching in the "regions of Africa [*Africae regiones*]" (*Letter* 13.2 [CCL 91:386]). Finally, for Ferrandus's references to Donatism, see Adamiak, "When did Donatist Christianity End?" 218–219.

67 Ferrandus's *Brevatio canonum* can be found in CCL 149:284–311.

68 Cf. Ferrandus, *Brevatio canonum* 42 and 66.

69 Ferrandus, *Brevatio canonum* 58, mentions "the apostolic see [*apostolicem sedem*]." Again, this is a shift from earlier African tradition. During Augustine's time, an African priest named Apiarius from Sicca was condemned by a council of African bishops. He appealed to Pope Zosimus, who defended his right to do so. The African bishops, however, denied such a right. See details in Mar Marcos, "Papal Authority, Local Autonomy, and Imperial Control: Pope Zosimus and the Western Churches (a.417–418)," in *The Role of the Bishop in Late Antiquity: Conflict and Compromise,* ed. Andrew Fear, José Fernández Ubiña, and Mar Marcos (London: Bloomsbury, 2013), 157–160.

70 Victor of Tunnuna, *Chronicle* 141.

71 See Patrick Amory, *People and Identity in Ostrogothic Italy, 489–554* (Cambridge: Cambridge University Press, 1997), for sources.

72 Markus, "Religious Dissent," 143–144.

73 For the text, see CCSL 173A: 3–55; for bibliography and discussion, see C. Cardelle de Hartmann's introduction in the same volume (2001).

74 For the text of his works, see CCL 93.

75 E.g. Otto Bardenhewer, *Patrology: The Lives and Works of the Fathers of the Church,* 2nd ed., trans. Thomas J. Shahan (St. Louis, MO: B. Herder, 1908), 641.

76 Due to the limits of space in this volume, the role of exegesis is only briefly mentioned here for Vercundus and in the next paragraph for Primasius. For a study of the centrality of exegesis (and who can validly exegete) in the Three Chapters controversy, see Leslie Dossey, "Exegesis and Dissent in Byzantine North Africa," in *North Africa Under Byzantium and Early Islam,* ed. Susan T. Stevens and Jonathan P. Conant (Washington, DC: Dumbarton Oaks, 2016), 251–267.

77 *Commentary on Revelation,* prol.24 (CCL 92; my trans.)

78 *Commentary on Revelation,* prol.7.

79 See Burns, Jensen, et al., *Christianity in Roman Africa*, 79.
80 For a fuller discussion, see R. B. Eno, "Doctrinal Authority in the African Ecclesiology of the Sixth Century: Ferrandus and Facundus," *Revue des etudes augustiniennes* 22 (1976), 95–113. His writings are available in CCL 90A. Also see the text (and French trans.) of *Defense of the Three Chapters* in SC 471, 478, 479, 484, 499.
81 For his early resistance, see his preface to *Defense of the Three Chapters*.
82 Facundus, *Letter on the Catholic Faith* 7.
83 Markus, "Reflections on Religious Dissent," 143, citing Facundus, *Against Mocian*: "the persecutors, from whom we flee [*persecutorum quos fugimus*]" (my trans.; PL 67:855C).
84 Conant, *Staying Roman*, 323.
85 *Against Mocian* 53–54.
86 *Against Mocian* 55. Augustine's reception of Cyprian was discussed on p. 217.
87 *Defense of the Three Chapters* 12.3.
88 Text in CCL 90A: 417–434.
89 Markus, "Religious Dissent," 147.
90 *Saeculum: History and Society in the Theology of St. Augustine*, rev. ed. (Cambridge: Cambridge University Press, 1989), 131.
91 Which Markus knows, see his essay, "Reflections on Religious Dissent," 145–146.
92 Text in CCL 90A:399–416.
93 *To the Emperor Justinian* (PL 67:996).
94 See bibliography and discussion in Uta Heil, "Liberatus von Karthago und die 'Drei Kapitel,' Anmerkungen zum *Breviarium causae Nestorianorum et Eutychianorum*," *Zeitschrift für antikes Christentum* 14 (2010), 8–10; and Désirée Scholten, "Cassiodorus' *Historia tripartite* Before the Earliest Extant Manuscripts," in *Resources of the Past in Early Medieval Europe*, ed. Clemens Gantner, Rosamond McKitterick, and Sven Meeder (Cambridge: Cambridge University Press, 2015), 44–46.
95 *A Short Report on the Nestorian and Eutychian Controversies* (text in ACO 2.5:98–141).
96 Philippe Blaudeau, "Liberatus de Carthage ou l'historiographie comme service diaconal," *Augustinianum* 50 (2, 2010), 551.
97 *A Short Report* 24.169. See discussion in Markus, "Religious Dissent," 143.
98 *Secret History* 20: Ἰούνιλον δὲ Λίβυν γένος . . . γράμματα δὲ Λατῖνα μὲν ἐξεπιστάμενον, Ἑλληνικῶν μέντοι ἕνεκα οὐδὲ πεφοιτηκότα πρὸς γραμματιστοῦ πώποτε, οὐδὲ τὴν γλῶσσαν αὐτὴν ἑλληνίζειν δυνάμενον (πολλάκις ἀμέλει φωνὴν Ἑλληνίδα προθυμηθεὶς ἀφεῖναι πρὸς τῶν ὑπηρετούντων γέλωτα ὦφλεν).
99 *Handbook of the Basic Principles of Divine Law* (text/trans. in Mass, *Exegesis and Empire*, 118–235).
100 Junillus, *Handbook of the Basic Principles of Divine Law* pref. (Mass, *Exegesis and Empire*, 118–119).
101 For Augustine, see chapter eight. For Primasius, see his *Commentary on Revelation*, pref.7.
102 *Handbook of the Basic Principles of Divine Law* 2.3–10.
103 The dissenters explicitly see themselves as heirs to Cyprian, according to Markus, "Religious Dissent," 146.
104 "Doctrinal Authority," 112.
105 Frend, "The Christian Period in Mediterranean Africa," 2:487.
106 See the debate over the twenty-eighth canon of the council of Chalcedon (451) which the west rejected, although the east unanimously accepted; cf. Yves Congar, *After 900 Years: The Background of the Schism* (New York: Fordham University Press, 1998), 55–56.

107 For a detailed study of this exchange, see Yvette Duval, "Grégorie et l'Église d'Afrique," in *Gregorio Magno e il suo tempo* (Studia Ephemeridis "Augustinianum" 33; Roma: Institutum Patristicum "Augustinianum," 1991), 1:129–158.

108 See bibliography in John R. C. Martyn, *The Letters of Gregory the Great* (Medieval Sources in Translation 40; Toronto: Pontifical Institute of Mediaeval Studies, 2004), 1:36 n.89. Frend, "The Christian Period in Mediterranean Africa," 2:487, who normally speaks of a "re-emergence" of Donatism (since he believes Donatism was in fact defeated in 411) provides one statement that offers a more promising paradigm for understanding late Donatism:

> Byzantine churches that have been excavated in southern Numidia, with their dedications to non-canonical martyrs, their reliquaries and their inscriptions relating to persecution, show continuity in rite and outlook with the churches of two centuries before. Southern Numidia had lain outside Vandal control except for occasional punitive expeditions against the Aures mountaineers. The return of the Byzantines meant the return to exploitation by absentee landlords and grasping officials, factors to encourage the resurgence of Donatism. So far as the religious life of the people was concerned, only the importation of some specifically Eastern saints in the Numidian martyrology distinguished their chapels from those of two centuries before (2:487).

109 See the evidence catalogued in Adamiak, "When Did Donatist Christianity End?" 223–225; also cf. Cameron, "Byzantine Africa," 51.

110 Cf. Markus, "The Problem of 'Donatists' in the Sixth Century," in *Gregorio Magno e il suo tempo* (Rome: 1990), 164, reprinted in *Sacred and Saecular: Studies on Augustine and Latin Christianity* (Aldershot, UK: 1994).

111 *Christianity in Roman Africa*, 81–82.

112 An "exarch" was a military title developed in late antiquity. This office functioned as both governor and military commander of a region.

113 *Letter* 1.72: *adversariis catholicae ecclesiae.*

114 *Letter* 1.72: *resistendi donatistis.*

115 *Letter* 1.73: *bella vos frequenter appetere non desiderio fundendi sanguinis sed dilatandae causa rei publicae, in qua deum coli conspicimus . . . quatenus christi nomen per subditas gentes . . . circumquaque discurreret.* Martyn, *The Letters of Gregory the Great*, 1:187 n.348, comments "Again, Gregory uses the emotive 'republic.' To ancient Romans, glory very much consisted in winning wars against foreigners, to spread Roman peace, law and baths; for Gregory, the sequel is the spread of Christianity."

116 See the archaeological evidence in Pringle, *Defence of Byzantine Africa*, 1:102.

117 See details in Caudel, *Les premières invasions Arabes dans l'Afrique du nord*, 3.2:12.

118 *Letter* 1.75: *universis episcopis Numidiae.*

119 *Letter* 1.75: *vestrae consuetudinem.*

120 *Letter* 1.75: *ex Donatistis.*

121 *Letter* 1.82; cf. *Letter* 2.39.

122 *Letter* 1.82.

123 This letter has largely been ignored in the secondary literature about Gregory's correspondence with the African Christians.

124 *Letter* 2.43.

125 *Letter* 2.43: *de trium capitulorum.*

126 *Letter* 2.43: *in urbe regia . . . ad matrem.*

127 *Letter* 2.43, citing *On the Unity* 14.

128 For Gregory's other letters on this controversy, see Martyn, *The Letters of Gregory the Great*, 1:87 n.237.

129 *Letter* 2.31: *Afros passim vel incognitos peregrinos ad ecclesiasticos ordines tendentes nulla ratione suscipias, quia Afri quidem aliqui Manichaei, aliqui*

rebaptizati, peregrini vero plurimi etiam in minoribus ordinibus constituti fortiori de se praetendisse honori saepe probati sunt.

130 *Letter* 2.39.

131 *Letter* 2.39: *etsi hoc anterior usus permitteret, manere atque persistere fides catholica prohiberet;* cf. *Letter* 1.72 (discussed on p. 303).

132 *Letter* 2.43: *Porro autem praesentium latorum insinuatione didicimus Donatistarum haeresem pro peccatis cotidie dilatari, et valde plures, data per venalitatem licentia, post Catholicum baptisma a Donatistis denuo baptizari.*

133 See *Letters* 2.40; 5.3; 6.19; 6.63; 7.32; 8.31; 10.20; 12.1.

134 *Letter* 2.40: *ecclesiasticis . . . privilegiis.*

135 *Letter* 3.47: *beato Petro apostolorum principi.*

136 *Letter* 3.47: *primatem synodi tuae.*

137 *Letter* 3.48.

138 *Letter* 4.13. Crementius himself will later (c.598) be expelled by the bishops of Byzacium; see *Letters* 9.24; 9.27; 12.12. The outcome of his case is not known, but it seems that Gregory cannot do anything to restore him.

139 *Letter* 4.7: *Numidiae contra patrum tramitem atque canonum statuta committi.*

140 *Letter* 4.32: *Donatistarum . . . audacia . . . rebaptizare.*

141 *Letter* 4.35.

142 *Letter* 5.3.

143 *Letter* 6.36.

144 *Letter* 6.36: *a clero sit modis omnibus alienus.*

145 *Letter* 6.62. For Paul, see *Letters* 4.32; 4.35; 7.2; 7.3; 7.14; 8.13; 8.15; 8.24.

146 *Letter* 6.63.

147 *Letter* 6.64: *ex Africana provincia.*

148 *Letter* 7.2: *Quod enim multorum vos inimicitias ob hoc, quod nostris vos frequentius visitamus epistulis.*

149 Although their correspondence does continue; e.g. *Letters* 12.3; 12.8.

150 *Letter* 7.32: *quocumque voluerint, vagantes.*

151 *Letter* 8.13 to Adeodatus and Maurentius; *Letter* 8.14 to Victor and Columbus; and *Letter* 8.15 to Columbus.

152 *Letter* 8.31: *in Africanis partibus.*

153 *Letter* 10.20: *in Africanis partibus.*

154 *Letter* 11.7: *in locis suis violentias multa que alia contra edicti morem Africanos iudices exercere.*

155 *Letter* 12.9.

156 See discussion and details in Conant, *Staying Roman*, 324–330.

157 "Donatism: the Last Phase," 123.

158 Markus, "The Problem of 'Donatists' in the Sixth Century," 162. Markus compares the sixth century to 411, where there existed "church against church, altar against altar," whereas in the sixth there "were no rival ecclesial communities" (163).

159 Martyn, *The Letters of Gregory the Great*, 40.

160 Markus, "The Problem," 164–165; Markus, "Donatism: The Last Phase," 125. As evidence, he cites only the outdated work of Monceaux. For a slightly more nuanced explanation of the Donatist party in the Vandal period, see Markus, "The Imperial Administration and the Church in Byzantine Africa," 18.

161 "Donatism: The Last Phase," 125.

162 *Staying Roman*, 329.

163 *Staying Roman*, 330.

164 "Reflections on Religious Dissent," 146.

165 Markus's major weakness is in his attempt to explain why Paul was hindered by local officials and excommunicated by the local synod. His claim that Paul was "distrusted for his fussy intransigence" and for being a "busybody" (Markus,

"The Imperial Administration and the Church in Byzantine Africa," *Church History* 36 (1967), 18–23 21; cf. Markus, "Donatism: the Last Phase, 121) is unconvincing at best. Why would the local "Catholic" synod excommunicate Paul, who was "defending the catholic faith" just because he was "fussy"? Instead, perhaps we should assume he was defending the Catholic faith as Gregory was promoting it, which meant ultramontanism (to use an anachronistic phrase), or Roman primacy in local affairs. This resulted in his excommunication by the Donatists, whose only unifying quality that makes them "Donatist" is their anti-Romanism, or at least their sense of local autonomy. Markus is at his best when he stipulates, "Neither the Church (even, as I have argued, the African Church) nor the government can be treated as monolithic in this respect." (Markus, "The Imperial Administration," 23). It seems to me that the same should have been said for "Donatism" all along.

166 See *Staying Roman*, 186–190, where Conant insists that to be Roman at this time in no way implies being not African. The question is regarding how to understand the African identity of these Christians.

167 For a helpful introduction, see Louth, *Maximus the Confessor*, 3–18, and for a more recent treatment and bibliography, see Blowers, *Maximus the Confessor: Jesus Christ and the Transfiguration of the World* (Oxford: Oxford University Press, 2016), 25–42. For previous studies, see Mikonja Knežević, *Maximus the Confessor (580–662): Bibliography* (Bibliographia serbica theological 6; Belgrade: Institute for Theological Research, 2012).

168 Maximus, *To Peter the Illustrious* (PG 91:142). For details about the location, see *The Syriac Life of Maximus* 19, and the later *Greek Life of Maximus* 7–14.

169 Most famously, his *Questions and Responses for Thalassius*, written to an African abbot; for "Thalassius the African" and his works, see Marek Jankowiak and Phil Booth, "A New Date-List of the Works of Maximus the Confessor" in *The Oxford Handbook of Maximus the Confessor*, ed. Pauline Allen and Bronwen Neil (Oxford: Oxford University Press, 2015), 25. Also, one of his correspondents, Anastasius, was said to be "well known in these regions [i.e. Africa], having been born there"; see *The Syriac Life of Maximus* 19 (Sebastian P. Brock, "An Early Syriac Life of Maximus the Confessor," *Analecta Bollandiana* 91 [1975], 310 and 317; reprinted in Brock, *Syriac Perspectives on Late Antiquity* [London: Variorum, 1984]). The later Greek *Life of Maximus* 14, claims Maximus

> met with the bishops in Africa. . . . By putting forward his own arguments to them, and letting loose his tongue which flowed with holy words, he both made them stronger in the faith and taught and instructed them in particular how they could escapte the traps of the enemies and avoid their sophistries [πρῶ μὲν τοῖς ἐν Ἀφρικῇ ἐπισκόπος συγγίνεται . . . οἷς καὶ λόγους προθεὶς τοὺς οἰκείους, καὶ γλῶσσαν τὴν τὰ Θεῖα πελαγίζουσαν ἐπαφείς, βεβαιοτέρους τε περὶ τὴν πίστιν καθιστᾷ, καὶ ὅπως ἂν ἔχοιεν τὰς τῶν ἐναντίων διαδιδράσκειν λαβάς, καὶ λόγους αὐτῶν τοὺς σοφιστικοὺς ὑπεκκλίνειν, ἐδίδασκε μάλα καὶ ὑπετίθει].

170 For discussion, see Daley, "Making a Human Will Divine: Augustine and Maximus on Christ and Human Salvation," in *Orthodox Readings of Augustine*, ed. George E. Demacopoulos and Aristotle Papanikolaou (Crestwood, NY: St. Vladimir's Seminary Press, 2008), 101–126.

171 *The Syriac Life of Maximus* 20 (Brock 311 and 318).

172 See the details about the council with Pope Theodore on p. 310.

173 See details in Cameron, "Byzantine Africa," 54–55. For the chronology, see Blowers, *Maximus the Confessor*, 34.

174 For Sophronius's life and role in the theological controversies of the time, see Pauline Allen, *Sophronius of Jerusalem and Seventh-Century Heresy: The*

Synodocial Letter *and Other Documents* (Oxford: Oxford University Press, 2009), 15–23.

175 See discussion in Gerrit J. Reinink, in "Heraclius, the New Alexander: Apocalyptic Prophecies During the Reign of Heraclius," in *The Reign of Heraclius (610–641): Crisis and Confrontation*, ed. Gerrit J. Reinink and Bernard H. Stolte (Groningen Studies in Cultural Change 2; Leuven: Peeters, 2002), 81–94.

176 See further discussion in Gerald O'Collins, *Christology: A Biblical, Historical, and Systematic Study of Jesus* (Oxford: Oxford University Press, 2009), 200; and Cyril Hovorun, *Will, Action and Freedom: Christological Controversies in the Seventh Century* (Leiden: Brill, 2008), 163.

177 For an explanation of the theological significance of these formulae, see Wilhite, *The Gospel According to Heretics*, 184–193.

178 One detail worth noting is how Sophronius agreed to hand over Jerusalem to the Muslims. He had earlier declared that the Muslims were "unwitting representatives of God's inevitable chastisement of weak and wavering Christians" (according to Averil Cameron and Lawrence I. Conrad, "Introduction," in *The Byzantine and Early Islamic Near East*, ed. Averil Cameron, et al. [Princeton, NJ: Darwin Press, 1992], 21). Later, Anastasius of Sinai would claim the Muslim invasion was God's judgment on the emperor, because of the treatment of Pope Martin I and the bishops who met with him in 649, which would have included African bishops (see the source and discussion in Paul Blowers, *Maximus the Confessor*, 22).

179 The dialogue is available in the English translation by Joseph P. Farrell, *The Disputation With Pyrrhus of our Father Among the Saints Maximus the Confessor* (South Canaan, PA: St. Tikhon's Seminary Press, 1990). For critical editions and studies of Maximus's works, see Blowers, *Maximus the Confessor*, 336–337.

180 Louth, *Maximus*, 17.

181 See especially the letter of the African bishops to Theodore (in PG 87:81–84). Other letters were known at the synod of Rome in 649; see details in Burns, Jensen, et al., *Christianity in Roman Africa*, 83.

182 Cf. *The Life of Maximus* 53.

183 For discussion about Maximus's part in encouraging Gregory's role, see Kaegi, *Muslim Expansion*, 90; and see Conant, *Staying Roman*, 355–356, for further details. Also, see Phil Booth, *Crisis of Empire Doctrine and Dissent at the End of Late Antiquity* (Berkeley, CA: University of California Press, 2014), esp. chapter 7 "Rebellion and Retribution" (p. 278 ff.); section 1 = "Maximus from Africa to Rome" and section 3 = "Rebellion and Trial." Maximus certainly did have extensive communication with the African generals and political leaders; see Daniel Sahas, "The Demonizing Force of the Arab Conquests: The Case of Maximus (*ca.* 580–662) as a Political 'Confessor,'" *Jahrbuch der österreichischen Byzantinistik* 53 (2003), 98–110.

184 Theophanes, *Chronicle* 6138; cf. the Syriac *Life of Maximus* 18.

185 Cited in Kaegi, *Muslim Expansion*, 87.

186 Blowers, *Maximus the Confessor*, 334, ends his monograph by noting how Maximus's theology developed in the "'South' (Africa)," and so Blowers commends Maximus for "today's postcolonial churches of the 'Global South.'"

187 "Reflections on Religious Dissent," 149.

11 The Arab conquests in Africa

According to one *Life of Muhammad* written by a medieval Christian, Muhammad was trained by Simon Magus, the person rebuked by Peter (in Acts 8:9–24). Simon Magus, according to this *Life*, had gone to "Libya," where he met Muhammad. Under this tutelage, Muhammad became the governor of all Libya, and after his death, Simon Magus used false magic to trick everyone there into worshipping Muhammad as a god.

This obviously false and negative propaganda about Muhammad (who was never in Africa, nor lived during the time of Simon Magus), told by an otherwise unknown writer named Embrico of Mainz around 1100, illustrates how some Christians in Europe believed that all of "Libya" had become followers of Muhammad.[1] In modern times, historians described the Christian decline in North Africa as sudden, resulting not from false magic but from the military conquest of Arab expansion.[2] This view, as we will discuss later in this chapter, has been heavily criticized. In fact, Christians remained in North Africa for centuries after its conquest by Muslims, but it is true that the number of Christians did decline from the first arrival of the Arab armies until Christians disappeared altogether from the African landscape.

Understanding the sources and background

Historians struggle with this period of African Christian history more than any other.[3] The reason for the view that Christianity simply disappeared in seventh- and eighth-century Africa is due to the fact that African Christian voices fall silent at this time.[4] The literary record ceases almost entirely, and there is certainly nothing like the bodies of literature produced in the earlier periods. Therefore, any fragments of evidence such as surviving archaeological records will be vital to understanding this history.

When looking to the Muslim sources for the conquest of North Africa, there are equally significant difficulties. The evidence survives in much later accounts, and the earliest sources (recorded in the later accounts) are all from writers outside of Africa in places like Egypt and Syria. Even then, the Arabic sources offer relatively little information about the local populations who "submitted" to Islam, such as the *Naṣārā* (i.e. the "Nazarenes" or Christians).[5] These accounts focus on the military victories as signs of Allah's blessing of the Muslims over their enemies. Furthermore, the accounts of North Africa, written later, bear the marks of later agendas, such as touting the values of the Abbasid dynasty, which replaced the Ummayad dynasty in 750.[6] The *Book of the Conquests of Egypt and of Maghrib*, for example, was written by Ibn Abd al-Hakam around 870, and it is the oldest known Arabic source about this area. It depends on oral tradition, and when later accounts expand on al-Hakam's details, they do so with conflicting and therefore dubious conclusions.

With such sparse material from this era, we need to correct any potential misunderstandings about the spread of Islam in general. Whereas many people today may think of Islamic conquest as a jihad involving forced conversions and religious intolerance, those more informed with Islam's history know this to be a distortion. The Qur'an is clear that forced conversions are impermissible, and it even speaks of protecting synagogues, churches, and monasteries.[7]

There were at this time some Christians in many parts of the world who appreciated Muhammad's call to worship the one true God and to live according to his justice. This applies in particular to our study of North Africa when we consider the distinction between Arabization and Islamization. These two concepts, while distinct, should not be entirely separated. In one way, the late seventh and early eighth century in Africa was about military conquest, the expansion of the rising Arab empire, and bloody battles. There is no doubt that many Africans would have understood the events in much the same way that earlier generations had experienced the Punic, Roman, Vandal, and Byzantine conquests of North Africa. At the same time, the Arab conquerors certainly understood their actions in religious terms, and we should assume they were sincere in their religious convictions. In what follows, phrases like "Arab conquest" and "Muslim expansion" will be used largely interchangeably, but with the awareness that the distinction between the two should be kept in mind and that a more in-depth study would require much more nuance. One of the major questions involved in how best to describe the Islamization of Africa is in regard to how distinct and well-defined "Islam" was at this time.

Part of the difficulty in understanding the conversion of Christians and a Christian region to Islam is our preconceived notion of conversion itself and how these two distinct religions were understood in the middle ages. For one thing, we will have to revise the fundamental idea that they were "two distinct religions." While this is how they appear to modern historians, in the early period of the Arab conquest the boundary was not always so clear. Scholars who undertake a critical study of Islam's history often distinguish "early Islam" from "traditional Islam," which is a way of acknowledging how the later medieval tradition within Islam came to tell the story of its origin in such a way that may not corroborate with the earlier evidence.

This historical distinction can be seen in three areas.[8] First, whereas the traditional life of Muhammad is accepted as orthodox by the vast majority of Muslims today, historians question whether the later accounts are accurate. For example, was Muhammad spoken of as "the" prophet or "a" prophet in the seventh century? Second, the Qur'an itself is understood by most Muslims today as an eternal word from God, but many scholars apply historical criticism to the Qur'an, assuming that it has its own textual history wherein it depended on earlier sources and came together in a finalized form only sometime after the death of Muhammad. Third, the early spread of Islam is understood by most Muslims to have involved the spreading of Muhammad's teachings to which non-believers should submit. However, historians find that Arab conquerors, while certainly spreading Islam as part of their mission, had incentives not to encourage conversions since non-believers could be taken as slaves and "people of the Book" (i.e. Jews and Christians) would be forced to pay a higher tax. Furthermore, early Muslim beliefs and practices were still developing at the time of North Africa's conquest and so the exact points of conflict may have differed from later centuries.

If one accepts this revisionist history of "early Islam," then Islam itself in its earliest centuries becomes much more porous and open to allowing Christians to be somehow "within" Islam (and vice versa). The term *Islam* itself in Arabic means "submit," and *Muslim* likewise is the word for "one who submits." To what were Christians asked to submit? Arab rule? If so, many Christians likely understood the Arab conquest as simply the latest political shift in North Africa's long history of foreign rule. Some may even have welcomed the Arabs as a better alternative to the Byzantines. To Muhammad's teachings? If Muhammad taught monotheism and just living, then many Christians likely saw him as one more sectarian leader who could be accommodated at some level within Christianity.[9] Were the Christians in North Africa asked to submit to the Qur'an's teachings? This assumes that the Qur'an was complete in its final form and transported to Africa by this time, which may or may not have been the case according to some historians. Furthermore, even if the Qur'an was known in Africa, could it be read and compared to the Christian scriptures? How many Christians in Africa could even read their own Christian scriptures? (This is an especially difficult question when thinking of the many Punic speakers in Africa who may not have known Latin.) The Qur'an, it should also be remembered, has much to say about both Jesus and Mary. While Jesus is not the "son" of God according to the Qur'an (for this would imply "biological offspring" in Arabic), he is described in very elevated terms: his birth was foretold, he is the Word of God cast into Mary's womb, he is a great prophet whom the Jews wanted to crucify, and God took him up into heaven whence he will return for the day of judgment. How many Christians would initially be aware of the differences that remain between this view of Jesus and their own?

One other complication in how Christianity compared with Islam at the time of the Arab conquest of North Africa is the amount of diversity within each religion and the possible overlap of these two diverse religions. Christianity in North Africa allegedly still consisted of sects like the Manicheans, and it possibly still involved rival Catholic, Donatist, and Arian communions. Likewise, Islam itself was more diverse than often thought. Even beyond the well-known Sunni and Shia groups, there were other factions within Islam such as the Ibadis and the Kharajites.[10] These groups, it should be noted, were prevalent in North Africa.

Many scholars believe that these heterodox Muslim groups became the home of many African Christians who syncretized the two faiths in various ways.[11] While the history of Islam and its various factions is beyond the scope of our discussion, we should consider some examples of how divided Muslims were among themselves in the early centuries of the Arab conquest of Africa. For example, it is tempting to look for the last remnants of Christian Africans in the history of Muslim groups like the Rustamid dynasty, which ruled over central North Africa from 767 to 909. This short-lived empire made its capital in Tahart (in modern Algeria), a city known to have tolerated Christians well into the Arab period of African history.[12] Unfortunately, virtually all of the primary sources about this dynasty were lost when the Rustamids were defeated in 909 and the library of Tahart was burned.[13] The remnant of this group fled to M'zab, an oasis in what is today central Algeria, and the "Libyan-Phoenician style"[14] of architecture they built at this time was later declared a UNESCO World Heritage Site. Despite the fact that its inhabitants fled to there from all over North Africa, "the common feature to all these immigrants was that they were Berbers and schismatics."[15] If we had more information about these immigrants, we would likely learn much about the remnants of Christianity at the time.

More internal divisions of Islam can be found in Africa. The Fatimids, who had defeated the Rustamids, formed their own caliphate in 909.[16] This was itself a Shi'ite rebellion against the Sunni Abbasid Caliphate in Baghdad. The Fatimids based their headquarters in Mahdia, a port city (in modern Tunisia) that dates back to the Punic era. The Fatimids later (969) moved their capital to Cairo, and in so doing they appointed the "Berber" Zirids to rule *Ifriqiya* (the Arabic transliteration of Roman *Africa*) in their stead. The Zirids later broke with the Fatimid caliphate and aligned with the Abbasids. Their rejection of Shi'itism and embracement of the Sunni form of Islam caused further unrest in North Africa because many local tribes (some independent, others siding with the Fatimids) fought against the Zirids. In one of history's strange turns, the Zirids were finally defeated by Norman raiders who plundered the North African coastline around 1147.

By this point, Africa had become very fragmented in terms of government. More to the point for our purpose, this political fragmentation reflects the fragmentation of various forms of Islam in North Africa (and elsewhere) at this time. If Christianity and Islam each included diverse factions, there must have been some instances where the boundary between the two religions was not so clear.

All of this should be remembered when attempting to understand what happened to "Christianity" in North Africa during the spread of Islam. Furthermore, there likely was not one single Christianity or one consistent phenomenon that applied to all Christians. We should instead look for the many variables among diverse Christian and Muslim groups across the region.

When the Arabs first looked to conquer *al-Maghrib* ("the west" in Arabic, which refers to all the lands west of Egypt), they did so in military terms, and these details are relatively well documented. How they understood the religious conversion of those conquered, and how those who "submitted" understood their own actions, becomes a much more difficult question to answer. Therefore, we will first review the history of the conquest before returning to the question about African Christianity's disappearance in the middle ages.

History of the conquest

When studying "Byzantine Africa," one is likely to be impressed by the magnificent remains of *Romanitas* left throughout the region. The archaeological footprint of the empire was significant and indicates widespread economic development.[17] Nevertheless, a word of caution is in order:

> When confronted with the gallery of monuments to Roman civilization, that survive from Roman Africa, literary and intellectual, artistic and architectural, it is easy to forget that Africa was one of the least throughly [sic] Romanized of all the western dioceses of the later Roman empire. . . . native tribes continued to exist, speaking their own languages, worshipping their own gods and preserving their own tribal structures.[18]

As we will see in what follows, the African landscape at this time included the remnants of the Byzantine citizens, an influx of new Arab conquerors, and an array of people groups that the Romans called "Mauretanians" and the Arabs called "Berbers."[19]

While we will look specifically into the African identities of this period (as we have done in previous chapters), we will also need to use caution in understanding these "Berbers." For one thing, even the Arabic term is derived from the Latin "barbarian (*barbari*)," and so the name carries a stigma of being un-civilized. Furthermore, while contemporary *Imazighen* (i.e. the name "Berbers" prefer to call themselves today)[20] may have a largely cohesive social identity that spans regions and nations (if not centuries), the "Mauretanians" in the Roman, Byzantine, and Arab periods consisted of many different groups that did not always see themselves as one social unit.

Many sided with the Byzantines while others sided with the Arabs. Other switched their allegiances at some point in their history, while many more avoided both foreign powers altogether. The ethnic/linguistic demarcation does not do justice to the diversity of self-understandings among the various Mauretanian/"Berber" peoples at the time.

This brings us to the political and military events of this period, which were briefly introduced in the opening chapter. Here it is worth recounting in further detail the series of events that unfolded at this time. The background to this period is Muhammad's conquest of much of Arabia before his death in 632. His followers would continue to spread their control, with Damascus falling in 636 and Jerusalem in 637. By 642 both Syria and Egypt were completely under Arab control. That same year, Arabs began raiding further west into Libya, easily conquering Cyrenaica by 645 and even reaching to Tripolitania.

In 645 the exarch of Africa, Gregory, declared Africa independent of Constantinople, and declared himself emperor – not of Rome, but of Africa.[21] In the words of one chronicler, he "raised a rebellion together with the Africans."[22] While this likely generalizes and assumes all "Africans" were co-conspirators with Gregory, his support does seem to have been widespread, and we should remember from the last chapter that the dyothelites of Africa and those who supported them, like Theodore of Rome and Maximus the Confessor, were accused of treason by the Byzantine emperor, which is to say they supported Gregory's rebellion.

Gregory made his capital in the city of Sufetula in Byzacena (modern Sbeitla, Tunisia), which is centrally located – approximately 100 miles south of Carthage and 70 miles west of the coast. Sufetula had been a well-established Roman city, the ruins of which still stand impressively today. Although many traces of its Punic heritage survive in the records, the landscape became dominated by the three temples built to Rome's Capitoline triad: Jupiter, Juno, and Minerva. The city's Christian population is known from the archaeological remains of numerous Byzantine basilicas, many of which would have been built upon earlier sites. This location, it seems, placed Gregory in a better position to coordinate with the many inland "Berber" peoples with whom he had formed an alliance.

In 648 Gregory was killed in battle. His allied forces were nearly equal to the size of the 20,000 Arab troops led by Abdallah Ibn Saad, the new governor of Egypt. When even more Arab reinforcements arrived, Gregory was utterly defeated. After plundering the region, the Arab forces returned east, but they required an annual tribute from the Africans. Meanwhile, the emperor in Constantinople continued taxing Africa as well, which created animosity among local Africans.[23] Even in Carthage, which had largely remained loyal to the emperor, the local population rejected Byzantine rule and elected to pay tribute only to the Arabs, which provided them with approximately twenty years of peace.

In 661 more Arabs raided Africa, spreading from Egypt west along the coast. Then, in 683, Uqba Ibn Nafi, the newly appointed governor of Africa, led a major conquest further west into Byzacena. He had earlier established a new city, Kairouan, which would become the capital of Africa and is still an important city in Tunisia. The religious significance of the city stems from a story of how one of Uqba's soldiers found a goblet in the sand there. It turned out to be the one that had gone missing in Mecca, and when it was pulled up, a spring of water appeared that was said to have the same water flowing from it as the well in Mecca.[24] The "Great Mosque" of Kairouan became a pilgrimage site, attracting many devoted Muslims. In addition to the religious significance, Kairouan functioned as a strategic location for Arab forces. Rather than staging sporadic raids, Arabs were able to permanently maintain a presence in the region from which they could expand further west.

With Kairouan as his base of operation, Uqba conquered vast areas inland, advancing all the way across Numidia and Mauretania. He allegedly even reached the Atlantic. However, on his return to Kairouan he encountered an alliance of local groups under the leadership of a king named Kusayla, or in its more Latinized form, Caecilius.[25] Kusayla had earlier been defeated by Uqba, but this time the Arab forces had been depleted by their long march and were vulnerable. In 690 Kusayla himself was defeated, but the Arab forces did not yet take control of Africa. It was not until 697 when the newly appointed governor of the Maghreb, Hasan Ibn an-Nuuman al-Ghasani, led a more widespread conquest of Africa. The Byzantine strength still lay in its navy, but by this time the Arabs had acquired enough ships to counter the Byzantines even on the sea. This made it possible to conquer Carthage, which was reinforced via its port. After a successful blockade, Hasan defeated the last of the Byzantine forces at Carthage in 698.[26]

The last major resistance to Arab rule over North Africa came from a queen named Dihya, who organized another alliance of indigenous groups. She was known as "Kahina" in the Arab sources, which is an Arabic word meaning "seer" or "diviner."[27] This title was no compliment; it implied that she was a witch who could foresee their military plans. Ibn Khaldun claims she and her "tribe" were Jewish, but this has been shown by historians to have problems and she and her people are now thought to have been Christian.[28]

Similar to this claim about the Jewish background of these "Berber" groups, Ibn Khaldun also reports that the indigenous peoples of North Africa were (at least understood as) Punic. It is worth citing Ibn Khaldun's lengthy statement to illustrate this point:

> Possibly some of the Berbers practiced Judaism, which they had received from their powerful Israelite neighbors in Syria. Among the Jewish Berbers were the Djeraoua, who inhabited Aurès, the tribe of Kahina, who

was killed by the Arabs in their first conquests. Other Jewish tribes were the Nefouca of the African Berbers, the Fendelaoua, the Medioun, Behloula, Giatha and the Berbes of the extreme Maghreb, the Fazaz. Idris the First of the Beni el-Hassan, son of El-Hassan who reached the Maghreb, wiped out all traces of the religions that persisted in his territory and crushed the independence of the tribes.[29]

Shlomo Sand comments on this passage to say, "Ibn Khaldun apparently assumed that at least some of the Berbers, North Africa's longtime inhabitants, were descendants of the ancient Phoenicians or some other Canaanite population that originated in the vicinity of Syria and converted to Judaism."[30] Another statement from Ibn Khaldun can further corroborate Sand's point, for the medieval historian also said, "The Berbers were in Palestine. Their king was Jalut [= Goliath]. He was killed by David, peace be upon him. They then left for the Maghrib."[31] In other words, in the late fourteenth century many still believed the Africans were descended from the ancient Phoenicians. It is probable that Ibn Khaldun learned this from "Berbers" who still understood themselves in such terms.

Another modern scholar concluded from these sources that "the great majority of the Christians who remained had more Moorish that Roman blood in their veins."[32] While such conclusions are important, they require much further study and analysis because much of the information about "the Kahina" and her compatriots is shrouded in exaggeration and legend. For example, in one memorable story, this sorceress queen had dark skin and when angered her eyes would turn red while her hair stood straight.[33] She is also said to have committed suicide – a fitting tale for this last queen of Africa, since this is a common theme in African history dating back to the first queen of Carthage, Dido. According to another source, however, she lived to be 127 years old. Whatever the exact manner of her death, after many military successes, Dihya was finally defeated by Hasan around 703.

Other, smaller, groups continued to resist the Arab conquest, and many of these were known to be Christian. One Arab source explains why so many "Berbers" joined a 739 uprising as due to the promise that Jesus himself was going to join the battle.[34] Another uprising was defeated in Tripolitania in the 740s, and many Christians were publicly crucified in the market of Oea (modern Tripoli) as punishment.[35]

For at least a century, Islam was present in North Africa almost exclusively in coastal towns and in a few fortified cities.[36] From there, as the Arabs had more contact with the so-called Berber tribes and recruited many to fight in their armies, the teachings of Islam spread further into Africa. As Arabs intermarried with local Africans, there emerged a growing sense of independence among even Muslims in the region: "the Muslim states of the Maghrib defied the Arab authority of Bagdad and maintained a stout independence from the East."[37] This independence can be seen in the formation of an independent caliphate (= the Fatimid dynasty) and in how many converts to Islam were part of dissenting groups within Islam, such as the Shi'ites, the Ibadi, and the Kharajites – as mentioned on p. 324.[38] Furthermore, the Sufi Islamic tradition, with its emphasis on saints, among other distinctives, fit well in North Africa, where it thrived in various forms throughout much of the middle ages.[39]

With major conflict now over, the rest of Africa was subdued with relatively little resistance. According to both Arab and Byzantine sources, the battles themselves had been brutal and the conquest included widespread plundering and capturing of slaves.[40] The local population must have suffered greatly in the late seventh century. The next century of African history then witnessed a relatively peaceful period when Arab civilization developed in the region. The governors of Africa recruited and developed their own standing army and navy, which served the caliph. New cities like Tunis and Kairouan, built from the ruins of Carthage and Sufetula respectively, meant that the Arab societal structures were easily established, and economic development spread from these centers through trade.

Although forced conversions are not documented in the early years of Arab rule in Africa, economic incentives to convert would have been significant. Many Africans would have wanted to join the new army and navy, or at least avoid the poll tax. Furthermore, many would have accepted Arab rule for political reasons as much as or even over against religious reasons. One other factor to consider about the Arab conquest of Africa is how varied the reaction was from the so-called Berber tribes.

Throughout the whole history of the Muslim era, the "Berber" groups valued their independence. Their self-description, *Imazighen*, simply means "the free people." From the seventh century onward, such groups responded to the Arab empire in various ways, ranging from alliances to outright rebellions. Especially in regions not easily governed by the caliphs, such as the mountainous regions inland and the far western areas like Morocco, these groups retained their autonomy and established their own dynasties.

To be sure, the so-called Berbers all eventually accepted Islam. The question remains as to how this occurred in the earliest centuries of Islam's introduction into North Africa. As Elizabeth Savage concluded, "Many Berbers became Muslim, possibly not Muslims in a strictly religious sense, but rather in terms of throwing in their lot with Muslim leaders who seemed most likely to protect their interests."[41] One example Savage provides is that of Ibrāhīm al-Nasrānī ("Abraham the Nazarene" or "Abraham the Christian") who helped the Muslim ruler while remaining a Christian.[42] Did some forms of Christianity continue to be practiced in regions where the "Berbers" retained their independence? Tourists today can still visit the Moroccan village of Bhalil in the Atlas mountains, where locals will host them for tea in their modern houses that are built over the cave dwellings of their ancestors' homes. This village and others like it, according to folklore, were first inhabited by Christians who fled to the highlands in order to preserve their faith. The evidence, however, is slim to none, and so this kind of quest quickly becomes one of pure speculation. Nevertheless, there may be ways forward for our discipline. Just as we recommended that future studies of Christianity in the early Roman period could benefit from additional research into the Punic/Phoenician backgrounds, so here it is suggested that future studies of Christianity in medieval Africa may benefit from scholars willing to incorporate the findings of social anthropologists who have done their fieldwork among the *Imazighen*.

Even admitting that the evidence for Christianity's survival among the so-called Berber groups is slim, the fact that we can identify any traces of Christianity among these groups at all indicates the kinds of options available to Christians upon Islam's arrival in North Africa. Historians find that some Christians remained strictly Christian, while others converted to Islam (even in a religious sense), while others remained Christian while "submitting" to Arab rule, and still others submitted to certain factions within Islam, such as the Ibadis and Kharajites, who were mentioned on p. 324 as being prevalent in North Africa.

This diversity of responses is a point that we will reiterate in our conclusion to this chapter. As for the Christian communities in particular, Christianity in Africa would certainly decline in the following centuries; the only question is at what rate.[43] We can now turn to the last artifacts of Christianity's survival in order to see how late and in what condition Christianity continued under Arab rule in Africa.

Survival of evidence and evidence of survival

Since no major literary work survives from Africa after around 650, we must look to scraps of evidence for any signs of ongoing Christianity.[44] These will be listed here, and although the items that follow allow precious little information about the African Christians from this period, they do allow us to catch glimpses of Christianity's survival for centuries after the Arab conquest.[45] We will list these glimpses in roughly chronological order.

One piece of Christian literature is sometimes dated to the late seventh century. It is a compilation of church laws produced by an otherwise unknown writer named Cresconius "the African (*Africanus*)."[46] His work is usually dated to the end of the seventh century, so it is an important artifact for our discussion, but the text unfortunately does not offer much information about the state of African Christianity at the end of the seventh century.

In 684, the fourteenth Council of Toledo met to address the ongoing Monophysite controversy. This council included at least one African, a certain Potentinus, bishop of Utica. Possibly, he represented the African tradition of defending two-nature Christology (see discussion on pp. 295–301 in Chapter 11).

Another controversy is referenced by Pope Gregory II (r.715–731). In 722 he wrote a letter, usually cited as expressing concern that Donatists are still a problem in Africa.[47] More precisely, Gregory urges Boniface not to accept any "Africans [*Afros*]" claiming to be ordained, because many of them are "Manicheans and rebaptizers [*rebaptizati*]."[48] This last description likely does imply Donatism for Gregory, but it should be remembered that the practice called rebaptism was a traditional practice for African Christians dating back at least to Cyprian that continued in Africa in later centuries in other groups like the Vandals. Gregory's "rebaptizers," therefore, may be Donatists, but they likely did not identify as such. They may be some other (more traditional?) form of African Christianity.

Sometime later, after Pope Adrian died in 795, a certain poet named Silverius celebrated this pope's many accomplishments. Even "Africa rejoices [*Africa laetatur*]" because of the many captives ransomed from there and because the pope had appointed new clergy there.[49] Even if this is hagiographic exaggeration, such a claim would be plausible only if Roman Christians knew of African Christians still in their homeland.

In the late eighth century, an envoy from Bagdad, representing the emerging Abbasid dynasty, made contact with the king of the Franks in Gaul. The caliph at the time was Harun al-Rashid (d.809), who was later made famous by the stories in *1,001 Arabian Nights*. The Frankish king, Charlemagne, would soon be crowned Holy Roman Emperor by the pope, and the two rulers formed an alliance to counter what remained of those supporting the previous Umayyad caliphate. As part of one envoy sent through Africa, Harun al-Rashid allegedly gave Charlemagne an elephant and the relics of Cyprian (i.e. the symbol of Africa and the patron saint of Africa).[50] A contemporary poet, Florus of Lyon, celebrated this event: in the first poem about Cyprian's relics, which is full of allusions to Virgil's references to Carthage in the *Aeneid*, Florus tells of "the fall of Carthage" (which one?) and of how God intervened to rescue Cyprian's bones from the "barbarians (*barbaricis*)" (again, which ones?)[51] Given the penchant in Islam for venerating holy men, it is possible that Muslims and Christians (and those who likely inhabited both identities) continued to honor Cyprian's memory in Africa.[52]

In 813 Pope Leo III wrote to Charlemagne, reporting news about the Arab navy that came from "a Christian friend from Africa."[53] Unfortunately, no other information is given about Africa or about the Christian community there in this letter, but we know that such a community continued after this time. A few decades later, Pope Leo IV (r.847–855) issued a statement on the correct calculation of Easter, which he said was recognized by numerous Christians across the world, including the "Carthaginians and the Africans."[54]

Another source from outside of Africa provides an indication of an ongoing Christian presence in Carthage. As part of a pilgrimage around the Mediterranean to holy sites, a certain Frotmund and his brothers

> turned their steps toward Africa to visit the tomb of St Cyprian, archbishop and martyr of Christ, who lies at rest near the sea, at the second

milestone from the city of Carthage, where many great works and many miracles are very often revealed by the Lord. After four years Frotmund and his two brothers returned once again to Rome.[55]

The amount of detail regarding the location of the *Memoria Cypriani* basilica could indicate that this account is reliable. If so, then this text demonstrates that the site was still preserved in Carthage (by Christians?).[56]

Similarly, Eulogius of Cordoba (d.859) tells how George, a monk traveling from Palestine to Spain, witnessed how "in Africa . . . the church of God" was persecuted.[57] Once in Spain, George became one of the many Christian pilgrims there who volunteered themselves for martyrdom. Hagiographic accounts like this notoriously provide secondhand information, and so this text may simply report what was assumed to be going on in Africa.[58]

An Arabic source from Africa records another glimpse into Christianity in Carthage. Ibd 'Ahd-al-Hakam (803–871), the Arab governor of Carthage, began taxing Christians and Jews in North Africa, which of course indicates there were such groups still in existence at this time.[59] Furthermore, Christians and Jews were significant enough of a population to be seen as a revenue stream.

Outside of Carthage, we have very little information about other Christians, but we do know that Christian communities were present. Well into the eighth and ninth centuries, many cities and towns from Tripolitania to Mauretania retained churches[60] and some bishop's names survive, such as Qustās (= "Constans"), who was even allowed to build a church in Kairouan.[61] One group of Christians in Tahart (in modern Algeria) reportedly remained active in the ninth century, were allowed to keep their own church, and continued to play a role in the civic government.[62] Matthew Gaumer describes this "still-resilient church" as "clinging to its Donatistic 'collecta' ways."[63]

In the last decade of the ninth century, Pope Formosus (whose infamous "cadaver trial" after his death marked his controversial papacy) received representatives from "the African territories" who sought his intervention regarding "a schism among the bishops of the African provinces."[64] Once again, the source tells us nothing about the nature of this schism, but this event may help us interpret some of the data found in later sources, and so we will return to this item in a moment.

In the tenth century, Christian churches still existed in Tunis, but this is partly known in Arabic sources that relate the measures taken to suppress them.[65] Despite such calls to suppress Christianity, some of the other surviving evidence suggests that Christians thrived in this century, or at least were tolerated by some of their Muslim neighbors. One inscription from a Mosque dated to this time even spoke of "the equality of divine truths revealed" both to Muhammad and to Jesus.[66] Other mosques have been found that were converted churches, and one from southern Tunisia even retained an icon of Jesus carved into its wall.[67] There are also known bishoprics in the cities of Sousse (modern Tunisia) and Tlemcen (modern

Algeria) at this same time.[68] After the Fatimid caliphate was formed (909), one Arabic source tells its history and references Christians in North Africa who still have the "Epistles of Paul."[69]

At the end of the tenth century, many signs continue to point to Christianity in the region. Several funeral inscriptions have been found from around this time (c.945–1003) in the town of En Gila (in modern Libya). One quotes from the prophet Ezekiel to say, "Dry bones, you will rise up, you will live and see the glory of the Lord."[70]

Another indication of Christianity in Africa comes from the writings of later popes. Around 980, "from Africa the clergy and people of Carthage" wrote to Pope Benedict VII, requesting that he consecrate their own Jacob as archbishop, and thereby aid their "afflicted and desolate African city, which has been driven to nothingness."[71] Nothing is known about the problems mentioned in this letter, but a clue may come from a few decades later in 1053 when Pope Leo IX (r.1049–1054) wrote to Christians in Africa. The bishop of Gummi (in Byzacena) had claimed metropolitan status for the region, but Leo sided with Thomas, the bishop of Carthage. Leo decisively declares, "The bishop of Carthage is the first archbishop and metropolitan of all Africa."[72] In another letter, this same pope reminds other bishops in Africa of the tradition of Carthaginian primacy going back to "the blessed martyr Cyprian" and Aurelius (bishop of Carthage during Augustine's time – see Chapter 8).[73] The obvious implication of Leo's letter is that not everyone in Africa still viewed Carthage as the head of the church in Africa.[74] It seems that Leo knows of only a few bishops in Africa at all,[75] but I think it is worth considering the fact that the "schism" mentioned a few decades before this time (by Pope Formosus – see the previous page) could limit the number of bishops that Leo counted as valid in his letter. There could be other Christian communions that he refuses to acknowledge.

The same is true of the letters by Pope Gregory VII (r.1073–1085) written to Christians in Africa: there are not enough bishops in Africa to consecrate a new bishop – even though canon law required only three bishops to be present.[76] There are Christians still in Hippo, but Gregory mentions no bishop in his letter to them.[77] The most apparent reason for a lack of other bishops, according to most historians, is the pressure from Muslim rulers in Africa at this time.[78] For evidence of this, one can see Gregory's letter to King Anzir of the Mauretanians, who has only recently released some of his Christian prisoners. Pope Gregory thanks him for this action, and invokes the fact that they worship the same God: "we who believe and confess one God, albeit in different ways."[79] The case, I suspect, is more complicated. Perhaps there are other Christian bishops in Africa, only none still in communion with Cyriacus of Carthage. After all, even "the clergy and the Christian people of Carthage" have found their bishop guilty of some crime, and so they have handed him over to the "Saracens (*Saracenos*)" to be flogged.[80] The pope, nevertheless, still expects "the African church" to survive, as evidenced in his exhortation to Cyriacus himself.[81]

Moving into the eleventh century, many sources still indicate the wide-spread presence of Christians in Africa. For example, complaints arise from Arab leaders about Muslims celebrating Christmas and Easter.[82] Also, three inscriptions from Kairouan can be dated exactly to 1007, 1019, and 1064, because they use the phrase "in the year of the Lord [*anno domini*]."[83] In addition to this Christian dating, funerary epitaphs mark the date by using the phrase "in the year of the unbelievers [*anno infidelium*]," which refers to the Muslim dating of "in the year of the Pilgrimage [*anno hegirae*]." This clearly indicates the ongoing presence of Africans who self-identify as Christians, and not Muslims. These inscriptions from Kairouan also exhibit a decline (or at least an adaptation) of Latin because of the use of spelling that corresponds to sound rather than to classical writing.[84] Latin names can also be found in the Arabic sources describing Ibadi communities among "the Berbers," who were known to be more tolerant of Christians.[85] A small village in the Nafusa mountain range (near modern Aljimmari, Libya) was named *Idūnat*, which has been shown to derive its name from the plural form of the Latin *Donatus*, suggesting that it was known as a place where "Donatists" still resided well into the Arab conquest.[86]

In 1159 the Arab ruler of Africa decreed that Christians in Tunis must convert to Islam or be put to death.[87] It should be added, however, that such a declaration assumes that Christians were still present at the time. Furthermore, one can only guess as to how quickly or successfully such a mandate was enforced. There was likely an ongoing presence via an underground church, but such a Christian presence unfortunately disappears from the historian's view.[88] In the year 1192, an official list of the church of Rome only knows of one bishopric "*In Africa*," which is "Carthage [*Carthago*]," but even then no names are given in this list, and so it may simply reflect earlier information about the last known see in this region.[89]

When King Louis IX of France landed at Carthage in 1270 on what is remembered as the eighth Crusade, he apparently found no Christians remaining. That, however, tells us little: because of a sickness in his camp, neither he nor his army made contact with any Africans. Louis died, and his army returned to France.

Similarly, Raymon Lull believed there were no Christians in Africa in his day. He travelled to Tunis four times (in 1285, 1304, 1308, and 1314) with the intent of evangelizing the African Muslims. Instead, he was forced to return immediately each time except for the last, during which he was allegedly stoned. This is the last Christian source for North Africa until modern times. Nevertheless, Arab sources still identify those who spoke "the Latin language of Africa" as late as the fourteenth century, and so these are likely Christians who still speak Latin in the area.[90]

With those reports, we come to the end of any evidence of Christianity in Africa. What happened to the Christians? These scraps of evidence simply do not provide enough information to answer that question. Before turning to the various answers given by scholars, it will be helpful to take a step back from the details found in these sources, and try to survey the overarching trends of African Christianity in the time of Islam.

Characteristics of late African Christianity

The previous discussion of the surviving evidence needs to here be supplemented. While the details of what happened are of course essential to understanding the story, there is also a sense in which we can lose sight of the forest for the trees. Several important characteristics of late African Christianity could be missed if we were to focus solely on surviving evidence. It will be important, therefore, to pause to consider some of the key phenomena of African Christian history in its last stages.

These phenomena will be summarized here in order to provide a more holistic picture of the African Christian landscape at this time. However, we must be careful not to let these general trends become generalizations that would skew the actual evidence. When speaking, for example, of the many Christians who emigrated from Africa during the spread of Islam, we should not overstate the case and think that "most" African Christians fled to Europe at this time. Similarly, the conversions to Islam – which we will discuss on pp. 340–341 and 345–348 – did occur, but at what rate is all but impossible to establish. Instead of allowing these characteristics to override actual evidence, they will be treated as phenomena that did occur and that require further analysis before making more general claims. The claims and any theories as to what contributed to Christianity's disappearance from North Africa will be assessed in the next section. For now, let us take each of these phenomena in turn.

To begin with, one has to consider the history of wars that plagued Africa in late antiquity. On the one hand, there were recurring internal wars between various African groups like the Mauretanians, who sometimes fought each other and often attacked the more Romanized areas. On the other hand, there was the series of conquests that have been noted throughout this work, but are worth recounting here: the ancient Punic colonization of the North African coastline, the Roman victory in the Punic wars followed by widespread Roman colonization of Africa, the Vandal invasion of the fifth century, the Byzantine reconquest of the sixth century, and finally the Arab expansion of the eighth and ninth centuries. Each wave of war must have had a significant impact on the local populations.

These frequent wars and conquests have been understood as catalysts for the disappearance of Christianity in Africa in terms of two different phenomena. The first phenomenon assumed to have occurred in the Arab conquest of North Africa is that adherents of Christianity would have been forced, or at least pressured, to convert. Forced conversions, however, have been questioned in recent studies (as will be discussed on 340–341 and 345–348), and so this phenomenon must be carefully nuanced. Suffice it to say that Islam's presence in North Africa put pressure on Christians in some way, and we must consider what it would mean to resist the pressure to convert under Muslim rule. The second phenomenon that would have occurred in response to these various invasions of Africa would have been the flight of many Christians who emigrated across the Mediterranean.[91] We know this occurred en masse when the Vandals invaded, and there is evidence of many refugees fleeing from Africa during the Arab conquest as well. One famous example is a man named Hadrian (c.635–710) who immigrated to Italy, and from there was sent by the pope to the British Isles.[92] In Canterbury he became the abbot of Saint Peter's monastery – later renamed after Augustine of Canterbury. Bede states that Hadrian was "a man of the African nation [*vir natione Afir*]."[93] On a related note, Bede, writing just sometime near 709, also knows of Tyconius – the Donatist writer, discussed in Chapter 7 – and his commentary on Revelation.[94] Similarly, Pope Gregory II's letter (cited on p. 330) likely reflects an influx of African Christians into Italy and other provinces.[95] Therefore, while Christians did not altogether undertake an exodus from Africa when Muslims invaded, many Christians – especially those with the monetary means to do so – did move to other places in Europe, which must have left a diminished and weakened population of Christians in Africa.

Another important aspect to consider from this period is how fractured and divided Christianity was in North Africa when Muslims first arrived. As has been noted throughout this study, African Christianity continuously experienced schisms throughout its history. Beyond the early possible schismatic or diverse communities, such as Valentinianism and Novatianism, the Christian churches in North Africa aligned themselves along party or schismatic lines that could be considered long lasting, such as with Donatism and Arianism. As discussed in previous chapters, using these labels does little justice to the self-understanding and heritage of those so-called Donatists and Arians, but the point here is to recognize that many cities in North Africa had three distinct parties, or at least three (if not more) different basilicas – all with independent clergy and even bishops. In other words, if one visited a given town in North Africa, one could find three different bishops presiding in three different basilicas. Just how these parties interrelated over time, or even merged, is a matter that requires very meticulous study, for we cannot assume that things unfolded the same way in every locale. Nevertheless, when historians look to the last centuries of Christianity in North Africa, they must take into account how divided Christianity was and consider how this affected the stability of Christians who were confronted by the new presence of Islam.

Another factor to consider is how independent African Christianity was compared to other regional forms of Christianity, even in terms of local churches. Regionally, as we have discussed throughout this book, African Christians had defended their own tradition from the time of Tertullian and Cyprian, and this partly explains the Donatist controversy over rebaptism.[96]

Even after the Byzantine reconquest of North Africa, many African Christians who considered themselves "Catholic" and in line with the worldwide church felt at liberty to criticize and dissent from the decisions of Rome and Constantinople.[97] While this tendency to claim independence should not be exaggerated as an isolationist strategy, there was an element of isolation that occurred when Islam arrived and furthered the difference between what Christians experienced in Africa from the experiences of Christians across the Mediterranean.

At the level of the individual towns and cities, it has often been noted how this value of independence can be detected in how the local diocese governed. Whereas most provinces outside of Africa (including Egypt), had developed large dioceses so that the hierarchy of bishops were well-organized under the metropolitan of the region, African churches kept their dioceses very small so that even small towns and villages had their own bishop and did not answer to a bishop from a neighboring municipality. Cyprian had earlier insisted that even as bishop of Carthage he had no governing authority over other bishops in Africa. Instead, Cyprian relayed how the bishops should cooperate in councils. This Cyprianic model continued throughout African Christian history. Even the "primate" in the African provinces did not belong automatically to the bishop of the largest metropolis (= the metropolitan). When bishops from a local province, such as Numidia, met in council, the bishop who had reigned the longest presided, and then the others spoke in order of seniority. Just how such local autonomy affected Christians when Islam spread is still unclear, but it should be considered when studying this period, since this was one of the factors that set African Christianity apart from other regions around the Mediterranean, such as Egypt and Syria.

One last characteristic to consider about North Africa at this time is the demographics. Throughout this work, we have asked about the relationship between Roman identity and the various groups who had a non-Roman self-identity. In this late period of African Christian history there would have been even more Christians who understood themselves as "Rūm" (as the Arabs called them) or Roman – even though the city of Rome's influence had waned significantly compared to Constantinople. Even with Constantinople's loss of power in North Africa, many Africans seemed to have identified themselves as full-fledged members of the empire.[98] Nevertheless, it should also be remembered that the Africans who most likely could be described with such ties to the empire were "the Latin-speaking elite of Roman Landowner (Romano-Africans) . . . who held distinctive views and cherished a long-developed identification with and commitment to Roman cultural ideals, namely, Romanness or *Romanitas*."[99] This does not, however, describe the whole or even the majority of North Africans, as witnessed by the many so-called Berber tribes who sometimes did and sometimes did not support the efforts of the emperor. In short, "Byzantine relations with the autochthonous North Africans were never good."[100]

Just how many or what percentage of the African Christians would self-describe as Roman and how many would implicitly reject such an identity (and how many would embrace both Roman and non-Roman identities) is difficult to say.[101] Walter Kaegi sets up five categories for people from this context: "With respect to ethnic divisions one cannot make any reasonable estimate of the Latin versus Greek versus assimilated autochthonous versus non-assimilated autochthonous populations and Jews on the eve of the Muslim Conquest of North Africa."[102] Although he admits the sources are too sparse for any certain conclusions, Kaegi concludes that the Byzantines never succeeded in winning over the allegiances of the indigenous African groups like the "Berbers" (= "non-assimilated autochthonous populations"), whereas the Muslims ultimately were able to allow these groups a sense of autonomy while still requiring their ultimate "submission."[103] Conclusions such as this admittedly move us beyond the realm of "facts" and "evidence," and into the area of hypothesis and theory. We should, therefore, review the various theories about "the end of African Christianity" in order to make explicit the kinds of assumptions and questions involved in any study of this period.

Reasons for African Christianity's disappearance

What happened to the Christians in Africa? Since they disappear from the historical record and eventually disappear from North Africa altogether, historians – strictly speaking – do not know the answer to this question. Instead, scholars offer various conjectures as to what most plausibly explains the disappearance of African Christianity after the time of Islam. Perhaps Christians were forced to convert to Islam, or perhaps they simply fled across the Mediterranean in order to avoid religious persecution and/or political oppression. African Christians may have been vulnerable because of the way the churches were administered in the region, or they may have been so divided among themselves by schisms and heresies that they could not stand against the new religious presence in their midst. The African Christians may have aligned themselves too much with the foreign rulers in Rome and Constantinople so that they never fully Christianized the African peoples, or conversely they may have syncretized so much of their faith with other religious practices that they easily absorbed, and were absorbed into, Islam. Each of these possibilities will be discussed in turn, but first we need to acknowledge a problematic assumption in these theories.

In a recent essay, Mark A. Handley criticizes all these theories for explaining the history in terms of Christianity's "failure" instead of considering Islam's "success."[104] Handley offers a necessary correction of what he thinks is a Eurocentric assumption about the superiority of Christianity to Islam. He is correct that such assumptions have clouded past studies. One example of Eurocentric racism skewing the thought of a historian can be found in a comment by Julius Lloyd, an Anglican minister from the late nineteenth century. In his 1880 study entitled *The North African Church*, Lloyd criticized King Louis IX of France (d.1270) for his foolish attempt to evangelize a Muslim leader in Africa:

> The King had exchanged embassies with the Sultan of Tunis, and had listened with credulous enthusiasm to the sultan's message that he desired to receive Baptism. . . . That such a message was given in good faith is hardly credible; for the faith of Islam benumbs that higher spiritual intelligence to which the Christian revelation appeals; and sincere conversions are extremely rare.[105]

Generally speaking, overt racist comments like this are thankfully absent from contemporary discussions about the disappearance of African Christianity. Nevertheless, any investigation into this question will need to be aware of such problematic assumptions about what religion or people may be more "primitive," "violent," or "extreme."[106]

In addition to assumptions like these, I suspect theological commitments have also affected some Christian historians: the Matthean passage promising the church's survival has likely influenced the way this story is told.[107] Christians believe that Jesus's "kingdom shall have no end," according to the Nicene Creed. Furthermore, it was an African Christian who famously said, "The blood of the martyrs is seed."[108] Although such statements of faith need not be disavowed, the historian must be careful not to replace empirical evidence with theological assumptions.[109] After all, even theologically speaking, none of these statements promise that the church, the kingdom, or the martyrs' blood will perpetually survive in any given region.

With such criticisms acknowledged, there still remains work to be done. Criticism of how the question has been wrongly articulated does not make the question go away. Even apart from theological commitments, the historical question remains as to why Christianity did not survive in North Africa while it did in Egypt, Syria, and other Muslim-controlled regions. In what follows I will review the various theories offered to explain the disappearance of Christianity in North Africa, offering evaluations of the strengths and weaknesses of each. After this review, I will offer my own suggestion about what happened to Christianity in the region.

The following seven theories are listed distinctly for the sake of clarity. For each of the theories I will point to scholars who invoke the theory to explain African Christianity's disappearance. These citations, however, will not be comprehensive analyses of each scholar's work, and therefore I must stipulate that criticisms of the theories themselves are not necessarily criticisms of the scholars cited. Most historians point to multiple causes when talking about Christian disappearance during the time of Muslim rule in Africa. The citations of these scholars are meant to point the reader to help in further exploring each theory. With this caveat in place, let us now turn to the first possible explanation.

Political power theory

In 1555 German princes signed a treaty with Charles V, the Holy Roman Emperor. In the aftermath of the Protestant Reformation, this treaty established the principle *Cuius regio, eius religio* ("He who rules, his religion"). According to this principle, the subjects in any given region will adhere to the religion of their local ruler. Protestant principalities will have Protestant churches, while Catholic rulers will enforce their "religion" in their domains. Can this principle be generalized as a natural law that governs societies? If so, then one would expect North Africans to convert eventually when North Africa comes under Muslim rule.

Many scholars discuss the end of ancient African Christianity in ways that assume this political power theory.[110] On the surface, the conquest of North Africa by Arab rulers seems to be the most straightforward explanation of what happened to the Christians. The Byzantine armies lost many lives in the fight against the Arab invaders, and when Arabs finally drove out those forces, the plunder of the countryside was brutal (as discussed on p. 329). Any remaining Christians must have been pressured in various ways to become Muslim. The Arab conquest must also be set in the context of the broader history, where this kind of conquest occurred repeatedly in North Africa, namely by the Vandals, then the Byzantines reclaiming Africa from the Vandals. Such a succession of wars must have taken its toll on the population, especially the Christian population aligned with the Roman Empire. While this explanation must be part of any attempt to answer our question, it also must be admitted that this explanation has its problems.

To begin with, Christianity arrived in Africa quite in contradiction to this theory. The earliest records testify to the staunch resistance many Christians displayed to the Roman pantheon. Even if Rome's tolerance for foreign deities is taken into account, this general stance by Roman rulers was certainly overturned in some extreme instances under emperors like Decian and Diocletian wherein the Christians were pressured to abandon or at least syncretize their faith.[111]

Furthermore, even when Christians ruled as Roman emperors, they rarely were able to impose their "religion" on the African Christians (or many others for that matter). The Trinitarianism of the councils of Nicaea and Constantinople was not always enforced in Africa (among the Donatists and the Vandals), and the apparent monophysite sympathies of Justinian and other emperors met an unbending resistance in Africa during the Three Chapters controversy.

Another problem with this theory is that it assumes Muslims forced Christians to convert, which has been shown on pp. 322–323 to be untrue in the earliest centuries of the Arab conquests. Finally, it must also be added that even under lengthy rule by Muslims, Egyptian and Syrian Christianity survived whereas African Christianity did not. Therefore, the spread of Islam and the rule by Muslims does not satisfactorily explain Christianity's disappearance in Africa.

Christian exodus theory

Rather than face certain persecution and possible death from the new conquerors, perhaps most Christians – or at least those with means to do so – simply fled Africa in search of a Christian land of refuge. This theory goes hand in hand with the previous one in that it explains Christianity's disappearance from Africa in terms of the military conquest.[112] The difference is that instead of military force used directly against the African Christians, this theory focuses on the threat of such force and the willingness of the Christians themselves to flee Africa permanently.

Earlier in this chapter we surveyed evidence of African Christians fleeing abroad, and therefore this theory has merit. As with the previous theory, this phenomenon is especially compelling when considered in light of the evidence of earlier scenes in Africa's history, such as the Vandal invasion when many Christians – or at least Caecilianist/Catholic Christians – fled to the northern shores of the Mediterranean. Then, the Byzantine reconquest took many decades of war with the various Mauretanian uprisings, and we can assume that many (Romanized?) Christians would have fled Africa at this time as well.

Against this theory, it must be admitted that the evidence for such flight is relatively slim given how prevalent Christianity was in Africa. There is certainly no evidence of a mass exodus at this time, and even in the so-called Dark Ages one would expect more literary records were such an event or events to have taken place. The theory is more plausible if understood in terms of long-term attrition by way of numerous small-scale emigrations of Christian families spread out over the last centuries of African Christian history. Even so, given the numbers of Christian bishops and churches known from the Byzantine period in the literary and archaeological records, this explanation still requires more evidence.

Another problem with this theory lies in its implication about the Christians thought to have fled Africa. As we will see on pp. 344–345, some scholars assume that the Christians in Africa were not really African, and so they could easily uproot and move to more Romanized areas when the Arabs took over. While this may have been true of some Christians in Africa, we have shown throughout this work that Christianity was not monolithic in Africa, and many Christians in this region would have had a sense of Africa as their ancestral homeland. Therefore, this theory remains unpersuasive when taken as the singular or even principal cause of Africa's disappearance from North Africa.

Decapitation theory

"Strike the shepherd, and the sheep will be scattered."[113] This maxim may be thought by some to be another sort of natural law when it comes to social groups. When routing out any religious ideology, perhaps rulers naturally try to remove the religious leader(s) as a way of weakening the religious body. In virtually every persecution of Christians in Africa (e.g. by Roman officials, by Caecilianists/Catholics, by Vandals), there is evidence of bishops and clergy being targeted.[114] It would seem reasonable to assume the same occurred when Muslim rulers took control of Africa.

Curiously, there is very little evidence that Christian clergy were targeted during the Arab conquest of North Africa. This point might be noteworthy, except for the fact that the sources are virtually silent about any persecution at all. The Christian sources focus on the military conquest of Arab expansion, and the later Arabic sources describe the events as one singular victory – both military and religious – guided by God.[115]

Those who have advocated this theory do so by drawing on larger trends in African Christianity that can fill in the gaps in our evidence. Specific aspects of the African clergy from late antiquity explain why African Christianity disappeared in the middle ages. One such explanation is given by Averil Cameron, who points to the shift from Latin to Greek in the Byzantine reconquest of North Africa.[116] The primarily Latin-speaking church of Africa could not engage the contemporary issues, as evidenced by the lack of literary production at this time from African clergy. The Byzantine period produced no literary heir to Tertullian, Cyprian, Augustine, or Ferrandus. Therefore, the church was ill-equipped to face new theological challenges, such as those presented by Islam.

Another variation of the decapitation theory can be found in the work of Maureen Tilley.[117] She points to the unique role of the bishops in African Christianity and how this was undermined in the last two centuries before Islam. As we have seen in previous chapters, each bishop in Africa retained an autonomy from other bishops, although the bishops as a whole attempted to act as "colleagues" by frequently meeting in councils. Unlike other regions, in Africa even the smallest towns and villages had a bishop, not a presbyter serving under a bishop in a larger city like most of the western provinces, and not a *chorepiskopos* or "country-bishop" serving under a city-bishop like the eastern provinces. Tilley believes the authority of these African bishops was undermined by (1) the Vandal persecution that targeted them, (2) the Byzantine enforcement of foreign church practice and doctrine, and (3) the interference from Roman popes, like Gregory the Great, which undermined their authority. The weakened bishops allowed for a decentralized and demoralized African church at the time of Islam's arrival.

One other form of this decapitation theory relates not to bishops but to monks. According to W.H.C. Frend, in other regions like Egypt and Syria, the monastic heroes of the faith served as spiritual leaders to lay Christians.[118] In Africa, however, monasticism was a late and foreign phenomenon. Augustine had attempted to establish monasticism in Numida in the late fourth and early fifth centuries, and evidence of more monasteries is available during the Byzantine period, but these have ties to the Greek east. For example, Thalassius "the African," who led a monastic community in Carthage at this time, wrote in Greek and had clear ties to eastern Christianity.[119]

Admittedly, this theory, especially in this last form regarding the lack of monasticism, is difficult to test. What exactly is missing from North African Christianity that monasteries would have provided? More literacy? A stronger champion of Christian identity? Even so, how did these things help preserve Christianity in places like Syria and Egypt? The theory may help supplement our understanding of this period of history, but on its own it still cannot fully explain Christianity's disappearance. Therefore, in addition to this decapitation theory, still more are offered by scholars.

House divided theory

Another theological claim that has become somewhat of a maxim of the history of religion is that "A house divided against itself cannot stand." Jesus, of course, made this claim in response to questions about his own inner state, and later Augustine used this statement with the same individual meaning.[120] Much later, Abraham Lincoln famously borrowed this remark to defend the American "Union."[121] Lincoln, however, had applied this more in the sense used by Thomas Hobbes, which is to think in terms of an institutional body.[122] Should historians follow suit and think of this as a natural principle at work in the ancient African Church?

Given the fact that African Christianity had experienced numerous long-lasting schisms, one could easily expect it to become weaker and further fragmented in its last years. The early sources indicate that there were various "Gnostic" groups, like the Valentinians in North Africa, and in Cyprian's time known schisms included the Laxists and Rigorist/Novatianists.[123] The major event in African Christianity is the Donatist schism, since after this event the majority of cities and towns were known to have had rival bishops leading rival churches.[124] The Vandal invasion only further complicates and fragments the North African church. While many historians believe that most remaining Donatists reunited with the Caecilianist/Catholic party, the evidence is not so clear. There were certainly some Donatist churches that continued after the Vandal invasion, and perhaps some even continued until the time of the Arab invasion. Therefore, some – perhaps many – cities would have had three rival communions: Donatist, Caecilianist/Catholic, and Vandal/Arian. Furthermore, it is difficult to know how prevalent the Manicheans still were in North Africa, since the fleeting references to them throughout the Byzantine period may be due to standard formulae borrowed from earlier sources.

How might this state of affairs have affected African Christians at the time of the Arab conquest? From the perspective of a common layperson, the new religion also speaks highly of Jesus (see p. 323). Perhaps the Muslim faith was viewed simply as another alternative in the array of Christians sects, and therefore many Christians would not have understood their "submission" to the new rulers as a betrayal of their Christian faith, any more than a conversion from a Donatist to a Caecilianist communion, or from a Catholic to a Vandal faith.

While this theory sounds plausible, it too is difficult to test with evidence. Furthermore, we could again cite the examples of Syria and Egypt where the churches were also divided along the lines of Nestorians, Chalcedonians, Monophysites, and other schismatic groups. For the house divided theory to be persuasive, we would have to demonstrate other variables that explain the survival of Christianity in some regions and its disappearance in Africa.

Cultural gap theory

A common trope in contemporary missiology is to speak of the need for Christianity to be contextualized and to become an authentic expression of the indigenous people. If foreign missionaries impose their culture as much as their faith on new people groups, then their work is as much about colonialism as it is evangelism. Did the Christians in ancient Africa make this same mistake? Was Christianity in Africa so identified with Roman and Latin culture that when the Roman power was finally replaced in the Arab conquest Christianity simply disappeared with it?

W.H.C. Frend, who was cited on p. 342 as acknowledging several factors as contributing to Christianity's decline, argued that this was the fundamental cause of African Christianity's disappearance.[125] The Donatist church, for Frend, was the authentic African Church in two ways. First, in Africa Proconsularis and Byzacena, it was the theological heir to Cyprian. Second, in Numidia and Mauretania, it was the church of the indigenous "Berbers." Therefore, Frend concludes, "The destruction of this society . . . contributed in no little way to the ultimate destruction of Christian and Roman north Africa."[126] Thus, for Frend the gap between "Berber" culture and the Roman culture led to Christianity's disappearance from North Africa.

Another version of this theory can be found in an article by C. J. Botha, who offered one major caveat to this point: some "Berbers" were Romanized and therefore Christianized, while others were not.[127] Those "Berbers" who were never evangelized, therefore, were easily converted to Islam when the Romans retreated from Africa and when the Roman/-ized population fled before the Arab conquest.

It should be noted that this theory at times seems to assume that the Donatists were simply African "nationalism in disguise," which is a claim that has been shown to be entirely anachronistic and unsubstantiated by the sources.[128] Alternatively, this theory has also been invoked a way that it is not concerned with nationalist/ethnic identity, but instead with a focus on language.[129] Whereas the Syrian church had historically used Aramaic (and its descendant, Syriac), and the Coptic church translated the Greek sources into the native tongue of Egyptians, the African church always remained Latin in its literature and liturgy. Perhaps this gap between the church's official language and the common tongue of the people resulted in Christians' inability to articulate their faith properly in the face of a new religious presence. Notice that this version of the cultural gap theory especially makes sense in tandem with others: if there was a lack of trained bishops (decapitation theory) and if Islam appeared to be one of many choices of communities who revere Jesus (house divided theory), then how would a Christian (even a literate one) test which theology is correct, if both Latin and Arabic scriptures are foreign to said Christian?

The primary weaknesses of this theory are as follows. The theory risks slipping back into a nationalistic/ethnic view of the Christian landscape, and this is a reductionistic view of religion that risks denying the sincerity of the African Christians. Also, as we have seen throughout the previous chapters, there were numerous instances when African Christians exhibited some form of an "indigenous" identity, and so the gap between Christianity and the local culture was not universally present. Nevertheless, the relationship between Christianity and Romanization is a valid question for this time period, and the linguistic gap does have explanatory power, especially when coupled with other theories mentioned in this section. The last two theories that can be added to our list understand the problem not in terms of a gap between Christianity and the local culture, but in terms of blurring of lines between Christianity and new social factors. These will be discussed in terms of theological syncretism and then political pragmatism.

Theological syncretism theory

With the advance of Arab rulers into North Africa, African Christians may not have seen the need to enforce a theological boundary between their faith and that of the new conquerors. Since Christians and Muslims were seen to worship the same God, the only question about "submitting" to Muhammad's teachings had to do with finding out what exactly Muhammad taught.[130] The five pillars – if they were recognized as such in early Islam – provide us with specific beliefs and practices that can be considered here.

The first pillar is to confess (*shahāda*) that there is (depending on how one translates the Arabic) "no god but God" – with which all Christians would agree. Furthermore, the traditional confession states that "Muhammad is the prophet of God." Was this originally taught as the final revelation of God? Or, would North Africans – especially Latin speakers without a definite article in their language – have understood this to mean that Muhammad was *a* prophet? What then, does Muhammad teach? If his message is fundamentally one of rejecting idols, turning to the one true God, and living according to God's teachings about a just society, then this prophet's message is remarkably consistent with the many African Christian apologists of previous generations. What Muhammad says about Jesus is of course a more pertinent question for Christians at this time. As we mentioned on p. 323, the Qur'an in fact has a very high view of Jesus, even though it denies Jesus was "divine" (which in Arabic would have meant "a god"). We will return to this Christological question in a moment.

The second pillar of Islam is to pray (*salāh*) five times a day, something Christians were already doing at this time.[131] The third pillar is to give alms (*zakāh*), which Christians in theory have always affirmed. The fourth pillar is the pilgrimage (*hajj*) to Mecca, but there have always been exceptions for those who are to ill, old, or poor to make such a pilgrimage. The fifth is to fast during Ramadan, which also has more overlap with Christianity than is often acknowledged. Although Ramadan as such would have been novel to Christians in terms of when this occurs and the story being celebrated, Christians by this time already had designated seasons of fasting, such as Advent and Lent.

Could a Christian submit to these practices? Perhaps Christians did so with the sincere belief that the new rulers were blessed by God and had come to establish justice and order. Perhaps many Christians agreed to be a "Muslim" (= one who submits), but also continued as a Christian. This, of course, still ignores the question of Islam's view of Jesus.

In his 1960 *Church History* article C. J. Speel put forward a very specific argument that assumes this theory and tries to explain Christianity's disappearance from Africa in terms of syncretistic Christology.[132] According to Speel, the Vandals succeeded in converting – by all means necessary – most African Christians to their form of "Arianism." That is to say, the Vandals and their African converts denied that Jesus was "truly God," and instead viewed him as subordinated to the Father. Speel believed that unlike other practitioners of forms of "Arianism" common at the time, the Vandals clung to their Germanic heritage, which set the All-Father categorically above all lesser spiritual beings, but they saw Jesus as an honored and perhaps even "divine" champion. This would be a much closer step toward Islam's view of Jesus.

Speel's argument has come under sharp criticism, and to be sure he exaggerates how "Germanic" the Vandals' subordinationism was along with how successful their conversion rate was.[133] Nevertheless, his underlying premise may have something to offer, especially when paired with other theories (like the house divided theory). If Arianism was still part of the African Christian landscape, then why couldn't Islam be seen as compatible with Christian beliefs? I would add a piece of evidence from a coin found from North Africa, dating from 736. It reads "God is One . . . He does not beget nor is He begotten, and none is like unto Him."[134] This exact sentence could have been said by an Arian (in any century). This theory then cannot be entirely dismissed, although it does not satisfactorily explain the entire phenomenon of Christian disappearance in Africa – especially in the form articulated by Speel. The next and last theory to be mentioned here also assumes that Christianity could overlap with a new order, but this time the primary concern is not theological but political.

Political pragmatism theory

In the pre-modern world, no one would have recognized theology and politics as two distinct spheres. Rarely was there a separation between the church and the state. Even if intellectuals could distinguish the two, the two would not be thought of as independent of the other. We already discussed on p. 322 how the "Arab conquest" was in some ways one and the same as the "spread of Islam."

Even though religion was inherently enmeshed in politics (and vice versa), we would like to balance the previous theory by isolating political motivation for the sake of analysis. The reason for this stems from the recognition by scholars that the conquered were not passive recipients of a new culture, religion, or political order – a concern found especially among postcolonial theorists.[135]

When we discussed Romanization in previous chapters, we rejected the notion that the conquerors simply imposed *Romanitas* by force upon the indigenous Africans. No laws required Africans, for example, to wear the toga. The new political presence no doubt did pressure the local population, especially the elites, to take an active role in the new order, and doing so included actions like embracing the Roman social norms, such as dress. This subtle shift of seeing the conquered as having an active role in negotiating their response to the new political order allows the historian to appreciate how some of the local population decided to accept *Romanitas* as being in their best interest while others did not. The population as a whole need not have responded in the same way. We suggest that the same view be allowed during the Arab conquest. Perhaps African Christians assessed their options in light of the new political power, and some simply found that "submission" was the most expedient option; others would have submitted in political terms for pragmatic reasons but retained their own theological convictions and practices. Others still likely would have resisted, fled, or even accepted extreme punishment for their unwillingness to accept Islam (i.e. enslavement or death).

In a recent book on Christian practice in North Africa, a group of scholars explained African Christianity's disappearance as follows:

> The reasons for its ultimate extinction may not be so puzzling, however, in light of those previous centuries of struggle to maintain identity in

the context of successive internal divisions, colonial occupations, and doctrinal controversies. Each new ruler required some level of religious conformity, and perhaps in the great scheme of things, this last arrival was no more "foreign" than any of the others. In fact, it may have seemed more like traditional African Christianity than any of the others in certain respects – including its emphasis on rigorous individual and communal purity; the importance of heroic martyrs and saints; and the perception that one true community guarded and guaranteed authentic religious faith. Perhaps at least the character (if not the theology) of African Christianity survived in some respect, after all, by being absorbed into the Islam of the Maghreb.[136]

The first thing to note about this quote is how several different theories are espoused as part of a multifaceted explanation. These authors have championed an approach that attempts to take the African Christians' theological motivation seriously, and so reject any reductionistic explanation of African history in terms of pure social trends or political expediency. Their statement is helpful here because they also recognize how "foreign" political and theological orders do not negate or eclipse the previous religious community's values and characteristics. I take their statement to help explain how African Christians did not simply disappear: they negotiated ways to retain their "character" even if the surviving sources suggest they were "absorbed" into the new reality. As discussed on pp. 328–329, the Islam of North Africa was as changed as the Christianity it allegedly superseded.

When faced with new rulers, I would suggest that some African Christians viewed their "submission" as primarily a politically expedient action. Even so, they likely knew that such a submission would involve a theological syncretism (as discussed with the previous theory) – but the Christians should be understood as active agents who negotiated what and how any syncretism took place. As noted on p. 334, many in North Africa continued to celebrate Christmas and Easter for centuries after Christianity's alleged disappearance. With this example, we can perhaps catch a glimpse of how Christians believed that they could be "absorbed" into Arab rule while still holding to their Christian allegiances.

This theory should not be understood as applying to all African Christians in the time of Islam. Nor should it be used reductionistically to claim that African Christians simply abandoned their beliefs for pragmatic reasons. Instead, it can help supplement the other theories listed here as one more factor that helps explain why Christianity in Africa eventually disappeared as a recognizably distinct religion.

Tentative conclusions on African Christianity's end

All the theories discussed so far have their merits as well as their weaknesses. Historians have long recognized that in the absence of evidence one must offer an "educated guess," hopefully one that is well informed and theoretically plausible. It is suggested here that no single explanation of African Christianity's disappearance sufficiently explains what happened. Instead, the various theories can be used to understand what must have been a variety of factors that affected the history of this period.

This treatment of African Christianity's disappearance is by no means exhaustive, and my conclusion is of course provisional. We may hope that more evidence will come to light that will help us better understand this period of Africa's history: may there be a Qumran, Oxyrhynchus, or Nag Hammadi in the future of North African archaeology. In the meantime, what few sources are extant for this late period of Africa's history deserve further analysis by scholars. Additional scrutiny and debate of this material can certainly help us better understand the history.

Christianity in Africa deserves to be understood in light of its uniquely African context, as has been argued throughout this book, and with more studies along these lines we may find that a new understanding of this region's history emerges. Then, the story of African Christianity under Arab rule can be better compared to the stories of Christian communities in neighboring regions like Spain and Egypt.

Notes

1 Text available in Guy Cambier, *Embricon de Mayence La Vie de Mahamet* (Collection Latomus 52; Bruxelles: Latomus, Revue d'etudes Latines, 1961). See discussion in John V. Tolan, "Anti-hagiography: Embrico of Mainz's Vita Mahumeti," *Journal of Medieval History* 22 (1996), 25–41; and Alberto Ferreiro, *Simon Magus in Patristic, Medieval and Early Modern Traditions* (Leiden: Brill, 2005), 221–240.

2 E.g. A. Schwarze, "North African Church," in *The New Schaff-Herzog Encyclopedia of Religious Knowledge*, ed. Samuel Macauley Jasckson, et al. (New York: Funk and Wagnalls, 1910), 8:193.

3 See the collection of essays on this period in general, which only devotes a few pages to North Africa in Michael Bonner (ed.), *Arab-Byzantine Relations in Early Islamic Times* (The Formation of the Classical World 8; Aldershot, UK: Ashgate, 2004).

4 For details and discussion of the sources, see Pringle, *The Defence of Byzantine Africa*, 1:1–8; and Vassilios Christides, *Byzantine Libya and the March of the Arabs Towards the West of North Africa* (British Archaeological Reports 851; Oxford: BAR, 2000), 71–77; and Kaegi, *Muslim Expansion*, 29–40. The Arabic primary sources, unfortunately, are mostly not available in an English translation (although some have been collected in J.F.P. Hopkins [trans./ed.] and Nehemia Levtzion [ed.], *Corpus of Early Arabic Sources for West African History* [Cambridge: Cambridge University Press, 1981]). For the difficulties with the sources from this period in general, see the essays in Averil Cameron, et al. (eds.), *The Byzantine and Early Islamic Near East: Problems in the Literary Source Material* (Princeton, NJ: Darwin Press, 1992).

5 The Arabic sources are listed in Isabella Sjöström, *Tripolitania in Transition: Late Roman to Islamic Settlement With a Catologue of Sites* (Aldershot, UK: Avebury, 1993), 22–23. One of the most extensive albeit later sources was Ibn

Khaldun (1332–1406), who was born in Tunisia and who is important for many disciplines in addition to historiography, such as sociology.

 6 For example, one agenda that scholars have found in these sources is the need to justify the enslavement of the "Berbers." Since, according to these sources, these Berbers had originally converted to Islam but then recanted the faith, they were validly enslaved. See Michael Brett, "The Arab Conquest and the Rise of Islam in North Africa," in *The Cambridge History of Africa*, ed. J. D. Fage (Cambridge: Cambridge University Press, 1978), 2:506.

 7 E.g. Qur'an 22:40. In fact, it was the Christians at this time forcing the conversions of others, such as the Jews; see Maximus the Confessor's disapproval of this practice in Africa (discussed in Cameron, "Byzantine Africa," 56) and the *Teachings of Jacob*, written in Palestine but set in Carthage.

 8 For a bibliography and extended discussion on the points raised in the following paragraphs, see Wilhite, *The Gospel According to Heretics*, 217–243.

 9 For example, John of Damascus, *On Heresies* 101, thought Muhammad was an Arian Christian. Would North African Christians with their history of contacts with Arians see him the same way?

10 To be sure, these groups would not see themselves as associated with Christianity today. The point here is that Africa under Islam witnessed many different forms of both faiths.

11 Fred Donner, *Muhammad and the Believers* (Cambridge, MA: Harvard University Press, 2010), has demonstrated this for the Muslim conquest of Syria. Furthermore, Walter Emil Kaegi, "Seventh-Century Identities: The Case of North Africa," in *Visions of Community in the Post-Roman World: The West, Byzantium and the Islamic World, 300–1100*, ed. Walter Pohl, Clemens Gantner, and Richard E. Payne (Farnham, Surrey: Ashgate, 2012), 167, believes that Donner's model best explains what happened in North Africa. For the Ibadis, see Elizabeth Savage, *A Gateway to Hell, A Gateway to Paradise: The North African Response to the Arab Conquest* (Studies in Late Antiquity and Early Islam 7; Princeton: Darwin Press, 1997), who can even refer to "Christians Ibadis" (see esp. pp. 89–105 in Chapter 5 "Christian 'Ibādīs": Equality of the Divine Truths").

12 Savage, *Gateway to Hell*, 101.

13 For the known theological sources from this community, see Mohammed Ech-Cheikh, "Ignored Pages of the History of the Ibādī Theology in North Africa during the Middle Ages: The *Wājiz* (Summary) of 'Abd al-Kāfī and the *Dalīl* (Proof and Demonstration) of al-Warjlānī," in *Ibadi Theology: Rereading Sources and Scholarly Work*, ed. Ersilia Francesca (Hildesheim: Georg Olms, 2015), 103–114. For an introduction to the history of these various groups, see Roman Loimeier, *Muslim Societies in Africa: A Historical Anthropology* (Bloomington, IN: Indiana University Press, 2013), 35–53 (= Chapter 2 "The Bilād al-Maghrib: Rebels, Saints, and Heretics").

14 See Marcel Mercier, "Mzab," in *The Encyclopaedia of Islam: A Dictionary of the Geography, Ethnography and Biography of the Muhammadan Peoples* (Leiden: Brill, 1938), 166.

15 Mercier, "Mzab," 166. Others, both Christians and Muslims, fled to Ouargla (also in modern Algeria); see Talbi, "Le Christianisme maghrébin," 321.

16 They were not the first to operate independently; the Aghlabids recognized the Baghdad Caliph's theoretical supremacy, but retained their own autonomy. See Kenneth J. Perkins, "Aghlabid Amirate of Afriqiya (800–909)," in *The Encyclopedia of African History*, ed. Kevin Shilington (London: Routledge, 2005), 35–37.

17 For archaeological and epigraphical evidence from this time, which indicate ongoing development, see Kaegi, *Muslim Expansion*, 69–71.

18 Pringle, *The Defence of Byzantine Africa*, 1:13.
19 For details on these groups and their internal diversity as well as their interrelations and acculturation with each other, see Christides, *Byzantine Libya*, 4–14. The most detailed study for this period is Modéran, *Les Maures*.
20 See helpful background information in the opening chapter of Bruce Maddy-Weitzman, *The Berber Identity Movement and the Challenge to North African States* (Austin, TX: University of Texas Press, 2011).
21 For a helpful timeline of events in North Africa, see Kaegi, *Muslim Expansion*, 11–15.
22 Theophanes, *Chronicle* 645/6: σὺν τοῖς Ἄφροις (de Boor, *Theophanes Chronographia*, 343; Mango and Scott, *The Chronicle*, 477).
23 Kaegi, *Muslim Expansion*, 268.
24 Not the first time such an event was said to occur in the region; cf. Procopius, *History of the Wars* 3.15.34–35; *Buildings* 6.6.
25 For details, see Modéran, "Kusayla: l'Afrique et les arabes," in *Identités et cultures dans l'Algérie antique*, ed. Claude Briand-Ponsart (Rouen and Le Havre: Publications des universités de Rouen et du Havre, 2005), 423–457, who questions much of the traditional account.
26 This final destruction of Carthage, however, has been called into question. Susan T. Stevens, "Carthage in Transition," in *North Africa Under Byzantium and Early Islam*, ed. Susan T. Stevens and Jonathan P. Conant (Washington, DC: Dumbarton Oaks, 2016), 89–103, notes how the medieval literary evidence for this event clearly uses Rome's destruction of Punic Carthage as a motif, and then shows how the archaeological evidence counters the notion of a sudden and total destruction of the city.
27 For the primary sources, see Pringle, *The Defence of Byzantine Africa*, 2:382 notes 65 and 66. For details – or at least what details can be known from the sources, see Modéran, "De Mastiès à la Kâhina," *Aouras* 3 (2006), 159–183.
28 Jacob Abadi, *Tunisia Since the Arab Conquest: The Saga of a Westernized Muslim State* (Reading, UK: Ithaca Press, 2013), 12. For further details about Kahina's Christian identity, see Talbi, "al-Kāhina," in *Encyclopedia of Islam*, 2nd ed. (Leiden: 1978), 4:422–423.
29 Ibn Khaldun, *Histoire des Berbères et des dynasties musulmanes de l'Afrique septentrionale* (Paris: Geuthner, 1968), 208–209; cited/translated by Shlomo Sand, *The Invention of the Jewish People* (London: Verso, 2009), 202. Shlomo refers to this same work (p. 198) for "the war of the Berbers' ancestors in Syria against the Israelites, and their subsequent migration to the Maghreb."
30 Sand, *The Invention*, 202.
31 Ibn 'Abd al-Hakam cited in Abdelmajid Hannoum, *Colonial Histories, Post-Colonial Memories: The Legend of the Kahina, a North African Heroine* (Studies in African literature; Portsmouth, NH: Heinemann, 2001), 9.
32 Holmes, *The End of African Christianity*, 229.
33 Abadi, *Tunisia*, 12.
34 Cited in Savage, *A Gateway to Hell*, 99.
35 Savage, *A Gateway to Hell*, 100.
36 Even so, there was much continuity for these cities after the defeat of the Byzantines; see Paul Reynolds, "From Vandal *Africa* to Arab *Ifrīgiya*: Tracing Ceramic and Economic Trends through the Fifth to the Eleventh Centuries," in *North Africa Under Byzantium and Early Islam*, ed. Susan T. Stevens and Jonathan P. Conant (Washington, DC: Dumbarton Oaks, 2016), 129–172; and Cécile Morrisson, "*REGIO DIVES IN OMNIBUS BONIS ORNATA*: The African Economy from the Vandals to the Arab Conquests in the Light of Coin Evidence," in *North Africa Under Byzantium and Early Islam*, ed. Susan T. Stevens and Jonathan P. Conant (Washington, DC: Dumbarton Oaks, 2016), 173–200.

37 Shillington, *History of Africa*, 75.
38 For details, see Frage, "Arab Conquest and the Rise of Islam in North Africa," 513–522 and 540–542; and see discussion in Christides, *Byzantine Libya*, 65. Shillington, *History of Africa*, 76, adds:

> The Kharajite movement was reminiscent of the Donatist Christian movement in its rejection of alien authority. . . . A number of Kharajite Berber states rose and fell in the Maghrib during the eighth and ninth centuries, each asserting varying degrees of independence from the Caliphs of Bagdad.

Savage, *A Gateway to Hell*, 97–98, also asserts the link between Donatism and the Kharajites and the later Ibadis.
39 For further details of these various expressions of Islam and their history in North Africa, see Jamil M. Abun-Nasr, *A History of the Maghrib in the Islamic Period* (Cambridge: Cambridge University Press, 1987), 26–70.
40 E.g. Theophanes, *Chronicle* 668/9, reports that the "Saracens" took 80,000 Africans as slaves in one raid.
41 *A Gateway to Hell*, 90.
42 Savage, *A Gateway to Hell*, 90 n.8.
43 Richard Boulliet, *Conversion to Islam in the Medieval Period: An Essay in Quantitative History* (Cambridge, MA: Harvard University Press, 1979), 92–103.
44 While the archaeological remains have proven difficult to date, recent studies have returned to this material to find more continuity between the periods prior to and after the Arab conquest; see Corisande Fenwick, "From Africa to Ifrīqiya: Settlement and Society in Early Medieval North Africa (650–800)," *Al-Masāq* 25 (1, 2013), 9–33.
45 The following section is heavily indebted to the essay by Michael Handley, "Disputing the End of African Christianity." However, the primary sources cited this chapter are my own readings of them unless otherwise noted.
46 *Concordia canonum* (in PL 88).
47 *Letter 4*, to Boniface (text available in Maier, *Le dossier* 2:394–396).
48 *Letter 4* (my trans.).
49 Silverius 9.47–48 (*MGH: Poetae latini aevi Carolini* 1:114).
50 Marios Costambeys, Matthew Innes, and Simon Maclean, *The Carolingian World* (Cambridge: Cambridge University Press, 2011), 372. For details on dates and interaction, see Michael Greenhalgh, *Marble Past, Monumental Present: Building With Antiquities in the Mediaeval Mediterranean* (Leiden: Brill, 2009), 359–360. For the primary source, see Matthew Gabriele, *An Empire of Memory: The Legend of Charlemagne, the Franks, and Jerusalem Before the First Crusade*. Oxford: Oxford University Press, 2011), 26.
51 Florus 13.15 and 3.17: *Cartago . . . ruina* (*MGH: Poetae latini aevi Carolini* 2:544).
52 Florus says otherwise: "the neglected coffin of the bones of Cyprian the martyr [*Cypriane martyr / . . . loculus neglectus ossa*]" 13.23–24 [*MGH: Poetae latini aevi Carolini* 2:544]. However, the abandonment of Cyprian's shrine altogether makes the gift from the caliph a miraculous event. David Whitehouse, "An Early Mosque at Carthage?" *Annali dell'Istituto Universario Orientale* 43 (1983), 161–172, believes that Cyprian's church, the same basilica at which Monica prayed for Augustine (see p. 254 in chapter eight), was converted into a mosque, which would explain the Muslim's acquisition of his relics and the ongoing cult of Cyprian. It may also indicate some form of Christian/Muslim syncretism in the early years of the Arab conquest of Africa.
53 Leo III, *Letter 7: christianus amicus . . . ab Africa* (*MGH: Epistolarum* 5.3:98).
54 Leo IV, *Letter 8: Carthaginensium, Africanensium* (= "To the Bishops of Britany"; PL 115:668).

55 *Gesta Sanctorum Rotonensium* 3.8: *direxerunt gressum ad Africam visitare sepulchrum sancti Cypriani archiepiscopi et martyris Christi, qui secundo miliario ab urbe Carthaginensi requiescat iuxta mare, ubi multae virtutes et multa miracula a Domino saepus ostenduntur. Post autem quatuor annos iterum Frotmundus cum duobus fratribus suis Romam reversi* (text/trans. Caroline Brett, *The Monks of Redon:* Gesta sanctorum Rotonensium *and* Vita Conuuoionis [Wolfeboro, NH: Boydell Press, 1989], 206–209).

56 Handley, "Disputing the End of African Christianity," 305–306, finds this source reliable; he is also to be credited as the first (to my knowledge) to use this source as evidence for the ongoing existence of Christians in Africa.

57 See the account in Eulogius, *Memorialis sanctorum* 2.10.23: *Africam . . . Dei Ecclesiam* (PL 115:787); Handley, "Disputing the End of African Christianity," 306, is – as far as I can tell – the first to utilize this source for evidence of ongoing Christianity in Africa.

58 For two other sources from this time, which also serve as Byzantine propaganda about Sicilians and Italians being raided by Muslims from Africa, see Jonathan Conant, "Anxieties of Violence: Christians and Muslims in Conflict in Aghlabid North Africa and the Central Mediterranean," *Al-Masāq* 27 (1, 2015), 7–23.

59 Gaumer, "*Ad Africam visitare sepulchrum sancti Cypriani*" (forthcoming).

60 Savage, *A Gateway to Hell*, 107–110, for thirty-three towns known to have Christian communities at this time; Savage, it should be noted, lists only those with connection to the Ibadis.

61 M. Talbi, "Le Christianisme maghrébin de la conquête musulmane à sa disparition une tentative d'explication," in Michael Gervers and Ramzi Jibran (eds.), *Conversion and Continuity: Indigenous Christian Communities in Islamic Lands – Eight to Eighteenth Centuries* (Toronto: Pontifical Institute of Medieval Studies, 1990), 316–317.

62 See Savage, *A Gateway to Hell*, 101, for sources.

63 "*Ad Africam visitare sepulchrum sancti Cypriani*" (forthcoming).

64 Recorded by Flodoard of Reims, *History of the Church of Reims* 4.2: *regionis Africanae . . . inter episcopos ipsarum provinciarum schismate* (PL 135:267).

65 Talbi, "Le Christianisme," 321–324.

66 Savage, *A Gateway to Hell*, 105, 205–206, and figure 10.

67 Savage, *A Gateway to Hell*, 205, and figure 9.

68 Savage, *A Gateway to Hell*, 110.

69 Ibn al-Haytham, *Kitāb al-Munāzarāt* (trans. Wilferd Madelung, and Paul Ernest Walker, *The Advent of the Fatimids: A Contemporary Shi'i Witness* [London: I. B. Tauris, 2000], 140).

70 Cited/trans. in Decret, *Early Christianity in North Africa*, 200: *Ossa arida resurgetis et vivetis et videbitis majestatem Domini.*

71 Recorded in Pope Sylvester II (r.999–1003), *Letter* 42: *clerus et populous Cartaginensis . . . miserae et desolatae Africanae civitati, qui ita ad nichilum redacta est* (PL 139:342–343).

72 Leo IX, *Letter* 83: *primus archiepiscopus et totius Africae maximus metropolitanus est Carthaginensis episcopus* (PL 143:728).

73 Leo IX, *Letter* 84: *beati martyris Cypriani* (PL 143:729).

74 In fact, while the bishop of Carthage always presided over African councils held in Carthage as the highest ranking see, there is little to no tradition in Africa of assuming that the bishop of Carthage has jurisdiction over other sees. Of course, the bishops of Rome at this time are very concerned with jurisdiction: the so-called Great Schism between Rome and Constantinople will occur the very next year.

75 Handley, "Disputing the End of African Christianity," 305.

76 Gregory VII, *Letter* 3.19 (PL 148:449).

77 *Letter* 3.20 (PL 148:449–450).

78 This is the time when Constantine the African was exiled from Carthage for allegedly practicing magic. According to the twelfth-century source, this African with a Christian name converted to Christianity only after his arrival in Italy. See Peter the Deacon, *Life of Constantine the African* (translated in Herbert Bloch, *Monte Cassino in the Middle Ages* [Rome: Edizioni di Storia e Letteratura, 1986], 1:127–129). For further discussion of Constantine and the importance of the works he transmits to Europe, see the essays in Charles Burnett, *Constantine the African and 'Alī Ibn-Al-'Abbās Al-Maǧūsī: The* Pantegni *and Related Texts.* Leiden, Germany: Brill, 1994).

79 *Letter* 3.21: *qui unum Deum, licet diverso modo, credimus et confitemur* (PL 148:451).

80 *Letter* 1.22: *clero et plebe Christianae Carthaginensi* (PL 148:305–306).

81 *Letter* 1.23: *Ecclesiam Africanam* (PL 148:308).

82 Handley, "Disputing the End of African Christianity," 304, citing Hadi Roger Idris, "Fêtes chrétiennes célébrées en Ifriquiya à l'époque ziride," *Revue africaine* 98 (1954), 261–276.

83 See Amar Mahjoubi, "Nouveau témoignage épigraphique sur la communauté chrétienne de Kairouan au XIe siècle," *Africa* 1 (1966), 85–103.

84 E.g. the Vs are replaced with Bs (i.e. *vocem* as *bocem*, *vita* as *bita*, etc.).

85 Savage, *A Gateway to Hell*, 103.

86 Savage, *A Gateway to Hell*, 104.

87 See the sources, cited in Talbi, "Le Christianisme," 328.

88 Peter von Sivers, "Egypt and North Africa," *The History of Islam in Africa*, ed. Nehemia Levtzion and Randall Lee Pouwels (Athens: Ohio University Press, 2000), 26, concludes, "Thus it is only from the thirteenth century and the establishment of Sunni orthodoxy onward that we can speak of the full Islamization of the Maghrib."

89 *Liber censuum romanae ecclesiae* (Muratori, *Antiquitates Italicae medii aevi* 5:900).

90 Handley, "Disputing the End of African Christianity," 304, citing Al-Idrisi, *Opus Geographicum* and Ibn Khaldun, *Muqaddimah*.

91 See Conant, *Staying Roman*, 67–129, for details and analysis of earlier flights from Africa.

92 Bernhard Bischoff and Michael Lapidge, *Biblical Commentaries from the Canterbury School of Theodore and Hadrian* (Cambridge: Cambridge University Press, 1994), 82–92, suggest that Hadrian was from Cyrenaica. Perhaps Carthaginian expatriates in the British Isles at this time could also explain some of the references to Augustine and "Carthage" (the alleged "Carthaginian circle" of monks) found in certain manuscripts in Ireland: see M. Herren, "The Pseudonymous Tradition in Hiberno-Latin: An Introduction," in *Latin Script and Letters A.D. 400–900: Festschrift Presented to Ludwig Bieler on the Occasion of his 70th Birthday*, ed. John J. O'Meara and Bernd Naumann (Leiden, Germany: Brill, 1976), 127–131. As an aside, it is tempting to inquire about the influence of Africans abroad in terms of later European history: if there was a "Carthaginian circle" in Ireland at this time, and if there was some truth to the notion that the "Irish saved civilization" (cf. Thomas Cahill, *How the Irish Saved Civilization* [New York: Nan A. Talese/Doubleday Press, 1995]), perhaps it was Africans in Ireland who did so.

93 *Ecclesiastical History* 4.1 (my trans.); also, cf. *Vita beatorum abbatum Benedicti, Ceofridi, Eosterwini, Sigfridi et Hwaetbert* 3.

94 *Explanation of Revelation* pref. Bede contrasts Tyconius with Augustine of Hippo, and yet he curiously neglects to label him as a "Donatist," but instead notes that he is considered "most learned among his own (people?) [*inter suos eruditissimi*]."

95 Adamiak, "When did Donatist Christianity End?" 233. It should be noted that Gregory II's letter to Boniface cannot prove that African Christians were in Germany or Italy. Nevertheless, the curious warning begs for some form of explanation.

96 Tertullian's opposition to the bishop of Rome can especially be found in *Against Praxeas*, and Cyprian opposed Stephen of Rome in the baptismal controversy (see previous discussion in chapters four and five). The Donatist controversy was not strictly in opposition to Rome, but the identity and tradition of Africans did include their understanding of Africa's history and tradition as distinct from Rome (see chapter seven).

97 I.e. during the Three Chapters controversy (see chapter ten).

98 For example, Heraclius, who became emperor in 610, had lived in Africa for ten years, and retained family ties by marriage to Africa (as discussed in chapter one).

99 Kaegi, *Muslim Expansion*, 65.

100 Kaegi, *Muslim Expansion*, 159.

101 For discussion, see Talbi, "Le Christianism maghrébin," 313–351.

102 Kaegi, *Muslim Expansion*, 66.

103 *Muslim Expansion*, 299–300.

104 "Disputing the End of African Christianity," 291–292. The following section is heavily indebted to Handley's essay, although the material has been rearranged to suit the present discussion. Also, the names and assessments of these various theories, most of which Handley discusses and critiques, are my own.

105 *The North African Church* (London: Society for Promoting Christian Knowledge, 1880), 379–380. Lloyd later calls this "Sultan" a "Moorish prince" (p. 380).

106 At various times in history, both Christians and Muslims in Africa acted with violence and extremism.

107 E.g. Matt. 16:18, "I will build my church, and the gates of Hades will not prevail against it"; and Matt. 28:20, "I am with you always, to the end of the age" (NRSV).

108 *Apology* 50.13: *semen est sanguis christianorum!*

109 E.g. Ulrich Schoen, "The Death of a Church: Remarks on the Presumed Reasons for the Disappearance of the 'First Church' in North West Africa," *Theological Review* 2 (1, 1979), 3–20, offers an admittedly subjective analysis (p. 15) for the purpose of constructing a missiology for future evangelization of the Maghreb.

110 Holme, *The Extinction of the Christian Churches of North Africa*, 4. It should be noted, however, that Holme also discusses other factors throughout his work.

111 See Ramsay MacMullen, *The Second Church: Popular Christianity A.D. 200–400* (Writings from the Greco-Roman World Supplements 1; Atlanta, GA: Society of Biblical Literature, 2009); and Rebillard, *Christians and Their Many Identities*.

112 Holme also points to evidence of Christians fleeing to Europe (*The Extinction*, 203).

113 Zech. 13:7 (NRSV); cf. Matt. 26:31.

114 E.g. Cyprian, *Letter* 59.6.1.

115 The exceptions have been cited on pp. 332 and 334.

116 Cameron, "The Byzantine Reconquest of North Africa and the Impact of Greek Culture," 153–165.

117 Tilley, "The Collapse of a Collegial Church," 3–22.

118 Frend, "The End of Byzantine Africa: Some Evidence of Transitions," *Colloque d'Histoire et Archéologie d'Afrique du Nord* 2 (1985), 387–397. More recently, see Kaegi, "Seventh-Century Identities," 167, who concurs: "Seventh-century North Africa significantly lacked any monastic authors comparable to Anastasius the Sinaite, and the absence of monastic constructors of identity may have facilitated the disappearance of Christian communities."

119 See details in Booth, *Crisis of Empire*, 154.

120 See *Confessions* 8.8.1.

121 Cf. Matt. 12:25/Mark 3:25 and Lincoln's "House Divided" speech (June 16, 1858).

122 Cf. *Leviathan* 18. This view can be found in American political discourse by way of Thomas Paine, "Common Sense," in *The Writings of Thomas Paine: Volume I 1774–1779*, ed. Moncure Daniel Conway (New York: G.P. Putnam's Sons, 1894), 73.

123 See previous discussions in chapters three, four, and five.

124 Frend, *The Donatist Church*, concludes his work by insinuating that the Donatist defeat at the council of 411 resulted in (a) a swift decline and eventual disappearance of Donatism, and (b) the weakening of African Christianity so that it became easy prey for Islam in later centuries. Both implications have been shown to be too simplistic, as Frend himself has shown in other studies.

125 Frend, *The Donatist Church*; and Frend, "Donatus, '*paene totam Africam decepit*' How?" *Journal of Ecclesiastical History* 48 (4, 1997), 611–627.

126 "Donatus, '*paene totam Africam decepit*' How?" 627.

127 Chris J. Botha, "The Extinction of the Church in North Africa," *Journal of Theology for Southern Africa* 57 (1986), 24–32.

128 See discussion in Wilhite, "Were the 'Donatists' a National or Social Movement in Disguise? Reframing the Question."

129 E.g. Philip Jenkins, *The Lost History of Christianity: The Thousand-Year Golden Age of the Church in the Middle East, Africa, and Asia – and How It Died* (New York: HarperOne, 2008), 229–230. Jenkins can elsewhere speak of the "native" and the "colonial" forms of Christianity, and so he does hold to more than merely a linguistic gap.

130 For an introduction to this phenomenon in general, see Wilhite, *The Gospel According to Heretics*, 217–243.

131 The sevenfold liturgy of the hours was not yet unanimous in Christian practice.

132 Charles Jarvis Speel, "The Disappearance of Christianity from North Africa in the Wake of the Rise of Islam," *Church History* 29 (1960), 379–397.

133 E.g. by Kaegi, *Muslim Expansion*, 39, "there is no evidence that Vandal-inspired Arianism predisposed the population of North Africa to receive Islam."

134 *A Gateway to Hell*, 203 and figure 2a; cf. Qur'an 112:1–4.

135 For an introduction to this issue and for a bibliography of outdated models, see T. H. Eriksen, *Small Places, Large Issues: An Introduction to Social and Cultural Anthropology*, 2nd ed. (London: Pluto Press, 2001), 252–253.

136 Burns, Jensen, et al., *Christianity in Roman Africa*, 85.

12 Conclusion

What was African about ancient African Christianity?

In this work we have attempted to tell the story of African Christianity from its inception to its disappearance, and we have attempted to do so while focusing on African Christianity as its own unique tradition or school. In doing so, several features come to the forefront that correct common assumptions about our subjects. In order to conclude this discussion, we will offer a brief summary of our findings, followed by sections that assess the importance of this study.

Summary of findings

In order to synthesize the many details covered in the previous chapters, we will offer several statements here that summarize the findings of this study. Although these generalizations risk losing the nuances stipulated in the preceding discussions, they will help to illustrate the emphasis given here for each period of African Christian history. These emphases can be summarized as follows.

Christianity comes to Africa early. While the earliest datable evidence belongs to the late 170s, this same evidence points to an already well-established Christian community. Most scholars who have considered this material find that Christianity must have arrived in Africa by the early second century. Furthermore, although the scattered early references to Christianity in this region from outside of Africa consist more of hearsay than firsthand information (such as in Acts, Irenaeus, and Hippolytus), it is plausible that Christians resided in Africa as early as the first century.

The earliest African Christians share, if not establish precedent for, the concerns found in the later African Christian tradition. The African Christians associated with the early martyrdom accounts can be found to value the following items: the elevation of martyrs and possibly even the practice of dining with the dead; the concern with betrayal by compatriots; and the fear of contagion from idolatry. Furthermore, the militant language established in these martyrdoms between the Roman government and the Christian church should be seen as establishing a precedent for the later African Christians, who display a distrust of the government's interference in Christian affairs. This can even be seen in the Christians who come very late in the empire's history (e.g. Lactantius [at least before Constantine's sole rulership], Augustine [at least after the fall of Rome], those involved in the Three Chapters controversy, and those supporting Maximus the Confessor).

Tertullian should be appreciated as influential for later African Christians. Because he allegedly fell into the Montanist heresy late in life, modern scholarship has tended to dismiss, ignore, or downplay his role in influencing later African Christian writers. Later writers, such as Minucius Felix, Cyprian, Arnobius, Lactantius, and others all read Tertullian. Therefore, even after Augustine questions Tertullian's legitimacy, Tertullian's influence on the later African tradition is already well established. Augustine of course is the most expansive and careful writer to come from late antiquity, and his influence cannot be overstated. Nevertheless, Augustine should not eclipse the importance of earlier writers like Tertullian, especially for the "African school" of thought. Instead, the bishop of Hippo and even the later Augustinian tradition should be understood as indebted to (even if engaging with and at times challenging) the earlier African tradition stemming from Tertullian.

Cyprian was a man of his times, but he was also a man of his context. While historians rightly attempt to understand Cyprian as uniquely situated in the events and controversies of the Roman Empire in the 250s, Cyprian faced those events and controversies while trying to be true to the burgeoning African Christian tradition. The important place of precedence, such as the council under Agrippinus, has been well documented in Cyprian's thought. Furthermore, it is well known that Cyprian strove to represent and adhere to the consensus of bishops in his region, even when those African bishops came into direct conflict with other regional synods. This centrality of African tradition and African solidarity should be further appreciated in Cyprian, since Cyprian himself in turn becomes in many ways the most influential figure in later African tradition. All who follow will claim to be faithful to Cyprian, and this is especially important for the Donatist party.

The Donatist controversy began long before Donatus. While scholars debate whether the controversy began in the first or second decade of the fourth century, and while scholars acknowledge the attempt by both sides to claim Cyprianic teaching in this controversy, the story of Donatism should be seen as one continuous story dating back to Cyprian himself. Telling the story in this way brings into sharp relief the fact that the Donatist party represents Cyprian and the African tradition, while the Caecilianists represent those more aligned with the Roman tradition.

The Donatist party, furthermore, did not simply surrender and fold into the "Catholic" party. While Augustine and his collaborators portrayed the Donatists as a faction that began around 312 and ended at 411, the surviving sources provide a different picture altogether. The Donatists, even accounting for their diversity, represent the Christians who defended their African tradition against the Roman tradition, and when the Vandals removed this Roman tradition in Africa (or at least its position of prominence in Africa), then the "Donatists" simply went back to identifying themselves as Christians. They, therefore, consist of African Christians whose identity for some time was defined by opposition to the party associated with Rome.

Augustine belonged to African Christian tradition, even if he intentionally tried to supplant that tradition with the "Catholic" tradition from across the Mediterranean. Even though Augustine disagreed with the Donatists' apparently isolationist stance, Augustine could identify as an African, and he attempted to harmonize his African Christian tradition with the "Catholic" teaching he had learned while in Italy. His identity, therefore, was complex in that he could identify as both an African and as a member of the Roman Empire. Even so, Rome's centrality had already waned in the imperial politics of Augustine's day, and he clearly drew on an African tradition of suspicion regarding Roman hegemony after the sacking of Rome in 410. Augustine, therefore, needs to be understood as both "Catholic" and African.

The Vandal period of African Christianity is better understood in light of the Donatist controversy that precedes it. Rather than partitioning the Donatist controversy from the Vandal invasion, the continuities of these two periods of African history should be underscored. The discontinuity of course is significant in that Rome's control of Africa ends, and it should be recognized that the "Roman" empire never fully regained control of Africa after the Vandals. Furthermore, we can no longer assume that the Donatists assimilated themselves into the Caecilianist party when faced with Vandal "Arianism."

The Byzantine period in Africa should be seen in terms of the tenuous hold that Constantinople had over Africa. Not all of Africa was truly regained by the empire, and the local population was likely sharply divided in their loyalty to the new regime. While the Christianity from the larger empire certainly impacted the local Christians in Africa, much of the Christianity from the wider empire was seen to be Greek and foreign by the local Christians. The African Christians retained their sense of autonomy throughout this period, as evidenced by their willingness to critique both the bishop of Rome and the Roman emperor. This is even true for those Christians affiliated with the Catholic and imperial cause, for the African "Catholic" Christians criticized the foreign errors whenever they found it necessary.

Finally, Christianity in Africa continued much longer than is normally acknowledged. Even though Christianity began to wane in the seventh century, there is evidence for its survival into the twelfth century, and there must have been some sort of lingering Christian presence in the many different expressions of Islam in the region after that time. Christianity's end could be attributed to many different causes, and no single theory sufficiently explains its disappearance from North Africa.

Elements found in the "African School"

As discussed in the opening chapter, a previous generation of scholars once spoke of ancient African Christianity in terms of certain "characteristics" found among African Christians that were embedded in their race. Here, we have replaced such ethno-centric assumptions with an attempt to trace how the Christians from this region self-identified. While we must not revert to speaking of any sort of characteristics as if they were inherent to Africans, we can recount certain elements that were found to be recurring themes in African Christianity's history. These elements should be attributed to the fact that African Christians wrote with an awareness of their own unique tradition.

Many African Christians can be identified with the Punic heritage of Africa. Sometimes this heritage simply surfaces as an awareness of their own African identity, which was caricatured by the epic past of the Punic wars. At other times, writers from this region could explicitly oppose their own heritage with the heroes of Rome. Furthermore, there were even times when their anti-Roman statements implied a clear rejection of *Romanitas*. This identity with the Punic past, however, did not always imply such a rejection of *Romanitas*, for many African Christians embraced both.

Sometimes the African identity can be detected as implicit in the sources. Clear examples of this can be found in instances where the Punic language was used or ties to the Punic religion were found. Other examples include times where writers identified with the south or with Africa. Often, the identification with Africa came in response to outsiders who stereotyped the Punic and African heritage. Even in these instances, however, the self-identity as African was reinforced by the opposition made between African and Roman identities.

This opposition between Roman and African tradition can be found specifically for the opposing Christian traditions found in each region. While nothing directly links the antagonism toward the Roman Christian tradition found in writers like Tertullian, Cyprian, the Donatists, and later Byzantine writers, the frequent conflict between African and Roman Christians did at times entail a self-conscious "school" of African Christian thought opposed to the Roman practice. Even when Augustine contested the claim that the Donatists were heirs to Agrippinus and Cyprian, he betrays the fact that Christians at this time intentionally identified with their own regional tradition.

Further considerations

One major shortcoming of this work relates to the tension between the general and the specific. For example, we have constantly repeated the caveat that Africa and African Christianity are generalizing categories that should not cause us to gloss over the diversities within Africa and African

Christianity. The need for a focus on "African Christianity" as a general category has been due to past approaches where this context is subsumed even more generally under the headings "Latin" and "western Christianity." Hopefully, we have accomplished our aim of pointing out aspects of African Christianity that are unique because of the African context.

In addition, this study has often been Carthage-centered due to the centrality of Carthage in most of the literary sources. Additional work will need to be done to examine Cyrenaean, Tripolitanian, Byzacenan, Numidian, and Mauretanian Christianity. We have mentioned how the Roman presence extended far into what is modern-day Morocco, such as the cities of Lixus and Volubulis, both of which had a Christian community. These sites can still be visited today. Future scholarship will benefit from studies that narrow the focus to one region or city while also tracing the whole history of Christianity in that locale.[1] African Christians, furthermore, kept ongoing communication with those who lived in Iberia.[2] This is unsurprising, since African Christians attempted to stay in communication (and communion) with Christians from around the Mediterranean. With the Iberian Christians, however, there may be more to the story: the northwestern Mediterranean was Punic before the fall of Carthage; the contacts with Iberia found in African Christians like Cyprian and Parmenian may indicate ongoing ties between these regions; and many African Christians fled to the old Punic harbors in these regions during the various hostile incursions during the Vandal, Byzantine, and Arab periods. The possible historic connections to old Punic trade routes is worth exploring further.

Moving in the other direction, the precise relationship of African Christians in places like Carthage with those found in the regions closer to Egypt needs to be better understood. Was there a clear and consistent dividing line between Egyptian Christianity and the region of Cyrenaica? What kinds of influence can be found between Cyrenaica and other African regions? Since the sources from this region are sparse, they have not been given extended attention in this present work, but these questions deserve further attention in future studies.

It should also be admitted that a sweeping history such as the one offered here has not been able to devote sufficient attention to the nature of all the sources. While the previous chapters applied a critical reading and traditional historical methodologies to the primary texts, many of these primary texts need to be scrutinized even more closely in order to identify rhetorical tropes and underlying agendas. Much of the non-African sources cited for the background of African Christianity intentionally paint the indigenous populations as barbaric. Many of the sources for Septimius Severus and other Romanized Africans come from later times and represent – at best – secondhand information and various themes one would expect from the historiography of late antiquity. Even many of the sources written by Africans invoke stereotypes and caricatures of their own region, such as in regard to the Punic wars, and they even do so by borrowing from quintessential

Roman sources, like Virgil, and so they in fact tell us little to nothing about the actual Punic society of their own day. Augustine, for example, likely refers to Donatists as Punic speaking as a way of discrediting his opponents as uncivilized and violent barbarians. Future studies, therefore, will need to continue to question these sources and apply additional methodologies that can bring to light more helpful interpretations.

Potential implications

The early African Christians were Africans. Over the past few years, as I have presented this claim in various venues, I have often received a two-part reaction. The initial reaction is incredulity, a rejection of the thesis altogether: "you can't say they were Africans." This incredulity is often due to a variety of objections: "'African' implies something different today"; "they were Roman"; etc., etc. These concerns, then, are fairly easily addressed and alleviated: we have to define what "African" meant in Roman times; Roman and African were not mutually exclusive identities; etc., etc. The second reaction then often comes from the same person, except the next response swings to the opposite posture: indifference, an acceptance of the thesis as too obvious and so inconsequential. I would contend, however, that the first reaction belies the second. If it is so obvious, then why the knee-jerk negative reaction to the thesis in the first place? One contribution this volume should make is to provide the proper categories for us to speak about ancient African Christians: we should recognize them as Africans and attempt to understand better what their identity implies.

Why does it matter that we identify ancient African Christians as Africans? I would first stipulate that a historical project's validity is not derived from its implications for the future. The merit of a historical thesis is based on its ability to explain the data from the past. By focusing on the African identities in the sources, the current study has been able to highlight many aspects of this material that has too often been neglected in previous studies. Furthermore, the future implications of this project cannot be predicted. I certainly do not claim to know all of the particular ramifications that will result from this research, and I obviously cannot anticipate all of the objections of others who study this field. Nevertheless, those who are skeptical of this thesis have a right to question its implications, and so in what follows I will offer some suggestions about possible implications of this project.

The first significance should be obvious in that any historical project benefits from better understanding of context. If ancient African Christians self-identified as Africans, then we are better served by understanding what influenced that identity. Allow me to offer a parallel example: in the modern era, many scholars influenced by the Enlightenment interpreted Paul's remarks about the "Law" as speaking to the moral law of the universe. While it is true that contemporary readers may interpret Paul's letters as applicable to ethics via natural reason, it now goes without saying that when we hear

"Law" in Paul we should think "Torah," at least in addition to whatever else we are going to say. The particular historical heritage influences Paul as a "Hebrew of Hebrews." Another example would be Jesus's triumphal entrance into Jerusalem. Most historically informed readers see this scene not only as a fulfillment of scripture (Zech. 9:9), but also as an echo of Judas Maccabeus's triumphal entry (cf. 1 Maccabees 10:7 and 2 Maccabees 10:7) after defeating the Greeks. Was Jesus signaling that he would likewise drive out the Roman armies? Was he subverting the common expectations about power? Whatever we make of Jesus's actions in terms of ushering in a peaceful kingdom (cf. John 18:11, 36), by knowing the heritage of the Maccabees in Judah at this time we can see why his entry was interpreted as a political statement, both by the Judeans and by the Romans.

To return to North Africa, we can find numerous parallel examples of how the context and background shapes what we find in the Christian writings. In Chapter 2 we gave a quote from Lactantius that is worth repeating here. Speaking to a certain "Donatus" who has been tortured for his faith, Lactantius exclaims, "How pleasing the spectacle to God, when He beheld you a conqueror, yoking in your chariot not white horses, nor enormous elephants, but those very men who had led captive the nations!"[3] The scene refers to the Roman leader, Pompey, who was celebrating his defeat of Africans by attempting to ride an elephant-drawn chariot, and our knowledge of this historical background makes Lactantius's statement – at least potentially – politically charged. In fact, analyzing this statement in light of the centuries of political upheaval in North Africa, where numerous uprisings fought against an empire that "led captive the nations," makes Lactantius's statement look incredibly subversive. Even if Lactantius is not invoking a militant sentiment, his statement likely evokes political sentiments for those in an Africa colonized by Rome. To reiterate, the point here is not to claim too much about Lactantius's intentions; the point is that we should not claim too little. Much like the crowd at Jesus's triumphal entry, Lactantius's audience would almost certainly have interpreted the statement in terms of its political overtones. Let us remember that not too long after this text, Donatists (who probably have no connection to the Donatus addressed by Lactantius) are accused of taking up arms against Roman soldiers in Africa (in the 340s under Macarius and then later under Firmus and Gildo). Moreover, it must be repeated that "political" need not mean either military action or an unreligious sentiment. Jesus's actions were certainly political (he is King, not Caesar) and religious (he is the promised Messiah who cleansed the temple). The comparison with Jesus and Paul illustrates how easily we can allow for context, even political context, to inform our understandings of ancient Christian writings; the same should be allowed for ancient African Christians.

Another implication of this study has to do strictly in terms of historiography, the discipline of writing history. That is, this current study can be programmatic, enabling additional research projects that analyze the ancient African Christians to be better informed by their unique African context. Throughout the previous chapters, I have noted areas where more research is needed. Some of these areas I intend to pursue on my own, while I also welcome others to take up the baton in all of these areas and further our understanding of the many different nuances of ancient African Christianity. The more methods and viewpoints brought to bear upon this material, the more informed we will be about this history.

Another possible implication of this study has to do with historical theology in general. Regarding my discussion of Paul and Jesus in the last paragraph, few would question the importance of understanding their historical context and its relevance for today. However, when we turn from examples from scripture to examples from Christian history, the "implications" may not be so readily apparent to all. Even so, most would agree that Augustine's works have significantly impacted the thought of many people today – whether Roman Catholics who consider him a saint, Protestants who consider him an influential Christian, or westerners who inevitably are indebted to his worldview. If we can learn more about the context and influence of Augustine and his compatriots, then we will better understand our own heritage, in whatever form that heritage may be.

One additional ramification of recognizing the ancient African Christians as Africans is that the claim counters the myth that Christianity is a European religion. This myth should already be rejected by any well-read individual, since the history of Christianity in the Middle East (where it began) and Asia (wherein it quickly expanded) is now well documented. Not only was Christianity non-western, it was also non-European. Additionally, it should now be clear that Christianity was just as much a religion of the south from very early times, which this study tries to underscore for the Roman provinces generally deemed African, but which is also true of Coptic and Ethiopian Christianity. Even for those who know that Christianity has a rich non-European tradition, it should be further acknowledged that many of the most influential "western" Christians – such as Tertullian, Cyprian, and Augustine – were all Africans. The primary direction of Christian development in the early centuries was from south to north.[4] To say this, of course, is to say nothing new. The real contribution found in the present study is that even "western" Christianity needs to be further studied in terms of regional variations. Allowing the various provinces and regions to be seen in the local particularity and not simply as parts of a monolithic Roman Empire will provide further avenues of research for future studies of late antiquity.

Finally, beyond the matters of historiography and academic theology, I should acknowledge the fact that the story of African Christianity belongs to a living tradition. Many practitioners of Christianity today look to these ancient Christians as saints who belong to the great cloud of witnesses. Hopefully, the present study has been respectful of its subjects, even if it has had to apply the critical methodology of a historian. Furthermore, it is hoped that the present study has shed further light on these saints of old so that they can be further appreciated by those who look to them for inspiration.

Along these same lines, I would also be remiss if I did not acknowledge how many Christians in and from Africa today look to the past for ancestors of their faith as expressed particularly in Africa. "African Christianity" and "African Theology" are alive and well today in various forms, and even though it is beyond the scope of the present work (and beyond the capacity of the present author) to suggest how these ancient Christians fit within contemporary discussions of these so-called contextual theologies, I hope that the current study can serve as a resource for anyone who wishes to do so. This hope must be acknowledged even in a study that has for the most part been one of strict historical inquiry because today we are all too aware of the various forms of violence taking place in Africa. Much of this violence has a strong religious sectarian element to it, and such religious motivations are not new. They in fact belong to a story that has been unfolding since ancient times. Therefore, a study of ancient African Christianity that ends with the region's overall conversion to Islam certainly will have ramifications for how we understand the relationship between these two religions, both in the past and in the present.

Notes

1 See, for example, Yvette Duval, *Lambèse chrétienne: La gloire et l'oubli: de la Numidie romaine à l'Ifriqiya* (Paris: Institut d'etudes augustiniennes, 1995).
2 See Clarke, *The Letters*, 4:143, for a bibliography on Iberian Christian interaction with Africa – especially Carthage.
3 *On the Death of the Persecutors* 16.
4 This has been the argument championed recently by Thomas Oden. Oden, however, is largely ignored by historians because of his explicit theological agenda. See my review of Oden's recent works on Africa in *Augustinian Studies* 44 (1, 2013), 127–130.

Bibliography

Abbreviations

ACO	*Acta Conciliorum Oecumenicorum*
ACW	Ancient Christian Writers
AE	*L'Année Épigraphique*
ANF	Ante-Nicene Fathers
CCL	Corpus Christianorum Series Latina
CIL	*Corpus Inscriptionum Latinarum*
CPL	*Clavis Patrum Latinorum*
CSEL	Corpus Scriptorum Ecclesiasticorum Latinorum
FC	Fathers of the Church
LCL	Loeb Classical Library
NPNF	Nicene and Post-Nicene Fathers
NPNF²	Nicene and Post-Nicene Fathers, Series 2
NRSV	New Revised Standard Version of the Bible
PG	Patrologia Graeca
PL	*Patrologia Latina*
PLS	*Patrologia Latina Supplementum*
SC	Sources Chrétiennes
WSA	Works of Saint Augustine

Ancient sources cited (and critical editions and translations, when used)

Acta Purgationis Felicis

Acts of the Abitinian Martyrs 1 (text Jean-Louis Maier, *Le dossier du Donatisme, Tome 1: Des origines à la mort de Constance II (303–361)* [Berlin: Akademie-Verlag, 1987]; trans. Maureen A. Tilley, *Donatist Martyr Stories: The Church in Conflict in Roman North Africa* [Liverpool: Liverpool University Press, 1996]).

Acts of Cyprian (text/trans. Herbert Musurillo, *The Acts of the Christian Martyrs* [Oxford: Clarendon Press, 1972]).

The Acts of Maximilian (text/trans. Herbert Musurillo, *The Acts of the Christian Martyrs* [Oxford: Clarendon Press, 1972]).

Acts of Perpetua and Felicity

Acts of the Scillitan Martyrs (text/trans. Herbert Musurillo, *The Acts of the Christian Martyrs* [Oxford: Clarendon Press, 1972]).

Al-Idrisi, *Opus Geographicum*

Ammianus Marcellinus, *History* (LCL 300)

Anthologia Latina (text in D. R. Shackleton Bailey, *Anthologia Latina* [Stuttgart: Teubner, 1982]; partial trans. in Morris Rosenblum, *A Latin Poet Among the Vandals* [New York: Columbia University Press, 1961]; and in Nigel M. Kay, *Epigrams from the Anthologia Latina: Text, Translation, and Commentary* [London: Bloomsbury, 2006]).

Apostolic Tradition

Appian, *The Punic Wars* (LCL 2)

Apuleius, *Apology* (text in Paul Vallette, *Apulée: Apologie, Florides* [Collection des universités de France; Paris: Les belles lettres, 2002]; trans. Vincent Hunink in *Apuleius: Rhetorical Works*, ed. Stephen J. Harrison [Oxford: Oxford University Press, 2001]; and cf. trans. Harold Edgeworth Butler, *The Apologia and Florida of Apuleius of Madaura* [Oxford: Clarendon Press, 1909]).

Apuleius, *Florida* (text in Paul Vallette, *Apulée: Apologie, Florides* [Collection des universités de France; Paris: Les belles lettres, 2002]; trans. in John Hilton, *Apuleius: Rhetorical Works*. ed. Stephen J. Harrison, [Oxford: Oxford University Press, 2001]).

Apuleius, *Metamorphosis* (text G.F. Hildebrand, *L. Apuleii Opera Omnia* [Leipzig 1842])

Aristotle, *Politics* (LCL 264)

Arnobius, *Against the Nations* (ACW 87)

Athanasius, *To the Africans*

The Augustan History (*Scriptores Historiae Augustae*): *Clodian Albinus* (LCL 139), *Severus* (LCL 139), *The Three Gordians* (LCL 140)

Augustine, *Against the Academics*

Augustine, *Against Adversaries of the Law and the Prophets*

Augustine, *Against Cresconius*

Augustine, *Against Gaudentius*

Augustine, *Against Julian*

Augustine, *Against the Letter of Parmenian*

Augustine, *Against the Letters of Petilian*

Augustine, *Against Lying*

Augustine, *Against the Skeptics*

Augustine, *Brief Meeting With the Donatists*

Augustine, *City of God* (text CCL 48)

Augustine, *Expositions on the Psalms*

Augustine, *Concerning the One Baptism, Against Petilian*

Augustine, *Confessions* (trans. in Henry Chadwick, *Saint Augustine: Confessions* [Oxford: Oxford University Press, 2008])

Augustine, *Enchiridion/Handbook on Faith, Hope, and Love*

Augustine, *Harmony of the Gospels*

Augustine, *Incomplete Explanation of the Epistle to the Romans* (CSEL 84)

Augustine, *Incomplete Works Against Julian* 6.18 (CSEL 85)

Augustine, *Letters* (trans. NPNF 2–12; and WSA 2.1, 2.2)

Augustine, *Letter to the Catholics*

Augustine, *On Adulterous Marriages*

Augustine, *On the Agreement of the Evangelists*
Augustine, *On Baptism, Against the Donatists* (NPNF 4)
Augustine, *On the Care of the Dead*
Augustine, *On Christian Doctrine*
Augustine, *On the Christian Struggle*
Augustine, *On Continence*
Augustine, *On the Creed to Catechumens*
Augustine, *On the Divination of Demons*
Augustine, *On Eight Questions From Dulcitius*
Augustine, *On Eight Questions From the Old Testament*
Augustine, *On the Excellence of Widowhood* (trans. WSA 1/9)
Augustine, *On Faith and the Creed*
Augustine, *On Faith and Works*
Augustine, *On Holy Virginity*
Augustine, *On the Good of Marriage*
Augustine, *On the Good of Widowhood*
Augustine, *On the Greatness of the Soul*
Augustine, *On the Happy Life*
Augustine, *On Heresies*
Augustine, *On the Instruction of Beginners*
Augustine, *On Lying*
Augustine, *On the Merits and Forgiveness of Sins and Infant Baptism* (WSA 1.20)
Augustine, *On Music*
Augustine, *On Order*
Augustine, *On Patience*
Augustine, *On the Presence of God*
Augustine, *On the Trinity*
Augustine, *On Seeing God*
Augustine, *On the Value of Fasting*
Augustine, *On the Work of Monks*
Augustine, *Proceedings With Emeritus*
Augustine, *Psalm against the Donatist Party*
Augustine, *Questions on the Gospels*
Augustine, *Questions on the Heptateuch*
Augustine, *Responses to Januarius*
Augustine, *The Rule: Monastic Order*
Augustine, *The Rule: Precepts*
Augustine, *The Rule: A Rebuke*
Augustine, *Sayings in the Heptateuch*
Augustine, *Sermons*
Augustine, *Sermon to the People of the Church of Caesarea*
Augustine, *The Soliloquies*
Augustine, *The Teacher*
Augustine, *Ten Homilies on the Epistle of John to the Parthians* (SC 75)
Augustine, *To Cresconius*
Augustine, *To Simplicianus*
Augustine, *Tractate Against the Jews*
Augustine, *Tractates on the First Letter of John*
Augustine, *Tractates on the Gospel According to Saint John*

Aurelius Victor, *The Book of the Caesars*

Bede, *Ecclesiastical History* (text and trans. in Bertram Colgrave and R.A.B. Mynors, *Bede's Ecclesiastical History of the English People* [Oxford: Clarendon Press, 1969]).

Bede, *Explanation of Revelation* (text in CCL 121A).

The Book of Epigrams (part of the *Anthologia Latina* – see p. 367)

The Book of the Popes (text Louis Duchesne, *Liber Pontificalis: Texte, introduction et commentaire*, ed., 2 vols. [Paris: Ernest Thorin,1886–1892]; trans. Raymond Davis, *The Book of Pontiffs [Liber pontificalis]: The Ancient Biographies of the First Ninety Roman Bishops to AD 715* [Liverpool: Liverpool University Press, 2000]).

Caesar, *The African War*

Carthaginian Computus of 455 (PL 59)

Cicero, *On the Commonwealth*

Cicero, *On Divination*

Cicero, *On Ends*

Cicero, *On the Orator*

Cicero, *The Republic* (LCL 213)

Cicero, *To Gaius Herennius: On the Theory of Public Speaking*

Claudian, *On the Consulship of Stilicho* (LCL 136)

Claudian, *The War Against Gildo* (LCL 135)

Commodian, *Instructions* (CCL 15; ANF 4:203–218)

Commodian, *The Apologetic Song Against the Jews and Against the Nations* (or *Song Against Two Peoples*) (CCL 15)

Conference of Carthage 411 (CCL 149A)

Corippus, *In Praise of the Younger Justin* (text/trans. in Averil Cameron, *Flavius Cresconius Corippus: In laudem Iustini Augusti minoris (In Praise of Justin II)* [London: Athlone, Press, 1976]).

Corippus, *Iohannes* (text in Jacob Diggle and F.R.D. Goodyear, *Flavii Cresconii Corippi Iohannidos seu De Bellis Libycis LIbri VIII* [Cambridge: Cambridge University Press, 1970]; trans. in George W. Shea: *The Iohannis or de Bellis Libycis of Flavius Cresconius Corippus* [Studies in Classics 7; Lewiston, NY: Edwin Mellen, 1998]).

Councils of Carthage (CCL 149)

Cyprian, *Letters* (text in CCL 3–3E; trans. ACW 43, 44, 46, 47)

Cyprian, *On the Dress of Virgins*

Cyprian, *On the Good of Patience*

Cyprian, *On Jealousy and Envy*

Cyprian, *On the Lapsed*

Cyprian, *On the Lord's Prayer*

Cyprian, *On Mortality*

Cyprian, *On Works and Almsgiving*

Cyprian, *To Demetrian*

Cyprian, *To Fortunatus*

(Pseudo-)Cyprian, *On the Calculation of Easter* (text in CSEL 3.3; trans. in George Ogg, *The Pseudo-Cyprianic* De pascha computus [London: SPCK, 1955])

Dracontius, *On the Praises of God* (text [and French trans.] in Claude Moussy, Colette Camus, Jean Bouquet, and Étienne Wolff, *Dracontius: Oeuvres*, 4 vols. [Paris: Les Belles Lettres, 1985–1996]; trans. partially in James F. Irwin, *Liber I*

Draconitii de Laudibus Dei With Introduction, Text, Translation, and Commentary [PhD dissertation for the University of Pennsylvania, 1942]).

Dracontius, *Satisfaction* (text [and French trans.] in Claude Moussy, Colette Camus, Jean Bouquet, and Étienne Wolff, *Dracontius: Oeuvres*, 4 vols. [Paris: Les Belles Lettres, 1985–1996]; trans. in M. St. Margaret, *Dracontii Satisfactio with Introduction, Text, Translation, and Commentary* [PhD dissertation for the University of Pennsylvania, 1936]).

Ecumenical Councils (text in ed. Eduard Schwartz, et al., *Acta conciliorum oecumenicorum* (Berlin: De Gruyter, 1927-); partial text/trans. in Norman P. Tanner, *Decrees of the Ecumenical Councils* [Washington, DC: Georgetown University Press, 1990]; and cf. trans. in NPNF² 14).

Embrico of Mainz, *Life of Muhammad* (text in Guy Cambier, *Embricon de Mayence La Vie de Mahamet* [Collection Latomus 52; Bruxelles: Latomus, Revue d'etudes Latines, 1961]).

Epiphanius, *Panarion*

Epitome de Caesaribus

Eusebius, *Church History* (trans. Paul L. Maier, *Eusebius: The Church History* [Grand Rapids, MI: Kregel Publications, 2007]; cf. NPNF² 1).

Eusebius, *Life of Constantine*

Evagrius, *Church History*

Facundus, *Against Mocian* (CCL 90A)

Facundus, *Epistle on the Catholic Faith* (CCL 90A)

Facundus, *Defense of the Three Chapters* (CCL 90A)

Ferrandus, *Brevatio canonum* (CCL 149)

Ferrandus, *Letters* (text in CCL 90)

Ferrandus, *Life of Fulgentius* (text in CCL 92; trans. in FC 95)

Filastrius, *Book of Various Heresies*

Flodoard of Reims, *History of the Church of Reims* (PL 135)

Florus, *The Epitome of Roman History* (LCL 231)

Fronto, *Letter to the Mother of Caesar* (LCL 112)

Fronto, *On the Loss of His Grandson*

Fulgentius the Mythographer, *The Mythologies* (text in Rudolf Helm, *Fulgentii Opera* [Leipzig, 1898; reprint. Stuttgart, 1970]).

Fulgentius the Mythographer, *The Explanation of Obsolete Words* (text in Rudolf Helm, *Fulgentii Opera* [Leipzig, 1898; reprint. Stuttgart, 1970]).

Fulgentius the Mythographer, *The Explanation of Virgilian Continence* (text in Rudolf Helm, *Fulgentii Opera* [Leipzig, 1898; reprint. Stuttgart, 1970]).

Fulgentius the Mythographer, *On the Ages of the World and of Man* (text in Rudolf Helm, *Fulgentii Opera* [Leipzig, 1898; reprint. Stuttgart, 1970]).

Fulgentius of Ruspe, *Letters* and *Sermons* (CCL 91; trans. of letters partially available in FC 126)

Gelasius, *Letters* (text in Andreas Thiel, *Epistolae romanorum pontificum genuinae* [Braunsberg: Edward Peter, 1868]; trans. Bronwen Neil and Pauline Allen, *The Letters of Gelasius I (492–496): Pastor and Micro-Manager of the Church of Rome* [Turnhout: Brepols, 2014]).

(Pseudo-)Gelasius, *Gelasian Decree* (text Ernst von Dobschütz, *Das "Decretum Gelasianum de libris recipiendis et non recipiendis"* [Texte und Untersuchungen 38.4; Leipzig, 1912]).

Gennadius, *The Lives of Illustrious Men* (PL 58; NPNF² 3)

George of Pisidia, *On Heraclius's Return From Africa*

Gregory the Great, *Letters* (text in CCL 140, 140A; trans. in John R.C. Martyn, *The Letters of Gregory the Great*, 3 vols. [Medieval Sources in Translation 40; Toronto: Pontifical Institute of Mediaeval Studies, 2004]).

Gregory VII, *Letters* (PL 148)

Herodotus, *Histories*

Hippolytus, *The Refutation of All Heresies* (ANF 5)

(Pseudo-?)Hippolytus, *On the Seventy Apostles* (ANF 5)

Hydatius, *Chronicle*

Ibn 'Abd al-H'akam (trans. J.F.P. Hopkins, *Corpus of Early Arabic Sources for West African History*, rev. ed. [Princeton, NJ: Markus Wiener Publishers, 2000]).

Ibn al-Haytham, *Kitāb al-Munāzarāt* (trans. Wilferd Madelung, and Paul Ernest Walker, *The Advent of the Fatimids: A Contemporary Shi'i Witness* [London: I.B. Tauris, 2000], 140).

Ibn Khaldûn, *The Muqaddimah* (trans. Franz Rosenthal, *The Muqaddimah: An Introduction to History*, vol. 2, rev. ed. [Princeton, NJ: Princeton University Press, 1967]).

Ignatius, *To the Romans*

Irenaeus, *Against Heresies*

Jerome, *Chronicle* (PL 27)

Jerome, *Commentary on Galatians*

Jerome, *Lives of Illustrious Men* (trans. NPNF² 3)

John of Damascus, *On Heresies*

Julius Quintus Hilarianus, *On the Day and Month of Easter* (PL 13)

Julius Quintus Hilarianus, *On the Duration of the World* (PL 13)

Junillus Africanus, *Handbook of the Basic Principles of Divine Law* (text/trans. in Michael Maas, *Exegesis and Empire in the Early Byzantine Mediterranean: Junillus Africanus and the* Instituta Regularia Divinae Legis (Studien und Texte zu Antike und Christentum 17; Tubingen: Mohr Siebeck, 2003]).

Justinian, *Body of Civil Laws* (text in Theodor Mommsen, et al., *Corpus Iuris Civilis*, 3 vols. [Cambridge: Cambridge University Press, 2014 [orig. 1872–1895]).

Juvenal, *Satires* (LCL 91)

Lactantius, *The Epitome of the Divine Institutes*

Lactantius, *The Divine Institutes* (FC 49)

Lactantius, *On the Death of the Persecutors* (FC 54)

Lactantius, *On God's Workmanship* (FC 54)

Lactantius, *On the Phoenix* (FC 54)

Lactantius, *On the Wrath of God* (FC 54)

Leo, *Letters* (NPNF² 12)

Leo IX, *Letters* (PL 143)

Liber censuum romanae ecclesiae (Muratori, *Antiquitates Italicae medii aevi* 5)

Liberatus of Carthage, *Letters* (text PL 53; cf. Schwarz, ACO 1.1.2)

Liberatus of Carthage, *A Short Report on the Nestorian and Eutychian Controversies* (Schwartz, ACO 2.5)

Life of Maximus (Syriac version text/trans. in Sebastian P. Brock, "An Early Syriac Life of Maximus the Confessor," *Analecta Bollandiana* 91 [1975], 302–319; reprinted in Brock, *Syriac Perspectives on Late Antiquity* [London: Variorum, 1984]; Greek version text/trans. in Neil Bronwen and Pauline Allen, *The Life of Maximus the Confessor: Recension 3* [Early Christian Studies 6; Strathfield: St Pauls Publication, 2003]).

Livy (LCL 233, 367)

Lucan, *On the Civil War* (LCL 220)

Marius Victorinus, *Against Arius* (text in CSEL 83.1; trans. FC 69)

Marius Victorinus, *The Art of Grammar* (CCL 132)

Marius Victorinus, *Commentaries* (CSEL 83.2)

Marius Victorinus, *Explanations on Cicero's Rhetoric* (CCL 132)

Marius Victorinus, *Hymns on the Trinity* (text in CSEL 83.1; trans. FC 69)

Marius Victorinus, *On Definitions* (PL 64)

Marius Victorinus, *On the Generation of the Divine Word* (text in CSEL 83.1; trans. in FC 69)

Marius Victorinus, *The Necessity of Accepting the* Homoousion (text in CSEL 83.1; trans. in FC 69)

(Pseudo-)Marius Victorinus, *On Physics* (PL 8)

Martial, *Epigrammaton*

Martyrdom of Crispina (text/trans. Herbert Musurillo, *The Acts of the Christian Martyrs* [Oxford: Clarendon Press, 1972]).

Martyrdom of Felix (text/trans. Herbert Musurillo, *The Acts of the Christian Martyrs* [Oxford: Clarendon Press, 1972]).

Martyrdom of Marculus (text in Jean-Louis Maier *Le dossier du Donatisme*, 2 vols. [Berlin: Akademie-Verlag, 1987]; and Maureen A. Tilley, *Donatist Martyr Stories: The Church in Conflict in Roman North Africa* [Liverpool: Liverpool University Press, 1996]).

Martyrdom of Marian and James (text/trans. Herbert Musurillo, *The Acts of the Christian Martyrs* [Oxford: Clarendon Press, 1972]).

Martyrdom of Maxima, Donatilla, and Secunda

Martyrdom of Maximian and Isaac

Martyrdom of Montanus and Lucius (text François Dolbeau, "La Passion des saints Lucius et Montanus: Histoire et édition du texte," *Revue des etudes augustiniennes* 29 (1983), 39–82; cf. text/trans. Herbert Musurillo, *The Acts of the Christian Martyrs* [Oxford: Clarendon Press, 1972]).

Martyrdom of Polycarp

Maximus the Confessor, *Disputation With Pyrrhus* (text in PG 90; trans. in Joseph P. Farrell, *The Disputation With Pyrrhus of Our Father Among the Saints Maximus the Confessor* [South Canaan, PA: St. Tikhon's Seminary Press, 1990]).

Maximus the Confessor, *Letters* (PG 91)

Maximus the Confessor, *Questions and Responses for Thalassius*

Maximus the Confessor, *To Peter the Illustrious* (PG 91)

Minucius Felix, *Octavius* (text/trans. LCL 250; cf. Bernhard Kytzler, *M. Minuci Felicis Octavius* (Bibliotheca scriptorum Graecorum et Romanorum Teubneriana; Leipzig: B. G. Teubner Verlagsgesellschaft, 1982); and ACW 39).

Notitia provinciarum et civitatum Africae (CSEL 7)

Optatus of Milevis, *Against the Donatists* (SC 412, 413; trans. Mark J. Edwards, *Optatus, Against the Donatists* [Translated Texts for Historians 27; Liverpool: Liverpool University Press, 1997]; cf. O. R. Vassall-Phillips, *The Work of St. Optatus* [London: Longmans, Green, and Co., 1917])

Orosius, *History Against the Pagans* (trans. Roy J. Deferrari [Washington: Catholic University of America Press 1964]).

Ovid, *The Book of Days* (LCL 253)

Pacian, *Letters* (FC 17)

Papias/*Fragments of Papias* (text/trans. in Michael Holmes, *The Apostolic Fathers*, 3rd ed. (Grand Rapids, MI: Baker, 2007]).

Passion of the Martyrs at Agaune (CSEL 31)

Passion of Perpetua and Felicity (J. Amat, *Passion de Perpétue et de Félicité suivi des Actes* [SC 417; Paris: 1996]; trans. [with text] Herbert Musurillo, *The Acts of the Christian Martyrs* [Oxford: Clarendon Press, 1972]; and cf. text/trans. Thomas J. Heffernan, *The Passion of Perpetua and Felicity* [Oxford: Oxford University Press, 2012]).

Paulus, *The Sentences*

Peter the Deacon, *Life of Constantine the African* (trans. in Herbert Bloch, *Monte Cassino in the Middle Ages* [Rome: Edizioni di Storia e Letteratura, 1986]).

Plautus, *The Little Carthaginian* (LCL 26)

Pliny the Elder, *Natural History* (LCL 352, 353)

Pliny the Younger, *Letters*

Plutarch, *Pompey*

Polybius, *Histories* (LCL 30).

Pontianus, *To the Emperor Justinian* (PL 67)

Pontius, *Life of Cyprian* (text in CSEL 3, and trans. FC 21)

Primasius of Hadrumetum, *Commentary on Revelation* (CCL 92)

Procopius, *Buildings* (LCL 343)

Procopius, *The History of the Wars* (LCL 81)

Procopius, *Secret History* (LCL 290)

Prudentius, *Crowns of Martyrdom* (LCL 398)

Quintillian, *The Orator's Education* (LCL 127)

Quodvultdeus, *Against Five Heresies* 1 (= Homily 10; text in CCL 60)

Quodvultdeus, *The Barbaric Age* (= Sermons 11–12; text CCL 60; trans. R. G. Kalkmann, *Two Sermons De tempore barbarico Attributed to St. Quodvultdeus, Bishop of Carthage: A Study of Text and Attribution With Translation and Commentary* [PhD dissertation for Catholic University of America, 1963]).

Quodvultdeus, *The Book of Promises and Prophecies of God* (text in CCL 60)

Quodvultdeus, *On the Flood* (= Homily 7) (text in CCL 60)

Quodvultdeus, *Homilies* (or *Sermons*) (text in CCL 60; trans. partially available in ACW 60)

Qur'an (text/trans. in Ahmed Ali, *Al-Qu'rān: A Contemporary Translation* [Princeton, NJ: Princeton University Press, 2001]).

Sallust, *The War With Cateline* (LCL 116)

Sallust, *The War With Jugurtha* (LCL 116)

Salvian, *On the Government of God* (text [and French trans. [in SC 176, 220; trans. Jeremiah H. O'Sullivan, *The Writings of Salvian, the Presbyter* [FC 173; Washington, DC: Catholic University of America Press (orig. 1947) 2008]; and cf. Eva M. Sanford, *On the Government of God* [New York: Octagon Books, 1966]).

Sentences of the Eighty Seven Bishops (ANF 5)

Sermo in natali sanctorum innocentium (in PLS 1:289–294)

A Sermon on the Passion of Saints Donatus and Advocatus

Silius Itallica, *Punica*

Sozomen, *Church History*

Statius, *Silvae*

Strabo, *Geography*

Suetonius, *Life of Nero*

Sylvester II, *Letters* (PL 139)

Tacitus, *Annals*

Tacitus, *Germania*

Teachings of Jacob

Terence, *Phormio*

Tertullian, *Against Hermogenes* (C).

Tertullian, *Against the Jews* (CCL 2; trans. Geoffrey D. Dunn, *Tertullian* [London: Routledge, 2004]).

Tertullian, *Against Marcion* (CCL 1; Ernest Evans, *Tertullian: Adversus Marcionem*, 2 vols. [Oxford: Clarendon Press: 1972])

Tertullian, *Against the Nations* (CCL 1; ANF 3)

Tertullian, *Against Praxeas* (CCL 2)

Tertullian, *Against the Valentinians* (CCL 2)

Tertullian, *Apology* (CCL 1; FC 10)

Tertullian, *Exhortation to Chastity* (CCL 2)

Tertullian, *On the Apparel of Women* (SC 173)

Tertullian, *On Baptism* (CCL 1; trans. Ernest Evans, *Tertullian's Homily on Baptism* [London: SPCK, 1964]).

Tertullian, *On Fasting* (CCL 1)

Tertullian, *On the Cloak* (text/trans. in Vincent Hunink, *Tertullian*, De Pallio: *A Commentary* ([Amsterdam: J.C. Gieben, 2005]; cf. trans. ANF 4).

Tertullian, *On Fleeing Persecution* (CCL 2)

Tertullian, *On the Flesh of Christ* (CCL 2)

Tertullian, *On Idolatry* (CCL 2)

Tertullian, *On the Military Crown* (CCL 2; ANF 3)

Tertullian, *On Monogamy* (CCL 2)

Tertullian, *On Patience* (CCL 1)

Tertullian, *On Penance* (CCL 1)

Tertullian, *On Prayer* (CCL 1)

Tertullian, *On the Resurrection of the Flesh* (CCL 2)

Tertullian, *On the Shows* (CCL 1; ANF 3)

Tertullian, *On the Veiling of Virgins* (CCL 2)

Tertullian, *On the Soul* (CCL 2)

Tertullian, *Prescript Against the Heretics* (CCL 1; Thomas Herbert Bindley, *On the Testimony of the Soul and On the 'Prescription' of Heretics* [London: SPCK, 1914]; cf. ANF 3).

Tertullian, *The Scorpion's Sting* (CCL 2; ANF 3)

Tertullian, *Testimony on the Soul*

Tertullian, *To the Martyrs* (CCL 1)

Tertullian, *To the Nations* 1.2 (CCL 1; trans. ACW 499; cf. ANF 1)

Tertullian, *To Scapula* (CCL 2; trans. ANF 3)

Tertullian, *To the Wife* (CCL 1)

That Idols Are Not Gods (CSEL 3.1; trans. ANF 5)

Theodoret of Cyrrhus, *Compendium of Heretical Accounts*

Theodosian Code

Theophanes, *Chronicle* (text in Carl de Boor, *Theophanes Chronographia* [Lipsiae: B. G. Teubnneri 1883]; trans. in Cyril Mango and Roger Scott, *The Chronicle of Theophanes Confessor: Byzantine and Near Eastern History AD 284–813* [Oxford: Clarendon Press, 1997]).

Treatise on Rebaptism (Text in CSEL 3; trans. in ANF 5)

Valerius Maximus, *Memorable Doings and Sayings* (LCL 492)

Varro, *On the Latin Language*

Victor of Vita, *The History of the Vandal Persecution* (text in Serge Lancel, *Victor de Vita: Histoire de la persecution vandale en Afrique* [Paris: les Belles Lettres, 2002]; trans. John Moorhead, *Victor of Vita: History of the Vandal Persecution* [Liverpool: Liverpool University Press, 1992]).

Victor of Tunnuna, *Chronicle* (CCSL 173A)

Virgil, *Aeneid* (LCL 64)

(Pseudo-)Virgil, *Moretum*

Vita beatorum abbatum Benedicti, Ceofridi, Eosterwini, Sigfridi et Hwaetbert (text in Charles Plummer, *Vita beatorum abbatum Benedicti, Ceolfridi, Eosterwini, Sigfridi atque Hwaetberhti* [Oxford: Clarendon Press, 1896]; trans. in David Hugh Farmer, *Bede: Lives of the Abbots of Wearmouth and Jarrow* [London: Penguin Classics, 1983]).

Zeno of Verona, *Sermons* (text in CCL 22; partial trans. in Gordon P. Jeanes, *The Day Has Come! Easter and Baptism in Zeno of Verona* [Collegeville, MN: Liturgical Press, 1995]).

Zosimus, *New History* (text François Paschoud, *Zosimus: Histoire nouvelle*, 3 vols. [Paris: Les Belles Lettres, 1971–1989]; trans. Ronald T. Ridley [Canberra: Australian Association for Byzantine Studies, 1982]).

Secondary sources

Abadi, Jacob. *Tunisia Since the Arab Conquest: The Saga of a Westernized Muslim State* (Reading, UK: Ithaca Press, 2013).

Adam, Jean-Pierre. *Roman Building: Material and Techniques* (London: Routledge, 2005).

Adamiak, Stanslaw. "When Did Donatist Christianity End?" in *The Uniquely African Controversy: Studies on Donatist Christianity*, ed. Anthony Dupont, Matthew Gaumer, and Mathijs Lamberigts (Leuven: Peeters, 2014), 211–236.

Adams, James Noel. *Bilingualism and the Latin Language* (Cambridge: Cambridge University Press, 2003).

Albrecht, Michael von and Gareth L. Schmeling. *A History of Roman Literature: From Livius Andronicus to Boethius*, rev. ed. (Leiden: Brill, 1997).

Albu, Emily. "Disarming Aeneas: Fulgentius on *Arms and the Man*," in *The Power of Religion in Late Antiquity*, ed. Andrew Cain and Noel Lenski (Farnham, UK: Ashgate, 2009), 21–30.

Ali, Ahmed. *Al-Qu'rān: A Contemporary Translation* (Princeton, NJ: Princeton University Press, 2001).

Allen, Pauline. *Sophronius of Jerusalem and Seventh-Century Heresy: The Synodocial Letter and Other Documents* (Oxford: Oxford University Press, 2009).

Allen, Pauline, and Bronwen Neil, *Crisis Management in Late Antiquity (410–590 CE): A Survey of the Evidence From Episcopal Letters* (Supplements to Vigiliae Christianae 121; Leiden: Brill, 2013).

Amat, Jacqueline. "Images du Martyre dans les Passions Africaines du IIIe Siècle," in *L'imaginaire religieux gréco-romain*, ed. Joël Thomas (Perpignan: Presses universitaires de Perpignan, 1994), 273–281.

Ameling, Walter. "*Femina Liberaliter Instituta* – Some Thoughts on a Martyr's Liberal Education," in *Perpetua's Passions*, ed. Jan N. Bremmer and Marco Formisano (Oxford: Oxford University Press, 2012), 78–102.

Amory, Patrick. *People and Identity in Ostrogothic Italy, 489–554* (Cambridge: Cambridge University Press, 1997).

Ashcroft, Bill, Gareth Griffiths, and Helen Tiffin, *The Empire Writes Back: Theory and Practice in Post-Colonial Literatures* (London: Routledge, 1989).

Aubet, Maria Eugenia. *The Phoenicians and the West: Politics, Colonies, and Trade*, 2nd ed. (Cambridge: Cambridge University Press, 2001).

Bagnall, Nigel. *The Punic Wars 264–146 BC* (New York: Routledge, 2003).

Bainton, Ronald H. *Christian Attitudes Toward War and Peace: A Historical Survey and Critical Re-Evaluation* (New York: Abingdon, 1960).

Bakker, Henk, Paul van Geest, and Hans van Loon (eds.) *Cyprian of Carthage: Studies in His Life, Language, and Thought* (Leuven: Peeters, 2010).

Bakker, Henk, Paul van Geest, and Hans van Loon, "Introduction: Cyprian's Statute and Influence," in *Cyprian of Carthage: Studies in His Life, Language, and Thought*, ed. Henk Bakker, Paul van Geest, and Hans van Loon (Leuven: Peeters, 2010), 1–27.

Balfour, Ian. "Tertullian and Roman Law: What Do We (Not) Know?", *Studia Patristica* (forthcoming).

Bardenhewer, Otto. *Patrology: The Lives and Works of the Fathers of the Church*, 2nd ed., trans. Thomas J. Shahan (St. Louis, MO: B. Herder, 1908).

Barnes, Michel R. "Anti-Arian Works," in *Augustine Through the Ages*, ed. Allan Fitzgerald (Grand Rapids, MI: Eerdmans, 1999), 31–34.

Barnes, Timothy David. "Legislation Against the Christians," *Journal of Roman Studies* 58 (1–2, 1968), 32–50; reprinted in *Church and State in the Early Church*, ed. Everett Ferguson (New York: Garland Publishing, 1993).

Barnes, Timothy David. "The Beginnings of Donatism," *Journal of Theological Studies* 26 (1, 1975), 13–22.

Barnes, Timothy David. *Constantine and Eusebius* (Cambridge, MA: Harvard University Press, 1981).

Barnes, Timothy David. *Tertullian: An Historical and Literary Study*, rev. ed. (Oxford: Clarendon Press, 1985; orig. 1971).

Barnes, Timothy David. "Pagan Perceptions of Christianity," in *Early Christianity: Origins and Evolution to AD 600*, ed. Ian Hazlett (London: SPCK, 1991), 231–241.

Barnes, Timothy David. "Monotheists All?", *Phoenix* 55 (1/2, 2001), 142–162.

Barnes, Timothy David. *Early Christian Hagiography and Roman History* (Tübingen: Mohr Siebeck, 2010).

Baron, Arkadiusz. "Candidus: Marius Victorinus' Fictitious Friend and His Doctrine of the 'Logos,'" *Theological Research* 1 (2013), 79–94.

Barth, Fredrik. "Introduction," in *Ethnic Groups and Boundaries*, ed. Fredrik Barth (Boston: Little, Brown and Co., 1969), 9–38.

Bauer, Walter. *Orthodoxy and Heresy in Earliest Christianity*, ed. Robert A. Kraft and Gerhard Kroedel (Philadelphia : Fortress Press, [orig. 1934] 1979).

Baxter, J.H. "The Martyrs of Madaura," *Journal of Theological Studies* (October 1924), 21–37.

Benabou, Marcel. *La résistance africaine à la romanisation* (Paris: Maspéro, 1976).

Bévenot, Maurice. " '*Hi qui sacrificaverunt*': A Significant Variant in Saint Cyprian's *De Unitate*," *Journal of Theological Studies* n.s. 5 (1954), 68–72.

Bévenot, Maurice. *St. Cyprian's De Unitate chap. 4 in the Light of the Manuscripts* (Analecta Gregoriana, 11; Rome: 1937).

Bhabha, Homi K. *The Location of Culture* (London: Routledge, 1994).

Bird, H.W. *Sextus Aurelius Victor: A Historiographical Study* (Liverpool: F. Cairns, 1984).

Birley, Anthony R. "Some Notes on the Donatist schism," *Libyan Studies* 18 (1987), 29–41.

Birley, Anthony R. *The African Emperor: Septimius Severus*, rev. ed. (London: B.T. Batsford LTD, 1988).

Birley, Anthony R. "Persecutors and Martyrs in Tertullian's Africa," *Bulletin of the Institute of Archaeology of the University of London* 29 (1992), 37–68.

Bischoff, Bernhard, and Michael Lapidge, *Biblical Commentaries From the Canterbury School of Theodore and Hadrian* (Cambridge: Cambridge University Press, 1994).

Blackhurst, Andy. "The House of Nubel: Rebels or Players?", in *Vandals, Romans and Berbers: New Perspectives on Late Antique North Africa*, ed. Andrew H. Merrills (Aldershot, UK: Ashgate, 2004), 59–75.

Blanchard-Lemée, Michèle, Mongi Ennaïfer, Hédi Slim and Latifa Slim, *Mosaics of Roman Africa: Floor Mosaics From Tunisia*, trans. Kenneth D. Whitehead (London: British Museum Press, [orig. 1995] 1996).

Blaudeau, Philippe. "Liberatus de Carthage ou l'historiographie comme service diaconal," *Augustinianum* 50 (2, 2010), 543–565.

Blowers, Paul. *Maximus the Confessor: Jesus Christ and the Transfiguration of the World* (Oxford: Oxford University Press, 2016).

Bobertz, Charles A. *Cyprian of Carthage as Patron: A Social Historical Study of the Role of the Bishop in the Ancient Christian Community of North Africa* (PhD Dissertation for Yale University, 1988).

Bobertz, Charles A. "The Historical Context of Cyprian's *De Unitate*," *Journal of Theological Studies* 5 (1990), 107–111.

Boeft, Jan den, and Jan Bremmer, "Notiunculae Martyrologicae II," *Vigiliae Christianae* 36 (4, 1982): 383–402.

Böhme, Hartmut. "The Conquest of the Real," in *Perpetua's Passions*, ed. Jan N. Bremmer and Marco Formisano, trans. Jeanne Riou (Oxford: Oxford University Press, 2012), 220–243.

Bonner, Gerald. "Anti-Pelagian Works," in *Augustine Through the Ages*, ed. Allan Fitzgerald (Grand Rapids, MI: Eerdmans, 1999), 41–47.

Bonner, Gerald. *St Augustine of Hippo: Life and Controversies* (Norwich: Canterbury Press, 2002).

Bonner, Michael (ed.) *Arab-Byzantine Relations in Early Islamic Times* (The Formation of the Classical World 8; Aldershot, UK: Ashgate, 2004).

Bonnet, Corinne. "Le culte de Melqart à Carthage: Un cas de conservatisme religieux," *Religio Phoenicia: Acta colloquii Namurcensis habiti diebus 14 et 15 mensis Decembris anni 1984*, ed. Corinne Bonnet, Edward Lipiński, and Patrick Marchetti (Namur: Société des études classiques, 1986), 218–221.

Bonnet, Corinne, Edward Lipiński, and Patrick Marchetti (eds.) *Religio Phoenicia: Acta colloquii Namurcensis habiti diebus 14 et 15 mensis Decembris anni 1984* (Namur: Société des études classiques, 1986).

Boodts, Shari, and Nicholas de Maeyer, "The *Collectio Armamentarii* (Paris, Bibliothèque de l'Arsenal 175): *Status questionis* and New Avenues of Research," in *Praedicatio Patrum: Studies on Preaching in Late Antique North Africa*, ed. Gert Partoens, Anthony Dupont, Shari Boodts, and Mathijs Lamberigts (Instrumenta Patristica et Mediaevalia; Turnhout: Brepols, forthcoming).

Booth, Phil. *Crisis of Empire Doctrine and Dissent at the End of Late Antiquity* (Berkeley, CA: University of California Press, 2014).

Borchardt, C.F.A. "Cyprian on Patience," *Studiae historiae ecclesiasticae* 18 (1992), 17–26.

Botha, C.J. "The Extinction of the Church in North Africa," *Journal of Theology for Southern Africa* 57 (1986), 24–32.

Braun, René. *Deus Christianorum* (Paris: Presses universitaires de France, 1962).

Braun, René. "Aux origines de la chrétienté d'Afrique: un homme de combat, Tertullien," *Bulletin de l'Association Guillaume Budé* 4th series (1965), 189–208.

Bray, Gerald. *Holiness and the Will of God: Perspectives on the Theology of Tertullian* (London: Marshal, Morgan, and Scott, 1979).

Bremmer, Jan N. "The Motivation of Martyrs: Perpetua and the Palestinians," in *Religion im kulturellen Diskurs: Festschrift für Hans G. Kippenberg zu seinem 65. Geburtstag*, ed. Brigitte Luchesi and Kocku von Stuckrad (Berlin: De Gruyter, 2004), 535–554.

Bremmer, Jan N. "Felicitas: The Martyrdom of a Young African Woman," in *Perpetua's Passions*, ed. Jan N. Bremmer and Marco Formisano (Oxford: Oxford University Press, 2012), 35–53.

Bremmer, Jan N., and Marco Formisano (eds). *Perpetua's Passions* (Oxford: Oxford University Press, 2012).

Brent, Allen. *Hippolytus and the Roman Church in the Third Century* (Lieden: Brill, 1995).

Brent, Allen. *Cyprian and Roman Carthage* (Cambridge: Cambridge University Press, 2010).

Brett, Michael. "The Arab Conquest and the Rise of Islam in North Africa," in *The Cambridge History of Africa*, ed. J.D. Fage (Cambridge: Cambridge University Press, 1978), 2:490–544.

Brett, Michael, and Elizabeth Fentress, *The Berbers* (Oxford: Blackwell, 1996).

Brisson, Jean-Paul. *Autonomisme et christianime dans l'Afrique romaine: Dans l'Afrique Romaine de Septime Sévère à l'invasion vandale* (Paris: Éditions E. de Boccard, 1958).

Brock, M. Dorothy. *Studies in Fronto and His Age; With an Appendix on African Latinity Illustrated by Selections From the Correspondence of Fronto* (Cambridge: Cambridge University Press, 1910).

Brock, Sebastian P. "An Early Syriac Life of Maximus the Confessor," *Analecta Bollandiana* 91 (1975), 302–319; reprinted in Brock, *Syriac Perspectives on Late Antiquity* (London: Variorum, 1984).

Brock, Sebastian P. *Syriac Perspectives on Late Antiquity* (London: Variorum, 1984).

Bronwen, Neil, and Pauline Allen, *The Life of Maximus the Confessor: Recension 3* (Early Christian Studies 6; Strathfield: St Pauls Publication, 2003).

Broughton, T.R.S. *The Romanization of Africa Proconsularis* (Baltimore: John Hopkins Press, 1929).

Brown, Michael K., Martin Carnroy, Elliot Currie, Troy Duster, David B. Oppenheimer, and Marjorie M. Shult, *Whitewashing Race: The Myth of a Color-Blind Society* (Berkeley: University of California Press, 2003).

Brown, Peter. *Augustine of Hippo: A Biography* (London: Faber and Faber, 1967).

Brown, Peter. "Christianity and Local Culture in Late Roman Africa," *Journal of Roman Studies* 58 (1968), 85–95.

Brown, Peter. "Religious Coercion in the Later Roman Empire: The Case of North Africa," *Journal of Roman Studies* 58 (1968), 85–95.

Brown, Peter. *The World of Late Antiquity* (London: Thames and Hudson, 1971).

Brown, Peter. "Religious Dissent in the Later roman Empire: The Case of North Africa," *History* 48 (1963), 282–305; reprinted in *Religion and Society in the Age of Augustine* (1972), 301–331.

Brown, Peter. *The Body and Society: Men, Women, and Sexual Renunciation in Early Christianity* (New York: 1988).

Bryce, Jackson. *The Library of Lactantius* (New York: Harvard University Press, 1974).

Bryce, Jackson. "*De Ave Phoenice* and the Religious Policy of Constantine the Great," *Studia Patristica* 19 (1989), 13–19.

Bühler, Pierre. "Tertullian: The Teacher of the *credo quia absurdum*," in *Kierkegaard and the Patristic and Medieval Traditions*, ed. Jon Stewart (Aldershot, England: Ashgate, 2008), 131–144.

Burnett, Charles. *Constantine the African and 'Alī Ibn-Al-'Abbās Al-Mag̃ūsī: The Pantegni and Related Texts*. (Leiden: Brill, 1994).

Burns, J. Patout. *Cyprian the Bishop* (London: Routledge, 2002).

Burns, J. Patout, Robin Margaret Jensen, et al. *Christianity in Roman Africa: The Development of Its Practices and Beliefs* (Grand Rapids, MI: Eerdmans, 2014).

Burns, Thomas S. *Barbarians Within the Gates of Rome: A Study of Roman Military Policy and the Barbarians, Ca. 375–425 A.D.* (Bloomington: Indiana University Press, 1994).

Burns, Thomas S., and John Eadie, *Urban Centers and Rural Contexts in Late Antiquity* (East Lansing, MI: Michigan State University Press, 2001).

Butler, Rex D. *The New Prophecy & "New Visions": Evidence of Montanism in* The Passion of Perpetua and Felicitas. Patristic Monograph Series vol. 18. Washington: The Catholic University of America Press, 2006.

Cadotte, Alain. *La romanisation des dieux: L'interpretatio romana en Afrique du Nord sous le Haut-Empire* (Religions in the Graeco-Roman World; Leiden: Brill, 2007).

Cahill, Thomas. *How the Irish Saved Civilization* (New York: Nan A. Talese/ Doubleday Press, 1995).

Cameron, Averil. "Byzantine Africa: The Literary Evidence," in *Excavations at Carthage*, vol. 7, ed. John H. Humphrey (Ann Arbor: University of Michigan, 1982), 29–62.

Cameron, Averil. "The Byzantine Reconquest of North Africa and the Impact of Greek Culture," *Graeco-Arabica* 5 (1993), 153–165.

Cameron, Averil, and Lawrence I. Conrad (eds.) *The Byzantine and Early Islamic Near East* (Princeton, NJ: Darwin Press, 1992).

Cameron, Averil, and Lawrence I. Conrad, "Introduction," in *The Byzantine and Early Islamic Near East*, ed. Averil Cameron and Lawrence I. Conrad (Princeton, NJ: Darwin Press, 1992).

Cane, Anthony. *The Place of Judas Iscariot in Christology* (Hampshire, UK: Ashgate Publishing, 2005).

Caputo, John D. *Radical Hermeneutics: Repetition, Deconstruction, and the Hermeneutic Project* (Bloomington: Indiana University Press, 1987).

Caputo, John D. *More Radical Hermeneutics: On Not Knowing Who We Are* (Bloomington: Indiana University Press, 2000).

Carnelly, Elizabeth. "Tertullian and Feminism," *Theology* 92 (1989), 31–35.

Caron, Pier Giovanni. "Les 'seniores laici' de l'Église africaine," *Revue international des Droits de l'Antiquité* 6 (1951), 7–22.

Castelli, Elizabeth A. "Heteroglossia, Hermeneutics, and History: A Review Essay of Recent Feminist Studies of Early Christianity," *Journal of Feminist Studies in Religion* 10 (Fall 1994), 73–98.

Caudel, Maurice. *Premières invasions Arabes dans l'Afrique du nord* (Paris: Ernest Leroux, 1900).

Chadwick, Henry. *Saint Augustine: Confessions* (Oxford: Oxford University Press, 2008).

Champion, Craige B. (ed.) *Roman Imperialism: Readings and Sources* (Oxford: Blackwell, 2004).

Champlin, Edward. *Fronto and Antonine Rome* (Cambridge, MA: Harvard University Press, 1980).

Chandra, Kanchan (ed.) *Constructivist Theories of Ethnic Politics* (Oxford: Oxford University Press, 2012).

Chapot, Frédéric. "Tertullian," *Augustine Through the Ages*, ed. Allan Fitzgerald (Grand Rapids, MI: Eerdmans, 1999), 822–824.

Chapot, Frédéric. Review of Wilhite, *Tertullian the African* (2007) in *Chronica Tertullianae et Cyprianae* in *Revue des Études augustiniennes et patristiques* 54 (2, 2007), 326–327.

Chapot, Frédéric. *Virtus veritatis. Langage et vérité dans l'Oeuvre de Tertullien*. Paris: Etudes augustiniennes, 2009).

Charles-Picard, Gilbert. *Les religions de l'Afrique antique* (Paris: Plon, 1954).

Charles-Picard, Gilbert. *La Civilisation de l'Afrique romaine* (Paris: Etudes Augustiniaennes, 1990).

Charles-Picard, Gilbert, and Colette Charles-Picard, *Daily Life in Carthage at the Time of Hannibal*, trans. A.E. Foster (London: Ruskin House, 1961).

Cherry, David. "Marriage and Acculturation in Roman Algeria," *Classical Philology* 92 (1, 1997), 71–83.

Cherry, David. *Frontier and Society in Roman North Africa* (Oxford: Clarendon Press, 1998).

Cho, Dongsun. "Review of Wilhite, *Tertullian the African* (2007)," *Southwestern Journal of Theology* 52 (2, 2010), 245–246.

Christides, Vassilios. *Byzantine Libya and the March of the Arabs Towards the West of North Africa* (British Archaeological Reports 851; Oxford: BAR, 2000).

Church, F. Forrester. "Sex and Salvation in Tertullian," *Harvard Theological Review* 68 (1975), 83–101.

Clark, Gillian. "Pastoral Care: Town and Country in Late-Antique Preaching," in *Urban Centers and Rural Contexts in Late Antiquity*, ed. T. Burns and J. Eadie (East Lansing, MI: 2001), 265–284.

Clark, Elizabeth. *History, Theory, Text: Historians and the Linguistic Turn* (Cambridge, MA: Harvard University Press, 2004).

Clarke, Graeme W. *The Octavius of Marcus Minucius Felix* (ACW 39; New York: Newman Press, 1974).

Clarke, Graeme W. *The Letters of Cyprian of Carthage*, 4 vols. (ACW 43, 44, 46, 47; New York: Newman Press, 1984–1989).

Clark, J. Desmond, *Cambridge History of Africa*, vol.1 *From the Earliest Times to c.500 BC* (Cambridge: Cambridge University Press, 1982).

Clifford, Richard J. "Phoenician Religion," *Bulletin of the American Schools of Oriental Research* 279 (1990), 55–64.

Clover, Frank M. *The Late Roman West and the Vandals* (Aldershot: Variorum, 1993).

Colgrave, Bertram, and R.A.B. Mynors. *Bede's Ecclesiastical History of the English People* (Oxford: Clarendon Press, 1969).

Conant, Jonathan. *Staying Roman: Conquest and Identity in Africa and the Mediterranean, 439–700* (Cambridge: Cambridge University Press, 2012).

Conant, Jonathan. "Anxieties of Violence: Christians and Muslims in Conflict in Aghlabid North Africa and the Central Mediterranean," *Al-Masāq* 27 (1, 2015), 7–23.

Conant, Jonathan. "Donatism in the Fifth and Sixth Centuries," in *The Donatist Schism: Controversy and Contexts*, ed. Richard Miles (Liverpool: Liverpool University Press, 2016), 345–361.

Congar, Yves. *After 900 Years: The Background of the Schism* (New York: Fordham University Press, 1998).

Cooper, Kate. "Marriage, Law, and Christian Rhetoric in Vandal Africa," in *North Africa Under Byzantium and Early Islam*, ed. Susan T. Stevens and Jonathan P. Conant (Washington, DC: Dumbarton Oaks, 2016), 237–249.

Cooper, Stephen Andrew. *Marius Victorinus' Commentary on Galatians: Introduction, Translation, and Notes* (Oxford early Christian studies; Oxford: Oxford University Press, 2005).

Courtois, Christian. *Victor de Vita et son oeuvre* (Algiers: Imprimerie Officielle du gouvernement général de l'Algérie, 1954).

Coxe, Arthur Cleveland. *Institutes of Christian History: An Introduction to Historic Reading and Study* (Chicago: A.C. McClurg and Company, 1887).

Coyle, J. Kevin. "Anti-Manichean Works," in *Augustine Through the Ages*, ed. Allan Fitzgerald (Grand Rapids, MI: Eerdmans, 1999), 39–41.

Coyle, J. Kevin. "The Self-Identity of North African Christians," in *Augustinus Afer: saint Augustin, africanité et universalité*, ed. Pierre-Yves Fux, Jean-Michel Roessli, and Otto Wermelinger (Fribourg: Editions Universitaires, 2003), 61–73.

Crawley, Josephine Mary. *Imperialism and Culture in North Africa: The Hellenistic and Early Roman Eras* (PhD dissertation for the University of California, Berkeley, 2003).

Crawley, Josephine Mary. "Roman Africa?" "Romanization"?, ed. Jonathan Prag and Andrew Merryweather *Digressus* Supplement 1 (2003), 7–34.

Cross, F. L. "History and Fiction in the African Canons," *Journal of Theological Studies* 12 (1961), 227–247.

Daguet-Gagey, Anne. "Septime Sévère, un empereur persécuteur des chrétiens?" *Revue des études augustiniennes* 47 (2001), 3–32.

Daley, Brian E. *The Hope of the Early Church: A Handbook of Patristic Eschatology* (Cambridge: Cambridge University Press, 1991).

Daley, Brian E. "Making a Human Will Divine: Augustine and Maximus on Christ and Human Salvation," in *Orthodox Readings of Augustine*, ed. George E. Demacopoulos and Aristotle Papanikolaou (Crestwood, NY: St. Vladimir's Seminary Press, 2008), 101–126.

Daniel-Hughes, Carly. *The Salvation of the Flesh in Tertullian of Carthage: Dressing for the Resurrection* (New York: Palgrave Macmillan, 2011).

Daniélou, Jean. *The Origins of Early Christianity*, vol. 3 *The Origins of Latin Christianity*, trans. David Smith and John Austin Baker (London: Darton, Longman and Todd, 1977).

Davidson, Ivor J. "Review of Wilhite, *Tertullian the African* (2007)," *Scottish Journal of Theology* 66 (February 2013), 120–121.

Dean, Richard. *A Study of the Cognomina of Soldiers in the Roman Legions* (PhD Dissertation for Princeton University, 1916).

Dearn, Alan. "The Abitinian Martyrs and the Outbreak of the Donatist Schism," *Journal of Ecclesiastical History* 55 (1, 2004), 1–18.

Dearn, Alan. "Donatist Martyrs, Stories and Attitudes," in *The Donatist Schism: Controversy and Contexts*, ed. Richard Miles (Liverpool: Liverpool University Press, 2016), 70–100.

Decret, François. *Early Christianity in North Africa*, trans. Edward L. Smither (Eugene, OR: Wipf and Stock Publishers/Cascade Books, 2009 [French orig. 1996]).

Delattre, Alfred. *Gamart ou la nécropole juive de Carthage* (Lyon: Imprimerie Mougin-Rusand, 1895).

Deléani, Simone. *Christum sequi: Etude d'un thème dans l'oeuvre de saint Cyprien* (Paris: Etudes augustiniennes, 1979).

De Lubac, Henri. *The Christian Faith: An Essay on the Structure of the Apostles' Creed* (San Francisco: Ignatius Press, 1986).

Demacopoulos, George E., and Aristotle Papanikolaou (eds.) *Orthodox Readings of Augustine* (Crestwood, NY: St. Vladimir's Seminary Press, 2008).

Derrida, Jacques. "Différance," in *Margins of Philosophy*, trans. Alan Bass (Chicago: University of Chicago Press, 1986), 1–28.

Digeser, Elizabeth DePalma. "Lactantius and Constantine's Letter to Arles: Dating the *Divine Institutes*," *Journal of Early Christian Studies* 2 (1, 1994), 33–52.

Digeser, Elizabeth DePalma. *The Making of a Christian Empire: Lactantius & Rome* (Ithaca, NY: Cornell University Press, 2000).

Dixon, Susan. *Reading Roman Women: Sources, Genres, and Real Life* (London: Duckworth, 2000).

Dolbeau, François. "La Passion des saints Lucius et Montanus: Histoire et édition du texte," *Revue des etudes augustiniennes* 29 (1983), 39–82.

Donner, Fred. *Muhammad and the Believers* (Cambridge, MA: Harvard University Press, 2010).

Dossey, Leslie. *Peasant and Empire in Christian North Africa* (Berkeley: University of California Press, 2010).

Dossey, Leslie. "Exegesis and Dissent in Byzantine North Africa," in *North Africa Under Byzantium and Early Islam*, ed. Susan T. Stevens and Jonathan P. Conant (Washington, DC: Dumbarton Oaks, 2016), 251–267.

Douglass, Laurie. "Voice Re-Cast: Augustine's Use of Conversion in *De ordine* and the *Confessions*," *Augustinian Studies* 27 (1996): 39–54.

Dunn, Geoffrey D. *Tertullian* (London: Routledge, 2004).

Dunn, Geoffrey D. "Heresy and Schism According to Cyprian of Carthage," *Journal of Theological Studies* 55 (2, 2004), 551–574.

Dunn, Geoffrey D. "The White Crown of Works: Cyprian's Early Pastoral Ministry of Almsgiving in Carthage," *Church History* 73 (4, 2004), 715–740.

Dunn, Geoffrey D. "Mavilus of Hadrumetum, African Proconsuls and Meiaeval Martyrologies," in *Studies in Latin Literature and Roman History*, vol. 12, ed. Carl Deroux (Collection Latomus 27; Brussels: Latomus, 2005), 433–446.

Dunn, Geoffrey D. *Cyprian and the Bishops of Rome: Questions of Papal Primacy in the Early Church* (Strathfield, NSW, Australia: St Pauls, 2007).

Dunn, Geoffrey D. "Review of Wilhite, *Tertullian the African* (2007)," *Bryn Mawr Classical Review* (16 February 2008). http://bmcr.brynmawr.edu/2008/2008-02-16.html

Dunn, Geoffrey D. *Tertullian's Aduersus Iudaeos: A Rhetorical Analysis* (Patristic Monograph 19; Washington, DC: The Catholic University of America Press, 2008).

Dunn, Geoffrey D. "Rhetoric and Tertullian: A Response," *Studia Patristica* 65 (2013), 349–356.

Dunn, Geoffrey D. "Tertullian, Paul, and the Nation of Israel," in *Tertullian and Paul*, ed. Todd D. Still and David E. Wilhite (London: T&T Clark, 2013), 79–97.

Dupont, Anthony, and Matteo Dalvit, "From a Martyrological '*Tabernacula Pastorum*' towards a Geographical '*In Meridie*': Augustine's Representation and Refutation of the Donatist Exegesis of Sg. 1, 6–7," *Revue d'histoire ecclésiastique* 109 (1–2, 2014), 5–34.

Dupont, Anthony, Matthew Gaumer, and M. Lamberigts (eds.) *The Uniquely African Controversy: Studies on Donatist Christianity* (Leuven: Peeters, 2014).

Duval, Yvette. *Loca sanctorum Africae: le culte des martyrs en Afrique du IVe au VIIe siecle*, 2 vols. (Rome: École française de Rome, 1982).

Duval, Yvette. "Grégorie et l'Église d'Afrique," in *Gregorio Magno e il suo tempo* (Studia Ephemeridis "Augustinianum" 33; Roma: Institutum Patristicum "Augustinianum," 1991), 1:129–158.

Eastman, David L. *Paul the Martyr: The Cult of the Apostle in the Latin West* (Atlanta: Society of Biblical Literature, 2011).

Ech-Cheikh, Mohammed. "Ignored Pages of the History of the Ibādī Theology in North Africa during the Middle Ages: The *Wājiz* (Summary) of 'Abd al-Kāfī and the *Dalīl* (Proof and Demonstration) of al-Warjlānī," in *Ibadi Theology: Rereading Sources and Scholarly Work*, ed. Ersilia Francesca (Hildesheim: Georg Olms, 2015), 103–114.

Edwards, Catharine, and Greg Woolf. *Rome the Cosmopolis* (Cambridge: Cambridge University Press, 2006).

Ellingsen, Mark. *The Richness of Augustine: His Contextual and Pastoral Theology* (Louisville, KY: John Knox, 2005).

Elliot-Binns, Leonard Elliott. *The Beginnings of Western Christendom* (London: Lutterworth Press, 1948).

Elm, Susanna. "New Romans: Salvian of Marseilles on the Governance of God," *Journal of Early Christian Study* (forthcoming).

Eno, Robert B. "Doctrinal Authority in the African Ecclesiology of the Sixth Century: Ferrandus and Facundus," *Revue des etudes augustiniennes* 22 (1976), 95–113.

Eriksen, Thomas Hylland. *Small Places, Large Issues: An Introduction to Social and Cultural Anthropology*, 2nd ed. (London: Pluto Press, 2001).

Evans, Ernest. *Tertullian: Adversus Marcionem*, 2 vols. (Oxford: Clarendon Press: 1972).

Evans, Robert F. *One and Holy: The Church in Latin Patristic Thought* (Church Historical series 92; London: SPCK, 1972).

Evers, Alexander. "A Fine Line: Catholics and Donatists in Roman North Africa," in *Frontiers in the Roman World: Proceedings of the Ninth Workshop of the*

International Network Impact of Empire (Durham, 16–19 April 2009), ed. Olivier Hekster and Ted Kaizer (Leiden: Brill, 2011), 175–198.

Fage, John Donnelly. *The Cambridge History of Africa* vol. 2 *From c.500 BC to AD 1050* (Cambridge: Cambridge University Press, 1979).

Fantar, M'hamed-Hassine. "Death and Transfiguration: Punic Culture After 146," in *A Companion to the Punic Wars* (West Sussex: Wiley Blackwell, 2015), 449–466.

Farmer, David Hugh. *Bede: Lives of the Abbots of Wearmouth and Jarrow* (London: Penguin Classics, 1983).

Farrell, Joseph P. *The Disputation With Pyrrhus of Our Father Among the Saints Maximus the Confessor* (South Canaan, PA: St. Tikhon's Seminary Press, 1990).

Farrell, Joseph P. "The Canonization of Perpetua," in *Perpetua's Passions: Multidisciplinary Approaches to the Passio Perpetuae et Felicitatis*, ed. Jan N. Bremmer and Marco Formisano (Oxford: Oxford University Press, 2012), 300–320.

Fear, Andrew, José Fernández Ubiña, and Mar Marcos (eds.) *The Role of the Bishop in Late Antiquity: Conflict and Compromise* (London: Bloomsbury, 2013).

Fenwick, Corisande. "From Africa to Ifrīqiya: Settlement and Society in Early Medieval North Africa (650–800)," *Al-Masāq* 25 (1, 2013), 9–33.

Ferguson, Everett. *Backgrounds to Early Christianity* (Grand Rapids, MI: Eerdmans, 1987).

Ferguson, Thomas S. "Fulgentius of Ruspe," in *Biographical Dictionary of Christian Theologians*, ed. Patrick W. Carey and Joseph T. Lienhard (Westport, CT: Greenwood Press, 2000), 204.

Ferjaoui, Ahmed. "Le témoignage de Tertullien sur le sacrifice d'enfants à Saturne à la lumière des données ostéologiques du sanctuaire de Henchir el-Hami (Tunisie)," *Rivista di Studi Fenici* 40 (2012), 245–250.

Ferreiro, Alberto. *Simon Magus in Patristic, Medieval and Early Modern Traditions* (Leiden: Brill, 2005).

Février, Paul. "Africa – Archeology," in *Encyclopedia of the Early Church*, ed. Angelo Di Berardino (Oxford: Oxford University Press, 1992), 1:116.

Finn, Thomas Macy. *Quodvultdeus of Carthage: The Creedal Homilies. Conversion in Fifth-Century North Africa* (ACW 60; New York: The Newman Press, 2004).

Fitzgerald, Allan (ed.) *Augustine Through the Ages* (Grand Rapids, MI: Eerdmans, 1999).

Fournier, Éric. *Victor of Vita and the Vandal "Persecution": Interpreting Exile in Late Antiquity* (PhD Dissertation for the University of California, Santa Barbara, 2008).

Fournier, Éric. "Rebaptism as a Ritual of Cultural Integration in Vandal Africa," in *Shifting Cultural Frontiers in Late Antiquity*, ed. David Brakke, Deborah Deliyannis, and Edward Watts (Burlington, VT: Ashgate, 2012), 243–254.

Fournier, Éric. "The Vandal Conquest of North Africa: Origins of a Historiographical Persona," *Journal of Ecclesiastical History* (forthcoming).

Francesca, Ersilia (ed.) *Ibadi Theology: Rereading Sources and Scholarly Work* (Hildesheim: Georg Olms, 2015).

Frankfurter, David. *Religion in Roman Egypt: Assimilation and Resistance.* Princeton, NJ: Princeton University Press, 2000.

Fredouille, Jean-Claude. *Tertullien et la Conversion de la Culture Antique* (Paris: Études Augustiniennes, 1972).

Frend, William Hugh Clifford. *The Donatist Church* (Oxford: Clarendon Press, 1952).

Frend, William Hugh Clifford. "*Seniores laici* and the Origins of the Church in North Africa," *Journal of Theological Studies* 12 (2, 1961), 280–284.

Frend, William Hugh Clifford. *Martyrdom and Persecution in the Early Church: A Study of a Conflict from the Maccabees to Donatus* (Oxford: Blackwell, 1965).

Frend, William Hugh Clifford. "Heresy and Schism as Social and National Movements," in *Schism, Heresy and Religious Protest*, ed. D. Baker (Cambridge: Cambridge University Press, 1972), 37–56.

Frend, William Hugh Clifford. "Open Questions Concerning the Christians and the Roman Empire in the Age of the Severi," *Journal of Theological Studies* n.s. 25 (2, 1974), 333–351.

Frend, William Hugh Clifford. "The Christian Period in Mediterranean Africa, c. AD 200 to 700," in *The Cambridge History of Africa*, ed. J. D. Fage (Cambridge: Cambridge University Press, 1979), 2:410–489.

Frend, William Hugh Clifford. "Jews and Christians in Third Century Carthage," in *Paganisme, Judaïsme, Christianisme* (Paris: Éditions E. De Boccard, 1978), 185–194; reprinted in *Town and Country in the Early Christian Centuries* (London: Variorum, 1980).

Frend, William Hugh Clifford. "The End of Byzantine Africa: Some Evidence of Transitions," *Colloque d'Histoire et Archéologie d'Afrique du Nord* 2 (1985), 387–397.

Frend, William Hugh Clifford. "Prelude to the Great Persecution: The Propaganda War," *Journal of Ecclesiastical History* 38 (1, 1987), 1–18.

Frend, William Hugh Clifford. "The Family of Augustine: A Microcosm of Religious Change in North Africa," in *Atti del Congresso internazionale su S. Agostino nel XVI centenario della conversione (Roma, 15–20 settembre 1986) I* (Studia Ephemeridis "Augustinianum," 24 Rome, 1987), 140, reprinted in *Archaeology and History in the Study of Early Christianity* (London: Variorum, 1988).

Frend, William Hugh Clifford. "Donatus, '*paene totam Africam decepit*' How?," *Journal of Ecclesiastical History* 48 (4, 1997), 611–627.

Frend, William Hugh Clifford. "From Donatist Opposition to Byzantine Loyalism: The Cult of Martyrs in North Africa 350–650," in *Vandals, Romans and Berbers: New Perspectives on Late Antique North Africa*, ed. Andrew H. Merrills (Aldershot, UK: Ashgate, 2004), 259–269.

Fux, Pierre-Yves, Jean-Michel Roessli, and Otto Wermelinger (eds.) *Augustinus Afer: saint Augustin, africanité et universalité* (Fribourg: Editions Universitaires, 2003).

Gaisser, Julia Haig. *The Fortunes of Apuleius and the Golden Ass: A Study in Transmission and Reception* (Princeton, NJ: Princeton University Press, 2008).

Gantner, Clemens, Rosamond McKitterick, and Sven Meeder (eds.) *Resources of the Past in Early Medieval Europe* (Cambridge: Cambridge University Press, 2015).

Gardner, Jand, and Thomas Wiedemann. *The Roman Household: A Sourcebook* (London: Routledge, 1991).

Gaumer, Matthew Alan. "The Evolution of Donatist Theology as Response to a Changing Late Antique Milieu," *Augustiniana* 58 (3–4, 2008), 201–233.

Gaumer, Matthew Alan. "Dealing With the Donatist Church: Augustine of Hippo's Nuanced Claim to the Authority of Cyprian of Carthage," in *Cyprian of Carthage*, ed. Henk Bakker, Paul van Geest, and Hans van Loon (Leuven: Peeters, 2010), 181–201.

Gaumer, Matthew Alan. *Augustine's Cyprian: Authority in Roman Africa* (Leuven: Brill, 2016).

Gaumer, Matthew Alan. "'*Ad Africam visitare sepulchrum sancti Cypriani*': Concerning the Indelible Donatist Character of North African Christianity, 411–1159 CE," in *Religion in Carthage*, ed. Jane Merdinger (Leiden: Brill, forthcoming).

Gavrilyuk, Paul L. *The Suffering of the Impassible God: The Dialectics of Patristic Thought* (Oxford: Oxford University Press, 2004).

Gervers, Michael, and Ramzi Jibran Bikhazi (eds.) *Conversion and Continuity: Indigenous Christian Communities in Islamic Lands – Eight to Eighteenth Centuries* (Toronto: Pontifical Institute of Medieval Studies, 1990).

Gibbon, Edward. *The History of the Decline and Fall of the Roman Empire*, 6 vols. (New York: Harper Brothers, 1879).

Goldsworthy, Adrian Keith. *The Punic Wars* (London: Cassell, 2001).

Gonzalez, Eliezer. *The Fate of the Dead in Early Third Century North African Christianity: The Passion of Perpetua and Felicitas and Tertullian* (Tübingen: Mohr Siebeck, 2014).

González, Justo L. *The Mestizo Augustine: A Theologian Between Two Cultures* (Downers Grove, IL: IVP Academic, 2016).

Goudriaan, Koen. *Ethnicity in Ptolemaic Egypt* (Amsterdam: J.C. Gieben, 1988).

Graham, Alexander. *Roman Africa: An Outline of the History of the Roman Occupation of North Africa Based Chiefly Upon Inscriptions and Monumental Remains in that Country* (London: Longmans, Green, and Co., 1902).

Greenslade, Stanley Lawrence. *Early Latin Theology* (London: SCM Press, 1956).

Grig, Lucy. *Making Martyrs in Late Antiquity* (London: Duckworth, 2004).

Gruen, Erich S. (ed.) *Cultural Identity in the Ancient Mediterranean* (Los Angeles: Getty Research Institute, 2011).

Gruen, Erich S. *Rethinking the Other in Antiquity* (Princeton: Princeton University Press, 2011).

Gsell, Stéphane. *Histoire ancienne de l'Afrique du Nord*, 8 vols. (Paris: Hachette et Cie., 1913–1929).

Gsell, Stéphane. *Inscriptions latines de l'Algerie*, 2 vols. (Paris: Librairie ancienne Honoré Champion, 1922–1957).

Gumerlock, Francis X. *Fulgentius of Ruspe on the Saving Will of God: The Development of a Sixth-Century African Bishop's Interpretation of 1 Timothy 2:4 During the Semi-Pelagian Controversy* (Lewiston, NY: Edwin Mellen Press, 2009).

Halsall, Guy. *Barbarian Migrations and the Roman West, 376–568* (Cambridge: Cambridge University Press, 2007).

Handley, Mark A. "Disputing the End of African Christianity," in *Vandals, Romans, and Berbers: New Perspectives on Late Antique North Africa*, ed. A.H. Merrills (Aldershot, UK: Ashgate, 2004), 291–310.

Hannoum, Abdelmajid. *Colonial Histories, Post-Colonial Memories: The Legend of the Kahina, a North African Heroine* (Studies in African literature; Portsmouth, NH: Heinemann, 2001).

Hanson, Richard Patrick Crosland. "Notes on Tertullian's Interpretation of Scripture," *Journal of Theological Studies* n.s. 12 (1961), 273–279.

Hanson, Richard Patrick Crosland. *The Search for the Christian Doctrine of God The Arian Controversy, 318–381* (Edinburgh: T&T Clark, 1988).

Harden, Donald. *The Phoenicians* (New York: Frederick A. Praeger Publishers, 1963).

Harries, Jill. *Law and Empire in Late Antiquity* (Cambridge: Cambridge University Press, 1999).

Harrison, Stephen J. *Apuleius: A Latin Sophist* (Oxford: Oxford University Press, 2004).

Hays, Gregory. "Date and Identity of the Mythographer Fulgentius," *Journal of Medieval Latin* 13 (2003), 163–252.

Hays, Gregory. "'*Romuleis Libicisque Litteris*': Fulgentius and the 'Vandal Renaissance,'" in *Vandals, Romans and Berbers: New Perspectives on Late Antique North Africa*, ed. Andrew H. Merrills (Aldershot, UK: Ashgate, 2004), 101–132.

Heather, Peter. *The Fall of the Roman Empire: A New History of Rome and the Barbarians* (Oxford: Oxford University Press, 2006).

Heck, Eberhard. "Pseudo-Cyprian, *Quod idola dii non sint* und Laktanz, *Epitome diuinarum institutionum*," in *Panchaia: Festschrift für Klaus Thraede*, ed. Manfred Wacht (Jahrbuch für Antike und Christentum Ergänzungsband 22; Münster, 1922), 148–155.

Heck, Eberhard. *Die dualistischen Zusätze und die Kaiseranreden bei Lactantius* (Heidelberg: Winter, 1972).

Heck, Eberhard. "Constantin und Lactanz in Trier-Chronologisches," *Historia: Zeitschrift für Alte Geschichte* 58 (1, 2009), 118–130.

Heffernan, Thomas J. *The Passion of Perpetua and Felicity* (Oxford: Oxford University Press, 2012).

Heil, Uta. "Liberatus von Karthago und die 'Drei Kapitel,' Anmerkungen zum *Breviarium causae Nestorianorum et Eutychianorum*," *Zeitschrift für antikes Christentum* 14 (2010), 31–59.

Heine, Suzanne. *Women and Early Christianity* (London: SCM Press, 1987).

Hekster, Olivier, and Nicholas Zair, *Rome and its Empire, AD 193–284* (Edinburgh: Edinburgh University Press, 2008).

Hemelrijk, Emily Ann. *Hidden Lives, Public Personae: Women and Civic Life in the Roman West* (Oxford: Oxford University Press, 2015).

Henrichs, Albert. "Pagan Ritual and the Alleged Crime of the Early Christians: A Reconsideration," in *Kyriakon: Festschrift Johannes Quasten* (Münster: Aschendorff, 1970), 18–35.

Hermanowicz, Erika T. *Possidius of Calama: A Study of the North African Episcopate at the Time of Augustine* (Oxford: Oxford University Press, 2008).

Herren, Michael. "The Pseudonymous Tradition in Hiberno-Latin: An Introduction," in *Latin Script and Letters A.D. 400–900: Festschrift Presented to Ludwig Bieler on the Occasion of His 70th Birthday*, ed. John J. O'Meara and Bernd Naumann (Leiden: Brill, 1976), 121–131.

Herring, Edward. "Ethnicity and Culture," in *The Blackwell Companion to Ancient History*, ed. Andrew Erskine (Blackwell Companions to the Ancient World 49; New York: John Wiley and Sons, 2009), 112–122.

Hill, Ingrid. "Valor," in *New Stories From the South: The Year's Best 2004*, ed. Shannon Ravenel (Chapel Hill, NC: Algonquin Books, 2004), 50–69.

Hilton, John. "Introduction by John Hilton to *Florida*," in *Apuleius: Rhetorical Works*, ed. Stephen J. Harrison (Oxford: Oxford University Press, 2001), 1–10.

Hingley, Richard. *Globalizing Roman Culture: Unity, Diversity and Empire* (London: Routledge, 2005).

Hoffman, Daniel L. *The Status of Women and Gnosticism in Ireneaus and Tertullian* (Studies in Women and Religion 36; Lewiston, NY: E. Mellen Press, 1995).

Hollingworth, Miles. *Saint Augustine of Hippo: An Intellectual Biography* (Oxford: Oxford University Press, 2013).

Holloway, Paul A. *Coping With Prejudice: 1 Peter in Social-Psychological Perspective* (Tübingen: Mohr Siebeck, 2009).

Holme, L. R. *The Extinction of the Christian Churches in North Africa* (New York: Burt Franklin, 1895).

Hoover, Jesse. *The Donatist Church in an Apocalyptic Age* (PhD Dissertation for Baylor University Press, 2015).

Hopkins, J.F.P., and Nehemia Levtzion (eds.) *Corpus of Early Arabic Sources for West African History* (Cambridge: Cambridge University Press, 1981).

Hovorun, Cyril. *Will, Action and Freedom: Christological Controversies in the Seventh Century* (Leiden: Brill, 2008).

Hunink, Vincent. *Tertullian, De Pallio: A Commentary* (Amsterdam: J.C. Gieben, 2005).

Hunink, Vincent. "St. Cyprian: A Christian and Roman Gentlemen," in *Cyprian of Carthage: Studies in His Life, Language and Thought*, ed. Henk Bakker, Paul van Geest, and Hans van Loon (Leuven: Peeters, 2010), 29–41.

Hurst, Henry R. *The Sanctuary of Tanit at Carthage in the Roman Period: A Reinterpretation* (JRA Supplement series 30; Portsmouth, RI: JRA, 1999).

Hurst, John Fletcher. *History of the Christian Church* (New York: Eaton & Mains, 1897).

Huskinson, Janet. "Looking for Culture, Identity and Power," in *Experiencing Rome: Culture, Identity and Power in the Roman Empire*, ed. Janet Huskinson (London: Routledge, 2000), 3–27.

Hutchinson, John, and Anthony D. Smith (eds.) *Ethnicity* (Oxford: Oxford University Press, 1996).

Hutchinson, John, and Anthony D. Smith, "Concepts of Ethnicity: Introduction," in *Ethnicity*, ed. John Hutchinson and Anthony D. Smith (Oxford: Oxford University Press, 1996).

Idris, Hadi Roger. "Fêtes chrétiennes célébrées en Ifriquiya à l'époque ziride," *Revue africaine* 98 (1954), 261–276.

Ilevbare, J.A. *Carthage, Rome, and the Berbers: A Study of Social Evolution in Ancient North Africa* (Ibadan, Nigeria: Ibadan University Press, 1981).

Jankowiak, Marek, and Phil Booth. "A New Date-List of the Works of Maximus the Confessor" in *The Oxford Handbook of Maximus the Confessor*, ed. Pauline Allen and Bronwen Neil (Oxford: Oxford University Press, 2015), 19–83.

Janssen, L.F. "'Superstitio' and the Persecution of the Christians," *Vigiliae Christianae* 33 (1979), 131–159, reprinted in *Church and State in the Early Church*, in the series *Studies in Early Christianity Series*, ed. Everett Ferguson (New York: Garland Publishing, Inc., 1993), 79–107.

Jeanes, Gordon P. *The Day Has Come! Easter and Baptism in Zeno of Verona* (Collegeville, MN: Liturgical Press, 1995).

Jenkins, Philip. *The Lost History of Christianity: The Thousand-Year Golden Age of the Church in the Middle East, Africa, and Asia – and How It Died* (New York: HarperOne, 2008).

Jones, Edward L. *Profiles in African Heritage* (Seattle: Frayn Printing Co., 1972).

Jongeling, Karel. *Late Punic Epigraphy: An Introduction to the Study of Neo-Punic and Latino-Punic Inscriptions* (Tübingen: Mohr Siebeck, 2005).

Kaegi, Walter Emil. *Byzantium and the Early Islamic Conquests* (Cambridge: Cambridge University Press, 1992).

Kaegi, Walter Emil. *Heraclius: Emperor of Byzantium* (Cambridge: Cambridge University Press, 2003).

Kaegi, Walter Emil. *Muslim Expansion and Byzantine Collapse in North Africa* (Cambridge: Cambridge University Press, 2010).

Kaegi, Walter Emil. "Seventh-Century Identities: The Case of North Africa," in *Visions of Community in the Post-Roman World: The West, Byzantium and the Islamic World, 300–1100*, ed. Walter Pohl, Clemens Gantner, and Richard Payne (Farnham, Surrey: Ashgate, 2012), 165–179.

Kajanto, Iiro. "Peculiarities of Latin Nomenclature in North Africa," *Philologus* 108 (1964), 310–312.

Kalkmann, R.G. *Two Sermons* De tempore barbarico *Attributed to St. Quodvult-deus, Bishop of Carthage: A Study of Text and Attribution With Translation and Commentary* (PhD Dissertation for Catholic University of America, Washington, D.C., 1963).

Kaufman, Peter Iver. "Donatism Revisited: Moderates and Militants in Late Antique North Africa," *Journal of Late Antiquity* 2 (1, 2009), 131–142.

Kay, N.M. *Epigrams From the Anthologia Latina: Text, Translation, and Commentary* (London: Bloomsbury, 2006).

Kerr, Robert M. *Latino-Punic Epigraphy: A Descriptive Study of the Inscriptions* (Tübingen: Mohr Siebeck, 2010).

Kitzler, Petr. "*Passio Perpetuae* and *Actae Perpetuae*: Between Tradition and Innovation," *Listy Filologické* 130 (1–2, 2007), 1–19.

Kitzler, Petr. *From "Passio Perpetuae" to "Acta Perpetuae" Recontextualizing a Martyr Story in the Literature of the Early Church* (Berlin: De Gruyter, 2015).

Kneževikič, Mikonja. *Maximus the Confessor (580–662): Bibliography* (Bibliographia serbica theological 6; Belgrade: Institute for Theological Research, 2012).

Koch, Hugo. "Zu Arnobius und Lactantius," *Philologus* 80 (1925) 467–472.

Kraemer, Ross S., and Shira L. Lander. "Perpetua and Felicitas," in *Early Christian World*, ed. Philip F. Esler (London: Routledge, 2000), 2:297–314.

Krostenko, Brian. "Beyond (Dis)belief: Rhetorical Form and Religious Symbol in Cicero's *de Divinatione*," *Transactions of the American Philological Association* 130 (2000): 353–391.

Kurita, Nabuko. "The '*Libri Punici*', King Hiempsal and the Numidians," *Kodai: Journal of Ancient History* 5 (1994): 37–46.

Kytzler, Bernhard. *M. Minuci Felicis Octavius* (Bibliotheca scriptorum Graecorum et Romanorum Teubneriana; Leipzig: B.G. Teubner Verlagsgesellschaft, 1982).

Labriolle, Pierre de. *The History and Literature of Christianity: From Tertullian to Boethius*, trans. Herbert Wilson (London: Routledge, 2013; orig. 1924).

Labrousse, Mireille. *Optat de Milèv: Contre les Donatistes*, 2 vols. (SC 412, 413; Paris: Éditions du Cerf, 1996).

Lagouanere, Jérôme. "Tertullien et la littérature chrétienne d'Afrique: problématiques et enjeux," in *Tertullianus Afer: Tertullien et le littérature Chrétienne d'Afrique (IIe-Vie siècles)*, ed. Jérôme Lagouanere and Sabine Fialon (Turnhout: Brepols, 2015), 5–10.

Lagouanere, Jérôme, and Sabine Fialon (eds.) *Tertullianus Afer: Tertullien et la literature chrétienne d'Afrique (IIe-Vie siècles)* (Instrumenta Patristica et Mediaevalia 70; Turnhout: Brepols, 2015).

Lamberigts, Mathijs. "The Italian Julian of Aeclanum about the African Augustine of Hippo," in *Augustinus Afer: saint Augustin, africanité et universalité*, ed. Pierre-Yves Fux, Jean-Michel Roessli, Otto Wermelinger (Fribourg: Editions Universitaires, 2003), 83–93.

Lancel, Serge. *Actes de la conference de Carthage en 411*, 4 vols. (SC 194, 195, 224 and 373; Paris: Éditions du Cerf, 1972).

Lancel, Serge. *Saint Augustine*, trans. Antonia Nevill (London: SCM Press, 2002).

Lancel, Serge, and Paul Mattei. *Pax et Concordia: chrétiens des premiers siècles en Algérie (IIIe-VIIe siècles)* (Paris: Marsa, 2003).

Lang, Bernhard. *Sacred Games: A History of Christian Worship* (New Haven, CT: Yale University Press, 1997).

La Piana, G. "The Roman Church at the End of the Second Century," *Harvard Theological Review* 18 (1925), 201–277.

Laroui, Abdullah. *L'histoire du Maghreb: un essai de synthèse* (Paris: Maspero, 1970).

Laroui, Abdullah. *The History of the Maghreb: An Interpretive Essay*, trans. Ralph Manheim (Princeton: Princeton University Press, 1979).

Leal, Jéronimo. *Actas Latinas de Mártires Africanos* (Fuentes Patrísticas 22; Madrid: Editorial Ciudad Nueva, 2009).

Le Bohec, Yann. "L'onomastique de l'Afrique romaine sous le Haut-Empire et les cognomina dits 'Africains,'" *Pallas* 68 (2005): 217–239.

Leclercq, Henri. *L'Afrique Chretienne*, 2 vols. (Paris: Librairie Victor Lecoffre, 1904).

Leglay, Marcel. *Saturne africain: Histoire* (Paris: Arts et Métiers Graphiques, 1966).

Leglay, Marcel. *Saturne africain: Monuments*, 2 vols. (Paris: Arts et Métiers Graphiques, 1961, 1966).

Lee, A.D. *From Rome to Byzantium AD 363 to 565: The Transformation of Ancient Rome* (Edinburgh: Edinburgh University Press, 2013).

Lee, Benjamin Todd, Ellen D. Finkelpearl, and Luca Graverini (eds.) *Apuleius and Africa* (London: Routledge, 2014).

Lenski, Noel. "Imperial Legislation and the Donatist Controversy: From Constantine to Honorius," in *The Donatist Schism: Controversy and Contexts*, ed. Richard Miles (Liverpool: Liverpool University Press, 2016), 166–219.

Leone, Anna. *The End of the Pagan City: Religion, Economy, and Urbanism in Late Antique North Africa* (Oxford: Oxford University Press, 2013).

Leone, Anne, and Farès K. Moussa, "Roman Africa and the Sahara," *The Oxford Handbook of African Archaeology*, ed. Peter Mitchell and Paul Lane (Oxford: Oxford University Press, 2013), 777–788.

Lepelley, Claude. *Les cités de l'Afrique romaine au bas-empire*, 2 vols. (Paris: Études augustiniennes, 1979).

Leyerle, Blake. "Blood Is Seed," *The Journal of Religion* 81 (1, 2001), 26–48.

Leynaud, Augustin-Ferdinand. *Les catacombs africaines: Sousse-Hadrumète* (Alger: Jules Carbonel, 1922).

Leyser, Conrad. "'A Wall Protecting the City': Conflict and Authority in the *Life of Fulgentius of Ruspe*," in *Foundations of Power and Conflicts of Authority in Late-Antique Monasticism*, ed. Alberto Camplani and Giovanni Filoramo (Leuven: Peeters, 2007), 175–192.

Leithart, Peter. *Defending Constantine: The Twilight of an Empire and the Dawn of Christendom* (Downers Grove, IL: InterVarsity, 2010).

Lipinski, Edward. *Iteneraria Phoenicia* (Orientala Lovaniensia Analecta; Leuven: Peeters, 2004).

Lipiński, Edward. *On the Skirts of Canaan in the Iron Age: Historical and Topographical Researches* (Orientalia Lovaniensia Analecta 153; Leuven: Peeters, 2006),

Lloyd, Julius. *The North African Church* (London: Society for Promoting Christian Knowledge, 1880).

Lo Cascio, Elio. "Una possibile testimonianza sul valore dell' *antoninianus* negli anni di Decio?" in *Consuetudinis Amor: Fragments d'histoire romaine (IIe-Vie siècles) offerts à Jean-Pierre Callu*, ed. François Chausson and Étienne Wolff (Rome: L'Erma di Bretschneider, 2003), 299–309.

Lof, L.J. van der. "The Plebs of the *Psychici*: Are the *Psychici* of *De Monogomia* Fellow-Catholics of Tertullian?" in *Eulogia: Mélanges offerts à Antoon A.R. Bastiaensen à l'occasion de son soixante-cinquième anniversaire*, ed. Gerhardus Johannes Marinus Bartelink, Antonius Hilhorst, and Corneille H. Kneepkens (Steenbrugis: In Abbatia S. Petri, 1991), 353–363.

Loimeier, Roman. *Muslim Societies in Africa: A Historical Anthropology* (Bloomington, IN: Indiana University Press, 2013).

Loomis, Louise Roepes. *The Book of the Popes* (Liber Pontificalis) (New York: Columbia University Press, 1916).

Loon, Hans van. "Cyprian's Christology and the Authenticity of *Quod idola dii non sint*," in *Cyprian of Carthage*, ed. Henk Bakker, Paul van Geest, and Hans van Loon (Leuven: Peeters, 2010), 127–142.

Lorcin, Patricia M.E. "Rome and France in Africa: Recovering Colonial Algeria's Latin Past," *French Historical Studies* 25 (2, 2002): 295–329.

Lott, John Bert. *The Neighborhoods of Augustan Rome* (Cambridge: Cambridge University Press, 2004).

Lott, John Bert. "Regions and Neighbourhoods," in *The Cambridge Companion to Ancient Rome*, ed. Paul Erdkamp (Cambridge: Cambridge University Press, 2013), 169–204.

Louth, Andrew. *Maximus the Confessor* (London: Routledge, 1996).

Maas, Michael. *Exegesis and Empire in the Early Byzantine Mediterranean: Junilius Africanus and the* Instituta Regularia Divinae Legis (Studien und Texte zu Antike und Christentum 17; Tubingen: Mohr Siebeck, 2003).

McCarty, Matthew M. "Africa Punica? Child Sacrifice and Other Invented Traditions in Early Roman Africa," in *Religion in the Roman Empire* (forthcoming).

McCarty, Matthew M. "French Archaeology and History in the Colonial Maghreb: Inheritance, Presence, and Absence," in *Unmasking Ideology: Archaeology and Colonialism*, ed. Bonnie Effros and Guolong Lai (Los Angeles: Cotsen Institute of Archaeology, forthcoming).

McCarty, Matthew M. "Transforming Religion Under the Roman Empire," in *Companion to Roman Africa*, ed. Bruce Hitchner (Oxford: Wiley-Blackwell, forthcoming).

McCkracken, George E. *Arnobius of Sicca: The Case Against the Pagans Volume 1* (ACW 87; Westminster, MD: Newman Press, 1978).

MacDonald, Eve. *Hannibal: A Hellenistic Life* (New Haven, CT: Yale University Press, 2015).

McDonald, Mary Francis. *Lactantius: Minor Works* (FC 54; Washington, DC: Catholic University of America Press, 1965).

McGill, Scott. "Rewriting Dido: Ovid, Virgil, and the *Epistula Didonis ad Aeneam* (AL 71 SB), in *Classica et mediaevalia* 60 (2009), 177–199.

McGowan, Andrew. "Tertullian and the 'Heretical' Origins of the 'Orthodox' Trinity," *Journal of Early Christian Studies* 14 (4, 2006), 437–457.

McInerny, Jeremy (ed.) *A Companion to Ethnicity in the Ancient Mediterranean* (Oxford: Wiley Blackwell, 2014).

MacKendrick, Paul L. *The North African Stones Speak* (Chapel Hill: University of North Carolina Press, 1980).

Mackie, Gillian Vallance. *Early Christian Chapels in the West: Decoration, Function and Patronage* (Toronto: University of Toronto Press, 2003).

McLynn, Neil. "The Conference of Carthage Reconsidered," in *The Donatist Schism: Controversy and Contexts*, ed. Richard Miles (Liverpool: Liverpool University Press, 2016), 220–248.

MacMullen, Ramsay. *Romanization in the Time of Augustus* (New Haven, CT: Yale University Press, 2000).

MacMullen, Ramsay. *The Second Church: Popular Christianity A.D. 200–400* (Writings from the Greco-Roman World Supplements 1; Atlanta, GA: Society of Biblical Literature, 2009).

Maddy-Weitzman, Bruce. *The Berber Identity Movement and the Challenge to North African States* (Austin, TX: University of Texas Press, 2011).

Madigan, Kevin, and Carolyn Osiek. *Ordained Women in the Early Church: A Documentary History* (Baltimore, MD: Johns Hopkins University Press, 2005).

Maier, Jean-Louis. *L'Episcopat de l'Afrique romaine, vandale et byzantine* (Rome: Institut Suisse de Rome, 1973).

Maier, Jean-Louis. *Le dossier du Donatisme*, 2 vols. (Berlin: Akademie-Verlag, 1987).

Maier, Paul L. *Eusebius: The Church History* (Grand Rapids, MI: Kregel Publications, 2007).

Malamud, Margaret. "Black Minerva: Antiquity in Antebellum African American History," in *African Athena: New Agendas*, ed. Daniel Orrells, Gurminder K. Bhambra, and Tessa Roynon (Oxford: Oxford University Press, 2011), 71–89.

Malkin, Irad (ed.) *Ancient Perceptions of Greek Ethnicity* (Harvard, MA: Harvard University Press, 2001).

Mandouze, André. "Encore le donatisme: Problèmes de méthode posés par la thèse de Jean-Paul Brisson, *Autonomisme et christianisme dans l'Afrique romaine de Septime Sévère à l'invasion vandale*," *L'Antiquité classique*, 29 (1, 1960): 61–107.

Mandouze, André. *Prosopographie chrétienne du Bas-Empire. I: Prosopographie de l'Afrique chrétienne (303–533)* (Paris: Éditions du Centre National de la Recherche Scientifique, 1982).

Mandouze, André. "Les donatistes entre ville et campagne," *Histoire et archéologie de l'Afrique du Nord: Actes du IIIème Colloque international réuni dans le cadre du CXè Congrès national des sociétés savantes, Montpellier, 1er–15 avril 1985* (Paris, 1986), 193–217.

Mandouze, André. "Cloture de la session d'Alger," in *Augustinus Afer: saint Augustin, africanité et universalité*, ed. Pierre-Yves Fux, Jean-Michel Roessli, and Otto Wermelinger (Fribourg: Editions Universitaires, 2003), 385–388.

Marcos, Mar. "Papal Authority, Local Autonomy, and Imperial Control: Pope Zosimus and the Western Churches (a.417–418)," in *The Role of the Bishop in Late Antiquity: Conflict and Compromise*, ed. Andrew Daunton-Fear, José Fernández Ubiña, and Mar Marcos (London: Bloomsbury, 2013), 145–166.

Marion, Jean-Luc. *In the Self's Place: The Approach of Saint Augustine*, trans. Jeffrey L. Kosky (Stanford, CA: Stanford University Press, 2012).

Markschies, Christoph. "The *Passio Sanctarum Perpetuae et Felicitatis* and Montanism?", in *Perpetua's Passions: Multidisciplinary Approaches to the Passio Perpetuae et Felicitatis*, ed. Jan N. Bremmer and Marco Formisano (Oxford: Oxford University Press, 2012), 277–290.

Markus, Robert A. "The Imperial Administration and the Church in Byzantine Africa," *Church History* 36 (1967), 18–23.

Markus, Robert A. "Carthage – Prima Justiniana – Ravenna: An Aspect of Justinian's Kirchenpolitik," *Byzantion: Revue international des etudes byzantines* 49 (1979), 227–302; reprinted in Markus, *From Augustine to Gregory the Great: History and Christianity in Late Antiquity* (London: Variorum, 1983).

Markus, Robert A. "Country Bishops in Byzantine Africa," in *The Church in Town and Country*, ed. Derek Baker (Oxford: Ecclesiastical History Society and Blackwell, 1979, 1–15; reprinted in Markus, *From Augustine to Gregory the Great: History and Christianity in Late Antiquity* (London: Variorum, 1983).

Markus, Robert A. "Markus, "Reflections on Religious Dissent in North Africa in the Byzantine Period," in *Schism, Heresy, and Religious Protest*, ed. Derek Baker (Studies in Church History 16; Cambridge: Cambridge University Press, 1979) 144–149; reprinted as essay VII in *From Augustine to Gregory the Great: History and Christianity in Late Antiquity* (London: Variorum, 1983).

Markus, Robert A. *Saeculum: History and Society in the Theology of St. Augustine*, rev. ed. (Cambridge: Cambridge University Press, 1989).

Markus, Robert A. "The Problem of 'Donatists' in the Sixth Century," in *Gregorio Magno e il suo tempo* (Rome: 1990), 159–166; reprinted in *Sacred and Saecular: Studies on Augustine and Latin Christianity* (Aldershot, UK: Variorum, 1994).

Marshall, Eirean. "The Self and the Other in Cyenaica," in *Cultural Identity in the Roman Empire*, ed. Ray Laurence and Joanne Berry (London: Routledge, 1998), 49–63.

Martyn, John R.C. *The Letters of Gregory the Great*, 3 vols. (Medieval Sources in Translation 40; Toronto: Pontifical Institute of Mediaeval Studies, 2004).

Matisoo-Smith, Elizabeth A., Anna L. Gosling, James Boocock, Olga Kardailsky, Yara Kurumilian, Sihem Roudesli-Chebbi, Leila Badre, Jean-Paul Morel, Leïla Ladjimi Sebaï, and Pierre A. Zalloua, "A European Mitochondrial Haplotype Identified in Ancient Phoenician Remains From Carthage, North Africa," *Plos One* 11 (5, 2016), e0155046; doi: 10.1371/journal.pone.0155046.

Mattingly, David J. and R.B. Hitchner, "Roman Africa: An Archaeological Review," *Journal of Roman Studies* 85 (1995), 165–213.

Mattingly, David J. "From One Colonialism to Another: Imperialism and the Maghreb," in *Roman Imperialism: Post-Colonial Perspectives*, ed. J. Webster and N.J. Cooper (Leicester Archaeology Monographs 3; Leicester: University of Leicester, 1996), 49–69.

Mattingly, David J. *Tripolitania* (London: Routledge, 2003).

Mattingly, David J. *Imperialism, Power, and Identity: Experiencing the Roman Empire* (Princeton, NJ: Princeton University Press, 2011).

Médina, Gabriel. "Le christianisme dans le nord d l'Afrique avant l'Islam," *Revue Tunisienne* 8 (1901), 7, 156, 293, 407.

Mercier, Marcel. "Mzab," in *The Encyclopaedia of Islam: A Dictionary of the Geography, Ethnography and Biography of the Muhammadan Peoples*, ed. Martijn Theodoor Houtsma (Leiden: Brill, 1938), 164–167.

Merdinger, Jane. "Before Augustine's Encounter With Emeritus: Early Mauretanian Donatism," *Studia Patristica* 70 (2013), 371–380.

Merdinger, Jane. "In League With the Devil? Donatist and Catholic Perspectives on Prebaptismal Exsufflation," in *The Uniquely African Controversy: Studies on Donatist Christianity*, ed. Anthony Dupont, Matthew Gaumer, and M. Lambergts (Leuven: Peeters, 2014), 153–178.

Merdinger, Jane. "Roman North Africa," in *Early Christianity in Contexts: An Exploration Across Cultures and Continents*, ed. William Tabbernee (Grand Rapids, MI: Baker, 2014), 223–260.

Merdinger, Jane (ed.) *Religion in Carthage* (Leiden: Brill, forthcoming).

Merrills, Andrew H. "Introduction: Vandals, Romans and Berbers: Understanding Late Antique North Africa," in *Vandals, Romans and Berbers: New Perspectives on Late Antique North Africa*, ed. Andrew H. Merrills (Aldershot, UK: Ashgate, 2004), 3–28.

Merrills, Andrew H. "The Perils of Panegyric: The Lost Poem of Dracontius and its Consequences," in *Vandals, Romans and Berbers: New Perspectives on Late Antique North Africa*, ed. Andrew H. Merrills (Aldershot, UK: Ashgate, 2004), 145–162.

Merrills, Andrew H. (ed.) *Vandals, Romans and Berbers: New Perspectives on Late Antique North Africa* (Aldershot, UK: Ashgate, 2004)

Merrills, Andrew H., and Richard Miles, *The Vandals* (Malden, MA: Wiley-Blackwell, 2010).

Mesnage, Joseph. *Romanisation de l'Afrique* (Paris: B. Beauchesne, 1913).

Miles, Richard. "Communicating Culture, Identity and Power," in *Experiencing Rome: Culture, Identity and Power in the Roman Empire*, ed. Janet Huskinson (London: Routledge in association with the Open University, 2000), 29–62.

Miles, Richard. "The *Anthologia Latina* and the Creation of a Secular Space in Vandal Carthage," *Antiquite Tardive: revue internationale d'histoire et d'archeologie* 13 (2005), 305–320.

Miles, Richard. "Rivaling Rome: Carthage," in *Rome the Cosmopolis*, ed. Catharine Edwards and Greg Woolf (Cambridge: Cambridge University Press, 2006).

Miles, Richard. *Carthage Must be Destroyed* (London: Allen Lane, 2010).

Miles, Richard (ed.) *The Donatist Schism: Controversy and Contexts* (Liverpool: Liverpool University Press, 2016).

Millar, Fergus. "Local Cultures in the Roman Empire: Libyan, Punic and Latin in Roman Africa," *Journal of Roman Studies* 58 (1968), 126–134.

Millar, Fergus. *Rome, the Greek World, and the East*, ed. Hannah Cotton, and Guy MacLean Rogers (Chapel Hill, NC: University of North Carolina Press, 2004).

Mitchell, Peter, and Paul Lane (eds.) *The Oxford Handbook of African Archaeology* (Oxford: Oxford University Press, 2013).

Mitchell, Stephen, and Geoffrey Greatrex (ed.), *Ethnicity and Culture in Late Antiquity* (London: Duckworth, 2000).

Modéran, Yves. "La chronologie de la vie de saint Fulgence de Ruspe et ses incidences sur l'historire de l'AFrique vandale," *Melanges de l'Ecole francaise de Rome antiquite* 105 (1993), 135–188.

Modéran, Yves. "Fulgence de Ruspe," in *Encyclopédie berbère* (Peeters, 1998), 2939–2944.

Modéran, Yves. *Les Maures et L'Afrique romaine* (Bibliothèque des écoles françaises d'Athènes et de Rome 314; Rome: Ecole française de Rome, 2003).

Modéran, Yves. "Kusayla: l'Afrique et les arabes," in *Identités et cultures dans l'Algérie antique*, ed. Claude Briand-Ponsart (Rouen and Le Havre: Publications des universités de Rouen et du Havre, 2005), 423–457.

Modéran, Yves. "De Mastiès à la Kâhina," *Aouras* 3 (2006), 159–183.

Modéran, Yves. *Les Vandales et l'empire Romain*, ed. Michel-Yves Modéran (Arles: Éditions Errance, 2014).

Moffatt, James. "Aristotle and Tertullian," *Journal of Theological Studies* 17 (1915–1916), 170–171.

Moll, Sebastian. *The Arch-Heretic Marcion* (Wissenschaftliche Untersuchungen zum Neuen Testament 250; Tübingen: Mohr Siebeck, 2010).

Monceaux, Paul. *Histoire littéraire de l'Afrique chrétienne depuis les origins jusqu'a l'invasion arabe*, 7 vols. (Paris: Leroux, 1901–1923).

Moore, Jennifer P. *Cultural Identity in Roman Africa: The 'La Ghorfa' Stelae* (PhD Thesis for McMaster University, Hamilton, Ontario, 2000).

Moore, Rebecca. "O Mother, Where art Thou? In Search of Saint Monnica," in *Feminist Interpretations of Augustine*, ed. Judith C. Stark (University Park, PA: Pennsylvania State University Press, 2007), 147–166.

Moorhead, John. *Victor of Vita: History of the Vandal Persecution* (Liverpool: Liverpool University Press, 1992).

Morrisson, Cécile. "*REGIO DIVES IN OMNIBUS BONIS ORNATA*: The African Economy from the Vandals to the Arab Conquests in the Light of Coin Evidence," in *North Africa Under Byzantium and Early Islam*, ed. Susan T. Stevens and Jonathan P. Conant (Washington, DC: Dumbarton Oaks, 2016), 173–200.

Moscati, Sabatino (ed.) *The Phoenicians* (New York: Rizzoli International Publications, 1999).

Moss, Candida. *Ancient Christian Martyrdom: Diverse Practices, Ideologies, and Traditions* (New Haven, CO: Yale University Press, 2012).

Moss, Candida. "Martyr Veneration in Late Antique North Africa," in *The Donatist Schism: Controversy and Contexts*, ed. Richard Miles (Liverpool: Liverpool University Press, 2016), 54–69.

Mosshammer, Alden A. *The Easter Computus and the Origins of the Christian Era* (Oxford: Oxford University Press, 2008).

Moussa, Farès. "Berber, Phoenicio-Punic, and Greek North Africa," *The Oxford Handbook of African Archaeology*, ed. Peter Mitchell and Paul Lane (Oxford: Oxford University Press, 2013), 765–776.

Mueller, Hans-Friedrich. "*Vita, Pudicitia, Libertas*: Juno, Gender, and Religious Politics in Valerius Maximus," *Transactions of the American Philological Association* 128 (1998), 221–263.

Muhlberger, Steven. *The Fifth-Century Chroniclers: Prosper, Hydatius, and the Gallic Chronicler of 452* (Leeds: Francis Cairns Ltd., 1990).

Mukhtar, Muhammad Jamal al-Din. *General History of Africa* vol. 2 *Ancient Civilization of Africa* (Berkley: University of California Press, 1981).

Murray, Peter, Linda Murray, and Tom Devonshire Jones, *The Oxford Dictionary of Christian Art and Architecture*, 2nd ed. (Oxford: Oxford University Press, 2013).

Musurillo, Herbert. *The Acts of the Christian Martyrs* (Oxford: Clarendon Press, 1972).

Neil, Bronwen, and Pauline Allen. *The Letters of Gelasius I (492–496): Pastor and Micro-Manager of the Church of Rome* (Turnhout: Brepols, 2014).

Nicholson, Oliver. "*Civitas Quae Adhuc Sustentat Omnia*: Lactantius and the City of Rome," in *The Limits of Ancient Christianity: Essays on Late Antique Thought and Culture in Honor of R. A. Markus*, ed. William E. Klingshirn and Mark Wessey (Ann Arbor: University of Michigan Press, 1999), 7–25.

Nicholson, Oliver. "Arnobius and Lactantius," in *The Cambridge History of Early Christian Literature*, ed. Young, Ayres and Louth (Cambridge: Cambridge University Press, 2004), 259–265.

Niebuhr, H. Richard. *Christ and Culture* (New York: Harper & Brothers, 1951).

O'Collins, Gerald. *Christology: A Biblical, Historical, and Systematic Study of Jesus* (Oxford: Oxford University Press, 2009).

Oden, Thomas C. *How Africa Shaped the Christian Mind* (Downers Grove, IL: InterVarsity Press, 2008).

Oden, Thomas C. *The African Memory of Mark: Reassessing Early Church Tradition* (Downers Grove, IL: InterVarsity Press, 2011).

Oden, Thomas C. *Early Libyan Christianity: Uncovering a North African Tradition* (Downers Grove, IL: InterVarsity Press, 2011).

O'Donnell, James J. *Augustine* (Boston: G.K. Hall, 1985).

O'Donnell, James J. *Augustine: A New Biography* (San Francisco: HarperCollins, 2005).

Ogg, George. *The Pseudo-Cyprianic* De pascha computus (London: SPCK, 1955).

Ogilvie, Robert Maxwell. *The Library of Lactantius* (Oxford: Clarendon Press, 1978).

O'Meara, John Joseph. *The Young Augustine: An Introduction to the Confessions of St. Augustine* (London: Longman, 1980).

Oort, Johannes van. *Jerusalem and Babylon: A Study into Augustine's City of God and the Sources of His Doctrine of the Two Cities* (Supplements to Vigiliae Christianae 14; Leiden: E.J. Brill, 1991).

O'Reilly, Donald F. "The Theban Legion of St. Maurice," *Vigiliae Christianae* 32 (1978), 195–207.

Orloff, N. "Notes," *Journal of Theological Studies* 2 (1901), 417–420.

Orrells, Daniel, Gurminder K. Bhambra, and Tessa Roynon (eds.) *African Athena: New Agendas* (Oxford: Oxford University Press, 2011).

Osborn, Eric. *Tertullian: First Theologian of the West* (Cambridge: Cambridge University Press, 1997).

O'Sullivan, Jeremiah H. *The Writings of Salvian, the Presbyter (FC 173*; Washington, DC: Catholic University of America Press [orig. 1947] 2008).

Otten, Willemien. "Tertullian's Rhetoric of Redemption: Flesh and Embodiment in *De carne Christi* and *De resurrectione mortuorum*," *Studia Patristica* 65 (2013), 331–348.

Paine, Thomas. "Common Sense," in *The Writings of Thomas Paine: Volume I 1774–1779*, ed. Moncure Daniel Conway (New York: G.P. Putnam's Sons, 1894).

Palmer, James T. *The Apocalypse in the Early Middle Ages* (Cambridge: Cambridge University Press, 2014).

Papandrea, James. *The Trinitarian Theology of Novatian of Rome: A Study in Third-Century Orthodoxy* (Lewiston, NY: Edwin Mellen Press, 2008).

Papandrea, James. *Novatian: On the Trinity, Letters to Cyprian of Carthage, Ethical Treatises* (Corpus Christianorum in Translation 22; Turnhout: Brepols, 2015).

Parsons, Jonathan K. *The African Catholic Church under the Vandals, 429–533* (Doctoral Thesis for the University of London, 1994).

Pepino, John M. *St. Eucherius of Lyons: Rhetorical Adaptaion of Message to Intended Audience in the Fifth Century Provence* (PhD Dissertation for Catholic University of America, 2009).

Perkins, Kenneth J. "Aghlabid Amirate of Afriqiya (800–909)," in *The Encyclopedia of African History*, ed. Kevin Shilington (London: Routledge, 2005), 35–37.

Pervo, Richard I. *The Making of Paul: Constructions of the Apostle in Early Christianity* (Minneapolis: Fortress, 2010).

Plummer, Charles. *Vita beatorum abbatum Benedicti, Ceolfridi, Eosterwini, Sigfridi atque Hwaetberhti* (Oxford: Clarendon Press, 1896).

Pohl, Walter. "Introduction: Strategies of Distinction," in *Strategies of Distinction: The Construction of Ethnic Communities, 300–800*, ed. Walter Pohl and Helmut Reimitz (Leiden: Brill, 1998).

Pohl, Walter. "Telling the Difference: Signs of Ethnic Identity," in *Strategies of Distinction: The Construction of Ethnic Communities, 300–800*, ed. Walter Pohl and Helmut Reimitz (Leiden: Brill, 1998), 17–70.

Pohl, Walter, and Helmut Reimitz (eds.) *Strategies of Distinction: The Construction of Ethnic Communities, 300–800* (Leiden: Brill, 1998).

Pottier, Bruno. "*Circumcelliones*, Rural Society and Communal Violence in Late Antique North Africa," in *The Donatist Schism: Controversy and Contexts*, ed. Richard Miles (Liverpool: Liverpool University Press, 2016), 142–165.

Pottier, René. *Saint Augustin le Berbère* (Paris: Publications techniques et artistiques, 1945).

Powell, Douglas. "Tertullianists and Cataphrygians," *Vigiliae Christianae* 29 (1975), 33–54.

Pringle, Denys. *The Defence of Byzantine Africa From Justinian to the Arab Conquest: An Account of the Military History and Archaeology of the African Provinces in the Sixth and Seventh Centuries*, 2 vols. (British Archaeological Reports 99; Oxford: John and Erica Hodges, 2001).

Quasten, Johannes. "'*Vetus Superstitio et nova Religio*': The Problem of *Refrigerium* in the Ancient Church of North Africa," *Harvard Theological Review* 33 (1940), 253–266.

Quasten, Johannes. *Patrology*, 4 vols. (Westminster, MD: Christian Classics, 1986 [orig. 1950]).

Quinn, Josephine Crawley, and Nicholas C. Vella (eds.) *The Punic Mediterranean: Identities and Identification From Phoenician Settlement to Roman Rule* (Cambridge: Cambridge University Press, 2014).

Quinn, Josephine Crawley, and Matthew M. McCarty, "Echos puniques: langue, culte, et gouvernement en Numidie hellénistique," in *Massinissa, au Coeur de la consecration d'un premier Etat numide*, ed. Didi Badi (Algiers: 2015), 167–198.

Quispel, Gilles. "African Christianity before Minucius Felix and Tertullian," in *Gnostica, Judaica, Catholica: Collected Essays of Gilles Quispel*, ed. Johannes Oort (Leiden: E. J. Brill, 2008), 389–459.

Radcliff, Jason Robert. *Thomas F. Torrance and the Church Fathers: A Reformed Evangelical and Ecumenical Reconstruction of the Patristic Tradition.* (Cambridge: James Clarke & Co., 2015).

Ramelli, Ilaria. "Review of Wilhite, *Tertullian the African* (2007)," *Review of Biblical Literature* 9 (2009), 1–7.

Rankin, David. *Tertullian and the Church* (Cambridge: Cambridge University Press, 1995).

Rankin, David. "Tertullian and the Imperial Cult," *Studia Patristica* 34 (2001): 204–216.

Raven, Susan. *Rome in Africa* (London: Routledge, 1993).

Rebillard, Éric. *Christians and Their Many Identities in Late Antiquity, North Africa, 200–450 CE* (Ithaca: Cornell University Press, 2012).

Rebillard, Éric. "William Hugh Clifford Frend (1916–2005): The Legacy of the Donatist Church," *Studia Patristica* 53 (2013), 55–71.

Rebillard, Éric. "Late Antique Limits of Christianness: North Africa in the Age of Augustine," *Group Identity and Religious Individuality in Late Antiquity*, ed. Eric Rebillard and Jorg Rupke (Washington: CUA Press, 2015), 293–318.

Rebillard, Éric. "Popular Hatred Against Christians: The Case of North Africa in the Second and Third Centuries," *Archiv für Religionsgeschichte* 16 (1, 2015), 283–310.

Rebillard, Éric. "Augustine in Controversy With the Donatists Before 411," in *The Donatist Schism: Controversy and Contexts*, ed. Richard Miles (Liverpool: Liverpool University Press, 2016), 297–316.

Rebillard, Éric. "Early African Martyr Narratives," *Studia Patristica* (forthcoming).

Rebillard, Éric, and Jorg Rupke (eds.) *Group Identity and Religious Individuality in Late Antiquity* (Washington: CUA Press, 2015).

Reinink, Gerrit J. "Heraclius, the New Alexander: Apocalyptic Prophecies During the Reign of Heraclius," in *The Reign of Heraclius (610–641): Crisis and Confrontation*, ed. Gerrit J. Reinink and Bernard H. Stolte (Groningen Studies in Cultural Change 2; Leuven: Peeters, 2002), 81–94.

Reinink, Gerrit J., and Bernard H. Stolte (eds.) *The Reign of Heraclius (610–641): Crisis and Confrontation* (Groningen Studies in Cultural Change 2; Leuven: Peeters, 2002).

Reyn, Geert van. "Hippo's Got Talent: Augustine's *Psalmus contra partem Donati* as Pop(ular) Song," in *The Uniquely African Controversy: Studies on Donatist Christianity*, ed. Anthony Dupont, Matthew Alan Gaumer, and Matthijs Lambertigts (Leuven: Peeters, 2015), 251–268.

Reynolds, Joyce. "Libyans and Greeks in Rural Cyrenaica," *Quaderni di archeologia della Libya* 12 (1987), 379–384.

Reynolds, Paul. "From Vandal *Africa* to Arab *Ifrīgiya*: Tracing Ceramic and Economic Trends through the Fifth to the Eleventh Centuries," in *North Africa Under Byzantium and Early Islam*, ed. Susan T. Stevens and Jonathan P. Conant (Washington, DC: Dumbarton Oaks, 2016), 129–172.

Riesenweber, Thomas. *C. Marius Victorinus, Commenta in Ciceronis Rhetorica: Prolegomena und kritischer Kommentar*, vol. 1 (Berlin: De Gruyter, 2015).

Ripoll, Gisela. "Ceramics (West)," in *Late Antiquity: A Guide to the Postclassical World*, ed. G.W. Bowersock, Peter Brown, and Oleg Grabar (Cambridge, MA: Belknap Press, 1999), 368–369.

Rives, James B. *Religion and Authority in Roman Carthage From Augustus to Constantine* (Oxford: Clarendon Press, 1995).

Rives, James B. "The Piety of a Persecutor," *Journal of Early Christian Studies* 4 (1, 1996), 1–25.

Rives, James B. *Religion in the Roman Empire* (London: Blackwell, 2007).

Robeck, Cecil M. *Prophecy in Carthage: Perpetua, Tertullian, and Cyprian* (Cleveland: Pilgrim Press, 1992).

Roberts, Robert E. *The Theology of Tertullian* (London: Epworth Press, 1924).

Rosenblum, Morris. *A Latin Poet Among the Vandals* (New York: Columbia University Press, 1961).

Rouse, Richard, and Charles McNelis, "North African Literary Activity: A Cyprian Fragment, the Stichometric Lists and a Donatist Compendium," *Revue d'histoire des textes* 30 (2000), 189–238.

Rowan, Clare. *Under Divine Auspices: Divine Ideology and the Visualisation of Imperial Power in the Severan Period* (Cambridge: Cambridge University Press, 2012).

Rushworth, Alan. "From Arzuges to Rustamids: State Formation and Regional Identity in the Pre-Saharan Zone," in *Vandals, Romans and Berbers: New Perspectives on Late Antique North Africa*, ed. Andrew H. Merrills (Aldershot, UK: Ashgate, 2004), 77–98.

Sahas, Daniel. "The Demonizing Force of the Arab Conquests: The Case of Maximus (*ca.* 580–662) as a Political 'Confessor,'" *Jahrbuch der österreichischen Byzantinistik* 53 (2003), 98–110.

Said, Edward. *Orientalism* (London: Routledge & Kegan Paul, 1978).

Salama, P. "The Roman and Post-Roman Period in North Africa, Part II: From Rome to Islam," in *General History of Africa*, vol. 2 *Ancient Civilizations of Africa*, ed. G. Mokhtar (Heinemann, CA: Unesco, 1981), 499–510.

Salisbury, Joyce E. *Perpetua's Passion: The Death and Memory of a Martyr* (London: Routledge, 1997).

Savage, Elizabeth. *A Gateway to Hell, a Gateway to Paradise: The North African Response to the Arab Conquest* (Studies in Late Antiquity and Early Islam 7; Princeton: Darwin Press, 1997).

Schaff, Philip. *History of the Christian Church*, 8 vols. (New York: C. Scribner's Sons, 1882–1910).

Schoen, Ulrich. "The Death of a Church: Remarks on the Presumed Reasons for the Disappearance of the 'First Church' in North West Africa," *Theological Review* 2 (1, 1979), 3–20.

Schöllgen, Georg. *Ecclesia sordida? Zur Frage der socialen Schichtung frühchristlichen Gemeinden am Beispiel Karthagos zur Zeit Tertullians* (Münster: Aschendorff, 1984).

Scholten, Désirée. "Cassiodorus' *Historia tripartite* Before the Earliest Extant Manuscripts," in *Resources of the Past in Early Medieval Europe*, ed. Clemens Gantner, Rosamond McKitterick, and Sven Meeder (Cambridge: Cambridge University Press, 2015), 44–46.

Schott, Jeremy M. *Christianity, Empire, and the Making of Religion in Late Antiquity* (Philadelphia: University of Pennsylvania Press, 2008).

Schwarcz, Andreas. "The Settlement of the Vandals in North Africa," in *Vandals, Romans and Berbers: New Perspectives on Late Antique North Africa*, ed. Andrew H. Merrills (Aldershot, UK: Ashgate, 2004), 49–57.

Schwartz, Seth J., Koen Luyckx, and Vivian L. Vignoles (eds.) *Handbook of Identity Theory and Research*, 2 vols. (New York: Springer, 2011).

Schwarze, A. "North African Church," in *The New Schaff-Herzog Encyclopedia of Religious Knowledge*, ed. Samuel Macauley Jasckson (New York: Funk and Wagnalls, 1910), 8:193.

Scullard, H.H. "Carthage and Rome," in *The Cambridge Ancient History*, vol. 7 part 2: *The Rise of Rome to 220 B.C.*, 2nd ed., ed. F. W. Wallbank, A. E. Astin, M. W. Frederiksen, R. M. Ogilvie, and A. Drummond (Cambridge: Cambridge University Press, 1970), 486–569.

Sebastian, J. Jayakiran. ". . .*baptisma unum in ecclesia sancta* . . .": *A Theological Appraisal of the Baptismal Controversy in the Work and the Writings of Cyprian of Carthage* (Hamburg: Lottbeck Jensen, 1997).

Setzer, Claudia. "The Jews in Carthage and Western North Africa, 66–235 CE," in *The Cambridge History of Judaism: Vol. 1: Introduction, The Persian Period*, ed. W. D. Davies, A. E. Astin, M. W. Frederiksen, R. M. Ogilvie, and A. Drummond (Cambridge: Cambridge University Press, 1984), 68–75.

Shanzer, Danuta. "Intentions and Audiences: History, Hagiography, Martyrdom, and Confession in Victor of Vita's *Historia Persecutionis*," in *Vandals, Romans and Berbers: New Perspectives on Late Antique North Africa*, ed. Andrew H. Merrills (Aldershot, UK: Ashgate, 2004), 285–290.

Shaw, Brent D. "The Elders of Christian Africa," in *Mélanges offerts à R.P. Etienne Gareau*, Numéro spéciale de cahiers des études anciennes (Ottowa, Editions de l'Université d'Ottowa, 1982), 207–226; reprinted in Shaw, *Rulers, Nomads and Christians in Roman North Africa* (Aldershot: Variorum, 1995).

Shaw, Brent D. "The Structure of the Local Society in the Early Maghrib: the Elders," *The Maghreb Review* 16, nos. 1–2 (1991), 18–54; reprinted in Shaw, *Rulers, Nomads and Christians in Roman North Africa* (Aldershot: Variorum, 1995).

Shaw, Brent D. "The Passion of Perpetua," *Past and Present* 139 (1993), 3–45.

Shaw, Brent D. "African Christianity: Disputes, Definitions, and 'Donatists,'" originally in *Orthodoxy and Heresy in Religious Movements: Discipline and Dissent*, ed. Malcolm R. Greenshields and Thomas Arthur Robinson (Lampeter: The Edwin Mellen Press, 1992), 5–34; reprinted in *Rulers, Nomads and Christians in Roman North Africa* (Aldershot: Variorum, 1995).

Shaw, Brent D. *Environment and Society in Roman North Africa* (Aldershot, UK: Variorum, 1995).

Shaw, Brent D. *Rulers, Nomads, and Christians in Roman North Africa* (Aldershot, UK: Variorum, 1995).

Shaw, Brent D. *Sacred Violence: African Christians and Sectarian Hatred in the Age of Augustine* (Cambridge: Cambridge University Press, 2011).

Shaw, Brent D. "Who Are You? Africa and Africans," *A Companion to Ethnicity in the Ancient Mediterranean*, ed. Jeremy McInerny (Oxford: Wiley Blackwell, 2014), 527–540.

Sider, Robert D. *Ancient Rhetoric and the Art of Tertullian* (Oxford: Oxford University Press, 1971).

Sider, Robert D. "Credo quia absurdum?" *Classical World* 73 (1980), 417–419.

Simmons, Michael Bland. *Arnobius of Sicca: Religious Conflict and Competition in the Age of Diocletian* (Oxford: Clarendon Press, 1995).

Simmons, Michael Bland. *Universal Salvation in Late Antiquity: Porphyry of Tyre and the Pagan-Christian Debate* (Oxford: Oxford University Press, 2015).

Siniscalco, P. "Maximilian," in *Encyclopedia of Ancient Christianity*, ed. Angelo Di Berardino (Downers Grove: Intervarsity Press, 2014), 2:744.

Sivers, Peter von. "Egypt and North Africa," *The History of Islam in Africa*, ed. Nehemia Levtzion and Randall Lee Pouwels (Athens: Ohio University Press, 2000), 21–54.

Sjöström, Isabella. *Tripolitania in Transition: Late Roman to Islamic Settlement With a Catologue of Sites* (Aldershot: Avebury, 1993).

Slyke, Daniel Van. *Quodvultdeus of Carthage: The Apocalyptic Theology of a Roman African in Exile* (Early Christian Studies 5; Strathfield, Australia: St Paul's Publications, 2003).

Smith, Warren Thomas. *Augustine: His Life and Thought* (Louisville, KY: John Knox, 1980).

Snowden, Jr., Frank M. *Blacks in Antiquity: Ethiopians in the Greco-Roman Experience* (Cambridge, MA: The Belknap Press of Harvard University Press, 1970).

Snowden, Jr., Frank M., "Misconceptions About African Blacks in the Ancient Mediterranean World: Specialists and Afrocentrists," *Arion* 4 (3, 1997), 28–50.

Soren, David, Aïcha Ben Abed Ben Khader, and Hédi Slim, *Carthage: Uncovering the Mysteries and Splendors of Ancient Tunisia* (New York: Simon and Schuster, 1990).

Southern, Patricia. *The Roman Empire From Severus to Constantine*, 2nd ed. (London: Routledge, 2015), 231–238.

Spaeth, Barbette Stanley. *The Roman Goddess Ceres* (Austin: University of Texas Press, 1996).

Speel, Charles Jarvis. "The Disappearance of Christianity from North Africa in the Wake of the Rise of Islam," *Church History* 29 (1960), 379–397.

Stark, Rodney. *The Triumph of Christianity: How the Jesus Movement Became the World's Largest Religion* (San Francisco: HarperCollins, 2011).

Starks, John N., Jr., "Was Black Beautiful in Vandal Africa?", in *African Athena: New Agendas, Classical Presences*, ed. Daniel Orrells, Gurminder K. Bhambra, and Tessa Roynon (Oxford: Oxford University Press, 2011), 239–257.

Ste. Croix, Geoffrey Ernest Maurice de. "Aspects of the Great Persecution," *Harvard Theological Review* 47 (1954), 75–113.

Ste. Croix, Geoffrey Ernest Maurice de. "Why Were the Christians Persecuted?" in *Church and State in the Early Church*, ed. Everett Ferguson (New York: Garland Publishing, Inc., 1993), 16–48.

Stern, Karen B. *Inscribing Devotion and Death: Archaeological Evidence for Jewish Populations of North Africa* (Leiden: Brill, 2007).

Stevens, Susan T. "The Circle of Bishop Fulgentius," *Traditio* 38 (1982), 327–341.

Stevens, Susan T. "Carthage in Transition," in *North Africa Under Byzantium and Early Islam*, ed. Susan T. Stevens and Jonathan P. Conant (Washington, DC: Dumbarton Oaks, 2016), 89–103.

Stevens, Susan T., and Jonathan P. Conant (eds.) *North Africa Under Byzantium and Early Islam* (Washington, DC: Dumbarton Oaks, 2016).

Stewart-Sykes, Alistair. "Ordination Rites and Patronage Systems," *Vigiliae Christianae* 56 (2002), 115–130.

Stone, Harold S. "Cult of Augustine's Body," in *Augustine Through the Ages*, ed. Allan Fitzgerald (Grand Rapids, MI: Eerdmans, 1999), 256–259.

Sumruld, William A. *Augustine and the Arians: The Bishop of Hippo's Encounters With Ulfilan Arianism* (London: Associated University Presses, 1994).

Swain, Simon. *Hellenism and Empire: Language, Classicism, and Power in the Greek World, AD 50–250* (Oxford: Oxford University Press, 1996).

Syme, R. "Donatus and the Like," *Historia* 27 (4, 1978), 588–603.

Tabbernee, William. *Montanist Inscriptions and Testimonia: Epigraphic Sources Illustrating the History of Montanism* (Patristics Monograph Series 16; Macon, GA: Mercer University Press, 1997).

Tabbernee, William. "Perpetua, Montanism, and Christian Ministry," *Perspectives in Religious Studies* 32 (2005), 421–441.

Tabbernee, William. *Fake Prophecy and Polluted Sacraments: Ecclesiastical and Imperial Reactions to Montanism* (Leiden: Brill, 2007).

Tabbernee, William. *Prophets and Gravestones: An Imaginative History of Montanists and Other Early Christians* (Peabody, MA: Hendrickson Publishers, 2009).

Tabbernee, William. *Early Christianity in Contexts: An Exploration Across Cultures and Continents* (Grand Rapids, MI: Baker, 2014).

Talbi, M. "Le Christianisme maghrébin de la conquête musulmane à sa disparition une tentative d'explication," in *Conversion and Continuity: Indigenous Christian Communities in Islamic Lands – Eight to Eighteenth Centuries*, ed. M. Gervers and R. Bikhazi (Toronto: Pontifical Institute of Medieval Studies, 1990), 313–351.

Tefler, W. "The Origins of Christianity in Africa," *Studia Patristica* 4 (1961), 512–517.

Tengström, Emin. *Donatisten und Katholiken: soziale, wirtschaftliche, und politische Aspekte einer nordafrikanischen Kirchenspaltung* (Götenborg: Acta Universitatis Gothoburgensis, 1964).

Thiel, Andreas. *Epistolae romanorum pontificum genuinae* (Braunsberg: Edward Peter, 1868).

Thompson, James Westfall, and Bernard J. Holm, *A History of Historical Writing: From the Earliest Times to the End of the Seventeenth Century*, 2 vols. (New York: Macmillan, 1942).

Thompson, Lloyd J. *Romans and Blacks* (London: Routledge Press, 1989).

Thümmel, Wilhelm. *Zur Beurtheilung des Donatismus: Eine kirchengeschichtliche Untersuchung* (Halle: Ehrhardt Karras, 1893).

Tilley, Maureen A. "Scripture as an Element of Social Control: Two Martyr Stories of Christian North Africa," *Harvard Theological Review* 83 (4, 1990), 383–397.

Tilley, Maureen A. "Dilatory Donatists or Procrastinating Catholics: The Trial at the Conference of Carthage," *Church History* 60 (1, 1991), 7–19.

Tilley, Maureen A. "Understanding Augustine Misunderstanding Tyconius," *Studia patristica* 27 (Louvain: Peeters, 1993), 405–408.

Tilley, Maureen A. "The Passion of Perpetua and Felicity," in *Searching the Scriptures*, vol. 2 *A Feminist Commentary*, ed. Elisabeth Schüssler Fiorenza (New York: Crossroad, 1994), 829–858.

Tilley, Maureen A. *Donatist Martyr Stories: The Church in Conflict in Roman North Africa* (Liverpool: Liverpool University Press, 1996).

Tilley, Maureen A. *The Bible in Christian North Africa: The Donatist World* (Minneapolis: Fortress Press, 1997).

Tilley, Maureen A. "Sustaining Donatist Self-Identity: From the Church of the Martyrs to the Collecta of the Desert," *Journal of Early Christian Studies* 5 (1, 1997), 21–35.

Tilley, Maureen A. "From Separatist Sect to Majority Church: The Ecclesiologies of Parmenian and Tyconius," in *Studia patristica* 33 (Louvain: Peeters, 1997), 260–265.

Tilley, Maureen A. "Anti-Donatist Works," in *Augustine Through the Ages*, ed. Allan Fitzgerald (Grand Rapids, MI: Eerdmans, 1999), 34–39.

Tilley, Maureen A. "The Collapse of a Collegial Church: North African Christianity on the Eve of Islam," *Theological Studies* 62 (1, 2001), 3–22.

Tilley, Maureen A. "Augustine's Unacknowledged Debt to the Donatists," in *Augustinus Afer: saint Augustin, africanité et universalité : actes du colloque international, Alger-Annaba, 1–7 avril 2001*, ed. Pierre-Yves Fux, Jean-Michel Roessli, Otto Wermelinger, and Michael von Graffenried (Paradosis, 45; Fribourg, Suisse: Editions Universitaires, 2003), 141–148.

Tilley, Maureen A. "North Africa," in *Cambridge History of Early Christianity: Origins to Constantine*, ed. Margaret Mitchell and Frances Young (Cambridge: Cambridge University Press, 2006), 1:380–396.

Tilley, Maureen A. "From Schism to Heresy in Late Antiquity: Developing Doctrinal Deviance in the Wounded Body of Christ," *Journal of Early Christian Studies* 15 (1, Spring 2007), 1–21.

Tilley, Maureen A. "Redefining Donatism: Moving Forward," *Augustinian Studies* 42 (1, 2011), 21–32.

Tilley, Maureen A. "African Asceticism: The Donatist Heritage," in *The Uniquely African Controversy: Studies on Donatist Christianity*, ed. Anthony Dupont, Matthew Gaumer, and M. Lamberigts (Leuven: Peeters, 2014), 127–140.

Tilley, Maureen A. "Donatist Sermons," in *Preaching in the Latin Patristic Era: Sermons, Preachers, Audiences*, ed. Anthony Dupont, Shari Boodts, Gert Partoens, Johan Leemans (Leiden: Brill, forthcoming).

Tolan, John V. "Anti-hagiography: Embrico of Mainz's Vita Mahumeti," *Journal of Medieval History* 22 (1996), 25–41.

Torjesen, Karen Jo. "Tertullian's 'Political Ecclesiology' and Women's Leadership," *Studia patristica* 21 (Louvain: Peeters, 1989), 277–282.

Trevett, Christine. *Montanism: Gender, Authority and the New Prophecy* (Cambridge: Cambridge University Press, 1996).

Trout, Dennis. "Re-Textualizing Lucretia: Cultural Subversion in the City of God," *Journal of Early Christian Studies* 2 (1, 1994), 53–70.

Tucker, J. Brian, and Coleman A. Baker (eds.) *T&T Clark Handbook to Social Identity in the New Testament* (London: T&T Clark/Bloomsbury Publishing, 2014).

Turcan, Marie. "Être femme selon Tertullien," *Vita Latina* 119 (September 1990), 15–21.

Van Nijf, Onno. "Athletics, Festivals and Greek Identity in the Roman East," *Proceedings of the Cambridge Philological Society* 45 (1999): 176–200.

Várhelyi, Zsuzsanna. "What Is the Evidence for the Survival of Punic Culture in Roman North Africa?" *Acta Antiqua Academiae Scientiarum Hungaricae* 38 (1998), 391–403.

Vassall-Phillips, Oliver Rodie. *The Work of St. Optatus* (London: Longmans, Green, and Co., 1917).

Vliet, Edward van der. "The Romans and Us: Strabo's Geography and the Construction of Ethnicity," *Mnemosyne* 56 (3, 2003): 257–272.

Voelker, John. "Marius Victorinus' Exegetical Arguments for Nicene Definition in *Adversus Arium*," in *Studia Patristica* 38 (2001), 496–502.

Vokes, F.E. "Zeno of Verona, Apuleius, and Africa," in *Studia Patristica* 8.2 (1966), 130–134.

Walpole, A.S. *Early Latin Hymns* (Hildesheim: Georg Olms, 2004).

Walsh, P.G. *Cassiodorus: Explanation of the Psalms* (ACW 51; New York: Paulist Press, 1990).

Weigel, Sigrid. "Exemplum and Sacrifice," in *Perpetua's Passions*, ed. Jan N. Bremmer and Marco Formisano, trans. Joel Golb (Oxford: Oxford University Press, 2012), 180–200.

Whelan, Robin. "African Controversy: The Inheritance of the Donatist Schism in Vandal Africa," *Journal of Ecclesiastical History* 65 (3, 2014), 504–521.

Whitehouse, D. "An Early Mosque at Carthage?" *Annali dell'Istituto Universario Orientale* 43 (1983), 161–172.

Whitehouse, John. "The Course of the Donatist Schism in Late Roman North Africa," in *The Donatist Schism: Controversy and Contexts*, ed. Richard Miles (Liverpool: Liverpool University Press, 2016), 173–133.

Whitehouse, John. "The Scholarship of the Donatist Controversy," in *The Donatist Schism: Controversy and Contexts*, ed. Richard Miles (Liverpool: Liverpool University Press, 2016), 34–53.

Whitmarsh, Tim. *The Second Sophistic* (New Surveys in the Classics, 35; Oxford: Oxford University Press, 2005).

Whitmarsh, Tim. "Thinking Local," in *Local Knowledge and Microidentities in the Imperial Greek World* (Cambridge: Cambridge University Press, 2010), 1–16.

Whitmarsh, Tim. "The Romance between Greece and the East," in *The Romance between Greece and the East*, ed. Tim Whitmarsh and Stuart Thomson (Cambridge: Cambridge University Press, 2013), 1–19.

Wijnendaele, Jeroen W.P. *The Last of the Romans: Bonifatius-Warlord and Comes Africae* (London: Bloomsbury, 2015).

Wilhite, David E. *Tertullian the African Theologian: A Social Anthropological Reading of Tertullian's Identities* (Ph.D. Thesis for the University of St. Andrews, 2006).

Wilhite, David E. *Tertullian the African: An Anthropological Reading of Tertullian's Context and Identities* (Berlin: Walter De Gruyter, 2007).

Wilhite, David E. "Identity, Psychology, and the *Psychici*: Tertullian's 'Bishop of Bishops,'" *Interdisciplinary Journal for Research on Religion* (Fall 2009), Article 9: 1–26.

Wilhite, David E. "Patristic Pastoral Exegesis: Cyprian's Biblical Hermeneutic of Identity," in *Horizons in Biblical Theology* 32 (2010), 58–98.

Wilhite, David E. "Black Augustine," in *Oxford Guide to the Historical Reception of Augustine*, ed. Karla Pollmann and Willemien Otten (Oxford: Oxford University Press, 2013), 126–133.

Wilhite, David E. "Tertullian and the Spirit of Prophecy," in *Tertullian and Paul*, ed. Todd D. Still and David E. Wilhite (London: T&T Clark, 2013), 45–71.

Wilhite, David E. "True Church or True Basilica?: Parmenian's Ecclesiology Revisited," *Journal of Early Christian Studies* 22 (3, 2014), 399–436.

Wilhite, David E. "Augustine the African: Post-Colonial, Postcolonial and Post-postcolonial Readings," *Journal of Postcolonial Theory and Theology* 5 (2014), 1–34; repr./trans. in *Mayéutica* 41 (2015), 53–75.

Wilhite, David E. *The Gospel According to Heretics: Discovering Orthodoxy Through Early Christological Conflicts* (Grand Rapids, MI: Baker Press, 2015).

Wilhite, David E. "Donatism in Carthage until 411," in *Religion in Carthage*, ed. Jane Merdinger (Leiden: Brill, forthcoming).

Wilhite, David E. "Marcionites in Africa: What did Tertullian Know and When Did He Invent It?", *Perspectives in Religious Studies* 4 (2016), 437–452.

Wilhite, David E. "Were the 'Donatists' a National or Social Movement in Disguise?" *Studia Patristica* (forthcoming)

Wilken, Robert L. *The Christians as the Romans Saw Them* (New Haven, CT: Yale University Press, 1984).

Williams, Craig. "Perpetua's Gender: A Latinist Reads the *Passio Perpetuae et Felicitatis*," in *Perpetua's Passions*, ed. Jan N. Bremmer and Marco Formisano (Oxford: Oxford University Press, 2012), 54–77.

Willis, Geoffrey Grimshaw. *Saint Augustine and the Donatist Controversy* (London: SPCK, 2005).

Wilson, Andrew. "Romanizing Baal: The Art of Saturn Worship in North Africa," in *Proceedings of the 8th International Colloquium on Problems of Roman Provincial Art, Zagreb 2003*, ed. M. Sanader, et al. (Zagreb: Opuscula archaeologica, 2005), 403–408.

Wilson, Andrew. "Neo-Punic and Latin Inscriptions in Roman North Africa: Function and Display," in *Multilingualism in the Graeco-Roman Worlds*, ed. Alex Mullen and Patrick James (Cambridge: Cambridge University Press, 2012), 265–316.

Wilson, Stephen. *The Means of Naming: A Social and Cultural History of Personal Naming in Western Europe* (London: University College London Press, 1998).

Wolfe, Eric R. *Europe and the People Without History* (Berkeley: University of California Press, 1982).

Wypustek, Andrzej. "Magic, Montanism, Perpetua, and the Severan Persecution," *Vigiliae Christianae* 51 (3, 1997): 276–297.

Subject Index

Abbasid dynasty 322, 331
Abitinian martyrs 20–1
Abraham the Christian 329
Abraham the Nazarene 329
Adeodatus (primate of Numidia) 305, 318n151
Adeodatus (son of Augustine) 54–5, 241, 243, 251
Aemilian 159
Aeneas 12, 61, 90–1, 124, 155, 179, 185, 187–8, 191n79, 208, 231n116, 254, 257, 274, 285n144, 290–1
Aesculapius 137, 191n71
Aethiops 64
Afer ventus 221
Afra 50, 64, 69n24
Africanity 7, 10, 48, 148, 253, 255
Africa Proconsularis 2, 12, 33n3–4, 91, 272, 344
Africus 221, 237n252
Agape meal 88, 112
agonistici 201–2
Agrippinus 130n33, 217, 358, 360
Alexandria, Alexandrian, Alexandrians 3, 25–6, 34n6, 200, 269, 282n63, 295–7, 309
Alexandrian School 3, 25–6, 295
Algeria 10, 14, 16, 136, 173, 203, 207, 240, 244, 269, 272, 324, 332–3
Alypius 255
Ambrose 58, 172, 209, 215–16, 242, 251
Ameling, Walter 89, 99n30, 103n100–1
Anacharsis the Scythian 54, 71n60, 253
Anthony 242
Antiochene School 3
Antonius Julianus 140
Anulinus 174–5, 185, 190n46, 198–9, 203

Anzir 333
apocalypse, eschatology 210, 255–6, 299
apocryphal 151, 156, 166n153
Apollinarius 178
Apollo 178
Apollonius 178
Appian 34n9, 70n42, 74n113, 89, 103n98
Apuleius of Madauros 4, 16, 34n8, 51, 53–7, 61, 94, 110, 184, 210, 235n211, 250, 253–5, 262n88, 268
Arab, Arabian 26–8, 49, 154, 264, 279n6, 310–12, 320n183, 321–56, 361
Arabia 27, 326, 331
Arcadius 20
Archadius 209
Argentius of Lamigenum 304
Arian, Arianism 23, 200–1, 208, 216, 225, 228n47, 228n57, 244, 248–9, 258n20, 267, 269–71, 273, 275, 282n63, 290, 293, 302, 312n12, 324, 336, 343, 346–7, 350n9, 356n133, 359; *see also* Arius
Aristotle 109, 111, 118, 129n23
Arius 200, 208, 282n63
Arles 167n160, 175, 199, 217, 227n32
Arnobius 21, 102n86, 135n107, 141, 151, 156, 170, 174, 176–83, 190n34, 191n77, 191n80, 193n125, 209, 358
Artaxius 81
Artemis 63
Arzuges 206, 220, 230n106
asceticism 243, 245
Asheroth 61, 90
Asia Minor 84, 87, 109, 151
Asper 173

Astarte 61, 75n119, 137
Athanasius 200
Atlantic 28, 327
Atlas 61
Atlas mountains 61, 329
Augustine of Canterbury 336
Augustine of Hippo 1, 3–5, 10, 16,
    21–3, 27, 31–3, 42n157, 43n162,
    52, 54–9, 62, 65, 69n40, 70n40, 97,
    103n98, 112, 114, 121, 125, 131n36,
    133n77, 147–8, 152, 154, 165n131,
    175, 177, 182, 188, 191n59, 197–8,
    201–2, 204–9, 212–26, 231n120,
    234n195, 234n198, 235n201,
    235n224, 238n264, 239n275,
    240–63, 264, 266–7, 271, 273–4,
    279n6, 279n10, 281n55, 293, 297,
    299–301, 311, 315n69, 333, 342–3,
    354n92, 354n94, 358–60, 362, 364
Aurelius (Bishop of Carthage) 27, 254,
    266, 268, 311, 333
Aurelius Victor 188n2
Aures Mountains 28, 317n108, 327
authority 13, 23–5, 83, 87, 100n39,
    113, 134n106, 137, 148, 152–3,
    173, 175, 199, 204, 214, 243, 270,
    295, 297, 301, 306, 328, 337, 342,
    352n38
autonomy 8, 153, 307–8, 319n165,
    329, 337–8, 342, 350n16, 359
Awrabas 28

Baal 53–4, 59–60, 90, 103n103, 113,
    115, 135n107, 139–41, 178, 181–2,
    184, 238n265, 238n267, 267,
    313n38, 314n38; *see also* Jupiter;
    Saturn; Zeus
Babylon 157–8, 209
Bacchus 61, 250; *see also* Dionysius;
    Liber Pater
Bagai 201, 210, 224, 234n184
Baghdad 324, 350n16
Bainton, Roland H. 69n40, 256,
    262n101
baptism 88, 112, 117, 119, 127–8,
    133n79, 145–7, 151, 153–4, 199,
    203, 205–6, 209, 215–17, 220,
    228n37, 235n214, 237n242, 241–3,
    247, 258n6, 251, 267, 270, 272–3,
    293, 299, 301–2, 304–6, 331, 336,
    339
barbarians, barbaric 4, 12, 20, 22,
    34n9, 54, 65, 109, 120, 149,
    231n116, 241, 244, 255, 265, 275,
    284n123, 286n160, 288, 325, 361

basilica of Saint Euphemia 298
basilicas 74n106, 101n61, 112, 154,
    167n172, 198, 200, 203–4, 207,
    210–11, 215–16, 222, 268, 277,
    298, 332, 352n52
Basilique Saint Augustin 244
baths 88, 276, 317n115
Bauer, Walter 32
Bede 336, 354n94
Behloula 328
Bel 137
Belisarius 287–8
Benedict 301
Benedict VII 333
Beni el-Hassan 328
Beni Mansour 272
Berber, Berbes 6, 8, 46, 52, 72n80–1,
    236n223, 253, 260n62, 236n113,
    267, 307–8, 311, 324, 326–30, 337,
    344, 352n38
Bhalil 329
bishop of Rome 16, 26, 85, 113, 127,
    145, 148, 153, 199, 204–5, 230n90,
    261n269, 298, 301–2, 304–6, 308,
    355n96, 359; *see also* pope, papacy
bishop/s 18–19, 21, 23, 26, 58, 66,
    82, 85, 88, 101n61, 112–13, 120,
    133n33, 141–2, 144–6, 149, 151–3,
    162n67, 162n73, 163n96, 165n115,
    167n163, 170–1, 173, 175–6,
    195–9, 201, 203, 205, 207, 209–12,
    223–4, 234n188, 236n227–8,
    242–3, 245, 253–6, 266–70, 273,
    275–6, 279n6, 282n65, 284n127,
    293–4, 296, 298–300, 303–6, 310,
    330, 333, 337, 342, 353n74, 358
Bithynia-Pontus 63
Blossus Emilius Dracontius 274
bone, bones 176, 215, 244, 331,
    352n52; *see also* relic, relics
Boniface 22–3, 226, 271, 330, 355n95
Boniface II 278
Bonifacius 275
Bosphorus 298, 308
Botrus 197
British Isles 243, 336, 354n92
Brown, Peter 32–3, 47, 54, 56, 196,
    213, 251, 254, 257
Brutus 22, 91
Byzacena 33n4, 74n110, 76n145,
    220, 272, 275, 293, 298–300, 310,
    326–7, 344, 361
Byzantium, Byzantine 25–9, 49,
    130n29, 232n150, 244, 264, 276,
    278, 284n120, 286n166, 287–320,

322–3, 325–7, 329, 335, 337–8, 340–4

Caecilian 21, 32, 39n97, 104n132, 170, 175, 195–200, 214–15, 228n38
Caecilianists 175, 196–7, 201–2, 204, 206–7, 210–12, 214–18, 224, 243, 251, 269, 273, 278, 292–4, 302, 341, 343–4, 359; *see also* Catholics
Caecilius 136–8, 140, 150–1, 161n29, 166n43, 327
Caelestis 61, 75n120, 90, 265, 268
Caelestius 197
Caesar Augustus 22, 46, 51, 125, 145, 172–3, 194n165, 257
Cainites 119
Cairo 324
Caius 155
Calama 211, 218, 222, 243
caliph, caliphate 154, 324, 328–9, 331, 333, 350n16, 352n38, 352n52
Candidus 81, 99n31, 208
Capellianus 18
Cappadocia 80
Capreolus 226
Caracalla 18, 102n75
Carneades 182
Cartenna 224
Carthage 1, 4, 11–15, 18–21, 23–7, 29–30, 34n9, 36n53, 37n59, 42n158, 51–2, 54, 56–7, 59, 61, 65–6, 69n32, 69n40, 73n88, 74n106, 74n113, 76n140, 76n148, 79–80, 82–3, 85–91, 96–7, 97n6, 99n26, 99n29, 101n59, 109, 112, 114, 116, 118, 123–5, 125n2–3, 130n33–4, 133n88, 133n90, 136, 139, 141–6, 148–52, 154, 158, 163n86, 163n95, 165n126, 167n158, 167n163, 167n172, 170–4, 183–5, 188, 195, 197–200, 203, 205, 211, 215, 222–4, 227n30, 228n38, 231n116, 234n184, 237n249, 238n267, 238n275, 239n277, 241–2, 251, 253–4, 263n111, 264–6, 268, 272–6, 278, 279n5–6, 279n10, 280n17, 288–94, 297–8, 300, 303–6, 208–310, 313n37, 326–9, 331–4, 337, 343, 350n7, 351n26, 353n74, 354n78, 361, 365n2
Carthaginians 5, 13, 24, 57, 66, 73n88, 97n4, 118, 123, 129n5, 138, 223, 257, 266, 268, 288, 331
Cassiciacum 243, 258n12

catechumens 88, 94, 128
Catholic (party), Catholics, Catholicism 21, 23–4, 31–3, 113–14, 127, 148, 173, 175, 195–6, 198–9, 201, 203, 206–7, 209, 211–15, 217, 219, 222, 225, 226n3–4, 234n188, 236n227, 237n254, 243, 246, 251–2, 260n62, 261n69, 265–6, 268–77, 249n6, 279n9, 280n27, 281n55–6, 283n99, 289, 292–4, 302–3, 305–7, 319n165, 324, 337, 340–4, 359, 364
Cato 1, 10–11, 14, 180, 184, 190–1n56, 222, 249n5, 291
Caudel, Maurice 7
celibacy 113, 204, 214, 243, 249
Cereres 61, 90, 103n108
Ceres, Demeter 61, 90, 137
Chalcedon, Chalcedonians 25, 295–300, 344
Chaldaeans 137
Charlemagne 154, 331
chiliasm 156
chorepiscopus 153, 342
Chrestus 175
Christ, Jesus 15, 19–20, 23, 45, 82, 85, 92, 104n132, 118, 120–1, 124–7, 130n28, 133n79, 143–4, 147, 152–3, 155–7, 159, 177, 183, 203, 211, 213, 217, 220, 234n188, 242, 249, 254–7, 285n135, 295–6, 303, 309–10, 323, 328, 331–2, 339, 343–6, 363–4
Christmas 334, 348
Christology 154, 310, 330, 346
Cicero 109, 118, 169n219, 182, 238n264, 242
Circumcellions 42n161, 201–4, 207, 214, 216, 218, 228n62, 229n62, 229n69, 234n197, 262n95, 270, 306
circus, circuses 121, 265, 276
Cirta 4, 15, 136, 138, 140, 158–9, 264, 279n6
Cittinus 91
civilizing mission 7, 256, 303
Claudian 65
Claudius 138
Cleopatra 125, 135n106
Clodius Albinus 64, 68n21, 77n153
clothes, clothing 46, 48, 53, 55, 65–7, 73n89, 77n167, 90, 115, 117–19, 121, 123–4, 133n79, 150, 266, 277, 292, 347
colonization 7, 14, 46, 65, 106n150, 116, 125, 335
Columbus 305–6, 310

Commodian 151, 155–8
Condianus 92
confessor 27, 158, 310
Consentius 221
Constans 201, 228n57, 332
Constans II 311
Constantine 19, 33, 42n158, 136,
    154, 167n168, 170, 173–6,
    181–3, 185–8, 193n141, 194n160,
    194n165, 194n168, 198–201, 205,
    213, 227n32, 228n43
Constantine, Algeria 136
Constantine the African 354n78
Constantinople 24–8, 272, 278n1,
    287–9, 294–5, 297–301, 307–11,
    313n33, 314n42, 314n56, 326,
    337–8, 340, 353n74, 359
Constantius 171, 173, 193n159, 266
contagion 121–2, 133n80, 142, 146–7,
    174, 197–8, 204, 206, 215, 267, 357
conversion 39n90, 47, 106n158, 108,
    114, 124, 162n65, 174, 176, 182–3,
    186, 188, 207–8, 210, 243, 245,
    249, 257, 322, 325, 344, 346, 365
Coptic 345, 364
Cornelius 144–5, 151
Corsica 12
Council of Arles 175, 217, 235n214
Council of Chalcedon 26, 283, 296,
    298, 316n106
Council of Ephesus 244, 266, 295–6
Council of Nicaea 167n160, 200, 208
Council of Serdica 149, 200
creatio ex nihilo 246
Crementius 305
Cresconius 206
Cresconius The African 330
Crispus 181, 192n98
culture 5, 8, 12, 29–30, 34n5, 35n23,
    41n152, 45–9, 56–7, 63, 71n53,
    71n62, 110–11, 133n88, 256,
    263n113, 267, 284n120, 290,
    344–5, 347
Curubis 145, 164n109
Cyprian 3, 8, 15, 18–21, 27, 32, 66,
    112–14, 121, 127–8, 130n33,
    135n108, 136–71, 174, 183, 185,
    193n150, 195, 199, 205, 210,
    215–17, 226n4, 230n105, 247, 252,
    276, 278, 288, 299, 302, 304, 311,
    316n103, 331, 333, 336–7, 343–4,
    352n52, 355n96, 358, 360–1, 364
Cyprian (Pseudo-) 154, 167n173,
    168n176
Cypriana 167n169, 288

Cyrenaica 2, 11, 99n28, 221, 326,
    354n92, 361
Cyriacus 333
Cyril of Alexandria 295

Daia Maximinus 186
Dalmatia 255
Damascus 326
Dativus 21
David 328
deacon, deacons 21, 39n97, 141,
    169n216, 198, 266, 284n129, 297,
    300
Decius 18, 142, 162n74
Demetrian 149, 155
Demetrianus 185
demons 121–2, 146–7, 155
Deogratias 268, 273
Deo gratias 86, 214, 234n196
devil 17, 93, 114, 127, 146, 155,
    158–9, 185, 187
Diana 137, 191n64
Dido 12, 36n53, 41n141, 61, 74n109,
    90, 124–5, 185, 187–8, 216,
    239n277, 254, 285n144, 290–1, 328
Dihya 327–8; *see also* Kahina
Dinocrates 90
diocese 167n164, 211–13, 325, 337
Diocletian 2, 50, 170–6, 181, 184,
    186–8, 193n153, 195–6, 200,
    236n238, 340
Dionysius 61; *see also* Bacchus; Liber
    Pater
Dioscorus 296
dissident 159, 196, 237n254, 304
divorce 31, 113, 170
Djeraoua 327
Dominic 305–7
dominus 15, 91
Donata 91
Donatilla 172, 235n210
Donatism, Donatists, Donatist
    Controvery 6, 19–22, 27, 31–3,
    36n44, 42n157–8, 42n161, 47, 57,
    59, 67, 72n80, 121, 125, 127–8,
    130n29, 147–51, 154, 156–7,
    167n173, 170, 172–6, 179, 185–8,
    193n151, 195–239, 243–4, 246–7,
    251–2, 254, 258n20, 260n59,
    260n62, 266–71, 273, 278,
    279n6, 279n9, 281n53, 281n56,
    281n59–60, 282n63, 282n69,
    293–4, 298–9, 301–7, 314n48,
    314n56, 315n66, 317n108, 319n165,
    324, 330–2, 334, 336, 340, 343–4,

352n38, 354n94, 355n96, 356n124, 358–60, 362–3
Donatus of Bagaia 201, 226n3
Donatus of Carthage 27, 50, 53, 149, 151, 170, 185–8, 188n1, 195–6, 198–200, 203, 212, 215–17, 220, 223, 226n3, 227n30, 228n38, 239n277, 299, 311, 334, 358, 363
Donatus of Mutagenna 216
dragons 119, 284n117
Dyophysites, dyothelite 309–10, 326

Easter 210, 243, 281n53, 331, 334, 348
ecclesiology, *ecclesia* 112–13, 127, 144–6, 152–3, 198, 200, 204, 215, 237n244, 237n247, 247, 273, 318n158
Edict of Milan 173–4, 185–6
Edom 221
Egypt, Egyptian, *Aegyptius* 2, 11, 17, 27–8, 34n5, 61, 65, 68n17, 71n62, 72n81, 76n145, 96, 137–8, 140, 145, 151, 157, 172, 181, 200, 203, 231n124, 242, 269, 275–6, 285n135, 295, 321, 326–7, 337, 339, 341–5, 349, 361
El Alia 310
elders, *seniores laici* 20, 112, 129n20, 151, 173, 189n23, 198, 288
elephants 13, 50–1, 68n23, 69n25, 69n28, 186, 363
Eleusinians 137
Elias 157
El Kef 176
El Ksar el Kebir 203
Embrico of Mainz 321
energy 141, 307, 309
En Gila 333
Epaenetus 82
Ephesus 63, 244, 266, 295–6
Epidaurians 137
equestrian 89, 132n48, 159
Ethiopia 50, 64–5, 77n159, 276–7, 297, 364
ethnic identity 6, 34n14, 47, 67n10, 76n140–1, 253, 345
ethnicity 9, 30, 45–7, 64, 67n10, 256, 272, 277, 308
Eucharist 112, 147, 215
Eucherius of Lyons 171
Eugenius 273, 275–6
Eulogius of Cordoba 332
Eusebius of Caesarea 109, 173–4, 188
Eutyches 300

Eve 114, 247
evil 94, 121, 127, 147, 157, 171, 177, 183, 185, 188, 189n10, 200, 241–2, 245, 270–1, 291
exorcism 146, 241

Facundus 26–7, 299, 311
fallen angels 119, 291
fallenness, fall of humanity 119, 241–2, 244, 247
fasces 184
fasting 117, 121, 346
Fatimids 324, 328, 333
Faustus Basilica 277
Fazaz 328
Felicissimus 156, 164n98
felicity 15, 30, 53, 63, 79–81, 87–9, 93–4, 123, 125, 127–8, 158, 267, 278
Felix 172–4
Felix (Arian priest) 275
Felix I 275
Felix of Abthugni 197–8
Fendelaoua 328
Ferrandus 27, 275, 284n129, 297–8, 311, 315n66, 342
Firmus 19–20, 22, 41n141, 207, 216, 225, 231n120, 263, 363
Flaminius 138
Flavius Cresconius Corippus 291
Florus of Lyon 331
Formosus 332–3
Formula of Reunion 296
Fortunatus 310
free will 177, 244
Frend, W. H. C. 6, 72n80, 82, 179, 189n13, 261n63, 280n27, 301, 342, 344, 356n124
Fronto 4–5, 15–16, 37n62, 54, 56, 71n62, 94, 110, 136, 138, 140, 160n22, 250, 253
Frotmund 331–2
Fulgentius of Ruspe 275, 290
Fulgentius the Mythographer 290
Fussula 218

Gaetuli/ian 4, 16, 54–5, 134n100, 176
Gaius 110
Galerius 171, 173–4
Gallus 144, 164n99
Garamantean 65, 77n159, 276–7, 285
Garden of the Hesperides 61
Gaudentius 207, 216

Gaul, Gauls 13, 64, 82, 127, 137, 140, 151, 172, 199, 203, 227n32, 265, 270, 331
Geiseric 23–5, 40n135, 264–6, 269, 272–4, 276, 281n53, 288
Gelasius 151, 155–6, 166n154, 274, 284n123
Gelimer 276, 287, 289
Gennadius 155–6, 206, 303, 305–6
gentiles 4, 157, 159, 231n114
George (monk) 332
George of Pisidia 309
German, Germany 7, 167n174, 277, 286n160, 340, 346, 355n95
Geta 17–18, 77n151, 87, 96, 98n13, 102n75, 106n154
Giatha 328
Gibbon, Edward 148, 266
Gildo 20, 22, 41n141, 207, 216, 225, 231n116, 231n120, 363
golden apples 61, 90
Goliath 328
Gordian I 18, 41n141
Gordian II 18, 39n83
Gordian III 18
Goths 29, 157, 201
grace 61, 109, 111, 122, 143, 244, 247–9, 266, 274
grain 14, 20, 22–4, 26, 46, 110, 176–7
Gratus 215
Great Mosque 327
Great Mother 137
Greek, Greeks 2–4, 11–12, 16, 38n67, 45, 53, 55–6, 59–61, 64–6, 71n62, 72n71, 74n108, 82, 84, 99n27, 100n48, 103n101, 109, 111, 113, 119–20, 123, 125–6, 137, 143, 149, 179, 184, 193n123, 208–9, 249, 253, 263n113, 273, 288, 290, 294, 297, 300, 314n57, 315n63, 338, 342–3, 345, 359, 363
Gregory (exarch of Africa) 27–8, 41n141, 310, 326
Gregory I, Gregory the Great 27, 232n50, 287, 301–8, 317n115, 317n123, 317n128, 318n138, 319n165, 320n183, 342
Gregory II 330–1, 336, 355n95
Gregory VII 279n6, 333
Guilia Runa 271
Gummi 333
Gunthamund 274–5

Hades (hell) 157, 185, 246–7, 355n107
Hadrian 336, 354n92

Hadrumetum 68n21, 77n153, 81–2, 99n29, 298, 300
Hannibal 13, 41n141, 50–1, 54, 60–1, 69n32, 75n117, 77n169, 138, 165n130, 181, 207, 216, 231n116, 251–2, 261n67, 272
Haroun al-Rashid 154
Hasan Ibn an-Nuuman 327–8
Hasdrubal 14, 34n9
Hasdrubal's wife 41, 125, 216
Hebrew 61–2, 75n119, 118, 156, 206, 249, 252
Henchir es-Souar 197
Hera, Juno 61, 90, 139, 185, 222, 267, 326
Heraclius 26, 40n136, 308–10, 355n98
Heraclius the elder 309
Hercules 53, 61–2, 75n133, 91, 184, 223, 239; *see also* Melqart
heretic, heresy 2, 3, 7, 21, 26, 32, 42n157, 42n160, 83, 108–11, 114, 117–18, 120, 127, 131n36, 146, 151, 153, 156, 179, 193n151, 199, 201, 203, 205, 211, 216–17, 221, 224, 245, 247, 266–7, 269–70, 273, 278, 282n60, 292, 296–9, 305–6, 310, 324, 338, 358
Hermiane 26
Hermionem 299
Hermogenes 117–18
Herod 203
Hesperides 61, 91
Hesychius 255
hierarchy 84, 86, 153, 250, 276, 288, 302–3, 337
Hilarianus (persecutor) 80, 98n12
Hilary 231n124, 304
Hilderic 275–6
Hippo 23, 32, 137n173, 197, 213, 215, 218, 236n227, 243–4, 254, 260n47, 264, 266–7, 271, 279, 333, 358
Hippolytus of Rome 82, 357
holiness 83, 121, 126, 128
Holy Roman Emperor 331, 340
Holy Spirit 200, 232n137; *see also* Paraclete
Homer, homeric myths 16, 59
homoousia, or same-substance 208, 273
Honorius (Bishop) 224
Honorius (emperor) 20, 22, 211, 223
human soul 117–18, 177, 246, 248–9
Huneric 273, 275

Iatanbaal 54, 251
Ibadis 324, 330, 352n38, 353n60

Ibas of Edessa 40n132, 296–7, 299
Iberia, Iberian 12–13, 151, 203, 221, 230n99, 244, 264, 266, 304, 361
Ibn Abd al-Hakam 322, 332
Ibn Khaldun 327–8
Ibrahim al Nasrani 329
identity 1–2, 4–10, 30, 33, 34n14, 37n60, 42n161, 45, 47–51, 53–7, 60–2, 64, 66, 67n10, 67n12, 68n13, 76n140, 85, 91–3, 95, 98n18, 103n101, 104n126, 115–16, 124–6, 136–8, 140, 142, 147–9, 151, 157–60, 174–5, 179–80, 183–4, 196, 209, 218, 220–1, 223–5, 232n155, 234n195, 235n201, 240, 250–1, 253–5, 257, 274, 276–8, 288–92, 294, 302, 308, 325, 331, 337–8, 345, 347, 355n96, 355n118, 359–60, 362
idolatry 48, 122, 177
idols 94, 121, 143, 146–7, 154–7, 171, 174, 177, 181, 198, 214, 346
Idris the First 328
III Augustan Legion 11, 81, 99n31, 171
Illyricum 24
Imazighen 325, 329–30
incarnation 117, 295–7
incense 88, 226n11
India 50–1, 116, 138
Innocent (pope) 307
interpretatio Romana 59, 63, 90, 178, 222, 238n265, 250–1
Irenaeus of Lyon 32, 82, 98n23, 101n67, 117, 357
Isidore of Seville 244
Isis 61
Islam 2, 59, 62, 322–5, 328–31, 334–9, 341–2, 344–8, 350n6, 350n10, 352n39, 354n88, 356n124, 359, 365

Jerome 39n108, 111, 114–15, 130n29, 131n35–6, 150, 162n62, 177–9, 183, 200, 209, 237n252, 249, 252, 261n65
Jerusalem 83, 110–11, 122, 157, 188n1, 220, 234n188, 309, 320n178, 326, 363
John (bishop of Squillacium) 304
John the Usurper 22
John Troglita 25, 291–2
Josephus 140
Joshua 289
Jovinian 249
Jubaleni 19

Jucundus 81, 274
Judaism (Jews, Jewish, etc.) 4–5, 8, 11–12, 34n5, 45, 68n19, 76, 83–4, 96, 100n43, 103n98, 106n158, 140, 155, 157–8, 179, 210, 231n124, 249, 281n53, 289, 293, 323, 332, 327–8, 350n7, 351n29, 363
Judas Maccabeus 363
Judea 83, 363
Julian of Eclanum 252
Julian the Apostate 207
Julius Caesar 14–15, 22, 46, 51, 139
Julius Paulus 96
Julius Quintus Hilarianus 210
Junillus Africanus 129n5, 300
Junius 138
Juno 90, 135n106, 139, 185, 222, 267, 326; *see also* Hera, Juno
Jupiter 60, 74n113, 75n116, 139, 192n90, 267, 314n38, 326; *see also* Baal; Saturn
Justin II 299–300, 313n33
Justinian 25–7, 276, 287–91, 293, 295–301, 304, 314n42, 340
Justin Martyr 117, 123, 141

Kahina 28, 327–8
Kairouan 327, 329, 332, 334
Kataphrygians 84, 87
Kharajites 324, 329–30, 352n38
Kronos (saturn/Bal Hammon) 60; *see also* Saturn
Kusayla 28, 327

Lacinium 61
Lactantius 50–1, 98n11, 141, 151, 154, 156, 164n99, 170, 173–4, 176, 178, 181–8, 193n125, 193n141, 193n151, 194n165, 194n168, 207, 210, 231n124, 257–8, 363
Lambaesis 82
lapsed 143–7, 163n81, 163n94, 195, 269, 275
Lateran Council (649) 310
Latin 2, 5–6, 12, 14–15, 21, 30, 38n67, 39n108, 46–9, 52–6, 58–62, 71n56, 71n61–2, 73n89, 77n169, 82, 90, 104n126, 104n131, 108–9, 111, 115–17, 126, 136, 146, 149–50, 152, 156–7, 159, 178–9, 183, 197, 202, 208, 220–1, 242, 249–51, 253, 256, 262n101, 267, 271, 274–6, 287, 291, 297–8, 300, 312n13, 323, 325, 334, 337–8, 342, 344–5, 361
Latium 5, 184

law 45, 89–90, 96, 106n158, 109–10,
  112, 139, 174, 182, 205, 224, 251,
  314n47, 317n115, 333, 340, 342,
  362–3
Laxists 144–6, 164n98, 343
L. Caelius Firmianus 183
Lebanon 12
Leo I 24, 285n135, 296, 302
Leo III 331
Leo IV 331
Leo IX 333
Leptis Magna 17, 55, 62, 72n70, 116
Liber 178, 191n78
Liberatus of Carthage 300
Liber genealogus 230n112, 269,
  282n62
Liber Pater 61–2, 75n133, 250; *see also*
  Bacchus; Dionysius
Libya, Libyan 2, 4–6, 12, 14, 16–17,
  19, 34n11, 36n52, 37n59, 46, 49,
  52–4, 57, 59, 61–2, 64–5, 70n44,
  71n60–1, 73n97, 76n148, 91,
  98n23, 98n26, 99n27, 110, 116,
  129n7, 150, 164n106, 192n90,
  200, 221, 236n223, 238n262, 251,
  260n46, 263n113, 269, 288–92,
  295, 300, 312n14, 314n42, 321,
  324, 326, 333–4
Licinius 173, 185–6, 193n141, 228n43
light 17, 137, 241
lion 50, 238n274
liturgy 58, 80, 197, 243, 345, 356n131
Livy 61, 75n117, 179, 238n264,
  238n264
Lixus 61, 361
Lombards 301
Louis IX 334, 339
Lucilla 197, 215
Lucretia 91, 125, 134n106, 135n106,
  257
Lull, Raymon 334
lust 121, 249, 265
L. Vesperonius Candidus Sallustius
  Savinianus 81

Macarians 202–3
Macarius 201, 203, 219, 228n37, 363
Maccabees 158, 363
Macrinus 18, 39n81
Madauros 4, 16, 56, 185, 219,
  236n237, 240, 254
Maghrib 29, 325, 328, 352n38,
  354n88
Mahdia 324
Majorinus 195, 197–9

Maktar 90
Manicheans 241, 243, 245–6, 273,
  205, 324, 331, 343
Manius Aquilius 139
Mappala 218
Marcellinus 211, 254
Marcion 86, 100n51, 101n63, 101n67,
  104n132, 109–10, 113, 117–18,
  120, 232n135
Marcus Atilius Regulus 139
Marcus Aurelius 65, 98n16, 268
Marcus Cornelius Fronto 15, 136, 180
Marcus of Mactaris 21–2
Marius Victorinus 207, 242
Markus, Robert A. 27–8, 33, 213, 295,
  299, 307–8, 311, 318n158, 319n165
marriage 41n141, 113, 117, 216, 241,
  249–51, 355n98
martial 55, 134n94
Martin I 310, 320n178
Mary 118, 267–8, 280n34, 295, 323
Mascazel 20
Masuna 274
Mauretania 18–19, 23–6, 33n3–4,
  39n81, 62, 64–5, 73n93, 76n145,
  82, 91, 97n7, 130n29, 155, 160n27,
  172, 190n35, 210, 220, 224,
  229n84, 264, 271–2, 274, 325; *see
  also* Moors
Mauretania Caesariensis 33, 220
Maurice 7, 26–7, 172, 306
Mavilus of Hadrumetum 81
Maxima 172, 235
Maximian 171–5, 186–7, 189n9–10,
  189n17, 190n55, 205, 211, 224,
  233n164, 235, 305
Maximianist 205–6, 220, 234n184
Maximilian 171–2, 174
Maximilla 87, 112, 114
Maximinus 173, 186
Maximinus Thraz 18
Maximus of Madauros 219, 254
Maximus the Confessor 27, 287, 308,
  311, 326, 350n7, 358
Mecca 327, 346
Medinet-el-kedima 275
Mediterranean 11–13, 16, 24, 26, 29,
  45, 58, 61, 76n140, 84, 141, 180,
  210, 255, 272, 291, 331, 336–8,
  341, 359, 361
Megalius of Calama 243
Melitian Schism 200
Melqart 61–2, 75n133, 223, 238n274;
  see also Hercules
Memnon 77n159, 277, 285n148

Memoria Cypriani 154, 332
mensa 58, 154
Mensa Cypriani 154
Mensurius 21, 197–8
Mercury 137
Mesopotamia 138, 184
Metropolitan 86, 152, 167n163, 294,
  303, 333, 337
Mezentius 274
Milan 56, 58, 172–4, 185–6, 207,
  215–16, 228n38, 241–3
Millenarianism 210, 233n158; *see also*
  chiliasm
Miltiades 175, 199, 205, 227n25,
  227n35
Minerva 326
Minucius Felix 136–8, 140–1, 147,
  151, 155–7, 160n3, 185, 358
Mocian 299
modesty 110, 117, 134n106
Mon 54, 251
monasticism 3, 201, 229n62, 241,
  243, 245, 265, 275, 288, 301, 306,
  342–3, 354n92, 355n118
Monica, mother of Augustine 54–6, 58,
  154, 207, 209, 215, 231n122, 241,
  243, 250–1, 254, 256, 352n52
monogamy 113
Monophysite, Monophysites 27,
  295–6, 300, 309, 330, 340, 344
monothelite 27, 309–11
Montanists 84, 87–8, 100n49, 100n51,
  102n78, 112–13, 115, 130n28,
  130n29, 193n151, 204–5; *see also*
  Kataphrygian
Montanus (martyr) 158
Montanus (Phrygian prophet) 87–8,
  112, 114
Moors 64, 68n23, 134n100, 172,
  177, 190–1n56, 231n116, 266,
  273, 285n134, 288–9, 291–2, 328,
  355n105; *see also* Mauretania
morality, moral law 52, 184, 241,
  265–6, 269, 290–1, 362
Morocco 61, 329, 361
mortal sin 215, 249
Mucius Scaevola 139, 286n154
Muhammad 26, 321–3, 326, 332,
  345–6
Muslim 28–9, 154, 309–10, 320n178,
  356
M'zab 324

Nabor 172
Nafusa 334

Nag Hammadi 349
Nartzalus 91, 102n89
Nasara 322
Navigius 241
Nebridius 243
Nebuchadnezzar 271
Nectarius 222, 238n262
Nefouca 328
Neptune 59–60; *see also* Poseidon
Nero 93, 134n101, 157
Nestorius, Nestorianism 266, 295–6,
  300
New prophecy *see* Montanists
Nicasius 270
Nicene Creed 201, 208, 273, 339
Nicomedia 181, 183
nobility 27, 55, 65, 77n153, 87, 89–90,
  94–5, 180, 255
nomadic, nomads 4, 9, 12, 16, 54, 65,
  149, 177, 190–1n56, 201, 229n62
Normans 324
Novatian 145, 164n101
Novatians, Novatianism, Novatianist
  131n36, 149, 193n151, 205,
  228n50, 336, 343
Nubel 19
Numidia, Numidian 2, 4–5, 13–16,
  18–19, 25, 33n3–4, 36n52–4,
  42n161, 54–5, 76n145, 81, 91,
  138, 142, 145, 151, 158–9, 171,
  189n17, 197–8, 203, 213, 218,
  230n106, 234n184, 243, 252,
  260n48, 262n85, 264, 272, 293,
  301–7, 310, 317n108, 327, 337,
  344, 361

Octavius 136–41
Oea 328
Old Testament 62, 86, 109, 120, 151,
  157, 223, 232n135, 267, 271, 289,
  298
onomatology 54, 183, 251
Optatus of Milevis 32–3, 42n158,
  74n100, 197–8, 201–2, 204, 207,
  213, 215, 223, 227n16, 228n37,
  229n69, 230n90, 231n124,
  235n205, 276
ordination 197, 199, 204, 206, 214–15,
  236n224, 243, 305
orientalism 63
Origen 126, 178, 246, 249
orthodoxy 2, 32–3, 148, 214, 297,
  308, 354n88
Ostia 137, 243
Oxyrhunchus 349

Paccia Marciana 53
Pacian 149, 151
Pagan 90, 92, 121, 123, 143, 159, 180,
    183–4, 189n19, 209, 216, 218–19,
    222–3, 260n62, 262n89, 271–2,
    290–1
Palestine 27, 82–4, 308, 328, 332,
    350n7
pallium 65–6, 123–4, 133n90
Pantaleo 305
Papias 156, 168n190
Paraclete 113, 232n137; *see also* Holy
    Spirit
Parmenian 27, 203, 205–6, 311, 361
patria 53–4, 73n88, 85, 109, 115, 120,
    124, 222, 253
Patricius 54, 71n56, 175, 240, 250–1,
    256, 260n48
Paul (Bishop) 306
Paul (Roman official) 201, 203
Paul (the Apostle) 3–5, 38n76, 63, 83,
    85–6, 113, 121, 125, 130n25, 208,
    224, 333, 362–4
Paul of Nisibis 300, 318n165
Pavia 244
Pelagius 220, 243–4, 261n69
Pelagius II 304
Pelagius (of Rome) 299
Perpetua 15, 17, 30, 55, 74n106, 81,
    84, 87–91, 93–7, 99n30, 100n48–9,
    103n96, 103n101, 125, 127–8,
    134n102, 163n80, 267, 278
persecution 20, 63, 79–81, 86, 91,
    93–4, 96, 98n18, 99n32, 105n133,
    105n137, 109, 117, 125–6, 141–7,
    155, 158, 162n73, 163n80, 164n99,
    173–5, 181, 185–7, 195, 198,
    200–3, 236n238, 268–9, 273–4,
    281n55–6, 292, 297, 302, 317n108,
    338, 341–2
Persia, Persians 26–7, 184, 272, 287,
    300, 308
Peter (Apostle) 83, 125, 153, 166n157,
    204–5, 305, 321
Peter (Bishop) 306
Petilian 206, 211, 230n109
Pharaoh 271
Philistines 83
philosophy 45, 109–11, 208, 240, 242
Phocas 26, 309
Phoenician 12, 36n53, 37n56, 53, 61,
    69n37, 90, 134n93, 156, 182, 184,
    206, 223, 288–9, 330
Phrygia 84, 87, 100n51, 112
piety 215, 242, 251, 306

Placidia 23, 273
Plato 111
Platonism, Neoplatonism, etc. 208,
    242, 245–6, 258n26, 259n26
Pliny the Younger 63
Plotinus 242
poetry 109, 240
polemics 42n158, 73n92, 117, 120,
    233n177, 252
Polybius 13
Polytheism 139, 151, 203
Pompeiana 171
Pompey 50–1, 69n28, 139, 155, 186,
    363
Pompilius 180
Pontepolis 221, 269
Pontianus 300
Ponticianus 209
Pontius 141–2, 146, 150, 154,
    162n62–3
Pontius Pilate 155, 211
Pontus 63, 109–10, 120
Pope, papacy 24, 26–7, 166n154,
    175, 205, 232n150, 244, 274–5,
    278, 279n6, 284n123, 287, 296–8,
    301–2, 304–10, 315n69, 319n172,
    320n178, 330–3, 336, 342, 353n71;
    see also bishop of Rome
Porphyry 180, 190n33, 242
Portugal 12
Poseidon 59–60; *see also* Neptune
Possidius 211, 240, 249, 264, 279n6
Potentinus of Utica 330
Praesens 92
prayer 74n100, 75n116, 87, 91, 117,
    154, 157, 187, 202, 223, 240, 254,
    307, 346, 352n52
Priam 277
priests, priestesses, priestly status 16,
    62, 63, 66, 83, 88, 90, 103n96,
    111–12, 140, 143, 146, 151, 153,
    159, 164n115, 173, 198, 205,
    238n265, 243, 245, 255, 267, 271,
    275, 315
Primasius 298–300, 315n76, 316n101
Priscilla 87, 112, 114
Procopius 53, 266, 271, 289–90, 300,
    312n14, 314n42
Proculus 110
Prudentius 149, 154
Punic 6, 16, 53–4, 66, 70n49, 89, 148,
    219, 236n236, 236n237, 252, 254,
    277, 312n13
Punic Wars 1, 4, 10, 13–15, 24, 51–2,
    60, 112, 123, 138–9, 169n220, 183,

252, 222, 263n111, 264, 290, 335, 360–1
Puppianus 150–1
purple 65, 119, 139, 184
Pyrrhus 309–10

Q. Caecilius Natalis 136
quaestor 300
Quintillian 109, 118, 129n5
Quintus 81
Qumran 349
Quodvultdeus 23, 253, 266–8, 280n27, 281n46, 281n60
Qustas 332

Ravenna 211, 221, 224, 278n1
refrigerium 58, 74n101
Regulus 138, 155, 184, 257
relic, relics 90, 154, 167, 197, 244, 331, 352n52; *see also* bones
Remus 139, 151, 155, 257, 277, 313n31
Reparatus 26, 293, 298, 310
resurrection 110–11, 117, 133n79, 155, 182, 246
Revocatus 87, 95
rhetoric 7, 16, 19, 56, 97n7, 109, 115, 118–20, 124, 126, 176, 180–1, 207–8, 214, 241, 254
rigorism, rigorists 144–4, 147, 205, 343
Romanitas, Romanization, etc. 6, 9, 15–16, 30, 40n128, 45–9, 51, 55, 60–2, 65–6, 67n4, 73n90, 74n114, 115–16, 139, 142, 223, 236n236, 250–1, 254–5, 261n67, 263n113, 325, 337, 345, 347, 360
Romano-African x, 56, 94, 96, 277, 283n88, 337
Romanus 19, 39n93
Rome 1–2, 4–5, 8–9, 11–16, 18–20, 23–4, 26–9, 32, 34n11, 37n55, 42n161, 45, 49–54, 59–62, 65–6, 68n21, 69n32, 69n40, 71n62, 75n133, 82–3, 85–6, 89–91, 93, 95, 97n7, 100n39, 100n52, 104n132, 109–10, 113, 116, 118–19, 122–3, 125–8, 133n88, 133n90, 135n106, 136–40, 144–5, 147–51, 155, 157–8, 160n3, 163n87, 163n95, 166n157, 167n158, 172–7, 179–81, 183–4, 188, 191n77, 193n125, 195, 199, 204–5, 207–9, 212, 214, 216, 220–5, 231n116, 238n264, 238n275, 241, 243–4, 251, 254–7,

262n89, 263n111, 264–5, 272–5, 277, 279n10, 291–2, 294, 297–9, 301–2, 304–11, 313n31, 320n181, 326, 332, 334, 337–8, 353n74, 355n96, 358–60, 363
Romulus 139, 151, 155, 180, 191n79, 257, 277, 313n31
Rule of Faith 83
Ruspe 275
Rustamid dynasty 324

sacerdos 152, 255
saeculum 121–2, 128, 147
Saint, saints 10, 51, 122, 146, 151, 154, 161n40, 172–3, 202, 215, 219, 223, 236, 247, 298, 317n108, 329, 331, 348, 364–5
Sallust 52, 257
salvation 66, 104n132, 126–7, 144, 146, 220, 237n242, 247, 297
Salvian 265–6, 280n17
Sand, Shlomo 328
Sardinia 12, 244, 275
Saturn 53–4, 59–60, 74n108, 75n118, 90, 113, 115, 140, 156, 178, 181–2, 184, 238n265; *see also* Baal
Saturninus 21, 53, 80–1, 87, 89, 91–2, 94–5, 104n126
Saturus 53, 87–9, 100n48, 128, 281n51
Sbeitla 326
Scapula 81, 97n6, 118–19
Schaff, Philip 7, 148
schismatic 42, 112, 114, 145–6, 151, 156, 175, 195–6, 198–9, 201, 206, 211–12, 217, 247, 270, 324, 336, 344
Scilli 79, 82, 85–6, 101n61
Scipio Africanus 13–14, 34n9, 40n136, 69n32, 257
scripture 21, 69n25, 86, 111, 113, 118, 121, 124–5, 128, 140, 142, 157, 173–4, 197–8, 206, 208–11, 220, 236n238, 237n244, 242, 245, 248–9, 268, 300, 304, 323, 345, 363–4
Scythian 54, 71n60, 253
second marriages 113, 117, 131n36
Second Sophistic Movement 6, 16, 38n70, 56
Secunda 91, 172, 235n210
Secundinus 252, 261n67
Secundulus 87
Secundus of Tigisus 198

senate, senator 1, 14–15, 17–18,
39n83, 47, 62, 71n62, 89, 96, 136,
145, 150, 184, 186, 222, 275
Septimius Severus 16–17, 50, 53, 55–6,
62, 64–5, 68n21, 77n153, 87, 96,
98n13, 116, 137, 251, 361
Septuagint 249, 252
Serdica 149, 200
Sergius 309
Severus of Africa 16
sex 110, 121, 134n106, 165n129,
240–1, 249
Sextus Tarquinius 257
Shadrapa 61–2, 75n133
Shepherd, shepherds 138, 153, 221,
342
Shia, Shi'ite 324, 329
Sicca 176, 181, 190n48, 315n69
Sicily 12–13, 272, 293
Sidonius 272
Silverius 331, 352n49
Simon Magus 321
Simon the Cyrene 221
Simplicianus 208
sin 144, 177, 216, 246–7, 249, 265
slavery 14, 78n173, 87, 255, 271,
280n27, 289, 297, 323, 329, 347,
350n6, 352n40
Smyrna 82
Sol Invictus 174, 182–3
Solomon 25, 124, 220
Sophronius 309, 319n174, 320n178
Souk Ahras 240
soul 111, 113, 117–18, 132n64,
133n79, 177, 181, 220, 241, 246,
248–9, 259n38, 265, 290
Sousse 99n29, 161n45, 332
Spain 12, 23, 189n10, 190n55, 332,
349
Speratus 85, 91–2, 94, 96, 104n131
spiritual 8, 17–18, 31, 113, 118, 121,
246, 339, 343, 346
Squillacium 304
Statius 55
Stephen (bishop of Rome) 145, 152–3,
166n157, 174, 195, 199, 217,
355n96
Stephen (martyr) 125
Stephen of Byzacena 310
Stoics, stoicism 126, 132n64, 184, 242,
245
Strabo 65
subordinationism 201, 282n63, 346
substance 118, 208, 245, 248, 273
Sufes 222–3

Sufetula 27–8, 279n9, 326, 329
suicide 18–20, 41n141, 124–5, 128,
173, 184, 187, 216, 328
Sultan 339, 355n105
Sunni 324, 354n88
superstitio 93–4, 137
Syballine Oracles 183
Symmachus 275
Syracuse 175
Syria 13, 64, 137, 155, 182, 321,
326–8, 339, 341–5, 350n11,
351n29

Tahart 324, 332
Tanit 61, 90, 139, 222, 238n266, 265,
267–8; *see also* Juno
Taurians 137
Tebessa 136
Teman 221
temple 60–2, 74n113, 83, 120, 140,
177, 180, 190n48, 223, 268, 326,
363
Terence 53, 185, 188
Tertullian x, 1, 5–8, 10, 15–17, 21, 27,
31, 36n48, 38n71, 46, 51–2, 56, 66,
69n37, 73n88, 79–84, 86, 89, 97,
97n6–7, 98n13–14, 98n18, 99n29,
100n48, 100n51, 101n67, 102n78,
103n97, 104n132, 105n132–3,
108–35, 136, 138–9, 142–3, 145–7,
156–7, 173, 178–80, 182, 185,
188n1, 188n6, 208, 210, 227n33,
232n135, 232n137, 236n236,
238n267, 291, 299–300, 302, 306,
311, 336, 342, 355n96, 358, 360,
364
tetrarchy 171–3, 187, 194n166
Thagora 173
Thalassius 343
Thamugadi 207
theatre 121, 265, 267
Theban 172
Thelepte 275
Thenae 300
Theodore I 310
Theodore of Mopsuestia 40n132, 296
Theodoret of Cyrrhus 40n132, 279n8,
296
Theodosius (general) 19–20
Theodosius I 20
Theodosius II 22–3, 266, 272
Theognetus 218
theology 31, 66, 86, 108–9, 115,
119, 126–7, 132n68, 141, 151,
174, 176–8, 182–3, 194n168, 201,

208, 213, 218, 285n139, 298, 301, 320n186, 345, 347–8, 364–5
Theotokos 295
Thibilis 54
Thibiuca 173
Thomas (bishop of Carthage) 333
Thrasamund 275–6
Three Chapters Controversy 25, 287, 295–302, 309, 315n76, 340, 355n97, 358
Thuburbo Minus 79, 82, 99n30, 103n100
Tiberius 104n132, 115
Tiberius II 303
Tilley, Maureen 42n162, 45, 99n29, 203, 217, 342
Timgad 207
Tinguitani 176
Tipasa 82
Tlemcen 332
Toga 1, 49, 62, 65–6, 77n169, 78n173, 123, 134n94, 139, 142, 149–50, 238n264, 347
traditor, traditores 20–2, 39n108, 128, 197–9, 206, 214, 269
Trajan 63, 93–5, 207
Trasimene 138
Trinity, Trinitarian 128, 208, 232n137, 248–9, 269, 293, 297, 340
Tripolitania 19, 33n3, 62, 75n132, 91, 230n106, 272, 326
Trojans 77n159, 179, 238n262
Trojan War 179, 277
Troy 12, 124, 223, 277
Tunisia 14, 27, 69n24, 99n29, 161n45, 176, 197, 275, 310, 314n53, 324, 326–7, 332, 350n5
Turkey 296
Turnus 91
Tyconius 151, 156, 206, 298–9, 336, 354n94
tyrants 21, 91, 157, 180, 189n17
Tyre 12, 61, 223, 239n277, 280n17, 296

Umayyad, Umayyad dynasty 322, 331
unity 146, 148, 152–3, 155, 172, 199, 201, 224, 273, 302
Uqba Ibn Nafi 28, 327
Urbanists 206, 230n106

Valentinian III 22–3, 272
Valentinians 84, 100n51, 118, 193, 336, 343
Valerian 145, 158–9, 184
Valerius Maximus 65, 134n106, 135n106
Vandals 22–4, 224, 258, 264–86, 307, 335, 341, 343, 359
Venus 179, 190n48
Verecundus of Junca 298
Verona 209
Vestia 91
Via Scillitanorum 101n61, 173
Victor (bishop of Rome) 16, 85
Victor (primate of Numidia) 306, 310
Victoria 216
Victorianus of Uzalis 310
Victor Maurus 172
Victor of Garba 204
Victor of Tunnuna 298
Victor of Vita 24, 268, 271, 273–4, 277
Vigellius Saturninus 80, 101n59
Vigilius 26, 297–9, 301, 304
viper 119, 131n43
Virgil 12, 61, 64 (= Pseudo-Virgil) 75n120, 91, 123–4, 185, 208, 222, 257, 291, 362
virgin 63, 118, 120, 216, 257, 267–8
virtue 133n79, 274, 291
Visigoths 188, 244
visions 87–8, 102n82, 113, 158
Vitalis 266
Vitellius the African 206
Volubulis 361
Vulgate 39n108, 237n252, 249

witness 19, 87, 94–6, 111, 122, 137, 143, 147, 153, 158, 172, 289
women 30, 85, 90, 110, 114–15, 125, 130n29, 189n9, 190n48
Word of God 266, 296, 323
worship 58–63, 73n94, 94, 104n132, 137, 155, 176–8, 180, 209, 219, 223, 268, 303, 322, 333, 345

Zammac 19
Zeno (Bishop of Verona) 209–10
Zeno (emperor) 273–4, 295
Zeus 60, 75n117; *see also* Baal
Zirids 324

Ancient Source Index

Acta Purgationis Felicis 74n100
Acts of Cyprian 39n88, 166n145, 193n150
The Acts of Maximilian 39n89, 188n3
Acts of the Abitinian Martyrs 20–1, 49n98, 49n100–6, 189n19, 190n46, 227n24, 235n210
Acts of the Scillitan Martyrs 53, 63, 79–81, 85, 88, 93–4, 96, 98n17, 101n61–2, 101n64–6, 101n69–70, 104n121–3, 104n125, 104n127–8, 104n130, 105n146–7, 127, 174, 190n28
Al-Idrisi, Opus Geographicum 354n90
Ammianus Marcellinus, History 39n92, 39n94
Anthologia Latina 77n157–9, 276, 283n88, 285n143
Apostolic Tradition 163n95
Appian, The Punic Wars 34n9, 70n42, 74n113, 103n98
Apuleius, Apology 16, 34n8, 38n79, 70n47, 71n64, 72n66, 261n75, 355n108
Apuleius, Florida 34n8, 69n33, 71n65, 73n84, 261n79
Apuleius, Metamorphosis 75n122, 235n211, 281n48
Aristotle, Politics 129n23
Arnobius, Against the Nations 39n107, 102n86, 160n2, 176–9, 190n49, 190n52–4, 190n49, 190n52–4, 190–1n56, 191n59–65, 191n68, 191n59–65, 191n68, 191n79–85, 191n86, 191–2n89–90, 192n91–3, 226n11
Athanasius, Letter to the Africans 200
Athanasius, To the Africans 200, 228n53

The Augustan History 38n73–4, 68n21–2, 72n65, 72n67–8, 75n133, 77n152–5, 77n164–5, 77n167, 106n158, 107n162, 261n57, 313n36
Augustine, Against Adversaries of the Law and the Prophets 131n36
Augustine, Against Cresconius 165n136, 229n69, 230n106, 233n162, 233n164, 234n184, 235n209
Augustine, Against Gaudentius 231n121
Augustine, Against Julian 261n73
Augustine, Against Lying 259n27
Augustine, Against the Academics 258n2, 260n51
Augustine, Against the Letter of Parmenian 229n69, 229n79, 230n107
Augustine, Against the Letters of Petilian 229n70, 229n72, 230n99, 230n109–10, 234n184, 258n18–19
Augustine, Against the Skeptics 258n25
Augustine, Brief Meeting With the Donatists 229n76
Augustine, City of God 69n40, 71n61, 72n78, 131n36, 133n75, 188, 236n227, 237n249, 240, 244, 255–6, 259n34, 262n97, 262n100, 263n103–7, 263n109–11, 279n10
Augustine, Commentary on Romans 223
Augustine, Concerning the One Baptism, Against Petilian 230n109
Augustine, Confessions 71n56, 74n103, 103n98, 167n172, 209, 231n125–6, 232n129, 232n140–2, 232n144–6, 240–5, 249, 254, 258n3–5,

258n7–8, 258n10, 258n13, 259n32, 260n49, 260n56, 260n60, 261n78

Augustine, *Enchiridion/Handbook on Faith, Hope and Love* 259n27

Augustine, *Expositions on the Psalms* 33n4, 228n61, 230n101, 236n231, 259n43

Augustine, *Harmony of the Gospels* 74n108

Augustine, *Incomplete Explanation of the Epistle to the Romans* 192n106, 239n277

Augustine, *Incomplete Works Against Julian* 165n131, 252, 261n72

Augustine, *Letters* 39n113–14, 40n115–16, 98n22, 197, 229n72, 240, 243, 249, 255, 259n44, 262n90, 297

Augustine, *Letter to the Catholics* 217, 230n100, 239n277

Augustine, *On Adulterous Marriages* 259n27

Augustine, *On Baptism, Against the Donatists* 226n6, 234n195

Augustine, *On Christian Doctrine* 229n67, 230n107, 231n124, 259n28

Augustine, *On Continence* 259n30

Augustine, *On Eight Questions From Dulcitius* 259n27

Augustine, *On Eight Questions From the Old Testament* 259n27

Augustine, *On Faith and the Creed* 259n27

Augustine, *On Faith and Works* 259n27

Augustine, *On Heresies* 133n77, 228n51, 228n55, 236n227, 236n232, 259n31, 267

Augustine, *On Holy Virginity* 259n45

Augustine, *On Lying* 259n27

Augustine, *On Music* 258n25

Augustine, *On Order* 72n74, 258n25, 260n55, 271n77

Augustine, *On Patience* 259n27

Augustine, *On Seeing God* 259n27

Augustine, *On the Agreement of the Evangelists* 259n29

Augustine, *On the Care of the Dead* 259n27

Augustine, *On the Christian Struggle* 259n27

Augustine, *On the Creed to Catechumens* 259n27

Augustine, *On the Divination of Demons* 259n27

Augustine, *On the Excellence of Widowhood* 131n36

Augustine, *On the Good of Marriage* 259n45

Augustine, *On the Good of Widowhood* 259n30

Augustine, *On the Greatness of the Soul* 258n25

Augustine, *On the Happy Life* 258n25

Augustine, *On the Instruction of Beginners* 259n28

Augustine, *On the Merits and Forgiveness of Sins and Infant Baptism* 237n241–2

Augustine, *On the Presence of God* 259n27

Augustine, *On the Trinity* 248, 259n39, 259n41

Augustine, *On the Value of Fasting* 259n27

Augustine, *On the Work of Monks* 259n30

Augustine, *Proceedings With Emeritus* 239n281

Augustine, *Psalm Against the Donatist Party* 234n183, 259n36

Augustine, *Questions on the Gospels* 259n29

Augustine, *Questions on the Heptateuch* 259n29

Augustine, *Responses to Januarius* 259n27

Augustine, *Retractions* 240, 249

Augustine, *Sayings in the Heptateuch* 259n29

Augustine, *Sermons* 154, 213, 240, 243, 249, 259n43

Augustine, *Sermon to the People of the Church of Caesarea* 230n108

Augustine, *Ten Homilies on the Epistle of John to the Parthians* 260n47

Augustine, *The City of God* 72n78, 240, 279n10

Augustine, *The Rule: A Rebuke* 259n30

Augustine, *The Rule: Monastic Order* 259n30

Augustine, *The Rule: Precepts* 259n30

Augustine, *The Soliloquies* 258n25

Augustine, *The Teacher* 72n73, 258n25, 261n64

Augustine, *To Cresconius* 228n52, 258n18
Augustine, *To Simplicianus* 259n29
Augustine, *Tractate Against the Jews* 259n31
Augustine, *Tractates on the First Letter of John* 259n29
Augustine, *Tractates on the Gospel According to Saint John* 235n209, 259n29
Aurelius Victor, *The Book of the Caesars* 188n2

Bede, *Ecclesiastical History* 354n93
Bede, *Explanation of Revelation* 354n94
The Book of the Popes 38n65, 101n53, 166n154, 228n50, 230n102–4, 284n121, 284n126–7, 286n167

Caesar, *The African War* 69n28
Carthaginian Computus of 455 281n53
Cicero, *Hortensius* 241
Cicero, *On Divination* 104n132, 160n26
Cicero, *On Ends* 263n107
Cicero, *On the Commonwealth* 69n32
Cicero, *On the Orator* 238n264
Cicero, *Republic* 169n219, 182, 263n107
Cicero, *To Gaius Herennius: On the Theory of Public Speaking* 132n61
Claudian, *On the Consulship of Stilicho* 231n116
Claudian, *The War Against Gildo* 77n156, 231n116–17, 231n120
Commodian, *Instructions* 156, 168n191, 168n194, 168n196, 168n198
Commodian, *Song Against Two Peoples* 156, 168n201–3, 168n205
Commodian, *The Apologetic Song Against the Jews and Against the Nations* 156
Commodian, *The Instructions* 156, 168n194
Conference of Carthage 411 42n158, 101n61, 228n41, 230n98, 233n168, 233n171–3, 233n176, 238n269
Corippus, *In Praise of the Younger Justin* 313n33
Corippus, *Iohannes* 40n131
Councils of Carthage 215, 235n207, 285n142, 298, 302

Cyprian, *Letters* 18, 39n86, 136, 141, 143, 150, 152, 162n60, 162n65, 162n72, 163n73, 163n79–80, 163n82–4, 163n86–7, 163n89, 164n99, 164n101, 164n107, 164n114, 165n140, 166n149
Cyprian, *On Jealousy and Envy* 164n112
Cyprian, *On Mortality* 142, 162n71, 165n123, 166n141
Cyprian, *On the Dress of Virgins* 164n112
Cyprian, *On the Good of Patience* 164n112, 165n123
Cyprian, *On the Lapsed* 146, 163n80, 163n89–90, 163n92, 165n116–20
Cyprian, *On the Lord's Prayer* 164n112
Cyprian, *On the Unity of the Church* 146
Cyprian, *On Works and Almsgiving* 142, 164n112, 165n123
Cyprian, *To Demetrian* 155, 165n124, 165n137–9, 190n52
Cyprian, *To Fortunatus* 163n94, 165n122, 169n210
Cyril, *Letters* 282n62

The Didache 88
Donatus, *On the Holy Spirit* 200
Dracontius, *On the Praises of God* 274, 284n117
Dracontius, *Romulea* 274
Dracontius, *Satisfaction* 274

Ecumenical Councils 26, 167n160, 200, 208, 244, 266, 283n88, 295–8, 300, 310, 315n62, 316n106
Embrico of Mainz, *Life of Muhammad* 321
Epiphanius, *Panarion* 228n50, 228n54
Epitome de Caesaribus 72n70
Eusebius, *Church History* 38n65, 73n94, 101n53, 128n2, 131n35, 164n106, 165n116, 168n190, 174, 190n37–9, 190n41–3, 190n45, 193n142, 227n25, 228n36, 228n50, 230n95, 319n165
Eusebius, *Life of Constantine* 228n46, 228n48–50
Evagrius, *Church History* 315n61

Facundus, *Against Mocian* 299, 316n83, 316n85–6

Facundus, *Defense of the Three Chapters* 40n133, 299, 316n80–1, 316n87
Facundus, *Epistle on the Catholic Faith* 40n133, 299
Ferrandus, *Brevatio canonum* 315n67–9
Ferrandus, *Letters* 315n63
Ferrandus, *Life of Fulgentius* 275, 284n129, 285n129–30, 285n132–8, 297
Filastrius, *Book of Various Heresies* 230n94
Flodoard of Reims, *History of the Church of Reims* 353n64
Florus, *The Epitome of Roman History* 135n106
Fragments of Papias 168n190
Fronto, *Letter to the Mother of Caesar* 34n7, 71n61
Fronto, *On the Loss of His Grandson* 260n52
Fulgentius, *Explanation of Virgilian Continence* 290, 313n19, 313n21
Fulgentius, *Mythologies* 290, 313n19–20
Fulgentius of Ruspe, *Letters and Sermons* 284n129, 285n131, 285n137, 235n141, 315n64–6
Fulgentius the Mythographer, *On the Ages of the World and of Man* 313n19
Fulgentius the Mythographer, *The Explanation of Virgilian Continence* 313n19

Gelasius, *Letters* 284n122–3
Gennadius, *The Lives of Illustrious Men* 230n90, 230n107, 231n114
George of Pisidia, *On Heraclius's Return From Africa* 309
Gregory VII, *Letters* 279n6, 333
Gregory the Great, *Letters* 27, 232n150, 302–6, 308, 317n108, 317n113–15, 317n118–29, 318n130–55

Herodotus, *Histories* 34n11, 71n60, 75n126, 75n129, 229n67
Hydatius, *Chronicle* 279n7, 279n9, 282n64, 283n91
Hyppolytus, *The Refutation of All Heresies* 99n27

Ibn Abd al-Hakam, *Book of the Conquests of Egypt and of Maghrib* 322
Ibn Khaldun, *The Muqaddimah* 41n148
Ignatius, *To the Romans* 133n82
Irenaeus, *Against Heresies* 42n156, 98n23, 99n24, 101n67

Jerome, *Chronicle* 130n29, 131n35, 131n46, 132n54, 190n50, 191n73, 192n100, 231n125
Jerome, *Commentary on Galations* 232n149
Jerome, *Lives of Illustrious Men* 38n65, 101n53, 129n15, 129n18, 131n37, 131n46, 160n3, 160n10, 162n62, 162n64, 165n125, 166n43, 168n189, 191n72, 192n94, 192n97, 192n99, 192n121, 227n15, 228n15, 232n148
John of Damascus, *On Heresies* 350n9
Julius Quintus Hilarianus, *On the Day and Month of Easter* 210
Julius Quintus Hilarianus, *On the Duration of the World* 210
Junillus Africanus, *Handbook of the Basic Principles of Divine Law* 316n99–100, 316n102
Junvenal, *Satires* 169n220
Justinian, *Body of Civil Laws* 189n18

Lactantius, *Letters* 182
Lactantius, *On God's Workmanship* 185, 192n103, 192n107, 193n147
Lactantius, *On the Death of the Persecutors* 69n26, 162n74–5, 168n204, 182, 187, 189n9–10, 190n54–5, 193n126–8, 193n141, 193n143–5, 193n148, 193n153–9, 167n160–5, 229n70, 365n3
Lactantius, *On the Phoenix* 182, 186
Lactantius, *On the Wrath of God* 192n103, 192n108, 192–3n122–3
Lactantius, *The Banquet* 183
Lactantius, *The Divine Institutes* 131n35, 160n3–4, 187, 192n103, 192n110, 193n129–32, 193n134–40, 193n150, 194n160, 194n170–3
Lactantius, *The Epitome of the Divine Institutes* 192n103
Leo, *Letters* 24
Leo IX, *Letters* 333, 353n72–3

Liberatus of Carthage, *A Short Report on the* Nestorian and Eutychian *Controversies* 258n21, 280n25, 316n95

Liber censuum romanae ecclesiae 354n89

Life of Maximus 319n168–9, 319n171, 320n182, 320n184

Lucan, *On the Civil War* 161n35

Luxurious, *The Book of Epigrams* 77n157, 77n159, 285n144–6, 285n148, 286n151–6

Marcion, *Antitheses* 86

Marcion, *Apostolikon* 86

Marcion, *Euangelion* 86

Marius Victorinus, *Against Arius* 208, 232n147

Marius Victorinus, *Commentaries* 208, 232n139

Marius Victorinus, *Explanations on Cicero's Rhetoric* 231n127

Marius Victorinus, *Hymns on the Trinity* 232n137

Marius Victorinus, *On Definitions* 232n128

Marius Victorinus, *On the Generation of the Divine Word* 208

Marius Victorinus, *The Art of Grammar* 231n127

Marius Victorinus, *The Necessity of Accepting the Homoousion* 208

Martial, *Epigrammaton* 134n94

Martyrdom of Crispina 173, 190n28–32, 190n34, 190n44

Martyrdom of Felix 101n61, 189n21–6, 190n44

Martyrdom of Marculus 130n29, 228n57, 229n54, 235n209

Martyrdom of Marian and James 130n29, 158, 169n214, 169n216–18, 169n220–7

Martyrdom of Maxima, Donatilla, and Secunda 189n19, 189n26, 190n46, 235n210

Martyrdom of Maximian and Isaac 130n29, 203, 235n209

Martyrdom of Montanus and Lucius 39n89, 130n29, 158, 168n208–9, 169n211–12

Martyrdom of Polycarp 236n239

Maximus the Confessor, *Disputation With Pyrrhus* 320n179

Maximus the Confessor, *Letters* 320n181

Maximus the Confessor, *Questions and Responses for Thalassius* 319n169

Maximus the Confessor, *To Peter the Illustrious* 319n168

Minucius Felix, *Octavius* 73n92, 104n132, 135n113, 136–41, 155, 160n1, 160n3, 160n6–7, 160n10, 160n13–15, 160n17–21, 160n23–5, 160n27–8, 161n29–37, 161n39–42, 161n46–52, 162n53–6, 162n58, 168n184, 313n38

Notitia provinciarum et civitatum Africae 283n99

Optatus of Milevis, *Against the Donatists* 42, 130n29, 131n35, 188n1, 189n17, 190n44, 192n106, 226n12–13, 227n17–18, 227n20–3, 227n27–8, 227n31–4, 228n37–8, 228n40, 228n45, 228n58–60, 229n63, 229n65, 229n69–71, 229n77, 229n79, 229n81–2, 230n89, 230n91–2, 234n199, 235n203, 235n205, 235n209, 239n177–9

Orosius, *History Against the Pagans* 70n41, 231n120

Ovid, *The Book of Days* 134n106

Pacian, *Letters* 149, 165n135

Passion of Perpetua and Felicity 53, 63, 70n53, 79–81, 87, 89, 93–4, 127–8, 134n101, 158, 281n50, 283n110

Passion of the Martyrs at Agaune 189n12

Paulus, *The Sentences* 107n161, 167n166

Peter the Deacon, *Life of Constantine the African* 354n78

Plato, *Timaeus* 178

Plautus, *The Little Carthaginian* 75n116

Pliny the Elder, *Natural History* 34n11, 68n23, 69n27, 69n32, 71n64, 74n109–10, 75n120, 76n145, 135, 263n102

Pliny the Younger, *Letters* 63, 93, 105n143, 134n101

Plutarch, *Pompey* 69n27–8

Polybius, *Histories* 37n57, 75n117, 75n126

Pontianus, *To the Emperor Justinian* 316n93

Pontius, *Life of Cyprian* 130n29, 154, 162n61, 162n63–5, 162n67–9, 164n108, 164n110, 166n142–3, 166n146–7

Possidus, *Life of Augustine* 249, 279n5, 282n64

Primasius of Hadrumetum, *Commentary on Revelation* 298, 315n77–8, 316n101

Procopius, *Buildings* 312n4, 351n24

Procopius, *History of Wars* 70n48, 167n169, 286n161, 289

Procopius, *Secret History* 289, 312n15–16, 316n98

Procopius, *The History of the Wars* 40n117, 40n121, 40n127, 40n130, 40n134–5

Prosper of Aquitane, *Chronicle* 40n117, 40n121, 298

Prudentius, *Crowns of Martyrdom* 165n134, 167n175

Pseudo-Cyprian, *On the Calculation of Easter* 233n161

Pseudo-Gelasius, *Gelasian Decree* 156, 166n154

Pseudo-Hippolytus, *On the Seventy Apostles* 99n25

Pseudo-Marius Victorinus, *On Physics* 231n27

Pseudo-Virgil, *Moretum* 76n143

Quintillian, *The Orator's Education* 125n5

Quodvultdeus, *Against Five Heresies* 282

Quodvultdeus, *Homilies* 279n5

Quodvultdeus, *On the Flood* 281n60

Quodvultdeus, *The Barbaric Age* 40n119, 267, 279n5, 280n34, 280n37–41, 281n42

Quodvultdeus, *The Book of Promises and Prophecies of God* 268, 281n47, 282n30

Qur'an 322–3, 346, 350n7, 356n134

Sallust, *The War with Cateline* 69n39

Sallust, *The War with Jugurtha* 72n82

Salvian, *On the Government of God* 40n112, 40n127, 265, 279n11–13, 280n14–20

Sentences of the Eighty Seven Bishops 166n158, 137n166

Sermo in natali sanctorum innocentium 229n75

A Sermon on the Passion of Saints Donatus and Advocatus 227n25, 228n39

The Shepherd of Hermas 88

Silius Itallica, *Punica* 69n32, 75n124–5

Sozomen, *Church History* 228n54

Statius, *Silvae* 69n32, 72n69

Strabo, *Geography* 33n2, 71n64, 74n109, 75n127–8, 77n162, 77n167, 129n7

Suetonius, *Life of Nero* 105n138

Sylvester II, *Letters* 353n71

Tacitus, *Annals* 105n138

Tacitus, *Germania* 74n111

Teachings of Jacob 350n7

Terence, *Phormio* 194n171

Tertullian, *Against Hermogenes* 132n59, 132n64

Tertullian, *Against Marcion* 98n9, 101n67, 104n132, 105n132, 109, 113, 120, 129n6, 130n27, 132n59, 232n135

Tertullian, *Against Praxeas* 104n124, 132n60, 232n137, 355n96

Tertullian, *Against the Jews* 83, 98n9, 104n132, 105n132, 118, 132n59, 134n100, 134n103

Tertullian, *Against the Nations* 36n48

Tertullian, *Against the Valentinians* 132n59

Tertullian, *Apology* 17, 97n4, 97n7, 104n129, 104n132, 105n138, 115, 129n16, 129n21, 131n36, 132n51, 132n55, 132n66, 133n72, 133n81, 138, 160n21, 190n52, 191n78

Tertullian, *Exhortation to Chastity* 130n27, 132n58

Tertullian, *On Baptism* 100n48, 102n85, 119, 131n43, 132n59, 133n78–9, 164n102

Tertullian, *On Fasting* 121, 130n28, 132n60, 133n80

Tertullian, *On Fleeing Persecution* 132n58, 163n80, 163n88–9

Tertullian, *On Idolatry* 132n58

Tertullian, *On Monogamy* 121, 130n28, 133n80, 237n249

Tertullian, *On Patience* 129n16, 132n58

Tertullian, *On Penance* 129n16, 132n58

Tertullian, *On Prayer* 132n58

Tertullian, *On the Apparel of Women* 78n175, 129n11, 131n39, 131n45, 132n58, 132n69, 133n79

Tertullian, *On the Cloak* 34n15, 66, 67n3, 69n35–7, 78n171–2, 78n174–5, 123, 132n49, 132n55, 133n86–7, 133n89–90, 134n91, 134n93–5, 236n236

Tertullian, *On the Flesh of Christ* 129n9, 129n14, 132n59, 132n62

Tertullian, *On the Military Crown* 17, 38n80, 39n107, 100n48, 132n58, 188n6, 189n25

Tertullian, *On the Resurrection of the Flesh* 129n16, 132n59

Tertullian, *On the Shows* 132n58, 133n73, 133n76, 133n83–4

Tertullian, *On the Soul* 98n14, 129n17, 131n44, 132n59, 132n64, 134n102

Tertullian, *On the Veiling of Virgins* 78n175, 78n177, 100n48, 132n52, 132n62

Tertullian, *Prescript Against the Heretics* 83, 99n33, 100n38–41, 129n8, 132n59, 188n1, 227n33

Tertullian, *Testimony on the Soul* 132n59

Tertullian, *The Scorpion's Sting* 103n103

Tertullian, *To Scapula* 76n98, 97n5–6, 98n13, 98n15, 98n18, 98n20, 99n29, 99n31–2, 101n59, 102n90, 104n129, 105n133, 106n158, 118, 129n16, 132n55–7, 132n65–6, 134n102, 155, 190n52, 235n207

Tertullian, *To the Martyrs* 132n58, 133n72, 133n74, 134n102, 134n104–5, 135n116–19, 139

Tertullian, *To the Nations* 97n4, 104n132, 105n138, 118, 131n36, 132n55, 132n67

Tertullian, *To the Wife* 132n58

That Idols Are not Gods 154, 156–7, 168n177–83, 168n185–8, 191n78

Theodoret of Cyrrhus, *Compendium of Heretical Accounts* 228n54

Theodosian Code 189n19, 205, 229n83, 230n96–7

Theophanes, *Chronicle* 41n138, 220n184, 351n22, 352n40

Treatise on Rebaptism 166n157

Tyconius, *Commentary on Revelation* 336

Tyconius, *Commentary on Romans* 230n107

Valerius Maximus, *Memorable Doings and Sayings* 77n163, 134n106, 190n48

Varro, *On the Latin Language* 101n54

Verecundus, *On Penitential Satisfaction* 298

Victorinus, *Commentary of Ephesians* 208

Victorinus, *Commentary of Galatians* 208, 231n123, 232n138

Victorinus, *Commentary of Philipians* 208

Victor of Tunnuna, *Chronicle* 315n70

Victor of Vita, *A History of the Vandal Persecution* 268

Victor of Vita, *History of the Vandal Persecution* 24, 40n121, 40n127, 40n129, 101n61, 130n29, 268, 278n4, 279n6, 280n28, 281n43–4, 281n50, 281n52, 281n54, 282n69, 282n77

Victor of Vita, *The History of the Vandal Persecution* 40n121, 40n129, 101n61

Virgil, *Aeneid* 75n120, 91, 103n112, 104n117, 123–4, 134n91, 134n94, 161n45, 185, 187–8, 193n147, 194n162, 208, 222, 232n143, 237n261, 238n262, 263n102, 274, 284n114, 291, 331

Vita beatorum abbatum Benedicti, Ceofridi, Eosterwini, Sigfridi et Hwaetbert 354n93

Vitellius, *Against the Nations* 206

Vitellius, *On Ecclesiastical Procedure* 206

Vitellius, *Why the Servants of God are Hated by the World* 206

Zeno of Verona, *Sermons* 209–10, 232n151

Zosimus, *New History* 39n82, 39n84, 39n91, 39n96, 192n98

Scripture Index

1 Corinthians 232n139
1 Corinthians 3:1–3 130n25
1 Corinthians 9:21–22 4
1 Corinthians 10:21 147
1 Corinthians 15:22 247
1 John 14:6 248
1 Maccabees 10:7 363
1 Peter 2:11 130n25, 230n91
1 Peter 2:13–17 104n129
1 Timothy 3:6 142
1 Timothy 6:15 104n130
2 Corinthians 232n139
2 Corinthians 1:12 130n25
2 Maccabees 10:7 363
2 Timothy 3:16 111
2 Timothy 4:7 228n61

Acts 134n103
Acts 2:9–10 99n26, 104n132,
    134n103
Acts 4:32 258n15
Acts 8:9–24 321
Acts 19:23–27 63 105n144
Acts 22–23 224

Daniel 158

Ephesians 4:5 145
Ephesians 6:10 38n76
Ephesians 6:11–17 127
Exodus 33:11 267
Exodus 33:21 267
Ezekiel 221, 333
Ezekiel 28: 223, 239n277, 280n17

Galatians 3:27 133n79
Genesis 119, 246, 262n93
Genesis 22:16–18 262n93
Genesis 26:3–4 262n93

Habakkuk 3:3 221

Isaiah 224
Isaiah 23:1 224

John 14:6 248
John 18:11 363
John 18:36 363
Joshua 289
Jude 1:23 130n25

Luke 86
Luke 10:1 82
Luke 11:31 134n97
Luke 12:33 142
Luke 14:23 213, 247
Luke 17:22–37 217

Mark 3:25 356n121
Mark 15:21 221
Matthew 10:23 163n89
Matthew 10:33 144, 163n94
Matthew 12:25 356n121
Matthew 12:42 134n97, 237n249
Matthew 15 223
Matthew 16:18–19 163n93,
    355n107
Matthew 19:8–9 130n28
Matthew 24:4 217
Matthew 26:31 355n113
Matthew 28:20 355n107

Philippians 2:25 38n76
Philippians 3:5 4
Psalm 1:1 211
Psalm 82.8 192n106, 239n276
Psalm 83 223, 239n276
Psalm 83.7 192n106, 223,
    239n276

Psalm 89:4 183
Psalm 90.4 183
Psalms 179, 244

Revelation 157, 269, 298
Revelation 6:2 159
Revelation 6:9 143–4
Revelation 17:1–6 168n199
Revelation 17:14 104n130
Revelation 17–20 183
Revelation 19:6 104n130
Romans 232n139
Romans 5:12 247

Romans 7:14 130n25
Romans 11:13 4
Romans 12:19 200
Romans 13:1–7 104n129
Romans 13:13–14 258n11
Romans 15:27 130n25
Romans 16:5 99n25

Song of Songs 220–1
Song of Songs 1:5–7 220, 237n246

Zechariah 9:9 363
Zechariah 13:7 355n116